PRODUCING ISLAM(S) IN CANADA

On Knowledge, Positionality, and Politics

Edited by Amélie Barras, Jennifer A. Selby, and Melanie Adrian

During the last twenty years, public interest in Islam and how Muslims express their religious identity in Western societies has grown exponentially. In parallel, the study of Islam in the Canadian academy has grown in a number of fields since the 1970s, reflecting a diverse range of scholarship, positionalities, and politics. Yet, academic research on Muslims in Canada has not been systematically assessed.

In *Producing Islam(s) in Canada*, scholars from a wide range of disciplines come together to explore what is at stake regarding portrayals of Islam(s) and Muslims in academic scholarship. Given the centrality of representations of Canadian Muslims in current public policy and public imaginaries, which effects how all Canadians experience religious diversity, this analysis of knowledge production comes at a crucial time.

AMÉLIE BARRAS is an associate professor in the Department of Social Science at York University.

JENNIFER A. SELBY is an associate professor in the Department of Religious Studies and an affiliate member of the Department of Gender Studies at Memorial University.

MELANIE ADRIAN is an associate professor in the Department of Law and Legal Studies at Carleton University.

Producing Islam(s) in Canada

On Knowledge, Positionality, and Politics

EDITED BY AMÉLIE BARRAS, JENNIFER A. SELBY, AND MELANIE ADRIAN

UNIVERSITY OF TORONTO PRESS
Toronto Buffalo London

Toronto Buffalo London
utorontopress.com
Printed in the U.S.A.

ISBN 978-1-4875-0500-4 (cloth)
ISBN 978-1-4875-2788-4 (paper)
ISBN 978-1-4875-3133-1 (EPUB)
ISBN 978-1-4875-3132-4 (PDF)

Library and Archives Canada Cataloguing in Publication

Title: Producing Islam(s) in Canada : on knowledge, positionality, and politics / edited by Amélie Barras, Jennifer A. Selby, and Melanie Adrian.
Names: Barras, Amélie, editor. | Selby, Jennifer A., editor. | Adrian, Melanie, editor.
Description: Includes bibliographical references and index.
Identifiers: Canadiana (print) 20210339136 | Canadiana (ebook) 20210339144 | ISBN 9781487505004 (cloth) | ISBN 9781487527884 (paper) | ISBN 9781487531331 (EPUB) | ISBN 9781487531324 (PDF)
Subjects: LCSH: Islam – Research – Canada. | LCSH: Islam – Study and teaching – Canada. | LCSH: Islam – Canada. | LCSH: Muslims – Canada. | LCSH: Canada – Religion.
Classification: LCC BP43.C3 P76 2021 | DDC 297.0971 – dc23

This book has been published with the help of a grant from the Federation for the Humanities and Social Sciences, through the Awards to Scholarly Publications Program, using funds provided by the Social Sciences and Humanities Research Council of Canada.

University of Toronto Press acknowledges the financial assistance to its publishing program of the Canada Council for the Arts and the Ontario Arts Council, an agency of the Government of Ontario.

Canada Council for the Arts | Conseil des Arts du Canada

Funded by the Government of Canada | Financé par le gouvernement du Canada | Canada

Contents

Section 2: Charting the Study of Islam(s) and Muslims in Canada

Section 3: Positioning Selves

Preface

Having reached the end of my poor sinner's life, my hair now white, I grow old as the world does, waiting to be lost in the bottomless pit of silent and deserted divinity, sharing in the light of angelic intelligences; confined now with my heavy, ailing body in this cell in the dear monastery of Melk, I prepare to leave on this parchment my testimony as to the wondrous and terrible events that I happened to observe in my youth, now repeating verbatim all I saw and heard, without venturing to seek a design.

– Umberto Eco, *The Name of the Rose*

My mentor was the blessed Wilfred Cantwell Smith (1916–2000), the greatest Canadian scholar of religion in the twentieth century. In 1939, he completed an undergraduate degree in Oriental languages at the University of Toronto. In those days, the "Orient" was the Near East, so his focus was on Hebrew, Arabic, and other Semitic languages. As someone who has lived for the past quarter-century in Los Angeles, where China is to the West, I am interested in how those relative terms of "East" and "West" are defined.

Wilfred wanted to learn more about Islam and Muslims, and at that time, there were fewer than 1,000 Muslims in all of Canada (645 in the 1931 census). So in 1940, he and his wife Muriel moved to the country with the most Muslims, India. They lived in Lahore (coincidentally, the city of my birth) until 1946. After their return to Canada, and the completion of a doctorate at Princeton (the thesis that was rejected a few years earlier at Cambridge became his first book, *Modern Islam in India*), Wilfred became the Birks Professor of Comparative Religion at McGill University in 1948, where in 1951 he founded the Institute of Islamic Studies. It is important to remember Wilfred and his contributions as a Canadian, in Canada, to the study of Islam and Muslims. His legacy is examined in a collection edited by Ellen Aitken and Arvind Sharma (2017). Wilfred was, to put it most simply, our greatest Canadian scholar of Islam in the twentieth century. I know that he would be delighted with this book and the work that is being done by scholars of Islam in Canada (whether or not they are physically located within the country) in the twenty-first century.

When I began graduate work on Canadian Muslims in 1988 at the University of Toronto under the direction of the blessed Will Oxtoby, there were very few of us working in this area. One could, in those days before the internet, still be connected to the very small group of scholars doing that work across the country and in the United States. I was also fortunate to be able to get to know some of our grandmothers and grandfathers, such as Talat and Muin Muinuddin, Dr. Lila Fahlman, Dr. M. Qadeer Baig, and Dr. Fuad Shahin (may God be pleased with them all), who were key figures in the development of various Muslim groups in Canada. Thankfully, Murray Hogben is still with us and has published his memoir of some of those key figures, *Minarets on the Horizon: Muslim Pioneers in Canada* (2021). Since the 1980s, there has been enough of an increase in the work done, especially the work published, that as an older man I look back in wonder at those days of my youth.

In the fall of 1986, at a movie theatre in Toronto, I saw Jean-Jacques Annaud's film version of Umberto Eco's novel *The Name of the Rose* (Eco 1983). I am sure that's where I encountered the word "palimpsest" for the first time, as the opening credits called the film a palimpsest of the novel (Annaud 1986). Christian Slater, in what I think was only his second feature-film role, played the part of Adso of Melk, who began the film by narrating as an older man the events that he had witnessed in his youth. The epigraph, from Eco's novel, captures that scene and is a reminder as much of my introduction to hermeneutics as of my current intimations of mortality.

Professors Melanie Adrian, Amélie Barras, and Jennifer A. Selby are to be commended for this splendid volume. In 2018, Professors Selby, Barras, and Lori G. Beaman did their first volume on Canadian Muslims (Selby et al. 2018). The present volume brings in other voices, including interviews with some key researchers. It helps us to increase our understanding and carries on the legacy of those who helped to pave the way.

Amir Hussain
Chair and Professor of Theological Studies,
Loyola Marymount University, Los Angeles

REFERENCES

Aitken, Ellen Bradshaw, and Arvind Sharma (Eds.). 2017. *The legacy of Wilfred Cantwell Smith*. State University of New York Press.

Annaud, Jean-Jacques (Director). 1986. *The name of the rose*. Les Films Ariane, Neue Constantin, and Cristaldifilm.

Eco, Umberto. 1983. *The name of the rose*. Harcourt Brace Jovanovich.

Hogben, Murray. 2021. *Minarets on the horizon: Muslim pioneers in Canada*. Mawenzi House.

Selby, Jennifer A., Amélie Barras, and Lori G. Beaman (Eds.). 2018. *Beyond accommodation: Everyday narratives of Muslim Canadians*. University of British Columbia Press.

Acknowledgments

Academic literature on Islam and Muslims in Canada has burgeoned in the last two decades. We knew intuitively that the range was significant, but with this project, we have aimed to take a critical snapshot of the state of the field. We hope that in reading these contributions, readers can gauge what has been prioritized and why and consider what remains to be explored.

This edited volume began as a workshop at Carleton University in September 2017. We called it *Producing Islam(s) in Canada* to denote our shared critical reflection on knowledge production on Muslims and Islam in Canada to date.[1] We invited scholars working on Islam and Muslims in Canada to discuss and debate the state of the field. Together, we compiled the first bibliography of scholarly work on Islam and Muslims in Canada.[2] We produced three podcasts, led by Carleton University journalism students – Lauren Sproule, Salma Mahgoub, and Jordan Omstead – in which participants developed ideas discussed at the workshop.[3] We subsequently invited participants to expand on their ideas in written form in this volume.

First and foremost, we extend our sincere gratitude to the contributors for their time, intellectual generosity, and patience needed for an ambitious volume such as this. We acknowledge their labour, particularly as we completed final revisions in the early months of the COVID-19 pandemic. We thank the two anonymous reviewers for the University of Toronto Press for their stamina and substantive feedback.

We thank our research assistants who provided essential help at various stages of the production of this volume. Cory Funk did much to assist in the preparation of the workshop. Rehan Sayeed, Mehmet Ali Basak, Sara Hamed, and Sahver Kuzucuoglu conducted research and interviewed the key scholars featured in the volume. We thank IrisDawn Casselman and Colette Stoeber for their meticulous editorial assistance and Kimiya Missaghi for coordinating author revisions.

The workshop and the publication of this edited collection were made possible by generous funding from the Canadian Social Sciences and Humanities

Research Council, the Awards to Scholarly Publication Program, the Faculty of Public Affairs at Carleton University and the Faculty of Liberal Arts & Professional Studies at York University, Toronto, Canada. We are also grateful to our respective institutions for their support: the Department of Social Science at York University (Barras), the Department of Religious Studies at Memorial University (Selby), and the Department of Law and Legal Studies at Carleton University (Adrian).

A handful of the chapters in this volume were presented on a panel at the meeting of the 2018 American Academy of Religion in Denver, Colorado. We thank the audience for their engagement and thoughtful comments. Special thanks go to Ruby Ramji for her generous support at various stages and to Amir Hussain for his thoughtfulness and encouragement.

Our appreciation goes out to Jodi Lewchuk, our editor, for her initial enthusiasm for the project. Many thanks to Barbie Halaby for her eagle-eye copyediting, to UTP Managing Editor Robin Studniberg for her impressive organization in the final steps towards publication, and to Elena Gwynne for her adept work on the index.

We sincerely thank Iman Sattar, who allowed us to reproduce her work "From Light to Truth" on the title page. Iman Sattar is a Canadian visual artist based in Ottawa, who has worked with Arabic calligraphy since she was thirteen. In Sattar's words, "From Light to Truth attempts to discern the spiritual awakening, induced by the meditative state, that one may experience during *dhikr*, or the act of remembering God. As a recurrent depiction, the round composition of the Arabic letter *waw* comes to symbolize the relationship of creation with Creator, and its ability to manifest through an ongoing process of enlightenment and a growing consciousness of God's infinite love, mercy, and truths." We encourage readers to engage with Sattar's impressive larger body of work.

Finally, we wish to express our gratitude to our respective communities who, directly or indirectly, provided support for this project. We dedicate the volume to future scholars on these topics who will, rightfully, critique our contributions and move scholarship in new and exciting directions.

Parts of the interview with Anver Emon featured in this volume have previously appeared as: Anver M. Emon (2019), "The 'Islamic' deployed: The study of Islam in four registers," *Middle East Law and Governance*, *11*(3), 347–403. We are grateful to Janine Clark, the editor of the journal, and to Brill for allowing us to reproduce these sections.

NOTES

1 For more on the workshop, please see "Producing Islam(s) in Canada Workshop," Memorial University, Department of Religious Studies, 2017, https://www.mun.ca/relstudies/more/producingislams.

2 To access the bibliography, see "Bibliography Project," Memorial University, Department of Religious Studies, https://www.mun.ca/relstudies/more/producingislams/biblio.php.

3 To listen to the three podcasts featuring the themes through which we framed the workshop, see *Producing Islams in Canada* [Audio podcast], Memorial University, Department of Religious Studies, https://www.mun.ca/relstudies/more/producingislams/podcasts.php.

PRODUCING ISLAM(S) IN CANADA

General Introduction: Producing Islam(s) and Muslims in Canada

JENNIFER A. SELBY, AMÉLIE BARRAS, AND MELANIE ADRIAN

Knowledge production is central to what we do in the academy. It is political, it is positioned, and it requires examination. Authors in this volume have gathered and analysed academic work on Islam and Muslims in Canada to interrogate the production of knowledge on this topic. Together, we think critically about what kinds of knowledge scholars have produced to date on these topics. We ask: What *has* been studied and published? What *has not* been researched? By whom? In which disciplines? When? And why?

Muslims have lived in Canada since before Confederation, but the bulk of published scholarly work addressing their lives and experiences has been recent. Despite making up approximately 3 per cent of the population, Muslims have – as the reader is surely aware – been increasingly featured in the Canadian press, in the courts, and in policy and legal projects. As we will see, data show they have also been increasingly surveilled by the state and other actors, and also by academics. Indeed, this rise in interest has had a parallel life in the academy, as multidisciplinary scholarship has concurrently grown, especially since 2001.

This volume marks a first attempt to discuss and analyse this work. We believe a meta-critique of the output is a useful exercise: first, we can see what the corpus of knowledge entails at this particular point in history; and second, we can critically assess that body of work with an eye to identifying trends. Throughout the volume different politics, positionalities, and approaches are evident.

An important piece of our shared analysis draws on the systematic compilation, in bibliographical form, of what has been published about Islam(s) and Muslims in Canada. Authors aim to map and consider how academics have thought about, researched, interpreted, and written on these subjects to consider the politics, assumptions, and stakes in this academic work. *Producing Islam(s) in Canada* is not, therefore, a descriptive volume about Islam(s) and Muslims in Canada. The postmodern punctuation we use in the title – the "(s)" – signals the breadth and multiplicity of the traditions of Islam evident in this overview; it is not meant as a declarative theological statement against the notion of one true Islam as a unified set of beliefs and doctrines.

In general, contributors take a constructionist approach, understanding expressions of Islam not as "proper" or normative concepts but as sociopolitical and changing ones. In the field of religious studies, scholars, including Jonathan Z. Smith (1982), Russell McCutcheon (1999), and Catherine Bell (1996), have long critiqued the category of "religion." Some, including Asad (1994, 2003), Mahmood (2009), Sullivan et al. (2015), Beaman (2010), and Keane (2007), argue that unexamined categories of religion often reveal Protestant-cum-liberal influence. Taking a more constructionist approach, Smith (1982) famously argues that "*there is no data for religion*" [emphasis in original]. Religion is solely the creation of the scholar's study" (xi). Of course, not all scholars – including some of those featured in this volume – take this approach. Still, we see the constructionist tension as generative and locate it in broader emic/etic and insider/outsider orientations, which themselves have been critiqued for their dualistic rigidity (Coutin and Hirsch 1998). As editors, we situate Islam(s) as a discursive tradition (cf. Asad 1986) to acknowledge how power, privilege, and status are socially defined and authenticated (also see Fadil 2011, 93; Schielke and Debevec 2012; Ahmed 2015).

At the same time, drawing on Abdul Hamid el-Zein's (1977) anthropological thinking on "islams," the volume invites readers to think broadly about the variety of authoritative structures laden in the singular "Islam" so as to move away from ahistorical or static categorizations. While we recognize its omission in the qualitative research to date (see "Who Are 'Muslims in Canada'?") and can see how theological ideas inform concepts underpinning our work, this volume does not analyse the theological content of the traditions of Islam. We mostly take an intersectional approach in considering those who are Muslim, those who self-identify as Muslim, and, as the literature on Islamophobia and anti-Muslim racism suggests, those who are perceived as Muslim and the discriminations they experience.

In this introduction, thinking through our co-generated bibliography, we briefly examine the corpus of the literature. In general terms, as we will discuss momentarily, the scholarship to date is not cohesive. It is marked by noteworthy theoretical and methodological differences. Following an overview of the theoretical contexts for our shared work, we introduce the chapters within the volume's four sections: Examining Knowledge Production on Islam, Charting the Study of Islam(s) and Muslims in Canada, Positioning Selves, and Future Trends.

Scholarship on the Politics of Knowledge Production

Our investigation is influenced by scholars who have long thought about the connections between knowledge and power in scholarship on Islam(s) and Muslims (see, for example, Amiraux 2012; Amir-Moazami 2016; Asad 1986, 1994, 2003; Deeb and Winegar 2015; Masud and Salvatore 2009; Said 1978;

Yegenoglu 1998). Edward Said's (1978) seminal critique of seventeenth- and eighteenth-century cultural production in Britain, France, and the United States in *Orientalism* is often positioned by scholars as foundational to thinking through the politics laden in how we know what we know. Said's (1978) definition of Orientalism is umbrella-like, broadly introducing the term as one with particular scholarly significance:

> The most readily accepted designation for Orientalism is an academic one … Anyone who teaches, writes about, or researches the Orient – and this applies whether the person is an anthropologist, sociologist, historian or philologist – either in its specific or its general aspects, is an Orientalist, and what he or she says or does is Orientalism. (2)

He describes how Orientalism is

> the corporate institution for dealing with the Orient – dealing with it by making statements about it, authorizing views of it, describing it, teaching it, settling it, ruling over it: in short, Orientalism [can be read] as a Western style for dominating, restructuring and having authority over the Orient. (3)

Said thus takes a post-Enlightenment Foucaultian approach to the politics and power laden in knowledge and draws on a large corpus of art and literature to show how conceptualizing the so-called Orient objectifies and politicizes the "East." His work does not specifically address Islam as a field of study or as a religious tradition, but Said's critique of Orientalist scholarship has been generative to how scholars have since thought about their geopolitical positionality in relation to the world and how this positionality affects the knowledge they produce. Said ultimately shows that although it purports to be an objective, disinterested, and esoteric field, Orientalism functions to serve political ends. He is clear about this causal sequence: "To say simply that Orientalism was a rationalization of colonial rule is to ignore the extent to which colonial rule was justified in advance by Orientalism, rather than after the fact" (39). Orientalism led the "West" to see Islamic culture as static in both time and place, as "eternal, uniform, and incapable of defining itself" (301).

Contemporary scholars continue to build on Said's work to think about the politics of knowledge production. Talal Asad's (1986) essay on the anthropology of Islam is cited by many in this volume and similarly draws on a Foucaultian approach to point to the politics and construction of the categories of Islam and Muslim. Gil Anidjar (2006) takes Said in a different direction, arguing for how Orientalist visions of the world constitute a form of Christian imperialism (56). Others have taken Said's lens and extended it in intersectional ways to reflect on how gender, race, and class work alongside pejorative depictions of Islam to produce an essentialized "other" (see Abu-Lughod 2001, 101; Hussain 1984, 7; Yegenoglu 1998). Many of these works explore the consequences of these representations for the everyday lives of individuals who self-identify as Muslim.

Methodological tools have also been effectively critiqued in how they shape what we know. Amir-Moazami challenges the tendency to uncritically believe the so-called truths of quantitative statistical data. Her chapter in this volume considers scholarship in the contemporary German context. She notes:

> In the case of the statistical measurement of Muslim forms of social life and religious practice, we need to raise questions about the functions of measuring, and we need to ask why research of the social by numbers – "the strongest languages of all" (Asad 1994, 78) – has so stubbornly survived despite postmodern, post-structuralist, and postcolonial critique.

Like Amir-Moazami, who explores the politics of producing statistics, most contributors to this volume take up questions regarding the implications of their methodological approach(es).

As Deeb and Winegar elegantly put it in relation to their analysis of the politics laden in scholarship on the Middle East, these are far from navel-gazing exercises. A focus on knowledge production "brings a key insight of post-WWII humanities and social science research – that knowledge and power are co-constituted – to bear not just on the scholarship we produce, but on *how* we produce it" (Deeb and Winegar 2015, 4). In relation to the work in this volume, awareness of power invites examination of the corpus of published research on Islam(s) and Muslims in Canada, namely on which subjects scholars have focused their energies and which they have overlooked. We hope the exercise might entail genuine self-reflection on our research. As Deeb and Winegar (2015) argue, a central goal to analysing knowledge is "to expose important, yet often hidden, dynamics" (4).

Following Deeb and Winegar's line of enquiry, authors in this volume more specifically question: How is knowledge produced? Which methods are most commonly used? Which funding sources enable this production? When has knowledge about Islam(s) and Muslims in Canada been produced most prolifically? How do political contexts influence the directions of research? Who produces different kinds of research or is seen as authorized to do so? And how do these scholars shape the directions knowledge takes and the questions that are posed? On a more practical level, we seek to respond to these questions productively to reflect on the past and promote new possibilities for studying Islam(s) and Muslims in Canada.

The Canadian academic context further shapes our analysis of Islam. Much of the scholarship on Muslims and Islam(s) has been published in the last twenty years. In contrast, in their study of the English-language academic work published on Islam from the 1950s to the 1970s that focused on European contexts, Masud and Salvatore (2009, 51) observe a significant shift from Orientalist-informed textually based interpretations to greater sociological analysis of Muslims contemporarily. This shift is reflected in the scholarly work analysed in this volume: for the most part, it too is sociologically informed. In his chapter, Paul Eid analyses contemporary sociological analysis of Muslims in Quebec that has, in different decades, primarily focused on interlocutors' ethnicity, race, and, more recently, religion.

Initial Thinking

For Barras and Selby, many of these questions build on a preliminary review of the scholarly literature in *Beyond Accommodation: Everyday Narratives of Muslim Canadians* (Selby et al. 2018). With Lori G. Beaman, in this book's chapter "Who Are 'Muslims in Canada'?," they map and overview the Canadian corpus's range of disciplines, methodological approaches, and theoretical vantage points in relation to Canadian Muslim life. They argue that despite the richness of the bibliography, until recently only a relatively small number of scholars have published actively on Islam(s) and Muslims. Canadian scholars had often used the lens of immigration or ethnicity to examine Muslims, but not necessarily with a privileged focus on their religiosity or on the impacts of anti-Muslim racism. Today, as Muslimness is increasingly politicized in the public sphere, scholars are taking note.

Adrian charted similar trends in *Religious Freedom at Risk: The EU, French Schools and Why the Veil Was Banned* (2016) and in her comparative legal work between the EU and Canada. She found that while excellent research has been published, no bibliographic compilation or systematic analysis of work in this field had been done. Thus, questions on the vantage points from which Islam and Muslims in Canada have been studied and how this has shifted over time were difficult to answer. Spurred by these shared observations, the three of us sought to bring together scholars in the field who could help advance these considerations. Collectively, we applied for funding, organized a two-day workshop, formulated the book outline, and sought out contributors. This work is the culmination of our shared intellectual enterprise.

That the field in Canada is relatively small made it possible to imagine bringing scholars working on Islam(s) and Muslims together to reflect more systematically and collectively on the state of the field. The workshop *Producing Islam(s) in Canada*, co-organized by Adrian, Barras, and Selby with Karim H. Karim at Carleton University in September 2017, was an opportunity to begin this conversation. This volume reflects the continuation of this thought experiment.[1] We conceived of a two-day gathering with a non-traditional format.[2] Given the range of disciplinary and empirical foci, as well as divisive theoretical debates, we sought to foster a shared conversation. We therefore did not request single-authored, work-in-progress submissions. Instead, we prepared four case studies that we asked participants to think about and be ready to engage when we met. Our hope was that reading, mulling over, discussing, and re-discussing the corpus would foster a more organic and theoretically grounded conversation on knowledge production. This format pushed many of us outside of our comfort zones. We are appreciative of the support among our colleagues in the workshop space for embarking on this non-traditional route, which we believe has translated into the rich writing that follows (and is also evident in the podcasts created for the three last cases[3]). The case studies focused on the following areas:

(1) *A bibliography of scholarly work on Islam(s) in Canada:* In preparation for our gathering, we co-created a chronological bibliographical document to initiate reflection on the topics and methods that had been covered in the scholarship on Islam(s) in Canada to date.[4] While such a project on Islam in Europe or in the United States would have been difficult to compile given the breadth and size of the field, we were in the unique position in Canada to collect citations of most of the published work to date. Participants were asked to read for trends in the literature (methodological, theoretical, empirical), how and whether Islamic texts were featured, and whether there were oversights in the corpus. The initial document we circulated was not an exhaustive bibliography but a working document to which workshop participants were encouraged to add references. Our goal was to co-create a shared living list of references.

(2) *Depictions of people who wear niqabs, with attention to the case of Zunera Ishaq:* Zunera Ishaq won a Federal Court (and Federal Court of Appeal) decision in October 2015, allowing her to wear her niqab in a Canadian citizenship ceremony. As Natasha Bakht reflects in her chapter, Ishaq's niqab became the object of significant policy debates, as well as Islamophobia and anti-Muslim racism, during the 2015 federal election. The former prime minister of Canada's popularity rose briefly following his characterization of the garment as "anti-woman." The 2012 Supreme Court of Canada's *R. v. N.S.* decision and Bills 94, 60, 62, and 21 in Quebec further shaped debate about the acceptability of the niqab in the public sphere (see Bakht's chapter for more details regarding this case and these bills). Key questions that guided our workshop conversation included: What does it mean that veiling and Islamic dress receive so much attention in scholarly literature? What are the connections between the political/media focus on these garments and scholarly production of them? What images of Muslim women does this gaze engender? Can we imagine other areas related to Muslim dress that have received less or no attention? Sadaf Ahmed's contribution, "Time for a 'Hijab Ban'?," provocatively addresses these questions.

(3) *Depictions of Muslim men as Canadian foreign fighters with Daesh (2014–2017):* The war in Syria has been a game changer on several fronts, including the number of Canadians who have travelled to fight and the way social and traditional medias have publicized their actions. At the time of our workshop in 2017, twenty-one Canadian men were estimated to have died in the conflict; approximately 180 were still there, and sixty had returned to Canada (Public Safety Canada 2016). Despite these relatively low numbers, the spectre of terrorism has had significant pejorative affects for racialized, visibly Muslim men in Canada. In the workshop, we considered gendered discourses related to young Canadian Muslim men. We asked how current events have shaped scholarship and funding possibilities. Why, for instance, have scholars rarely studied the experiences of Muslim men, with the exception of those deemed radical? Do recent well-funded research projects on radicalization participate – even inadvertently – in reproducing this association between Muslim masculinity and terror? Aaron Hughes's investigation into which projects related to Islamic and Muslim studies have been funded by the Canadian Social Sciences and Humanities Research Council (SSHRC) in "Research Funding and the Production of Knowledge about Islam" is revelatory of some of these trends.

(4) *Narratives about requests for accommodation at Quebecois sugar shacks (shacks for tapping maple trees for syrup) between 2007 and 2017:* In the province of Quebec, sugar shack visits are a ubiquitous spring outing. Maple syrup–focused businesses are occasionally asked to adapt their "French Canadian" menu items to accommodate a variety of groups, including those with dietary requirements such as those Muslims who avoid pork. In our workshop discussion, we looked at academic, policy, and media narratives that focused on controversial accommodation requests at sugar shacks (e.g., Barras 2016; Bouchard and Taylor 2008) but that overlooked how most of these transactions between owners and clients occurred without fuss. We deliberated on different imaginative strategies crafted around food and prayer space requests that are depicted in the scholarly literature. Finally, we also considered why many of these cases are framed around the language of reasonable accommodation and appear to focus on Quebec.

Alongside discussion of these cases, we sought to weave in more theoretical enquiries.[5] Aiming to keep the group discussion iterative, we included questions such as:

- If some readings of the traditions of Islam are given prescriptive legitimacy over others in the public imaginary and in scholarly work in Canada (i.e., some sects, interpretations, groups, and individuals receive more attention and hold more authority than others), do scholars have a responsibility to address this imbalance and document overlooked ways of being Muslim? If yes, which approaches facilitate this task?

- Which theoretical perspectives are most useful or politically necessary in thinking about the category of Islam in scholarly work (e.g., postcolonial, anti-colonial, anti-racist, theological, feminist, critical race, and critical legal studies)? What do these perspectives reveal and obscure?
- Who has the legitimacy and authority to write about Islam(s) and Muslims in Canada? To what extent is identifying as Muslim important? Is the "insider/outsider" debate (e.g., Coutin and Hirsch 1998; McCutcheon 1999) important in the field? Participants in the workshop were divided on this question (see for example Selby et al. 2018, 188n13; Zine 2012, 27).
- Are there causal links between a scholarly trend of studying conservatism and the securitization of Muslim communities? In the same vein, are some communities/individuals over-solicited by our research? How do we address these concerns (and should we)?

Chapters in this volume, in both traditional and interview formats, take up these queries from different angles.

Methodologies and Positionalities

We come to this project as scholars and editors with different interdisciplinary backgrounds. Barras has a background in political science and now works in a law and society program. She is particularly interested in the relations between law, politics, and Islam and in the value of a comparative approach. Selby has religious studies and anthropology training, and much of her work draws on ethnographic methods to think about state intervention in the lives of Muslims in Canada and France. Adrian, trained in social anthropology and the study of religion, works in a Department of Law and Legal Studies and focuses on the intersections of law, human rights, and lived religiosity. We hope that the combination of this training and these approaches has allowed us to think about questions of knowledge production from a range of perspectives. As we will see, the study of Islam(s) and Muslims reflects a diversity of scholars, including those contributing to this volume. More significantly, we hope that bringing these voices together has laid the foundations for a productive and engaging reflection on the state of the field, especially where there are tensions.

Besides methodological and theoretical diversity, we must also reflect on our identities as White, perceived-Christian, cisgender, settler, and tenured women. In addition to being cognizant of the importance of locating this project in a particular political and socio-economic climate, which has surely facilitated its funding (again, see Hughes's chapter on this point), we know that our positionalities influence some of the questions that initially drove this project and the issues we agreed were worthy of attention. Our aim during the workshop and in shepherding this volume has been to foster a constructive dialogue between participants who come from a range of positional backgrounds. We do not all agree. The questions that run through this volume and the content of its chapters are the product of this conversation and, at times, of debate. Several participants chose to reflect on questions of positionality in their contributions in section 3 (Positioning Selves), reminding the reader of the importance of self-reflexivity and, at the same time, questioning the productivity of the rigid binary that structures the insider/outsider debate (see Tiflati and Djaout, Brown, Jahangeer, and Mossière on how their positionalities impacted their work).

Knowledge Production

Before we turn to specific chapters, in this section we present some of our thinking drawn from the workshop discussion and our quantitative analysis of the shared bibliography. More specifically, we think through some of the quantitative data we created by coding the bibliography.[6] We note a few of the most striking trends related to the year of publication, the primary scholarly discipline of the author (or first author), and the primary themes examined in the literature to date. The bibliography was compiled by Selby prior to the workshop, at which point participants reviewed it and added materials. We then discussed its contents as one of our four case studies (see above). The bibliography includes "scholarly production" on Islam(s) and Muslims in Canada in French and English, including theses, dissertations, and reports. We compiled more than 350 sources.[7]

In the first place, we thought it useful to remark on the publication date of most of the literature on Islam and Muslims in Canada (figure 1). While we expected to see a steady increase following 9/11, scholarly literature with a Canadian focus peaks in 2012. A number of explanations are possible, some coincidental, some political. First, two edited volumes that focused on Canada (by Korteweg and Selby 2012 and Zine 2012) were published that year. Second, several master's theses were completed that year. And last, several scholars wrote on Bill 94 proposed in the province of Quebec, which sought to ban women wearing niqabs from providing and receiving public services.

This pie chart (figure 2) shows our interpretation of the primary disciplinary foci in the literature. We appreciate that many scholars employ a range of tools and that some disciplines are especially methodologically diverse in their approaches. For this reason, when in doubt, we coded according to the scholar's

Figure 1. The literature by publication date (1980–2017)

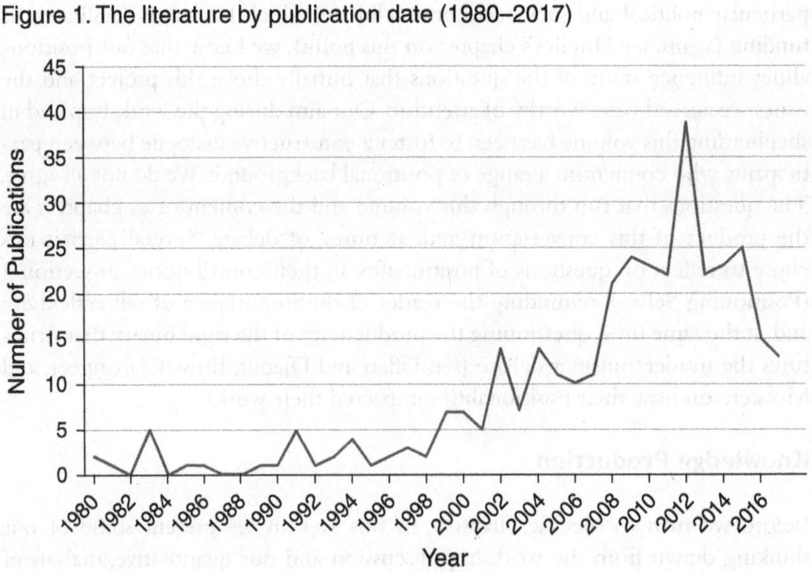

field of study, except in publications where the scholar was clearly publishing in a journal in a different field.

The pie chart (figure 2) reveals a few noteworthy trends. Most of the scholarship is qualitative in nature. Sociologists and religionists cited in the bibliography rely primarily on qualitative methods (see more on this methodological approach and qualitative research in Selby, Barras, and Beaman's chapter). In this area, it is striking that far more sociologists than anthropologists have engaged in this work (32 per cent versus 6 per cent). We also note the limited work undertaken on the history of the Muslim community or Islam in Canada (4 per cent). Although we do not have a list of unfunded work, in his chapter, Aaron Hughes explains that historical projects have been granted less funding, showing how funding priorities shape research. Moreover, while scholarship on Islam(s) and Muslims in Canada that falls primarily in the field of gender studies is limited (2 per cent), as the reader can see from figure 3 and in the analysis of the qualitative literature on Islam(s) and Muslims in Canada in this volume (see Selby, Barras, and Beaman and Ahmed), many of the works in other disciplines (e.g., political science, sociology, anthropology, law) focus on gender-specific questions. The delineation of these categories therefore entails a good deal of interpretation.

The majority of the literature is multidisciplinary and multi-focused (see figure 3). Coding for primary theme required significant interpretation. For instance, we coded Naved Bakali's *Islamophobia: Understanding Anti-Muslim Racism through the Lived Experiences of Muslim Youth* (2016) under "Islamophobia"

Figure 2. The literature by primary discipline of the author or by the field of the journal of publication

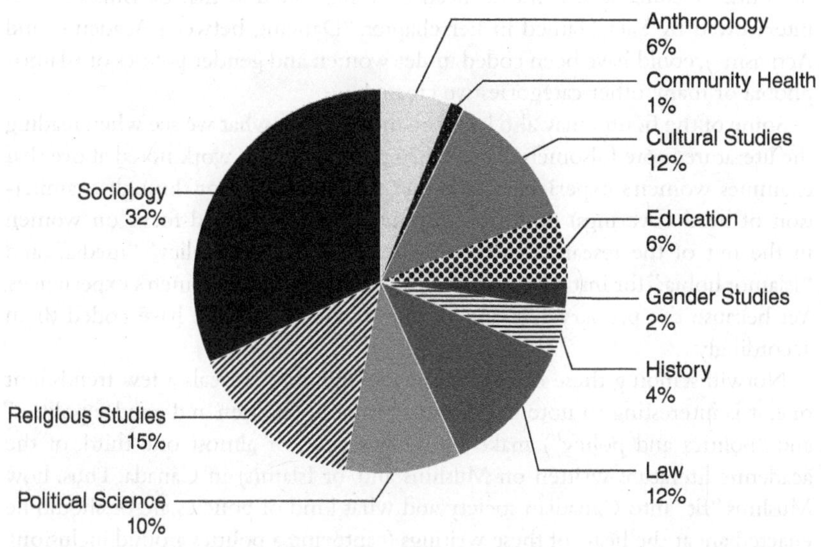

Figure 3. The academic literature by primary theme

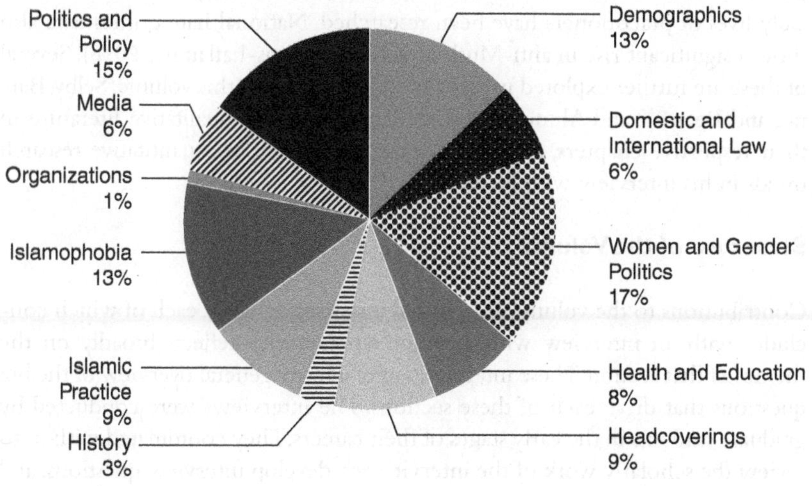

given that it was his chosen focus in the title; but clearly the content could have allowed it to fall under a number of the categories we created, such as politics or youth or education. Work on head coverings, such as that by Bullock (also interviewed by Sara Hamed in her chapter, "Dancing between Academia and Activism"), could have been coded under women and gender politics or Islamophobia or many other categories we created.

Some of the figures may also be more modest than what we see when reading the literature more fulsomely. For one, 26 per cent of the work noted above that examines women's experiences (whether more generally or through examination of head coverings) does not account for the gendered focus on women in the rest of the research. In the areas of "politics and policy," "media," and "Islamophobia," for instance, much of the data focuses on women's experiences. Yet because the primary foci are on one of these areas, we have coded them accordingly.

Notwithstanding these caveats, the graph (figure 3) reveals a few trends. For one, it is interesting to note that political topics ("women and gender politics" and "politics and policy") make up 32 per cent, or almost one-third, of the academic literature written on Muslims and/or Islam(s) in Canada. Thus, how Muslims "fit" into Canadian society and what kind of policies are or should be enacted are at the heart of these writings (capturing a politics around inclusion). Secondly, demographic considerations are another large slice of the pie at 13 per cent. Understanding how many Muslims there are and where they are located more quantitatively is a topic to which considerable time has been devoted.

Equal to the demographic piece at 13 per cent of the total, Islamophobia and anti-Muslim racism have been the focus of much attention, most of it recent. Questions around how and when Islamophobia manifests itself, what Islamophobia means for Canadian Muslims, and (more recently) how it affects the daily lives of practitioners have been researched. National hate crimes data also show a significant rise in anti-Muslim racism (Wilkins-Laflamme 2018). Several of these are further explored in various contributions to this volume. Selby, Barras, and Beaman and Ahmed, for instance, critique the qualitative literature in their respective chapters, and Abdie Kazemipur discusses quantitative research trends in his interview with Hamed.

Structure of the Volume

Contributions to the volume are divided into four sections, each of which concludes with an interview with a senior scholar, who reflects broadly on the themes of that section. These interviews offer a more general overview of the big questions that drive each of these sections. The interviews were conducted by graduate students in the early stages of their careers. They coordinated with us to review the scholarly work of the interviewees, develop interview questions, and write short introductions for the interviews. Additionally, we hope the interviews render some of the ideas accessible to a different type of audience than the traditionally written chapters, like for undergraduate students or policymakers.

The volume opens with theoretical discussions about what reflecting on knowledge production on Islam(s) and Muslims entails, the types of questions it engenders, and the consequences of this framework for studying this topic in and outside of Canada. Contributors to this first section also situate this conversation on knowledge production within a wider academic discussion that is taking place in Europe and the United States. In the first chapter, Schirin Amir-Moazami sheds light on the epistemologies, methodologies, and disciplinary practices that shape discourses on Islam in Europe. In so doing, she locates knowledge production on Islam(s) and Muslims well before the common 9/11 marker and charts the historical trends and mechanisms that inform the production of the figure of the Muslim. Muslims, she argues, are objects of study for scholars and of intervention by policymakers. Amir-Moazami urges readers to think about the implications and impact of this focus. While her analysis centres on Europe, her argument about the importance of "blend[ing] historical and contemporary analyses [in order] to grasp the longer-term legacies of knowledge production on Muslims" resonates transnationally.

Amir-Moazami's piece is followed by Aaron Hughes's chapter, which shows how research-granting agencies produce the material conditions to enable the production of certain types of knowledge on Islam(s) and Muslims while disabling others. Hughes examines trends in the projects that have been funded by the SSHRC in the post-9/11 era. He argues that funding decisions are oriented by questions such as: What knowledge of Islam "meets the needs of Canadians"? And how do these "needs – or fears – structure topics to be funded and thereby determine what is (or is not) valid knowledge about Islam?" He shows that the majority of recently funded projects have looked at the interactions between Islam and the state, particularly those that stress the ability of Islam to "fit" in the Canadian context. In contrast, historically focused archival projects have been more rarely funded (although this funding agency does not provide data on unfunded projects). This tendency, he ably argues, unavoidably pulls "scholarship in certain areas."

The first section concludes with two interviews with scholars who reflect on the politics of knowledge production on Islam in their work. In her interview with Sahver Kuzucuoglu, Lara Deeb reflects on her analysis of how the politics of knowledge production shape the work of anthropologists addressing the Middle East but who are located in the United States. In so doing, Deeb eloquently echoes a number of the arguments made in the preceding chapters. She theorizes on the "visible and invisible forces" that shape knowledge production. Deeb also links this academic work with other considerations, namely that the intersection between "specific political climate, degree and form that anti-Muslim racism [takes], and career stage" should be a central consideration for everyone, including early-career scholars as they shape their research agendas. Deeb underscores that scholars should be accountable for the knowledge they produce. She poses a question that resonates with our larger collective project: "Who are we writing for, and how do we decide which politics, which context, and which priorities to honour when those priorities, politics, or contexts come into conflict with one another?"

In his interview with Rehan Sayeed, Anver Emon reflects on how the "Islamic" and "Muslims" should be adjectivized so as to see them as constructed, including within academic disciplines, and how these constructions are deployed in the service of different projects of governance. Emon's reflection grapples with how the epistemic conditions of knowledge production relate to broader material consequences. Not unlike Amir-Moazami's and Hughes's arguments, Emon encourages readers to think about the empirical significance of knowledge production – with attention to politics laden in philological- and ethnographic-based research – for the lives of individuals identified as Muslims.

If the first section addresses some of the theoretical questions that inform consideration of knowledge production, the second section focuses on more specific case studies and empirical data. Charting the Study of Islam(s) and Muslims in Canada offers an empirically grounded discussion of trends in the literature since the 1970s. It aims to provide readers with a picture of the state of the field. The section opens with a chapter by Selby, Barras, and Beaman that analyses trends in seventy-seven published works within the qualitative literature on Islam(s) and Muslims in Canada from 1997 to 2017. The chapter shows how "Canada" and "Muslims" are imagined in this literature and identifies what these common assumptions overlook. In undertaking this exercise, the authors point to theoretical and empirical gaps in the research to date, namely a lack of attention to interpretations of theology and theoretical weakness in considering Islamophobia and anti-Muslim racism.

In the chapter "Studying Muslim Minorities in Canada," Paul Eid reflects on a change he charts in the literature on Canadian Arab-Muslim minorities after 9/11. He argues that this work shifted from a focus on Arab identity and anti-Arab racism to one centred on Muslim identities and Islamophobia. Drawing on his qualitative research on Muslim and Christian youths (2007), Eid notes how, regardless of their academically perceived identities, his respondents reject singular identities, whether religious or ethnic. He concludes by urging researchers to be cautious not to contribute, even inadvertently, to reinforcing these social categorizations with their methodological choices. Scholars, he argues, must be more expansive than reductive in their approaches.

In the next chapter, Sadaf Ahmed engages with the literature on Islam and Muslims in Canada. She critically assesses the proliferation of research on Muslim women's veiling practices in a post-9/11 era. Drawing on a rigorous review of the literature with this focus, Ahmed argues that this research carries the risk of flattening the experiences and lives of Muslim Canadian women. Ahmed concludes by calling on researchers to "refuse hijab-talk as somehow natural to Muslims in Euro-American contexts" and to "instead … begin by historicizing how veiled Muslim women become particularly visible to them." So doing would allow scholars not only to reflect on the politics of the knowledge they produce but also to focus on other, more fertile, questions that have been largely overlooked to date.

The chapter "Expressions of Sufism in Canada" offers a critique and overview of expressions of Sufism in Canadian scholarship on Islam(s) and Muslims, notably with regard to its underrepresentation in scholarship thus far. Meena Sharify-Funk and Jason Idriss Sparkes show that research has emphasized Sunni Islam for a number of political reasons. Drawing on their own qualitative research, Sharify-Funk and Sparkes convey some of the richness of Canadian Sufism, including analysis of its traditions' genealogies, practices, and cultural influences. They call on scholars of Muslims in Canada to better capture the multiplicity of Islam(s) to include Sufism. This broader engagement is essential, as "any representation of Islam in Canada which ignores Sufism is incomplete."

The second section concludes with two interviews. The first, conducted by Mehmet Basak, features Karim H. Karim, professor at Carleton University in the School of Journalism and Communication. Karim considers his personal academic trajectory over forty years and reflects on what it means to study Islam as a plural tradition. Karim articulates some of the challenges laden in the study of religious groups and the importance of self-reflexivity, in his case as a Muslim and Ismaili. Among other topics, he points to ways the study of Islam(s) in Canada has privileged a "North American Self" perspective and the lacunae and stereotypes that inform much of print media's coverage of Muslim life in Canada.

Finally, in his interview with Sara Hamed, Abdie Kazemipur, professor and chair of ethnic studies at the University of Calgary, thoughtfully reflects on his quantitative work on Islam(s) and Muslims in Canada. He considers new research directions, including "studying the nature of the relationships between Muslim and non-Muslim Canadians" and generating new data – "mostly quantitative, but also qualitative – on Canadian Muslims that could show the big picture and the trends over time." His insights move the discussion offered by the chapters in this section from a qualitative perspective to a rarer quantitative one.

Section 3, Positioning Selves, explores methodological and theoretical conundrums faced by scholars working on related research, including thinking productively and critically about the insider/outsider question and the challenges raised by particular methods. The section begins with a chapter by Hicham Tiflati and Abdelaziz Djaout. Tiflati and Djaout engage in an autoethnographic analysis of their "permanent insider" statuses as Muslim-identified researchers in Montreal. They discuss how this position shapes "what we see, what we conclude … and the ways in which we interpret our data." With attention to the pre-, during, and post-ethnographic periods within much qualitative research, including their own, Tiflati and Djaout critique the rigid insider-outsider and subjective-objective categories.

In the following chapter, Rachel Brown also examines how positionality impacts the research we undertake, with insightful attention to gender. In relation to her research on foodways among Muslims of North African origin in Montreal (and Paris), she critiques an implicit expectation among researchers that research focusing on food and Islam will primarily discuss women's experiences, given that the domestic sphere is "the domain of women" and that she, who identifies as a woman, would necessarily examine women's experiences. Brown critiques the insider/outsider dichotomy and beautifully captures the fluidity of identity in the field and subsequent scholarship.

Drawing on transnational qualitative research in France and Quebec, Roshan Arah Jahangeer continues consideration of the insider/outsider debate in relation to her own knowledge production. Like Tiflati and Djaout, she uses an autoethnographic approach to reflect on her fieldwork in Montreal, theorizing two specific incidents in her fieldwork. This approach enables her to subtly complicate the common insider/outsider divide in qualitative research methodology. She also effectively reorients academic scholarship within anti-Islamophobia activism.

In her chapter, Géraldine Mossière also tackles this insider/outsider question by drawing on her qualitative research with converts in France and Quebec. She critiques recurring patterns in the personal testimonies she collected and evaluates the methodological challenges of conducting empirical research among Muslim populations as a so-called outsider. She argues that her interlocutors' personal and political situations made traditional anthropological observation and thick description tricky. In order to mitigate her concern with the construction of the testimonials she collected, Mossière concludes by introducing a triangulation theory as one way to reposition her data.

In the last contribution to this section, Mehmet Basak interviews Jasmin Zine, professor at Wilfrid Laurier University and co-founder of a Muslim studies option in its Department of Religion and Culture. In this interview Zine reflects on some of the central components of her career to date: her work as a public intellectual responding to anti-Muslim racism and Islamophobia in the Canadian context and her contributions as an intellectual in the area of critical Muslim studies, among others. Zine usefully demarcates the politics laden in all scholarly work.

In the final section of the volume, we present and examine areas that have been under-researched. These areas present avenues for future research, including methodological and empirical directions. The section opens with Catherine Holtmann, who advocates for mixed-method (qualitative and quantitative) and comparative approaches to the study of Islam(s) in Canada. In her research on Muslim and Christian immigrant women in Atlantic Canada and their support networks, Holtmann discusses how analysing large data sets has allowed her to provide an overview of the characteristics that make up these different groups. It has not, however, been helpful in capturing the diversity within these groups. It is only by combining quantitative findings with qualitative research, she argues, that richer data emerge on the type of formal and informal religious support networks to which her female interlocutors turn. Her Muslim-Christian comparative research findings are significant because they show that, contrary to public discourse, the experiences of Muslim women and other female religious newcomers are not vastly different. Few scholars in the broad field under examination here undertake this kind of mixed methodological approach.

Melanie Adrian's chapter examines an issue that was entirely overlooked by the academic community in Canada, reminding readers that, of the multitude of events that shape the public imaginary on Islam(s) and Muslims in Canada, only some of these are studied. Adrian discusses the case of *Montreal Islamic School v. Benhabib*. This case took up statements made by Djemila Benhabib, a writer and well-known critic of Islam, about a private Islamic school in her Montreal neighbourhood. Benhabib claimed that the school observed "gender apartheid" and practised "indoctrination worthy of a camp … in Afghanistan or Pakistan." In the court case that followed, the issue was framed as pitting the right not to be defamed against the right to free speech. Adrian shows how the rhetoric of the defence of free speech invigorated an "us" versus "them" perspective. In the last section of the chapter she analyses scholarly counter-narratives, showing that no one spoke up in the press to offer a more academically informed and nuanced vision of Muslims in Canada and Quebec. Adrian thoughtfully demonstrates that the case and its lack of systematic analysis further ingrained a negative image of Islam in the Canadian public imaginary, forming part of what we "know" about Muslims in Canada.

In her chapter entitled "2(B) or Not 2(B): The Expressive Value of the Niqab," Natasha Bakht makes a case for researchers and the larger public to approach the rights of women who wear hijab or niqab not solely as a right to religious freedom and/or equality (i.e., section 2a of the Canadian Charter of Rights and Freedoms) but also as a right to freedom of expression (as captured in section 2b). For her, an approach that considers freedom of expression can also be translated into academic knowledge production. Bakht argues that scholars can and should engage with "the full array of these women's experiences" to better capture the complexity of their ways of being in a manner that current legislation ignores. This broadening, she shows, can "reframe our understanding of Muslim women and better serve our relations with them" both within and beyond the academy.

In the next chapter, Parin Dossa encourages researchers to consider storytelling when studying and writing about Canadian Muslims. Drawing theoretically on this genre, Dossa captures how her first-generation racialized women interlocutors remake their homes in British Columbia and reimagine their relationships to Islam. As she insightfully argues, thinking through their everyday narratives allows her to effectively interrogate politicized boundaries between nation states and how these influence the everyday lives of her participants.

This section concludes with an interview by Sara Hamed with Katherine Bullock, a scholar, activist, and community leader in the Greater Toronto Area. Bullock reflects on her academic work and the complexities of juggling academia and activism. Bullock discusses how wearing different hats has offered unique opportunities to dispel myths and negative stereotypes related to Islam(s) and Muslims in Canada, especially those related to Muslim women. In fact, Bullock notes how one of the driving forces behind her decision to establish the Tessellate Institute, a national independent not-for-profit research institute, was precisely to produce rigorous and "academically sound material" for individuals and groups outside of academia (e.g., policymakers, journalists) on Islam and Muslims in Canada.

Last, we thank Amir Hussain for generously introducing the volume and situating it in relation to pioneering scholars of Islam and Muslims in Canada, namely Wilfred Cantwell Smith (1916–2000). Hussain also recalls his own journey as a young scholar working on Canadian Muslims in the late 1980s, and how small and connected the field in Canada and the United States was at the time. He generously concludes by noting that *Producing Islam(s)* "carries on the legacy of those [we note, including Hussain himself] who helped to pave the way."

NOTES

1 We thank the Social Sciences and Humanities Research Council of Canada for their support of this work through a Connections Grant. We also thank the Centre for the Study of Islam, the Faculty of Public Affairs, and the Department of Law and Legal Studies at Carleton University, the Department of Religious Studies and the Vice-President Academic's Scholarship in the Arts fund at Memorial University, York University's Department of Social Science, York University Faculty of Liberal Arts & Professional Studies, the Religion and Diversity Project at the University of Ottawa, and the Canada Research Chair in Religion, Pluralism, and the Rule of Law at the University of Toronto for their support.

2 We worked hard to include non-scholarly voices in our deliberations, and concluded the workshop with a roundtable to which policymakers, journalists, local imams, and Muslim leaders were invited to share in a discussion on Islam(s) and Muslims in

Canada. Carleton University was an ideal spot for our meeting, not only because of its Centre for the Study of Islam run by Karim, but for the number of government individuals who could attend a two-hour gathering. We envisioned this public gathering as a preliminary peer and community review of our collective findings. We also thought of it as a bridging and networking moment to connect individuals who study, engage with, or practise Islam in Canada.

Despite our best intentions and efforts, we found it difficult to connect substantively and we feel that we were largely unsuccessful in relaying the central stakes in the cases or gathering feedback. In part, the challenge may have been because, in an effort to not overburden invited roundtable participants, we did not send them the case studies beforehand. Instead, four scholar-participants (Beaman, Bakht, Emon, and Amarasingam) from the workshop presented overviews of the cases and key points of discussion. Alternatively, the implicit power dynamics (that of a group of academics, even if of different ranks, presenting academic-based ideas in an academic venue) may have played a role.

3 Podcasts related to these cases are available online: *Producing Islams in Canada* [Audio podcast], Memorial University, Department of Religious Studies, https://www.mun.ca/relstudies/more/producingislams/podcasts.php.

4 The bibliography is available online: "Bibliography Project," Memorial University, Department of Religious Studies, http://www.mun.ca/relstudies/more/producingislams/biblio.php. While we aim to include all the literature to date, there are surely omissions. Please get in touch through the website with any missing work.

5 A number of these questions have been publicly debated among scholars, as with Aaron Hughes's 2015 book on the insider/outsider question and what he calls a "crisis" in the study of Islam (see also Rippin 2012; Tite 2014; Zempi and Awan 2017, who have taken up these questions).

6 We thank Rafaa Chehoudi for his able assistance in creating these graphs.

7 The combined bibliography is a work in progress, updated biannually (see https://www.mun.ca/relstudies/more/producingislams/biblio.php). Our quantitative analysis is too large to be shared in this chapter; readers are encouraged to contact Selby for enquiries on how we chose to code the literature.

REFERENCES

Abu-Lughod, Lila. 2001. "Orientalism and Middle East feminist studies." *Feminist Studies*, *27*(1), 101–15. https://doi.org/10.2307/3178451

Adrian, Melanie. 2016. *Religious freedom at risk: The EU, French schools and why the veil was banned*. Springer.

Ahmed, Shahab. 2015. *What is Islam? The importance of being Islamic*. Princeton University Press.

Amiraux, Valérie. 2012. "État de la littérature: L'islam et les musulmans en Europe; Un objet périphérique converti en incontournable des sciences sociales." *Critique International*, *56*, 141–57. https://doi.org/10.3917/crii.056.0141

Amir-Moazami, Schirin. 2016, 18 April. "Secular power and the predicaments of knowledge production on Muslims in Europe." *TRAFO – Blog for Transregional Research.* https://trafo.hypotheses.org/3980

Anidjar, Gil. 2006. "Secularism." *Critical Inquiry, 33*(1), 52–77. https://doi.org/10.1086/509746

Asad, Talal. 1986. *The idea of an anthropology of Islam.* Center for Contemporary Arab Studies. https://www.jstor.org/stable/20685738

– 1994. "Ethnographic representation, statistics, and modern power." *Social Research, 61*(1), 55–88. https://www-proquest-com.qe2a-proxy.mun.ca/scholarly-journals/ethnographic-representation-statistics-modern/docview/1297287483/se-2?accountid=12378

– 2003. *Formations of the secular: Christianity, Islam, Modernity.* Stanford University Press.

Barras, Amélie. 2016. "Exploring the intricacies and dissonances of religious governance: The case of Quebec and the discourse of request." *Critical Research on Religion, 4*(1), 57–71. https://doi.org/10.1177%2F2050303216630066

Beaman, Lori G. 2010. "Is religious freedom impossible in Canada?" *Law, Culture and the Humanities, 6*(3), 1–19. http://dx.doi.org/10.1177/1743872110366653

Bell, Catherine. 1996. "Modernism and postmodernism in the study of religion." *Religious Studies Review, 22*, 179–90. https://doi.org/10.1111/j.1748-0922.1996.tb00309.x

Bouchard, Gérard, and Charles Taylor. 2008. *Building the future: A time for reconciliation.* Quebec Commission de Consultation sur les Pratiques d'Accommodement Reliées aux Differences Culturelles. http://collections.banq.qc.ca/ark:/52327/bs1565996

Coutin, Susan Bibler, and Susan F. Hirsch. 1998. "Naming resistance: Ethnographers, dissidents, and states." *Anthropological Quarterly, 71*(1), 1–17. https://doi.org/10.2307/3317600

Deeb, Lara, and Jessica Winegar. 2015. *Anthropology's politics: Disciplining the Middle East.* Stanford University Press.

el-Zein, Abdul Hamid. 1977. "Beyond ideology and theology: The search for the anthropology of Islam." *Annual Review of Anthropology, 6*, 227–54. https://doi.org/10.1146/annurev.an.06.100177.001303

Eid, Paul. 2007. *Being Arab: Ethnic and religious identity building among second generation youth in Montreal.* McGill-Queen's University Press.

Fadil, Nadia. 2011. "Not-/Unveiling as an ethical practice." *Feminist Review, 98*, 83–109. https://doi.org/10.1057%2Ffr.2011.12

Hughes, Aaron W. 2015. *Islam and the tyranny of authenticity: An inquiry into disciplinary apologetics and self-deception.* Equinox.

Hussain, Asaf. 1984. "The ideology of Orientalism." In Asaf Hussain, Robert Olson, and Jamil Qureshi (Eds.), *Orientalism, Islam and Islamists* (pp. 5–22). Amana Books.

Keane, Webb. 2007. *Christian moderns: Freedom and fetish in the mission encounter.* University of California Press.

Korteweg, Anna C., and Jennifer A. Selby (Eds.). 2012. *Debating sharia: Islam, gender politics, and family law arbitration*. University of Toronto Press.

Mahmood, Saba. 2009. "Religious reason and secular affect: An incommensurable divide?" In Talal Asad, Wendy Brown, Judith Butler, and Saba Mahmood, *Is critique secular? Blasphemy, injury and free speech* (pp. 836–62). The Townsend Papers in the Humanities No. 2. University of California Press. https://www.jstor.org/stable/10.1086/599592

Masud, Muhammad Khalid, and Armando Salvatore. 2009. "Western scholars of Islam on the issue of modernity." In Muhammad Khalid Masud, Armando Salvatore, and Martin van Bruinessen (Eds.), *Islam and modernity: Key issues and debates* (pp. 36–53). Edinburgh University Press.

McCutcheon, Russell T. (Ed.). 1999. *The insider/outsider problem in the study of religion: A reader.* Cassell.

Public Safety Canada. 2016. "2016 public report on the terrorist threat to Canada." http://s3.documentcloud.org/documents/3034556/2016-Report-on-the-Terrorist-Threat-to-Canada.pdf

R. v. N.S., Supreme Court of Canada, SCR 726 (2012, 20 December).

Rippin, Andrew. 2012. "Provocation and its responses." *Method & Theory in the Study of Religion, 24*(4–5), 408–17. https://doi.org/10.1163/15700682-12341247

Said, Edward. 1978. *Orientalism*. Vintage Books.

Schielke, Samuli, and Liza Debevec. 2012. "Introduction." In Samuli Schielke and Liza Debevec (Eds.), *Ordinary lives and grand schemes: An anthropology of everyday religion* (pp. 1–16). Berghahn.

Selby, Jennifer A., Amélie Barras, and Lori G. Beaman. 2018. *Beyond accommodation: Everyday narratives of Muslim Canadians*. University of British Columbia Press.

Smith, Jonathan Z. 1982. *Imagining religion: From Babylon to Jonestown*. University of Chicago Press.

Sullivan, Winnifred Fallers, Elizabeth Shakman Hurd, Saba Mahmood, and Peter G. Danchin (Eds.). 2015. *Politics of religious freedom*. University of Chicago Press.

Tite, Philip. 2014. "Debating a discipline, contesting identities, and the future of Islamic studies." *Bulletin for the Study of Religion, 43*(4), 1–2. https://dx.doi.org/10.1558/bsor.v43i4.1

Wilkins-Laflamme, Sarah. 2018. "Islamophobia in Canada: Measuring the Realities of Negative Attitudes Toward Muslims and Religious Discrimination." *Canadian Review of Sociology, 55*(1), 86–110. https://doi.org/10.1111/cars.12180

Yegenoglu, Meyda. 1998. *Colonial Fantasies.* Cambridge University Press.

Zempi, Irene, and Imran Awan. 2017. "Doing 'dangerous' autoethnography on Islamophobic victimization." *Ethnography, 18*(3), 367–86. https://doi.org/10.1177%2F1466138117697996

Zine, Jasmin. 2012. "Introduction: Muslim cultural politics in the Canadian hinterlands." In Jasmin Zine (Ed.), *Islam in the hinterlands: Muslim cultural politics in Canada* (pp. 1–38). University of British Columbia Press.

SECTION 1

Examining Knowledge Production on Islam

Epistemologies of the "Muslim Question" in Europe: On the Politics of Knowledge Production in a Minefield

SCHIRIN AMIR-MOAZAMI

Introduction

The "Muslim question," as formulated by political theorist Salman Sayyid (2014), "refers to a series of interrogations and speculations in which Islam and/or Muslims exist as a difficulty that needs to be addressed. Thus, the Muslim question is a mode of enquiry that opens a space for interventions: cultural, governmental and epistemological" (3). If taken seriously, Sayyid's claim about cultural, governmental, and epistemological interventions raises questions about the connections between these spheres. In this chapter I will expand on Sayyid's claim, discussing the issue of "producing Islams" by enquiring into the nexus of knowledge and/as power, which Sayyid also alludes to in passing.

In doing so, I line up with the recent scholarship on Islam in Europe which has begun to analyse the complexities of power involved in producing Muslim subjectivities beyond discipline, repression, or segregation, as most prominently revealed in the paradigm of integration (Amir-Moazami 2011; Fadil 2009; Fernando 2014; Mas 2006; Peter 2008; Tezcan 2012). By focusing on epistemologies, however, I push these works further in two ways. First, I focus more explicitly on the nexus of knowledge and power, and second, I suggest a different temporality: The starting point for the emergence of a Muslim question in the European context (as articulated by Sayyid) is habitually linked to 9/11, and the production of Muslims as a suspicious religious community is then interpreted as an effect of global terror and the ways terrorism has been discursively framed (Bigo 2002; Bigo and Tsoukala 2008; Morsi 2017). I would not deny that terrorism in the name of Islam has, indeed, increased the discursive incitement on Muslims and animated different kinds of interventions into Muslim milieux. The analysis, however, remains ahistorical if the contemporary Muslim question is understood as effected merely by recent processes of securitization or post-war migration. The focus on epistemologies, I claim, can help us redirect our attention to the historicity of the contemporary Muslim question.

I even argue that the production of knowledge about Muslims (i.e., also the production of Islam in Europe) brings to the forefront ingrained epistemological practices predicated on older paradigms of regulation of religious minorities in a nation-state framework and on what Walter M. Mignolo (2009) called the "colonial matrix of power."

At the same time, when trying to understand the contemporary Muslim question in Europe as rooted in longer-term epistemologies, I do not suggest a stable, abstract, or disembodied notion of epistemology. I am instead guided by Foucault's understanding of epistemologies as *practices*, enabled and enacted by particular political, social, and economic circumstances (Foucault 1979/2006, 15). The question is therefore why and under which conditions certain epistemological practices (i.e., practices of knowledge production and their underlying assumptions about what counts as proper and legitimate knowledge) are more prevalent than others.[1] Because epistemologies are neither stable nor abstract, their grammar necessarily changes over time and according to political conditions. Therefore, I am not able to systematically tackle the relationship between continuities and breaks in the production of knowledge on Muslims in Europe. A closer look at the epistemological practices of knowledge production on Muslims in contemporary Europe could, however, trace a tentative path to thinking genealogically through the power/knowledge nexus inscribed in today's Muslim question in Europe.

This chapter cannot offer a detailed account of the sweeping variety of formats, methodologies, and disciplines involved in the production of knowledge on Muslims in Europe. Instead, I formulate a few points of departure that are meant to denaturalize those epistemological practices, which have become normal and habitualized to the extent that the epistemic violence they might cause tends to be opaque. My analysis is structured by the argument that the assumptions about what counts as proper knowledge in this field are intimately bound by assumptions about what counts as proper religion – bracketed by a secular matrix.

Surveying and Surveilling Normality and Deviance

Throughout Europe over the past two decades, Muslims have often been framed as having gradually become "visible."[2] Moreover, 9/11 and other terrorist attacks in the name of Islam globally have encouraged all kinds of actors to investigate and prevent the causes of Islamic radicalization. The increased use of survey data on Muslim social life and religious practices in most European countries with sizeable numbers of Muslims is related exactly to this momentum (Johansen and Spielhaus 2012). However, the topics of these investigations have gradually expanded to encompass all spheres of life. Survey questions addressed to Muslims range from routines of religious practices in daily life, through questions of gender and sexuality, to Muslims' attitudes towards liberal and/or democratic orders. There is very little that escapes the statistical view.

Take, for example, the commissioned studies of the Deutsche Islam Konferenz (DIK n.d.), a state-initiated integration measure directed exclusively towards Muslims.[3] One of the most immediate conclusions drawn from the first encounters at the DIK in 2006 was that Germany needed "reliable data" on Muslim forms of social life and religious practices. Many of these studies have thus been praised for providing representative data, and their numbers regularly circulate in the German public sphere. What qualifies these studies is their broad experience in quantitative data gathering – and rarely any expertise on Islam. Moreover, while many of the survey studies spend a lot of time explaining the strengths of the methods they apply, they often say very little about how the categories of measurement came about. Additionally, they remain entirely silent once it comes to normative and epistemological presumptions, not to mention questions of positionality. The legitimacy and authority of this research, on the contrary, depend to a large degree on the claim to generalizable knowledge, universalizable theories, and categories abstracted from concrete political contexts. They also depend on the invisibility of the researcher who fulfils the request to provide objective data, independent from their own presuppositions and sensibilities. The depiction of the findings in curves and pie charts turns them into easily consumable small packages. The analytical tools, in contrast, remain rather weak.

The example of the often-quoted study *Muslimisches Leben in Deutschland* (Brettfeld and Wetzels 2007; for a critical analysis see Dornhof 2009)[4] from Germany is telling in this regard. Its central rationale was to measure Muslims' degrees of religiosity and to correlate these with their degrees of integration into German society. The interviewees were asked to respond on a scale from 1 to 6 if they agree or disagree with predefined statements such as "Foreigners should keep their culture" (Brettfeld and Wetzels 2007, 155); "Different ethnic groups should be separated from each other to avoid conflicts" (154); "I believe that the Qur'an is the true revelation of God" (117); "Islam is the only true religion" (250); "Islam is the only religion which can solve the problem of our times" (250); and "In Western societies the sexual morality is corrupted" (380). Depending on the answers, the study classified Muslims' religiosity into categories like "orthodox religious," "strongly religious," "remotely religious," "fundamentalist," or "traditional-conservative."

Similarly, the study of the Wissenschaftszentrum Berlin, funded by the European Commission, compared degrees of "religious fundamentalism" among Muslims and Christians in six European countries.[5] The commission and study coordinator, Ruud Koopmans, regularly appears in the media and is not hesitant to publicly claim that "46% of Muslims across Europe are fundamentalists" (Astheimer 2016), given that the interviewees agreed with statements like

"Muslims should return to the roots of Islam," "The West as an enemy is out to destroy Islam," or "I don't want homosexual friends" (Koopmans 2015). The productive force of allegedly distant representation in such studies consists in the act of contouring a Muslim subject into a countable unity, and it consists in the act of constituting and replicating an unmarked national entity, which is mostly characterized by empty signifiers like equality, democracy, freedom, or secularity, to which Muslims are asked to respond in scales or compact answers.

In their pioneering and detailed analysis of quantitative data gathering on Muslims in different European countries, Birgitte Johansen and Riem Spielhaus (2012) come to three conclusions relevant to my own argument: First, both independent academic and politically commissioned studies are centrally driven by the same topics which also preoccupy political authorities – most notably radicalization, security, and integration. Second, the authors observe a frequent equation of Muslims and immigrants and hence a naturalized conflation between ethnicity, descent, and religion (see also Brubaker 2012; Tezcan 2012). Third, the framework in which Muslims are interrogated in these surveys is almost unanimously the nation state. Johansen and Spielhaus (2012) convincingly discuss their criticism of the categories used in most of these studies. They also remind us of the productive force involved in turning Muslims into a quantifiable and manageable religious community.

In what follows, I push Johansen and Spielhaus's (2012) analysis further, arguing that the practice of measuring normality and deviance is predicated on a deeper-rooted epistemic framework which has gained new salience in relation to today's Muslim question. Taking up Johansen and Spielhaus's critique of the equation of ethnicity and religion, I argue finally that it is necessary to look at the co-constitutive nature of modern categories of race and religion, which exceed specific methodologies beyond the quantification of Muslims in Europe.

Measuring Populations, Viewing from Nowhere

While the call for "objective" and "representative" data on Muslims in Europe is part of broader mechanisms of securitization and surveillance, its epistemological underpinnings need to be related to the rise of statistics as a means to measure and govern populations and sub-populations both inside and outside of nation-state borders. To start with, I recall Ian Hacking's work on statistics, the rise of quantitative sociology and probability. Hacking points to the intimate relationship between what is often called "reliable," "representative," "objective" data and policy aims and the productive force of numbers: "New slots were created in which to fit and enumerate people. Even national and provincial censuses amazingly show that the categories into which people fall change every ten years. Social change creates new categories of people, but the counting is no mere report of developments. It elaborately, often philanthropically, *creates* new ways for people to be" (Hacking 2002, 100).

In his attempt to relate Hacking's observations to the imperial legacy of anthropological research, Talal Asad points more explicitly to the connection between the emergence of modern nation states and the centralization of national statistics:

> They constitute social wholes that do not depend logically either on the intimate experience of a given region or on the assumption of typical social actors. They encourage and respond to individualized agents making individual choices in a variety of social situations. Ways of statistical calculation, representation, and intervention have become so pervasive that capitalist social economies and liberal democratic politics are inconceivable without them. (Asad 1994a, 74)

Both Hacking's and Asad's reflections are all the more important for my argument as they emphasize that the counting of populations has never been a generic act but has since its inception been coupled with divisions and hierarchizations of differences within populations. It is no coincidence that the success of taxonomic methods was paralleled by the success of modern theories of racial differences (Supik 2014, 55–60). It therefore needs to be connected to the realm of national and imperial politics and its related tools of measuring, counting, and thereby categorizing people into civilized and less civilized, that is, "backward," units of analysis.

The flourishing of statistics on Jewish life and conduct at the end of the nineteenth and beginning of the twentieth century in Germany succinctly illustrates such connections. This case also shows that the belief in the truth of numbers was to a large extent pushed by Jewish scientists themselves. For example, Arthur Cohen, one of the founding fathers of the Verein für Jüdische Statistik (Association for Jewish Statistics) in 1914, stated with enthusiasm, "Statistics bring rhythm, proportion and order into the diversity of social appearances: They line up in file and become only a number of the social group to which they belong" (Cohen, quoted in Diner 2014, 584). In his entry on Jewish statistics, Dan Diner (2014) observes that statistical measurement also transformed the scales of causal explanations:

> Statistically driven interpretations marginalized, for example, questions related to the morality of individuals, and instead social factors and anatomy as well as biological criteria of race became dominant research features. Both adherents of the Zionist movement and their Jewish opponents willing to assimilate attributed strong relevance to statistics. The central question for both was the hypothesis of degeneration in the turn of the century; all kinds of data about birth and death rates, the spread of certain diseases, and the number of suicides were consulted in this debate. (Diner 2014, 583; my translation from German)

By trying to counter the negative findings about their inability to assimilate into "German culture" with "objective facts," Jewish academics were thus trapped in the game of counting and measuring culture and religion, normality, and deviance with the same methodological framework. This example pertinently reveals the relationships between modern institutions, techniques of knowledge production, and national projects. The regulative instruments of the nation-state framework are thus structurally bound to instruments of scientifically inspecting, regulating, and hence producing minorities as dividable units of analysis who are assigned either conformity to or deviance from an unmarked norm.

Recalling these historical antecedents is crucial, as they mark the beginning of a paradox which has not yet been resolved, despite the institutionalization of liberal freedoms. Elaborating on the gardening, engineering, and ordering forces of modernity, social theorist Zygmunt Bauman (1991) compellingly analyses this paradox in his chapters on the assimilative force of modern nation states (chap. 4 and 5). It is not accidental that the notion of assimilation first appeared in the newly developed science of biology (see also Lettow 2014) and originally meant the absorption of one element by another. Its meaning gradually moved from the realm of plants and organic substances to the realm of the human. Bauman (1991) also complicates the often-made dichotomy between nationalist and liberal versions of the project of assimilation: "What made the standing invitation particularly alluring and morally disarming was the fact that it came in the disguise of benevolence and tolerance, indeed, the assimilatory project went down in history as a part of the liberal political program, of the tolerant and enlightened stance that exemplified all the most endearing traits of a 'civilized state'" (107).

Through the example of Jewish assimilation in nineteenth-century Germany, Bauman (1991) shows that assimilation was ultimately an unreachable goal, for the measurement of assimilation by the established national elite remained a shifting vantage point:

> The assimilating Jews acted under the pressure to prove their Germanhood, yet the very attempt to prove it was held against them as the evidence of their duplicity and, in all probability, also of subversive intentions. The circle was bound to remain vicious, for the simple reason that the values to which the Jews were told to surrender in order to earn acceptance were the very values which rendered acceptance impossible (121).

Assimilation therefore needs to be understood as a functional mechanism of the modern nation state: the instruments of its scientific measurement with modern techniques of knowledge production, its necessary consequence. This of course does not reveal to what extent the paradox of assimilation is reconfigured in new ways in the politics of integration. What is certain, however, is that integration has become the leading paradigm which currently guides the politics of coming to terms with cultural and religious plurality across Europe. Integration has also been praised as an antidote after multiculturalism received its death sentence before being carefully thought through (Amir-Moazami 2005; Lentin and Titley 2011).[6] Whatever its concrete implications are (and they are wide in range), it is undisputable that the paradigm of integration is also bound to unspecific and shifting criteria (Castro Verela 2013; Hess, Binder, and Moser 2009). Integration remains an ambivalent goal, even if it is not about ambitions to squeeze minorities into a "national culture" but is articulated in universal principles like democracy, liberty, and equality, whose content can be stretched to the extent that they turn into empty signifiers. Consequently, the notion of the "integrated Muslim" (often accompanied by other attributes like liberal, secular, enlightened, etc.) does not overcome the recurrent interpellation of Muslims as "exceptional citizens" (Amir-Moazami 2016b; Fernando 2009; Topolski 2017).

If we take this paradox seriously, we have to be attentive to the epistemological underpinnings of positivistic methodologies and their regimes of truth, rather than primarily focusing on the conclusions themselves. Even if it matters politically, if the numbers confirm or contest the compatibility or incompatibility between Islamic and liberal norms, we need to question the regime of truth (Foucault 1979/2006, 62) which scientifically reifies these norms.[7] In the case of the statistical measurement of Muslim forms of social life and religious practice, we need to raise questions about the functions of measuring, and we need to ask why research of the social by numbers – "the strongest language of all" (Asad 1994a, 78) – has so stubbornly survived despite postmodern, post-structuralist, and postcolonial critique (see Steinmetz 2005, 4). A first, even if insufficient, answer could be that objectivist and realist truth claims are often detached from the subjective and historical context within which research is located. Relations of power and the unavoidable entwinement of research and politics can, in other words, more easily be concealed with reference to "scientific autonomy" or "objectivity." Paradoxically, the more politicized the field gets, the stronger the claims to objectivism and realism are voiced.

Objectifying and Governing: The Geo- and Body-Politics of Antiseptic Research

To gain a better understanding of the connection between the often-praised virtue of objectivism and the will to knowledge and power, it is important again to distance ourselves from the immediate present and from the concrete research field in question. The authority of ontological divisions between the knowing subject and an object of research conceived of as a "thing" to be approached independently from the viewer has a long history in Enlightenment philosophy. Its genealogy, its point of departure in natural sciences, and its unquestioned transition into the humanities and social sciences have been interrogated at length from different perspectives (Espeland and Stevens 2008; Feyerabend 1975/2010; Foucault 1982; Gadamer 1960/1990; Hacking 1975/2006; Haraway 1988; Hindess 1977).

The assumption that Muslims could be studied as if they were a unified and passive object reveals Donna Haraway's (1988) feminist critique of the "view from nowhere." Haraway, more specifically, analyses how this view from nowhere is predicated on epistemologies and politics of visibility and transparency. Inscribed in these is a correlation between seeing and not-being-seen, which provides authority to the knowing and seeing subject, whose own subjectivity lies outside of their scope because it is merged into objectified and standardized methods.

The examination of certain populations in their most intimate spheres of life actualizes what Haraway calls the "leap out of the marked body into the conquering gaze from nowhere. A gaze which inscribes all marked bodies, that makes the unmarked category claim the power to see and not to be seen, to represent, while escaping representation" (Haraway 1988, 581). The abstract viewer, entitled to gaze at the other, is thus turned invisible precisely through exposing and marking the other as different and particular.

Haraway's elaborations are especially interesting if we take the relationship between the marked body and the unmarked gaze from nowhere as a vantage point to think about the bodily dimensions of knowledge production on Muslims in Europe. I claim that it is no coincidence that Muslim bodily practices have been so obsessively discussed by political and legal authorities, by the media, and increasingly by researchers – such as veiling, praying, or more recently, male circumcision. These bodily practices are not so much scrutinized because they unexpectedly render Muslim bodies visible in European public spheres (Göle and Amman 2004) or because they transgress inscribed and largely embodied ideals of privatized, invisible religiosity. Rather, the excessive interest in the body of the other also needs to be read as based on an inscribed epistemic scheme which *requires* the other's body to sustain or reconfigure a specific regime of truth: the abstract viewer from nowhere necessitates a Cartesian mind-body split, in which the mind – as the seeing and unseen gaze – is detached from the sensorial realm, from the body, and from concrete experience to claim disembodied universality.

As postcolonial theorists have extensively shown, the panoptic view from nowhere has, since its inception, been coupled with a geopolitical division of the world into what Walter M. Mignolo (2009) called the *humanitas* and the *anthropos*. These metaphors refer to the distinction between the allegedly disembodied and universal mind and the particular, tribal, exotic, or endangering body. While the first is the unmarked knowing mind that determines the conditions of how to properly know from the privileges of a particular geographical location (Europe, North America, or currently the Global North), the second represents the to-be-inspected and to-be-told body (the Orient, Asia, Africa, South America, or currently the Global South). *Humanitas* and *anthropos* are thus intimately bound by the relationship between geopolitics and body-politics of knowledge, which have been institutionalized through the colonial matrix of power, or as Mignolo (2009) puts it, through "a racial system of social classification that invented Occidentalism ... , that created the conditions for Orientalism; distinguished the South of Europe from its center ... and, on the long history, remapped the world as first, second, and third during the Cold War" (161). Islamic bodily practices are also extensively inspected throughout Europe because this very body-mind split is predicated on what we could call "secular embodiments" (Amir-Moazami 2016a; Hirschkind 2011) – the paradoxical claim to a disembodied view from nowhere and embodied social conventions, sensibilities, and affects which feed into the state regulation of religious practices.

It is not accidental that Mignolo couples his elaborations on the geopolitical and body-political divisions of the world into *humanitas* and *anthropos* by reminding us that its framework has moved from a Christian theology to a secular episteme (Mignolo 2009, 176). Mignolo thus raises the central question as to how and why Eurocentric epistemologies managed to conceal their own geohistorical and biographical locations and succeeded to create the idea of universal knowledge based on the assumption of the universal knowing subject:

> By locating knowledge in the mind only, and bracketing "secondary qualities" (affects, emotions, desires, anger, humiliation, etc.), social actors who happened to be white, inhabiting Europe/Western Christendom and speaking specific languages assumed that what was right for them in that place and which fulfilled their affects, emotions, fears and angers was indeed valid for the rest of the planet and, consequently, that they were the depositor, warrantor, creator and distributor of universal knowledge. In the process of globally enacting the European system of belief and structure of knowledge, human beings who were not Christian did not inhabit the memories of Europe, from Greece through Rome, were not familiar with the six modern imperial European languages and, frankly, did not care much about all of that until they realized that they were expected and requested to submit to the European (and in the twentieth century to the United States also) knowledge, belief, life style and world view. (Mignolo 2009, 177)

It would definitely be simplistic to claim that the epistemic framework described by Mignolo has univocally and coherently persisted from its emergence with the colonial matrix of power until today. The contemporary production of knowledge on Muslims in Europe contains different and additional dynamics of entanglements between *humanitas* and *anthropos*, not the least as a result of labour and postcolonial migration, which have increased encounters. The power relations between minorities and established majorities, moreover, have become much subtler with the consolidation of liberal freedoms within Western European societies than at the inception of an expanding nation-state framework, which Bauman or Mignolo refer to in different ways. The present situation is different too, because the scientific justification of Western hegemony has been substantially contested. The *anthropos* has started to resist being merely the object of study, to be confined to an epistemic framework, to be moulded by someone else and hence disobeying, to be ranked in relation to the ideals of *humanitas* (cf. Mignolo 2009, 161). Bold distinctions and hierarchizations between cultures, races, or religions are not easily justifiable any longer. The nexus of power and knowledge is thus not solely animated by the will to domination, degradation, paternalism, or hierarchy.

Despite these obvious shifts, there are persisting epistemic silences which a geo- and body-political order of knowledge production has enabled and institutionalized. Or, as Mignolo (2009) puts it, despite resistances to the divisions into *humanitas* and *anthropos*, "since the 16th century from all over the globe, imperial theo- and ego-politics of knowledge managed to prevail through economically sustained institutions (universities, museums, delegations, state officers, armies, etc.)" (177). What has thus predominated is a specific mechanism of investigating external or internal others in their difference or similarity on the grounds of a constantly shifting scale and hence a mechanism of marking and unmarking.

For our field of investigation, the epistemic silences and the related reactivation and naturalization of the "view from nowhere," which this scheme reproduces, consist particularly in normative assumptions about what religion is or should be. I tentatively suggest that these assumptions are predicated on what Luca Mavelli (2012) calls the "secular episteme" on the one hand and ingrained entanglements of modern categories of race and religion on the other. In the last section of this chapter, I therefore return to Johansen and Spielhaus's (2012) concern about the classification of Muslims along ethnic lines and delve more deeply into the epistemic framework which animates such equations. This epistemic framework expands particular methodologies such as statistical data gathering on Muslims in Europe. Incidentally, qualitative methodologies are not immune from positivist assumptions, even if they differ from standardized methods because they are often based on personal encounters.[8]

On the Entanglements between Race and Religion as Modern Categories of Knowledge

When addressing the problematic production of Islam and Muslims in Europe as a religious and racialized minority, it is necessary to always ask which notion of religion underpins knowledge production. The answers will definitely be broad and partly contradictory. The question is crucial, however, because these understandings ultimately matter for the results but also because they are constitutive for the backbone of the questions addressed. We should be alert, for example, if key categories moulded by disciplines like sociology of religion or religious studies – such as individualization, privatization, functional differentiation, secularization, heterodoxy, orthodoxy, orthopraxy, etc. – constitute the unquestioned framework to study Muslim forms of religiosity in Europe (Amir-Moazami and Salvatore 2003; Asad 1986), even if these forms are, of course, shaped by the respective societies. This conceptual repertoire, deriving from a Christian legacy, is inscribed into the canon of various disciplines and informs the production of knowledge regarding Muslims and Islam in Europe, though often tacitly (Amir-Moazami 2018). It is then not surprising that Muslims are typologized into registers of "strictly religious," "traditionalist," "orthodox," or "fundamentalist," once they claim that Islam structures their daily lives or that they meticulously try to follow each and every Islamic duty.

To better understand the very practice of squeezing religion into a clear-cut category, it is important to interrogate the archives of the sociology of religion and religious studies (including Islamic studies) about the racist and Orientalist baggage they carry (Boatcă 2013; Salvatore 1999; Turner 1974; Zimmermann 2013).[9] We also have to ask more substantially why and how the entitlement to understand religion in terms of a compact and clearly definable notion has so doggedly survived, even though its epistemological repertoire as predominantly based on Christian experiences has been criticized from various angles (Asad 1993; Bergunder 2011; Salvatore 1999). In an interview on the twentieth anniversary of his book *Genealogies of Religion* (1993), Talal Asad (2014) sharply illuminates some of the problems emerging from pre-constituted and predefined notions of religion:

> I argued that to define "religion" is to circumscribe certain things (times, spaces, powers, knowledges, beliefs, behaviors, texts, songs, images) as essential to "religion," and other things as accidental. This identifying work of what belongs to a definition isn't done as a consequence of the same experience – the things themselves are diverse, and the way people react to them or use them is very different. Put it this way: when they are identified by the concept "religion," it is because they are seen to be significantly similar; what makes them similar is not a singular experience common to all the things the concept brings together (sacrality, divinity, spirituality, transcendence, etc.); what makes them similar is the definition itself that persuades us, through what Wittgenstein called a "captivating picture," that there is an essence underlying them all – in all instances of "religion." (12)

The unquestioned universalization of modern concepts of religion is particularly problematic if these specifically Christian experiences with all their historical entanglements remain outside of the analysis (Ahmed 2016; Asad 1986,

2003). Scholars like Gil Anidjar (2003, 2008), Tomoko Masuzawa (2005), and Theodore Vial (2016) have shown that a Christian legacy and its conveyance into conceptual tools have at no moment in history been moulded in isolation but always in correspondence with, or more frequently in demarcation from, other "world religions" or "world regions." Masuzawa (2005), for example, illustrates how the formation of modern disciplines like religious studies, sociology of religion, philology, or Oriental studies in the course of the nineteenth century were coupled with colonial and imperial projects.[10] The scientific study of religion, Masuzawa goes on, within the emerging European nation states was paralleled by the classification of other "world religions" into friends or – more often – enemies.[11]

More importantly, these classifications were largely inspired by the then-flourishing theories on human races and language groups. Scholars of the emerging discipline of religious studies scientifically proofed alliances between Christianity, Aryan, and certain Asian language groups (think of "Indo-European") and Buddhism (which turned from a philosophy into a "religion" in the modern sense). Under the aegis of the emerging disciplines of comparative religious studies and Oriental philology, Islam and Judaism, on the contrary, were classified as "Semitic religions," mired in ethnicity and based on rough and unrefined language systems. While Christianity and Buddhism were conceptualized as peaceful and universalizable world religions, Judaism and Islam were treated as being incapable to expand peacefully and to therefore qualify as truly worldly. Judaism either spread into a "diaspora" or became a "minority" and gradually a "race." Islam, in turn, was conceptualized as an expanding religion – yet one that had failed to internalize self-critique and the rules of enlightenment and hence was unable to become a "proper" world religion.

Again, we cannot simply draw a linear causality between the nineteenth century and today's knowledge production on Muslims in Europe. However, what is important to capture from such analyses is that the epistemological repertoire undergirding recurrent conceptualizations of Islam as violent, suspicious, or at least disproportionately orthodox has been moulded much earlier and quite independently from events like 9/11, which often serve as proofs for this very understanding. More importantly, it is surprising that the connections between race *and* religion as co-constitutive modern categories of classification often remain opaque while scholars continually express their discomfort about the recurrent processes of racialization of Muslims across Europe. If we want to understand the deeper ingrained mechanisms undergirding the interrogation of people with Islamic backgrounds as naturally Muslims, it is not enough to critique a racial regime which marks and hierarchizes minorities as inferior. We also need to interrogate religion as a concept that classifies and hierarchizes people not only along their "ethnic descent" but also along their beliefs and practices.[12]

Such investigations should not only be critical of the production of Muslims as disproportionately fundamentalist, excessively pious, or otherwise deviating from what is considered normal within European societies. Rather, an analysis of the epistemologies underpinning knowledge production on Muslims in Europe also needs to be attentive to the more benevolent gestures through which Muslims are incorporated into a liberal-secular order. We should, for example, be vigilant when political scientist Olivier Roy (2010) in his research on global Islam benignly declares that for the majority of Muslims, European Islam was "just one amongst many other markers of identity" and that Islam in Europe is therefore "turning into a religion, just a religion."[13] To become one religion among others, for Roy, means to transcend and internalize one's religious markings.

Similarly, the findings about processes of secularization or individualization of Islam in Europe (for a critique see Amir-Moazami and Salvatore 2003; Peter 2006) should be looked at with caution. Such analyses often read like counter-narratives to the dominant discourse, which focuses extensively on radical or, more recently, Salafi Muslims. Muslims in Europe are then declared to be able to secularize and individualize or freely choose their religiosity (see Babès 1997; Boubaker 2004; Klinkhammer 2000; Venel 1999).[14] Islam is turning into a religion proper, once it is immunized from problematic forms of communitarianism or excessive piety. It becomes compatible with a scientific understanding of religion and hence also with liberal sensibilities. Islamic practice then is considered mere belief, internalized and privatized; Islamic bodily rituals turn into "signs" which Muslims externalize in their search for identity.

Likewise, scholars concerned with racialization tend to call for an understanding of Muslims as not merely "religious" subjects but as citizens or individuals like anyone else with heterogeneous, dynamic, and partly contradictory identities (see Tezcan 2012). Even if this call is comprehensible and probably politically urgent at first glance, it is problematic at second. Such results ultimately tend to leave unaddressed the subtle techniques of power through which subjects are turned into "ordinary citizens." If we want to take the complex mechanisms of subjectification seriously, perpetuated also in research on Muslims in Europe, it is not enough to conjure happy hybrids, multiple identities, or secularized, individualized Muslims that are compatible with liberal norms. Especially if we take the aforementioned legacies of knowledge production on Islam within Europe into account, Muslims are already marked and constituted as subjects before they can freely choose or dispose of their identifications. Their religious practices, moreover, cannot always be grasped with a vocabulary deriving from liberal projects or secularized religion (Mahmood 2005).

Also, in such approaches to Muslims in Europe, Islamic practices are ultimately reduced to their legibility by emancipatory, liberal, or modern projects. Such analyses are thus complicit with liberal-secular sensibilities and unavoidably reproduce a conceptual repertoire whose own historicity they rarely reflect. The discomfort with essentializing the other is here replaced by their normalization (see Amir-Moazami and Salvatore 2003). Even if politically necessary, the attempt to normalize Muslims in Europe reproduces the inadequacy of an existing epistemic framework, instead of making it part of the investigation. Or as put by Mignolo (2009), "it is not enough to change the content of the conversation … , it is of the essence to change the *terms* of the conversation" (162).

While I fundamentally agree with Mignolo, in my view the terms of the conversation in the field of knowledge production on Islam in Europe are not yet sufficiently understood in order to be changed. More specifically, what is called the secular matrix has rarely been scrutinized in both its freedom-enacting and its norm-shaping powers in the context of the discursive production on Muslims in Europe, for it is this matrix that ultimately moulds the terms in which Muslims refer to and articulate their relationship to an Islamic discursive tradition. My last point is therefore that we cannot understand the predicaments of knowledge production in this field without also interrogating the secular as its operative matrix which pervades the will to knowledge, truth, and power.

When speaking about a secular matrix, I refer to a specific understanding of reason and science as having gradually been detached from and superseded transcendence and as having given rise to a specific notion of subjecthood as autonomous, self-contained, and detached from the transcendent (God).[15] The secular, however, also comprises the contingent regulative force of formally secular nation states under the rule of law to guard and determine the borders between the religious and the secular in public and thereby necessarily also in private (Agrama 2010; Asad 2003; Mahmood 2015).[16] This guarding and defining, even if contingent and dynamic, requires practices of denoting what falls under the rubric of religion. In this sense, the scientific ambitions to define religion are paralleled by secular orders which *have to* define religion in order to know what is to be embraced or contained. Finally, the secular needs to be understood as more tacit and often unmarked social conventions (i.e., embodied practices).[17] Precisely because of this largely habitualized and unmarked character, the embodied forms of secularism paradoxically sustain the assumptions about the disembodied "view from nowhere," operative in many paradigms undergirding knowledge production on Islam and Muslims in Europe and largely responsible for the kinds of questions that scholars both (re)produce and are caught in.

The powers of the secular matrix, thus understood, do not consist in formulating one singular and fixed norm about what religion is or should become. Rather they consist in its capacity of setting the framework of questions (remember Mignolo's "terms of the conversation") within which Muslims have to position themselves and whose own normative presumptions remain untouched:

Are Muslim forms of social life and religious practices compatible with secular lifestyles and sensibilities? Can Islam be reformed and tamed like Christianity? Where is the Islamic Luther? Are Islamic gender norms becoming egalitarian or do they remain oppressive?[18] As I showed, this set of questions condenses into the question which implicitly or explicitly also drives knowledge production on Islam in Europe: Can Muslims be integrated into European secular nation states? This very framework constantly gets re-enacted *through* the interrogation and inspection of Muslims as differing from or conforming to it. Accordingly, Islam is either an invasive force or it is disappearing; Muslims either assimilate and merge into a given national framework or they are framed in terms of radical alterity; in short, either Islam in Europe is becoming a religion proper or it remains outside of the European imagination. The assimilative forces of the nation state, in other words, finds a correspondence with the assimilative and universalizing epistemologies undergirding knowledge production, in which we as academics are often complicit.

Conclusions

The labour I programmatically suggest for further analyses of the epistemological genealogies of the "Muslim question" in Europe is threefold. On a general level, rethinking the one-sided focus on Muslims as a denotable object of research would imply to turn the gaze from the object to the context of research. By this shift I mean more than a critical examination of one's own positionality. It also implies to deal with the "effected history" (Gadamer 1960/1990, 305ff) in which one's knowledge is situated. This kind of historicization raises the question why and under which conditions a specific phenomenon has become a problem and a field of research at all.

More specifically, shifting the gaze implies marking and denaturalizing different stocks of knowledge production in this field. This would, of course, also imply disclosing more systematically the formation and reproduction of disciplinary divisions, which have – at least partly – institutionalized the practices of dividing the *humanitas* from the *anthropos*. We would need, for example, to look more systematically into the archives of social sciences and the related connections between empiricism and imperialism or neo-imperialism (Steinmetz 2005, 2015).

We could ask, for example, why and how disciplines surrounding so-called Oriental studies could survive until today, despite inherent problems (Marchand 2010; Masuzawa 2005; Said 1978), and why, in turn, disciplines like Christian or Occidental studies would be unthinkable in the centres of what has come to be called the Islamic world – at least in Mignolo's sense as *anthropos*. The elaboration of theories and concepts, furthermore, still takes place predominantly in the academic centres of the Global North. It still belongs to the privileges of the

"First World" to predefine the epistemic orders. The fact that Islam is predominantly studied under the rubric of a modern classificatory system of "religion," for example, alludes precisely to these privileges.

Finally, in order to change the terms of the conversation, it would be important to more carefully blend historical and contemporary analyses and to grasp the longer-term legacies of knowledge production on Muslims in Europe. Genealogically oriented analyses and practices of reflexivity would of course not prevent the dilemmas entailed in the production of knowledge on Islam in Europe. But they could at least strengthen awareness of existing asymmetric power structures to which also the uneven distribution of the resources of knowledge belongs.

NOTES

1 Reflecting on epistemological practices in the context of empire, Ann Laura Stoler (2008) alluded to the instability of epistemologies and emphasized that also in the colonial context, epistemologies did not have a pre-constituted architecture but were generated through the practice of categorization, classification, and hierarchization, in Stoler's case of human races. Stoler is interested in particular in the inconsistencies, instability, and contradiction which occur in the process of knowledge production.

2 This very framing is of course by no means innocent. The turn to a "visible minority" bears the question: visible in which terms, how, and for whom? Especially if we think of this in terms of a shift, the question arises how Muslims were *seen* before by those who now consider them as more visible than before.

3 For critical analyses of the DIK as a governmental technique see Amir-Moazami 2011; Peter 2008; Tezcan 2012.

4 The study was republished and revised two years later by Sonja Haug, Sephanie Müssig, and Anja Stichs (2009).

5 The scholars of this study depicted their "Muslim" and "Christian" interlocutors primarily through telephone books: People whose names sounded German, Dutch, British, French, etc. were interrogated as Christians, whereas people with names that sounded Turkish, Arabic, etc. were interrogated as Muslims.

6 I am not suggesting here that multiculturalism per se is a more appropriate way of dealing with plurality, given its inherent problems of producing and freezing culture and enacting state sovereignty as the distributor of the good of recognition (see Markell 2003). Recognition is, however, based on a different epistemological legacy than the idea of a constituted whole into which minorities are considered to merge.

7 Indeed, a lot of the quantitative surveys tend to conclude compatibility (Johansen and Spielhaus 2012).

8 Asad (1994a), for example, addresses fieldwork and ethnography as practices prone to reinscribe data in an uncontested way on the characters and types of people through the "real," "experienced" gaze of the anthropologist.

9 I find Armando Salvatore's (1999) seminal critique of Max Weber intriguing, as it elucidates how a modern notion of religion shaped the ways in which "other religions" were investigated. Salvatore (1999) illuminates how the rationalization of religion within Christian theology gradually contributed to the construction of religion as a "compact notion" (24). Furthermore, he works out how certain generalizable methodologies and supposedly universal categories surrounding the study of Islam operated as both Orientalizing and secularizing forces.

10 The question of how this knowledge was translated by political authorities to serve national interests can not be answered in a unified way. It is nevertheless obvious that a quite direct connection was established between state-administered colonial institutes and scholars working in the service of the state, indeed in the same moment in which the dictum of scientific neutrality and objectivity was coined.

11 Interestingly enough, as a result of enlightenment philosophy, "religion" was increasingly conceptualized as belief and hence something subjective and situated outside of the realm of the empirical testable and factual (Johansen 2013, 10). Paradoxically, the study of religion as an object of scientific investigation emerged in the same moment in which the postulates of separation between science and belief or transcendence and immanence took shape. Similarly, the very scientific study of religion paradoxically began to take contours in the moment when "religion" turned into secularism's counterpart, while at the same time being inscribed into it through a specific Christian legacy.

12 Tellingly, especially in the context of Germany, race is often put in quotation marks while religion is not and tends to pass unnoticed as an unproblematic category.

13 Roy (2002) simultaneously belongs to those authors who on other occasions had claimed that processes of individualization of Islam were not as successful as in Western Christianity because of its "dogmatic affirmation of immutable principles" (90).

14 The recurrent juxtaposition of "organized Muslims" and "ordinary Muslims" (see Akca 2020) as well as the juxtaposition of "Islamic piety" and "everyday Islam" are similarly problematic (see Fadil and Fernando 2015).

15 Mavelli traces the gradual transcendence of the senses from Aquinas via Descartes to Kant and later the founding figures of sociology of religion, Weber and Durkheim. He notes that especially Descartes inaugurated a new epistemic framework with his call to liberate oneself from the burden of the body and from God as a prerequisite to turn to the real intellect. Recalling Foucault, Mavelli speaks about the "Cartesian moment" which was marked by the withdrawal of man in the individual space of the cogito. Mavelli connects these modern ideals of a secular subject and its withdrawal from the "transcendental other" (God) to what he calls the "withdrawal from the empirical other": "The moral impoverishment of the secular subject, it was suggested, can be accounted for as the result of the secular separation of knowledge and faith. By postulating a self-sufficient knowledgeable subject who no longer needs to become 'other than herself' in order to access the truth, the

possibility is open for a progressive withdrawal of the self from the transcendent Other/God and from the empirical other" (Mavelli 2012, 45). This withdrawal, Mavelli goes on, was one reason for the contemporary lack of engagement with Islamic norms in Europe in any dialogical manner, which would imply the transformation and not only the confirmation of oneself: "Europe … has overall neglected the possibility that its transformation could be a necessary and possibly enriching component of its encounter with Islam" (Mavelli 2012, 63).

16 Key to this understanding of secularism is that it is constituted by a set of built-in contradictions: the promise to universality and its simultaneous particular (i.e., Christian-Protestant) legacy; the claim to guarantee religious liberty and the necessary reliance on particular notions of what counts as proper religion; the state's claim to neutrality and its inescapable involvement in shaping religious life, sometimes in its most intimate spheres.

17 In her book on the relationship between secularism and the minority question, Saba Mahmood distinguishes between "political secularism" as the political and legal regulation of religion and "secularity" as sensibilities, emotions, social conventions, and habitualized practices. Moreover, secularity, Mahmood (2015) argues, constitutes "the epistemological and cultural ground on the basis of which religious claims can be authorized and validated" (206).

18 In an illuminating article on the debates on veiling in Belgium, Sarah Bracke and Nadia Fadil (2012) argue that this scheme of interrogation is centrally structured around the question of whether the headscarf is emancipatory or oppressive. This framing, the authors go on, leaves covered women in a deadlock: It scrutinizes *their* views on gender roles and relations and *their* agency or lack thereof, while imposing the ways in which the questions, and therefore necessarily also the answers, are framed. Bracke and Fadil (2012) impressively show how much they themselves as scholars have become captured by this very framing. They revealingly speak about their own discomfort when constantly being manoeuvred into the position to either defend or condemn veiling, while they were inclined to voice a critique of the discursive structures which sustain the very act of exceptionalizing the veil as a problem to be scrutinized politically, culturally, and epistemologically.

REFERENCES

Agrama, Hussein. 2010. "Secularism, sovereignty, indeterminacy: Is Egypt a secular or a religious state?" *Comparative Studies in Society and History, 52*(3), 1–29. https://www.jstor.org/stable/40864787

Ahmed, Shahab. 2016. *What is Islam? The importance of being Islamic.* Princeton University Press.

Akca, Almila. 2020. *Moscheeleben in Deutschland: Eine Ethnographie zu Islamischem Wissen, Tradition und religiöser Autorität.* transcript.

Amir-Moazami, Schirin. 2005. "Buried Alive: Multiculturalism in Germany." *ISIM Review, 16*, 22–3.

– 2011. "Dialogue as a governmental technique: Managing gendered Islam in Germany." *Feminist Review, 98*(1), 9–27. https://doi.org/10.1057%2Ffr.2011.8

– 2016a. "Investigating the secular body: The case of male circumcision." *ReOrient, 1*(2), 25–48.

– 2016b. "Die 'muslimische Frage' in Europa: Aporien der Anerkennung unter liberal-säkularen Bedingungen." In Marie-Luisa Frick and Philip Hubmann (Eds.), *Politische Aporien: Akteure und Praktiken des Dilemmas* (pp. 109–34). Turia + Kant.

– 2018. "Epistemologien der 'muslimischen Frage' in Europa." In Schirin Amir-Moazami (Ed.), *Der inspizierte Muslim: Zur Politisierung der Islamforschung in Europa* (pp. 91–124). transcript.

Amir-Moazami, Schirin, and Armando Salvatore. 2003. "Gender, generation, and thereform of tradition: From Muslim majority societies to Western Europe." In Stefan Allievi and Jørgen S. Nielsen (Eds.), *Muslim Networks and Transnational Communities in and across Europe* (pp. 52–77). Brill.

Anidjar, Gil. 2003. *The Jew, the Arab: A history of the enemy*. Stanford University Press.

– 2008. *Semites: Race, religion, literature*. Stanford University Press.

Asad, Talal. 1986. "*The idea of an anthropology of Islam.*" *Qui Parle, 17*(2), 1–30. https://www.jstor.org/stable/20685738

– 1993. *Genealogies of Religion: Discipline and Reasons of Power in Christianity and Islam*. Johns Hopkins University Press.

– 1994a. "Ethnographic representation, statistics, and modern power." *Social Research, 61*(1), 55–88. http://www.jstor.org/stable/40971022

– 1994b. *Genealogies of religion: Discipline and reasons of power in Christianity and Islam*. Johns Hopkins University Press.

– 2003. *Formations of the secular: Christianity, Islam and modernity*. Stanford University Press.

– 2014. "Genealogies of religion, twenty years on: An interview with Talal Asad." *Bulletin for the Study of Religion, 43*(1), 12–17. https://doi.org/10.1558/bsor.v43i1.12

Astheimer, Sven. 2016, *29* April. "Migrationsforscher im Gespräch: 'Die meisten Menschen wollen unbequeme Fakten nicht hören.'" *Frankfurter Allgemeine Zeitung*. http://www.faz.net/aktuell/wirtschaft/migrationsforscher-koopmans-haelt-multikulti-fuer-fatal-14202950.html

Atman, Ferda. 2015, 30 June. "Zwei Drittel der Muslime Fundamentalisten – wirklich?" *Mediendienst Integration*. https://mediendienst-integration.de/artikel/wzb-studie-koopmans-zu-fundamentalismus-muslime-und-christen-im-europaeischen-vergleich.html

Babès, Laïla. 1997. *L'islam positif: La religion des jeunes musulmans de France*. L'Harmattan.

Bauman, Zygmunt. 1991. *Modernity and ambivalence.* Cambridge University Press.

Bax, Daniel. 2016, 10 April. "Der Parallelforscher." *Taz.* http://www.taz.de/!5340970/

Bergunder, Michael. 2011. "Was ist Religion? Kulturwissenschaftliche Überlegungen zum Gegenstand der Religionswissenschaft." *Zeitschrift für Religionswissenschaft, 19*(1/2), 3–55. https://doi.org/10.1515/zfr-2011-0001

Bigo, Didier. 2002. "Security and immigration: Towards a critique of the governmentality of unease." *Alternatives, 27,* 63–92. https://doi.org/10.1177%2F03043754020270S105

Bigo, Didier, and Anastassia Tsoukala. 2008. *Terror, insecurity and liberty: Illiberal practices of liberal regimes after 9/11.* Routledge.

Boatcă, Manuela. 2013. "'From the standpoint of Germanism': A postcolonial critique of Weber's theory of race and ethnicity." *Postcolonial Sociology, Political Power and Social Theory, 24,* 55–80. https://doi.org/10.1108/S0198-*8719*(2013)0000024009

Boubaker, Amel. 2004. *Le voile de la mariée: Jeunes musulmanes, voile et projet matrimoniale en France.* L'Harmattan.

Bracke, Sarah, and Nadia Fadil. 2012. "'Is the headscarf oppressive or emancipatory?': Fieldnotes from the multicultural debate." *Religion and Gender, 2*(1), 36–56. https://doi.org/10.1163/18785417-00201003

Brettfeld, Katrin, and Peter Wetzels. 2007. *Muslime in Deutschland – Integration, Integrationsbarrieren, Religion und Einstellungen zu Demokratie, Rechtsstaat und politisch-religiös motivierter Gewalt.* Universität Hamburg.

Brubaker, Rogers. 2012. "Categories of analysis and categories of practice: A note on the study of Muslims in European countries of immigration." *Ethnic and Racial Studies, 36(1),* 1–8. https://doi.org/10.1080/01419870.2012.729674

Castro Varela, Maria do Mar. 2013. *Ist Integration nötig? Eine Streitschrift.* Lambertus.

Deutsche Islam Konferenz (DIK). n.d. "Results and Recommendations." Retrieved 20 July 2021 from https://www.deutsche-islam-konferenz.de/SiteGlobals/Forms/Suche/Ergebnisse-Empfehlungen-Suche_Formular.html?nn=598592.

Diner, Dan. 2014. "Statistik." In Dan Diner (Ed.), *Enzyklopädie jüdischer Geschichte und Kultur,* vol. 5, 580–5. J.B. Metzler.

Dornhof, Sarah. 2009. "Germany: Constructing a sociology of Islamist radicalization." *Race & Class, 50*(4), 75–82. https://doi.org/10.1177%2F0306396809102999

Espeland, Wendy N., and Mitchell L. Stevens. 2008. "A sociology of quantification." *European Journal of Sociology, 49*(3), 401–36. https://doi.org/10.1017/S0003975609000150

Fadil, Nadia. 2009. "Managing affects and sensibilities: The case of not-handshaking and not fasting." *Social Anthropology / Anthropologie Sociale, 17*(4), 439–54. https://doi.org/10.1111/j.1469-8676.2009.00080

Fadil, Nadia, and Mayanthi Fernando. 2015. "Rediscovering the 'everyday' Muslim: Notes on an anthropological divide." *Journal of Ethnographic Theory, 5*(2), 59–88. https://doi.org/10.14318/hau5.2.005

Fernando, Mayanthi. 2009. "Exceptional citizens: Secular Muslim women and the politics of difference in France." *Social Anthropology, 17*(3), 379–92. https://doi.org/10.1111/j.1469-8676.2009.00081.x

– 2014. *The republic unsettled: Muslim French and the contradictions of secularism*. Duke University Press.

Feyerabend, Paul. 2010. *Against method*. Verso. (Original work published 1975)

Foucault, Michel. 1982. *The archeology of knowledge: And the discourse on language*. Vintage.

– 2006. *Die Geburt der Biopolitik: Geschichte der Gouvernementalität II*. Suhrkamp. (Original work published 1979)

Gadamer, Hans-Georg. 1990. *Wahrheit und Methode: Grundzüge einer philosophischen Hermeneutik*. Suhrkamp. (Original work published 1960)

Göle, Nilüfer, and Ludwig Amman. 2004. *Islam in Sicht: Der Auftritt von Muslimen im öffentlichen Raum*. transcript.

Hacking, Ian. 2002. *Historical ontology*. Harvard University Press.

– 2006. *The emergence of probability: A philosophical study of early ideas about probability, induction and statistical inference*. Cambridge University Press. (Original work published 1975)

Haraway, Donna. 1988. "Situated knowledges: The science question in feminism and the privilege of partial perspective." *Feminist Studies, 14*(3), 575–99. https://doi.org/10.2307/3178066

Haug, Sonja, Stephanie Müssig, and Anja Stichs. 2009. *Muslimisches Leben in Deutschland*. Bundesamt für Migration und Flüchtlinge.

Hess, Sabine, Jana Binder, and Johannes Moser (Eds.). (2009). *No integration?! Kulturwissenschaftliche Beiträge zur Integrationsdebatte in Europa*. transcript.

Hindess, Barry. 1977. *Philosophy and methodology in the social sciences*. Harvester Press.

Hirschkind, Charles. 2011. "Is there a secular body?" *Cultural Anthropology, 6*(4), 633–47. https://doi.org/10.1111/j.1548-1360.2011.01116.x

Johansen, Birgitte. 2013. "Post-secular sociology: Modes, possibilities and challenges." *Approaching Religion, 3*(1), 4–13.

Johansen, Birgitte, and Riem Spielhaus. 2012. "Counting deviance: Revisiting a decade's production of surveys among Muslims in Western Europe." *Journal of Muslims in Europe, 1*(1), 81–112. https://doi.org/10.1163/221179512X644060

Klinkhammer, Gritt. 2000. *Moderne Formen islamischer Lebensführung: Eine qualitativ-empirische Untersuchung zur Religiosität sunnitisch geprägter Türkinnen der zweiten Generation in Deutschland*. diagonal.

Koopmans, Ruud. 2015. "Religious fundamentalism and hostility against out-groups: A comparison of Muslims and Christians in Western Europe." *Journal of Ethnic and Migration Studies, 41*(1), 33–57. https://doi.org/10.1080/1369183X.2014.935307

Lentin, Alana, and Gavan Titley. 2011. *The crises of multiculturalism: Racism in a liberal age*. Zed Books.

Lettow, Susanne. 2014. "Generation, genealogy, and time: The concept of reproduction from Histoire naturelle to Naturphilosophie." In Susanne Lettow (Ed.), *Reproduction, race and gender in philosophy and the early life sciences* (pp. 21–43). State University of New York Press.

Mahmood, Saba. 2005. *Politics of piety: The Islamic revival and the feminist subject.* Princeton University Press.

– 2015. *Religious difference in a secular age: A minority report.* Princeton University Press.

Marchand, Suzanne L. 2010. *German Orientalism in the age of empire: Religion, race and scholarship.* Cambridge University Press.

Markell, Patchen. 2003. *Bound by recognition.* Princeton University Press.

Masuzawa, Tomoko. 2005. *The invention of world religions: Or, how European universalism was preserved in the language of pluralism.* University of Chicago Press.

Mas, Ruth. 2006. "Compelling the Muslim subject: Memory as post-colonial violence and the public performativity of 'Secular and Cultural Islam.'" *Muslim World, 96*(4), 585–616.

Mavelli, Luca. 2012. *Europe's encounter with Islam: The secular and the postsecular.* Routledge.

Mignolo, Walter D. 2009. "Epistemic disobedience, independent thought and decolonial freedom." *Theory, Culture & Society, 26*(7–8), 159–81. https://doi.org/10.1177%2F0263276409349275

Morsi, Yassir. 2017. *Radical skin, moderate masks.* Rowman and Littlefield.

Peter, Frank. 2006. "Individualization and religious authority in Western European Islam." *Islam and Christian–Muslim Relations, 17*(1), 105–18. https://doi.org/10.1080/09596410500400165

– 2008. "Political rationalities, counter-terrorism and policies on Islam in the United Kingdom and France." In Julia Eckert (Ed.), *The social life of anti-terrorism laws* (pp. 79–108). transcript.

Roy, Olivier. 2002. *L'islam mondialisé.* Éditions du Seuil.

– 2010. "It is time to have a more relaxed approach to religion." Video, 6:57. https://www.youtube.com/watch?v=zZ2Zsz434I8.

Said, Edward. 1995. *Orientalism: Western conceptions of the Orient.* Penguin. (Original work published 1978)

Salvatore, Armando. 1999. *Islam and the political discourse of modernity.* Ithaca.

Sayyid, Salman. 2014. *Recalling the caliphate: Decolonisation and world order.* Hurst.

Steinmetz, Georges. 2005. *The politics of method in the human sciences: Positivism and its epistemological others.* Duke University Press.

– 2015. *Sociology and empire: The imperial entanglements of a discipline.* Duke University Press.

Stoler, Ann Laura. 2008. "Epistemic politics: Ontologies of the colonial common sense." *Philosophical Forum, 39*(3), 349–69. https://doi.org/10.1111/j.1467-9191.2008.00303.x

Supik, Linda. 2014. *Statistik und Rassismus: Das Dilemma der Erfassung von Ethnizität.* Campus.

Tezcan, Levent. 2012. *Das muslimische Subjekt: Verfangen im Dialog der Deutschen Islam Konferenz*. Konstanz University Press.

Topolski, Anya. 2017. "Good Jew, bad Jew … good Muslim, bad Muslim: 'Managing' Europe's others." *Ethnic and Racial Studies*, *41*(12), 2179–96. https://doi.org/10.1080/01419870.2018.1391402

Turner, Bryan. 1974. *Weber and Islam*. Routledge.

Venel, Nancy. 1999. *Musulmanes Françaises: Des pratiquantes voilées à l'université.* L'Harmattan.

Vial, Theodore. 2016. *Modern Race, Modern Religion*. Oxford University Press.

Zimmermann, Andrew. 2013. "From internal colonization to overseas colonization." In Georges Steinmetz (Ed.), *Sociology and empire: The imperial entanglements of a discipline* (pp. 166–87). Duke University Press.

Research Funding and the Production of Knowledge about Islam: The Case of SSHRC

AARON W. HUGHES

Introduction

No research topic, whether in the humanities or social sciences, exists naturally in the world, simply waiting to be discovered, quantified, or categorized. Such topics instead come into focus by means of a host of personal, social, and institutional forces. These can include idiosyncratic aspects of the researcher (e.g., gender, class, ethnicity, religious background) or, as this chapter argues, various institutional ones. Of particular relevance to me in what follows is how and why granting agencies provide support for certain topics and not others. To be eligible for funding from such agencies, one has to shape, both consciously and unconsciously, one's work in a particular way, avoiding certain topics and gravitating towards others. Such forces exert pressure on research, shaping it indirectly, and yet these forces are surprisingly and frequently left unexamined and untheorized. This is especially the case in Canada, a country where most universities are publicly funded. The present chapter focuses on the second of these two forces, the institutional, and argues that granting agencies play a major role in the creation of research topics by guiding their formulation and by ultimately determining how and to whom it is disseminated. To do this, I focus my attention on the Social Sciences and Humanities Research Council/Conseil de recherches en sciences humaines (hereafter SSHRC), the major fellowship granting agency associated with the federal government of Canada.[1]

As the late theoretician of religion Jonathan Z. Smith (1982) once infamously quipped, "*there is no data for religion* [emphasis in original]. Religion is solely the creation of the scholar's study" (xi). This is perhaps another way of saying that we, as scholars of religion, do not find religion "out there"; on the contrary, we conjure it into existence by artificially removing it from various social, cultural, and intellectual contexts (see McCutcheon 2007, 68–71; and, more recently, Levene 2019). We do this, moreover, through an intricate set of choices (why "x," for example, and not "y" or "z"?), methodological moves, and rhetorical flourishes that simultaneously select and remove, just as they privilege and deny. Unfortunately, however, we rarely focus on these latter aspects that govern knowledge production and prefer to proceed on the assumption that the projects we work on derive simply from personal interest, ecumenical desire, or humanitarian need.

Such issues are especially germane when it comes to the academic study of Islam, a religion that is frequently in the news, often for the wrong reasons. Numerous polls reveal that Canadians are mistrustful of Islam and Muslims, and the latter's allegiance to Canada's values are often questioned. How, then, does a scholar of Islam represent this religion and its practitioners to students, to the media, and in the public square? How, in turn, do these constituencies shape research? Since the study of religion, as an academic field of study, is not about finding and interpreting a set of eternal meanings or symbols but about constant reflection on our own choice and selection, this chapter assumes that more time ought to be devoted to the various material conditions that attend to such choice and selection (see Bynum 2014, 341–5).

While Smith warned us of the epistemological problems of not reflecting on the why and the how of what we study, he rarely examined the larger institutional frameworks that exert a set of influences on what we do. In order to add to his insights, what follows explores some of the ways in which SSHRC helps to shape research projects, thereby indirectly, if not actually directly, shaping the production of knowledge. When such agencies are connected to the government and its policies, we should perhaps not be surprised to witness the funding of projects that reflect its concerns.

SSHRC: A Brief Overview

SSHRC is a federal research-funding agency that promotes and supports research and training at the post-secondary level in both the humanities and the social sciences. It was founded by an act of Parliament in 1977 and reports directly to the federal government though the Ministry of Innovation, Science, and Economic Development, which oversees the federal government's economic development and corporate affairs department.

SSHRC does not simply fund projects deemed good by a panel of peer reviewers. Rather, it creates policy, plans budgets, and directs priorities through a council established by the federal government that is responsible for charting "the direction of SSHRC and ensur[ing] that our grants and fellowships programs meet the needs of Canadians."[2] The appointed members to this council are a mix of academics and representatives from industry, and their role is to advise the minister of Innovation, Science, and Economic Development with the aim of representing the interests of academic, public, and private sectors. Council committees create and oversee SSHRC's programs, determine the distribution of funds, and handle the strategies for enacting the organization's policies.

While faculty adjudication is ultimately responsible for the selection of successful proposals at SSHRC, the terms of reference of funding are predetermined by a "Quality Committee" responsible for the "overall design, coherence and performance of SSHRC's suite of programs and program-related policies in the context of strategic direction."[3] SSHRC, in other words, is governed by a council that "promotes and assists research and scholarship in the social sciences and humanities," and whose main goal is "to set policy and program priorities, allocate budgets, and to advise the minister of Science and Parliament on research policy in these areas."[4] These priorities, at least when it comes to religion in general and Islam in particular, constellate around a set of values that promote "good" religion and seek to reduce its more nefarious aspects.

Of all the discrete religions (e.g., Hinduism, Christianity, Judaism) that make up the academic study of religion and that SSHRC funds, Islam receives by far the most federal funding dollars.[5] Suffice it to mention here, but to be examined in more detail later, in the 2017/18 competition, for example, of the 177 grants devoted to discrete religious traditions, 81 (46 per cent) were devoted to Islam. Moreover, given that roughly three-quarters of the projects deemed fundable when it comes to Islam are devoted to political Islam, sharia (Islamic law), Islamophobia, radicalization (especially of young Muslims), and fitting Islam into the multicultural state, it would seem that SSHRC is certainly attempting to set policy and "program priorities." If we take the concerns of Canadians when it comes to Islam and Muslims and then look at the types of projects funded by SSHRC in the years since 9/11, we see, again using SSHRC's language, the "multidirectional flow of research knowledge across academia and society as a whole." SSHRC, then, is attempting to provide money to research topics and programs devoted to the role and place of Islam and Muslims within Canadian society. While there is certainly nothing wrong with this, it is surely worth noting that this means that only certain kinds of topics are funded when it comes to Islam, or at least funded to a greater extent than more philological/textual and historical research (which, prior to 9/11, were funded to a much greater extent). It also means that, in a time of shrinking funding resources, SSHRC exerts the single biggest influence on the knowledge production of Islam in the Canadian academy.

Funding: A Discursive Site and Theoretical Prolegomenon

To be clear, this is not a straightforward process. I won't be so naive as to suggest that an important funding body like SSHRC simply provides financial aid to projects that the federal government deems important to its mandate. I instead want to go deeper and argue that it is, to invoke the language of Foucault, a much more subterranean process. SSHRC creates meaning systems that produce "truth," while simultaneously defining and organizing a particular social world reflective of Canadian society. SSHRC thus functions as a discursive site that shapes a particular discourse about Islam and its place in the social and political imaginary, which, in turn, makes a field of knowledge possible (see Foucault 1977, 222–5). The production of knowledge about Islam, like the production of knowledge about anything, is predicated "upon institutional support and distribution and tends to exercise a sort of pressure, a power of constraint upon other forms of discourse" (Foucault 1972, 219).

Governments, including their elaborate infrastructures, reproduce the values of state authority – what is constructed as either "good" or "bad" – using the legal and political institutions and the meta-institutions that enable them (Foucault 1977, 55–70). The production of knowledge, including the manufacture of truth claims, thus plays a significant role in the construction of authority and authorizing discourses (see Lincoln 1994, 1–15). Within this context, I contend that funding agencies like SSHRC provide a site wherein we witness how Islam is imagined, how facts about it, and Muslims, can be determined (or not), and how space (social, intellectual, and so on) is carved out in a manner that facilitates discourse about Islam in the public sphere. This triangulation, in turn, constructs truths, determines how they are maintained, and establishes a set of power relations that they reproduce (Lincoln 1994, 2). SSHRC is an arm of the government, is governed by a council comprising both academics and non-academics, and selects the projects deemed fundable by scholarly peer review. Yet I also wish to suggest that all play by the same unwritten rules about what gets to count as knowledge because all have internalized what constitutes good Islam (and, by extension, good religion) and how that ought to fit into the modern nation.

I certainly do not want to claim that SSHRC is an ideological institution, or at least any more ideological than any other.[6] My argument is, I hope, much more subtle, namely, that we need to focus on the dynamics of its authority as much as, if not more so than, its variety of institutional incarnations. SSHRC, then, is not a bureaucratic entity that funds research so much as it is as an effect and the capacity for producing that effect. Even though the odd historical and textual work on Islam is funded, the overwhelming majority of projects funded by SSHRC since 9/11, as we shall see, have been ones that reproduce a certain discourse not only about Islam but about religion more generally. SSHRC is primarily in the business of funding research that replicates its own authority, which, in turn, is derived from its perceived virtues (diversity, multiculturalism) and the civic laws that uphold them, regardless of the particular government or prime minister in charge.

Religion, the State, and the Public Funding of Scholarship

The way in which the Canadian government, through SSHRC, publicly funds university chairs and grants means that when it comes to religion there is a distinct emphasis on, to use current granting language, "public impacts" or "knowledge mobilization plans." Research, in other words, must be relevant, au courant, and compatible with governmental policy (see Kaell 2017, 263n22). This means that we see Canada Research Chairs (CRCs) in the humanities and social sciences, which incidentally are also funded under the auspices of SSHRC, dealing with religion topics such as "Religious Diversity and Social Change" (University of Ottawa), "Religion, Law, and Social Justice" (University of British Columbia), "Islam, Pluralism, and Globalization" (Université de Montréal), and Islamic law (not one but two at the University of Toronto).[7] Even more historical CRCs have a distinctly modern feel to them. A CRC at McGill University in the History of Science in the Islamic World, for example, is devoted to the topic of "Unravelling the History of Science in the Islamic World" but has the following as its description: "Traditional views portray science in Islam as standing little chance of surviving – much less thriving – in a religiously oriented civilization seen as hostile to rationalism."[8] The goal of this chair, among other things, is to show how Islam is rational (and thus compatible with the modern liberal nation state). Even though the topic is historical, the effects of scholarship on the topic are not. CRCs in religion, perhaps not surprisingly, differ remarkably from those in other disciplines in the humanities, where we see more topics like "Colonial North American History" (history),[9] "Esthetics and the Art of the Novel" (English),[10] and "Latin Poetry and Its Reception" (classics).[11] For the sake of comparison, there are no CRCs devoted to Judaism, Hinduism, or Buddhism except in the same general multicultural framework mentioned above. None, moreover, are devoted explicitly, say, to the legal traditions or to gender justice in other religions.

Unlike other areas in the humanities, then, religion CRCs clearly reveal a bias not seen in cognate departments. Most of the CRCs that deal with religion or Islam have a distinctly ecumenical or multicultural character to them. When it comes to Islam, we see an emphasis on law or social justice and on how Islam is compatible with Canadian multiculturalism. The study of religion, at least for the federal government, is seen as connected to diversity, social justice, and globalization, and this has consequences for the ways in which religion in general and Islam in particular are conceived and taught at Canadian universities. There is no emphasis on a particular religion (e.g., Islam or Buddhism), even though individual chairholders may well work on them, only on a generically conceived religion and how it is compatible with Canada and Canadian values. The CRC website currently lists four CRCs devoted to religion; one devoted to Islam (the aforementioned one at UBC), one to multiculturalism (the aforementioned at

Ottawa), and two at Trinity Western University – one devoted to the Dead Sea Scrolls and one to "Religious Identities of Ancient Judaism." It is perhaps worth noting that when we add to this number the two devoted to Islamic law and the one to modern Islam, all, with the exception of the two at Trinity Western (which in many ways function as outliers), revolve around Islam in one way or another.

There is certainly nothing wrong with this, and my comments are not meant to detract from the important work being carried out by chairholders. I only point out that the funding structure of humanities research in Canada means that the government is primarily willing to support certain kinds of projects. In terms of the study of religion (and Islam in particular), this means that religion (or Islam) is imagined rationally, inclusively, ecumenically, and as an important part of the modern world. In order for religion to be fitted within such a mandate, however, certain aspects of it have to be selected or emphasized at the expense of others. This often means arguing that religion is a force of good and that those who commit violence in its name are somehow not really religious but instead motivated by political concerns (see Orsi 2005, 188–9). "Good" religion – coinciding with democracy, liberalism, and diversity – is procured and disseminated at the expense of "bad" religion, namely, that which coincides with violence and extremism.[12]

The question now becomes how and why the federal government is interested in such a take on religion. A quick survey of SSHRC-funded projects devoted to Islam, discussed in greater detail later, over the past five years reveals that of the 232 doctoral and faculty funded projects,[13] only about 40 (i.e., under 20 per cent) were devoted to historical non-political topics, and the rest deal with Islam and the West (especially Canada), sharia, Islamism, radicalization, the Arab Spring, and Islamophobia. All of the latter subjects incidentally are not only familiar but of concern to both the federal government and all Canadians. Such issues are also exacerbated by the media and manifest themselves in recent polls that show how Islam is anxiety producing.

An Angus Reid poll in 2017, for example, reported that 46 per cent of Canadians view Islam, and the clothing associated with it, unfavourably.[14] This is especially interesting given the fact that 94 per cent of Muslims describe themselves as Canadian, and 83 per cent describe themselves as "very proud" to be Canadians (compared to 73 per cent in the non-Muslim population).[15] A majority of Canadians (54 per cent), rightly or wrongly is not the point here, are concerned with radical Islam (even more so than White supremacy);[16] many are concerned about the niqab and burqa;[17] and many are worried about the establishment of "sharia courts" and the inability or unwillingness of Muslims to fit into Canadian culture.

This is where SSHRC-funded research projects come in. Many of these projects are attempts either to understand political Islam "over there" or to show

how Islam is an integral part of multicultural fabric "over here." One cannot have such a large cross-section of Canadians – especially new Canadians – be regarded as "un-Canadian" or as not belonging to the nation in which they find themselves. CRCs and SSHRC grants thus function as a way to alleviate the unease on the part of Canadians when it comes to non-Christian religions in general and Islam in particular. The question becomes – for the government, for academics who specialize in Islam – how can the general public be made to see Islam in a more favourable light? Within this context, the present chapter works on the understanding that SSHRC helps produce a certain perception of Islam by, again, creating material conditions that encourage some projects over others.

To view this in greater detail, I first provide a brief framework for examining some of the problems besetting the academic study of Islam, especially in the post-9/11 world. After this, I turn to a statistical analysis of the types of projects that SSHRC funds.

The Study of Islam Post-9/11

There is no getting around the fact that much of the anxiety that currently surrounds Islam stems from the attacks of 11 September 2001 and their aftermath. These events have had a profound effect on the study of Islam as carried out in the academy, as indeed they have had on most Canadians.[18] In terms of the former, these attacks have led to a number of scholarly responses. For the sake of convenience and heuristic purposes, these can be bifurcated into two groups. The first are those, specifically in religious studies, who have used the attacks as a way to defend Islam and Muslims with claims such as those who perpetuated such attacks are not true or authentic Muslims but terrorists who have "hijacked" the beautiful religion of Islam for their own nefarious ends.[19] While this, especially in the immediate aftermaths of the attack, provided an important antidote to those who wanted to implicate the entire tradition – and, by extension, *all* Muslims – in the attacks, it does have the consequence of trying to present a vision of Islam that is overwhelmingly positive and free of criticism (see Hughes 2012). This vision, moreover, is one that would seem to coincide with the aims of the federal government. Such approaches usually involve stressing the importance of a peaceful Islam that can be differentiated from "political Islam" or Islamism. They can also lead to a focus on Islamophobia.

The other scholarly approach is one that is more interested in the repercussions of Islam – whether positive, negative, or somewhere in the middle – on the global order in general and Canada in particular.[20] This approach focuses on Islamic law and how it can fit within the Canadian legal framework (recall the two Canada Research Chairs at the University of Toronto) and is also interested in both the history and present of Muslims in non-Muslim countries.

If we return to those topics funded over the past five years, we see that both of these scholarly approaches take up a large share of funded projects. Under 20 per cent of such projects are devoted to historical and intellectual topics that seem to have very little to do with either politics or Canadian society. The rest focus on areas that are relevant to both the government and the Canadian taxpayer, which I shall discuss in greater detail in the following section. It is difficult to know what projects on Islam were not funded, and this would certainly aid in my analysis. But even without that information, it should be clear that, with the types of projects funded, more and more scholars have increasingly focused their research on political and multicultural topics as opposed to historical or textual ones because the former are more eligible for federal funding. In this, we get a clearer glimpse of the way in which SSHRC shapes the type of knowledge produced on Islam.

We thus witness competing paradigms for the study of Islam at the beginning of the twenty-first century, and regardless of the paradigm, certain traditions of Islam are given prescriptive legitimacy over others in the public imaginary and in scholarly work in Canada. This definitely has repercussions on the way Islam is studied in the Canadian context, as the following section will show in more detail.

SSHRC and the Study of Islam

When we use this federal mandate as a way to understand the production of knowledge about Islam, especially in the post-9/11 world, we would do well to note a number of important features. Perhaps most basic and germane is this: What knowledge of Islam, to return to SSHRC's locution, "meets the needs of Canadians"? Presumably it is the construction of an Islam that can counter negative portrayals in the media and, indeed, portrayals that the majority of Canadians seem to have. How, in turn, do those needs – or fears – structure topics to be funded and thereby determine what is (or is not) valid knowledge about Islam? An analysis of research topics deemed fundable by SSHRC include, as mentioned, an overwhelming number that deal with Islamism or political Islam, with sharia (especially within a Canadian context), with Islam's role in the multicultural state, with radicalization among Muslim youth in Canada, and with the successful integration of refugees from predominantly Muslim countries into Canada. Such topics, perhaps not surprisingly, are or have been frequently in both the national and local news. So then, how do the media, the "needs of Canadians," and SSHRC triangulate to determine what kinds of knowledge are valuable?

A "titles and keywords" search reveals that SSHRC funds more topics on Islam than it does any other religious tradition in religious studies.[21] In the 2017/18 competition, for example, of the 177 grants devoted to discrete religious traditions, 81 (46 per cent) were devoted to Islam – whereas 53 (30 per cent) were devoted to Christianity, 20 (11 per cent) to Buddhism, 17 (10 per cent) to Judaism, and 6 (3 per cent) to Hinduism. The year 2017/18 is in keeping with the general tenor over the past twenty years. From the years 1998/9 to 2017/18, for example, of the 2,325 topics on religion broadly defined, the majority, 960 (41 per cent), were devoted to Islam, with other religions receiving, in order of funding, Christianity (675 or 29 per cent), Judaism (357 or 15 per cent), Buddhism (254 or 11 per cent), and Hinduism (89 or 4 per cent).

With this in mind, it might be worth looking at a breakdown of the types of grants that SSHRC funds on Islam. Of the seventy-five projects and three CRCs[22] funded in the 2017/18 competition,[23] well over half are what we could call favourable to what the government is trying to achieve: general (i.e., non-Canadian) Islamism or political Islam (twenty-eight grants or 37 per cent), women and gender in Islam (nine grants or 12 per cent), Islam and multiculturalism (nine grants or 12 per cent), countering radicalization of Muslim youth (four grants or 5 per cent), and Islamophobia (five grants or 7 per cent). The remaining (twenty grants or 26 per cent) are devoted to topics that, by their description, seem to have little political or contemporary significance.

There seems to be an overwhelming propensity for funded projects that deal with various aspects of political Islam, albeit not necessarily in a distinctly Canadian context. The emphasis on the Islamism in other places, however, is ultimately an attempt to understand the repercussions of it on Canadian society. What is interesting is that the study of political Islam in other places is supplemented by studies on women and gender, particularly how women can reclaim the tradition of Islam for themselves, in a Canadian context. Indeed, the CRC devoted to Religion, Law, and Social Justice, as mentioned above, has as its raison d'être "Constructing a Feminist Shari'a."

If we compare these numbers to the situation before 2001, the contrast is striking, not only in terms of number of projects funded but also in terms of the types of research projects funded. A "titles and keywords" search of "Islam" in the 1998/9–1999/2000 competitions, for example, reveals that only nineteen projects were funded. Eleven (58 per cent) were historical – two in archaeology, two on Turkey in World War I, one in astronomy, one in Byzantine history, one in South Arabian ecology, one in economics, one on how Westerners are portrayed in Malaysian print media, and one on intellectual history. Four (21 per cent) were devoted to women and gender; three (16 per cent) to Islamism; and one (5 per cent) each on English and postcolonialism, Bosnia, and sacred spaces in Canada.

These numbers reveal a rather different situation than the present. Before 9/11, Islam was rarely on our radar; today, the religion is everywhere. If we look to the first two years after the 9/11 attacks – 2002/3 and 2003/4 – we see the beginning of this transformation. In this year 21 projects were funded; using the same rubrics used in the previous paragraph, we witness: 7 (33 per cent) devoted to Islam in Canada; 7 (33 per cent) to political Islam (including sharia); 5 (24 per cent) devoted to historical topics; and 2 (10 per cent) to women and gender. We thus begin to see a transformation from funding overwhelmingly historical topics to more politically "relevant" ones.

Just to show that this change in both number and type of fundable projects is not simply coincidental, let's look at one more set of random years, that of 2014/15–2015/16, using the same rubrics.[24] Of the eighty-nine projects on Islam funded in that year,[25] twenty-nine (33 per cent) are devoted to political Islam, terrorism, and/or sharia; twenty-five (28 per cent) to more historical topics; fifteen (17 per cent) to Islam in Canada (including radicalization and multiculturalism); ten (11 per cent) to women and gender; seven (8 per cent) to globalism and refugees; and three (3 per cent) to Islamophobia.

These numbers clearly show that an interest in the study of Islam and Muslims has increased with the exposure of the religion and those who subscribe to it. A look at the types of projects funded by SSHRC reveals that since 9/11 the overwhelming interest has been in studying projects that deal with Islamism, especially in the Middle East (since there is a fear that such political Islam might enter Canada), with the potential for radicalization among Muslim youth in Canada, and with the place of Islam in multicultural Canada.

With this, as I have tried to suggest, we witness federal resources devoted to humanities scholarship in general, and to Islam in particular, being channelled to certain topics as opposed to others. I do not necessarily want to suggest that the federal government has an agenda, but I do want to draw attention to the fact that such statistics show clearly that SSHRC shapes knowledge production about Islam.

Conclusions

Scholarship can be engaged or dispassionate, but it can never occur from some Archimedean point. Since scholarship is a matter of choice and selection, we have to be aware of the various theoretical motivations and methodological moods that bring research projects into existence. This chapter has suggested that we ought to focus not solely on the personal aspects of research but also on the broader institutional ones. These latter aspects, I suggested, play just as important a role in shaping research because they exert a set of pressures, often subterranean, that nevertheless have the potential to push and pull scholarship in certain areas (and not others) based on what is (and is not) and can (and cannot) be funded.

Within this context, the present chapter has assumed that knowledge production of Islam, like all knowledge production, is never a value-neutral enterprise, something done simply for the sake of what used to be imagined as an old-fashioned notion of objective scholarship. This Orientalist imaginary has been replaced in recent years with the notion that scholarship on Islam has always been invested in the political when it comes to Western scholarship and bias. Despite the fact that this should not come as a surprise to many in the modern age, we still need to be aware and self-conscious of how our research is both shaped and produced.

We are often content to focus on obvious issues such as the current political moment (which, in the case of Islam, is certainly vectored through all kinds of media, from the mainstream to the neoconservative), the demography of classrooms, and the positionality of researchers (see, for instance, the contributions of Jahangeer and Brown in this volume). I have instead suggested that we focus on the ways in which the government funds projects on Islam. This means examining the types of projects that are funded and the types of topics that are seen as relevant.

I certainly do not want to suggest that this is a straightforward process. It is not contingent, for example, on the fiat of the minister of Innovation, Science, and Economic Development, let alone reducible to the ideology of the particular government that happens to be in power; rather, it is based on the way in which religion in general, and Islam in particular, is imagined to fit into the modern nation state. Scholarly activity, shaped through the types of projects funded, is thus an apparatus of the modern nation state, rather than an activity that occurs solely within the confines of the ivory tower.

The present chapter has instead suggested that the federal government, through institutions such as SSHRC, does not play an insignificant role in shaping research on Islam. Within this context, the overwhelming type of projects that are funded by SSHRC emphasizes the place of Islam in the modern nation state and connection between Islam and violence (specifically, so-called radicalization). Historical and literary projects, by contrast, tend not to be funded, especially when compared to the years prior to 9/11. Instead, we witness the funding of many ecumenical projects that stress Islam's ability – but never its inability – to fit into the Canadian context.

NOTES

1 SSHRC has a significant budget, providing roughly $410 million per annum for programs and another $369 million for its Research Support Fund.

2 SSHRC (n.d.), *Organizational structure*, https://www.sshrc-crsh.gc.ca/about-au_sujet/governance-gouvernance/index-eng.aspx.

3 SSHRC (n.d.), *Programs committee*, http://www.sshrc-crsh.gc.ca/about-au_sujet/governance-gouvernance/committees-comites/programs-programmes-eng.aspx.

4 SSHRC (n.d.), *Council*, http://www.sshrc-crsh.gc.ca/about-au_sujet/governance-gouvernance/committees-comites/council-conseil-eng.aspx.

5 See the final section of this chapter.

6 SSHRC is certainly not unique in this. Other such agencies, with clearer goals, that I am personally familiar with include the John Templeton Foundation (religion and science) and the Tikvah Fund (Jewish studies). The former "provides small and large grants for research and public engagement in specific funding areas: Science & the Big Questions (including Philosophy & Theology); Charter Virtue Development; Individual Freedom and Free Markets; Exceptional Cognitive Talent and Genius; Genetics; and, Voluntary Family Planning" (John Templeton Foundation (n.d.), *Funding areas*, https://www.templeton.org/funding-areas). The latter funds projects that elucidate something that they refer to as "Jewish ideas" and how such ideas can function in the political governance of the modern State of Israel. Needless to say, no project critical of Zionism, for example, or critical of the intersection of religion and science will ever be funded by these two organizations. For criticism of Templeton, see Wiebe (2009, 126); for criticism of the Tikvah Fund, see Hughes (2013, 108–12).

7 It might be also worth noting in the present context that the Canada Research Chair at UBC works on a project titled "Constructing a Feminist Shari'a."

8 Online description may be found at http://www.chairs-chaires.gc.ca/chairholders-titulaires/profile-eng.aspx?profileId=2223 (link no longer valid, as the CRC appears to have ended.

9 "Allen R. Greer," *Canada Research Chairs*, Government of Canada, http://www.chairs-chaires.gc.ca/chairholders-titulaires/profile-eng.aspx?profileId=2614.

10 "Isabelle Daunais," *Canada Research Chairs*, Government of Canada, http://www.chairs-chaires.gc.ca/chairholders-titulaires/profile-eng.aspx?profileId=2841.

11 "Susanna Braund," *Canada Research Chairs*, Government of Canada, http://www.chairs-chaires.gc.ca/chairholders-titulaires/profile-eng.aspx?profileId=2137.

12 In this regard Public Safety Canada has recently been running its own competition on radicalization, to which scholars of Islam have been regularly invited to apply. The news release may be found here: Public Safety Canada (2018, 24 July), *Federal funding for research project to counter radicalization to violence* [News release], https://www.canada.ca/en/public-safety-canada/news/2018/07/federal-funding-for-research-project-to-counter-radicalization-to-violence.html. I would like to thank Jennifer Selby for these references.

13 To arrive at this number I searched the "Awards Search Engine" with the keyword "Islam" from 2012/2013 to 2017/2018. This gave me 417, from which I removed funding for journals, CRCs, and multiyear projects (which I only counted once).

14 The poll may be found at Angus Reid (2017, 16 November), "Faith and religion in public life: Canadians deeply divided over the role of faith in the public square," http://angusreid.org/faith-public-square/.

15 Environics Institute (2016, 30 April), *Survey of Muslims in Canada 2016*, https://www.environicsinstitute.org/projects/project-details/survey-of-muslims-in-canada-2016.

16 Angus Reid (2018, 12 July), "Radicalization and homegrown terrorism: Four-in -ten say radicalized individuals live in their communities," http://angusreid.org /radicalization-homegrown-terrorism.
17 The same poll found that only 32 per cent of Canadians supported the right of a woman to wear a niqab and 29 per cent a burqa. This compared to 88 per cent who supported a person wearing a nun's habit or 77 per cent those who wore a turban.
18 I have written about this in several studies. See, for example, Hughes (2007, 2012).
19 A survey of such scholars may be found in Hughes (2015, 75–93).
20 I say "scholarly" because these are the only responses that I am interested in here. Non-scholarly responses – such as Islamophobic attacks that want to portray Islam as an inherently violent religion – are beyond the scope of the present study.
21 Again, one can only get at the search engine (http://www.outil.ost.uqam.ca /CRSH/RechProj.aspx?vLangue=Anglais) through the SSHRC site (http://www .sshrc-crsh.gc.ca/results-resultats/recipients-recipiendaires/index-eng.aspx).
22 Though the three CRCs – one in "Religion, Pluralism, and the Rule of Law," one in "Religion, Law, and Social Justice," and one, less germane but still relevant, in "History of Science in Islamic Societies" – still coincide with the government's agenda.
23 I removed two on account of repetition and one because it was a scholarly aid to a journal (*Journal of the Canadian Society for Syriac Studies / Journal de la Société Canadienne des études Syriaques*).
24 As a comparison, it is worth noting that in the same years there were roughly sixty funded projects devoted to Christianity; twenty to Buddhism; fifteen to Judaism; and four to Hinduism.
25 Again, removed of CRC funding and duplications.

REFERENCES

Bynum, Carol Walker. 2014. "Avoiding the tyranny of morphology: Or, why compare?" *History of Religions, 53*(4), 341–68.

Foucault, Michel. 1972. "Discourse on language." In *The archaeology of knowledge: And the discourse on language* (A.M. Sheridan Smith, Trans.) (pp. 215–37). Pantheon.

– 1977. *Discipline and punish: The birth of the prison* (Alan Sheridan, Trans.). Pantheon.

Hughes, Aaron W. 2007. *Situating Islam: The past and future of an academic discipline.* Equinox Press.

– 2012. "The study of Islam before and after September 11: A provocation." *Method and Theory in the Study of Religion, 24*(4–5), 314–36. https://doi .org/10.1163/15700682-12341234

– 2013. *The study of Judaism: Authenticity, identity, scholarship.* State University of New York Press.

– 2015. *Islam and the tyranny of authenticity: An inquiry into disciplinary apologetics and self-deception*. Equinox.

Kaell, Hillary. 2017. "Introduction." In Hillary Kaell (Ed.), *Everyday sacred: Religion in contemporary Québec* (pp. 3–29). McGill-Queen's University Press.

Levene, Nancy. 2019. "Structure and history and X." *Method and Theory in the Study of Religion*, *31*(1), 40–56. https://doi.org/10.1163/15700682-12341461

Lincoln, Bruce. 1994. *Authority: Construction and corrosion*. University of Chicago Press.

McCutcheon, Russell T. 2007. *Studying religion: An introduction*. Equinox.

Orsi, Robert A. 2005. *Between heaven and earth: The religious worlds people make and the scholars who study them*. Princeton University Press.

Smith, Jonathan Z. 1982. *Imagining religion: From Babylon to Jonestown*. University of Chicago Press.

Wiebe, Donald. 2009. "Religious biases in funding religious studies research?" *Religio: Revue pro religionistiku*, *17*(2), 125–40.

Creating Ecologies of Knowledge as a MENA Scholar in North America: An Interview with Dr. Lara Deeb

SAHVER KUZUCUOGLU

Biography

Dr. Lara Deeb is professor of anthropology at Scripps College in Claremont, California. She received her PhD in anthropology in 2003 from Emory University in Atlanta, Georgia, and was a Harvard Academy Scholar from 2003 to 2004 and 2006 to 2007. As an anthropologist with a focus on Middle Eastern studies, Deeb includes among her research interests the politics of knowledge production, gender and sexuality, religion (Islam in particular), and transnational feminism, with a specific geographical focus on Lebanon.

Deeb's first book, *An Enchanted Modern: Gender and Public Piety in Shi'i Lebanon* (Princeton University Press, 2006), is based on two years of ethnographic research in Dahiya, the southern suburbs of Beirut. This work established Deeb's interest in understanding Islam, pious women's activism, and their integrated relationship with modernity. This complex integration was constructed through ongoing debates, contestations, and reformulations as Shi'i Muslims in this community negotiated piety, modernity, and cosmopolitanism both individually and collectively. Deeb concludes that piety and everyday politics, as demonstrated by the term "everyday Islamists," are inseparable from each other (Deeb 2006, 6).

Deeb's second book, *Leisurely Islam: Negotiating Geography and Morality in Shi'ite South Beirut* (Princeton University Press, 2013, co-authored with Mona Harb), focuses on the dynamics between morality, geography, politics, and the role of leisure and cafe culture for youth in Dahiya, or, as they refer to this area of the capital, South Beirut. The book highlights how gender, sexuality, religion, urban processes, and economic forces intersect as these young adults navigate their identities, traditions, neighbourhoods, and global influences, as well as their political and religious affinities. This multidisciplinary research brings another dimension to a region of Beirut that is often seen solely as a conservative Hizbullah stronghold. By so doing, Deeb and Harb challenge the negative stereotypes of Islam and young Muslims living in the Middle East and highlight the richness and diversity of youth culture in the area. Like much of Deeb's scholarship, this book allows the reader to engage with and understand the complexities laden in the everyday lives of youths who live in Dahiya.

Deeb's published work also reflects her concerns with the politics of knowledge production in academia. For example, her most recent book, *Anthropology's Politics: Disciplining the Middle East* (Stanford University Press, 2015, co-authored with Jessica Winegar), provides a critical assessment of the political and economic dimensions that shape and potentially impede United States–based scholars researching and teaching about the Middle East (MENA). Based on ethnographic data, including archives and media resources, participant observation, and over one hundred interviews with colleagues in Middle East anthropology, this book reveals the dynamics and hierarchies that have affected MENA scholars throughout their careers. Deeb and Winegar show how Islamophobia and "compulsory Zionism" (Deeb and Winegar 2016, 72) persist within the discipline. They conclude that US academic, national, and MENA politics have simultaneously opened spaces for new research and teaching about the region while stifling the production of critical knowledge by encouraging scholars to self-censor their public presentations and teaching.

Putting into practice what she studies and teaches, Deeb is also a scholar-activist. Her scholarly articles addressing subjects such as Muslim women's participation in the public realm, transnational feminism engagements with Islam, and Hizbullah's history and political role in Lebanon directly and indirectly confront Islamophobia, anti-Muslim racism, and compulsory Zionism. She also takes up these topics in her teaching and editorial work.

I see Dr. Lara Deeb's expertise on knowledge production as an integral contribution to the study of Islam(s) and Muslims in North America. As an anthropologist working in the United States who has navigated her role vis-à-vis students, funders, fellow faculty members, administration, and professional organizations, Deeb shares her experiences and insights through a series of interview questions, which guide us in our reflection on knowledge production.

Interview

Sahver Kuzucuoglu [SK]: In your most recent book with Jessica Winegar, *Anthropology's Politics* (2016), you stress the significance of considering how and why scholarly knowledge is produced and stated that politics and academia must be considered co-constitutive. What brought you to this line of questioning? How do you conceive of the link between historical-political contexts with knowledge production in your work? In your view, given the current political climate, are there particular considerations for scholars who study Islam(s) and Muslims in North America? What recommendations would you give to scholars working on Islam(s) and Muslims in Canada?

Lara Deeb [LD]: Questions around how and why scholarly knowledge is produced, or the politics of knowledge production in the academy, arose in both anthropology and Middle Eastern studies long before I began my academic career. Anthropology, specifically in its sociocultural formations, began addressing these questions in the 1970s and 1980s through postcolonial and post-structural critiques of the discipline, feminist interventions, and critiques of representational politics in ethnographic writing. Middle Eastern studies was of course shaken by Said's (1978) *Orientalism*, as well as similar feminist, postcolonial, and post-structuralist interventions. Scholars working at the intersection of these fields have contributed to a significant body of work about knowledge production in each of them. By the time I entered graduate school in 1996, the idea that scholars should think about the politics of knowledge production was almost taken for granted; at minimum, it had become a critical part of most graduate educations in both anthropology and Middle Eastern studies. In other words, these considerations were never *not* a part of my line of questioning, no matter what the specific topic at hand. Simply put, like most scholars of my generation, I do not think it possible to produce knowledge outside a historic-political context. Every scholar lives and works in a place and time, and the questions they ask, projects they propose, research they conduct, and writing they produce are all influenced by their location in that place and time. It is also important to keep disciplinary norms and histories in mind as we talk about knowledge production. My perspectives have been shaped not only by my research in the Middle East and with Muslim communities, and my vantage point as a scholar living and working in the United States and in a variety of US academic institutions in the late twentieth and early twenty-first centuries, but also by my disciplinary location in sociocultural anthropology.

Neither scholars nor scholarship are produced in a political vacuum. In our book *Anthropology's Politics*, Jessica Winegar and I show how the "disciplining" of academics and academic knowledge production takes place in two ways. Scholars are disciplined by blunt external agents that subject them to a range of pressures, with public defamation, job denial, and physical attack at the most extreme end of this range. And they are also disciplined through self-regulating, subjectivating processes. While these two forms are of course interrelated, we found that in the balance, the latter is far more frequent. Disciplining – of both ourselves as scholars and of the knowledge we share with students and other publics – is primarily enacted through self-preservation practices developed in order to navigate the intersections of national, global, and academic politics. Such self-censorship is particularly intense in relation to criticism of the state of Israel, although it emerges in relation to studies of Islam and Muslim communities in North America as well. Self-censorship joins external pressures on scholars not to study or talk about certain topics, the constraints and openings of funding initiatives that are sometimes linked to government interests, and the structural and political factors that make research in some places impossible or dangerous due to political repression or violence. When we think about the politics of knowledge production, we need to consider both visible and invisible forces that shape knowledge, the questions we ask, and the research we produce.

To answer your question about specific considerations and recommendations for scholars who study Islam and Muslims in North America, let me share my own early-career experience. I completed the fieldwork for my dissertation and first book in August 2001, at a political moment when US corporate media was describing Hizbullah, the political party supported by most of my Shi'i Muslim interlocutors in Lebanon, as a political Islamic group that maintained charitable organizations alongside its "guerrilla fighters." By the time I had returned to the US and begun writing my dissertation, Hizbullah had been labelled "the A-team of terrorists." The events of 11 September 2001 were the moment that prompted this shift, despite the party having no relationship to those attacks. That shift in representational politics created challenges that I had to learn to navigate while writing and while on the job market. The politics of knowledge production came into sharp relief for me as a point of stress and active engagement, where before, it had hovered in the background as a taken-for-granted aspect of all academic work on the region. It is crucial to note that anti-Muslim racism and Islamophobia were not new at the time. However, they spiked in particular ways that impacted me – and many of my colleagues (as we explain in *Anthropology's Politics*) at an early career stage. Earlier generations of scholars had been forced to learn to navigate spikes in racism and Islamophobia triggered by other events, such as the 1990 Gulf War, the Islamic Revolution in Iran, or the first intifada.

I share this experience in order to emphasize that the answer to your question about specific considerations for scholars of Islam and Muslims in North America hinges on this intersection of specific political climate, degree and form that anti-Muslim racism is taking, and career stage. While I am not familiar with the Canadian context, my advice would be the same as to those working in the United States: Observe and analyse the political context around you, think about how your work may be used, and pay attention to your audience, but also listen to your interlocutors and be true to their self-representations while taking steps to protect their identities and communities. Incidentally, I would give the same advice to scholars who do ethnographic work in other areas. The politics of knowledge production and representation are not unique to studies of the Middle East, or Islam, or Muslim communities. It is simply that the political moment in which we currently live and work highlights violence and racism impacting these communities, bringing them into more obvious visibility. But the lessons of awareness and deliberate engagement with the politics of knowledge production hold true for work in other historical and geographic contexts as well.

SK: You speak in *Anthropology's Politics* about the long-standing intersections of racism, sexism, and compulsory Zionism as the "sleeping giant of the discipline" (Deeb and Winegar 2016, 111). Despite scholars of anthropology and other branches of knowledge being committed to supporting the oppressed and challenging empire, you have received considerable resistance and criticism for your advocacy in lobbying the American Anthropological Association (AAA) to take a stand and join the Boycott, Divestment, and Sanctions (BDS) movement by boycotting Israeli educational institutions. How do you frame this advocacy within your thinking on the politics of knowledge? Given the unspoken expectations you have encountered on self-disciplining and self-censoring research in response to scholarly resistance to Middle Eastern studies (Deeb and Winegar 2016, 5), how does (or can) an academic circumnavigate the boundaries enforced by institutions, without compromising one's own academic and personal integrity or being branded a heretic, troublemaker, or outlier?

LD: For me, social justice advocacy grows out of anthropological knowledge and is intertwined with the discipline. Recall that I began my graduate training at a moment when the corner of academe in which I found a scholarly home had already embraced postcolonial and post-structuralist critiques of knowledge production and representations of the other. I also came of age during the anti-apartheid movement, which provided a model for transnational politics, and the 1990 Gulf War, which positioned the Middle East as the primary post–Cold War "enemy other" of the United States and "the West." It is not uncommon in my generation of scholars to understand political and academic commitments as intertwined. In *Anthropology's Politics*, we show that the vast majority of our colleagues trained after 1990 understand anthropology to be a discipline that should always be critical of power, especially state power, and supportive of human rights – an understanding shared with feminist scholars of earlier generations as well. In fact, many of us came to anthropology in the first place because we believed that the discipline, through its on-the-ground, ethnographic, "perspective of the interlocutor" method, was necessarily aligned with activism. Not all anthropologists would agree with that aspiration for the discipline. However, this perspective has grown more common with time, a shift that is linked to the prevalence of concerns about the politics of knowledge production and representational responsibility in the discipline.

Concerns about representation in particular have long been a part of this conversation for feminist scholars who write about Muslim communities, because they often feel a significant responsibility to correct negative stereotypes about Muslim women. Scholars who write about Islam are embedded in a climate of scholarly and popular interest in Muslim women dominated by the conflation of Islam with political conflicts. This produces tremendous pressure to counter stereotypes (including *within* the academy), no matter what the specific topic of one's work. This pressure persists as the "War on Terror" continues to produce and depend on misconceptions about Muslim women for its ideological justification. It also reflects a gendering of Islamophobia or anti-Muslim racism where the overdetermined category of "Muslim women" is used as the other that constructs White women as liberated and White liberal feminists as liberators.

You asked specifically about my support for BDS. The Boycott, Divestment, and Sanctions movement is the best way that people living and working outside Palestine-Israel can support Palestinian rights. That academics *should* support Palestinian rights seems obvious to me, especially for those of us who work in a nation state complicit with and funding the Israeli occupation, violence, and human rights abuses – we have a responsibility to speak out against these abuses. My perspective and knowledge of Palestine-Israel is shaped by my scholarly reading of ethnographies of Palestine and Palestinian communities. In fact, Palestine and Palestinian communities are among the most researched field sites in Middle East anthropology today (Deeb and Winegar 2012). This means that we have at our disposal a significant body of well-researched ethnographic analyses of a range of issues that elucidate life in Palestinian communities as well as Israeli settler colonialism and occupation. These scholarly works provide the information and knowledge scholars need to be able to take a knowledgeable political stance in support of Palestinians. Such solidarity with people against state violence and against settler colonialism is a hallmark of contemporary anthropology due to its method, which emphasizes attention to on-the-ground perspectives, daily lives, and experiences.

In my view, it would be irresponsible to answer the last question in a generalized way, because whether or how an academic can circumnavigate institutional boundaries depends on a number of factors including but not limited to the scholar's positionality, institutional location, and level of precarity in terms of employment but also in terms of life situation, finances, family, and so on. No matter what one's location, it is crucial to seek co-conspirators, allies, comrades – likeminded colleagues, whatever you choose to call them. It is also important to research your institution, to understand its specific relationship to the political questions at hand and the ways in which administrators have responded in the past. And it is incumbent upon those of us with the privilege of tenure to use that security to protect others, students and colleagues alike.

SK: The lived religion/piety debate has over the past few years dominated discussions among anthropologists of Islam. Some state that an overemphasis on similarities is necessary to rehumanize the Muslim, while others emphasize that this focus on sameness not only may erase diversity but can also construct Muslims as "aberrational, unnatural, and even inhuman" (Fadil and Fernando 2015, 82). Can you expand on one of your arguments in "Thinking Piety and the Everyday Together: A Response to Fadil and Fernando" (Deeb 2015)? How can we move from binaries (such as fundamentalist or everyday Muslims) to the study of Muslims and Islam(s) as ecologies of knowledge (a fully integrated, multirelational web of disciplines and knowledges) that account for intersections, continuums, and broader sociological relationships? Or, as you say, that piety and lived religion are co-produced in "both directions" (Deeb 2015, 96). What theoretical and empirical shifts does this approach require?

LD: In my view, the "lived religion versus piety" debate often relies on straw man arguments on both sides. It remains unclear to me how the alleged sides in the debate grew so opposed to one another, because I think we would all agree that there is no single way of approaching "Islam" and no single "Muslim community." Once again, context is everything, and we need to both listen carefully to our interlocutors and understand our audiences. That said, I do not think that catering to audiences by overemphasizing similarities is necessarily the answer. I stand by my call for a focus on "ecologies of knowledge" that account for "intersections, continuums, and broader sociological relationships." To do so requires a focus on people's situated lives, rather than rhetoric or doctrinal perspectives. Even the most ideologically committed person is situated in an ever-changing social context, which affects how they practise their religion and apply its values in other areas of life. Self-understandings also change over time, sometimes from year to year, sometimes from moment to moment. Put bluntly, human beings – pious or not – are complex messes who don't always articulate accurate explanations for what they do and why and don't always live up to their own notions of morality, values, or a good life. Capturing this messiness and how it is interpreted, shaped, corralled, and lived in context will lead us to better understand complex ecologies of knowledge and practice, whether in relation to Islam, other religions, or other ways of being in the world.

Take, for example, the self-described pious Muslim youth in South Beirut that Mona Harb and I described in our co-authored book *Leisurely Islam* (Deeb and Harb 2013). Our analysis of these youth aimed to show how they negotiated different and sometimes conflicting values and ideas of what it meant to live well, specifically in relation to their leisure lives. Understanding these negotiations was not merely about moving from one set of values to another in different moments, but it was deeply context specific, shaped by factors ranging from time of day and location to who was present and the person's mood. Furthermore, the values at hand were themselves subject to change and to be influenced by the various situations youth encountered and their experiences. This is what I meant by the co-production of piety and lived religion. The ideals that underlie one's understanding of oneself as a pious person, or the ideals one aims to attain, also emerge from social contexts. It is a mistake to assume that "what religion says" and "what people do" exist outside of relation to one another. What people do affects how they understand or hear or read "what religion says" and may in fact impact the "rules" or doctrine or interpretations of a text. This ability to attend to an ever-shifting social landscape in order to understand piety is one of the strengths of an ethnographic perspective.

SK: A common understanding of "Islamophobia" in broader society is that it is a fear of Muslims and Islam, which is basic and therefore inadequate. Scholars have been highlighting and emphasizing the connections between individual violent acts targeting Muslims and those who "look like" Muslims, the networks that feed these behaviours, and the manifestation of Islamophobia in institutions and systems in North America and across the globe. Yet resistance to systemic Islamophobia and intolerance in society is also growing in response. How do you define Islamophobia? Do you incorporate anti-Islamophobia and anti-Muslim racism approaches in your scholarship? If yes, how so?

LD: The best way for me to answer this question is to call upon other scholars who have done extraordinary work analysing and combating Islamophobia and anti-Muslim racism. I had the privilege of working with a group of these scholars in creating the "Islamophobia Is Racism" syllabus (Abdul Khabeer et al. n.d.), available at https://islamophobiaisracism.wordpress.com. My own definition of Islamophobia concurs with our approach in the syllabus, summed up in this extended quote from its introduction:

> Although "Islamophobia" is the term most recognizable in public discourse, it does not accurately convey the making of racial and religious "others" that fuels the forms of discrimination Muslims face in the United States. The term Islamophobia frames these forms of discrimination and their roots solely as a problem of religious discrimination. Calling this a "phobia" suggests that this discrimination is solely a problem of individual bias, which obscures the structural and systemic production of anti-Muslim racism.

In other words, Islamophobia must be understood as a form of racism rooted in the history of US and European empire and nation-state building. This structural understanding requires us to shift our focus away from the individual and towards the societal and state structures of violence and ideologies that constitute and perpetuate racism and Islamophobia. This is one of the reasons I believe it is crucial to think about anti-Muslim racism instead of Islamophobia, because we must avoid falling into the trap that this is a problem of individual prejudice that can be solved by teaching people more about Islam. This is not a matter of ignorance and fear and therefore people subsequently being biased against what they do not understand. Such an approach lets state power and histories of White supremacy off the hook. This is a structural problem, and it cannot be challenged without attending to the ways that structures of inequality, state practices, war, and violence have created racism and discrimination, even as they are practised by and impact individuals.

You also asked whether I incorporate anti-Islamophobia and anti-Muslim racism approaches in my scholarship. I strive to do so, and I hope that the ways I have approached my research does some of this work. As a whole, I view one of the goals of my scholarship as providing readers with better ways of understanding not only Islam and Muslim communities but also the political-economic and historical structures of power and violence, often colonial violence, that have shaped the communities about which I am writing. This is reflected even more strongly perhaps in my teaching, and I view the classroom as one of the key spaces in which scholars can do productive anti-racist work. For example, even courses that are not focused on Islam or Muslims can often include readings (and accompanying discussions) of some of the work on the Islamophobia syllabus mentioned above. In my own teaching, the vast majority of my courses – no matter what the topic – begin with several "framing" articles, and I try to choose combinations of these that lead to classroom discussions that connect racisms historically and across communities. With the caveat that this is by no means an exhaustive list, simply a list of what has worked well in my specific courses in recent years, these readings have included Lila Abu-Lughod's (2013) *Do Muslim Women Need Saving?*, excerpts from Said's (1978) *Orientalism* and Mahmood Mamdani's (2005) *Good Muslim, Bad Muslim*, J. Kēhaulani Kauanui's (2012) interview with Patrick Wolfe titled "Settler Colonialism Then and Now," and Andrea Smith's (2006) "Heteropatriarchy and the Three Pillars of White Supremacy." Because I teach at a small, private liberal arts college, my goal is to prompt students to engage with these materials in ways that make intersectional connections and instigate a different, critical understanding of their own experiences, approaches, and positionalities.

SK: Debates on positionality, power, and authority in the anthropology of Islam arise alongside discussions on insider/outsider status. To what extent do these debates, along with the co-constitution of academia and politics, influence scholars' foci and, more specifically, what they feel authorized (and not authorized) to write about? Who is authorized to write about Islam(s) and Muslims? Who is being spoken for, and who is being spoken to? Additionally, whose voices remain silent? Does this debate resonate with you? To what extent do these similar questions influence scholars working on the MENA region, and to which extent do you consider these questions in your own work?

LD: Yes, this debate does indeed resonate with me, but once again, it does so through the lens of anthropology, which complicates my perspective and experiences over the course of my career thus far. Because anthropology, for most of the discipline's history, privileged the idea of research from a perspective "outside" the community or group of people about which the scholar was writing, for years, so-called "heritage" or "native" or "halfie" scholars were often viewed as "too biased" or "too close" to their research to be able to produce quality scholarship. I have encountered or been informed of comments suggesting as much about my own work, for example, even though I have written mostly about communities in Lebanon that are quite different from that of my family. In our research for *Anthropology's Politics*, Jessica Winegar and I found that although it has become far more acceptable in anthropology to study "one's own" community (however defined) in recent decades, pushback persists. Scholars from the region described being encouraged to work "somewhere new" and expressed concerns that if they worked in the region they would not be taken as seriously as White scholars. White anthropologists, in turn, articulated worrying about being called an Orientalist or expressed erroneous assumptions that region-related scholars somehow had it easier. Within anthropology, these discussions about positionality and authoritative knowledge are far from over.

There is another important component to this problem of authority and authorship. In the current political climate, many scholars who identify as Middle Eastern or Muslim feel compelled to teach and speak publicly about Islam and gender in ways that upend stereotypes. Yet, like some feminists of colour, many of us also hesitate to "air our dirty laundry" in contexts where it is assumed that sexism and patriarchy are worse in Muslim societies than anywhere else. This is another old problem, one heard in countless conversations at conferences and workshops and about which women of colour have been writing for decades. One hopes that shedding light on an issue will dispel stereotypes but fears that audiences will hear only what they are listening for. While we have come to expect these stereotypes in public discourse, we forget that they infuse academic contexts as well. For this reason, in *Do Muslim Women Need Saving?*, Abu-Lughod reminds us that it is important to maintain a healthy scepticism about why we are interested in particular issues among particular people.

Let me give you another example from my own experience: Nearly a decade ago, I wrote a short piece on the e-zine *Jadaliyya* explaining how my colleague Mona Harb and I decided to drop a component of our project on youth and leisure that addressed temporary marriage among our young interlocutors (Deeb 2017). We did so because we did not want to contribute to a sensationalist context where temporary marriage was already over-represented in the English-language press in ways that combined exoticism with a colonial desire to save Muslim women. Moreover, variations of those same discourses were also present at the time in the Lebanese press, where they fuelled negative stereotypes about Shi'i Muslims that linked political fears and discrimination to sectarian difference in a national context. In that *Jadaliyya* piece, I argued that some of the focus on temporary marriage served to shift attention away from issues of political representation and legitimacy by reframing the conversation as one about essential moral difference. I stand by my analysis of the problem in that piece but am on the fence about the end result of representational paralysis leading to ethnographic refusal. We chose not to write about something that would have been an excellent example of youth-driven social change and the tensions between religious tenets and social norms, as well as a lens on the shifting terms of gender inequality and the practice's health and social consequences. We stumbled at the question of how to do that without providing fodder for the increasingly absurd and vociferous Islamophobic and sectarian political rhetorical machine. In doing so, we lost the opportunity to analyse a problem with potential social justice implications.

Questions of identity, audience, and authority remain at the forefront of my mind in my current project on social sectarianism or sect as a form of social difference in Lebanon. Frankly, acknowledging that many people in Lebanon discriminate against one another based on sect feels a bit like airing a family secret. I worry that writing about how sect matters to people on the ground will contribute to the intransigent assumption in the policy world that sectarianism explains everything that is wrong with the Middle East. But those worries have not led me to drop the question, for several reasons: Sectarianism's continued reign, among pundits and policymakers, as their favoured explanation for all the region's problems speaks to their own flawed thinking. It also speaks to the concept's utility to both US and regional actors as a discourse for justifying ideological perspectives and political ends (Makdisi 2017). While this context, where sectarianism is an all-too-legible concept available for ready manipulation by political actors, should be something of which, as scholars, we remain aware but that which should not suppress research. Second, paralleling the long-held arguments of feminist and anti-racist scholars, no matter how much one shows the constructed nature of the differences upon which any discrimination is based, that discrimination still has material and affective consequences in the world. Another key factor is my interlocutors' interest in the project and in talking about these patterns of discrimination and their hope that revealing these dynamics will assist in dispelling them.

Again, I think the decisions scholars make about what to research and write have to be made and understood in relationship to institutional and personal contexts. No matter our own positionalities, those of us who feel an ethical pull towards producing scholarship that we think, perhaps naively, will contribute to social justice in some way should always ask questions such as: How do we produce scholarship critical of injustice, critical of settler colonialism, including the Israeli settler colonial project, while fearing reprisal? How do we responsibly counter stereotypes without giving them importance and quell liberal desires to save the world without denying social problems where they exist? How do we produce writing that analyses difference critically without reproducing its categories? In the end, this is about accountability in relation to knowledge production. Who are we writing for, and how do we decide which politics, which context, and which priorities to honour when those priorities, politics, or contexts come into conflict with one another?

REFERENCES

Abdul Khabeer, Su'ad, Arshad Ali, Evelyn Alsultany, Sohail Daulatzai, Lara Deeb, Carol Fadda, Zareena Grewal, Juliane Hammer, Nadine Naber, and Junaid Rana. n.d. "Islamophobia is racism." Retrieved 30 August 2018 from https://islamophobiaisracism.wordpress.com

Abu-Lughod, Lila. 2013. *Do Muslim women need saving?* Harvard University Press.

Deeb, Lara. 2006. *An enchanted modern: Gender and public piety in Shi'i Lebanon.* Princeton University Press.

– 2015. "Thinking piety and the everyday together: A response to Fadil and Fernando." *HAU: Journal of Ethnographic Theory, 5*(2), 93–6.

– (2017, 14 September) "'Til sect do you part?': On sectarianism and intermarriage in Lebanon." *Jadaliyya.* http://www.jadaliyya.com/Details/34552/%E2%80%9CTil-Sect-Do-You-Part%E2%80%9D-On-Sectarianism-and-Intermarriage-in-Lebanon

Deeb, Lara, and Mona Harb. 2013. *Leisurely Islam: Negotiating geography and morality in Shi'ite South Beirut.* Princeton University Press.

Deeb, Lara, and Jessica Winegar. 2012. "Anthropologies of Arab-majority societies." *Annual Review of Anthropology, 41*, 537–58. https://doi.org/10.1146/annurev-anthro-092611-145947

– 2016. *Anthropology's politics: Disciplining the Middle East.* Stanford University Press.

– 2017. "Middle East politics in US academia." *Comparative Studies of South Asia, Africa and the Middle East, 37*(1), 103–12. https://doi.org/10.1215/1089201x-3821333

Fadil, Nadia, and Mayanthi Fernando. 2015. "Rediscovering the 'everyday' Muslim: Notes on an anthropological divide." *HAU: Journal of Ethnographic Theory, 5*(2), 59–88.

Kauanui, J. Kēhaulani, and Patrick Wolfe. 2012. "Settler colonialism then and now." *Politica & Societá, 2*, 235–58. https://doi.org/10.4476/37055

Makdisi, Ussama. 2017. "The mythology of the sectarian Middle East." Baker Institute for Public Policy, Rice University. https://www.bakerinstitute.org/research/mythology-sectarian-middle-east

Mamdani, Mahmood. 2005. *Good Muslim, bad Muslim.* Three Leaves Press; Doubleday.

Said, Edward. 1978. *Orientalism.* Penguin.

Smith, Andrea. 2006. "Heteropatriarchy and the three pillars of White supremacy." In Andrea Lee Smith, Beth E. Richie, Julia Sudbury, and Janelle White (Eds.), *The color of violence: The INCITE! anthology* (pp. 68–73). South End Press.

The Study of Islam(s) and Western Academia: An Interview with Anver Emon

REHAN SAYEED

Biography

Anver M. Emon is professor and Canada Research Chair in Islamic Law and History in the Faculty of Law at the University of Toronto. He is also appointed to the Department of History in the Faculty of Arts and Sciences and currently directs the university's Institute of Islamic Studies. Emon holds doctorates in history from the University of California, Los Angeles, and law from Yale University. He researches Islamic legal history to reflect on Islamic law in the past and in the present across different regions. His analysis engages Islamic law both as a subject of historical analysis and as a vehicle of critique. More specifically, taking a historical approach, he explores the nuances of legal argument, charting continuities and discontinuities in a diachronic fashion. He problematizes the idea of "Islamic law" in order to critique what is meant by the very concept of legal. Emon was the founding editor of *Middle East Law and Governance: An Interdisciplinary Journal* and currently serves as editor of the Oxford Islamic Legal Studies Series. The recipient of numerous research grants, Emon was named a 2014 Guggenheim Fellow in the field of law and awarded the 2017 Kitty Newman Memorial Award in Philosophy from the Royal Society of Canada.

Emon's first monograph, *Islamic Natural Law Theories* (2010), is an ambitious jurisprudential enquiry into an uncharted tradition of natural theory. It is ambitious in the sense that it attempts to bridge Islamic legal theory and its ethical theories with theology, an approach traditionally sidelined due to its complexities. Engaging with premodern Muslim jurists in the ninth and tenth centuries, Emon distinguishes between what he calls "Hard" (the Muʿtazilite) and "Soft" (Ash'arite) Naturalists, arguing that both, although theologically distinct, granted ontological authority to reason. Extending his doctoral research on natural theories, he developed another project investigating the question of tolerance in Islam.

This research led to his second monograph, titled *Religious Pluralism and Islamic Law: "Dhimmīs" and Others in the Empire of Law* (2012), in which he sheds light on the difficulties present in pursuing pluralism alongside the rule of law and effective governance. Analysing various Muslim jurists' discourses on the legal rights of *dhimmīs* (minorities), Emon offers an in-depth account of how Muslim jurists have traditionally developed frameworks to deal with the challenge of the "legal Other." Taking a comparative approach, he offers a critical analysis of recent legal debates from the US, the UK, and the European Court of Human Rights. He suggests that sharia be understood as a mode of regulating the polity and not so different from a "rule of law" (Emon 2012, 15). Problematizing the notion of "tolerance," Emon concludes that despite claims for legal pluralism, legal systems cannot escape being hegemonic against the interests of minorities. Adopting a legal frame of analysis, which is of course foundational to Emon's scholarship, *Religious Pluralism and Islamic Law* opens novel questions regarding the past and present of the Islamic legal tradition.

Emon's research interests, although focused on Islam, cut across multiple legal and religious traditions. His collaboration with scholars of Christian and Jewish legal thought led to *Natural Law: A Jewish, Christian, and Islamic Trialogue* (co-authored with David Novak and Matthew Levering, 2014) and an edited volume, *Islamic and Jewish Legal Reasoning: Encountering Our Legal Other* (2016a). In both of these books, Emon brings in scholars of other legal and religious traditions to draw attention to the inherent universality of natural law claims in Abrahamic religious traditions.

In addition to Emon's expertise in Islamic legal history, his scholarship also speaks to the politics of knowledge production on Islam in the North Atlantic world. His 2019 article, "The 'Islamic' Deployed: The Study of Islam in Four Registers," is one such contribution. In it, Emon argues that the approaches to studying Islam and Muslims, and thus the deployment of "Islamic," shares rhetorical similitude with the projects of governance, whether by the modern state or a premodern regime. Critical of philology's and anthropology's "narrow range of disciplinary approaches," Emon offers an analytical framework that considers the varied deployments of the "Islamic" across the four registers – time, space, rhetoric, and scale. The article is taken up in greater detail in the interview below.

Last, Emon has considerable experience leading collaborative efforts at the intersection of academic research and public engagement. He brings his scholarly background to his consultations for governments, NGOs, and legal advocacy groups. In 2013, Emon received a grant from Canada's Department of Justice to develop a high school curriculum project on forced marriage. The project was a partnership among the University of Toronto Faculties of Law and Social Work, the Ontario Justice Education Network (OJEN), Law in Action Within Schools, and the South Asian Legal Clinic of Ontario. These academic and non-academic partners were committed to advancing justice education. One output of the project was the creation of a digitized graphic novel.

In this interview, focused on his work on the politics of knowledge production, I engage Emon's critical take on philology and ethnography, drawing on "The 'Islamic' Deployed."[1] The interview also focuses on understanding how his intellectual trajectory, with backgrounds in both law and history, has shaped his views regarding the deployment of the "Islamic" in Western academia.

Interview

Rehan Sayeed [RS]: In your recent essay titled "The 'Islamic' Deployed: The Study of Islam in Four Registers" (2019), you argue for the game-changing role of September 11 and the ensuing "War on Terror" on the academic study of Islam. You write, "9/11 began to affect 'who' could study and produce research and to what ends" (Emon 2019, 349).

I have a few questions on this point. First, can you expand on how these events have impacted the study of Islam – at both methodological and theoretical levels? Put differently, what is the discursive power of 9/11 in shaping how Islam is studied and mobilized, especially in North American academic settings?

And second, there is a common perception that North American universities have become more militarized post-9/11. Arguably, however, American universities also became militarized with the Vietnam War and through the Cold War era, when some renowned American universities became laboratories for military experiments which continue today. What do you think?

Anver Emon [AE]: The events of that day launched new and enhanced state security and military projects, though to be fair, they had been with us for a longer period of time, well before 9/11. The difference is that 9/11 foregrounded those issues for a greater number of stakeholders and across a wider range of publics. For those of us in the North Atlantic academy, 9/11 offered a paradigmatic change (with epistemic implications to follow) as a new global threat took the place of the USSR and its communist ideology. Francis Fukuyama had declared the "end of history" in 1992, but with the new global presence of jihadism or whatever you want to call it, he had to walk that back.

In the halls of advanced research, the "War on Terror" had the effect (whether deserved or not) of signalling a sea change in the formation of research agendas (see Wagner-Pacifici 2010). For example, in law schools, scholars began to interrogate immigration and national security rules that guard against an "Islamic" threat (see Roach 2011). In psychology departments, researchers advanced or critiqued government programs that counter violent extremism (CVE) by using the "Islamic" extremist as paradigmatic.[2] In these and other instances, scholars began to engage, critique, support, or otherwise address state practices in the shadow of varying constructions of the "Islamic."

Also, as I describe in that 2019 article, 9/11 began to affect *who* could study and produce research and to what ends. The security-conscious environment that became the norm ushered in a regime of immigration restrictions in the United States, for one, that limited who could study and produce knowledge, where they could go, and which borders they could cross in pursuit of ideas. One can appreciate how immigration restrictions impact who can enter a country to study and produce knowledge; how such knowledge production should be framed; and how knowledge relates to projects of the state – together these lean towards a single outcome: knowledge produced in the service of the state by those loyal to it.[3]

I see therefore how the study of Islam, increasingly, is undertaken in service of the state as a project. Wherever one might stand on the political spectrum, the study of Islam is undertaken in the shadow of the state as a disaggregated project of law and justice, border control, national security, and overall regulation.

RS: You also argue in "The 'Islamic' Deployed" that epistemologically, both philology and ethnography can be understood to be at odds in their academic pursuit of the "Islamic." However, these approaches, you say, share a common thread: that the methodological rhetoric of the "Islamic" is deployed by both in ways that bolster state governance projects.

This is a claim that I think needs some parsing. I want to begin with the politics of ethnography, as I am an anthropologist in training. How do you see ethnography as a methodology – that, in your words, is "radically democratic" in relation to philology and which "pluraliz[es] the range of signifying possibilities" (Emon 2019, 388) – grasp the adjectival nature of "Islamic," especially in the context of how Western-trained anthropologists deploy it?

AE: In the field of Islamic studies, this everyday, lived approach to the study of Islam often takes the disciplinary form of anthropology and the methodological form of ethnography. If nineteenth- and twentieth-century philology was a methodological proxy for a historically positivist, authenticity-oriented approach to Islam, ethnography has served as a counterweight, radically redistributing authenticity in the subjectivities of the ethnographized Muslim. Ethnography infers the "Islamic" from the ordinary, day-to-day experiences of Muslims, thereby collapsing the "Islamic" and the "Muslim," which in turn explains why I want to use both in adjectival form.

The radicalness of ethnography lies in how it scales authority and authenticity democratically by presuming it as immanent in the lived experiences of a Muslim qua Muslim. Ethnographers have been especially influenced by the work of Talal Asad, who examines Muslim practices in order to identify the moral frameworks that inform how Muslims understand both themselves (in the world that they inhabit) and the world around them. Critical of then-existing approaches to the anthropology of Islam, Asad wrote in 1986 that "Islam as the object of anthropological understanding should be approached as a *discursive* tradition that connects variously with *the formation of moral selves* [emphasis added], the manipulation of populations (or resistance to it), and the production of appropriate knowledge" (Asad 2009, 10).[4] Asad (2009) casts Islam as a "tradition" and, in so doing, counters a discourse among adherents regarding the "correct form and purpose of a given practice that, precisely because it is established, has a history" (20). Examining such practices in real time allows Asad to incorporate, while at the same time collapsing, the past and future in the observable present of participant observation.

To draw upon the past by reference to a future mediated by the present, as Asad explains is the location of the Islamic discursive tradition, does not ignore the literary tradition, nor does it relegate it to the scrap bin of irrelevance. Rather, the meaningfulness of the literary tradition is mediated by reference to the practices of those who adhere to that tradition in the present. Instead of abiding by notions of orthodoxy and heterodoxy, which already imply the operation of an elite power in the construction of knowledge, if not the construction of the compliant subject, an anthropology of Islam begins with the "instituted practices ... into which Muslims are inducted as Muslims" (Asad 2009, 21).

The use of the passive tense here ("are inducted") signals the rhetorical shift from the presumed compliance of philology to a radical democratic sensibility regarding the Muslim subject. For instance, Charles Hirschkind (2006) encounters Muslims in Cairo who engage in the "common and valued" activity of listening to cassette tape sermons (4). These Muslims are not the radical extremists prosecuted in courts around the world or whose cassette tape listening habits are evidence for the prosecution. Rather, Hirschkind gives voice to complex, very human subjects "who hold regular jobs, study at the university, send their kids to public schools, and worry about the future of their communities" (4). Hirschkind's interlocutors in taxicabs, shisha parlours, and elsewhere listen to cassette tape sermons to inform their "religious sensibility" or moral selves, which in turn enable them to situate themselves within a politics of belonging that was both national and transnational. While the authoritarian Egyptian state always existed in the backdrop to Hirschkind's study, it often served as a foil for the radical, democratic "counterpublics" in which his subjects interacted, debated, and participated. Drawing upon Hannah Arendt, Hirschkind's (2006) counterpublic is a space of radical democracy given the "activities of ordinary citizens who, through the exercise of their agency in a context of public interaction, shape the conditions of their collective existence" by reference to an "Islamic" they deploy through cassette tape technologies (8).

In another exceptional anthropology of Islam in Egypt, Amira Mittermaier writes about the long-standing practices of dream interpretation by a group of Egyptian shaykhs and their students. Mittermaier (2011) recounts the work, practices, and narratives of dream interpreters to complicate the all-too-frequent image of a "monolithic Islam." Standing on the fringes of Hirschkind's reformist counterpublics, Mittermaier's (2011) dream interpreters are "dismissed by many reformist thinkers, but they are in continuous if ambivalent dialogue with reformism and constitute a vibrant aspect of the Islamic Revival" (5). Mittermaier does not psychoanalyse Egyptian Muslims for their psychic experiences. Rather, her "anthropology of the imagination" examines how they "tell, understand, interpret, and live their dreams" and thereby map the "landscapes of a particular imagination" (5). Dreams by their nature are obviously unobservable. But the interpretive practices around the dreams – their retelling, their interpretation, and their implications on creating a moral framework of being in the world – were the ethnographic stuff of Mittermaier's analysis.

For Mittermaier (2011), the radical democratic sense of the "Islamic" lay in the everyday "preludes and aftermaths" of dreams (21). If philology privileges the text in informing the "Islamic," the ethnographic approach radically relocates the "Islamic" in the ordinary, everyday practices of Muslims. Correlating if not collapsing the "Islamic" with the "Muslim," the anthropological study of Islam gives the impression of a discursive tradition in which the agency of content lies in the individual Muslim in community with other Muslims. This is in stark contrast to the philological study, in which the literary tradition potentially overdetermines the subjectivity of the "Muslim" by reference to a historically positivist cast of Islam's presumed "core."

Rhetorically, ethnography's radical democracy has two implications. First, ethnography's tendency to decentre the "Islamic" by diffusing it into the autonomous actions of individual Muslims collapses the "Muslim" with the "Islamic," thereby justifying my turn to the adjectival sense of "Islamic" and "Muslim." Second, contrary to the textualist deduction of philology, the ethnographic inferential model renders the ethnographized Muslim as representative of a collectivity that is not at the same time the state. In other words, once ethnographized, the subject is no longer single, individual, personal, but instead an ethnographically rendered representative of a collective that stands separate from the state. These two rhetorical features allow the ethnographer to situate his or her analysis as an implicit if not explicit critique of what Migdal (2001) problematizes as the idealized state, imagined along Enlightenment liberal ideals of the state and citizenship. While ethnography is certainly an important intervention in the field of Islamic studies, the fact that the state hovers in the backdrop, I argue, informs the politics of ethnography's methodological rhetoric.

RS: Moving away from the discursivity so inherent in ethnography, one can hardly ignore the historical centrality of philology in the study of Islam. In this same essay (Emon 2019), you show how the scholarly study of Islam in nineteenth- and twentieth-century Europe deployed philology. Despite contemporary criticisms of philology, especially those arising from proponents of ethnography, its heuristic importance cannot be underestimated. In what ways do you see the rhetoric of "Islamic" being promulgated within philology, and how does it speak to your critique of knowledge production with reference to Islam, especially in the North Atlantic world?

AE: Given the centrality of Arabic in the early study of Islam, it is not surprising that from the nineteenth century onwards, philology would assume such prominence in the study of Islam in Europe. Bernard Lewis (1979), identifying the centrality of "philology" to what he called Islamic "classical and scriptural studies," wrote that at that time, "major progress in Arabic and related scholarship was made in the West, especially in the fields of grammar and lexicography and, toward the end of the century, in the study of Muslim law, theology, and history" (365). Charles Adams (2001, viii) too remarked on the "strong, indeed, almost exclusive, textual and philological orientation of traditional Islamic studies" as he contrasted it with a broadly social scientific approach to the study of religion. Ironically, by the twenty-first century, scholars of Islam explained the marginality of Islamic studies in research universities by reference to the salience of philology to the disciplinary formation of Islamic studies. As Carl W. Ernst and Richard C. Martin (2010) recount, "what we today call Islamic studies emerged from Orientalism, the erudite study of texts and ideas that became a highly developed field in the nineteenth and twentieth centuries in Europe and the United States" (2–3).

The primacy of philology, though, remains wedded to the field of Islam, so it seems. Take, for instance, the late Shahab Ahmad's *What Is Islam?* Ahmed (2015) shifts the spatial register of the "Islamic" (e.g., Balkans-to-Bengal complex) and the temporal register of the "Islamic" (from the formative/classical to the post-formative or thirteenth century) to identify when and where the "Islamic" informed a cosmology of the "Islamic" life (75). But it nonetheless reflects, in its emphasis on texts and the literary tradition, an ongoing focus on elite-produced texts and commentary.

This methodological priority of philology in the study of Islam has significant rhetorical implications in its deployment across governance projects of variable scale. For instance, the global business of Islamic finance is premised upon a formal reading of premodern legal sources, as if Islamic finance is not also a construct doing political work in the service of enterprising capitalists (see El-Gamal 2006). Moreover, when self-proclaimed security experts such as Frank Gaffney and Sebastian Gorka cast the "Islamic" as threat, they reduce it to texts – scriptural or otherwise – that are read literally and ahistorically, which is ironically what many Islamist extremists such as Bin Laden and al-Baghdadi of ISIS have done as well (McCants 2015).[5] Of course, one might argue that these are instances of non-specialists utilizing Islamic sources for obvious, if not overt, political or economic gain.

Those naysayers ignore, however, that the very framing of a study is immersed in a politics that too often goes unstated and unaccounted for and arguably mistakes the "Islamic" for something else. For instance, consider Hiroyuki Yanagihashi's seminal study of early Islamic property law. In his look at the "first centuries of Islam regarding civil liability," Yanagihashi (2004) focuses on special types of sales and the prohibition of *ribā*. Importantly, he defines his study by reference to "property," though elsewhere he describes his research as pertaining to "civil liability" or "the Islamic law of obligations" (15). For a casual reader, these phrases may seem dull or merely descriptive. In contrast, a common-law-trained lawyer reading Yanagihashi's study would argue that his title makes a category mistake; rather than property, the subject matter concerns contract law. Yanagihashi's study is framed in the shadow of other European writers, such as Chafik Chehata, whose implicit understanding of law and legality was framed by the European civil law tradition. Presumably the same applies to Yanagihashi, as Japan implements the civilian legal tradition as well.

So what can or does "philology" signal rhetorically? As Suzanne Marchand (2009) explains in her masterful study on nineteenth-century German Orientalism, the philologist engaged in an "internalist source criticism, perfecting attempts to take texts apart from the inside, and to determine their authenticity, date, and authorship. Combined with 'external' testimony … these findings could be, if one dared, used to recreate lost worlds" (160). The power of philology was attractive for those looking to the Arabic literary tradition for hints about the Bible and the history of Christianity, as it was presumed that these old Arabic texts were windows into the cultural milieu from which they emanated. In other words, the nineteenth-century philological project rhetorically espoused a historical positivism as philology's enticing promise: "The lasting beauty of it was that at least in principle, one listened to the texts themselves, speaking in their own tongues, and even sometimes trusted their testimony over and against that of traditional authorities" (Marchand 2009, 160), such as those assuming canonical status in European academe (e.g., Herodotus).

While philology has an important role to play in the historical account of language, its standing in the academy has suffered. Latinist and medievalist Jan Ziolkowski recounts the polarizing effect of the term "philology" across various departments. For some, philology is "belittled as being a set of basic tools or data rather than as an approach valid in its own right" (Ziolkowski 1990, 2). Its historical positivist presumptions run contrary to the interpretive turn in the humanities and social sciences, leading some to suggest that philologists are unable or unwilling to "test their own presuppositions and to ask new questions," leading to studies that are little more than "stale and irrelevant" (Ziolkowski 1990, 3). Its adherents insist on its centrality to the humanistic endeavour (see Turner 2014), as a discipline of "refined techniques acquired through centuries of learned enterprise" (Ziolkowski 1990, 3). And certainly, there are innovative developments in the practice of philology (e.g., Menocal's *Arabic Role in Medieval Literary History*) that we cannot help but applaud for their critical engagements. In short, philology offers either a great deal or very little depending on the question being asked.

For my purposes, my concern with the primacy of philology in the early study of Islam in the academy is that who Muslims are and what they believe, all too often, has been simply defined by reference to a text. The rhetorical implications of this textual construction of the "Muslim" feeds into justifications for certain state projects. For instance, security studies on terrorism repeatedly cite verses from the Qur'an on jihad to intimate the threat Muslim citizens of the state may pose as neighbours, let alone as candidates for immigration. In contrast, one might see ethnography as a full-throated response against this rhetorical inclination of philology. Rather than constructing the "Muslim" through an elite textualist tradition, the ethnographer draws upon a discursive tradition of present practice; rhetorically, this method avoids rendering the Muslim's subjectivity vulnerable to the textual positivism of philology. It is in this sense that ethnography evinces a radical democracy that waits to hear from Muslims themselves, leaving it to them to make sense of their literary tradition as they otherwise live their lives.

RS: Identifying the limits of ethnography in its universalizing attempt to construct "Muslim" by subversively collapsing the Muslim with "Islamic," you write, "the ethnographization of the Islamic or the Muslim reveals a representative liberal-cum-Protestant mode of analysis" (Emon 2015; 2019, 380). I wondered if you could unpack this argument semantically and rhetorically and elaborate on what you mean by the terms "representative," "liberal," and "Protestant" in this context?

AE: By "liberal" I mean that the ethnographic subject, before being ethnographized, maps neatly onto the atomized rights-holder subjected to state law. By "representative," or more specifically "representative democratic," I mean that the views of individual subjects are generalized as applicable to a group. Methodologically, this speaks to the long-standing question across various fields of study of "representativeness." We all have archives or evidence from which we generalize. But the question of whether or how far we can generalize something as representative of the "Islamic" ought to constantly be a point of consideration for us as we produce new knowledge. Politically, this implies that the ethnographized "Muslim" interlocutor is one from whom the ethnographer can generalize to a group, thereby diffusing that construed "Islamic" across all Muslims.

On this approach to the "Islamic," the religious experience starts atomistically but is made to represent something more collective. By "Protestant" I mean that, in the context of religious belief, practice, and argument, the voices of individuals (whether many or few or even the one) stand for more than the particulars of any given ethnographic interlocutor. This rhetoric of the "Islamic" can be deployed by ethnographers for or against the state. For the political Right, that surveillance and scrutiny reflect a view of Muslims as potential threats, based on what a limited sample of Muslims have said or done. For the political Left, that surveillance and scrutiny are palpably unfair, again, based on what a limited sample of Muslims have said or done. To characterize these two arguments as representative liberal-cum-Protestant is thereby to reveal the relation between the rhetoric of the "Islamic" and the deployments to which it is put. Ethnographizing particular Muslims' experiences to generalize about Muslims as a group or Islam as a religion can either uphold or subvert the securitization narrative that has informed so many states since the events of 9/11. Consequently, when Muslims in North America and Europe (however few they may be) claim that ISIS is Islamic, or even commit lone-wolf acts of aggression, is it surprising that many view individual Muslim proponents of ISIS-like ideology as anything but individuals? These Muslims represent in their embodied performances and utterances the threat of more to come and thereby support political elites who demand policies to expand and enhance the already securitized state.[6]

RS: The goal of this edited volume, as I see it, is to question the epistemological and ontological premises that undergird knowledge production of Islam in Canada. How has your background in medieval history, law, and rhetoric influenced your thinking on method and theory?

AE: That is a question that I am constantly asking myself each day. I have no easy answers. My current appointment is split between the Faculty of Law and the Department of History, while I also direct the Institute of Islamic Studies in a public university in Canada. In the law school environment, we are committed to training tomorrow's lawyers. The professional nature of the curriculum raises questions for some about whether and to what extent the study of Islamic law belongs in a professional school committed to training legal practitioners. Yet my study of law and my study of medieval Islamic legal history consistently suggest to me that the two have much to learn from one another. In contrast, my approach to Islamic legal history no doubt strikes historians as far too doctrinal and even formalistic. I'm aware that my work reads for most historians as almost too legal given the tendency of history departments to view good history production as various forms of social and cultural history. At best, my work might be appreciated as an homage to an older style of intellectual history.

As much as the Islamic legal tradition may be considered legal and/or medieval, the fact is that law operates according to different temporal logics. In that sense, my training in these diverse fields help me think pluri-temporally, in other words, in relation to different and competing ideas of temporality and their implications for writing legal history today from an Islamic legal archive.

For instance, many years ago I was asked to provide expert analysis to the Government of Canada on why Muslim-majority states do not accede to the Hague Child Abduction Convention. As parents divorce and fight over child custody, it is not uncommon for the non-custodial parent to abscond with his or her child to a different country, leaving the other parent with little legal recourse. The Hague Child Abduction Convention was meant to solve that problem by automatically returning children to the state of residence from which they were abducted. Muslim-majority states have largely refused to accede to the convention on the grounds that it violates sharia. But what does that mean? Through our research, my colleague and I recognized that the concept of sharia in these states draws very much upon those premodern sources but is also entangled with modern multilateral treaties and takes new statutory forms.

The past remains present, but it is integrated in complex ways with public international law, private international law, and domestic family law. To understand such problems requires an appreciation of modern law, medieval Islamic law, and how both take shape politically and culturally in the modern state and its various institutions. When we wrote our study, which is soon coming out as a book, we recognized that what was happening was not so much a conflict between Islamic law and human rights or between Islamic law and public international law. Rather, we found that at issue were competing ideas about jurisdiction, ideas that stretched from the premodern period of Islamic imperial politics to the modern period of transnational trade and financial regulation.

RS: Thank you very much, Professor Emon.

NOTES

1 Passages of this interview are drawn from, with permission, Emon (2019).

2 See, for instance, the Public Safety Canada website highlighting psychology as a part of a broad research endeavour on countering violent extremism. Public Safety Canada, n.d., "Priority 1," *National Strategy on Countering Radicalization to Violence*, retrieved 20 September 2020 from https://www.publicsafety.gc.ca/cnt/rsrcs/pblctns/ntnl-strtg-cntrng-rdclztn-vlnc/index-en.aspx#s6.

3 See, for example, Warwick (2005), where he argues that 9/11 informed a more robust policing of academia, with "watchdog" organizations like Campus Watch featuring dossiers on faculty who espoused views deemed contrary to national values.

4 Reprinting Asad's 1986 contribution by the same title to the Occasional Paper Series of Georgetown University's Center for Contemporary Arab Studies.

5 See also Martin (1985/2001), where he highlights the relation between philological expertise and isolation from the rest of the academy.

6 See Simon (1990, 18), who recounts one view of philology as "having the capacity to retrieve the experiences of the past, of lost cultures, through close study of the written record."

REFERENCES

Adams, Charles. 2001. "Foreword." In Richard C. Martin (Ed.), *Approaches to Islam in religious studies* (pp. vii–ix). Oneworld Publications. (Original work published 1985)

Ahmad, Shahab. 2015. *What is Islam? The importance of being Islamic.* Princeton University Press.

Asad, Talal. 2009. "The idea of an anthropology of Islam." *Qui Parle, 17*(2), 1–30. https://doi.org/10.5250/quiparle.17.2.1

El-Gamal, Mahmoud A. 2006. *Islamic finance: Law, economics and practice.* Cambridge University Press.

Emon, Anver M. 2010. *Islamic natural law theories.* Oxford University Press.

– 2012. *Religious pluralism and Islamic law: "Dhimmīs" and others in the empire of law* (1st ed.). Oxford Islamic Legal Studies. Oxford University Press.

– 2015, 27 March. "Is ISIS Islamic? Why it matters for the study of Islam." *The Immanent Frame.* https://tif.ssrc.org/2015/03/27/is-isis-islamic-why-it-matters-for-the-study-of-islam

– (Ed.). 2016a. *Islamic and Jewish legal reasoning: Encountering our legal other.* Oneworld Publications.

– 2016b. "Shariʿa and the rule of law." In Robert W. Hefner (Ed.), *Shariʿa: Law and modern Muslim ethics* (pp. 37–64). Indiana University Press.

– 2019. "The 'Islamic' deployed: The study of Islam in four registers." *Middle East Law and Governance, 11*(3), 347–403. https://doi.org/10.1163/18763375-01103001

Emon, Anver M., Matthew Levering, and David Novak. 2014. *Natural law: A Jewish, Christian, and Islamic trialogue.* Oxford University Press.

Ernst, Carl W., and Richard C. Martin. 2010. "Introduction: Toward a post-Orientalist approach to Islamic religious studies." In Carl W. Ernst and Richard C. Martin (Eds.), *Rethinking Islamic studies: From Orientalism to cosmopolitanism* (pp. 1–20). University of South Carolina Press.

Hirschkind, Charles. 2006. *The ethical soundscape: Cassette sermons and Islamic counterpublics.* Columbia University Press.

Lewis, Bernard. 1979. "The state of Middle Eastern studies." *American Scholar, 48*(3), 365–81.

Mahmood, Saba. 2005. *Politics of piety: The Islamic revival and the feminist subject.* Princeton University Press.

Marchand, Suzanne L. 2009. *German Orientalism in the age of empire: Religion, race, and scholarship.* German Historical Institute.

Martin, Richard C. 2001. "Islam and religious studies: An introductory essay." In Richard C. Martin (Ed.), *Approaches to Islam in religious studies* (pp. 1–21). Oneworld Publications. (Original work published 1985)

McCants, William. 2015. *The ISIS apocalypse*. St. Martin's Press.

Migdal, Joel S. 2001. *State in society: Studying how states and societies transform and constitute one another*. Cambridge Studies in Comparative Politics. Cambridge University Press.

Mittermaier, Amira. 2011. *Dreams that matter: Egyptian landscapes of the imagination*. University of California Press.

Roach, Kent. 2011. *The 9/11 effect: Comparative counter-terrorism*. Cambridge University Press.

Simon, Eckehard. 1990. "The case for medieval philology." *Comparative Literature Studies*, 27(1), 16–20. https://www.jstor.org/stable/40246723

Turner, James. 2014. *Philology: The forgotten origins of the modern humanities*. Princeton University Press.

Wagner-Pacifici, Robin. 2010. "Theorizing the restlessness of events." *American Journal of Sociology, 115*(5), 1351–86. https://doi.org/10.1086/651299

Warwick, Shelly. 2005. "Will the academy survive 9/11? Scholarship, security, and United States government policy." *Government Information Quarterly, 22*, 573–93. https://doi.org/10.1016/j.giq.2006.01.004

Yanagihashi, Hiroyuki. 2004. *A history of early Islamic law of property*. Brill.

Ziolkowski, Jan. 1990. "'What is philology': Introduction." *Comparative Literature Studies*, 27(1), 1–12. https://www.jstor.org/stable/40246721

SECTION 2

Charting the Study of Islam(s) and Muslims in Canada

Who Are "Muslims in Canada"? An Analysis of the Qualitative Literature from 1997 to 2017

JENNIFER A. SELBY, AMÉLIE BARRAS, AND LORI G. BEAMAN

Introduction

A central aim of this volume is to interrogate the methodological, theoretical, and empirical moves made by scholars who produce knowledge on Muslims and Islam(s) in Canadian contexts. In this chapter, we analyse twenty years of qualitative-based literature in the corpus of scholarly publications. More specifically, we ask: How is "Canada" imagined in the methodologically qualitative work? How does this literature present "Muslim Canadians"? "Islam(s)"? What foci, theories, and empirical evidence are prevalent or largely absent in this literature?[1] And last, what does this literature tell us about the politics of qualitative-based knowledge production on Islam(s) and Muslims in Canada to date?

To address these questions, we examine seventy-seven qualitative-based scholarly dissertations, reports, articles, chapters, and monographs published between 1997 and 2017 to see what they tell us – and do not tell us – about Islam and Muslims in Canada.[2] Most of the scholarly literature produced in this twenty-year period – the most prolific period to date – takes a qualitative approach through focus groups, interviews (whether semi-directed or open-ended), and participant observation. Not surprisingly, we note in this review of the literature that the recent climate of increased securitization of Muslims Canadians has influenced the direction this literature has taken, in particular the theoretical underpinnings that shape how it imagines "Canada." Indeed, a number of scholars have started to look critically at the Canadian nation state, considering, among other things, how it is deeply implicated in the production and deployment of Islamophobia and anti-Muslim racism. Following our analysis of how Muslims, Canada, and Islam are commonly portrayed in this literature, we conclude by considering some of the voices we heard in our own qualitative research project with self-identified Muslims in St. John's, Newfoundland and Labrador, and Montreal, Quebec, to point to potential future directions for qualitative research (Selby et al. 2018). Our participants' narratives shed light on two lacunae in the scholarship in contemporary Canada: data on theological interpretations and theorization about race and Islamophobia.

How Is "Canada" Imagined in the Qualitative Literature?

In this section we argue that "Canada" in qualitative-based studies about Muslims is generally geographically limited to urban areas and that Canadian policies are applauded more than they are critiqued.

To be fair, with a handful of exceptions, the published literature parallels the demographic distribution of Muslims in Canada, insofar as much of it centres on the experiences of those living in the Greater Toronto Area, Greater Montreal, and, to a lesser extent, Metro Vancouver.[3] As demonstrated by figure 1, "Canada" in the qualitative scholarship does not parallel its geographic expanse. In what follows, we begin by quantifying the location of this recent social-scientifically oriented work. We then look at how "Canada" is imagined, noting a significant shift from scholarship that positions the nation state more neutrally or even commendably as multicultural and welcoming to, more recently, critiques of the country's securitization measures. Recent Statistics Canada data show the disproportional and significant impact of securitization measures and other anti-Muslim policies for Muslim Canadians (Statistics Canada 2018; Wilkins-Laflamme 2018).

Canadian Geography

A handful of scholars recognize the limitations of this overriding urban focus. The corpus reflects neither the breadth of sociocultural contexts within the country's provinces and territories nor the historical areas of settlement of Muslims to Western Canada. In her examination of the foodways (or the intersections of food in culture, history, and religion) and migration in the narratives of Muslim Montrealers of Maghrebian origin, Rachel Brown (2016b) explains how the cosmopolitan context of Montreal shapes her interlocutors' more "positive" interreligious encounters. Brown concludes that these encouraging experiences "are simply less possible in other regions of Québec, where Muslim populations are practically non-existent, allowing for the potential for overarching stereotypes to remain unchallenged" (197). However, as other work on diversity demonstrates, the rural experience differs from the urban, although in admittedly complex ways. For example, our study's Newfoundland respondents reported ways that the province's geographical challenges as more remote and as immigrant-scarce created an environment in which individuals fought to protect diversity and difference (Selby et al. 2018). We therefore need further data on these more rural locations.

Little scholarship exists which depicts smaller Canadian centres and none that accounts for more rural or northern experiences.[4] This gap makes sense given

Figure 1. Distribution of published qualitative literature by province (there is no qualitative literature based in Canada's three territories; fractions reflect multisited studies)

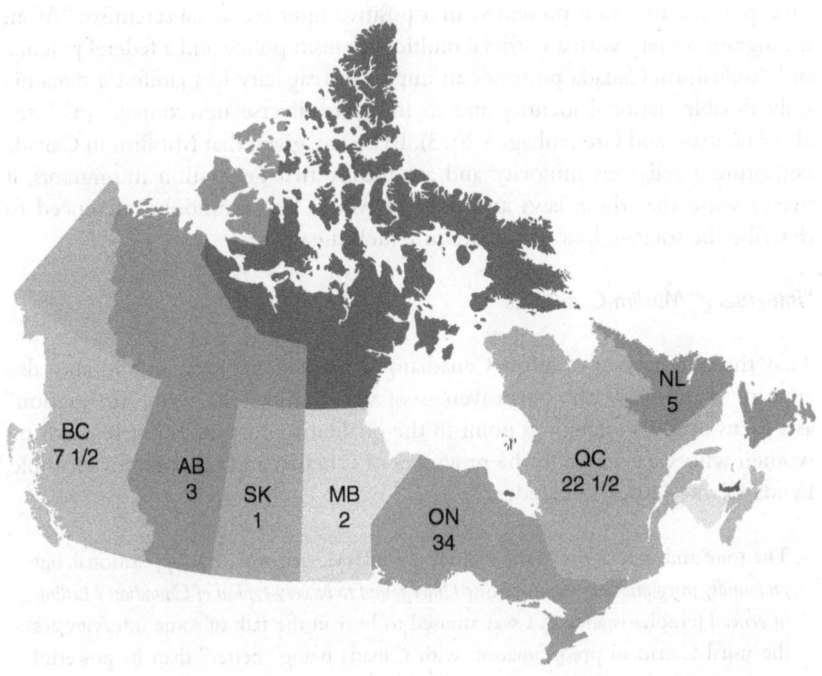

that most Muslim Canadians are first-generation immigrants who have settled in the country's metropolises. With few exceptions (i.e., Versi 2010; Waugh 2012, 2018; Waugh and Wannas 2003), qualitative scholarly research on the experiences of Albertan Muslims is notably absent.[5] This omission is relevant given the Western province's historical significance as home to Canadian Muslims since before Confederation. The Edmonton area was the first area of concentrated migration of first-generation Muslim Canadians and is where the first official Canadian Sunni mosque was built in 1938 (Selby et al. 2018, 61–4; Waugh 2018).

Canada as Multicultural and Welcoming

Political depictions of Canada as a nation state can also be mapped in the qualitative literature we have analysed. Indeed, "Canada" is rarely a benign backdrop. On the one hand, Canada's notion of multiculturalism (beginning as a policy in 1971 and established as an act in 1988) figures commonly in the literature until 2008 as an ethos that positively shapes how Muslim-identified minorities engage with and amidst non-Muslim Canadians. In contrast to this commonly referenced idea of multiculturalism, the 1982 Charter of Rights and Freedoms is very rarely mentioned as shaping the religious lives of Muslim Canadian interlocutors. This passage from Sharify-Funk (2010) captures how these multicultural policies are often presented in a positive light by social scientists: "As an immigrant society with an official multiculturalism policy and a federal practice of bilingualism, Canada possesses an impressive capacity to manifest a dynamically flexible national identity and to integrate diverse newcomers" (537; see also Anderson and Greifenhagen 2013). To be fair, given that Muslims in Canada constitute a religious minority and are mostly first-generation immigrants, it makes sense that these laws and policies would be commonly referenced to describe the socio-religious climate in which they live.

"Integrating" Muslim Canadians

That the majority of Muslim Canadians are first-generation immigrants also appears to influence the pervasiveness of variations of the term "integration" as a focus or as a concluding point in the qualitative corpus. In her research on women who wear niqab in the provinces of Ontario and Quebec, for example, Lynda Clarke (2013) concludes,

> The tone and statements of the women we interviewed were not oppositional, but *profoundly integrationist, a characteristic I have found to be very typical of Canadian Muslims in general* [emphasis added]. I was amused to hear in the talk of some interviewees the usual Canadian preoccupation with Canada being "better" than its powerful southern neighbour and jokes about the winter weather – including, inevitably, the burka being ideal for keeping out the cold. (59)

Clarke's qualitative interviews featured in this work are valuable given the paucity of research on people who wear full-face-covering hijabs that takes a qualitative approach. Clarke's informants joke about challenging winter weather conditions and, as individuals, are "profoundly integrationist." We mention this example of implicitly positively construed "integration" to question the normalizing politics latent in making this determination, even when the notion of being "integrated" is how interviewees themselves describe their Canadian experience. A core preoccupation in government policy is social integration. We do not dispute that it is important to query the ways that so-called positive integration manifests. However, a concomitant query is often missing – what are the costs to Canadian Muslims who might, for example, suffer discrimination but minimize it, or who may have needs that are not met and are silenced? Put differently, we can also think about the parameters within which Muslim interlocutors are questioned and how these lines of enquiry shape subsequent conclusions. What are the political implications of the "compatibility" of (an often-imagined-as-homogeneous) Muslim community with Canadian law and policy and their lack of threat to the nation state and its ideals? What are the implications of entrenching an "us" to which "they" must integrate? For these reasons, we posit that scholarship that addresses concerns with the so-called compatibility (i.e., ability to integrate) of Muslims in the Canadian nation state needs further engagement. "Integration" could be critiqued as an assumed desirable (and unquestioned) end goal.

This recurrent "positive" depiction of a welcoming nation state in the literature, often described in relation to the benefits of "integrating" within Canadian multiculturalism, is especially apparent in national comparative qualitative studies. Granted, some essentialization of the politics within "contexts of reception" is necessary for comparative purposes, but the nearly invariably positive characterization of Canada in this literature is striking. Canada is presented as more welcoming than France (as reflected in Barras 2018; Clarke 2013, 62; Mossière 2016; Selby 2012a), but also in comparisons with Finland (Riikonen 2016), the UK (Berns McGown 1999), and Afghanistan (Dossa 2008a).[6] Public opinion polls are also often referenced in qualitative scholars' presented data to portray Canada positively.[7]

Distinguishing Quebec from the Rest of Canada

Quebec is almost invariably understood in this corpus of literature as a very different sociopolitical context for Muslim Canadians. Charting differences between Quebec and the rest of Canada (ROC) is a common academic practice.[8] The distinction is unsurprising. French colonial history has meant that the French language and culture impacts the everyday lives of Muslims who live in that province. Moreover, a philosophy touted by some as "interculturalism" and the 1991 Canada-Québec Accord, which allows Quebec to control its immigration, are also distinctive factors. One of the direct consequences of this political climate is that it has encouraged more migration of Francophone Muslims to Quebec than elsewhere in Canada. More recently, academic knowledge production on Quebec has crescendoed following the province's 2007 debates on "Reasonable Accommodation" (Barras 2016; Côté 2008; Mahrouse 2010; Selby et al. 2018; Sharify-Funk 2010). These debates are most often framed through the Bouchard-Taylor Commission, a 2007 appointed government commission that sought to consult and make recommendations on how best to manage religious differences in the Quebecois public sphere. The resulting report (Bouchard and Taylor 2008) preceded a number of controversial bills (Bill 94 in 2011, 60 in 2013, 62, which passed in 2018 and, at the time of writing, has been stayed, and 21, passed in 2019) that have had significant impacts for Muslim Quebeckers, and Muslim women Quebeckers in particular. Figure 1 captures how approximately 22.5 per cent of the qualitative literature has a Quebecois focus.

The "Reasonable Accommodation" debates in Quebec have clearly marked the scholarly literature on Islam(s) and Muslims in Quebec. Several scholars begin their descriptions of the contemporary Quebec context in 2007 with the provincial elections following the "Hérouxville incident," a unanimously voted town charter against so-called barbaric cultural practices, which many scholars position as spurring the Bouchard-Taylor Commission. Others, like Pauline Côté (2008) and Solange Lefebvre (2008), also look to the 2006 *Multani* decision by the Supreme Court of Canada as prompting public debates on the "reasonability" of minority religious practices, in particular Muslims' practices (*Multani v. Commission scolaire Marguerite-Bourgeoys* 2006). Invariably, these events are referenced to characterize the province's "unique" approach to questions related to religious diversity (Sharify-Funk 2010, 537). So too the notion of "interculturalism" is earmarked to distinguish the province's understanding of diversity as distinct from the ROC's multiculturalism (Bakali 2016; Sharify-Funk 2010, 544; Jamil 2014; see also Lavoie 2018, 39). Interculturalism is an approach advocated by some politicians and scholars in the province of Quebec. Its paradigm emphasizes integration to Quebecois communal values and is often positioned in contrast to multiculturalism, imagined as less protective of the province's distinctive minority language, cultural concerns, and identity (Bouchard 2012; Bouchard and Taylor 2008, 19–20; Foblets and Schreiber 2013). In her research on young women's identities, Riikonen (2016) describes how interculturalism creates a different milieu for Muslim life in Quebec:

> Quebecois interculturalism promotes the idea that the francophone majority of the Quebecois population represents a minority nation of [individuals with] a French cultural background within Canadian federalism: this conception goes against the multicultural model that does not impose an official culture. (95; our translation)

Riikonen argues that Quebec's intercultural model privileges one cultural model over others, something that is perhaps substantiated by the 2019 passing of Bill 21 which disproportionately impacts Muslims, Jews, and Sikhs. The intercultural model she posits therefore looks different from the "multicultural" model in the ROC.

While there are obvious historical and political differences between Quebec and the ROC, there are also a number of important similarities that we see as often overlooked in the qualitative literature. Among others, these include growing Islamophobia and the legacies of Christianity, settler colonialism, and Christian privilege in all Canadian provinces and territories.[9] Qualitative comparative research between provinces has rarely been undertaken to verify an often-assumed difference between Quebec and the ROC or to examine provincial or territorial differences, like life in Saskatchewan compared to Nunavut. Our own study – published in *Beyond Accommodation: Everyday Lives of Muslim*

Canadians (Selby et al. 2018) – drew on qualitative interviews with ninety Muslim Canadians in Montreal and St. John's. When we completed our coding of interview data on narratives of daily life, we decided that obvious provincial differences, particularly related to differing population sizes, the number of visible minorities, and provincial bills in Quebec, did not have a significant impact on what we call everyday navigation and negotiation. For these reasons, we privileged the Canadian context more than the provincial one in our analysis (see Selby et al. 2018, 12–14). We note this point not to argue that all Canadian provincial jurisdictions share the same politics, linguistic or otherwise, but to question a common assumption that Muslim daily life necessarily differs significantly in Quebec compared to the ROC.

Canada as Restrictive in an Era of Surveillance

On the other side of the representation of Canada spectrum, several authors in our qualitative corpus are much more critical of how the Canadian nation state "integrates" Muslim Canadians. Generally, these studies were published after 2007. Anthropologist Parin Dossa (2008a, 13), for example, is attentive to how her first-generation female interlocutors of different backgrounds in the Greater Vancouver Area experience "here" (Canada) and "there." Dossa (2008a) critiques the power structures at play in how the women she interviewed engage with their country of reception. She evaluates Canada's lack of accountability in recognizing its contribution to creating refugee crises and its ineffective response to the needs of those they receive: "It [Canada] does not provide them with adequate services to settle down and rebuild their lives" (12). With her ethnographic research, Dossa (2008a)recognizes the politics that impact her interviewees' everyday lives:

> The [Afghan-origin, former refugee] women lived near a mall [close to Burnaby, BC] – a place of consumption and sociality – but the products sold were beyond their reach. Their social interactions were also limited; the language barrier and racism are salient in this regard. (20)

Like Dossa, other scholars draw on qualitative interview data and analysis of specific laws to show how federal post-2001 Canadian securitization policies and legal projects are Islamophobic and negatively impact the lives of Muslim Canadians. In her study of Muslim youth in Toronto and Vancouver, Nagra (2017) convincingly shows the impact of Canadian anti-terror legislation and surveillance on her interlocutors' lives (and the influence of American security forces). She discusses how border-crossings are especially problematic: "In addition to extra questioning, the young Muslims in this study believe that they and their belongings undergo extra searching at airports and border crossings"

(108). More generally, informants depicted in the larger corpus of qualitative texts unequivocally report facing an increase in experiences of Islamophobia and anti-Muslim racism, especially those who are women and are visibly Muslim (e.g., Lavoie 2018, 36; Mahrouse 2010; Selby et al. 2018b; Sharify-Funk 2010; Zine 2017).

How Securitization Impacts Qualitative Research

Canada's recent securitization laws and policies impact both the kinds of research that are regularly funded, as Aaron Hughes argues in this volume, and the recruitment of participants who may be reluctant to engage in further examination. Liam Harvey-Crowell (2015) considers this reluctance in his study of Canadian Muslim university students' usage of the internet. After completing fifteen interviews with student members of Memorial University's Muslim Students' Association (MSA), Harvey-Crowell (2015) explains that the then-new legislation that allowed for greater unrestricted surveillance as part of anti-terror measures (Bill C-51) impacted his research. Drawing on his field notes, he describes how

> this group of five people [who were student members of the MSA] informed me that they had heard of my project (and even read my pamphlet on the project) but were still suspicious of it, fearing that saying "the wrong thing" or having something taken out of context would get them or the MSA in trouble. (72)

This anecdote reveals how Muslim Canadians may wish to express themselves online or offline but are restrained in their participation by broader politics and surveillance, whether real or symbolic.

Other scholars find this climate of surveillance significant in motivating their participants' desire to engage in research. They often describe a desire to debunk stereotypes, for instance, about the proclivity of converts to become involved in terror-related activities. Flower and Birkett (2014) argue for the importance of their work based on semi-structured interviews with twenty-five converts in Ontario in 2014 because of the country's "contemporary securitized milieu post 9/11" (1). Theirs is one of the few qualitative studies on converts (see also Guzik 2017; Mossière 2010, 2013). Flower and Birkett (2014) explain that "the study represents an initial step toward correcting negative public media discourses on Muslim converts and provides the first empirical evidence for policy makers to reflect upon" (2). This goal of "debunking myths" undergirds a great deal of the scholarship in this period (for more on this trend in the study of contemporary Islam in the US, see Fuerst and Ayubi 2016).

In sum, in its characterization of "Canada," the qualitative literature from 1997 to 2017 maintains a geographic and political narrowness in describing the Canadian nation state. There are few historical archival-based analyses, likely because of the small number of self-identified Muslims during the pre-1967 "British Protestant" era and because academic interest in Muslim Canadians grew after 9/11. Related to this point is a likely erasure of early Black Muslims in Canada whose presence proceeded the Lebanese community in Alberta (see Jackson-Best 2019 for a helpful list of bibliographic sources on published and unpublished materials on Black Muslims in Canada; also Cooper 2006, 2007). Still, with few exceptions, only recently has the qualitative literature become critical of the impact of Canadian securitization policies. As interventions like Bill C-51 (which received royal assent in 2015), critiqued for breaching privacy and curtailing civil liberties, disproportionally impact Muslim Canadians, researchers too have taken notice and the scholarly literature has become increasingly critical of the Canadian nation state (see Nagra 2017; Nagra and Maurutta 2016; Forcese and Roach 2015). We suspect the adoption of Bill 21 in Quebec in 2019 will also receive a good deal of attention related to securitization.

How Are "Muslims" Described in This Literature?

In this section, we examine the corpus of qualitative studies over this period to see what it reveals about how Muslims are described. Quantitative data from Statistics Canada show that Muslim Canadians constitute the country's most ethnically heterogeneous religious communities (Bramadat 2005). Yet, despite this diversity, we will show that the composite picture emerging from the bulk of this literature is of a younger, conservative, middle-class and educated heterosexual woman wearing a headscarf. There are some ethno-geographical particularities as well. In line with the demographics and immigration patterns, the literature in the Greater Toronto Area emphasizes Muslims of South Asian origins and in Montreal those of Maghrebian origin.

As we note in figure 2, the corpus takes a gendered perspective. There is a notable focus on women's experiences, family life, and hijab – approximately 22 per cent of the qualitative-based research from 1997 to 2017 – which focuses on young, able-bodied, 1.5- or second-generation women's experiences.[10] Other foci listed in figure 2 like the law, youth, identity, and Islamophobia also emphasize female interlocutors and their perceptions of agency, but this is not apparent because we coded for one primary theme. Paralleling the current demography, in his work on Muslim women public servants, Bertrand Lavoie notes that the majority of his participants are between eighteen and thirty-five years old, that their average age is twenty-four, and that nearly half are born in Canada (Lavoie 2018, 28). Similarly, in her PhD dissertation, Riikonen (2016) focuses on how young female students in Finland and Quebec construct their Muslim subjectivities. Parts of our own research also centre on young female subjects (Selby 2016a; Selby et al. 2018a). Of course, there are variations in how women's

Figure 2. Qualitative literature on Muslims in Canada by primary theme

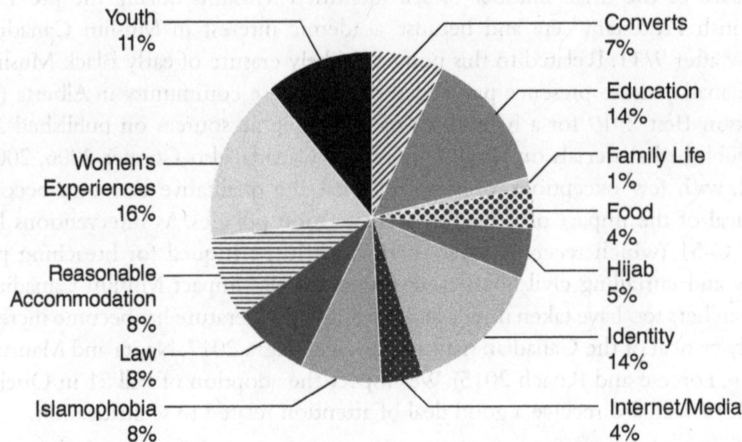

experiences are examined. Parin Dossa, for one, has largely focused on differently abled Muslim women in the Metro Vancouver area (Dossa 2008b), as well as the migration and displacement experiences of Afghan-origin women over thirty-five years old living in lower-income households (Dossa 2008a).

The lack of attention to men's experiences in the literature is notable. Interestingly, in her contribution to this volume, Sadaf Ahmed stresses that a good deal of qualitative scholarly production on women focuses on their headscarves. In part, in a context of post-9/11 "War on Terror" fetishization of headscarves and silencing of women who wear them, this scholarship has aimed to counteract these positions. In her examination of four Canadian veiled women's experiences,[11] Katherine Bullock (2010, 168) aims to respond to prevalent problematic and pejorative popular characterizations by arguing that "the 'false consciousness' assumption does violence to *hijabi* women's agency and intelligence."[12]

Bullock takes on theological assumptions implicit in scholarly work on hijabs by calling into question work that, in enquiring *why* women veil, interpret the Qur'an and determine that the command to veil is not clearly indicated (see also Bullock's comments in her interview in this volume). As we will discuss in the next section, theologically focused research in our corpus of qualitative work is rare. For Bullock (2010), determining that veiling is an optional practice has significant political and theological consequences: researchers, she says, then "call into question *hijabi* women's ability to interpret the Qur'an, so ultimately to question their own intelligence" (169). Bullock worries that this framing by academics can be translated into how Western states may feel it less necessary to accord accommodations if veiling were interpreted as optional. In her interview-based work, Bullock is one of the few scholars who engages her interlocutors on their theological understandings of Sunnah and the importance of veiling.

Lavoie's (2018) study similarly focuses on women who wear hijabs.[13] Publishing more than ten years after Bullock, he analyses reactions to the Charter of Values (or Bill 60 in 2013) in Quebec that aimed to ban individuals wearing visible religious signs from working for or receiving public services (28). Drawing on interviews with female Muslim government workers in Montreal, Lavoie argues that these interlocutors largely defend the notion of a secular state, as proposed by the ruling provincial party in 2013. Put differently, Lavoie shows how the women he interviewed combine their religious values with their commitment to citizenship, which allows them to combat Islamophobic ideas that see the hijab as the symbol of non-democratic values.

As mentioned, one exception to the prevalent hijab focus in research characterizing Muslim Canadians is ethnographic research by Parin Dossa (2008a, 2008b, as well as her contribution to this volume). Located in the discipline of anthropology, Dossa has chosen not to give a great deal of attention to the visible Muslimness of her female interlocutors. In an article on women of Afghan origin in Vancouver, she engages theoretical literature on migration, the body, and pain. She says her interlocutors generally pray three to five times per day and read Qur'anic passages, but she aims to "be attentive to social and political dimensions" that shape their experiences (Dossa 2008a, 18). Significantly, for many of her female informants who lack English-language fluency, to read or recite verses from the Qur'an "was one area where they could claim expertise and feel totally at home" (19), therein complexifying their engagement with their religious practice post-migration. In so doing, Dossa historicizes and contextualizes the hijab practices of her interlocutors as one element among many others that shapes their lives in Canada.

In this overview of veiling in the qualitative literature to date, we do not mean to suggest that this focus is inherently problematic. It is understandable in light of recent attempts by governments, including the Canadian federal and Quebecois provincial governments, to regulate or ban them. Equally pressing for many scholars are data showing that women who veil in Canada are most vulnerable to a variety of forms of Islamophobia (including hate crimes) and racism.[14] However, we wonder whether this emphasis on certain interlocutors in the qualitative scholarship overly emphasizes more conservative practices. This focus tends to flatten the range of experiences and ways of being Muslim in Canada. A number of scholars have raised this conundrum in their work on conservative practices, which receive disproportional academic attention (to read more broadly on this point, see Deeb and Harb 2013; Schielke 2009). Clarke, for one, in her study of women wearing niqabs, stresses the marginality of the practice. She astutely argues, "Women in Canada wearing niqab ultimately constitute a very small sub-culture, sustained, as the remainder of the study suggests, by determined individuals" (Clarke 2013, 31).

One response to this fetishism is academic work that aims to take a more comprehensive approach. In our own most recent work (Selby et al. 2018a), we have underscored the importance of documenting how religion is articulated in the lives of our participants, among a multitude of other commitments and priorities. This approach follows a trend of charting "lived religion" in the lives of participants and allowed us to capture a wide range of experiences of being Muslim in Canada, where, in a number of cases, religiosity was not the sole or the primary point of identification. Participant recruitment practices are rarely discussed but also shape the data generated (for an interesting discussion of these techniques and challenges faced by researchers, see Nagra 2017, 38–41). Likewise, in her PhD dissertation Riikonen (2016) explains the importance of recruiting female students with a range of religious experiences, including "secular Muslims" (27) or Muslims "who do not practice religion that much" (90). Riikonen notes how this broader focus also rendered the recruitment of participants more challenging. She therefore intentionally went beyond the traditional recruiting strategies – e.g., through Muslim student associations or mosques – to depict more breadth among her participants. Fewer studies of the unmosqued or the "non-pious Muslims" are part of the qualitative corpus. We return to this point in the next section.

Gaps in the Literature

We noted two significant omissions in our analysis of the qualitative literature on Islam and Muslims in Canada: first, how Canadian Muslims engage with and shape Islamic theology, and second, scholarly theorization on race and racism and how these concepts relate to Islamophobia.

First, few scholars reference the theological repertoires engaged by Muslim Canadians. These include the sources of authority with which they engage in how they live Islam in their everyday lives (notable exceptions are the work of Cutting 2012 and Macfarlane 2012 on the role of imams' interpretation of religious law in arbitrating Islamic divorce in Ontario). In fact, the qualitative literature rarely addresses the Islamic legal schools or interpretations thereof by their interlocutors. In part, this omission might be explained by a common methodological consideration of theological studies as textual studies (a binary discussed by Emon in his interview in this volume) and not in the scope of qualitative work. Within the qualitative literature, in her study of eighty-one Canadian women who wear niqab, for instance, Lynda Clarke (2013) touches briefly on the role of theology by explaining that while her participants generally did not "refer to Islamic texts or scholarly opinions," these texts played a role in informing their reasoning behind wearing the niqab: "The practice of covering the face has been subject to ongoing debate; grasping some of the material of that debate helps in understanding different Muslim perspectives" (4). Still, characteristic of this general omission, she does not expand or explore how her respondents navigate different Islamic opinions. Which sources or individuals do they find most authoritative? Why? How are these sources selected or deemed authoritative? Does the Canadian context impact theological interpretation? The literature focuses more on constructing Muslims vis-à-vis the Canadian state and its policies than on analysing whether and how they navigate theological concepts. In part, we posit that this omission is because, at least implicitly, much of the scholarship takes the category of "Islam" as a stable qualifier.[15] In so doing, it may leave the reader with the impression that practices and beliefs in the traditions of Islam are more rigid than they are for our interlocutors.

Second, we note how with important early exceptions (i.e., Haque 2010; Razack 2008; Zine 2006, 2008a), the qualitative literature until recently on Islam and Muslims in Canada (like Flower and Birkett 2014, 12) was more likely to engage questions of ethnicity than of race.[16] This tendency is increasingly changing as recent scholarship has begun to better address race and refer to anti-Muslim racism. Zine (2006), for instance, considers how Muslim girls in gender-segregated Islamic schools in Toronto negotiate the "dual oppressions" of the racism and Islamophobia in broader society and the "patriarchal forms of religious oppression" in their communities (239). In his work drawing on interviews with Muslim youths in Montreal, Naved Bakali (2016) also effectively demonstrates these intersections, grounding them in theory on racialization and race and attending to the specificities of the Quebecois context. Likewise, Nagra's (2017) most recent work, on Muslim youth understanding of national belonging in an increasingly securitizing era, offers a robust analysis of racialization.

We suggest, however, that qualitative scholars more rarely engage conceptual linkages and distinctions between race, racialization, and Islamophobia. For instance, in his earlier work, Bakali (2015b) considers his interlocutors' experiences with racism in education settings in Quebec. To do so, he draws on theoretical frameworks proposed by Razack to provide a conceptual discussion of anti-Muslim racism or "the social construction of the Muslim 'Other'" (2015b, 47; see also Karim 2002). Selby, Barras, and Beaman draw on the same author to consider the multiple "othering" processes experienced by their participants in their everyday lives (Selby et al. 2018a). Yet neither Bakali nor Selby et al. conceptualizes the differences between Islamophobia and anti-Muslim racism. A variety of data suggests that distinguishing these terms is significant. Lavoie (2018) points out that even if the literature on Muslims in Western contexts repeatedly uses the term "Islamophobia" to refer to the discrimination faced by Muslims in Canada and elsewhere, his female hospital-working participants in Montreal prefer describing their experiences as "racism" or "discrimination" (37).

Unfortunately, he does not elaborate on the differences and relations between these terms. The lack of theoretical attention to these categories, we suggest, is reflective of a broader trend in the literature whereby authors state that Islamophobia exists (as do discrimination and racism) and link it to structural inequalities, particularly in securitization policies, but do not systematically conceptualize the theoretical and political parameters of Islamophobia and anti-Muslim racism.[17] In our own study, even if our interlocutors did not frequently use the term "racism" (and indeed, despite the fact that race was not a focus on the study), we recognize the importance of better conceptualizing these distinctions.

More generally, this omission might reflect the fact that much of the qualitative scholarship remains more empirical than theoretical. Still, this theoretical conceptualization would, in our opinion, be an important contribution to the literature. Greater specificity would shed better light on the multiple ways Muslim Canadians experience discrimination – as gendered, embodied, racialized, and religionized – and how it manifests itself in entangled and shifting ways. In her recent qualitative research on Iranian American youths and the limits of Whiteness in the United States, sociologist Neda Maghbouleh notes why it is important to think about which concepts are used to describe discrimination. In relation to her qualitative research on race, racism, and Islamophobic experiences in the United States, Maghbouleh (2017) writes,

> The contemporary use of "Islamophobia" as a catchall term for discrimination against Iranian and other Middle Easterners in the United States efficiently but erroneously flattens the extent of genuine diversity within these groups and, more important, critically obscures the consistent racial valence of such harassment. Alongside South Asian Americans and other communities of color in the United States, Iranians and populations from the broad Middle East practice a variety of religions, hail from many separate nationalities, and attach importance to a wide range of ethnic identities. Nonetheless, together they are profiled, classed, and treated in everyday life as a "group" or "type" that is different from whites. (13)

We saw this potential for flattening as we coded our data from Montreal, Quebec, and St. John's, Newfoundland and Labrador, and in informal comments we heard at public events from Black Muslim youth especially.

Interpreting the experience of one of our participants, "Dina," a twenty-one-year-old Sunni-identified engineering student of Ethiopian origin, who lives in St. John's made this point clear (also cited in Selby 2018, 221).[18] As a Black immigrant young woman who wears a visibly Muslim religious sign (hijab), Dina describes discriminatory experiences in her three years in Canada to date, attributable to racism, sexism, Islamophobia, and xenophobia (see also Mugabo

2016, 162, for challenges among Canadian anti-Islamophobia activists to recognize Blackness). In an interview in a quiet corner of the university's Student Centre, she described this incident as Islamophobic:

> This lady, she was like … I was asking for a lot of vinegar or something at the [university] dining hall for a project that we were doing in the house for a[n engineering] competition. Anyways, so she's like, "Oh what are you gonna do with all that? Are you gonna make a bomb out of it or something?" And I really just laughed at it and left. But my [non-Muslim] friend was like, she was mad. She's like, "We're going to report her" and all that. And I don't think about things that, you know, in that way or whatever. That was just a comment and I left it. But then, she was like, "Did you hear what she said to you?" … I guess they don't realize what they are saying or sometimes they do and they're just doing it.

In this instance, Dina, like other participants in our study, preferred not to respond to this cafeteria employee, even if this moment remains a deeply hurtful one. Significantly, Dina did not reference her Blackness in describing any of her experiences of discrimination, perhaps because our interviews centred on Muslimness but also perhaps because we did not expressly ask her about her experiences of racism or because the interviewer was White.

Akeem, twenty-nine, also illustrates the complex ways assumptions around Islamophobia and his Muslimness appear in his daily life. Akeem is a graduate student from, as he calls it, a "traditional" family of Kuwaiti origin. In this narrative he describes an interaction with another young man he presumed was also of Middle Eastern origin at a takeout pizza place:

> I'm [a] vegetarian. So whenever I go to restaurants they always assume that, they always ask me "are you vegetarian for religious reasons?" I think they just confuse Buddhism with Islam. And then I said, "No. I'm not. I'm just vegetarian." I just, it just, I think just people are obsessed with, they just want to categorize every single thing. Just group everything and label it.
>
> And sometimes when I'm in St. John's I experience that when I go to, I went to a pizza place and the guy was from the Middle East. And I said, "Can I have, can I have a vegetarian pizza?" And he gave me a pizza with chicken. And I said, "No, I want a vegetarian pizza." And he said, "Don't worry, it's not pork."
>
> He just assumed that I'm Muslim so I'm ordering vegetarian because I don't want to eat meat. And I said, "No, I'm actually vegetarian." It's so, yeah it gets a bit annoying. You always have to explain.

We draw several points from this narrative. In part we believe this narrative emerged in the interview because our questions focused not on rigid notions of practice and un/belief but on ones that were more situationally oriented, such as, "How do you live your religiosity at work? On public transport? At school?" and so on. In addition, we also note how Akeem was recruited to this research through snowball sampling. He was initially reluctant to be interviewed, believing his experiences would not be representative because he had actively avoided attending a mosque since moving to Canada five years earlier. He recalls once "accidentally" going to a Muslim Students' Association event, which he had erroneously thought was a social gathering for Middle Eastern–origin students. He considers himself a non-practising Muslim. His Muslimness, nonetheless, remains an important part of his identity.

We also included his narrative because, in reflecting on the larger corpus of qualitative literature, non-practising Muslims have rarely been examined. This pizza parlour employee's lack of attention may inaccurately translate Akeem's vegetarianism as a necessary religious compulsion, whether Hindu or Muslim, erasing the possibility of other explanations. This omission might be directly related to the image of "Muslimness" projected in the current literature, as well as the rather limited theoretical apparatus to capture experiences that do not directly fall within dominant understandings of being Muslim, including those who self-identify as cultural Muslims, unmosqued, and atheist Muslims. As is the case for those who are pious and unable to practise fully, the imposition of imagined piety or assumptions about observance can be equally damaging.

Returning to the larger qualitative corpus, we argue that better conceptualizing and understanding how discrimination intersects with gender, religion, race, and class would help shed light on the different ways "othering" processes work and affect the lives of a variety of individuals across Canada. Although "Islamophobia" is the term most recognizable in public discourse, it does not necessarily convey the making of racial and religious "others" that fuels the forms of discrimination Muslim Canadians face. Moreover, as scholars have argued, calling this a "phobia" suggests that this discrimination is solely a problem of individual bias, which obscures the structural and systemic production of anti-Muslim racism. Engaging more closely with an important body of the literature in the US on this topic would be particularly helpful in this endeavour (see, for instance, Bayoumi 2006; Chan-Malik 2011; Jackson 2011; Maira 2014; Naber 2008; 2012, 111–55), a comparison that remains rare in the qualitative literature.

Put differently, we posit that the literature on Islam in Canada from 1997 to 2017 has not paid sufficient attention to intersectional identities when thinking about the diversity of "othering" processes, particularly in taking anti-Muslim racism seriously (aside from a few noteworthy exceptions, e.g., Bakali 2016; Nagra 2017; Zine 2006).[19] Most of this body of work also does not tackle the conceptual differences and similarities between Islamophobia and anti-Muslim racism, even if those concepts are often referred to. Engaging in this conceptual work would help scholars develop a more robust theoretical conversation around the extent to which "Islamophobia" is a productive term to capture this diversity. At the same time, this perspective would make us more attentive to the structural dimensions of anti-Muslim racism and how it is connected to a wider Canadian history of systematic racism, Whiteness, exclusions, and violence that is far from being about only individual religious discrimination. It is imperative, therefore, that scholars, ourselves included, better conceptualize the varied and intersectional forms of discrimination experienced against individuals identified as Muslims.

Conclusion: Future Trends for Qualitative Research on Muslims in Canada?

In this chapter, we analysed seventy-seven qualitative research publications and theses from 1997 to 2017 on Islam(s) and Muslims in Canada in order to reflect on the characterization of Canadian Muslims. Our analysis has provided a window into thinking about the types of research questions that have occupied researchers for the last two decades, and the opportunity to think of the questions that we see have not been asked or not been sufficiently explored. We have also sought to consider ways our own scholarship may contribute to the gaps we have identified.

We have argued that the literature tends to project a narrow story about Canada, whereby the country is often defined in terms of its multicultural character, which is described as facilitating the "positive" integration of Muslims and other minorities. While some scholars have begun critically analysing Canadian policies with regard to religious minorities, especially in post-9/11 securitized contexts, it seems that, particularly when the country is compared to other countries (e.g., France) or when the discussion focuses on differentiating Quebec from the rest of Canada, Canada is invariably portrayed as welcoming. Moreover, most of the empirical literature explores the lives of contemporary Canadian Muslims in urban environments, paralleling the demographic distribution of Muslims in Canada. Together, this work tends to project an urban, apolitical, and "ahistorical" image of Canada. Indeed, the qualitative work rarely draws on historical analysis and, beyond this qualitative corpus, historical studies on Canadian Muslims remain scarce.

The qualitative literature also participates in conveying a certain gendered image of Canadian Muslims. As we mentioned, it focuses on the lives of individuals who are young, able-bodied, 1.5- or second-generation women who identify as pious. Of course, they have, at the same time, received a good deal of public scrutiny and are disproportionally vulnerable to Islamophobia and anti-Muslim racism. Research questions appear to revolve around a narrow examination of Muslimness, whereby researchers seek to understand how wearing the headscarf affects young women's lives. Even if this goal is understandable given the policy focus in and beyond Canada on regulating Muslim headgear, we wonder what this examination of Muslimness overlooks and how it perpetuates a somewhat singular characterization of Muslim women. Far less scholarship has focused on Muslim men (exceptions include Beyer 2014; Cassin 2014). Likewise, we note that despite this emphasis on piety, there has been little attention to how Canadian Muslims engage (or do not engage) with theology, including whether and how they select or accept sources of authority. Finally, while the literature is increasingly paying attention to the racism and Islamophobia faced by Muslim Canadians, we underscored that these concepts were not systematically theorized or differentiated. This lacuna is one we experienced directly when we were coding our qualitative interviews with Muslim Canadians in St. John's and Montreal.

While the vast majority of our own participants, like Akeem or Dina, clearly experience discriminations and othering processes in their everyday lives, we suggest that scholars need to develop a more robust theoretical apparatus to think through the ways individuals who identify as Muslims experience discrimination in various ways related to their life stories and complex identities. This greater breadth would help us make better sense of the impact of the dominant trend among policymakers, scholars, and citizens (like Akeem's pizza parlour server) to collapse "Brown-ness" with piety and Muslimness, while at the same time it would facilitate shedding light on the diversity of religious identification and non-identification within groups constructed and labelled as "Muslims." We worry that defining Islamophobia and racism as interchangeable forms of discrimination without properly conceptualizing these notions projects the idea that anti-Muslim racism is mainly about individual religious discrimination and overlooks the fact that it is linked to structural and systematic racism and to colonial-influenced politics of exclusion that are deeply embedded in Canadian history and society.

NOTES

We thank the Social Sciences and Humanities Research Council for funding the workshop that led to this project, as well as Rafaa Chehoudi for his assistance in creating the chapter's graphs.

1 We do not address some of the critiques of qualitative methodological approaches more generally, including how researchers' politics and positionality necessarily impact research design, theorization, and outcomes (see Harding 1987; Naples 2007; Neitz 2011).

2 The qualitative corpus we examine is listed in full as "Primary Sources" in the References section. We apologize for any unintentional omission(s). The multidisciplinary and methodologically varied bibliography is a work in progress updated biannually (see https://www.mun.ca/relstudies/more/producingislams/biblio.php).

3 For the Greater Toronto Area: Berns McGown 1999; Chraibi and Cukier 2017; Gibb and Rothenberg 2000; Guzik 2017; Memon 2010; Zine 2000, 2001, 2006,

2007, 2008a; for Montreal: Bakali 2015a, 2015c, 2016; Brown 2016a, 2016b; Eid 2003; Jamil 2014; Mossière 2013; and for Vancouver: Dossa 2002, 2004.

4 See Anderson and Greifenhagen 2013 and Hameed 2015 on the prairies; Akter 2011, Harvey-Crowell 2015, and Selby 2016b on St. John's, Newfoundland and Labrador; and Cassin 2014 for her multisited ethnography.

5 Richard Awid (2000, 2010) is an amateur historian who has published on the Alberta community.

6 There is surprisingly little comparative work with the US (see Macfarlane 2012 as an exception).

7 While not our focus in this chapter, quantitative data also includes comparative analysis where Canada consistently is portrayed more positively by way of contrast, typically with Western European countries (Kazemipur 2014; see also Leuprecht and Winn 2011; Litchmore and Safdar 2015; Moghissi et al. 2009; Reitz et al. 2017).

8 Anglophone and Francophone bodies of literature cite one another surprisingly infrequently. This chasm, in our opinion, is an example of how silos in the "Canadian" literature are created and reinforced.

9 Elsewhere we have analysed the representations of so-called controversies involving Muslims and de-exceptionalized Quebecois public policies as unique compared to the ROC (see Barras et al. 2018).

10 1.5ers are those who immigrate as children or in their early teens. Significant is that with few exceptions (Lavoie 2018; Waugh and Wannas 2003), most of the qualitative literature on Muslim women is written by female scholars. When we presented some of our findings from this analysis at the 2018 American Academy of Religion meetings, an audience member asked whether we would also code the literature for Muslim vs. non-Muslim authorship to consider "insider" and "outsider" involvement in the scholarship. We have not done so because few authors religiously self-identify in their work. In addition, some scholars we know as practising Muslims, or as non-practising, or as married to Muslims or converts, do not publicly self-identify. Not only do we not want to publicly identify them on their behalf, but we also recognize that religious identities often change over time. Authors in this volume (see Tiflati and Djaout and Brown) suggest that authors' consideration of their positionality is methodologically and theoretically important but not exclusionary (see also Nagra 2017, 38–40; 2018).

11 The women were first interviewed in 1994; Bullock re-engaged four women in 2008 to follow up on their hijab experiences.

12 Bullock explains that she was similarly motivated to respond to a CBC program that asked whether the hijab was a "Canadian" garment (2010, 177–9).

13 We chose exceptionally to include Lavoie's book, published in 2018, in our sample, because it is largely based on his PhD dissertation defended in 2017, currently under embargo.

14 In an op-ed in the *National Post* newspaper, Jasmin Zine (2017) notes how a number of political moments contributed to a climate of hatred that may have motivated this surge in violence, including the Barbaric Cultural Practices Act and

proposal for a corresponding "tip line" Bill C-51/Anti-Terrorism Act, Security Certificates, and Bill 94, which sought to ban the niqab in Quebec and which was later replaced with Bill 21 in 2019. Nagra (2018) also shows how these interventions impact racialized Muslim women in particular.

15 In general, qualitative scholars reference the five pillars as a descriptor of how their participants engage with Islam (i.e., Brown 2016b, 190n10). Guzik (2017) does not describe the five pillars directly but mentions the recitation of the *shahadah* (17) and cites interviewees who note its importance in their conversion journey (65, 77, 158).

16 To be fair, in this study of Muslim converts, Flower and Birkett note that sixteen out of twenty-five participants could be labelled as "White" (2014, 8; see also McDonough and Hoodfar 2005).

17 These conceptual difficulties around defining Islamophobia and anti-Muslim racism are visible not only in scholarly work but also in public debates. Most recently, these were visible in 2017 during debates around Motion 103 that called upon the government of Canada to "condemn Islamophobia and all forms of systemic racism and religious discrimination."

18 In a similar vein, Shahzad's (2014) study of Canadian university students demonstrates the multitudinous ways the "War on Terror" and its discourse of fear – which she describes as "racism, Islamophobia, and social control" (467) – affect Canadian university students, no matter their religious background, who are repeatedly faced with situations where they are assigned a narrow identity with which they might not identify and where they are often othered or excluded.

19 Scholars like Bakht 2012 and Razack 2008 take a critical race lens, but their work is not among the qualitative-focused works under examination here.

REFERENCES

Primary Sources

Akter, Nasrin. 2011. *The religious lives of immigrant Muslim women in Canada: The case of Bangladeshi women in St. John's, Newfoundland*. Lambert Academic Publishing.

Al-Fartousi, May. 2013. "Unveiling Shi'i religious identities: A case study of hijab in culturally homogenous Canadian schools." PhD diss., Brock University.

Anderson, Brenda, and Franz Volker Greifenhagen. 2013. "Covering up on the prairies: Gender, Muslim identity and security perception in Canada." In Emma Tarlo and Annelies Moors (Eds.), *Islamic fashion and anti-fashion in Europe and North America* (pp. 55–72). Bloomsbury.

Bakali, Naved. 2015a. "Islamophobia in Québec secondary schools: Inquiries into the lived experiences of Muslim youth Post-9/11." PhD diss., McGill University.

– 2015b. "Muslim teachers' experiences with race and racism in Québec secondary schools." *Canadian Journal of New Scholars in Education*, *6*(1), 45–54.

– 2015c. "Québec identity politics and anti-Muslim bias in Québec secondary schools." In D. Napier (Ed.), *International perspectives on race (and racism): Historical and contemporary considerations in education and society* (pp. 339–58). Nova Science Publishing.

– 2016. *Islamophobia: Understanding anti-Muslim racism through the lived experiences of Muslim youth.* Sense Publishers.

Barras, Amélie. 2016. "Exploring the intricacies and dissonances of religious governance: The case of Québec and the discourse of request." *Critical Research on Religion, 4*(1), 57–71. https://doi.org/10.1177%2F2050303216630066

– 2018. "Reasonable Accommodation." In Catherine Holtmann (Ed.), *Exploring religion and diversity in Canada – people, practice and possibility* (pp. 183–205). Springer.

Barras, Amélie, Jennifer A. Selby, and Lori G. Beaman. 2016. "In/visible religion in public institutions: Canadian Muslim public servants." In Benjamin Berger and Richard Moon (Eds.), *Religion and the exercise of public authority* (pp. 95–110). Hart Publishing.

– 2018. "Rethinking Canadian discourses of Reasonable Accommodation." *Social Inclusion, 6*(2), 162–72. https://doi.org/10.17645/si.v6i2.1443

Berns McGown, Rima. 1999. *Muslims in the diaspora: The Somali communities of London and Toronto.* University of Toronto Press.

Beyer, Peter. 2014. "Securitization and young Muslim males: Is none too many?" In Paul Bramadat and Lorne Dawson (Eds.), *Religious radicalization and securitization in Canada and beyond* (pp. 121–44). University of Toronto Press.

Beyer, Peter, and Rubina Ramji (Eds.). 2013. *Growing up Canadian: Muslims, Hindus, Buddhists.* McGill-Queen's University Press.

Brown, Rachel. 2016a. "How gelatin becomes an essential symbol of Muslim identity: Food practice as a lens into the study of religion and migration." *Religious Studies and Theology, 35*(2), 89–113. http://doi.org/10.1558/rsth.v35i2.32558

– 2016b. "Immigration, integration and ingestion: The role of food and drink in transnational experience for North African Muslim immigrants in Paris and Montréal." PhD diss., Wilfrid Laurier University.

Bullock, Katherine (Ed.). 2005. *Muslim women activists in North America: Speaking for ourselves.* University of Texas Press.

– 2010. "Hijab and belonging: Canadian Muslim women." In Theodore Gabriel and Rabiha Hannan (Eds.), *Islam and the veil: Theoretical and regional contexts* (pp. 161–80). Continuum International Publishing Group.

– 2015. "Visible and invisible: An audience study of Muslim and non-Muslim reactions to Orientalist representations in *I Dream of Jeannie.*" *Journal of Arab and Muslim Media Research, 8*(2), 83–97. https://doi.org/10.1386/jammr.8.2.83_1

Bullock, Katherine, and Paul Nesbitt-Larking. 2013. "Becoming 'holistically indigenous': Young Muslims and political participation in Canada." *Journal of*

Muslim Minority Affairs, 33(2), 185–207. https://doi.org/10.1080/13602004.2013.810116

Bunting, Annie, and Shado Mokhtari. 2007. "Migrant Muslim women's interests and the case of 'shari'a tribunals' in Ontario." In Vigay Agnew (Ed.), *Racialized migrant women in Canada: Essays on health, violence, and equity* (pp. 233–64). Toronto University Press.

Cassin, Katelyn L.H. 2014. "A multifaith military: Religiosity and belonging among Muslim Canadian armed forces members." Master's thesis, McMaster University.

Chraibi, Radia, and Wendy Cukier. 2017. "Muslim women in senior management positions in Canada: Advancement, perceptions of success, and strategies for inclusive HRM." In Jasmin Mahadevan and Claude-Hélène Mayer (Eds.), *Muslim minorities, workplace diversity and reflexive HRM* (pp. 162–82). Routledge.

Clarke, Lynda. 2013. "Women in niqab speak: A study of the niqab in Canada." Canadian Council of Muslim Women. http://ccmw.com/wp-content/uploads/2013/10/WEB_EN_WiNiqab_FINAL.pdf

Cutting, Christopher. 2013. "Shari'a and constraint: Practices, policies, and responses to faith-based arbitration in Ontario." PhD diss., University of Waterloo.

Dossa, Parin A. 1999. "(Re)imagining aging lives: Ethnographic narratives of Muslim women in diaspora." *Journal of Cross-Cultural Gerontology, 14*(3), 245–72. https://doi.org/10.1023/A:1006659904679

– 2002. "Narrative mediation of conventional and new 'mental health' paradigms: Reading the stories of immigrant Iranian women." *Medical Anthropology Quarterly, 16*(3), 341–59. https://doi.org/10.1525/maq.2002.16.3.341

– 2004. *Politics and poetics of migration: Narratives of Iranian women from the diaspora.* Canadian Scholars' Press.

– 2008a. "Creating politicized spaces: Afghan immigrant women's stories of migration and displacement." *Affilia, 33*(1), 10–21. https://doi.org/10.1177%2F0886109907310462

– 2009. *Racialized bodies, disabling worlds: Storied lives of immigrant Muslim women.* University of Toronto Press.

– 2014. *Afghanistan remembers: Gendered narrations of violence and culinary practices.* University of Toronto Press.

Downie, Caitlin. 2012. "Negotiating perceptions and constructing identities: Muslim strategies in St. John's Newfoundland." Master's thesis, University of Ottawa.

Eid, Paul. 2002. "Ethnic and religious identity retention among second-generation Arab youths in Montréal, Québec." PhD diss., University of Toronto.

– 2003. "The interplay between ethnicity, religion, and gender among second-generation Christian and Muslim Arabs in Montréal." *Canadian Ethnic Studies, 35*(2), 30–61. https://www-proquest-com.qe2a-proxy.mun.ca/scholarly

-journals/interplay-between-ethnicity-religion-gender-among /docview/215638254/se-2?accountid=12378

– 2007. *Being Arab: Ethnic and religious identity building among second generation youth in Montreal*. McGill-Queens University Press.

Elsayed, Soha. 2009. "Exploring a sense of Canadianness: Canadian Muslims in Kitchener-Waterloo." Master's thesis, Wilfrid Laurier University.

Flower, Scott, and Deborah Birkett. 2014. *(Mis)understanding Muslim converts in Canada: A critical discussion of Muslim Converts in the contexts of security and society*. Canadian Network for Research on Terrorism, Security, and Society. Working Paper Series No. 14–06. https://www.tsas.ca/publications/misunderstanding -muslim-converts-in-canada

Funk, Cory. 2017. "Hashtagging Islam: #JeSuisHijabi, social media, and religious /secular identities in the lives of Muslims in Winnipeg and St. John's, Canada." Master's thesis, Memorial University of Newfoundland.

Gibb, Camilla, and Celia Rothenberg. 2000. "Believing women: Harari and Palestinian women at home and in the Canadian diaspora." *Journal of Muslim Minority Affairs*, *20*(2), 243–59. https://doi.org/10.1080/713680360

Guzik, Elysia. 2017. "Informing identities: Religious conversion experiences of Muslims in the Toronto area." PhD diss., University of Toronto.

Hameed, Qamer. 2015. "Grassroots Canadian Muslim identity in the prairie city of Winnipeg: A case study of 2nd and 1.5 generation Canadian Muslims." Master's thesis, University of Ottawa.

Harvey-Crowell, Liam. 2015. "The impact and perception of Islam and authority online among Muslim university students in St. John's, NL." Master's thesis, Memorial University of Newfoundland.

Hussain, Amir. 2001. "The Canadian face of Islam: Muslim communities in Toronto." PhD diss., University of Toronto.

Jamil, Uzma. 2014. "The impact of securitization on South Asian Muslims in Montréal." In Lorne Dawson and Paul Bramadat (Ed.), *Religious radicalization and securitization in Canada and beyond* (pp. 145–63). University of Toronto Press.

Lavoie, Bertrand. 2018. *La fonctionnaire et le hijab: Liberté de religion et laïcité dans les institutions publiques québécoises*. Presses de l'Université de Montréal.

Le Gall, J. 2013. "The meaning of prayer for young Muslim immigrants in Québec (Canada)." In G. Giordan and L. Woodhead (Eds.), *Annual review of the sociology of religion, Vol. 4: Prayer in religion and spirituality* (pp. 141–55). Brill.

Macfarlane, Julie. 2012. *Islamic divorce in North America*. Oxford University Press.

Memon, Nadeem. 2010. "Social consciousness in Canadian Islamic schools?" *Journal of International Migration and Integration*, *11*(1), 109–17. https://doi.org/10.1007 /s12134-009-0118-8

Mossière, Géraldine. 2008. "Reconnue par l'autre, respectée chez soi: La construction d'un discours politique critique et alternatif par des femmes converties à l'Islam en France et au Québec." *Les Cahiers du Gres, série Diversité urbaine, 8*(2), 37–59. https://doi.org/10.7202/000318ar

– 2010. "Des femmes converties à l'islam en France et au Québec: Religiosités d'un nouveau genre." PhD diss., Université de Montréal.

– 2011. "Devenir musulmane pour discipliner le corps et transformer l'esprit: L'herméneutique du sujet pieux comme voie de restauration du soi." *Ethnologies, 33*(1), 117–42. https://doi.org/10.7202/1007799ar

– 2013. *Converties à l'islam: Parcours de femmes au Québec et en France.* Presses de l'Université de Montréal.

– 2016. "The intimate and the stranger: Approaching the 'Muslim question' through the eyes of female converts to Islam." *Critical Research on Religion, 4*(1), 90–108. https://doi.org/10.1177%2F2050303216630067

Nagra, Baljit. 2011. "'Our faith was also hijacked by those people': Reclaiming Muslim identity in Canada in a post-9/11 era." *Journal of Ethnic and Migration Studies, 37*(3): 425–41. https://doi.org/10.1080/1369183X.2011.526781

– 2017. *Securitized citizens: Canadian Muslims' experiences of race relations and identity formation post-9/11.* University of Toronto Press.

Nagra, Baljit, and Paula Maurutto. 2016. "Security and surveillance among young Canadian Muslims." *Canadian Journal of Sociology, 41*(2), 165–94. https://doi.org/10.29173/cjs23031

Riikonen, Tanja. 2016. "Des identités musulmanes: Analyse discursive des négociations identitaires d'étudiantes universitaires et immigrantes en Finlande et au Québec." PhD diss., Université de Montréal.

Selby, Jennifer A. 2012a. "Construing the secular: Implications of the Ontario shari'a debate." In Anna C. Korteweg and Jennifer A. Selby (Eds.), *Debating shari'a: Islam, gender politics and family law arbitration* (pp. 351–76). University of Toronto Press.

– 2012b. "Suburban Muslims: 2004 debates outside of Toronto and Paris." In Lori G. Beaman (Ed.), *Religion and Canadian society: Traditions, transitions, and innovations* (2nd ed., pp. 115–36). Canadian Scholars' Press.

– 2013. "Promoting the everyday: Public relations and pro-shari'a advocacy in Ontario, Canada's 'shari'a debate.'" *Religions, 4*(3), 423–42. https://doi.org/10.3390/rel4030423

– 2016a. "'The diamond ring now is the thing': Young Canadian Muslim women negotiating *mahr* on the web." In Adeline Masquelier and Benjamin Soares (Ed.), *The 9/11 generation: Young Muslims in the new world order* (pp. 189–212). School for Advanced Research Press.

– 2016b. "Muslimness and multiplicity in qualitative research and in government reports in Canada." *Critical Research on Religion, 4*(1), 72–89. https://doi.org/10.1177%2F2050303216630298

– 2018. "Muslim Canadians." In Catherine Holtmann (Ed.), *Exploring religion and diversity in Canada: People, practice and possibility* (pp. 207–36). Springer.

Selby, Jennifer A., Amélie Barras, and Lori G. Beaman. 2018a. *Beyond accommodation: Everyday narratives of Muslim Canadians*. University of British Columbia Press.

Sharify-Funk, Meena. 2009. "Representing Canadian Muslims: Media, Muslim advocacy, organizations, and gender in the Ontario Shari'ah debate." *Global Media Journal–Canadian Edition, 2*(2), 73–89. http://gmj-canadianedition.ca/wp-content/uploads/2018/12/v2i2_sharify-funk.pdf

– 2010. "Muslims and the politics of 'Reasonable Accommodation': Analyzing the Bouchard-Taylor Report and its impact on the Canadian province of Québec." *Journal of Muslim Minority Affairs, 30*(4), 535–53. https://doi.org/10.1080/13602004.2010.533451

Versi, Salima. 2010. "Make this your home: The impact of religion on acculturation: The case of Canadian Khoja Nizari Isma'ilis from East Africa." Master's thesis. Queens University.

Waugh, Earle. 2012. "Muslim perspectives on a good death in hospice and end-of-life care." In Harold Coward and Kelli I. Stajduhar (Eds.), *Religious understandings of a good death in hospice palliative care* (pp. 77–98). State University of New York Press.

Waugh, Earle, and Jenny Wannas. 2003. "The rise of a womanist movement among Muslim women in Alberta." *Studies in Contemporary Islam, 1*, 1–15.

Zine, Jasmin. 2000. "Redefining resistance: Towards an Islamic subculture in schools." *Race, Ethnicity and Education, 3*(3), 293–316. https://doi.org/10.1080/713693042

– 2001. "Muslim youth in Canadian schools: Education and the politics of religious identity." *Anthropology Education Quarterly, 32*(4), 399–423. https://doi.org/10.1525/aeq.2001.32.4.399

– 2002. "Muslim women and the politics of representation." *American Journal of Islamic Social Sciences, 19*(4), 1–22. https://doi.org/10.35632/ajis.v19i4.1913

– 2004. "Staying on the 'straight path': A critical ethnography of Islamic schooling in Ontario." PhD diss., University of Toronto.

– 2006. "Unveiled sentiments: Gendered Islamophobia and experiences of veiling among Muslim girls in a Canadian Islamic school." *Equity and Excellence in Education, 39*(3), 239–52. https://doi.org/10.1080/10665680600788503

– 2007. "Safe havens or religious 'ghettos'? Narratives of Islamic schooling in Canada." *Race, Ethnicity and Education, 10*(1), 71–92. https://doi.org/10.1080/13613320601100385

– 2008a. *Canadian Islamic schools: Unravelling the politics of faith, gender, knowledge, and identity.* University of Toronto Press.

– 2008b. "Honour and identity: An ethnographic account of Muslim girls in a Canadian Islamic school." *Topia: Canadian Journal of Cultural Studies, 19*(39), 39–67. https://doi.org/10.3138/topia.19.35

Secondary Sources

Awid, Richard Asmet. 2000. *Through the eyes of the son: A factual history of Canadian Arabs*. Accent Printing.

– 2010. *Canada's first mosque: The Al Rashid*. High Speed Printing.

Bakali, Naved. 2016. *Islamophobia: Understanding anti-Muslim racism through the lived experiences of Muslim youth*. Sense Publishers.

Bakht, Natasha. 2012. "Veiled objections: Facing public opposition to the niqab." In Lori G. Beaman (Ed.), *Reasonable Accommodation: Managing religious diversity* (pp. 70–108). University of British Columbia Press.

Barras, Amélie. 2018. "Travelogue of secularism: Longing to find a place to call home." *European Journal of Women's Studies* (February), 1–16. https://doi.org/10.1177%2F1350506818755415

Bayoumi, Moustafa. 2006. "Racing religion." *CR: The New Centennial Review, 6*(2), 267–93. https:// doi.org/10.1353/ncr.2007.0000

Bouchard, Gérard. 2012. *L'interculturalisme: Un point de vue québécois*. Les Éditions du Boréal.

Bouchard, Gérard, and Charles Taylor. 2008. "Building the future: A time for reconciliation." *Québec Commission de Consultation sur les Pratiques d'Accommodement Reliées aux Differences Culturelles*. Retrieved 5 May 2016 from http://collections.banq.qc.ca/ark:/52327/bs1565996

Bramadat, Paul. 2005. "Beyond Christian Canada: Religion and Ethnicity in a Multicultural Society." In Paul Bramadat and David Seljak (Eds.), *Religion and Ethnicity in Canada* (pp. 1–19). Pearson Longman.

Chan-Malik, Sylvia. 2011. "Common cause: On the Black-immigrant debate and constructing the Muslim American." *Journal of Race, Ethnicity, and Religion, 2*(8), 1–39. http://www.raceandreligion.com/JRER/Volume_2_(2011)_files/Chan%20Malik%202%208.pdf

Cooper, Afua. 2006. *The hanging of Angelique: The untold story of Canadian slavery and the burning of old Montréal*. HarperCollins.

– 2007, Spring. "Acts of resistance: Black men and women engage slavery in Upper Canada, 1793–1803." *Ontario History, 99*(1), 5–17. https://doi.org/10.7202/1065793ar

Côté, Pauline. 2008. "Québec and Reasonable Accommodation: Uses and misuses of public consultation." In Lori G. Beaman and Peter Beyer (Eds.), *Religion and diversity in Canada* (pp. 41–65). Brill.

Cutting, Christopher. 2012. "Faith-based arbitration or religious divorce: What was the issue?" In Anna C. Korteweg and Jennifer A. Selby (Eds.), *Debating shari'a: Islam, gender politics, and family law arbitration* (pp. 66–87). University of Toronto Press.

Deeb, Lara, and Mona Harb. 2013. *Leisurely Islam: Negotiating geography and morality in Shi'ite South Beirut*. Princeton University Press.

Dossa, Parin. 2008b. "Creating alternative and demedicalized spaces: Testimonial narratives on disability, culture and racialization." *Journal of International Women's Studies, 9*(3), 79–98. https://vc.bridgew.edu/jiws/vol9/iss3/6

Foblets, Marie-Claire, and Jean-Philippe Schreiber (Eds.). 2013. *The round tables on interculturalism*. Larcier.

Forcese, Craig, and Kent Roach. 2015. "Legislating in fearful and politicized times: The limits of Bill C-51's disruption powers in making us safer." In Edward M. Iaccobucci and Stephen J. Toope (Eds.), *After the Paris attacks: Responses in Canada, Europe, and around the globe* (pp. 141–58). University of Toronto Press.

Fuerst, Ilyse, and Zahra Ayubi. 2016. "Shifting boundaries: The study of Islam in the humanities." *Muslim World, 106*(4), 643–54. http://doi.org/10.1111/muwo.12163

Harding, Sandra. 1987. *Feminism and methodology*. Indiana University Press.

Haque, Eve. 2010. "Homegrown Muslim and other: Tolerance, secularism, and the limits of multiculturalism." *Social Identities: Journal of the Study of Race, Nation and Culture, 16*(1), 79–101. https://doi.org/10.1080/13504630903465902

Harvey-Crowell, Liam. 2015. "The impact and perception of Islam and authority online among Muslim university students in St. John's, NL." Master's thesis, Memorial University of Newfoundland.

Islamophobia is Racism. n.d. "#IslamophobiaIsRacism Syllabus." Retrieved 2 July 2018 from https://islamophobiaisracism.wordpress.com

Jackson, Sherman A. 2011. "Islam, Muslims and the wages of racial agnosia in America." *Journal of Islamic Law and Culture, 13*(1), 1–17. https://doi.org/10.1080/1528817X.2012.693386

Jackson-Best, Fatimah. 2019, February. "Black Muslims in Canada: A systematic review of published and unpublished literature." Tessellate Institute and Black Muslim Initiative. http://tessellateinstitute.com/wp-content/uploads/2019/02/Black-Muslims-in-Canada-Systematic-Review-FatimahJacksonBest.pdf

Karim, Karim H. 2002. "Muslim encounters with new media: Towards an inter-civilizational discourse on globality?" In Ali Mohammadi (Ed.), *Islam encountering globalisation* (pp. 36–60). Routledge.

Kazemipur, Abdolmohammad. 2014. *The Muslim question in Canada: A story of segmented integration*. University of British Columbia Press.

Lefebvre, Solange. 2008. "Between law and public opinion." In Lori G. Beaman and Peter Beyer (Eds.), *Religion and diversity in Canada* (pp. 175–98). Brill.

Leuprecht, Christian, and Conrad Winn. 2011, November. "What do Muslim Canadians want? The clash of interpretations and opinion research." In *True north in Canadian public policy*. Macdonald-Laurier Institute.

Litchmore, Rashelle V.H., and Saba Safdar. 2015. "Young, female, Canadian and Muslim: Identity negotiation and transcultural experience." In Claude-Hélène Mayer and Stephan Wolting (Eds.), *Purple jacaranda: Narrations on transcultural identity development* (pp. 59–67). Waxmann.

Maghbouleh, Neda. 2017. *The limits of Whiteness: Iranian Americans and the everyday politics of race.* Stanford University Press.

Mahrouse, Gada. 2010. "'Reasonable Accommodation' in Québec: The limits of participation and dialogue." *Race and Class, 52*(1), 85–96. https://doi.org/10.1177%2F0306396810371768

Maira, Sunaina. 2014. "Surveillance effects: South Asian, Arab, and Afghan American youth in the War on Terror." In Suvendrini Perera and Sherene H. Razack (Eds.), *At the limits of justice: Women of colour on terror* (pp. 86–106). University of Toronto Press.

McDonough, Sheila, and Homa Hoodfar. 2005. "Muslim groups in Canada: From ethnic groups to religious community." In Paul Bramadat and David Seljak (Eds.), *Religion and ethnicity in Canada* (pp. 133–53). Pearson Education Canada.

Moghissi, Haideh, Saeed Rahnema, and Mark J. Goodman. 2009. *Diaspora by design: Muslims in Canada and beyond.* University of Toronto Press.

Mugabo, Délice. 2016. "On rocks and hard places: A reflection on antiblackness in organizing against Islamophobia." *Critical Ethnic Studies, 2*(2), 159–83. https://doi.org/10.5749/jcritethnstud.2.2.0159

Multani v. Commission scolaire Marguerite-Bourgeoys, 1 S.C.R. 256, 2006 SCC 6 (2006).

Naber, Nadine. 2008. "'Look, Mohammed the terrorist is coming!': Cultural racism, nation-based racism and the intersectionality of oppressions after 9/11." In Amanay Jamal and Nadine Naber (Eds.), *Race and Arab Americans before and after 9/11: From invisible citizens to visible subjects* (pp. 276–304). Syracuse University Press.

– 2012. *Arab America: Gender, cultural politics, and activism.* New York University Press.

Nagra, Baljit. 2018. "Cultural explanations of patriarchy, race, and everyday lives: Marginalizing and 'othering' Muslim women in Canada." *Journal of Muslim Minority Affairs, 38*(2), 263–79. https://doi.org/10.1080/13602004.2018.1466488

Naples, Nancy A. 2007. "Feminist methodology and its discontents." In W. Outhwaite and Stephen P. Turner (Eds.), *The SAGE Handbook of Social Science Methodology* (pp. 547–62). SAGE.

Neitz, Mary Jo. 2011. "Lived religion: Signposts of where we have been and where we can go from here." In Giuseppe Giordan and William H. Swatos (Eds.), *Religion, spirituality and everyday practice* (pp. 45–56). Springer.

Razack, Sherene. 2008. *Casting out: The eviction of Muslims from Western law and politics.* University of Toronto Press.

Reitz, Jeffrey, Patrick Simon, and Emily Laxer. 2017. "Muslims' social inclusion and exclusion in France, Québec, and Canada: Does national context matter?" *Journal of Ethnic and Migration Studies, 43*(15), 2473–98. https://doi.org/10.1080/1369183X.2017.1313105

Schielke, Samuli. 2009. "Being good in Ramadan: Ambivalence, fragmentation and the moral self in the lives of young Egyptians." *Journal of the Royal Anthropological Institute, 15*(s1), S24–S40. https://doi.org/10.1111/j.1467-9655.2009.01540.x

Selby, Jennifer, Amélie Barras, and Lori G. Beaman. 2018b. "Le Terroriste, l'Homme éclairé et le Patriarche: Les figures qui hantent le quotidien des musulmanes." *Anthropologie et Société, 42*(1), 155–82. https://doi.org/10.7202/1045128ar

Shahzad, Farhat. 2014. "The discourse of fear: The effects of the war on terror on Canadian university students." *American Review of Canadian Studies, 44*(4), 467–82. https://doi.org/10.1080/02722011.2014.976232

Statistics Canada. 2018. "Police-reported hate crime." https://www150.statcan.gc.ca/n1/daily-quotidien/200226/dq200226a-eng.htm

Waugh, Earle. 2018. *Al Rashid Mosque: Building Canadian Muslim communities.* Gutteridge Books Alberta.

Wilkins-Laflamme, Sarah. 2018. "Islamophobia in Canada: Measuring the realities of negative attitudes toward Muslims and religious discrimination." *Canadian Review of Sociology, 55*(1), 86–110. https://doi.org/10.1111/cars.12180

Zine, Jasmin. 2017, 9 May. "Let's worry more about violent Islamophobes – and less about writers who fear being called 'Islamophobic.'" *National Post.*

Studying Muslim Minorities in Canada: Pitfalls Facing Researchers Attempting to Turn a Racialized Category into a Category of Analysis

PAUL EID

Introduction

In this chapter, I want to reflect critically on the process by which scholars working on Islam and Muslims in Canada can contribute, whether they like it or not, to socially reinforcing the notion that there is one bounded and unitary Muslim Canadian "community." The point here is not to discredit the raison d'être of research on Islam and Muslim Canadians. The latter is indeed much needed, if only because Islam, as will be further discussed below, has gradually become the master category through which the otherness and dangerousness of people identified or self-identifying as Muslims are socially constructed by majority groups in Western societies. Yet this process of racialization (Garner and Selod 2015) makes it all the more important to be aware of certain epistemological and political challenges that, as scholars, we are bound to face when studying Muslim minorities in Canada. More specifically, considering that Muslim Canadians constitute an "imagined" community (Anderson 1983) with shifting identity boundaries, how can they be investigated *as Muslims* without giving credence, even inadvertently, to the deep-seated belief that Islam is this frozen, metacultural frame, overdetermining those categorized (and thus racialized) as such?

The Social Construction of "Muslimness" in the West after 9/11

Since 9/11, Muslim populations across the West have increasingly become construed as a social problem deserving immediate political attention. Numerous authors have documented the "securitization" of Islam and Muslims in Western states. Often, when Muslims and Islam are conjured up in Western media, it is to depict them as a security threat warranting either a military or a legislative response. And I am referring here not only to the "anti-terrorist" rhetoric portraying Muslims as a physical threat, exposing them to greater scrutiny and racial profiling both inside and outside of Canadian and US borders (Cesari 2002, 2011; Kundnani 2014; Nagra 2017; Razack 2008; Saeed 2016). In Europe and North America, Muslim minorities are also represented as a cultural threat, being frequently suspected of undermining "our" Western national(ized) values, particularly gender equality and secularism, which are deemed intrinsically incompatible with Islam's presumed propensity to foster patriarchy and religious orthodoxy (read: rigidity) (Andreassen and Lettinga 2012; Bilge 2013; Lentin and Titley 2011). As a result, since 9/11, Muslims and Islam have triggered, in the West, a sort of "moral panic" (Cohen 1972) that is certainly fuelled by far-right and openly Islamophobic movements and parties but upon which mainstream parties and politicians periodically attempt (and sometimes achieve) to capitalize electorally (Lentin and Titley 2011).

This process of social categorization (Massey 2007) and stigmatization certainly impacts heavily on identity formation among Muslim minorities in the West, as their religion has become the primary frame through which majority groups manufacture their otherness. In this context, not only do Muslim minorities tend to feel expelled from the realm of citizenship, as Nagra (2017) shows for Canada and Selod (2015) for the US, but it becomes hard for them to ignore or even downplay their religious affiliation, irrespective of their actual level of religious piety and devotion per se (Selby et al. 2018). In this sense, nowadays the power of individuals labelled as "Muslims" in the West to self-determine to which (if any) groups they belong, and when and where to avail themselves of this or that category drawn from their identity repertoire, is heavily constrained by a racialized process of assignation to otherness (Meer 2013; Nagra 2017; Selod 2015). As a result, those associated with Islam see their (real or imagined) "Muslimness" foregrounded when they attempt to broker their ethnocultural self in both informal day-to-day social interactions and more formal institutional settings (Nagra 2017; Selby et al. 2018). My own research (Eid 2007) has shown that, among the second-generation Muslim (and Christian) Arabs that I interviewed and surveyed in Montreal, religion tends to fuse with ethnicity in the delineation of distinct group boundaries. I am not saying that religious devotion per se is absent from these young people's relationship to religion. However, their attachment to religion should be understood not exclusively as a mere sign of piety but also, and perhaps most importantly, as a group identity provider and community binder, which signals the interweaving of their ethnic and religious selves (Eid 2003, 2007).[1] Of course, "Muslimness" is not the only cultural identity that, in the West, is heavily shaped by categorization. In the United States and Canada, for example, the same can be said about certain pan-ethnic labels such as "Asian" (Espiritu 1992; Lee and Zhou 2015), "Latino" (Chavez 2008; Massey and Sánchez R. 2010; Portes and MacLeod 1996), and "Arab" (Asal 2016; Boosahda 2003; Eid 2007; Suleiman 1988, 1999).

Certain actors play a pivotal role in the consolidation of these all-encompassing categories that lump together very culturally heterogeneous groups. The mass media, for instance, can be singled out as a major contributing factor to the coalescence of ethnic and racial categories among both majority and minority groups (Bouamama 2011; Van Dijk 2008). The state, mostly through its public policies and official census data and statistics, also contributes to bolstering the categorical frames through which racialized or ethnicized power relationships are produced and maintained (Nagel 1994).

In what follows, I want to focus on the role played by academics in such processes. Social scientists must not only be cognizant of their research's potential impacts on social categories; conversely, they must be aware that the way they frame their research topics, as well as the populations they are studying, is itself shaped by social categories that are historically situated and sometimes politically loaded (Martiniello and Simon 2005). The question I want to tackle here is how and at what cost can research on Muslim Canadians be conducted in a context where "Muslimness" as a social category and "Muslimness" as a category of analysis are continuously cross-fertilizing – or cross-contaminating, some would say – each other?

The Role of Social Scientists in the Reification of the Minority Groups They Are Studying

As social scientists, we need to ask ourselves to what extent the way we frame and delineate the contours of the populations we are studying contributes to superimposing categories and labels on our subjects that we presume to be determinant in their self-definitions. By doing so, we are always at risk of naturalizing the "imagined communities" we are researching, thus essentializing their identity boundaries, which are, in effect, multilayered and multifaceted. This sort of analytical reductionism can yield undesirable power effects, as it can reinforce the reifying categories whereby majority groups construct minority groups' otherness and, on this basis, relegate them to subaltern positions, both socioeconomically and symbolically (Martiniello and Simon 2005).

Of course, social researchers' categories of analysis are not modelled mechanically after the social categories of practice they are meant to explain, at least most of the time. However, because social scientists do not create their categories of analysis in a social vacuum, they, too, depend on the specific social locations they speak from and run the risk of naturalizing the dominant performative categories through which the social world is rendered intelligible to actors. This sort of epistemological pitfall has been rightfully flagged by authors such as Brubaker (2004), Martiniello and Simon (2005), and Wimmer (2013), just to name a few. Brubaker is certainly among those who emphasized this point most eloquently and convincingly. For Brubaker (2004), the main risk facing social scientists is to engage in what he refers to as "groupism," by which he means

> the tendency to take discrete, bounded groups as basic constituents of social life, chief protagonists of social conflicts, and fundamental units of analysis. I mean the tendency to treat ethnic groups, nations, and races as substantial entities to which interests and agency can be attributed. I mean the tendency to reify such groups, speaking of Serbs, Croats, Muslims and Albanians in the former Yugoslavia ... , of Jews and Palestinians in Israel and the occupied territories ... , or of Blacks, Whites, Asians, Hispanics, and Natives Americans in the United States as if they were internally homogeneous, externally bounded groups, even unitary collective actors with common purposes. (8)

Drawing on Fredrik Barth's (1969) seminal work, Brubaker (2004) warns researchers against treating ethnic groups as if they were discrete "things-in-the-world" (see also Wimmer 2013). Instead, Brubaker (2004) urges a focus on processes of ethnic identification and boundary formation, which are not only shifting and historically contingent but also shaped by "ethnopolitical entrepreneurs" who mobilize – and manipulate – certain cultural schemas and symbols so as to manufacture a sense of community. In other words, from this perspective, ethnic groups do not pre-exist the work of boundary formation performed by ethnic entrepreneurs; they stem from it. Group consciousness is thus engineered politically and ideologically. Brubaker does not deny that these imagined communities have real sociological consequences on actors, as they result in systems of classification sustaining "ethnic" conflicts (or framed as such) and unequal power relationships. He rightly points out, however, that social analysts should not think of ethnicity as a substance or a thing but rather explore the social conditions and mechanisms that bring about ethnic, "racial," class, religious, or any other form of group consciousness for that matter. This means, concretely, that they should turn their attention to "practical categories, situated actions, cultural idioms, cognitive schemas, discursive frames, organizational routines, institutional forms, political projects and contingent events" (Brubaker 2004, 11).

I too, like most researchers in the field of ethnic studies today, subscribe to this constructivist approach to group identity formation. Still, I think that Brubaker's Barthian framework overlooks an important dimension of ethnocultural identity construction in a migratory context. More specifically, Brubaker is not attentive enough to the fact that ethnicity, or any other form of groupness understood as an Us/Them boundary, can also be rooted, to varying degrees, in practices of socialization and communalization that produce a renewable reservoir of shared meanings and symbols (Juteau 1999/2015; Weber 1921/1971, 416). Put differently, although ethnic groups are not bound by a monolithic and unitary culture, we must acknowledge that group boundary formation is facilitated when group members – and not only ethnic entrepreneurs – can count on a large repertoire of shared cultural symbols and practices to (re)invent their ethnicity in a diaspora context. Of course, as Mary Waters (1990) has shown in her research on third- and fourth-generation Euro-Americans ("ethnic Whites"), group members can develop a strong ethnic self-concept that, nonetheless, is not sustained by socialization networks and cultural practices structured along ethnic lines, a phenomenon which, following Herbert Gans (1979), she refers to as "symbolic ethnicity." Similarly, in Canada, many second-generation Muslims self-identify strongly as "Muslims" but without being enmeshed in religious networks or showing outward signs of religious devotion (Eid 2003). Other second-generation Muslims, as Levitt et al. (2011) have shown for the United States, creatively reinvent and combine different religious norms, symbols, and practices drawn from various sources and sites, thus performing their own creolized rendition of what it means to be and act "Muslim" in North America.

In any case, if social scientists studying Muslim minorities in a migratory context are to take Brubaker seriously – and I think they should – they ought to be cautious, in their research, not to give credence to the political fiction that there is such a thing as a discrete, seamless, and monolithic Muslim "community," since the racialization of Muslims rests precisely on such an essentializing frame. I will grapple with this issue in the last section of this chapter. But if social scientists can inadvertently fuel social categorization, the other way around is also true: social categorization influences how researchers frame their research questions and how they define the boundaries of the population they are studying. In the next section, I will illustrate this latter process, taking my own research choices and trajectory as a case in point.

How Arabs Became Muslims, First in Popular Imagery … and Then in Research

In 1998–9, for my PhD research in sociology, I chose to study processes of ethnic and religious identity building among second-generation Arab Canadians in Montreal.[2] When recruiting participants for data collection, in 2000 and 2001 (before 9/11), I looked for Muslim and Christian youths who either were Canadian-born or arrived here at a young age, and whose parents both immigrated to Canada from an Arab country. Using questionnaires and in-depth interviews, I tried to determine, among many other things, to what extent the Arab category was a significant source of identification for them, whether they thought Arabs were misrepresented in the media, and whether they felt well "accepted as Arabs by Canadians in their personal life."[3] My primary concern was to explore how second-generation Arabs in Montreal performed their ethnicity and religiosity in a social context where, I presumed, "Arabness" was not only socially salient but also socially compromising. My main rationale for doing so was that "Arabness," although by no means exhausting the identity repertoire of my subjects, could not be ignored in the analysis, since

> in the Western world in general and in North America in particular, the importance of the "Arab" category in the formation of Arab minorities' ethnic identity tends to be magnified. Arab-origin minorities are ascribed a prefabricated "Arabness" that they can hardly disregard since the notion lies at the centre of the system of representations through which the majority group conceives of their ethnicity. (Eid 2007, xiv)

I thus assumed that, because of external categorization, Arab Canadians could hardly remain neutral towards the Arab category.

At the end of the 1990s, my choice to focus my research on Arab-origin youths made sense because Western-based minorities originating from Muslim-majority countries were more socially construed (and disparaged) as Arabs than as Muslims.[4] Several factors rooted in national and international politics accounted for this tendency. In the Arab world, up to the nineties, most anti-colonial, and later postcolonial, movements of resistance to Western imperialism mobilized a nationalist rhetoric that was generally secular and socialist and that very often conjured up "Arabness" as a (transnational) community binder. Indeed, Pan-Arabism, under Gamal Abdel Nasser's impulse, was a very influential ideology shaping not only political mobilization and resistance but also group consciousness and identities throughout the Arab world (Farah 1987). Furthermore, historically, since the first migratory cohorts started to settle in North America at the turn of the twentieth century, minorities originating from the Arab world were socially and politically categorized as Arabs or "Turks," and eventually as Arab Canadians (Abu-Laban 1980; Asal 2016) or Arab Americans (Suleiman 1988). From the 1950s until the late 1990s, the Arab-Israeli conflicts were highly instrumental in crystallizing the Western-made figure of the violent, backward, and sexist Arab Other and, reactively, an Arab-based solidarity and consciousness cutting across national and even religious allegiances, perhaps even more effectively among the Arab diaspora in the West. The US media coverage of the first Gulf War, in 1990–1, powerfully buttressed the stereotypical figure of the belligerent and violent Arab, full of hatred for "our" liberties and democracy (Gavrilos 2002, 432–3; Suleiman 1999). During this same period, Hollywood, and the mass media in general, contributed strongly to rigidifying the Arab category, and especially the stigma attached to it, through its depiction and representation of Arab villains in movies (Shaheen 2001, 2003).

However, the Iranian Revolution of 1979, and ten years later the fatwa called on Salman Rushdie for his book *The Satanic Verses*, heralded a gradual shift away from "Arabness" towards "Muslimness" as the master category through which the primary significant Other of the West was fantasized. Throughout the

1990s, this shift accelerated with the political growth of increasingly influential Islam-based political movements in the "Arab" world, of which a minority resorted to political violence and terrorism to destabilize postcolonial dictatorships and their Western allies and protectors, both domestically and abroad (e.g., the bombing of the World Trade Center in 1993, as well as the multiple terrorist attacks committed in Paris by the Algerian Groupe islamique armé in 1995).

As a result, by the mid-nineties onwards, especially in Europe and to a lesser extent in North America, minorities originating from predominantly Muslim countries started to become primarily othered as Muslims. In the UK, for example, since the fifties, racism suffered by South Asian minorities had always been framed by mainstream institutions as a "race relations" problem, which was addressed politically, for instance, by the Race Relations Act (1968, 1976) and the Commission for Racial Equality (1976). However, from the late nineties onwards, South Asian Muslims in the UK became more and more socially represented and stigmatized as Muslims, so much that, in 1997, the Commission on British Muslims and Islamophobia issued the well-known "Runnymede Report," which addressed Islamophobia as a pressing social problem to be urgently dealt with. In France, where North African migrants and their descendants had been primarily categorized and racialized as Arabs or Maghrébins since the 1950s, the veiling controversies that first erupted in 1989 were key contributing factors to the emergence of the "Muslim problem" in this country, that is, the notion that French "Muslims" were culturally unsuited to comply with French republican values, culture, and principles, namely secularism and gender equality (Delphy 2008; Hajjat and Mohammed 2013).

However, it was with the terrorist attacks committed on American soil on 11 September 2001, the ensuing invasion of Afghanistan by the United States and Canada, the US war waged in Iraq, and the numerous post-9/11 terrorist attacks committed in Europe and North America that Islam was unmistakably turned, in Western popular imagery, not only into a major security threat but also into this omnipotent "culture" overdetermining every individual categorized (and thus racialized) as Muslims. In Quebec, for example, since the 2006–8 Reasonable Accommodation debates, all the public controversies surrounding the place of religion in the public domain were powered in large part by the notion that Islam and Muslims are culturally unfit for both *laïcité* and gender equality (Bilge 2013; Eid 2016). The framing of Muslim minorities as culturally alien to feminism, and thus to shared national values, was particularly acute during the 2013–14 public debates around a bill championed by the Parti Québécois known as Bill 60 or the Charte des valeurs. Had it passed, the Charter of Values would have banned conspicuous religious symbols for public servants. Similarly, Bill 62, passed by the provincial Liberal Party in 2016, requires public services to be provided and received with an uncovered face. In June 2019, Quebec's current ruling party, Coalition Avenir Québec, passed Bill 21, which prohibits the display of "religious signs" (*signes religieux*) for certain categories of public servants, including primary and high school teachers. The use of gender equality as a vehicle for the racialization of Muslim minorities is by no means unique to Quebec; it has also been documented in Europe (Andreassen and Lettinga 2012; Lentin and Titley 2011) and in France in particular (Delphy 2008; Laborde 2008; Scott 2007). In France, for example, the Stasi Commission led to the passing of the 2004 bill prohibiting students from displaying conspicuous religious signs in public schools. Although this bill was neutral on the surface, its main purpose was to solve once and for all the veil controversy by purging hijabs from public schools (Lorcerie 2008). Various anti-veil bans were passed in Europe during the first two decades of the twenty-first century. For example, from 2003 onwards, several German *länders* passed laws to prevent teachers from wearing headscarves, while full-face veiling became illegal in all public places in France (2010), Belgium (2011), Austria (2017), Denmark (2018), and two Swiss cantons (2016, 2018). In the Netherlands, since 2018, full-face veiling is prohibited in public buildings, on public transport, in schools, and in hospitals.

Interestingly, the scholarly literature mimicked this gradual shift away from "Arabness" to "Muslimness" as the primary categorizing frame through which is imagined, in the West, the otherness of minorities originating from predominantly Muslim countries (Selby et al. 2018). Prior to the early 2000s, in the West, the latter groups were still more investigated as members of either nation-based communities or communities defined along ethnic or pan-ethnic lines, such as South Asians in the UK (Baumann 1996), Maghrébins or Beurs[5] in France (e.g., Begag 1990; Bloul 1998; Jazouli 1995; Lapeyronnie 1987), or Arab Americans (e.g., Abraham and Abraham 1983; Naff 1994; Suleiman 1999) and Arab Canadians (e.g., Abu-Laban 1980; Antonius and Bendris 1998; Hayani 1999) in North America. However, by the mid-nineties, "Muslimness" had already started to compete seriously with nation-, ethnic-, or pan-ethnic-based categories as the master frame through which minorities originating from Muslim-majority countries were investigated by Western scholars. But what was, at first, the beginning of a timid shift became a strong trend after the terrorist attacks of 9/11.

To test the hypothesis that 9/11 was a turning point beyond which research on Arab Canadians began to be superseded by research on Muslim Canadians, I ran two searches in the scholarly articles databases of the University of Toronto and the Université du Québec à Montréal (UQAM)[6]: one with "Arabs" and "Canada" in the title, and the other with "Muslims" and "Canada" in the title.[7] For each set of results, I computed the proportion of articles published before and after 2001. As shown in table 1, the results are quite conclusive. Both databases revealed that the majority of articles with "Arabs" and "Canada" in the title were published before 2001, whereas, inversely, a majority of articles with "Muslims" and "Canada" in the title were published after 2001.

Table 1. Percentages of scholarly articles about Muslims and Arabs in Canada published before and after 2001, according to University of Toronto's and UQAM's databases

		Publications before 2001	Publications after 2001	Total
University of Toronto's databases (all fields)	Scholarly articles with "Arabs" and "Canada" in the title	63.3% (62)	36.7% (36)	100% (98)
	Scholarly articles with "Muslims" and "Canada" in the title	16.5% (20)	83.5% (101)	100% (121)
UQAM's databases (field: sociology[a])	Scholarly articles with "Arabs" and "Canada" in the title	61.1% (11)	38.9% (7)	100% (18)
	Scholarly articles with "Muslims" and "Canada" in the title	16.7% (9)	83.3% (45)	100% (54)

[a] It was impossible to undertake a multidisciplinary search in UQAM's databases. I therefore decided to circumscribe my search to scholarly journals related to sociology.

I personally partook in this post-9/11 shift away from researching Arab-origin minorities towards researching Muslim minorities. Thus, in 2008–9, I conducted an interview-based study to explore how veiled and non-veiled Muslim female teenagers in Montreal negotiate the meanings embedded in the hijab and, more globally, their religious and cultural identities (Eid 2015). Like my previous research on Arab-origin youth, this research focused on identity building among children of immigrants, except this time, the common denominator shared by my interviewees was their ascribed or self-chosen "Muslimness," not their "Arabness." Once again, such a choice made perfect sense to me at the time, because in Quebec, since my previous fieldwork, those who were categorized at the end of the 1990s as "Arabs" by virtue of their name and/or appearance were, almost ten years later, much more likely to be categorized as "Muslims" based on the exact same markers. In other words, in Quebec, as elsewhere in Canada and in the Western world, the same signs that once signified primarily "Arabness" in popular imagery had been re-encoded, mainly but not exclusively, into symbols of Islam and "Muslimness." Thus, when I conducted my research in 2008–9, the figure of the Muslim Other was solidly ingrained in Quebecois' consciousness, because of 9/11 sure enough, but also because of the moral panic (Cohen 1972) surrounding the religious accommodations "crisis." As mentioned, during this highly mediatized debate, which started in 2006 and culminated with the public release of the Bouchard-Taylor Report in 2008, Muslim minorities were presented on a daily basis in the media as the bearers of a culture intrinsically inimical to gender equality and secularism and, by extension, to Western culture (Bilge 2013).

In this context, it can be hypothesized that the process whereby Islam and Muslims became the focus of increased sociological attention at the turn of the millennium echoed, and was even largely impelled by, the process by which Islam and Muslims were turned into a social problem in the public arena around the same time. In what follows, I will reflect on the epistemological and political implications of this (implicit) process, using my work on Muslim female teenagers in Montreal for illustrative purposes.

Studying Muslims without Essentializing "Muslimness"

Social scientists, irrespective of their field of study, must be careful not to model too closely their categories of analysis on the social categories of practice derived from common sense (Bourdieu 1990; Martiniello and Simon 2005). However, researchers concerned with racialized groups need to handle an additional challenge: Treating, say, Muslims, Arabs, Blacks, and Latinos as "groups" to be investigated can have the unintended effect of reinforcing the sociopolitical fiction that there is such a thing as a bounded and united Muslim, Arab, Black, or Latino "community." Furthermore, by selecting participants or respondents based on their common sense of identification as, say, Muslims – be this category understood as a religion per se, a cultural identity, or both – researchers can involuntarily contribute to validating the rigid categorizing frame through which this minority's otherness is socially produced and reproduced.

That does not mean that groupism (Brubaker 2004) – or the tendency to treat social groups as "things-in-the-world" – cannot be (at least partially) neutralized by researchers, but this can only be done following data analysis. More specifically, through empirical research, academics can and ought to deconstruct the preconceived one-size-fits-all categories that oversimplify the complex and multilayered selves of the group members under investigation. This de-reification process is all the more important in the case of racialized groups whose "members" are, by definition, more likely to be stripped of their individuality, as the majority group's standardizing gaze turns them into interchangeable specimens of their group.

Fortunately, for the past fifteen years or so, research has shown that Muslim identities in Canada are multifaceted and shaped contextually (e.g., Eid 2007, 2015; Marcotte 2010; Moghissi et al. 2009; Nagra 2017; Ramji 2008; Selby et al. 2018). These studies, among others, debunked the myth that there is such a thing as a homogeneous and cohesive Muslim "community" in Canada. In my own fieldwork conducted in Montreal, for example, I found that, when negotiating their ethnic and/or religious selves, both second-generation Muslim and Christian Arab youths (Eid 2007), as well as female Muslim teenagers (Eid 2015), selectively draw upon, and critically engage with, a large cultural repertoire providing them with various normative models, interpretative frames, and schemas of action, which they contextually either internalize, endorse, oppose, or even ignore.

However, although empirical research highlighting the manifold forms by which "Muslimness" is performed and experienced in Canada is socially and scientifically relevant, even indispensable, it can still contribute to disproportionately magnifying the importance taken by Islam in the lives of Muslim Canadians. Religion is only one of many identity options from which Muslim Canadians can, and do, choose from and, depending on the context, not even necessarily the most salient one. Thus, participants in both of my aforementioned studies shared a common denominator: Regardless of how strongly they identified as "Muslims" and/or "Arabs," the vast majority of them resented and resisted the majority group's tendency to perceive them exclusively as such, as if all their thoughts, behaviours, attitudes, and values ought to be by-products of their faith or culture (Eid 2007, 2015). For example, even though in general the (veiled and non-veiled) female Muslim teenagers I interviewed in 2008–9 considered their religion to be an important identity and meaning provider, most of them, including those wearing the hijab, also made clear that religion was rather peripheral in their interactions with their high school peers, be they Muslims or not. In fact, most participants, including veiled ones, reported that religion is rarely discussed within their circles of friends. The following comment made by a Muslim female teenager wearing the hijab is representative:

> Religion? It's a topic that we sometimes talk about, but we're in grade 11th, we're seventeen years old, and we don't always feel like talking about religion. I talk about religion in places where I feel like talking about it, when I go to the mosque or in meetings where religion is debated. When I go to the mosque, we have meetings where we talk about religion. But when I'm with my friends, we talk about other things.[8]

This latter finding was not reported in the scholarly publication in which this research resulted (Eid 2015). However, had I mentioned it, there would have been a certain irony in pointing out that "Muslimness" is only one of the many identity categories used by these youth in a research such as mine for which participants were selected based exclusively on their common sense of identification as Muslims. My point here is that even researchers working from a constructivist approach (such as I and many others) can unintentionally lend credence to the essentializing frame through which the minority group they investigate is socially racialized on a daily basis. They risk doing so when they (re)appropriate, for analytical purposes, the same categories as those used by majority groups to lock minority group members into some sort of irreducible otherness, thus disregarding all the multiple other and rich facets of their psyches and social selves.

Conclusion

In Western societies, the acute racialization – let alone demonization – of Muslims is a good reason in itself to study these populations as "Muslims." The challenge, however, is to remain attuned to what Islamophobia and anti-Muslim racism *do* to Muslim identities but without assuming the existence of an Islam-based groupness prior to empirical observation. Consequently, researchers studying Muslim minorities should treat "Muslimness" not as an objective reality waiting to be unveiled but rather as a fluctuating and socio-historically situated identity boundary whose formation and maintenance processes need to be critically unpacked. But even this constructivist approach, which has flourished over the past fifteen years or so, can end up reinforcing the same naturalized Us/Them boundaries on which rests the othering of Muslim minorities in a Western context. Scholars engaged in the production of knowledge on Islam and Muslims in Canada are not immune to this risk since, upon laying out the contours of the population they study, they have no choice but to duplicate the group boundaries of the imagined "community" into which non-Muslim Canadians tend to lock up their fellow citizens of Muslim faith.

That said, researchers would be ill advised to stop investigating how minorities identified or self-identifying as Muslims perform and relate to their religion in a Canadian (and Western) context. Indeed, to the extent that, in the West, the Muslim category shapes relationships of domination, processes of identification and ascription, and, possibly, life paths and trajectories, researchers need to validate, if only temporarily, the resulting group boundaries if they wish to understand when, why, and how this category becomes socially salient and relevant for some Muslims and not for others.

NOTES

1 In any case, these young people proved to have a very privatized and liberal relationship to religion, as do most people of their age.

2 My dissertation was eventually turned into a book entitled *Being Arab: Ethnic and Religious Identity Building Among Second-Generation Youth in Montréal* (see Eid 2007).

3 In the interview, I asked them an open-ended question to let them self-define their ethnic identity, but in the questionnaire, they were asked to choose which from the following labels best captured how they thought of themselves first and foremost: (a) as an Arab, (b) as a member of a national Arab group (e.g., Moroccans, Egyptians),

and if so which one, (c) as an Arab-Canadian (or Quebecois), (d) as a (national group)-Canadian (or Quebecois), (e) as either a Canadian or a Quebecois, and (f) other.

4 In any case, in 2001, 51.2 per cent of Arab Canadians were Christians (Eid 2007, 16).

5 *Beur*, in France, is a slang word referring to French-born children of North African immigrants. It originates from the phonetic inversion of the syllables forming the French word *Arabe*.

6 Like most universities, UQAM's and the University of Toronto's libraries pay significant amounts of money to a handful of large scholarly journal publishers, such as EBSCO, Taylor and Francis, and Wiley Blackwell, in order to provide their subscribers with online bundled access to thousands of scholarly journals from all disciplines.

7 Note that by searching for articles with the words "Arabs," "Muslims," and "Canada" in the title, I am certainly missing some relevant papers whose title does not include such keywords. However, searching with those same keywords as "subject terms" yielded an excessive number of articles that dealt only remotely or indirectly with the study of Arabs and Muslims in Canada. That is why I preferred searching by "words in the title."

8 Of course, the fact that my participants were recruited in two strikingly pluricultural Montreal high schools may account in part for their capacity to downplay their religious belonging so easily when interacting with their student peers. Indeed, ethnic and religious diversity was so ingrained in these schools' sociocultural fabric that no particular group stuck out as a "minority."

REFERENCES

Abraham, Sameer Y., and Nabeel Abraham, N. (Eds.). 1983. *Arabs in the new world: Studies on Arab-American communities.* Wayne State University, Center for Urban Studies.

Abu-Laban, Baha. 1980. *An olive branch on the family tree: The Arabs in Canada.* McClelland and Stewart.

Anderson, Benedict. 1983. *Imagined communities: Reflection on the origin and spread of nationalism*. Verso.

Andreassen, Rikke, and Doutje Lettinga. 2012. "Gender and gender equality in European national narratives." In S. Rosenberger and B. Sauer (Eds.), *Politics, religion and gender: Framing and regulating the veil* (pp. 17–36). Routledge.

Antonius, Rachad, and Naima Bendris. 1998. "Des représentations sociales aux transactions interculturelles: L'image des femmes arabes et son impact dans les situations de conflit personnel." In K. Fall and L. Turgeon (Eds.), *Champs multiculturel, transactions interculturelles: Des analyses, des théories, des pratiques* (pp. 215–39). L'Harmattan.

Asal, Houda. 2016. *Se dire Arabe au Canada: Un siècle d'histoire migratoire.* Presses de l'Université de Montréal.

Barth, Fredrik. 1969. "Introduction." In Fredrik Barth (Ed.), *Ethnic groups and boundaries: The social organization of cultural differences* (pp. 9–38). Little Brown.

Baumann, Gerd. 1996. *Contesting culture: Discourses of identity in multi-ethnic London.* Cambridge University Press.

Begag, Azouz. 1990. "The Beurs: Children of North African immigrants in France: The issue of integration." *Journal of Ethnic Studies, 18*(1), 1–13.

Bilge, Sirma. 2013. "Reading the racial subtext of the Québécois accommodation controversy: An analytics of racialized governmentality." *Politikon, 40*(1), 157–81. https://doi.org/10.1080/02589346.2013.765681

Bloul, Rachel. 1998. "From moral protest to religious politics: Ethical demands and Beur political action in France." *Australian Journal of Anthropology, 9*(1), 11–20. https://doi.org/10.1111/taja.1998.9.1.11

Boosahda, Elizabeth. 2003. *Arab-American faces and voices: The origin of an immigrant community.* University of Texas Press.

Bouamama, Saïd. 2011. *Les discriminations racistes: Une arme de division massive.* L'Harmattan.

Bourdieu, Pierre. 1990. *In other words: Essays towards a reflexive sociology.* Stanford University Press.

Brubaker, Roger. 2004. *Ethnicity without groups.* Harvard University Press.

Cesari, Jocelyne. 2002. "Islam in France: The shaping of a religious minority." In Y. Haddad (Ed.), *Muslims in the West: From sojourners to citizens* (pp. 36–52). Oxford University Press.

– 2011. "Islamophobia in the West: A comparison between Europe and the United States." In J.L. Esposito and I. Kalin (Eds.), *Islamophobia: The challenge of pluralism in the 21st century* (pp. 5–20). Oxford University Press.

Chavez, Leo R. 2008. *The Latino threat: Constructing immigrants, citizens and the nation.* Stanford University Press.

Cohen, Stan. 1972. *Folk devils and moral panics.* MacGibbon and Kee.

Delphy, Christine. 2008. "Antisexisme ou antiracisme: Un faux dilemme." In *Classer, dominer: Qui sont les "autres"?* (pp. 174–216). La Fabrique.

Eid, Paul. 2003. "The interplay between ethnicity, religion, and gender among second-generation Christian and Muslim Arabs in Montréal." *Canadian Ethnic Studies, 35*(2), 30–61.

– 2007. *Being Arab: Ethnic and religious identity building among second-generation Arab youth in Montréal.* McGill-Queen's University Press.

– 2015. "Balancing agency, gender and race: How do Muslim female teenagers in Quebec negotiate the social meanings embedded in the hijab?" *Ethnic and Racial Studies, 38*(11), 1902–17. https://doi.org/10.1080/01419870.2015.1005645

– 2016. "Les nouveaux habits du racisme au Québec: L'altérisation des arabo-musulmans et la (re)négociation du Nous national." In Diane Lamoureux and Francis Dupuis-Déri (Eds.), *Au nom de la sécurité! Criminalisation de la contestation et pathologisation des marges* (pp. 81–109). M Éditeur.

Espiritu, Yen Le. 1992. *Asian-American panethnicity: Bridging institutions and identities.* Temple University Press.

Farah, Tawfik (Ed.). 1987. *Pan-Arabism and Arab nationalism: The continuing debate.* Westview Press.

Gans, Herbert. 1979. "Symbolic ethnicity: The future of ethnic groups and cultures in America." *Ethnic and Racial Studies, 2*, 1–20. https://doi.org/10.1080/01419870.1979.9993248

Garner, Steve, and Saher Selod. 2015. "The racialization of Muslims: Empirical studies of Islamophobia." *Critical Sociology, 41*(1), 9–11. https://doi.org/10.1177%2F0896920514531606

Gavrilos, Dina. 2002, October. "Arab Americans in a nation's imagined community: How news constructed Arab American reaction to the Gulf War." *Journal of Communication Inquiry, 26*(4), 426–45. https://doi.org/10.1177%2F019685902236900

Hajjat, Abdellali, and Marwan Mohammed. 2013. *Islamophobie: Comment les élites françaises fabriquent le "probleme musulman."* La Découverte.

Hayani, Ibrahim. 1999. "Arabs in Canada: Assimilation or integration." In Michael W. Suleiman (Ed.), *Arabs in America: Building a new future* (pp. 284–303). Temple University Press.

Jazouli, Adil. 1995. "Les jeunes 'Beurs' dans la société française." *Migrations et société,* 7(38), 6–24.

Juteau, Danielle. 2015. *L'ethnicité et ses frontières* (2nd ed.). Presses de l'Université de Montréal. (Original work published 1999)

Kundnani, Arun. 2014. *The Muslims are coming: Islamophobia, extremism, and the domestic War on Terror.* Verso.

Laborde, Cécile. 2008. *Critical Republicanism: The hijab controversy and political philosophy.* Oxford University Press.

Lapeyronnie, Didier. 1987. "Assimilation chez les jeunes de la seconde génération de l'immigration maghrébine." *Revue française de sociologie, 28*, 287–318. https://doi.org/10.2307/3321679

Lee, Jennifer, and Min Zhou. 2015. *The American Asian achievement paradox*. Russell Sage Foundation.

Lentin, Alana, and Gavan Titley. 2011. *The crises of multiculturalism: Racism in a neoliberal age.* Zed Books.

Levitt, Peggy, Kristen Lucken, and Melissa Barnett. 2011. "Beyond home and return: Negotiating religious identity across time and space through the prism of the American experience." *Mobilities, 6*(4), 467–82. https://doi.org/10.1080/17450101.2011.603942

Lorcerie, Françoise. 2008. La 'loi sur le voile': Une entreprise politique." *Droit et société, 1*(68), 53–74. https://doi.org/10.3917/drs.068.0053

Marcotte, Roxanne. 2010. "Muslim women in Canada: Autonomy and empowerment." *Journal of Muslim Minority Affairs, 30*(3), 357–73. https://doi.org/10.1080/13602004.2010.515816

Martiniello, Marco, and Patrick Simon. 2005. "La catégorisation et la classification comme enjeux de pouvoir: Rapports de domination et luttes autour de la représentation dans les sociétés post-migratoires." *Revue européenne des migrations internationales, 21*(2), 7–17. https://doi.org/10.4000/remi.2484

Massey, Douglas S. 2007. *Categorically unequal: The American stratification system.* Russell Sage Foundation.

Massey, Douglas S., and Magaly Sánchez R. 2010. *Brokered boundaries: Creating immigrant identity in anti-immigrant times.* Russell Sage Foundation.

Meer, Nasar. 2013. "Racialization and religion: Race, culture and difference in the study of antisemitism and Islamophobia." *Ethnic and Racial Studies, 36*(3), 385–98. https://doi.org/10.1080/01419870.2013.734392

Moghissi, Haideh, Mark J. Goodman, and Saeed Rahnema. 2009. *Diaspora by design: Muslims in Canada and beyond.* University of Toronto Press.

Naff, Alixa. 1994. *Becoming American: The early Arab immigrant experience.* Southern Illinois University Press.

Nagel, Joane. 1994. "Constructing ethnicity: Creating and recreating ethnic identity and culture." *Social Problems, 41*(1), 152–75. https://doi.org/10.2307/3096847

Nagra, Baljit. 2017. *Securitized citizens: Canadian Muslims' experiences of race relations and identity formation post 9/11.* University of Toronto Press.

Portes, Alejandro, and Dag MacLeod. 1996. "'What shall I call myself?': Hispanic identity formation in the second generation." *Ethnic and Racial Studies, 19*(3), 523–47. https://doi.org/10.1080/01419870.1996.9993923

Ramji, Rubina. 2008. "Being Muslim and being Canadian: How second generation Muslim women create religious identities in two worlds." In Kristin Aune, Sonya Sharma, and Giselle Vincett (Eds.), *Women and religion in the West: Challenging secularization* (pp. 195–206). Ashgate.

Razack, Sherene. 2008. *Casting out: The eviction of Muslims from Western law and politics.* University of Toronto Press.

Saeed, Tania. 2016. *Islamophobia and securitization: Religion, ethnicity and the female voice.* Palgrave Macmillan.

Scott, Joan W. 2007. *The politics of the veil.* Princeton University Press.

Selby, Jennifer A., Amélie Barras, and Lori G. Beaman. 2018. *Beyond accommodation: Everyday narratives of Muslim Canadians.* University of British Columbia Press.

Selod, Saher. 2015. "Citizenship denied: The racialization of Muslim American men and women post-9/11." *Critical Sociology, 41*(1), 77–95. https://doi.org/10.1177%2F0896920513516022

Shaheen, Jack. 2001. *Reel bad Arabs: How Hollywood vilifies a people.* Olive Branch Press.

– 2003, July. "Reel bad Arabs: How Hollywood vilifies a people." *Annals of the American Academy, 588*, 171–93. https://doi.org/10.1177%2F0002716203588001011

Suleiman, Michael W. 1988. *The Arabs in the mind of America.* Amana Books.

– 1999. "Introduction." In Michael W. Suleiman (Ed.), *Arabs in America: Building a new future* (pp. 1–23). Temple University Press.

Van Dijk, Teun A. 2008. *Discourse & power.* Palgrave Macmillan.

Waters, Mary. 1990. *Ethnic options: Choosing identities in America.* University of California Press.

Weber, Max. 1971. *Économie et Société, vol. 1* (Julien Freund et al., Trans.). Plon. (Original work published 1921)

Wimmer, Andreas. 2013. *Ethnic boundary making: Institutions, power, networks.* Oxford University Press.

Time for a "Hijab Ban"? The Hypervisibility of Veiling in Scholarship on Islam in North America

SADAF AHMED

Introduction

In a working bibliography of research produced on the study of Islam in Canada comprising approximately 250 articles, book chapters, and graduate theses, at least 90 titles focus on hijab as a central topic or draw on it instrumentally towards other analysis (Selby et al. 2017).[1] This means that approximately one-third of such scholarship has pursued the hijab to reveal lines of enquiry relating to Muslims and Islam in the Canadian context, a scholarly inclination that in this chapter I argue both shapes the research produced and inadvertently re-flattens Muslim women as objects of research. Largely based on the post-9/11 research focus on agency and multiplicity of meaning, scholars aim to recover the voices of veiled Muslim women in Euro-American societies, resisting their silencing in policy and politics. But using hijab "as a lens" through which to access politics reiterates its hypervisibility, which I show reinscribes the very social dynamics this scholarship aims to destabilize. Instead, hijab-focused enquiries ought to historicize and particularize the assumption that hijab productively uncovers Islam in North America. Even when Muslim women discuss the topic of veiling unprompted by researchers, the ethnographic encounter itself remains shaped by the ways Muslim women are socially and politically interpellated outside of it. By highlighting the possibility of *refusing* hijab-talk as somehow natural to scholarly discussions about Muslims and Islam, I open up ways for scholars to grapple with the ongoing histories of compelling Muslim women to account for themselves in order to instead seek modes of Muslim life unconsidered.

Recovering Multiplicity and Agency after 9/11 in North America

The political conditions after 9/11 have elicited a particular methodological and analytical response in Canadian scholarship on Islam.[2] After 9/11, liberal states positioned Muslim women's veils as indicators of the "incompatibility" between Euro-Western values and Islam. Studies relate heightened policy talk on hijab to the rise in anti-Muslim social sentiment as well as increased instances of anti-Muslim harassment, which disproportionately affects visibly Muslim women (Arat-Koç 2012). The political focus on hijab informed various policy restrictions and bans on Muslim women's sartorial practices in public spaces in various liberal orders. In the Muslim-minority context of Canada, examples include the 2007 Bouchard-Taylor Commission, which implicitly put Muslim women at the centre of its debates, and the introduction of Quebec's Bill 94 in 2010, which banned women who wear the niqab from receiving basic services in public spaces and institutions.[3] In the academy, the response to these conditions has consisted of a proliferation of ethnographic work on the religious dimensions of Muslim women's dress choices, primarily focusing on those who veil. While the use of ethnographic methods to solicit Muslim women for accounts of their lived experience is not new (Bullock 2002; Roald 2001; Zine 2001), scholars writing in and about the post-9/11 period especially highlight how Muslim women are situated in policy discourses as objects of discussion rather than as participating subjects (Arat-Koç 2012; Bakht 2015; Razack 2008). Informed by the aim to recover voices that are often stifled in hostile political and policy debates, this scholarship shows Muslim women to be engaged in complex agentive reasoning processes that generate a multiplicity of meanings and signal myriad motivations.

These multiple meanings and motivations for veiling include publicly performing support for Islam by representing "positive images of one's religion" (Nagra 2011) and "the complex intersection of adhering to Islamic moral codes of modesty [while on] the quest for self-assertion" (Atasoy 2006) vis-à-vis Muslim communities and broader society. In the case of young Muslims, wearing hijab can ensure pious recognition among their Muslim counterparts and can permit various engagements in mixed-gender settings. For example, it can mitigate "parental fears concerning drinking, sexual activity ... [and moral] reputation ... [as it concerns] finding a husband" (Hoodfar 2003, 18); communicate a lack of romantic availability towards male non-Muslim peers; and confer religious authority (Spurles 2003). Hijab-wearers commonly draw on a discourse of "empowerment," whereby hijab releases them from "objectifying" male gazes. Women describe how they "derive a great amount of strength and dignity from the hijab ... [since] it cannot but help serve as a reminder that our worth lies not in whether a man finds us attractive, but rather in what we are doing in order to serve Islam" (McDonough 2003b, 108). At the same time, hijab can promote "confidence to not have to rely on other characteristics, but your own personality" (Ramji 2014, 110). Often situated within a lexicon of "either flaunting or shrouding [one's] sexuality" (McDonough 2003a, 125), this rendering of veiling as an articulation of various antipatriarchal commitments is widespread in the scholarship on Muslim women of all ages.[4]

The drive to enumerate and underline hijab's multiplicity – and its antipatriarchal force – emerges from a particular political situation. The post-9/11 rise of anti-Muslim sentiment led Muslims to attempt to increase their own religious literacy. Per the global effects of the Islamic revival, the practice of veiling across North America surged (Alvi 2003; Hamdon 2010; Mir 2014; Nagra 2011). Striving to restore agency to Muslim women, scholarship on North American Islam responded by increasingly framing this resurgence less as a tactic of resistance (Mernissi 1975) or an identity marker (El Guindi 1999) than as "complex social practices in which individuals exercise considerable personal freedom" (Alvi et al. 2003, xix; referencing Kelly Spurle). The fact of hijab's multiple meanings then becomes a tool for different purposes. Some use it to argue *against* a research focus on pious Muslim subjects: the fact of hijab's diverse meanings opens up the study of Muslims – even hijab-clad ones – as other than conservative religious subjects (Marcotte 2010). Others put hijab's multiplicity to work to argue that scholarship ought to treat hijab-wearers as *other* than religious subjects and engage them in terms of the allegedly non-religious ways they live their lives (Beaman 2017; Selby 2013).[5] Collectively, ethnographic studies of hijab-wearing in Canada push back against reductive depictions of Muslim women, painting vivid and varied pictures of the hows and whys Muslim women veil. Inseparable from the post-9/11 surveillance and stigmatization of Muslim life in North America, this scholarship offers a view of Islam as varied in meaning and Muslim women's practices as agentively motivated.

Hijab as Lens

When scholars bring forward nuances missed by a Western gaze, hijab often acts as a lens – one that can be turned back on the viewer. Hijab allows scholars to complicate dominant social imaginaries about Muslim life, but it also provides a means by which to challenge secular liberal structures of pluralism and inclusion or to unravel the category of "liberality" itself. Through hijab, researchers explore topics ranging from belonging and minority identity preservation (Bullock 2010; Le Gall 2003; Khan 2002; Marcotte 2010; Ramji 2008, 2014) to intergenerational or transnational effects in diaspora communities (Berns McGown 1999; Eid 2007, Litchmore and Safdar 2015; Werbner and Fumanti 2013). Drawing on the myriad differences among hijab-wearers, studies are replete with analyses of how Muslims "negotiate" and "construct" varied religious, ethnic, and gendered identities (Bucar 2017; Gabriel and Hannan 2010; Lewis 2015). But hijab also provides a lens through which to analyse the politics of accommodation and multiculturalism, demonstrating how these social and political structures impact Muslim women as well as Muslims in general (Hanniman 2008; Perry 2014;

Selby 2014, 2016; Sharify-Funk 2010; Smith 2002; Tirone 2000; Zine 2008). To this end, studies often make suggestions for more substantive modes of accommodation and "deep equality" (Beaman 2017) in order to advance equity and social justice in the domains of health (Jiwani and Rail 2010; Reitmanova and Gustafson 2008), education (Al-Fartousi 2013; Bullock 2002; Zine 2006), and law and policy (Korteweg and Selby 2012; Marcotte 2010; Selby 2014; Sharify-Funk 2010). As the trope of hijab "as lens" reveals, both questions about Muslim life in North America and debates about how to live better together among difference are often approached *through* the fact of veiling.

Hijab then signals, symbolizes, and wraps unto itself a number of scholarly questions and debates. This point can be illustrated by the number of scholarly works on Muslims and Islam that feature a hijab-clad woman on their book cover (Berns McGown 1999; Nouraie-Simone 2005; Roald 2001; Zuhur 1992). But even when scholarship that positions hijab as a lens onto the world does so in service of creating more equitable societies, this continual focus on Muslim women's dress choices reinforces the premise that there is indeed something special about veiling. The notion that beneath the veil lies a distinct particularism is hardly new. A Euro-Western focus on Muslim women's sartorial practices has roots in Europe's colonial encounter with Muslim regions (Ahmed 1992; Alvi et al. 2003; Scott 2007). From the writings of colonial officials to depictions in western European arts and literatures, the Muslim woman's veil was a ubiquitous reference by which to signal the moral depravity of the Orient, as a site of both undue stricture and excess.[6] Ultimately, it is through this history that the veil became a long-standing "Orientalist cliché" (Said 1978, 190), a prominent trope in the construction of the irreducible difference between Islam and the West. In due course, the cliché of the veil would provide the conditions for the emergence of contemporary discourses on the clash of civilizations and the War on Terror (Scott 2007). Contemporary scholarship on hijab overwhelmingly speaks out against and strives to undermine the conditions that render Muslim women's dress as external to Western pluralist states. But the persistent use of hijab as a lens risks reinforcing a culturally contingent conception of veiling as hypervisible.

Hijab as Hypervisible

Whether to continually clarify misconceptions about Muslim life or to turn back the reflexive gaze upon discourses of pluralism that fall short of their aspirations, scholarship drawing on hijab maintains its tacit hypervisibility. For example, in his attempt to reveal the limits of Canadian multiculturalist aspirations, Douglas E. Cowen (2008) writes,

> From our history of suspicion when it comes to new religious movements to the multitude of issues that constellate around religious prerogatives ranging from the

Sikh kirpan in a public school to the Muslim hijab in a voting booth, we have a latent sociophobic view of new or non-dominant religious cultures. (72)

Cowen (2008) casually lists hijab as an "obvious" example of a "fear"-based "disincentive" to multiculturalism. Similarly, Paul Bowlby (2014) draws on hijab to critique the public-private binary that he says dictates Canadian political discourse about the role of religion in the public sphere:

While there is some evidence for the aspiration to relegate all aspects of religion to the private sphere, religion's public participation has been both frequent and controversial … Issues like the niqab, the hijab … suggest that the wish to liberate the public sphere entirely of religion has not succeeded and probably cannot. (27)

Evidently, hijab reveals the murky line between public and private in liberal political orders. But this turn of the gaze continues to be funnelled through hijab and remains tethered to the premise of hijab's distinct particularism. Cowen and Bowlby are correct to point out how hijab debates expose the frayed seams of liberal modes of pluralism, but the ongoing mention – indeed, the repetition – of this point throughout scholarship ultimately produces a narrowed discursive space for how Muslims and Islam can be understood and positioned vis-à-vis the state and broader society.

Scholarship on Islam has much to gain from widening its purview. Discourse is inevitably bound by parameters that include or exclude certain topics and modes of thought (Foucault 1969/2002). The discursive framing of hijab as hypervisible in turn makes invisible other ways of Muslim life: funnelling through hijab filters out other questions about Muslim modes of being, including those in relation to various pressing social issues. For example, how do Muslims inhabit a world that faces climate change (Gade 2019)? What do Muslim modes of giving look like in a global circumstance of ever-increasing economic inequality (Mittermaier 2019)? Scholarship that relinquishes itself from the grip of hijab-based lines of questioning allows the ethnographic mode of *being with* people to do what it does best: to unexpectedly uncover ways of engaging with the world – such as attending to widespread social challenges of our time – and de-familiarizing Euro-Western hegemonies (Fernando 2014a). One way to counter the effect of funnelling and filtering is to historicize and particularize the hypervisibility of hijab, thinking through the secular sentiments and bodily attenuations that make hijab especially observable and apparent to others.

Historicizing Hypervisibility

In order to offer a more politically effective intervention and produce richer accounts of Muslim life, scholarship ought to lay bare the complex historical production of hijab's hypervisibility. Joan Scott (2009) excavates how the opposing poles of sexual equality and women's subordination are consistently articulated through the easy opposition of secularism and religion, particularly Islam. Pervasive at the level of both policy and social discourses, this opposition informs the rendering of Muslim women's veils as hypervisible across liberal states. Scott's analysis of debates about what ought to be the legal wording of French law banning religious symbols in public schools is a case in point. The term "visible," Scott writes, was considered but dropped because it would encompass too many religious markers, conflicting with court rulings that protect religious rights. The term "ostentatious" was suggested, but this could ascribe motives to the wearer that were difficult to prove. It was the term "conspicuous" that finally settled the debate, elucidating how hijab uniquely reintroduced gender subordination by way of religion into the laic state – a state that had already secured sexual equality precisely by separating itself from the church (Scott 2007, 134). What lawmakers aspired to capture in the legal lexicon was a certain secular affect: there was something about hijab that stood out. France's efforts to legally prohibit hijab's purported conspicuousness serve as an especially clear example of a tendency across liberal states (Amir-Moazami 2013; Scott 2007): to presume a linkage between secularism and sexual freedom that makes hijab a hypervisible emblem of otherness.

To widen the discursive framing available to Muslims in North America, ethnographic accounts might begin with an acknowledgment of this sex-secularism nexus, including the ongoing production of the secular body. Scholars of secularism have long noted how notions of secularity themselves require unpacking in the study of religion, especially because the secular body is often considered unmarked and inconspicuous. Secular embodiment comes into full sensory view, however, precisely in instances of offence, disapproval (Hirschkind 2011; Mahmood 2009), and even fascination (Amir-Moazami 2013). Scholarship must begin by adequately problematizing such offence or preoccupation, as some studies have done already (Korteweg and Yurdakul 2014; Selby 2014).[7] When the presumptive link between secularism and sexual freedom is not properly particularized, scholarship ends up taking veils to be ipso facto hypervisible – even while the aim is to undercut any notion of veiling's objective meaning or reflexively reconsider the liberal state's social and political forces of exclusion. Scholarship that takes hijab to be empirically available as a justification for analysis ultimately works against its own broader aspirations, contributing to a confining discourse about Muslims and Islam today.

Power and Answering for Hijab

But what of the question that hijab-talk is often initiated by Muslim interlocutors themselves, unprompted by researchers? Even apart from engaging in hijab-talk as ethnographic subjects, Muslim women in North America seem to constantly articulate their reasons for wearing hijab in a multitude of media platforms, including news vignettes (MacKenzie 2016), opinion pieces (Duffy and Gordon 2017; Nouh 2016), and blog posts (Zahran 2016). A web series called *The Secret Life of Muslims*, written and produced by a group of American Muslims, seeks to reveal the "fascinating careers, unexpected talents, and inspiring accomplishments" of Muslims (Secret Life of Muslims 2016). One of the first episodes launched is called "A Beginner's Guide to Hijabs." It features an array of American Muslim women who self-initiate explanations about wearing hijab. One states that putting on the hijab was "emancipation, because that was the moment I reclaimed my identity"; another clarifies that hijab "takes nothing away from my intellect, takes nothing away from my passions" (Secret Life of Muslims 2016).[8] Ghassan Hage's (2015) argument about minoritized subjects as "fixed" in their terms of engagement with the broader majority is instructive here. For Hage, minoritized subjects often end up presenting themselves in "oppositional" ways; they articulate how they are *not* what the dominant groups says they are. This notion illuminates some of the ways Muslim women engage with researchers on the topic of hijab, particularly as they offer, unprompted, "dis-proving" rationalizations of why they wear it.

Before considering Muslim women's emphasis on hijab in their self-narrativizations, however, researchers might pause at the way this framing can inoculate Islam from the contingencies of modern secular processes. Muslims are not, and have never been, outside of this history. Saba Mahmood's (2016) historical analysis of modern religious family law in Egypt comes up against the common-sense notion that patriarchal norms of kinship premised on religious doctrines signal a nation only partially secularized. To the contrary, she shows how the quotidian link between normative gender and proper religion in modern Muslim life is itself a product of modern secularism's privatization of both religion and sexuality (Mahmood 2016, 119). The literature on the Islamic revival similarly documents how Islamist political groups, religious clerics, and Muslim women integrate secularist assumptions in their proud promotion of hijab as a religiously mandated practice that subverts Westernization (Abu-Lughod 1993; Ahmed 1992, 2012; Mahmood 2005; Zuhur 1992). Leila Ahmed (1992) famously argues that the veil eventually came to represent *for Muslims themselves* the validity of native customs, particularly the ones under fiercest colonial attack (i.e., those relating to women). Such a resistance narrative "reversed but also accepted" the terms set in place by colonizers (Ahmed 1992, 164). While scholars often acknowledge the social circumstance of re-veiling in the Islamic revival (Mir 2014; Nagra 2011; Zuhur 1992), they do not necessarily point to the reconstruction of Muslim mores around gender and sex, including hijab-wearing, as informed by modernizing processes. Contemporary scholarship's uncritical recording of hijab's hypervisibility, then, not only forecloses other questions but also removes Muslims from their placement within the historical vectors that produced it. Resituating Muslims within this history makes fraught the claim that ethnographic studies should simply document the articulations of Muslim women themselves explaining why and how they veil.

How North American Muslim women understand and represent their veiling practices can also be historicized as the product of racialization processes both within Muslim communities and outside of them. Whether Othered or "humanized" through mass media, Islam became solidified in the North American imagination as a Brown religion[9] – part of neither White America nor Black America but a foreign elsewhere. As Kayla Wheeler (2017) shows, even ongoing "positive" representations of Islam that attempt to push back against anti-Muslim depictions particularly exclude Black Muslims and Black Islam. Media representations of Islam created by Muslims themselves often mirror these exclusions. Even when featuring the embodiments of Afrodiasporic cultures – such as veiling styles – on non-Black Muslims, Black Muslims themselves are often absented from these representations;[10] thus, despite appropriating Blackness in some ways, Muslims continually consolidate Muslimness as Brown in others. This absenting and appropriating is consonant with entrenched racial dynamics in North American Muslim communities. Scholars analysing the nexus between race and Islam show how broader notions of Blackness are enacted within Muslim communities in their own specific configuration. Veiling practices, for example, from Arab and Southwest Asian regions tend to be upheld as religiously normative, while Afrodiasporic ones are often rendered religiously improper (Abdul Khabeer 2016). This religious repudiation is continuous with a larger marginalizing of Black Islam within Muslim communities in the ways they narrate and understand Islam for themselves.[11]

Su'ad Abdul Khabeer (2016) notes that scholarship on hijab is framed as a site of encounter between Western and Islamic values, where the latter is a "metonym for racially, ethnically, and temporally specific Muslim practices" (137) that originate in an imagined "Islamic East" (138).[12] This metonym erases African American Muslims and their distinctive veiling practices from the picture researchers paint of Islam and its multiplicity.[13] These works exploring the intertwinement of race and religion offer an example of how to attend to the *production* of hijab's hypervisibility that I call for;[14] here, unpacking what is primarily identified as hijab in the first place – mutually reinforced in the public, the media, and Muslim communities – is shown as *itself* produced by processes of racialization. The self-representations of Muslims – however agentive – are then always entrenched in historical relations of power. Without accounting for racial dynamics entrenched in North American Muslim communities, hijab-talk in research reproduces a larger racial-religious formation. The phenomenon of associating normative Islam with an Islamic East then reflects and refracts between scholarship, broader society, and Muslim communities.

The question of Muslim women's own focus on hijab also shifts when the inherent asymmetry of the encounter between researchers and subjects is taken into account. The ethnographer is the one to ask her subject to divulge how she inhabits and perceives the politicized entity of Islam. Here, Mayanthi Fernando's (2014b) research on Muslim women in the French Republic, and her adaptation of the Foucauldian notion of an "incitement to discourse," proves informative. Fernando extends Scott's conceptual links between religion and sexuality to show how Muslim French women are summoned to *make private* their religious and sexual practices, which are rendered as beyond the purview of the state in liberal secularism, but also to *exhibit* them – through discursive rationalizations to the laic state. A key point here is that these women are always "already interpellated" as religiously and sexually "aberrant" (Fernando 2014b, 692), compelled by force *and* desire to prove their non-aberrancy. Fernando's analysis suggests that being commanded to explain oneself generates a "deontic" drive or desire to explain oneself (692). The researcher's position makes Fernando's notion of a double register of compulsion especially productive to consider: In what ways might North American Muslim women, positioned as research subjects asked to speak about their lives, experience a *compulsion* to give an account of themselves when solicited by researchers in the post-9/11 contemporary moment? It is evident that many Muslim women – at least sufficient in number to sustain this scholarship about them – not only *do not resist* responding to the solicitations of academic researchers, both revealing and clarifying how and why they dress as they do, but in fact *initiate* the matter of hijab unprompted. The carefulness with which they explain the various ways hijab does not indicate patriarchal Muslim oppression opens up a reading of their articulations as "dis-proving" their aberrancy.

This character of self-initiated explanations on hijab by Muslim women in social and media contexts then also surfaces in research. Ethnographies brim with turns of phrase on hijab as "a personal choice" not "forced" by anyone (Al-Fartousi 2013; Bullock 2002); something enabling wearers to be "a person" rather than "an object" (Tarlo and Moors 2013); and an iteration of a "feminist" statement, or one that properly places a woman's "dignity" elsewhere than her sexuality (Alvi et al. 2003). Even when prompted with relatively open-ended research questions about their lives as Muslims, they choose to address assumptions and stereotypes in broader society about the headscarf, articulating whether it is or is not patriarchal, whether it is or is not an expression of liberal choice or autonomy (Berns McGown 1999; Beyer 2014; Jiwani and Rail 2010; McDonough 2003a; Mir 2014; Ramji 2014). Of course, it might simply be the case that hijab is sufficiently significant to women to warrant explaining it when someone enquires after Muslim life in general. But given that self-initiated rationalizations are so often framed in terms of *undoing assumptions*, the causal story becomes less clear: Is it that the importance Muslims place on hijab comes to be duly reflected in scholarship or that the incitement to discourse about hijab comes to permeate the condition of being Muslim in North America? One way or another, Muslim women seem to be continually presenting their religious subjectivity according to dominant discursive terms. In spite of scholars' aspirations to recover Muslim women's own voices on the matter, my reading of hijab-as-lens suggests that academic research's unequal distribution of who determines what is relevant might inadvertently reproduce dominant interpellations.

Concluding Remarks

Even when hijab is used to uncover dominant social and political life – to turn the gaze back on forces of political power, "Islamophobia," or anti-Muslim racism – it retains its hypervisibility. "Hijab-talk" takes up much of the discursive space about who and what Muslims are, reproducing relations of power and removing from view other aspects of their subjectivities, including in the corpus of scholarship on Islam in Canada, under investigation in this volume. Even at the hand of sympathetic researchers who use hijab as a material to bring into focus secular knowledge politics, Muslim life is inevitably reflattened. Already held to account by the "incitements" of broader assumptions, Muslim women offer accounts, clarifications, and defences of these assumptions. Scholars, too, are "incited to discourse," never immune to the discursive pressures of the social field. This much is already evident in the citational practices of academic scholarship, which hold discursive density around certain topics and not others. These compulsions ought to be a starting point for self-reflection. If part of anthropology's commitment is to defamiliarize and destabilize the universalist sensibilities that animate the discipline, positioning hijab as a centre of gravity forecloses the possibility of learning from, and being transformed by, those aspects of Muslim life that remain un-thought and un-asked about in the academy. Remaining compelled to write about hijab as it continually resurfaces in policy debates – whether in Quebec or the broader geopolitical sphere – means that scholarship produces a mimicry of this broader social and political fixation, rather than a shift away from it.

To avoid trapping Muslims and Muslimness in the grammar of state discourses, I urge future ethnographic research to refuse hijab-talk as somehow natural to Muslims in Euro-American contexts. Instead, I propose that ethnographers begin by historicizing how veiled Muslim women become particularly visible to them and grapple more directly with the impact of state interpellation, or "incitement to discourse," on Muslim communities' self-understandings and subjectivities. After all, one expected outcome of explicating the multiple meanings and nuances of veiling is to call into question, and indeed diminish, the gaze upon it. The goal was, presumably, to render hijab banal. In light of this aspiration, I contend it is productive neither to continue to enumerate hijab's various meanings and agentive complexities nor to draw on it as a lens to view broader questions. Retaining the focus on veiling continually reinscribes its importance and precludes other research avenues that could destabilize hegemonic modes of viewing Islam in North America. Recognizing the effects of current modes of hijab-focused scholarship opens up possibilities to produce richer and layered accounts of Muslim life in North America.

NOTES

For their engagement and careful readings of various drafts, I am indebted to Suzanne Van Geuns and Ayan Kassim. For their critical comments, I thank Youcef Soufi, Jennifer Selby, Amélie Barras, Basit Iqbal, and two anonymous reviewers.

1 To determine this minimum number, I scanned the bibliography to look for any words referring to the practice of hijab and its synonyms of veiling and covering. I also scanned for words that would signal hijab as a possible topic within the work (gender, women), which I then pursued to check whether they engage hijab. Because I did not enquire after every single work in the bibliography, the actual figure is likely even higher.

2 Such a response also occurs in scholarship on Islam in North America and Islam in Western Europe. While I focus significantly (but not exclusively) on the body of literature on Islam in Canada and the United States, the overlap in subject matter and research interests is significant. This overlap is generally due to commonalities among the sociopolitical positions of Muslims in post-9/11 liberal democracies but is heightened further by the similarities between the political secular ethos of Quebec and the French laic state, including in its relationship with Muslim minorities.

3 For Quebec's most recent legal stipulation, see Bill 21, and particularly Article 8, which focuses on limiting the face veil within public space: National Assembly of Québec (2019).

4 For example, Tarlo and Moors's (2013) *Islamic Fashion and Anti-Fashion* bridges the disparity between political debates about Muslim women's dress and the "actual developments in Muslim dress practices" by showing that Islamic fashion does not necessarily show "alienation from … [North] American cultural norms as much as complex forms of critical and creative engagement with them" (2). This work also analyses how Islamic fashion *impacts* broader fashion norms among non-Muslim fashion designers and consumers, even while it broadly joins recent scholarship exploring Muslim women's sartorial choices. For more examples of this growing literature, see Reina Lewis's (2015) *Muslim* Fashion and Elizabeth Bucar's (2017) *Pious* Fashion.

5 Anthropologists of Islam working in Muslim-majority contexts develop this line of thought further by critiquing what they perceive as a reified focus on pious

subjectivities (Bangstad 2011; Schielke 2015; see also Deeb and Harb 2013). Critiques of this approach point out how the setting aside of piety risks the re-introduction of "good Muslim/bad Muslim" distinctions (Fadil and Fernando 2015; Mamdani 2004).

6 The latter theme was notable in depictions of the licentious sexuality of the Orient, particularly during the increasing "embourgeoisement" of nineteenth-century Europe (Said 1978); as sexuality became increasingly institutionalized in their own societies, Europeans read promiscuity onto the Other (Said 1978, 190).

7 These studies signal a crucial attunement to an ongoing history that informs any contemporary discourse on hijab, whether it be hijab debates that reveal and re-establish narratives of national belonging (Korteweg and Yurdakul 2014) or majoritarian sensibilities of gender and secularism (Selby 2014). I contend that the pursuit of other (non-hijab-based) research agendas on Muslims and Islam is to be encouraged, precisely *because* works like these have so substantially furthered scholarly analysis of hijab in this register.

8 See Anonymous 2015; Yusef 2015. See also Boesveld 2017. Fajar Khan is one of the Muslims interviewed, specifically for competing in a national cricket competition in Alberta. When describing her athletic trajectory, Khan herself raises the topic of hijab and her discussions with teammates about its meaning.

9 Here I draw on Kayla Wheeler's (2017) definition of Brown as either "Arab, South Asian, Iranian, Kurdish, and Turkish peoples" (145) who are normatively constructed as Muslim in mainstream media representations and can be rendered and interpellated as such in everyday life – whether they self-identify as Muslim or not (Love 2017). In her analysis of the "Browning of Islam" in media depictions, Wheeler (2017) shows how Black Muslim women YouTubers are foreclosed from entering the mainstream cosmetics industry; unlike their Brown Muslim counterparts, the aesthetic of Islam of these Black Muslim women is "not legible to the broader non-Muslim public" (124). Roshan Jahangeer, in her contribution in this volume, also discusses this ineligibility in the context of the difficulties faced by Black Muslim women to participate in the debates on Bill 60 in Quebec.

10 See analyses by Wheeler (2017) of a music video titled "Somewhere in America #MIPSTERZ" (154–5) and one called "100 Years of Hijab Fashion in One Minute," produced by the website *Muslim Girl* (148–9).

11 Historical narratives of how-Islam-came-to-be – whether its origins with the Prophet Muhammad or its arrival in America – routinely sideline Black African Muslim histories. Additionally, Islamic practices regional to Black Africa (and their diasporic instantiations in Black America) have been long treated as non-normative or peripheral to practices native to Arab, South Asian, and Persianate cultures. For analyses of disparate manifestations of this general phenomenon, see, for example, Abdul Khabeer 2016; Curtis 2014; Jackson 2005; Karim 2008; Ware 2014; Wheeler 2017.

12 See also Grewal (2014) for a discussion of how Islamic authority among American Muslims is constructed through a rendering of Muslim authenticity as locatable only outside of the United States and in selective Muslim-majority regions. See also Jackson (2005), specifically his concept of "Immigrant Islam."

13 See especially this section of Abdul Khabeer's (2016) analysis of how the practice of "hoodjab" contests ethno-religious hegemonies *within* American Muslim community life (138). See her chapter "Blackness as a Blueprint for the Muslim Self" (109–44) for a fuller elucidation of racial-religious formations of dress among American Muslim women.

14 Here I refer especially to Abdul Khabeer (2016) and Wheeler (2017).

REFERENCES

Primary Sources

Anonymous. 2015, 2 August. "4 things you've thought about hijabis that are completely wrong." *Everyday Feminism*. https://everydayfeminism.com/2015/08/wrong-thoughts-about-hijabis

Boesveld, Sarah. 2017, 16 February. "What it's actually like to be a Muslim girl in Canada." *Chatelaine*. http://www.chatelaine.com/living/what-its-actually-like-to-be-a-muslim-girl-in-canada

Duffy, Clare, and Annika Gordon. 2017, 21 April. "Muslim women answer: 'What does the hijab mean to you?'" *The Beacon*. http://www.upbeacon.com/article/2017/04/meaning-of-the-hijab

MacKenzie, Tina. 2016, 9 June. "The hijab is the 'centrepiece' of these outfits rocked by young Toronto Muslim women." *CBC News*. http://www.cbc.ca/news/canada/toronto/muslim-women-fashion-1.3668743

National Assembly of Québec. 2019, 16 June. *Bill 21: An act respecting the laicity of the state*. 1st Session, 42nd Legislature. http://www2.publicationsduquebec.gouv.qc.ca/dynamicSearch/telecharge.php?type=5&file=2019C12A.PDF

Nouh, Yasmin. 2016, 11 May. "The beautiful reasons why these women love wearing a hijab." *HuffPost Canada*. http://www.huffingtonpost.com/entry/the-beautiful-reasons-why-these-women-love-wearing-a-hijab_us_57320575e4b0bc9cb0482225

Secret Life of Muslims. 2016. "A beginner's guide to hijabs." Video, 1:53. https://workingnotworking.com/projects/100668-a-beginners-guide-to-hijabs-the-secret-life-of-muslims

Selby, Jennifer A., Amélie Barras, and Melanie Adrian. 2017. "Case study 1: Bibliography." Producing Islam(s) in Canada Workshop, Carleton University.

Yusef, Hanna. 2015, 8 July. "My personal decision to wear the hijab has nothing to do with me being oppressed." *Everyday Feminism*. https://everydayfeminism.com/2015/07/my-hijab-feminist-statement

Zahran, Baraah. 2016, 1 March. "Is hijab an obstacle for Muslim women living in Canada?" *Huff Post.* https://www.huffingtonpost.com/baraah-zahran/is-hijab-an-obstacle-_b_9355880.html.

Secondary Sources

Abdul Khabeer, Su'ad. 2016. *Muslim cool: Race, religion, and hip hop in the United States.* New York University Press.

Abu-Lughod, Lila. 1993. *Writing women's worlds: Bedouin stories.* University of California Press.

Ahmed, Leila. 1992. *Women and gender in Islam: Historical roots of a modern debate.* Yale University Press.

– 2012. *A quiet revolution: The veil's resurgence, from the Middle East to America.* Yale University Press.

Al-Fartousi, May. 2013. "Unveiling Shi'i religious identities: A case study of hijab in homogenous Canadian schools." PhD thesis, Brock University.

Alvi, Sajida Sultana. 2003. "Muslim women and Islamic religious tradition: A historical overview and contemporary issues." In Sajida Sultana Alvi, Homa Hoodfar, and Sheila McDonough (Eds.), *The Muslim veil in North America: Issues and debates* (pp. 145–80). Women's Press.

Alvi, Sajida Sultana, Homa Hoodfar, and Sheila McDonough (Eds.). 2003. *The Muslim veil in North America: Issues and debates.* Women's Press.

Amir-Moazami, Schirin. 2013. "The secular embodiments of face-veil controversies across Europe." In Nilüfer Göle (Ed.), *Islam and public controversy in Europe* (pp. 83–100). Ashgate.

Arat-Koç, Sedef. 2012. "Invisibilized, individualized, and culturalized: Paradoxical invisibility and hyper-visibility of gender in policy making and policy discourse in neoliberal Canada." *Canadian Woman Studies, 29*(3), 6–17.

Atasoy, Yildiz. 2006. "Governing women's morality: A study of Islamic veiling in Canada." *European Journal of Cultural Studies, 9*(2), 203–21. https://doi.org/10.1177%2F1367549406063164

Bakht, Natasha. 2015. "In your face: Piercing the veil of ignorance about niqab-wearing women." *Social and Legal Studies, 24*(3), 419–41. https://doi.org/10.1177%2F0964663914552214

Bangstad, Sindre. 2011. "Saba Mahmood and anthropological feminism after virtue." *Theory, Culture and Society, 28*(3), 28–54. https://doi.org/10.1177%2F0263276410396914

Beaman, Lori G. 2017. *Deep equality in an era of religious diversity.* Oxford University Press.

Berns McGown, Rima. 1999. *Muslims in the diaspora: The Somali communities of London and Toronto.* University of Toronto Press.

Beyer, Peter. 2014. "Regional differences and continuities at the intersection of culture and religion: A case study of immigrant and second-generation young adults in Canada." In Solange Lefebvre and Lori G. Beaman (Eds.), *Religion in the public sphere: Canadian case studies* (pp. 66–95). University of Toronto Press.

Bowlby, Paul. 2014. "Canadian social imaginaries: Re-examining religion and secularization." In Solange Lefebvre and Lori G. Beaman (Eds.), *Religion in the public sphere: Canadian case studies* (pp. 25–44). University of Toronto Press.

Bucar, Elizabeth. 2017. *Pious fashion: How Muslim women dress.* Harvard University Press.

Bullock, Katherine. 2002. *Rethinking Muslim women and the veil: Challenging historical and modern stereotypes.* International Institute of Islamic Thought.

– 2010. "Hijab and belonging: Canadian Muslim women." In Theodore Gabriel and Rabiha Hannan (Eds.), *Islam and the veil: Theoretical and regional contexts* (pp. 161–80). Continuum.

Cowen, Douglas E. 2008. "Fearing planes, trains and automobiles: Sociophobics and the disincentive to religious diversity." In Lori G. Beaman and Peter Beyer (Eds.), *Religion and diversity in Canada* (pp. 67–85). Brill.

Curtis, Edward E. IV. 2014. *The call of bilal: Islam in the African diaspora.* University of North Carolina Press.

Deeb, Lara, and Mona Harb. 2013. *Leisurely Islam: Negotiating geography and morality in Shi'ite South Beirut.* Princeton University Press.

Eid, Paul. 2007. *Being Arab: Ethnic and religious identity building among second generation youth in Montreal.* McGill-Queen's University Press.

El Guindi, Fadwa. 1999. *Veil: Modesty, privacy and resistance.* Berg.

Fadil, Nadia, and Mayanthi L. Fernando. 2015. "Rediscovering the 'everyday' Muslim: Notes on an anthropological divide." *HAU: Journal of Ethnographic Theory, 5*(2), 59–88. https://doi.org/10.14318/hau5.2.005

Fernando, Mayanthi L. 2014a. "Ethnography and the politics of silence." *Cultural Dynamics, 26*(2), 235–44. https://doi.org/10.1177%2F0921374014526025

– 2014b. "Intimacy surveilled: Religion, sex, and the secular cunning." *Signs: Journal of Women in Culture and Society, 39*(3), 685–708. https://doi.org/10.1086/674207

Foucault, Michel. 2002. *The archaeology of knowledge.* Trans. A.M. Sheridan Smith. Routledge. (Original work published 1969)

Gabriel, Theodore P.C., and Rabiha Hannan (Eds.). 2010. *Islam and the veil: Theoretical and regional contexts.* Continuum.

Gade, M. Anna. 2019. *Muslim environmentalisms: Religious and social foundations.* University of Columbia Press.

Grewal, Zareena. 2014. *Islam is a foreign country: American Muslims and the global crisis of authority.* NYU Press.

Hage, Ghassan. 2015. *Alter-politics: Critical anthropology and the radical imagination.* Melbourne University Press.

Hamdon, Evelyn Leslie. 2010. *Islamophobia and the question of Muslim identity: The politics of difference and solidarity.* Fernwood.

Hanniman, Wayne. 2008. "Canadian Muslims, Islamophobia and national security." *International Journal of Law, Crime and Justice, 36*(4), 271–85. https://doi.org/10.1016/j.ijlcj.2008.08.003

Hirschkind, Charles. 2011. "Is there a secular body?" *Cultural Anthropology, 26*(4), 633–47. https://doi.org/10.1111/j.1548-1360.2011.01116.x

Hoodfar, Homa. 2018. "More than Clothing: Veiling as an adaptive strategy." In Sajida Sultana Alvi, Homa Hoodfar, and Sheila McDonough (Eds.), *The Muslim veil in North America: Issues and debates* (pp. 3–40). Women's Press.

Jackson, Sherman A. 2005. *Islam and the Blackamerican: Looking toward the third resurrection.* Oxford University Press.

Jiwani, Nisara, and Genevieve Rail. 2010. "Islam, hijab, and young Shia Muslim Canadian women's discursive constructions of physical activity." *Sociology of Sport Journal, 27*(3), 251–67. https://doi.org/10.1123/ssj.27.3.251

Karim, Jamillah. 2008. *American Muslim women: Negotiating race, class and gender within the ummah.* NYU Press.

Khan, Shahnaz. 2002. *Aversion and desire: Negotiating Muslim female identity in the diaspora.* Women's Press.

Korteweg, Anna C., and Jennifer A. Selby (Eds.). 2012. *Debating sharia: Islam, gender politics, and family law arbitration.* University of Toronto Press.

Korteweg, Anna C., and Gökçe Yurdakul. 2014. *The headscarf debates: Conflicts of national belonging.* Stanford University Press.

Le Gall, Josiane. 2003. "Le rapport à l'islam des musulmanes shi'ites libanaises à Montréal." *Anthropologie et Sociétés, 27*(1), 131–47. https://doi.org/10.7202/007005ar

Lewis, Reina. 2015. *Muslim fashion: Contemporary style cultures.* Duke University Press.

Litchmore, Rashelle V.H., and Saba Safdar. 2015. "Young, female, Canadian and Muslim: Identity negotiation and transcultural experience." In Claude-Hélène Mayer and Stephan Wolting (Eds.), *Purple jacaranda: Narrations on transcultural identity development* (pp. 59–67). Waxmann.

Love, Erik. 2017. *Islamophobia and racism in America.* New York University Press.

Mahmood, Saba. 2005. *Politics of piety: The Islamic revival and the feminist subject.* Princeton University Press.

– 2009. "Religious reason and secular affect: An incommensurable divide?" *Critical Inquiry, 35*(4), 836–62. https://doi.org/10.1086/599592

– 2016. *Religious difference in a secular age: A minority report.* Princeton University Press.

Mamdani, Mahmood. 2004. *Good Muslim, bad Muslim: America, the Cold War, and the roots of terror.* Pantheon.

Marcotte, Roxanne D. 2010. "Muslim women in Canada: Autonomy and empowerment." *Muslim Minority Affairs, 30*(3), 357–73.

McDonough, Sheila. 2003a. "Perceptions of the *ḥijāb* in Canada." In Sajida Sultana Alvi, Homa Hoodfar, and Sheila McDonough (Eds.), *The Muslim veil in North America: Issues and debates* (pp. 121–42). Women's Press.

– 2003b. "Voices of Muslim women." In Sajida Sultana Alvi, Homa Hoodfar, and Sheila McDonough (Eds.), *The Muslim veil in North America: Issues and debates* (pp. 105–20). Women's Press.

Mernissi, Fatima. 1975. *Beyond the veil: Male-female dynamics in a modern Muslim society.* Schenkman.

Mir, Shabana. 2014. *Muslim American women on campus: Undergraduate social life and identity.* University of North Carolina Press.

Mittermaier, Amira. 2019. *Giving to God: Islamic charity in revolutionary times.* University of California Press.

Nagra, Baljit. 2011. "'Our faith was also hijacked by those people': Reclaiming Muslim identity in Canada in a post-9/11 era." *Journal of Ethnic and Migration Studies, 37*(3), 425–41. https://doi.org/10.1080/1369183X.2011.526781

Nouraie-Simone, Fereshteh. 2005. *On shifting ground: Muslim women in the global era.* Feminist Press at the City University of New York.

Perry, Barbara. 2014. "Gendered Islamophobia: Hate crime against Muslim women." *Social Identities, 20*(1), 74–89. https://doi.org/10.1080/13504630.2013.864467

Ramji, Rubina. 2008. "Being Muslim and being Canadian: How second generation Muslim women create religious identities in two worlds." In Sonya Sharma, Kristin Aune, and Giselle Vincett (Eds.), *Women and religion in the West: Challenging secularization* (pp. 195–205). Ashgate.

– 2014. "Maintaining and nurturing an Islamic identity in Canada – online and offline." In Solange Lefebvre and Lori G. Beaman (Eds.), *Religion in the public sphere: Canadian case studies* (pp. 97–120). University of Toronto Press.

Razack, Sherene. 2008. *Casting out: The eviction of Muslims from Western law and politics.* University of Toronto Press.

Reitmanova, Sylvia, and Diana L. Gustafson. 2008. "'They can't understand it': Maternity health and care needs of immigrant Muslim women in St. John's, Newfoundland." *Journal of Maternal and Child Health, 12,* 101–11. https://doi.org/10.1007/s10995-007-0213-4

Roald, Anne Sofie. 2001. *Women in Islam: The Western experience.* Routledge.

Said, Edward W. 1978. *Orientalism.* Penguin.

Schielke, Joska Samuli. 2015. *Egypt in the future tense: Hope, frustration, and ambivalence before and after 2011.* Indiana University Press.

Scott, Joan Wallach. 2007. *The politics of the veil.* Princeton University Press.

– 2009. "Sexularism." Gender and Europe, Ursula Hirschmann Annual Lectures. http://cadmus.eui.eu//handle/1814/11553

Selby, Jennifer A. 2013. "Promoting the everyday: Pro-sharia advocacy and public relations in Ontario, Canada's 'sharia debate.'" *Religions, 4*(3), 423–42. https://doi.org/10.3390/rel4030423

– 2014. "Unveiling women's bodies: Secularism and sexuality in full-face veil prohibitions in France and Québec." *Studies in Religion / Sciences Religieuses, 43*(3), 1–28. https://doi.org/10.1177%2F0008429814526150

– 2016. "Muslimness and multiplicity in qualitative research and in government reports in Canada." *Critical Research on Religion, 4*(1), 72–89. https://doi.org/10.1177%2F2050303216630298

Sharify-Funk, Meena. 2010. "Muslims and the politics of 'Reasonable Accommodation': Analysing the Bouchard-Taylor Report and its impact on the Canadian province of Québec." *Journal of Muslim Minority Affairs, 30*(4), 535–53. https://doi.org/10.1080/13602004.2010.533451

Smith, Jane I. 2002. "Introduction." In Yvonne Yazbeck Haddad (Ed.), *Muslims in the West: From sojourners to citizens* (pp. 3–16). Oxford University Press.

Spurles, Patricia Kelly. 2003. "Coding dress: Gender and the articulation of identity in a Canadian Muslim school." In Sajida Sultana Alvi, Homa Hoodfar, and Sheila McDonough (Eds.), *The Muslim veil in North America: Issues and debates* (pp. 41–70). Women's Press.

Tarlo, Emma, and Annelies Moors. 2013. *Islamic fashion and anti-fashion: New perspectives from Europe and America.* Bloomsbury Academic.

Tirone, S. (2000). "Racism, indifference and the leisure experiences of South Asian Canadian teens." *Journal of Applied Recreation and Research, 24*(1–2), 89–114. https://doi.org/10.1080/14927713.1999.9651260

Ware, Rudolph. 2014. *The walking Quran: Islamic education, embodied knowledge, and history in West Africa.* University of North Carolina Press.

Waugh, Earle, and Jenny Wannas. 2003. "The rise of a womanist movement among Muslim women in Alberta." *Studies in Contemporary Islam, 1*, 1–15.

Werbner, Pnina, and Mattia Fumanti. 2013. "The aesthetics of diaspora: Ownership and appropriation." *Ethnos, 78*(2), 149–74. https://doi.org/10.1080/00141844.2012.669776

Wheeler, Kayla Renée. 2017. "How YouTube made the hijab cool: Race, gender, and authority in the American ummah." PhD diss., University of Iowa.

Zine, Jasmin. 2001. "Muslim youth in Canadian schools: Education and the politics of religious identity." *Anthropology and Education Quarterly, 32*(4), 399–423. https://doi.org/10.1525/aeq.2001.32.4.399

– 2006. "Unveiled sentiments: Gendered Islamophobia and experiences of veiling among Muslim girls in a Canadian Islamic school." *Equity and Excellence in Education, 39*(3), 239–52. https://doi.org/10.1080/10665680600788503

– 2008. *Canadian Islamic schools: Unravelling the politics of faith, gender, knowledge, and identity.* University of Toronto Press.

Zuhur, Sherifa. 1992. *Revealing reveiling: Islamist gender ideology in contemporary Egypt.* SUNY Series in Middle Eastern Studies. State University of New York Press.

Expressions of Sufism in Canada

MEENA SHARIFY-FUNK AND JASON IDRISS SPARKES

Introduction

In 1871, only four years after the Dominion of Canada was established as a self-governing country, the first national census revealed the presence of Islam as reflected in the thirteen Muslims at the time, who were mainly of Middle Eastern origin (Karim 2002, 263). Nearly a century later, after immigration reform had opened Canada to diverse peoples seeking educational and economic as well as political and social freedoms, the country's Muslim community had expanded to almost 100,000 and was extremely multicultural. In addition to immigrants from different parts of the Arab world such as Jordan, Syria, Lebanon, Palestine, and Egypt, it also included members from India, Pakistan, Bangladesh, Turkey, Iran, Eastern Europe, East Africa, the Caribbean, and elsewhere. This diversity remains a hallmark of the Canadian Muslim community in the twenty-first century, which today composes over 3.2 per cent of the national population, making Islam the second-largest religion in the country (Statistics Canada 2011).

Whereas scholarship on Canadian Muslims has acknowledged their remarkable cultural as well as sectarian diversity (as reflected in Sunni and Shi'a traditions), one aspect of the Canadian Muslim experience that has received relatively little attention is the presence of Sufism amidst the many different Muslim subcultures. As the first academic survey of Sufism in Canada, this chapter introduces diverse Sufi expressions across the country, from the official and visible to the subtle and discreet. For this reason, the selected examples are purposely eclectic and evocative rather than thorough or representative. Other examples could have been chosen, but the intention here is to give a small taste of Sufi diversity in Canada with the hope of provoking an appetite for future research on the topic. Such research might eventually explore whether there exists a distinctly Canadian Sufism. However, a thorough examination of *Sufism in Canada* must be undertaken before it is possible to speculate about *Canadian Sufism.*

This chapter asks: Where is Sufism within statistics seeking to represent the religious and cultural landscape? What is Sufism's story in Canada? Though seemingly straightforward, such questions can be difficult to answer. Perhaps the infrequency with which they have been posed reflects the challenge of defining who and what is Sufi more than mere scholarly indifference. Many Muslims, after all, have been highly influenced by Sufism without necessarily identifying themselves as Sufis or practise Sufism in a way that is integrally related to broader cultural and religious traditions which are themselves associated with a localized or regional experience of Islam. At the same time, for many Muslims there is no difference between being a Sufi and being a Muslim, as they feel that Islam and Sufism are one and the same. For them, identifying as *a Sufi* is redundant. Sufism is an important aspect of Islam in Canada which is often ignored in public discourse by Muslim leaders, the media, and academics. To begin the process of uncovering the Sufi dimension of Islam in Canada, we make two proposals: (1) to shed light on the diversity of Sufi expressions in Canada; and (2) to explain the silence surrounding Sufism in scholarship on Islam and Muslims in Canada and in public discourse. The second point is important because greater awareness of this erasure is necessary for the discussion on Sufi expressions in Canada to continue beyond this chapter. We argue that any representation of Islam in Canada which ignores Sufism is incomplete and that Sufism therefore requires much more scholarly attention.[1]

After providing a brief overview of how Sufism developed historically within the broader Islamic tradition, we begin our survey of Sufism in Canada by considering the presence of formal Sufi orders, or tariqas. While some of these orders understand Sufism as an integral part of Islam, others understand it as a universal spirituality, not confined to the Muslim community. Then we examine informal Sufi networks as well as Sufi expressions within institutions and organizations not primarily or solely associated with Sufism. Indeed, the impact of what we have labelled "implicit Sufism" extends beyond Sufi centres and even mosques. For instance, Sufi musicians regularly perform in Canadian concert halls; museums present Sufi-related exhibitions and workshops; psychologists draw upon traditional Sufi practices of self-knowledge and discipline; and Muslim Students' Associations occasionally present conferences or talks on Sufi themes. Yet we observe that these diverse expressions of Sufism are often silenced in discourses about Islam in Canada, including in academic literature. To understand this tendency, we analyse the difficult historical context, characterized by widespread racism and Islamophobia, in which Islam and consequently Sufism developed in Canada. We argue that there appears to be a connection between the erasure of African Muslims in early Canadian and colonial history and the exclusion of Sufism in Canadian discourses on Islam. Furthermore, the contemporary Muslim community in Canada, which has expanded over the last century and a half principally thanks to waves of immigrants, seems generally reluctant to recognize the legitimacy of Sufism as a dimension of Islam. This contrasts with the more organic relation of Sufism to Islam in Muslim-majority societies such as Egypt. However, we also observe that this relation has been controversial across much of the Islamic world, especially among elites, in colonial and postcolonial eras. Several factors help explain the particularities of the Canadian context, including existing as an internally diverse religious minority in a context of bigotry and racism, and the impact of immigration policies on Canadian Muslim communities.

Historical Overview of Sufism

The difficulty of locating Sufism as a demographic phenomenon is hard to overstate. As William C. Chittick (2003) notes, Sufi practices can be traced to the formative period of Islam. They have taken on many different forms which have not always been described by their practitioners as "Sufi." As an integral aspect of the historical Islamic experience, Sufism is a far less bounded phenomenon than sectarian identity and manifests a fluid or variable character within distinct population groups:

> It is certainly not a sect within Islam. It has nothing to do with the two major denominations, Sunnism and Shi'ism, since it has been found in both from earliest times. Both men and women engage in Sufi practice, and it is common for some members of a single family to be Sufis, and for others not to be. A husband may be a Sufi, while his wife may not, or vice versa. Certainly, not every Muslim is a Sufi, but Sufism has been present wherever there have been sizable Muslim populations. This is especially obvious from about the thirteenth century, when clearly defined institutions associated with the word came to be established.
>
> It is, in short, extremely difficult if not impossible to draw a clear distinction between Sufis and other Muslims. Even if we take an anthropological perspective and say that a Sufi is someone who says that he is a Sufi, we may find that for historical or political reasons the word itself is not employed by people who would be called Sufis by most other definitions of the term. (Chittick 2003)

Sufi origins date to shortly after the death of the Prophet in 632 CE and are connected to dimensions of religious piety with an emphasis on *direct* and *personal experience* of God. *Dhikr*, meaning invocation and remembrance, is an important Sufi practice. It is believed that God revealed some of His Names in the Qur'an and sanctified them and that his presence is in the Names. *Dhikr* is combined with meditation (*fikr*) and is carried out alone, in retreats, in a group setting (with music or in unison), or in daily practices. It involves the repetition of a Divine Name or a formula based on revelation. The practice of *dhikr* is an act of piety that is central in Sufism. Although Sunni and Shi'ite Sufis also engage in the typical forms of worship practised by Muslims, they further engage in *dhikr* as a means of constantly remembering God, as interpreted by the Qur'anic statement that the remembrance of God is the greatest practice (29:45). Sufi practice also emphasizes the role of saints, known as "friends" of God, who are venerated and celebrated in rituals during which names of God are frequently recited. Sufi popular practices include commemoration of saints' birthdays or death anniversaries; visitation of shrines or graves; reciting poetry and singing to praise God; and devotional dancing.

Sufism is often organized as a tariqa (path) followed by members of a community, which can vary from a loose, inclusive association of people with shared reverence for a spiritual teacher to a more strictly bounded order whose members disclose their practices only to fellow initiates. Spiritual practice guided by a master-disciple relationship is at the core of most Sufi orders, though there are many differences between paths predicated on loyalty to different spiritual leaders (alive or deceased) and to distinct lineages of teachers through which blessings and practices have been transmitted across many generations. Sufi organizations vary considerably in structure and degree of formality, as well as in methods of teaching and distinctive practices and rituals that may have been formed within specific regional contexts.

Historically, Sufi institutions developed in parallel with other widely recognized Islamic institutions. As madrasas developed to provide centres for exoteric training in law and theology, the Sufis developed additional specialized spaces such as the *khanaqah* or *zawiya*, which might be variously described as rest houses, retreat centres, or lodges. The different Sufi tariqas, or orders, were usually associated with an original founder whose teachings were preserved and developed by subsequent generations to form a school of practice bearing the name of the founder. The founder of a given order or brotherhood would be revered for offering a distinctive style of teaching as well as mystical exercises and a rule of life.

Diverse Sufi Expressions in Canada

Literature about Islam in Canada generally indicates that Al Rashid Mosque, in Edmonton, was the first mosque to be established in Canada, in 1938. Most of these sources make no mention of Sufism in relation to this event. Yet, on the "History" page of the mosque's website, there is an old black-and-white photograph of people who appear to be the women and men who established the mosque, as described in the accompanying text (Al Rashid Mosque 2016). Among these dignitaries is an Indian Muslim known as Maulana 'Abdul 'Aleem Siddiqui al-Qadiri. The title "al-Qadiri" at the end of his name indicates affiliation to the Qadiri Sufi Order. But the website does not explain his presence in the photograph. With some digging, an article on Sufism in Toronto, published on another website, clarifies this mystery:

> The first well-known *sufi* saint to bring *baraka* (blessings) to Canada was Maulana 'Abdul 'Aleem Siddiqui al-Qadiri *Rahmatullahi 'alaih*. He performed the opening ceremony of the first mosque to be built in Canada in Edmonton in 1939. He also visited Toronto, the largest metropolis in Canada, where he presented Islam as a gift to a largely non-Muslim gathering. (Noormuhammad 1995)

Apparently, the first mosque in Canada was inaugurated by a Sufi. But he was not only a Sufi. Rather, Sufism was one of the several Islamic disciplines in which he was traditionally trained. While it is understandable that Sufism is not the central aspect remembered about the inauguration of Al Rashid Mosque, the complete silence about it is problematic. For instance, Earle H. Waugh, who has written extensively about Sufism in other contexts (Waugh 1989, 2005), does not explore this dimension in his monograph devoted to Al Rashid Mosque (Waugh 2018).

Sufi Tariqas in Canada

When trying to assess the importance of Sufism within a given context, one may seek to determine the scope of adherence to formally established Sufi orders. One may also try to evaluate how popular or influential the leaders of these institutions are, by how large their audience is on social media, how often they appear on radio or television, and how many books they sell. For instance, Frédéric Castel estimates that in 2001, in the province of Quebec, there were fewer than five Sufi centres among the hundred or so Muslim places of worship he surveyed, which ranged from college prayer rooms to major mosques (Castel 2010, 555). By 2010, he estimates that eight to ten Sufi orders were active in the province, but not always with a fixed address (565). These orders include the Qadiriya Boutchichiyya, Shadhili Bourhaniya, Oveyssi, Shahmaghsoudi, Muridiyya (Mourides), and Chishtiya Inayati.[2] This quantitative data indicates that a mere 5 per cent of Muslim places of worship in Quebec are Sufi.

Moreover, attendance of services at major urban mosques far exceeds participation in the activities of Sufi centres. Although more quantitative research of this sort needs to be undertaken in the rest of Canada, a preliminary assessment leads us to predict that the proportion of Sufi centres in relation to other Muslim places of worship would not be radically different in other provinces. For instance, in the tri-city Region of Waterloo, Ontario, with a population of over 530,000 (Region of Waterloo n.d.), we have found one Sufi place of worship, the Zawiya Fellowship, out of ten or so Muslim places of worship (including university prayer rooms). Moreover, most Sufi centres are concentrated in major urban centres.

However, quantitative research offers a useful but incomplete picture of Sufism in Canada. Indeed, when calculating the number of Sufis in a given location, one must begin with a working definition of who a Sufi is. Yet there is no broad agreement about this definition. The classic Islamic definition of a Sufi only applies to spiritually realized beings, such as the leaders of orders, not to disciples still in the stages of apprenticeship. A sociological definition might also include disciples, but should it include people who are not members of an order but reverentially visit Sufi saints or the tombs of saints? And how should people who participate in yearly festivals in honour of such saints be categorized? Quantitative research which proposes generalizations based on contested definitions can serve only a limited purpose. It would be wise to remember the wisdom, attributed in oral tradition to the legendary Sufi character Mullah Nasruddin, not to only look for one's lost keys under the street lamp, just because the light is better there. The street lamp in this analogy is quantifiable data (Wallerstein 2004, 19).[3]

Informal Sufi Networks and Discreet Sufism in Formal Settings

The extent of Sufism's presence in Canada cannot be measured by institutional Sufi centres alone, because Sufism can also be expressed through informal networks and non-Sufi institutions or organizations. Put differently, formal institutions should not be the only aspects of Sufism we examine. In Canada, Sufis have been struggling for decades to develop their institutions beyond the embryonic stage. It is true that, in bigger cities, some orders have established centres devoted entirely to Sufi activities. For instance, the Naqshbandi Nazimiyya operates such a centre in Montreal. And as the largest and most diverse city in Canada, Toronto is home to a growing number of Sufi orders, some of which have well-established centres, such as the Jerrahi Sufi Order of Canada. Yet most Sufi orders operate from residential basements or out of multipurpose spaces such as the Rumi Rose Garden Cafe and Market in Vancouver, which houses the local activities of the Naqshbandi Nazimiyya Sufi Order.

Other orders operate within mosques or other Islamic organizations, where Sufism constitutes a tacit undercurrent rather than an overt message. One such example is the Moroccan Shadhili-Darqawi-Alawi Order, based in Fez and led by Shaykh Abdallah al-Haddad. Shaykh Ramzy Ajem, who represents the order in Toronto, co-founded the Risalah Foundation in 2008. At the time, this organization comprised only a handful of members gathering in homes. But on 15 April 2018, it established Masjid Vaughan, a sizeable mosque in the suburban community of Vaughan, Ontario. Ajem is simultaneously a Muslim community leader, Islamic scholar, and representative of a Sufi order. Observers might understandably ignore the Sufi dimension of the Risalah Foundation and Masjid Vaughan, since it is discreet and seamlessly tied into a broader mission of service to the Muslim community. The same can be said of many other mosques in the region, such as Jamiat-ul-Ansar in Brampton, connected to a Shadhili branch called the Hashimiyya-Darqawiyya, and the Mississauga Muslim Community Centre, connected to the Qadiri Sufi lineage. The challenge of finding Sufi expressions unobtrusively embedded within broader Muslim institutions can be even greater when these institutions serve ethnically homogeneous minority communities. For instance, English-speaking academics from outside the community might easily ignore the Sufi activities in a mosque frequented by Muslims of Pakistani origin, in which Urdu is the main language of communication. That is one more reason not to look for our keys only near the street lamp.

Sufism as a Universalist Spirituality

Orders explicitly aiming to serve a multiethnic community are often easier to find. This is particularly true of many Sufi institutions that represent their teachings as a universal spirituality for people of all faiths, which are less closely associated with Muslim communities. To be certain, non-Muslims are welcome in nearly all Canadian Sufi centres, but they are generally understood to be honoured guests in an Islamic space. Universalist Sufis see things differently. For example, the website of Sufi Order International Toronto Centres explains,

> Sufism can best be described as a way of looking at the world and a way of living in the world. As Sufism is not an established religion or doctrine it is not made up of a body of dogma that one must follow. The Sufi Message, as brought to the West by Hazrat Inayat Khan in 1910, is universal in nature and joyfully welcomes people of all faiths, philosophies and heritages. The work of the Sufi Order International centres draws on the work and teachings of Hazrat Inayat Khan, his son Pir Vilayat, and his grandson Pir Zia, who is the current spiritual leader of the Order. (Sufi Order International n.d.)

Several other universalist Sufi organizations exist in Canada, such as the Caravan of the Heart in Vancouver, a local branch of the Inayati Order. While such institutions do not perceive their mission as principally for Muslims, they all recognize the importance of Islam in the historical development of Sufism. It would be wise to consider the differences between Islamic and universalist Sufism in Canada as a spectrum rather than a dichotomy, since most orders present some relation to Islam as well as teachings they see as universal. Moreover, they all adapt their teachings and practices to the Canadian and broader North American context to some degree (Dickson 2015).

"Implicit Sufism" in Canada

Surveys focused on Sufi institutions, leadership, membership, and attendance are inadequate for two main reasons. First, many Sufis worship in mosques and prayer spaces rather than specifically Sufi centres. For instance, in Waterloo, Ontario, several practitioners of Sufism pray at the Waterloo Masjid, run by the Muslim Society of Waterloo and Wellington Counties. They act in accordance with the classical understanding that Sufis are exceptionally pious members of the broader Muslim community to which they belong. Second, Sufi expressions are not limited to the realm of official orders. One must consider the impact of Sufism in such diverse areas as music, poetry, psychology, philosophy, dance, and visual arts. This impact is observable in Muslim communities but also among non-Muslims in Canada and globally. In short, one need not be a Sufi to be influenced by Sufism.

When Nusrat Fateh Ali Khan (d. 1997) travelled to Canada, his Sufi expression affected more than just Sufis. In the 1980s and 1990s, Khan became an international celebrity of what was then labelled "world music," thereby introducing new audiences to the South Asian musical style of Qawwali, connected to the Chishti Sufi Order. On 17 October 1992, Khan and his ensemble packed St. James United Church in Montreal. The audience comprised many Pakistanis but also a significant number of people from other backgrounds, including many Euro-Canadians. The virtuoso gave an energetic performance which lasted several hours, during which many Pakistani men approached the stage, whirling ecstatically, showering the performers with money, and handing over bits of paper with musical requests that were graciously received by Khan. During the intermission, a copious Pakistani buffet awaited the audience in the church basement. It was an extraordinary event in Montreal's increasingly cosmopolitan musical scene. Depending on their background and expectations, audience members could experience this concert as religious, spiritual, cultural, musical, or even all of the above. Three years later, on 1 October 1995, Khan returned to Montreal. This time he performed at the prestigious Place des Arts, in the Salle Wilfrid-Pelletier, "the largest multi-purpose concert hall in Canada … home to two world renowned resident companies: Les Grands Ballets Canadiens de Montréal and Opéra de Montréal," and known for hosting the likes of Bob Dylan, Luciano Pavarotti, and Ella Fitzgerald (Opera de Montréal, 2018). No Pakistani meal was served and the few audience members to attempt an ecstatic whirl could do so only in the aisles, far from the large stage.[4] Qawwali seemed far away from its popular devotional roots. Among the many Canadians experiencing this form of Sufi expression, in Montreal and other cities, only a small minority were Sufis or even Muslims. The same can be said for the readers of popular English and French translations of poetry by Turkish Sufi Jalal al-Din Rumi (d. 1273) (Sharify-Funk et al. 2018, 140–81).

In Canada, Sufi expressions can occur in a concert hall, a library, and a variety of other contexts. One can enjoy a bite to eat and a warm drink at Restaurant Rumi in Montreal. In Toronto, one can visit the Aga Khan Museum to register for courses on Sufi poetry or "participate in a Sufi whirling meditation session with members of Rumi Canada" inside a Mongolian yurt erected in the museum's courtyard (Aga Khan Museum 2018). Adherence to Islam or a Sufi order are not required. When Saudi Arabian psychologist Amal Elyas explores Sufi approaches in her doctoral research at the University of Victoria, she is engaged in an academic expression of Sufism in Canada (Elyas 2005). The intended readers of such research are not principally Muslim or Sufi. The same can be said of the research conducted by Faruk Arslan (2014) at Wilfrid Laurier University, who writes in his dissertation that "Fethullah Gülen's[5] action-oriented Sufi methods described in his book series 'The Emerald Hills of the Heart' provides the basis for a heart-based therapeutic intervention through self-journeying, which is the objective of this thesis" (2).

On university campuses, Sufi expressions can be observed not only in research or curriculum but also in Muslim chaplaincies and Muslim Students' Associations. This observation may come as a surprise to some. After all, the Muslim Students' Association of North America and Canada, also known as MSA National, was founded in 1963 and largely associated with foreign students sympathetic to Islamic currents deeply critical of contemporary Sufism:

> Most of its members – the majority of whom were students of engineering, the hard sciences, and medicine – saw themselves as participants in a historic Islamic "renaissance" ushered in by such Islamist thinkers as Abul A'la Mawdudi and Sayyid Qutb (1906–1966), the contemporary ideologues of Jama'at-i Islami and the Muslim Brotherhood respectively. Some of the founding members of the MSA were in fact members of these organizations. (GhaneaBassiri 2010, 266)

Although foreign organizations did not control the MSA, they inspired its mission to promote a "utopian, ideological, pan-Islamic society" (GhaneaBassiri 2010, 267). Given its genealogy, the MSA is a surprising place to look for Sufi expressions. However, the structure of the organization allows for greater diversity on the ground than one might expect. "Each MSA chapter is an independent student-run organization operating under the rules and regulations of their own respective campuses" (MSA National 2017). Over time, we have observed an increasing diversity within the MSA network, especially in recent decades, when the type of militant political Islam described above has become discredited among many North American Muslims.

An interesting example of this diversity is to be found at Université du Québec à Montréal, where the Association des étudiants musulmans (AEMUQAM) was presided over by Jawhar El Guermaï in 2016–17. El Guermaï sought this position after having attended the weekly lessons on the oeuvre of the famous

Sufi Abu Hamid Al-Ghazali (1058–1111), sponsored by AEMUQAM in 2015–16. He was deeply inspired by the lecturer, Shaykh Hamdi Ben Aissa, a Sufi scholar and community leader from Ottawa. During his mandate, El Guermaï continued to organize Ben Aissa's weekly lectures, videos of which began to attract thousands of viewers on YouTube. Both Ben Aissa and AEMUQAM were gaining an international following. At the time, Ben Aissa was also conducting weekly lessons in English for the MSA at McGill University; those recordings, however, did not achieve the same success online. Nevertheless, this example indicates that MSA sponsorship of Sufi lectures was not confined to one university. At the same time, the increasing success of the pro-Sufi AEMUQAM attracted some very vocal detractors, both online and on campus. In a letter written after he and his team were elected out of office by students with a much more negative view of Sufism, El Guermaï complained that he and Ben Aissa had been the victims of a smear campaign he described as "intellectual terrorism" (El Guermaï 2017). The controversies surrounding Sufi expressions on Montreal campuses demonstrate not only that there is a sometimes-chaotic diversity of approaches to Islam in MSAs, but also that these student organizations work in tandem with Muslim leaders who are not students, some of whom are Sufi or at least Sufi-friendly. These include Muslim chaplains such as Ustadh Amjad Tarsin at University of Toronto and Shelby Haque at University of Alberta.

The Silence on Sufism in Canada: Some Explanations

Having established that even the most universalist expressions of Sufism are still connected to Islam, and that many Sufis assume leadership roles in the Muslim community, our initial question remains: Why are expressions of Sufism silenced in popular and academic discourses about Islam in Canada? One might respond that these expressions are passively neglected rather than actively silenced. However, when there is an observable trend within a discourse to ignore or neglect certain voices, even unwittingly, silencing occurs. The good intentions of certain participants in the discourse community are of little consequence in this process. An explanation for the silencing is still needed. Perhaps the diversity of contexts in which such expressions of Sufism occur can partially explain this problem. Yet surely the same can be said of other types of Islamic expression. After all, Canadian Islam is extremely diverse in terms of ethnicity, language, social class, and of course religious understanding. This diversity has not prevented the publication of numerous writings about Islam in Canada, from academics, journalists, and Muslim apologists alike.

Silence in Literature on Sufism in Canada

There are many different types of books about contemporary Islam and the negotiation of identity within Western contexts (especially in America and

Europe). There is also a growing body of literature on the negotiation of Canadian Muslim identity in the twenty-first century.[6] Most of these books on Islam and Canada are mainly about controversial political issues impacting Canadian Muslims. To the extent that adherents of Sufi traditions might have distinctive perspectives on these issues, such perspectives are not generally sought or included in the analysis.

Two significant edited volumes are *Belonging and Banishment: Being Muslim in Canada* (Bakht 2008) and *Islam in the Hinterlands: Muslim Cultural Politics in Canada* (Zine 2012). Both of these books offer scholarly commentary on current controversial subjects (e.g., sharia debates in Ontario, integration, minority rights) from Canadian scholars and activists; however, as anthologies they do not provide an integrated perspective or aspire to present a sustained analytical focus. *Diaspora by Design: Muslim Immigrants in Canada and Beyond* (Moghissi et al. 2009) provides a helpful introduction to the diversity of the Canadian Muslim population but focuses more on integration issues than on the dynamic processes through which Muslim women have become major players and symbols in Canadian debates about cultural identity. But it does not address their participation in Sufism. In a more recent publication, *Beyond Accommodation: Everyday Narratives of Muslim Canadians* (Selby et al. 2018), the focus is on Islam as a lived religion in Canada rather than political controversies. This could be an excellent approach to include Sufi expressions in the daily lives of Muslims, but the topic is only briefly discussed.

Sufism is also largely absent from other books that focus specifically on Canadian Muslim women but are not consistently engaged with recent controversial issues that have come to dominate public discussions (e.g., Bill 94, the Bouchard-Taylor Commission and its final report, the sharia debate in Ontario, the North American women imams controversy). These books include *Aversion and Desire: Negotiating Muslim Female Identity in the Diaspora* (Khan 2002), *The Muslim Veil in North America* (Alvi et al. 2003), and *Muslim Women Activists in North America: Speaking for Ourselves* (Bullock 2005). They also do not analyse the "Islam and the West" literature that has developed in the wake of 9/11, which plays a powerful role in shaping the discourse used in current controversies.

It can be argued that Islam in Canada literature is still in its "formative stage," often presenting a somewhat homogenized view of Muslim experiences as a minority group in polarized and security-conscious times within which "otherness" is commonly perceived to be threatening. In addition to the scholarly analysis that utilizes a theoretical framework for understanding what it can mean to negotiate a Muslim identity in Canada, one also finds books authored by journalists, which articulate similar issues in a more descriptive and accessible format (Khan 2009; Siddiqui 2006). Once again, Sufism is absent from these analyses.

It is true that a number of edited volumes explore the subject of Sufism in the West, but they generally offer very little content on Sufism in Canada (Malik and Hinnells 2006; Westerlund 2004). Too often, Canada is assimilated into the American context or relegated to its margins. A notable exception is *Sufis in Western Society: Global Networking and Locality* (Geaves et al. 2009), in which Michael Frishkopf's (2009) chapter on Sufi music in the West is based on a Canadian case study and the sociopolitical Canadian context is examined. Canada is also given fair treatment in a recent monograph entitled *Living Sufism in North America* (Dickson 2015), but Canadian particularities are not explored in depth since the focus is continental. Despite the publication of several case studies of limited scope (Haddad 2008; LeBlanc 2013; Qureshi 2003) and works in which a section is devoted to Sufism in a Canadian context (Hermansen 2000, 176–7; Hussain 2001, 173–8; McDonough 1994, 321–2), there has been no major work broadly examining this issue. The present chapter is but a step in this direction.

Racism and Islamophobia

Since understanding the history of Islam in Canada is helpful for understanding the history of Sufism as well, it is important to remember that the early colonial powers, in the lands we now refer to as Canada, fostered a Christian-centric culture within which other religions such as Islam had only marginal status. In such a context, some Muslims might very well have perceived hiding their religious identity as beneficial. This would have been an especially attractive option for early members of the African diaspora, present in these lands since at least 1604 (Cooper 2006; Divine 2007). Most of the early members of this diaspora were enslaved. But even free Africans such as Mathieu Da Costa (d. c. 1619), had to contend with an extremely Eurocentric society. Da Costa served as an interpreter for French colonial explorers Pierre Dugua de Mons (d. 1628) and Samuel de Champlain (d. 1635) starting in 1608. It is important to remember the exclusively Catholic character of New France, especially after the 1627 charter granted to the Company of New France stipulated that only Roman Catholics should be allowed to settle in the colony. Enslaved or free Africans were unlikely to publicize their affiliation to any other religion in such circumstances. Moreover, when it came to the enslaved, European colonists were interested solely in the obedient productivity – not the diverse world views – of a population they considered private property, categorized alongside animals, furniture, and land.

Yet we know that a significant percentage of enslaved Africans in the Americas were Muslims, often belonging to West African Sufi orders (Diouf 2013). It seems unlikely that no Muslims or Sufis would have been counted among those who ended up in New France, often after spending time in places like Jamaica or other colonies (Elgersman 2016; Nelson 2016). Even after the abolishment of slavery, the officially Christian character of successive regimes in what is now called Canada may very well have encouraged people already marginalized for the colour of their skin to hide their adherence to Islam. There was no incentive for any Muslims establishing a prayer space (i.e., mosque) under these conditions to register with local authorities. Thus, there is reason to doubt official accounts that the first mosque was established in Canada in 1938 or that the first Muslims came to Canada from Syria and Lebanon in the late nineteenth century. Furthermore, there seems to be a connection between the erasure of African Muslims and the omission of Sufis, who are both marginalized in Canadian discourses on Islam. Perhaps the first Muslim to have come to the land now called Canada was a West African Sufi whose remains are buried in an unmarked grave. Of course, this is mere speculation, but educated guesses are necessary since the historical archive is incomplete.

Reformism, Migration, and the Loss of Local Traditions

Anti-Black racism may explain the erasure of any expressions of Sufism by members of the early African diaspora in these lands, but what of the more numerous waves of Muslims who have immigrated to Canada in the past century and a half? Their connection to Sufism can be analysed in relation to circumstances both in Canada and in their lands of origin. One nuanced and multifaceted explanation about the Canadian context is offered by the ethnomusicologist and specialist of Sufism Michael Frishkopf (2009). When conducting fieldwork in Egypt, he observed how Sufism was an integrated aspect of the dominant Islamic culture, just as Sufi music was a ubiquitous feature of the nation's "soundworld":

> Clear boundaries between "Sufi" and "orthodox" Islam, so carefully inscribed both by orientalist and Islamic reformist discourses, hardly exist in Egyptian Muslim practice. This ambiguity is best demonstrated in the soundworld, that affectively charged sonic-social intersubjectivity, where sharp boundaries between "Sufi" and "non-Sufi" sound and practice cannot be located. Rather, the whole of Islam is suffused with sonic practices, including tilawa (Qur'anic recitation), du'a' (supplication), adhan, ibtihalat, and inshad, mediated or live, as associated with daily prayer, lifecycle events, and religious holidays, as well as with liturgies of the Sufi orders, indicating the interpenetration of Sufi and "mainstream" Islam. (Frishkopf 2009, 49)

In Egypt, Frishkopf met Shaykh Mohamed el-Helbawy, whose expertise covers a range of traditional Islamic forms of sonic expression. Affiliated with the Hamidiyya Shadhiliyya Sufi Order, el-Helbawy is popular in Egypt for mastering Qur'anic recitation, the call to prayer, and diverse forms of religious song. He is a regular feature of Egyptian radio and television. Beyond the mosque and the Sufi lodge, el-Helbawy also performs concerts in Egypt and internationally, accompanied by a traditional musical ensemble.

> Aside from exceptional instances featuring unequivocally mystical texts, and outside of explicitly Sufi contexts, it is impossible to say whether Shaykh el-Helbawy's repertoire is "Sufi" or "orthodox," because the same recurrent themes (supplication, praise, exhortation, devotion) permeate all Islamic religious poetry and are featured in all Islamic performance contexts. These genres of Islamic vocal performance are highly melodic, powerfully expressive, and deeply affecting. The unarticulated, unremarkable prevalence of these sonic forms mediates social relations by linking individual and group experience in an integrated, affectively rich soundworld. (Frishkopf 2009, 49)

However, in 2005, when Frishkopf invited el-Helbawy to the University of Alberta in Edmonton, it became clear that a stark contrast existed between traditional Islamic cultures and the minority context of Muslims in Canada. According to Frishkopf, the rich "soundworld" of Egyptian mosques is nowhere to be found in the comparatively silent mosques of Edmonton and most other Canadian cities. Similarly, the presence of Sufism is mostly silenced. Whereas Frishkopf had hoped the local Muslim community might benefit as much as the university from the shaykh's presence, local Islamic institutions such as the mosques and the MSA were far from enthusiastic. Arab and Egyptian cultural associations were far more welcoming, as were many non-Muslims. For instance, "a local Christian college went furthest in providing a warm welcome to Shaykh el-Helbawy, featuring him as guest speaker, and even providing lunch" (Frishkopf 2009, 54).

These contrasts between Egypt and Canada, and between local Islamic and non-Islamic circles, led Frishkopf to analyse why Sufism and music are often viewed with such suspicion in Canadian Islamic spaces. According to Frishkopf, when Sufi music is presented to non-Muslims as an "exotic" or "authentic" form of "cultural" or "spiritual" expression, it is well received. It is also well received by first-generation immigrants eager to reconnect with their cultural heritage. Interestingly, these nostalgic immigrants might not welcome the same music in a religious context. Culture is one thing; religion is another. Frishkopf explains that much of the enthusiasm for Sufism outside the Muslim community in Canada is related to the capitalist commodification of Sufi music as "world music." He contrasts the holistic Islamic "soundworld" with the decontextualized "soundscape" of world music (Frishkopf 2009, 66). While he focuses on sound, Frishkopf's argument can be extended to Sufi literature packaged as "world literature" and Sufi metaphysics as "universal spirituality." In the capitalist world of market segmentation, these products are not intended for Muslims. Therefore, second- and third-generation immigrants, as well as converts and their children, may understandably be completely ignorant about Sufism. Yet other factors surely contribute to explaining why they are not listening to the music collections of first-generation immigrants (often their parents) or noticing how they often cite Sufi verses and proverbs in casual conversation. This topic merits further research.

Frishkopf suggests that several factors have converged to silence Sufism in Canadian mosques. One such factor is the challenge Canadian Muslims face of being both a relatively small minority and greatly diverse in terms of language, culture, and socio-economic status. This diversity may explain why Sufi institutions are more developed in bigger cities such as Toronto and Montreal, with larger Muslim populations (Frishkopf 2009, 64). Indeed, the natural tendency for minorities is to unite in solidarity when facing misunderstanding, suspicion, and even hostility from a majority group. But it is very difficult to unite an internally eclectic community. Those cultural aspects of Islam which have developed in local settings, since the very first generation of Muslims appeared in Arabia centuries ago, can create unwanted division in multicultural Canadian mosques. First-generation immigrants may be tempted to leave their cultural specificities at home, such as their recordings of Nusrat Fateh Ali Khan or Shaykh el-Helbawy, and focus on what unites them with their coreligionists at the mosque: Arabic scriptures. In more culturally homogenous contexts, oral traditions in local languages, including dialectical Arabic, permeate discussions about scripture. But in the multicultural Canadian mosque, the shared languages are modern standard Arabic, English, or French. Narrow literalist interpretations of scripture prevail in this context. Conservative reform movements, which are often persecuted in countries such as Egypt, thrive in such environments, to the extent that many young Muslims in Canada are ignorant of the deeply complex and often pluralistic expressions of Islam which, as Frishkopf observes, are mainstream elsewhere. Another factor silencing Sufism in the mosque, according to Frishkopf, is Canadian policy, which favours students and immigrants from "precisely those socio-occupational classes (mostly engineers) most partial to Islamic reformism, and least knowledgeable about local oral traditions (whether Sufi or otherwise)" (Frishkopf 2009, 63). Perhaps Sufism would be better represented if Canadian immigration policy favoured "intellectuals, artists, and the poor" (63). Further research would be useful to analyse the impact of immigration policies on the type of Islamic knowledge – or knowledge about Islam – produced in Canada.

Elitist Modernism

One must be careful not to overemphasize the national dimensions of the challenges facing Sufism in Canada. Frishkopf argues that the problems of Sufism in Canada are exacerbated by global and transnational trends such as postmodern capitalism and pan-Islamic reform movements. Therefore, situations in Islamicate countries remain crucial to understand the Canadian setting. His work can be connected to that of another scholar of Sufism who conducted extensive fieldwork in Egypt, Valerie Hoffman. Like Frishkopf, Hoffman observes that Sufi expressions are loud and clear in Egyptian Islam, but she also mentions that foreigners and upper-class Egyptians tend to present Sufism as a marginal phenomenon confined to the lower classes and slowly disappearing as society modernizes. She retorts that marginality and irrelevance better describe the elites who formulate such accusations (Hoffman 1995, 18). On the ground, she observes massive participation in Sufi-related activities by people of all social classes, including members of the elite.

Hoffman's account indicates that there is an attempt to silence Sufism by many among the dominant classes in Egypt. Moreover, many people are unaware or hardly aware of the Sufi dimensions of activities in which they partake. They do not realize that the lyrics of a folk song played at a wedding was written by a Sufi or that the saint being celebrated in a local festival was a Sufi. In the end, although Sufism is ubiquitous, "its influence is often subtle and unobserved" (Hoffman 1995, 377). This is partly because the primary mission of most Sufi orders is to help individuals reach spiritual enlightenment by combating their egos. Consequently, many Sufis are discreet, and they are commonly silent about their spiritual practice.

If official discourses on Islam frequently silence Sufism in Egypt, where millions of people adhere to well-established Sufi orders, it is not surprising to observe a similar trend in Canada, where Sufism is still struggling to develop strong institutions. The ignorance of many Muslims regarding Sufism is somewhat justifiable when hostility and suspicion from non-Sufi Muslims is met with silence by discreet Sufis. In Canada, this somewhat crushing combination of silences is compounded by Western Orientalist notions that Sufism is not truly Islamic. In fact, there are Sufi groups proclaiming that Sufism need not be experienced as part of an Islamic practice, a notion which would not resonate with most Sufis in Egypt or other Islamicate countries. Without contesting the right of universalist Sufis, as well as Muslims hostile to Sufism, to develop and promote their beliefs, we must recognize that these discourses can discourage the expression of the Sufi dimensions of Islam in Canada, making it more difficult for new generations of Muslims to recognize what previous generations accepted as an integral dimension of their religious culture.

Conclusion

Sufism has long been present in Canada, and yet a complex range of factors have impacted its expression and social acceptance as well as its representation in academic work. Little attention is given to the Sufi dimensions of historical events such as the presence of Maulana 'Abdul 'Aleem Siddiqui al-Qadiri at the inauguration of Canada's first recognized mosque. Factors to explain this absence of scholarly attention include the unique historical circumstances of

Muslim communities in the lands now called Canada evolving in a context of Eurocentric racism and Islamophobia; the commodification of Sufi art and literature as a universal spirituality in the age of globalized capitalism; the challenges of developing a sense of community as an internally diverse religious minority; Canadian immigration policy and its favouring of certain groups; and the controversies surrounding Sufism throughout the Islamic world in the colonial and postcolonial periods. Consequently, it is important for scholars of Islam in Canada to start seeing and hearing Sufism. This entails seeking out Sufis and giving them a voice in the academic discourse on Islam in Canada. Failure to do so results not just in a disservice to Sufis but also in an impoverished understanding of global Islamic experiences and of ways in which these experiences are being transmitted as well as transformed in the Canadian context. Scholarship that fails to note the presence of Sufism deprives its readership of access to an aspect of Islam in Canada that is less marginal than many scholars appear to believe.

Providing better accounts of Sufism in Canada will require attention to methodological challenges as well as the acquisition of the knowledge and experience required to recognize Sufism in Canadian settings. This means not just noting formal Sufi associations but also recognizing the impact of Sufism through informal networks and within the workings of formal institutions that accommodate discreet or implicit aspects of Sufi teachings. Sufism can also be recognized through diverse cultural expressions that, though not necessarily central to the corporate life of diverse immigrant Muslim communities, are still sources of meaning and connection to a homeland and its traditions. Attention should be paid to differences between rural, suburban, and urban contexts, regional and provincial particularities, and an intersection of factors including ethnicity, race, conversion, class, gender, and sexuality.

Recognizing Sufism may also require coming to terms with a tendency among many scholars and cultural modernists to devalue oral and vernacular traditions or to underestimate the extent to which forces such as colonialism, modern capitalism, and migration have destabilized traditional religious life and practices. Additionally, it should be clear that recognizing Sufi Muslim experiences in Canada need not come at the expense of other experiences. The problem which needs solving is not the diversity of voices but the underrepresentation of Sufis. Diverse Sufi expressions have been a dimension of Islam in Canada for a long time. They should not be neglected, erased, or silenced. By taking renewed interest in Sufism and its long-standing presence, scholars have an opportunity not just to acquire deeper insight into "what is really happening" to and within Muslim communities but also to foster more profound conversations about the present historical moment and the choices Muslims and others face in the search for meaning amidst rapid change.

NOTES

1 We base our conclusions on an intertextual analysis and regular interaction with Sufi communities in Canada.
2 This list uses Castel's spelling of names, for which there are often several versions romanized from languages such as Arabic or Persian.
3 Mullah Nasruddin's folk tales have been transmitted for centuries in such disparate places as Turkey, Iran, and India.
4 This description of Nusrat Fateh Ali Khan's performances is based on the recollections and notes of Jason Idriss Sparkes, who attended both the 1992 and the 1995 concert in Montreal.
5 Fethullah Gülen is a Turkish Islamic scholar based in the United States.
6 Although Canadian Muslims are mentioned in a variety of books that focus on the North American context more generally (e.g., Yvonne Haddad, Jane I. Smith, and Kathleen M. Moore's *Muslim Women in America: The Challenge of Islamic Identity Today*), the treatment of Canada is marginal and overshadowed by the American experience of being Muslim.

REFERENCES

Aga Khan Museum. 2018. *Rumi Canada: Sufi whirling meditation session*. https://www.agakhanmuseum.org/programs/rumi-canada-sufi-whirling-meditation-session

Al Rashid Mosque. 2016. *The history of Al Rashid Mosque*. https://alrashidmosque.ca/history

Alvi, Sajida Sultana, Homa Hoodfar, and Sheila McDonough (Eds.). 2003. *The Muslim veil in North America: Issues and debates*. Women's Press.

Arslan, Faruk. 2014. "A heart-based Sufi mindfulness spiritual practice employing self-journeying." Thesis, Wilfrid Laurier University.

Bakht, Natasha (Ed.). 2008. *Belonging and banishment: Being Muslim in Canada*. TSAR.

Bullock, Katherine (Ed.). 2005. *Muslim women activists in North America: Speaking for ourselves*. University of Texas Press.

Castel, Frédéric. 2010. "La dynamique de l'équation ethnoreligieuse dans l'évolution récente du paysage religieux québécois: Les cas du façonnement des communautés bouddhistes et musulmanes (de 1941 à aujourd'hui)." PhD diss., Université du Québec à Montréal.

Chittick, William C. 2003, May. *Mysticism in Islam*. A lecture delivered at the David M. Kennedy Center for International Studies, Brigham Young University. http://meti.byu.edu/mysticism_chittick.html.

Cooper, Afua. 2006. *The hanging of Angélique: The untold story of Canadian slavery and the burning of Montréal*. Harper Collins.

Dickson, William Rory. 2015. *Living Sufism in North America: Between tradition and transformation*. State University of New York Press.

Diouf, Sylviane A. 2013. *Servants of Allah: African Muslims enslaved in the Americas* (15th anniversary ed.). New York University Press.

Divine, David. (Ed.). 2007. *Multiple lenses: Voices from the diaspora located in Canada*. Cambridge Scholars Publishing.

Elgersman, Maureen G. 2016. *Unyielding spirits: Black women and slavery in early Canada and Jamaica*. Routledge.

El Guermaï, Jawhar. 2017, 29 June. Facebook post. https://www.facebook.com/jawhar.elguermai/posts/10155478164778599

Elyas, Amal. 2005. "Arwah abiya from the Arabian Peninsula: A narrative inquiry of seven women with fiery resistor spirits." PhD diss., University of Victoria, Victoria, Canada.

Frishkopf, Michael. 2009. "Globalizing the soundworld: Islam and Sufi music in the West." In Ron Geaves, Markus Dressler, and Gritt Klinkhammer (Eds.), *Sufis in Western society: Global networking and locality* (pp. 44–76). Routledge.

Geaves, Ron, Markus Dressler, and Gritt Klinkhammer (Eds.). 2009. *Sufis in Western society: Global networking and locality*. Routledge.

GhaneaBassiri, Kambiz. 2010. *A history of Islam in America: From the New World to the new world order*. Cambridge University Press.

Haddad, Mouloud. 2008. "Zawiya réelle, zawiya virtuelle: Soufisme, francophonie et nouvelles technologies au Québec." *Globe: Revue Internationale d'études Québécoise, 11*(1), 197–208. https://doi.org/10.7202/1000498ar

Hermansen, Marcia. 2000. "Hybrid identity formations in Muslim America: The case of American Sufi movements." *Muslim World, 20*(1–2), 158–97. https://doi.org/10.1111/j.1478-1913.2000.tb03686.x

Hoffman, Valerie J. 1995. *Sufism, mystics, and saints in modern Egypt*. University of South Carolina Press.

Hussain, Amir. 2001. "The Canadian face of Islam: Muslim communities in Toronto." PhD diss., University of Toronto.

Karim, Karim H. 2002. "Crescent dawn in the Great White North: Muslim participation in the Canadian public sphere." In Yvonne Yazbeck Haddad (Ed.), *Muslims in the West: From sojourners to citizens* (pp. 262–77). Oxford University Press.

Khan, Shahnaz. 2002. *Aversion and desire: Negotiating Muslim female identity in the diaspora*. Canadian Scholars' Press.

– 2009. *Of hockey and hijab: Reflections of a Canadian Muslim woman*. TSAR.

LeBlanc, Marie Nathalie. 2013. "Sufi Muslims in Montréal: Tensions between cosmopolitanism and the cultural economy of difference." *Anthropologica, 55*(2), 425–40. https://www.jstor.org/stable/24467347

Malik, Jamal, and John Hinnells (Eds.). 2006. *Sufism in the West*. Routledge.

McDonough, Sheila. 1994. "Muslims of Montreal." In Yvonne Yazbeck Haddad and Jane Idleman Smith (Eds.), *Muslim communities in North America* (pp. 317–33). State University of New York Press.

Moghissi, Haideh, Saeed Rahnema, and Mark J. Goodman. 2009. *Diaspora by design: Muslim immigrants in Canada and beyond*. University of Toronto Press.

MSA National. 2017. "About." https://www.msanational.org/about

Nelson, Charmaine A. 2016. *Slavery, geography and empire in nineteenth-century marine landscapes of Montréal and Jamaica*. Routledge.

Noormuhammad, S.O. 1995. *The Sufi tradition in Toronto*. Muslim Canada. http://muslimcanada.org/sufi/toronto.htm (link no longer available)

Opera de Montréal. 2018. *Salle Wilfrid-Pelletier*. https://www.operademontreal.com/en/visit/salle-wilfrid-pelletier

Qureshi, Regula. 2003. "Lineage, shrine, qawwali, and study circle: Spiritual kinship in transnational Sufism." *Religious Studies and Theology, 22*(1), 63–84. https://doi.org/10.1558/RSTH.V22I1.63

Region of Waterloo. n.d. *About Waterloo Region*. Retrieved 28 October 2018 from https://www.regionofwaterloo.ca/en/exploring-the-region/about-waterloo-region.aspx

Selby, Jennifer A., Amélie Barras, and Lori G. Beaman. 2018. *Beyond accommodation: Everyday narratives of Muslim Canadians*. University of British Columbia Press.

Sharify-Funk, Meena, William Rory Dickson, and Merin Shobhana Xavier. 2018. *Contemporary Sufism: Piety, politics, and popular culture*. Routledge.

Siddiqui, Haroon. 2006. *Being Muslim*. Groundwood Books.

Statistics Canada. 2011. National Household Survey. https://www12.statcan.gc.ca/nhs-enm/2011/dp-pd/prof/details/page.cfm?Lang=E&Geo1=PR&Code1=01&Data=Count&SearchText=Canada&SearchType=Begins&SearchPR=01&A1=Religion&B1=All&Custom=&TABID=1

Sufi Order International. n.d. *SOI Toronto Centres*. Retrieved 28 October 2018 from http://www.soitoronto.org

Wallerstein, Immanuel. 2004. *World-systems analysis: An introduction*. Duke University Press.

Waugh, Earle H. 1989. *The Munshidīn of Egypt: Their world and their song*. University of South Carolina Press.

– 2005. *Memory, Music, and Religion: Morocco's Mystical Chanters*. University of South Carolina Press.

– 2018. *Al Rashid Mosque: Building Canadian Muslim communities*. University of Alberta Press.

Westerlund, David. 2004. *Sufism in Europe and North America*. Taylor and Francis.

Zine, Jasmin (Ed.). 2012. *Islam in the hinterlands: Muslim cultural politics in Canada*. University of British Columbia Press.

Unpacking Media Coverage, Islam, and Ismaili Muslims in Canada: An Interview with Karim H. Karim

MEHMET ALI BASAK

Biography

Karim H. Karim is Chancellor's Professor at Carleton University and the director of Carleton University's Centre for the Study of Islam in Ottawa, Canada. He is a full professor in the School of Journalism and Communication, of which he was previously director, and serves as a board member of the *Canadian Journal of Communication* and the *Global Media Journal–Canadian Edition*. Karim has been a co-director of the Institute of Ismaili Studies (IIS) in the United Kingdom and a visiting scholar at Harvard University during sabbatical leaves from Carleton. He holds degrees from Columbia and McGill Universities in Islamic studies and communication studies. Prior to becoming an academic, he worked as a senior researcher and senior policy analyst in the Department of Canadian Heritage, as a reporter for Inter Press Service (Rome) and Compass News Features (Luxembourg), and as a religious education coordinator in the Ismailia Association for Canada.

Karim has been publishing material related to Islam and Muslims in Canada for more than four decades. *Islamic Peril: Media and Global Violence* (2003a; originally published in 2000), for which he won the Canadian Communication Association's inaugural Robinson Book Prize, provides detailed analysis of Western media coverage of violence involving Muslims, particularly in the Canadian press. It extensively charts the patterns in how the media report conflict between "Islam" and "the West." In *Re-Imagining the Other: Culture, Media, and Western-Muslim Intersections* (Eid and Karim 2014c) and in *Engaging the Other: Public Policy and Western-Muslim Intersections* (Karim and Eid 2014a), he and Mahmoud Eid employ Edward Said's clash of ignorance critical model to deconstruct Samuel Huntington's clash of civilizations theory. They argue that conflicts between Western and Muslim societies are not triggered by civilizational differences but are often due to their ignorance of historical engagements and collaborations.

Karim has contributed to Ismaili studies in both scholarly and administrative roles. When he served as co-director of the IIS in London from 2009 to 2011, his responsibilities included management of the institution's graduate studies and transnational training programs. In March 2017, he held the Second International Ismaili Studies Conference, *Mapping a Pluralist Space in Ismaili Studies*, at Carleton University. The conference was the largest international event on Ismaili studies, bringing together prominent scholars in this area. Karim is a leading authority on the contemporary global Ismaili community, and his contributions extend into numerous book chapters and articles examining this Muslim tradition in Canada and elsewhere. In "A Semiotics of Infinite Translucence: The Exoteric and Esoteric in Ismaili Muslim Hermeneutics" (2015b), he traces how the current communication practices of this Shi'a group have been influenced by its long-standing esotericism. "At the Interstices of Tradition, Modernity and Postmodernity: Ismaili Engagements with Contemporary Canadian Society" discusses how Ismailis in Canada interact with "a tripartite 'dialectic' of tradition, modernity, and postmodernity" (Karim 2011a, 287). Karim has discussed how the Ismaili community's members are prominently engaged within the Canadian public sphere (2011a, 2014a). In other work, he has analysed the public discourses on pluralism (2013) and ethics (2015c) of the current Ismaili imam, Aga Khan IV.

Karim's extensive work on the ways in which diasporas communicate has been critically acclaimed. His edited book *The Media of Diaspora* (2003c) has become an international reference on the topic. Karim's co-edited publication *Diaspora and Media in Europe: Migration, Identity, and Integration* (Karim and Al-Rawi 2018) provides further empirical data for the emerging area of digital migration studies. Both volumes have several case studies of Muslim diasporas. Karim's forthcoming monograph is on the clash of ignorance. These are but a few of his significant contributions to scholarship on Muslims, with particular attention to communication and Ismaili studies. Mehmet Ali Basak, a PhD student at the University of Ottawa, poses several questions based on his research of Karim's scholarly work.

Interview

Producing "Islam(s)"

Mehmet Ali Basak [MAB]: How do you view the "production" of Islam(s), which is the theme of this book?

Karim H. Karim [KHK]: A career spent examining the portrayals of Muslims makes one keenly aware of the misunderstandings that non-Muslims and Muslims have perpetuated through their presentations – i.e., their productions – of Islam.

They seem unaware that the historical and current manifestations of Islam are multifaceted; indeed, as Aziz Al-Azmeh (1993) notes, "there are as many Islams as there are situations that sustain it" (1). Similarly, Mohammed Arkoun (1990) said, "We can no longer use the word 'Islam' without quotation marks. It has been so misused and distorted by the media, Muslims themselves, and political scientists that we need a radical reworking of the concept" (50). In engaging with the religion, we deal with a very long period of time and a very large number of people who now live on six continents. Many books, articles, documentaries, and other materials on Islam have sought to produce an easily understandable account of the general topic. However, some attempts to simplify the narrative slide into the simplistic. For example, Islam is usually explained in terms of numerical standardizations of belief, particularly ideas such as five pillars and ninety-nine names of God, which come to be viewed inaccurately as immutable Islamic dogma that all Muslims follow. That these formulations appeared in specific periods after the Prophet's time and were often influenced by particular social, cultural, and political circumstances is often lost on the persons and institutions promoting these ideas as Islam's "official closed corpus" (Arkoun 2002, 62).

A primary challenge facing scholars who are also members of religious communities is to resist communal subjectivities. They are sometimes unaware of their defensiveness in dealing with some of the more prickly parts of their research. There is a propensity to slip into rationalization and apologetics stemming from an often-unconscious drive to protect one's community from uncomfortable questions. Such defensiveness fails to produce scholarly credibility and, ironically, does not uphold the integrity that the religion itself demands. I was alerted early in my academic career about such tendencies on my part. Advice from a member of my PhD committee was vital in making me aware of the need to practise the self-reflexivity that is essential for scholarly analysis. One has to endeavour relentlessly to recognize one's own human subjectivity and the biases that flow from it.[1] Our moral compass has to be striving constantly to point towards the truth that lies past our own inclinations.

MAB: In your book chapter "Sustaining and Enhancing Life" (2018b) you demonstrate how the

> shari'a is a human construct whose fundamental aim is to foster spiritual and material existence in an ethical manner. However, it is often reduced in popular culture to the formulaic binarism of what is permissible (halal) and what is not (haram), rather than being a sophisticated means of engaging with one's intellect and spirituality to address issues as a religious aspirant and as a citizen of society. (64–5)

How do you conceptualize the sharia in Canada? Are there particularities?

KHK: One of the most misunderstood aspects of Islam, in Canada and elsewhere, is the sharia. It is often essentialized as "Islamic law" and is presented as a fixed and unchanging institution to which all Muslims are bound. The reality is that the inherent nature of the sharia is much broader than law; it draws on culture, custom, and folk tradition along with the Qur'an and the Prophet's teachings. As a consequence, it enables varying "Islams" among Muslims living in different locations and circumstances. The initial development of the sharia unfolded from the work of numerous medieval Muslim scholars as "an amalgam of law, ethics and methodology" (Sardar 2003, 66). A key feature of this institution is the methodology it offers to respond to changing situations. The sharia's overriding intent from the outset has been to improve the quality of Muslims' material and spiritual lives under evolving circumstances rather than being a rigid set of laws about what is *halal* (permitted) and what is *haram* (prohibited). Such misperceptions about Islam are present among Muslims themselves and others trying to understand the religion.

Interactions between Western and Muslim-Majority Societies

MAB: In "Covering Muslims: Journalism as Cultural Practice," you argue that "there has emerged over three decades a set of journalistic narratives on 'Muslim terrorism' whose construction is dependent on basic cultural perceptions about the global system of nation states, violence and the relationship between Western and Muslim societies" (Karim 2011b, 132). How do your studies engage this relationship between "Western" and "Muslim" societies?

KHK: Before proceeding to respond to this question, let me state that whereas there have been Muslims in Western societies for centuries, I am contingently using the terms "European" and "Western" as non-Muslim here in order to discuss the relationships between the two groups of people. People of European and Muslim backgrounds have been engaging culturally, intellectually, and militarily for almost one and a half millennia. Yet, remarkably, most on both sides know relatively little about the other. Stereotypes are prominent in their reciprocal images. Negative discourses conceal the peaceful and productive aspects of their long relationship and highlight their quarrels (Selby et al. 2018). The dominant narratives make it seem that the normative relationship between Westerners and Muslims is one of unremitting conflict. Certain powerful institutions on both sides have had much to gain by promoting fear and hatred of the Other (Bail 2015). Ensuring that the supposed enemy continues to be dressed in villainous guises is politically useful in distracting people from the corruption besetting one's own community. There is a general impression that the animus which a number of Western people and Muslims hold against each other arose with the attacks of 11 September 2001 and their aftermath. This is incorrect. It is a historical fact that people of Western and Muslim backgrounds have had bouts of conflict with each other. But it is also incorrect to believe that the relationship between the two societies is unidimensional, that it is characterized only by clash. Whereas this complicated, multilayered story has had occasions of acrimony, betrayal, and contempt, it also features long periods of respect, mutual support, and deep friendship. However, the dominant discourses that underlie the production of knowledge about this complicated relationship have highlighted conflict over cooperation, as demonstrated by Edward Said (1978) and others. Canadian society, as a part of Western civilization and home to more than a million Muslims, is heir to this complex legacy.

Said's critique of Orientalism (the Western study of the East) has been instrumental in shaping my four-decade endeavour of unpacking the production of "Islams." His 1976 *New York Times* essay, which critically reviewed several prominent Orientalists' publications, provided an initial glimpse of his thought. He was a professor of literature at Columbia University, where I was an undergraduate majoring in Islamic studies – reading the Orientalist literature that was the object of his critique. Said's review (1976) was like a breath of fresh air in a place where people could no longer smell the polluted environment. It was a hint of liberation for a colonized mind that had not yet learned to deconstruct ethnocentrically and ideologically shaped narratives. Said, a Palestinian American intellectual, laid bare for scrutiny the Western scholarly discourses that had been used to describe Eastern peoples for two centuries. He audaciously challenged the sacred belief that well-established academics were immune from prejudice and political motivations, that the production of knowledge could lack integrity. However, in the very process of critiquing Western constructions of Islam, Said himself seemed to be reinforcing notions of a strict separation of "the West" and "Islam." He has been criticized for participating in an "Occidentalism" that is a mirror opposite of Orientalism (Buruma and Margalit 2005; also see Halliday 1996 and Young 1990).[2] Such nuances were to become apparent to me later.

Examining Media Depictions of Muslims

MAB: In your opinion, what can communication studies contribute to shaping or critiquing representations of Islam and Muslims in the so-called pluralist context of Canada?

KHK: I graduated with a major in Islamic studies from Columbia but with a state of mind that was increasingly troubled by the way that Islam was being examined in Western academia. The momentum that had propelled me since my youth in Kenya sent me next to McGill University to pursue a master's degree in the same field. I proposed a thesis on Western portrayals of Muslims, but the Institute of Islamic Studies' faculty members declined, saying that the department only studied Islam from within. We settled on a mutually agreeable MA topic, but my soul searching intensified. I eventually crossed the campus to pursue doctoral work at another program. Unlike Islamic studies, the relatively new discipline of communication studies seemed to provide an apt, if precarious, site from which to launch my scrutiny of the construction of "Islams." At that time communication studies was so engaged in intellectual reflexivity that it questioned its own legitimacy as an academic endeavour. This was the period when postmodernism was in full flower, questioning the modernist certainties of knowledge and challenging the very ground on which scholarly disciplines stood. I hung on for dear life in this turbulent environment that was set on centrifugally rearranging my brain's neural connections.

Said's work provided the intellectual framework for my research in the midst of this instability. The groundbreaking *Orientalism* (Said 1978), which presented a substantial exposition of his critique of Islamic and Middle Eastern studies, also challenged other areas of the humanities and the social sciences. More pertinently for me, Said had opened an enquiry into media presentations in his 1981 *Covering Islam*. Research into the representation of various groups was steadily gaining pace in communication studies. The field's inherent interdisciplinarity opened up space for new enquiries. Cultural studies, which is closely linked to the study of communication, provided me with the intellectual and methodological rigour to develop one of the earliest large-scale examinations of the representations of Muslims in the media. My doctoral thesis and later book, *Islamic Peril: Media and Global Violence* (2000b, 2003a), put forward a theoretical and analytical framework for studying journalistic productions of Muslims. Its empirical evidence, drawn from material covering two decades, presented an extensive body of findings. *Islamic Peril*, which was published in an updated edition in 2003, has become a standard international reference on the reporting of violence and terrorism. These developments helped provide confirmation that my academic journey was on the right track.

Even though the research for the award-winning *Islamic Peril* was conducted in the 1990s, its findings still appear to have currency, as evidenced in continuing citations of the book in new publications. Other writings of mine on this topic (Karim 1997, 2000a, 2002a, 2004, 2006a, 2008, 2011b, 2012) have strived to analyse carefully the patterns in the ongoing Western coverage of Muslims. In order to make a case about Western journalism's problems with respect to reporting on Muslims, it has been important to examine large and varied bodies of coverage methodically. This approach has helped to reveal particular tendencies in the use of language and imagery, the uneven treatment of the various religions' adherents, the systematic unwarranted attributions of Islam to politically or culturally motivated actions, the ideological and ethnocentric forms of coverage, and the resilience of dominantly negative discourses on Muslims.

This research has demonstrated the ingrained nature of centuries-old Western core stereotypes (topoi) about Muslims (violence, lust, greed, and barbarism), which had appeared in classic literature, Romantic-era paintings, silent films, and other media. These topoi were even more intensively reproduced by the mass media following the Cold War as the Muslim was made the primary Other. After the 9/11 attacks, the age-old frameworks for viewing Muslims were hyper-energized. There is a continuity that can be traced from medieval images of the Arab or Turk attacking Europeans with a sword in one hand and the Qur'an in the other to contemporary editorial cartoons of the Muslim extremist holding an automatic rifle and the holy book. The general figure of the terrorist has become conflated with that of Muslims to such an extent that terrorism by persons who are not Muslim is viewed as being abnormal. Terrorism's history is erased when terms such as "home-grown terrorists" are exclusively applied to local adherents of Islam carrying out political violence. Commentators forget that late twentieth-century groups such as the Front de libération du Québec in Canada, the Jewish Defense League in the US, the Irish Republican Army in Northern Ireland, the Red Army Faction in Germany, the Euskadi Ta Askatasuna in Spain, the Aum Shinrikyo in Japan, the Tamil Tigers in Sri Lanka, and the Sendero Luminoso in Peru were also home-grown terrorists. There also seems to be great reluctance in naming as terrorism the extensive political violence of contemporary far-right-wing groups and individuals in Western countries, which has grown exponentially. My more recent work has examined these issues in public discourses and has scrutinized the terminology used by media and government to speak about "Islam" and Muslims (Eid and Karim 2014a, 2014b, 2014c; Karim, 2010b; Karim and Eid 2014a, 2014b, 2014c).

MAB: In your short intervention in a *Producing Islam(s) in Canada* podcast (Omstead 2018), you briefly explain why you chose to study media coverage and practices of Islam in Canada. In *Islamic Peril: Media and Global Violence* (2003a), you more specifically note that a significant part of the Canadian mass media's coverage of Muslim societies involves an interpretation of Muslim responses to the North's, often American, cultural, ideological, economic, and military influence over those parts of the world.

KHK: The Western self is viewed as the actor from whom all important thought and actions originate; the other, who supposedly has little agency, merely reacts to them. The general tendency is for Canadians to understand "Islams" from the perspective of the dominant Canadian or North American Self, rather than from the viewpoint of Muslims. West-centric, and particularly US-centric, views tend to dominate Canadian coverage. It is commonplace for developments in Muslim societies to be covered by Washington-based Canadian correspondents, who foreground the White House's and Congress's perspectives. Muslims' own world views, their aspirations for a good life, their concerns about the future, and so on, often appear to be of minimal interest. Events taking place abroad in Muslim-majority societies (or in other southern countries) which are perceived as not having a bearing on North America or Europe are given little attention. The self's view of others, therefore, normatively takes place only through the calculation of its own interests. This is also a tendency among many Muslims in their perceptions of Western societies. However, Western perceptions of the Muslim other have much greater global influence than Muslims' views about the Western other.

It is important to emphasize, however, that I hold to the position that one cannot attribute these tendencies to a consciously orchestrated media conspiracy in which people are centrally directed how to present Muslims in their writings. The tendencies are rather the result of the ways in which mainstream journalism is structured and in the cultural practices of media workers, as I show in *Islamic Peril* and other writings on the topic, such as "Covering Muslims: Journalism as Cultural Practice" (Karim 2011b). The cultural studies scholar Stuart Hall's (e.g ., 1980) thought on this matter has informed my work. It is vital to understand the roles that capital, politics, and ideology (including nationalism and religion) play in the manners that information is assembled, interpreted, and disseminated. A dominant discourse does prevail – but it is not monolithic nor is it omnipotent. It continually has to compete with other kinds of narrative (oppositional, alternative, populist) to maintain its hegemony. Dominant discourses are usually successful in overcoming others because they are sustained by the resources of powerful interests and the resilience of age-old perceptions to support them. My work on this topic and similar endeavours by colleagues[3] in Canada and elsewhere are merely the beginning of a conversation which, due to persistent tendencies in coverage, will continue into the future. It has been particularly gratifying to have supervised several doctoral students who are now professors also engaged in this scholarly dialogue. Several dissertations that I am overseeing currently are addressing the production of "Islams" in digital media. Students' fresh insights, as well as the questions from journalists and audiences of public lectures that I deliver in various countries, continually challenge and sharpen my thinking.

The Clash of Ignorance Thesis

MAB: In "Clash of Ignorance" (Karim and Eid 2012) you criticize Huntington's (1996) clash of civilizations thesis. You highlight that "to present the hugely pluralist 'West' and 'Islam' as static, monolithic entities is to misunderstand the dynamics of culture" (9). In light of this point, can you describe how you understand and categorize West and Islam in your scholarly work? How do tensions about the clashes contribute to academic work on Islam and Muslims in a Canadian context?

KHK: The "clash of ignorance" has become a major area of research for me; it is a term that I first heard in the discourse of Aga Khan IV (2002). Edward Said (2001) appears to have coined it in a magazine article he published six weeks after the 9/11 attacks. It was a counterargument to Samuel Huntington's (1996) politically influential "clash of civilizations" thesis. There has emerged a general scholarly consensus that the latter idea does not provide an informed way to analyse the conflict between segments of Western and Muslim civilizations (Bulliet 2004; Fox 2002; Matlock 1999; Rubenstein and Crocker 1994).[4] Its causes can be understood as stemming largely from ignorance rather than being the natural and inevitable outcomes of cultural or religious difference. Clashes are often produced by fear of the other as well as by not knowing that good Western-Muslim relations have been the rule rather than the exception over many centuries. Even more troubling is that ignorance is actively manipulated by various actors to exacerbate conflict. Comments on my work on the clash of ignorance (Karim and Eid 2012) from colleagues and from students around the world who read it for their courses continue to help enhance my thinking on this topic.

The examination of Western media coverage of Muslim societies has required the scrutiny of dominant meanings attached to terms such as "the West" and "the Muslim world." Whereas both of these regions have dominant groups and tendencies, they are characterized by a rich internal diversity. The general idea of "the West" as a unitary civilization with an exclusive cultural connection to the history of Europe begins to break down when examined closely. In our times one can clearly see it as multicultural and multi-religious; but history also shows that non-European peoples and ideas have been present in Western societies, including Europe, for millennia. My work on the use of media by diasporas in Western societies, including those of Muslim backgrounds, has examined how they express their identities away from homelands (Karim 2002b, 2003c, 2006b, 2007, 2010a, 2018a). Such self-perceptions are of significance because Muslim diasporas living in Western societies are part of worldwide "Islams" as well as part of the "the West."

Like those of "the West," uses of the terms "Islam," "the Muslim world," or "the ummah" to mean a monolithic religious community, civilization, or geopolitical bloc are misleading. As noted previously, Aziz Al-Azmeh (1993) asserts that "there are as many Islams as there are situations that sustain it" (1). Whereas the followers of Islam generally adhere to a certain set of common beliefs, there is a vast plurality not only in cultural but also in religious behaviour among Muslims living around the world. Additionally, there is no country that is homogeneously Muslim. Nevertheless, "the Muslim world" and "the West" are generally imagined in dominant (Muslim and Western) discourses as fixed, clearly demarcated entities and as having monolithic sets of residents. John Hobson states that "rather than treating civilizations as autonomous and self-contained, self-generating entities that are often diametrically opposed, I shall treat the Muslim and Western worlds as promiscuous civilizations that are significantly 'other-generated' as they entwine in mutually co-constitutive and promiscuous ways" (Hobson 2014, 77). My own writing seeks to avoid applying terms such as "the West" and "the Muslim world" that seem to validate the idea of monolithic blocs or categories. It instead uses alternative terminology such as "Western societies" and "Muslim-majority countries" that encourage readers to conceive of them both as being multicultural and multi-religious entities, which is what they are in reality.

MAB: Do these issues occur in the study of Muslims in Canada?

KHK: An American scholar whom I will not name and who was looking for authors to pen chapters for a book that she was editing about Muslim communities in various Western countries in the early 2000s approached me to write one on Canada. One of the central questions she asked me to address was "Who in Canada speaks for Islam?" This struck me as deeply problematic, not just in the Canadian context but for any country – since there is significant diversity of Muslims in states around the world. No single group or organization can speak for Islam in its various forms. Yet there is no shortage of bodies that are named in such a way as to give the impression that they represent all Muslims in a particular country. Unfortunately, journalists and policymakers do not realize that some persons who present themselves as the heads of "Islamic" organizations are actually running outfits with tiny memberships. Conversely, a number of significant Muslim communities are left out of articles and books written by academics who ostensibly seek to provide an overview of the practice of Islam across Canada. It is vital that scholars not be caught up in forms of thinking that give exclusive validation only to certain Muslim groups and organizations and, as a consequence, increase the marginalization of others. As already discussed, integrity is vital to intellectual endeavours, as it is in other aspects of life. I have sought to ensure in my research and writing, in teaching and supervision of students, and in organizing initiatives at the Carleton Centre for the Study of Islam to be as inclusive of the multiplicity of perspectives on Islam as possible.

Ismaili Studies

MAB: In "Pluralism, Migration, Space and Song: Ismaili Arrangements of Public and Private Spheres," you claim that "pluralism is promoted as a primary value by Ismaili institutions" in Canada (2013, 148). You argue that pluralism is one of the main premises of Aga Khan's discourses. Moreover, in your book chapter, "At the Interstices of Tradition, Modernity and Postmodernity: Ismaili Engagements with Contemporary Canadian Society," you say "Ismailis in Canada find themselves engaged in a tripartite 'dialectic' of tradition, modernity and postmodernity ... Members of the community view their tradition as the source of guidance for the ethical conduct of their lives in Western contexts" (2011a, 289). In light of these contributions, how do you see Ismailis participating in shaping an image of Islam in Canada? How do you situate Canadian Ismailis and this project in the broader context of "Islams" in Canada?

KHK: Following a two-year sabbatical leave from 2009 to 2011, during which I served as co-director of the Institute of Ismaili Studies in the UK, I began conducting research on and publishing about the Shi'a Ismaili Muslim tradition in which I was raised (Karim 2011a, 2011c, 2013, 2014a, 2015a, 2015b, 2016). Its intellectual impulses had originally given me the incentive to pursue Islamic studies. The concerns that the Aga Khan (the hereditary Ismaili imam) expressed in the early 1980s about the depictions of Muslims (Aga Khan IV n.d.) steered me towards studying the production of "Islams." The challenge of being self-reflective in addressing one's subjectivities arose in a more specific way in the process of writing about Ismaili engagements with the contemporary world. One of the manners in which I have sought to deal with this issue is to apply the very standards with which the community has identified itself, like those of pluralism, ethics, and truth. For example, my book chapter "Pluralism, Migration, Space and Song" (Karim 2013) juxtaposes the Ismaili discourse on pluralism with its lack of attention to the amazing manifestation of pluralism in the community's own historical experience in South Asia; "Aga Khan Development Network: Shia Ismaili Islam" (Karim 2014a) addresses the apparent lapses in ethics; and the article "A Semiotics of Infinite Translucence: The Exoteric and Esoteric in Ismaili Muslim Hermeneutics" (Karim 2015b) enquires into the seeming contradictions of Ismaili institutions' public and private presentations of the communal self. The medieval Ismaili Fatimids referred to their proselytizing mission as *Da'wat al-Haqq* ("Call to Truth") (Klemm and Walker 2011, 1) and my own ancestral Indian Ismaili tradition is called Satpanth ("Path of Truth"). This engagement with truth led to the development of a number of discourses on ethics in Ismaili history. Addressing problems of subjectivity in this case therefore appears to be facilitated here by the object of study itself, which promotes the adherence to truth and ethics. These are the standards by which the group apparently wants to be judged. However, my critical analyses of the community are not appreciated by some of its members.

Multiculturalism

MAB: Before joining Carleton University as a faculty member in 1998, you worked in the Canadian federal government as a policy officer and researcher for a decade. You published several papers on topics relating to multiculturalism during that time. How did that experience contribute to your work in academia?

KHK: One way in which several countries have sought to deal with the fear of the other is through multiculturalism policies. While remaining contentious, they provide rich possibilities for the inclusion of marginalized cultural groups into the larger societal self. Canada has grappled with the often-contradictory impetuses of colonialism, British-French hegemony, and cultural pluralism. Prior to 9/11, the federal government's relations with its Muslim population had come into sharp focus during the 1991 Gulf War, in which Canada, among several other countries, was involved. I was tasked to work in a team that sought to ensure harmonious relations among Muslim, Jewish, Christian, and other Canadian communities. This involved organizing consultations with organizations and conducting research on portrayals of Muslims in Canada and elsewhere (Karim 1991). The government is obliged to respond to the concerns of community groups under the policy of multiculturalism. However, this has not always been smooth sailing. There were multiple abuses of Muslims by police and security agencies in the aftermath of the 11 September 2001 attacks (Abu-Laban and Nath 2007; Byers and Jones 2007).

I continue to draw on the knowledge and experience gained during my time in government from 1989 to 1998. During the 2015 federal election, Prime Minister Stephen Harper and his cabinet members pursued divisive tactics by promoting the view that certain practices which they termed "barbaric" were endemic among Muslim Canadians (Andrew-Gee 2015). Quebec's prohibition against wearing religious symbols in the public sector has also caused problems (Authier 2017). My research on this topic (2008) enquired into the ostensible separation of church and state and examined a series of controversies involving adherents of certain religions in various provinces. Apart from investigating controversies in Quebec such as those regarding prayer on school grounds, the wearing of kirpans by Sikh males in schools, the erection of succah huts by Orthodox Jews, the request by Hassidic Jewish males to have the YMCA conceal the sight of exercising women, the discomfort of Hassidic males in speaking to female police officers, privacy of swimming lessons for Muslim females, the wearing of hijabs by women engaging in certain sports, the accommodation of the religious dietary requirements of Muslims at a sugar shack, and requests from some Hindus, Muslims, and Sikhs for specific prenatal classes for women only, the study also looked at cases in other provinces. These included the proposal of some Ontario Muslim organizations to use the sharia in family arbitration, the exemption from wearing a helmet at Ontario amusement parks for Sikh males with turbans, government enquiries in British Columbia into sexual abuse in a polygamist Mormon community, the objections of Hutterites in Alberta to have their pictures on drivers' licences, and the Canadian Jewish Congress's objection to a Nova Scotia town declaring December to be the Christmas season.

Future Projects

MAB: Can you share thoughts about some of your future projects?

KHK: I will have the opportunity to consolidate my experience with multiculturalism as a government policy analyst and as an academic in a book that I have been commissioned to write by a British publisher for its prestigious "rethinking series" on public issues. I also plan to write about how some Muslims and adherents of other religions have misportrayed each other by manipulating the ignorance that exists in society. This work on ignorance as an epistemic problem and the current political turn towards what has been termed "post-truth" has propelled me to the study of how truth has been conceptualized in religious and secular thought. As an initial foray into this area, I delivered a conference paper (Karim 2019) on the confluence of Islamic and Vedic thought on truth in the Ismaili tradition of Satpanth and have taught undergraduate and graduate courses on communication and truth over the last two years.

Subjectivities

MAB: Any final thoughts?

KHK: Allow me to end by revisiting the issue of subjectivities. Should it be relevant whether a scholar of Islam is a Muslim or not? I do not believe it is. Some of the most insightful work in this area has been produced by non-Muslims. Despite his general critique of Orientalism, Edward Said (1978, 270) praised the non-hegemonic work of several of its major exponents, particularly Louis Massignon. Said, who died in 2003, himself was of Protestant Christian background. Yet some Muslim students hold that Islam can only be taught by Muslims, whose approach supposedly would be more authentic. A certain Muslim family that was considering a monetary donation to the Carleton Centre for the Study of Islam, of which I am the director, refused to fund lectures by non-Muslims. I ended our discussions at that point as the family's position went against Carleton University's policies and my own principles.

It causes me discomfort to be described as a Muslim (or an Ismaili) academic, which happens from time to time. I prefer to see myself as a scholar who studies Muslims and other topics. Of most significance to scholarly work is not the religious background of the researcher but the integrity that he or she brings to it. I have great respect for many non-Muslim colleagues who are engaged in the study of Islam. Their research, along with that of scholars with Muslim backgrounds, has added considerably to my understanding about the lives of Muslims. The Western study of Islam has come a long way in the forty years since Said published *Orientalism*.

NOTES

1 This does not necessarily mean the abandonment of empathy for the object of study. See Cabezón and Davaney 2004.
2 Said was indeed aware of the tendencies among Muslims to stereotype Western societies, but his critique's primary purpose was to examine how Orientalists framed Muslims.
3 For example, Ahmed Al-Rawi, Mahmoud Eid, Kai Hafez, Faiza Hirji, Yasmin Jiwani, Elizabeth Poole, and John Richardson.
4 Rubenstein and Crocker (1994) were responding to Huntington's earlier expression of his views on the clash of civilizations in a 1993 journal article.

REFERENCES

Abu-Laban, Yasmeen, and Nisha Nath. 2007. "From deportation to apology: The case of Maher Arar and the Canadian state." *Canadian Ethnic Studies, 39*(3), 71–98. https://doi.org/10.1353/ces.0.0049

Aga Khan IV. n.d. *Kalam-e-Imam-e-Zaman: Farmans to the Western world (1957–1991)*. N.p.

– 2002, 23 June. "Banquet in honour of the Governor of Texas (Houston, Texas, USA)." *The Nanowisdoms Archive of Imamat Speeches, Interviews & Writings*. http://www.nanowisdoms.org/nwblog/6256/

Al-Azmeh, Aziz. 1993. *Islams and modernities* (1st ed.). Verso.

Andrew-Gee, Eric. 2015, 2 October. "Conservatives vow to establish 'barbaric cultural practices' tip line." *Globe and Mail*. https://www.theglobeandmail.com/news/politics/conservatives-vow-to-establish-barbaric-cultural-practices-tip-line/article26640072

Arkoun, Mohammed. 1990. "Islamic cultures, developing societies, modern thought." In Hayat Salam-Liebich (Ed.), *Expressions of Islam in buildings* (pp. 49–64). Aga Khan Trust for Culture.

– 2002. *The unthought in contemporary Islamic thought*. Saqi.

Authier, Philip. 2017, 22 February. "Majority of Quebecers want ban on religious symbols: Poll." *Montreal Gazette*. https://montrealgazette.com/news/quebec/majority-of-quebecers-want-ban-on-religious-symbols-poll

Bail, Christopher. 2015. *Terrified: How anti-Muslim fringe organizations became mainstream*. Princeton University Press.

Bulliet, Richard W. 2004. *The case for Islamo-Christian civilization*. Columbia University Press.

Buruma, Ian, and Avishai Margalit. 2005. *Occidentalism: The West in the eyes of its enemies*. Penguin.

Byers, Bryan D., and James A. Jones. 2007. "The impact of the terrorist attacks of 9/11 on anti-Islamic hate crime." *Journal of Ethnicity in Criminal Justice, 5*(1), 43–56. https://doi.org/10.1300/J222v05n01_03

Cabezón, José Ignacio, and Sheila Greeve Davaney. 2004. *Identity and the politics of scholarship in the study of religion*. Routledge.

Eid, Mahmoud, and Karim H. Karim. 2014a. "Engaging the Other." In Karim H. Karim and Mahmoud Eid (Eds.), *Engaging the Other: Public policy and Western-Muslim intersections* (pp. 1–15). Palgrave Macmillan. https://doi.org/10.1057/9781137403698

– 2014b. "Public policy and the clash of ignorance." In Karim H. Karim and Mahmood Eid (Eds.), *Engaging the Other: Public policy and Western-Muslim intersections* (pp. 213–25). Palgrave Macmillan. https://doi.org/10.1057/9781137403698

– (Eds.). 2014c. *Re-imagining the Other: Culture, media, and Western-Muslim intersections*. Palgrave Macmillan.

Fox, Jonathan. 2002. "Ethnic minorities and the clash of civilizations: A quantitative analysis of Huntington's thesis." *British Journal of Political Science, 32*(3), 415–34. https://doi.org/10.1017/S0007123402000170

Hall, Stuart. 1980. "Encoding/decoding." In Stuart Hall, Dorothy Hobson, Andrew Lowe, and Paul Willis (Eds.), *Culture, media, language* (pp. 136–7). Routledge. https://doi.org/10.4324/9780203381182

Halliday, Fred. 1996. *Islam and the myth of confrontation: Religion and politics in the Middle East*. Tauris.

Hobson, John. 2014. "The clash of civilizations 2.0." In Mahmood Eid and Karim H. Karim (Eds.), *Re-imagining the Other: Culture, media, and Western-Muslim intersections* (pp. 75–97). Palgrave Macmillan.

Huntington, Samuel P. 1996. *The clash of civilizations and the remaking of world order*. Simon and Schuster.

Karim, Karim H. 1991. *Images of Arabs and Muslims: A research review*. Images of minorities: research reviews. Policy & Research, Multiculturalism Branch, Multiculturalism & Citizenship, Government of Canada.

– 1997. "The historical resilience of primary stereotypes: Core images of the Muslim Other." In Stephen Harold Riggins (Eds.), *The language and politics of exclusion: Others in discourse* (pp. 153–82). SAGE.

– 2000a. "Covering the South Caucasus and Bosnian conflicts." In Abbas Malek and Anandam P. Kavoori (Eds.), *The global dynamics of foreign news: Studies in international news coverage and news agenda* (pp. 177–96). Ablex.

– 2000b. *Islamic peril: Media and global violence* (1st ed.). Black Rose Books.
– 2002a. "Making sense of the Islamic peril: Journalism as cultural practice." In Barbie Zelizer (Ed.), *Journalism after September 11* (1st ed., pp. 101–16). Routledge.
– 2002b. "Muslim encounters with new media." In Ali Mohammadi (Ed.), *Islam encountering globalisation* (pp. 36–60). Routledge. https://doi.org/10.4324/9780203037584
– 2003a. *Islamic peril: Media and global violence* (2nd ed.). Black Rose Books.
– 2003b. "Mapping diasporic mediascapes." In Karim H. Karim (Eds.), *The media of diaspora* (pp. 1–17). Routledge.
– 2003c. *The media of diaspora*. Routledge.
– 2004. "War, propaganda, and Islam in Muslim and Western sources." In Yahya R. Kamalipour and Nancy Snow (Eds.), *War, media, and propaganda: A global perspective* (pp. 107–16). Rowman & Littlefield.
– 2006a. "American media's coverage of Muslims." In Elizabeth Poole and John E. Richardson (Eds.), *Muslims and the news media* (pp. 116–27). I.B. Tauris.
– 2006b. "Globalization, transnational communication and diaspora." In Paul Michael Attallah and Leslie Regan Shade (Eds.), *Mediascapes: New patterns in Canadian communication* (2nd ed., pp. 272–94). Thomson Nelson.
– 2007. "Media and diaspora." In Eoin Devereux (Ed.), *Media studies: Key issues and debates* (pp. 361–79). SAGE.
– 2008. "Press, public sphere, and pluralism: Multiculturalism debates in Canadian English-language newspapers." *Canadian Ethnic Studies Journal, 40*(1), 57–78. https://doi.org/10.1353/ces.0.0074
– 2010a. "Media and diasporas." In Kim Knott and Seán McLoughlin (Eds.), *Diasporas: Concepts, intersections, identities* (pp. 162–6). Zed Books.
– 2010b. "Self and Other in a time of terror." In Tareq Y. Ismael and Andrew Rippin (Eds.), *Islam in the eyes of the West: Images and realities in an age of terror* (pp. 160–76). Routledge.
– 2011a. "At the interstices of tradition, modernity and postmodernity: Ismaili engagements with contemporary Canadian society." In Farhad Daftary (Ed.), *A modern history of the Ismailis: Continuity and change in a Muslim community* (pp. 265–94). I.B. Tauris.
– 2011b. "Covering Muslims: Journalism as cultural practice." In Barbie Zelizer and Stuart Allan (Eds.), *Journalism after September 11* (2nd ed., pp. 131–46). Routledge.
– 2011c. "Muslim migration, institutional development and geographic imagination: The Aga Khan Development Network's transnationalism." In Joan DeBardeleben and Achim Hurrelmann (Eds.), *Transnational Europe: Promise, paradox, limits* (pp. 205–21). Palgrave Macmillan.
– 2012. "The legends of the 'assassins' in news coverage of Muslims." In Diane Winston (Ed.), *The Oxford handbook of religion and the American news media* (pp. 229–42). Oxford University Press.

– 2013. "Pluralism, migration, space and song: Ismaili arrangements of public and private spheres." In Susan L.T. Ashley (Ed.), *Diverse spaces: Identity, heritage and community in Canadian public culture* (pp. 148–69). Cambridge Scholars Publishing.

– 2014a. "Aga Khan Development Network: Shia Ismaili Islam." In Stephen M. Cherry and Helen Rose Ebaugh (Eds.), *Global religious movements across borders* (pp. 143–60). Routledge.

– 2014b. "Islamic, Islamist, moderate, extremist." In Mahmoud Eid and Karim H. Karim (Eds.), *Re-imagining the Other: Culture, media, and Western-Muslim intersections* (pp. 89–109). Palgrave Macmillan.

– 2015a. "A Muslim modernity: Ismaili engagements with Western societies." In Roberto Tottoli (Ed.), *Routledge handbook of Islam in the West* (pp. 244–58). Routledge.

– 2015b. "A semiotics of infinite translucence: The exoteric and esoteric in Ismaili Muslim hermeneutics." *Canadian Journal of Communication, 40*(1), 11–28. https://doi.org/10.22230/cjc.2015v40n1a2861

– 2015c. "Speaking to post-secular society: The Aga Khan's public discourse." In Nurjehan Aziz (Ed.), *The relevance of Islamic identity in Canada: Culture, politics, and self* (pp. 97–107). Mawenzi House.

– 2016. "Shia Ismaili leadership: Past and present." *American Journal of Islamic Social Sciences, 33*(2), 102–12. http://doi.org/10.12816/0037443

– 2018a. "Migration, diaspora and communication." In Karim H. Karim and Ahmed K. Al-Rawi (Eds.), *Diaspora and media in Europe: Migration, identity, and integration* (pp. 1–23). Palgrave Macmillan.

– 2018b. "Sustaining and enhancing life." In Amyn B. Sajoo (Ed.), *The shari'a: History, ethics and law* (pp. 59–79). I.B. Tauris.

– 2019, 30 January. *The quest for truth in Satpanth* [Conference paper]. Khōjā Studies Conference, University of Mumbai, Mumbai, India.

Karim, Karim H., and Ahmed Al-Rawi (Eds.) 2018. *Diaspora and media in Europe: Migration, identity, and integration*. Springer International Publishing.

Karim, Karim H., and Mahmoud Eid. 2012. "Clash of ignorance." *Global Media Journal, 5*(1), 7–27.

– 2014a. *Engaging the Other: Public policy and Western-Muslim intersections*. Palgrave Macmillan.

– 2014b. "Imagining the Other." In Mahmoud Eid and Karim H. Karim (Eds.), *Re-imagining the Other: Culture, media, and Western-Muslim intersections* (pp. 1–21). Palgrave Macmillan.

– 2014c. "Re-imagining the Other." In Mahmoud Eid and Karim H. Karim (Eds.), *Re-imagining the Other: Culture, media, and Western-Muslim intersections* (pp. 217–31). Palgrave Macmillan.

Klemm, Verena, and Paul Walker (Eds. and Trans.). 2011. *A code of conduct: A treatise on the etiquette of the Fatimid Ismaili Mission*. I.B. Tauris.

Matlock, Jack. 1999. "Can civilizations clash?" *Proceedings of the American Philosophical Society, 143*(3), 428–39.

Omstead, Jordan. 2018. "Foreign fighters and Muslim masculinities." *Producing Islam(s) in Canada* [podcast]. https://soundcloud.com/user-375255614/foreign-fighters-and-muslim-masculinities

Rubenstein, Richard E., and Jarle Crocker. 1994. "Challenging Huntington." *Foreign Policy, 96*, 113–28. https://doi.org/10.2307/1149220

Said, Edward. 1976, 31 October. "Arabs, Islam and the dogmas of the West." *New York Times*. https://www.nytimes.com/1976/10/31/archives/arabs-islam-and-the-dogmas-of-the-west-arabs.html

– 1978. *Orientalism*. Vintage Books.

– 1981. *Covering Islam: How the media and the experts determine how we see the rest of the world* (rev. ed.). Vintage Books.

– 2001. "The clash of ignorance." *The Nation, 273*(12), 11–13.

Sardar, Ziauddin. 2003. "The shari'ah as a problem-solving methodology." In Sohail Inayatullah and Gail Boxwell (Eds.), *Islam, postmodernism, and other futures: A Ziauddin Sardar reader* (pp. 64–80). Pluto Press.

Selby, Jennifer, Amélie Barras, and Lori G. Beaman. 2018. *Beyond accommodation: Everyday narratives of Muslim Canadians*. University of British Columbia Press.

Young, Robert. 1990. *White mythologies: Writing history and the West*. Routledge.

The Relational Approach to Integration in Canada: An Interview with Abdie Kazemipur

SARA HAMED

Biography

Abdolmohammad (Abdie) Kazemipur is a professor of sociology at the University of Calgary in Alberta, Canada, and the current president of the Canadian Sociological Association. Previously, he held the Stephen Jarislowsky Chair in Culture Change at Memorial University in Newfoundland and subsequently became a University Scholar Research Chair in the social sciences at the University of Lethbridge. Kazemipur has also founded two Statistics Canada Research Data Centres, one during his time at Lethbridge and the other during his post at Memorial University, and is currently the academic director of the University of Calgary's Research Date Centre. In addition to his various academic positions and affiliations, Kazemipur has authored eight monographs – the ninth is currently in press – and dozens of journal articles and book chapters on his two principal research contexts, the Middle East and Canada, writing in both English and Persian.

His work on the Middle East focuses on religious developments and socio-economic trends in Iran, and to a lesser extent in Egypt and Turkey. In Canada, his work centres on the socio-economic experiences of immigrants and minorities, with a special interest in Muslim integration. In his John Porter Award–winning book, *The Muslim Question in Canada: A Story of Segmented Integration* (2014), Kazemipur uses both interviews with Muslims and statistical data to underscore the socio-economic challenges facing contemporary Muslims in Canada. He concludes that academics and policymakers concerned with the successful integration of Muslim immigrants into broader Canadian society need to shift their attention to sociological explanations of Muslims' behaviours instead of trying to find the origins of those behaviours in Islamic theology. He argues that rather than seek to understand Muslims by demystifying, revising, and reinterpreting the doctrines and practices of Islam to make room for Canadian cultural mores, studies concerned with integration should focus on understanding the social and economic obstacles that Muslims face and respond to every day (Kazemipur 2014).

Building on the book's call to turn to sociological explanations, Kazemipur has written extensively on the advent of *Fiqh al-Aqalliyat* (Jurisprudence of Muslim Minorities) and its place in the lives of Canadian Muslims (Kazemipur 2016). In "Bringing the Social Back In: On the Integration of Muslim Immigrants and the Jurisprudence of Muslim Minorities," he discusses minority *fiqh* as an example of how Muslims' conceptualizations and formulations of their faith are constantly evolving in response to the social and economic demands of life in the West, and Canada more specifically. For Kazemipur, the discourses of minority jurisprudence demonstrate that Muslims' understanding of Islam is not simply a static force that unilaterally operates on passive recipients, but rather it is one of many social variables present in the lives of Muslims. More importantly, the contents of these discourses demonstrate Muslims' attempts to modify their *fiqh* as a result of their decision to interact with non-Muslims. Minority *fiqh*, Kazemipur argues, is driven in part by positive interactions between Muslim immigrants and a largely non-Muslim Canadian population. Thus, impediments to such positive interactions must be identified and resolved in order to create the conditions for successful Muslim immigrant integration.

To this end, Kazemipur identifies the social and economic problems facing Muslims in Canada and highlights their effects on the question of integration (Kazemipur 2014, 2016, 2017a, 2017b). His studies show that there has been a disproportionate preoccupation with the principle of freedom in discussions of Muslim integration in Canada at the expense of the equally important concepts of equality and solidarity. Further, he compellingly demonstrates that the freedom issue is inextricably linked to the de facto problems of equality and solidarity plaguing Canadian Muslim communities: Muslims in Canada experience persistent economic disadvantages (in comparison to the average Canadian population) such as higher unemployment rates and lower wages. Moreover, their communities are characterized by social isolation from the national majority. For Kazemipur, successful integration depends largely on a balance between considerations of freedom, equality, and solidarity but even more so on the creation of emotional bonds with the non-Muslim majority (Kazemipur 2014). In this way, his work offers both policymakers and Muslims alike an overview of Muslims' socio-economic realities as well as a compelling case for "the relational approach to integration" (Kazemipur 2013).

Besides his academic writing, Kazemipur is frequently called upon to address minority and immigrant matters in Canada as well as issues related to religion in the Middle East by various media outlets. His work has been featured in the *Globe and Mail*, the *Toronto Star*, *National Post*, *Christian Science Monitor*, *Asia Times*, *La Presse*, *El Confidencial*, and the *Star Calgary*, among others. Kazemipur's various academic and media interventions provide much-needed empirical clarity to the question of Muslim integration in Canada and the not-unrelated subject of Islamic religious developments in the Middle East.

Interview

Sara Hamed [SH]: Resoundingly, in your sociologically based research, you call for a move from focusing on "theology" to highlighting "the social" (Kazemipur 2014, 180). Instead of working to unpack and revise the fundamental tenets of Islam, you advocate looking at the social and economic factors that colour interactions between Muslims and non-Muslims in Canada to resolve "the Muslim question" of integration (180). Drawing on large-scale statistical data and face-to-face interviews, your 2014 book, *The Muslim Question in Canada*, underscores "successful integration" (189) as the desirable socio-economic end goal or state of affairs, implying that it has not yet fully occurred. How has your mixed-methodology (qualitative and quantitative) approach enabled you to undertake these analyses? In your opinion, what is the value of a mixed methodology when producing knowledge on Islam and Muslims in Canada?

Abdie Kazemipur [AK]: My call for the need to shift the focus of our thinking and theorizing about Muslim minorities from "theology" to "social" was directly based on the findings of both my quantitative and qualitative data. These data demonstrated the significant diversity that exists within Canadian Muslim communities with regard to their experiences as immigrant or religious minority groups in Canada; the changes that have or have not happened in these experiences over time; and the diverse, unique, and innovative ways in which individual Muslims are negotiating the teachings of their faith with the realities of their lives in Canada. This diversity and its dynamic quality run completely against the almost omnipresent assumption that to understand the lives and behaviours of Muslims in any context, one needs to understand Islam and, as a corollary, that any changes in those lives and behaviours have to start from a change in their religious beliefs. This is an unfortunate consequence of the post-9/11 environment in which people, policymakers, and even some academics were rushing to understand Muslim realities in a fast and simple way. As you might know, for many months after 9/11, the Qur'an was among the *New York Times* best-seller books in North America. I remember having had been invited to several community gatherings after 9/11 to talk about Muslims and the Muslim world, and almost 70 per cent of the attendees were holding an English translation of the Qur'an with many verses highlighted and pages bookmarked. This assumption was also partly the reason behind the proliferation of Islamic studies positions in various universities.

Paying attention to the social has another – methodological – component as well. If we accept that the opinions and behaviours of Muslims, like everybody else's, are shaped in response to, or in conversation with, their surrounding environment, then we need to have a methodology that would allow us to capture this broader environment. This analysis is not achievable using mere textual analysis or an exclusive reliance on qualitative methodologies. As we know, there is a division in the social sciences research community over the use of quantitative or qualitative methods – a division that I believe is both unhealthy and unproductive. Many researchers, at least in sociology departments that I am more familiar with, chose their methodologies in graduate school and they have simply continued with that choice. As a result, they only take on the research questions that could be studied qualitatively. I think we have to, first, think about our research questions on the basis of where the field is and what kind of issues are at the leading edges of the field; then, we need to choose the kind of data that are able to address those questions; and, finally, we should choose the right methodology for that kind of data. The current practice seems to follow an opposite process. So I would like to add a methodological suggestion to my previously mentioned conceptual proposition as well: that is, the need to shift from exclusively qualitative or quantitative methods to mixed methods. Given the current status of the field of research on Muslims in Canada (or what has been published to the greatest extent to date), this means a need for more quantitative research. This is a call not for abandoning qualitative, textual, and discourse analyses, which make up the bulk of the existing research on Muslims in Canada and elsewhere, but for complementing them with quantitative data.

SH: Relatedly, what does "successful integration" comprise, in your estimation? In terms of integration, according to the most recent quantitative data from Statistics Canada, how were Muslims faring in 2018, four years after the publication of your book *The Muslim Question in Canada: A Story of Segmented Integration*, in which you suggest the complementarity of equality, solidarity, and freedom (Kazemipur 2014, 188)? Can you share some of the trends you see?

AK: I have discussed in the book that the litmus test of integration is the development of "emotional attachment" between the minorities and the majority – in this case, Muslim and non-Muslim Canadians. The previous studies have focused on things such as securing the freedom of expression and religion, as well as improving the economic performances of the minorities, as signs of integration. For me, these are extremely important, but they do not constitute integration itself; they are simply means towards the development of emotional attachment, which I consider to be the true indicator of integration.

Now, the image that was provided in the book was based mostly on the data from the previous decade. The more recent data – including the new census data of 2011, the second survey of Canadian Muslims by Environics in 2016, and newly crafted combined immigration and taxation data (reported in Evra and Kazemipur 2019) – give a mixed image for the 2010s. While most of the indicators of social and economic integration have either worsened or remained the same, Muslims seemed to have developed a stronger sense of belonging to Canada. How could this paradoxical situation be explained?

In a 2018 publication, I argued that the improvement that has occurred has been due to two factors: the worse conditions of Muslims in other Western countries (including in Western Europe and in the US) and the worse conditions of Canadian Muslims under the Conservatives (2006–15). In other words, the sources of a more positive attitude among Muslims towards Canada have been exogenous to their day-to-day experiences and mostly the consequence of a "relative advantage" (the flip side of the "relative deprivation"). Therefore, I believe that, in the absence of real changes on the ground, such feelings will be short-lived.

SH: In your chapter "Religion in Canadian Ethnic Landscape: The Muslim Factor," you explain the importance of a shift from a "deterministic to relational perspective" to develop "a better understanding of the nature of the relationship between Muslims and non-Muslims in western liberal democracies" (Kazemipur 2018, 264). You write that this shift allows for the consideration of "economic, political, and social elements" (263) in the examination of inter-group relationships that are otherwise overlooked, creating the false impression that Muslims are moved and shaped only by their religion. While this shift underscores the importance of context, by depending on the Muslim/non-Muslim distinction, does it not also reinscribe the assumption you set out to challenge by categorizing all Muslim immigrants principally under their faith banner?

AK: The diversity of experiences "within" the Muslim population is an important issue that should be addressed in the research; and it would be a major mistake to overlook that. But the "within-group" diversity has to be added to, and not to replace, the "between-groups" differences. The main challenge in capturing the "within-group" differences, however, is the data limitation, particularly in quantitative research. By breaking down a group along too many subcategories, we soon arrive at small numbers in each combination of categories that would render the results unreliable. When such a limitation is not there, the "within-group" categories must certainly be added. In *The Muslim Question*, I have done that to some extent. But in a recent article on the income trajectory of various groups of immigrants to Canada between 2002 and 2016 (see Evra and Kazemipur 2019), I have done that much more thoroughly, as I had much more data to work with. Interestingly enough, the patterns that have emerged from this latter study show that the Muslimness of an immigrant is one of the most influential factors in determining his/her income, even after controlling for things such as immigration category, ethnic/racial background, region of origin, region of residence in Canada, the economic sector of employment, social networks, education, age, and gender. So the salience of religious background is not just a theoretical decision; rather, it is dictated by the realities on the ground. We should therefore be careful not to make the same mistake that some European countries like France have made, which is removing the variable "religion" from their data-gathering practices, simply because they think that it should not be an identity marker. But the realities on the ground show that, when it comes to issues such as treatment in the job market, in community, and in political environments, religion is an influential factor. Thinking that a feature "ought" not to play a role in one's socio-economic experiences is not quite the same as finding that it "is" not playing a role. Looking at the experiences of Muslims, in comparison to non-Muslims, is necessary and it does not mean a categorization of them or an imposition of an abstract identity on them and ignoring all their other traits – in the exact same way that looking at the experiences of visible minorities versus Whites, or women versus men, is a meaningful and necessary consideration in research.

SH: In "Reckoning with the Minority Status: On Fiqh al-aqalliyat al-Muslema (Jurisprudence of Muslim Minorities)" (2017b), you make a compelling case for the agency of Muslim communities in Canada and other Western countries. Specifically, you argue that minority jurisprudence is a vehicle through which Muslim communities push religious authorities to revise their religious interpretations in ways that appear more inclusive (Kazemipur 2017b, 31). Your intervention is an important addendum to what seems like a competing idea: the notion that minority *fiqh* has been a means for religious scholars to restore Muslims in Western societies to their religious roots (Caeiro 2011, 217). Caeiro's argument was born out of a study centred on the views of Muslim *ulama* (religious scholars), while your study draws primarily on the perspectives of members of the general Muslim population in Canada.

Is there a way to square these seemingly competing views of minority *fiqh*? Can you comment on how the production of different knowledges on Muslims and Islam is shaped by the various perspectives on Islamic law?

AK: I think both of these arguments share two common themes: (a) Muslims are not passive recipients of their religious teachings; and (b) those teachings are not an omnipotent force in shaping the Muslim lives, whether as minorities or in Muslim-majority countries. The assumptions that both of these arguments refute are the ones developed mostly by people who have not had the experience of living in Muslim-majority countries and, therefore, have not been in a position to see the intricate and dynamic relationship that exists between people and their own faith. In many of these countries, different segments of the general

Muslim population, as well as the competing factions within the ranks of the Muslim *ulama*, compete to advance their own version of what sharia and *fiqh* should look like. Depending on the effectiveness of their strategies, they may win or lose in this competition, totally or partially.

Just as an example, we need to remember the case of mujahidin in Afghanistan over the past four decades. During the Soviet occupation of Afghanistan, Western countries, including the United States, managed to present themselves to mujahidin as the "God-believer Christian" allies in the fight against the "infidel communists." Two decades later, they found themselves as the targets of a bloody campaign by many of the same mujahidin organizations. In the first period, the Westerners' campaign succeeded; in the next, it failed; during the first period, they were a part of the "faithful"; in the latter, they became the new "infidels." Another example is the concept of "religious tricks" (*hileh shar'ee*) in many Muslim countries, which refers to the ways in which people give a religiously acceptable appearance to a practice that is not necessarily consistent with the spirit of religious teachings; and by doing this, they satisfy both their own and others' religious sensibilities. In his research on Egypt, Asef Bayat (2007) shows how some Egyptian youth become more religiously disciplined in certain areas as a compensation for their laxity in other areas.

So once we start seeing religion among Muslims, like among non-Muslims, as a social phenomenon – as opposed to an abstract force standing outside history and geography – we would be able to make sense of all the above dynamics, without viewing them as contradictory. And, more importantly, it is only then that we could come up with real and realistic solutions for the problems that may be associated with Muslims.

SH: As someone who studies the social and economic experiences of Muslims in Canada and based on your recent work on minority *fiqh*, is there anything exceptional or particular about the phenomenon that has been termed the Islamic revival in the Canadian context?

AK: There are some studies, like Nagra's (2017), that suggest the presence of some kind of "Islamic revivalism" among the Canadian Muslim youth in the immediate post-9/11 environment, in a form that could be similar to the development of a "reactive ethnic identity." But this research has also shown that, first, this "reactive Muslim identity" has coexisted with a strong sense of Canadian identity in their minds; and, second, this wave has faded away gradually as we got farther away from 9/11.

It is hard to give an empirically based answer to this question, due to a lack of systematically gathered data. My theoretically based response in accordance with the sociological perspective that I mentioned before, however, tells me that such a phenomenon would be extremely limited in Canada compared to what we see in Europe or even in the US, simply because of the different socio-economic experiences of Canadian Muslims. That said, and despite a better institutional and media treatment of Muslims in Canada, I am worried about the persistence of Canadian Muslims' economic disadvantages and social isolation, which can potentially result in an intensified sense of Muslim identity at the expense of, rather than a supplement to, their Canadian identity.

SH: One of the conclusions of your study detailed in "Religion in Canadian Ethnic Landscape: The Muslim Factor" (2018) is that less emphasis should be placed in scholarly work on rectifying Canadian institutional practices and misrepresentation of Muslims in the media. Rather, more energy should be directed at "the situation of Muslims in the Canadian economy and in the community" (279). This recommendation follows from your findings that (1) Muslims report overall fair treatment in Canadian schools and other public institutions, (2) Canadian media is not markedly biased towards Muslims, and (3) Muslims' negative experiences in Canada centre on the job market and discrimination in general.

Why is challenging non-Canadian media misrepresentations in your view futile given the interconnectedness of social media and its impact on discrimination in Canada and around the world? Do you see your work playing a part in the "fine-tuning" of the Canadian economy and community you mention briefly in the conclusion (279)? Can you elaborate on what such "fine-tuning" might look like?

AK: The "fine-tuning" that I think needs to happen is in the scholarly treatment of this issue. I am aware that the university environments in Canada, and most likely in other countries as well, have a moral/philosophical/ideological bent that is more liberal and social-justice-oriented. I share those philosophies and orientations as well, but I think we should be careful to let them inform only our ideas about how things "should be," not our understanding of how things "are." The latter should be informed by the logic of objective scientific discovery, as much as it is humanly possible. The lack of caring about this distinction can result in arriving at imprecise pictures in which the possible differences between Canada and other countries, and between different domains of societal life in Canada, as well as the possible existence of positive narratives and experiences, are systematically ignored. A "fine-tuning" like this would also allow for sharper policy actions and social interventions.

Now, applying this to the issue of media representation of Muslims, the data, including the views of some umbrella Muslim organizations in Canada, suggest that Canadian media have been treating Muslims in a fairer and more balanced way, and that most of the negative contents are coming from non-Canadian media outlets. The recognition of this dual reality will have very specific implications for the strategies to choose in dealing with this problem, including creating public awareness to counter those negative media images, without pressuring Canadian media to fix a problem that may not exist. Furthermore, the above approach does not suggest that the Canadian media will always act in the same way; so our research should develop tools that would capture any possible changes in the media environment. Now, an ideologically informed view that presents the situation as one wholesome global anti-Muslim phenomenon does not take into account any such details and various possibilities and, hence, it cannot provide any specific and precise suggestions for remedial actions.

SH: In a number of publications (e.g., Kazemipur 2017b, 32; 2018, 279) you gesture at the implications of your findings on economic and social (multicultural) policymaking in Canada. However, you also have suggestions for Muslim community members, such as not over-emphasizing cultural heritage transmission (in the form of insulated Islamic schools or closed Muslim neighbourhoods [Kazemipur 2014, 182, 183]) at the expense of social interaction with non-Muslims. As you point out, your work can be used to inform both policymakers in the government and community activists (Kazemipur 2014,187).

In your opinion, what are the most significant ways in which policymakers and community activists have used your work to shape and support their various projects? Oftentimes, researchers worry about how their work might be misused and unintentionally contribute to the perpetuation of further discrimination against Muslims. Has this ever been a concern for you?

AK: Answering this question would be much easier if I had only one concern, that is, the welfare of the Muslim community. That of course is one of my concerns, but I have a bigger concern as well, and that is the issue of social justice in general, both in Canada and elsewhere. That makes me concerned about not only the welfare of the Muslim community but also the welfare of some minorities within the Muslim community, the future of the Canadian society at large, and, eventually, humanity's ability to find solutions to its current problems. I see the factually based research as the first step towards addressing all these concerns. As a human entity and like any other community, the Muslim community has its own problems that need to be addressed and discussed as well. Alongside the issue of discrimination and racism against Muslims, for instance, one should address some strands of racism and discrimination *within* the Muslim communities/societies, elements of gender inequality, religious intolerance, and so on. The only way out of this maze of competing concerns is a commitment to the facts, to the reality, and to the honest reporting of genuine findings, as well as a sensitivity to human suffering in all its forms, to the extent that it is humanly possible.

This, of course, should not be taken as a suggestion to downplay the concerns about the possible misuse or misinterpretation of research findings. But those concerns should be addressed and dealt with outside the realm and beyond the process of scientific discovery; they should influence neither the outcomes of research nor the communication of the results. If we study a social problem, we should address all aspects of the problem to the best of our knowledge and ability, without any self-censoring. There are lots of partial images out there, including in academia, which have been informed by commitments to particular ideologies, certain communities, political agendas, particular governments, and so on. To give a partial account, even out of a noble fear about the possible misuses, would undermine the credibility of the whole research enterprise. In this regard, I think we should subscribe to the old Weberian paradigm, in which our values and preferences can, and perhaps should, influence the choice of the topics for our research and the application of the findings, but not the process through which those findings are produced. The epistemological disagreements over what constitutes an objective enquiry and how this goal could be achieved should not result in the total removal of that goal from our perspectives.

SH: Regarding Muslims in Canada, what new research directions do you envision for yourself moving forward?

AK: I feel that the future research in this area, including my own research, can/should move in several new directions, including:

(a) studying the nature of the relationships between Muslim and non-Muslim Canadians, the factors that influence those relationships, and the scenarios that bring about positive outcomes in inter-group relationship;
(b) developing a deeper understanding of the ways in which Muslims are treated in the economy, particularly the mechanisms through which Muslims may be discriminated against in the job market;
(c) the issue of the possible diversity of experiences within the Muslim population, taking into account attributes such as gender, generation, branch of Islam, national/ethnic background, race, etc.;
(d) how to generate new data – mostly quantitative, but also qualitative – on Canadian Muslims that could show the big picture and the trends over time;
(e) the study of the religious leadership in the Muslim community and the nature of the relationship between *ulama* and ordinary Muslims.

SH: Thank you, Dr. Kazemipur, for sharing your thoughts on these new directions for research and on the impacts of methodology on our findings.

REFERENCES

Bayat, Asef. 2007. *Making Islam democratic: Social movements and the post-Islamist turn*. Stanford University Press.

Caeiro, Alexandre. 2011. "Theorizing Islam without the state: Minority fiqh in the West." In Marinos Diamantides and Adam Gearey (Eds.), *Islam, law and identity* (pp. 209–35). Routledge.

Evra, Rose, and Abdolmohammad Kazemipur. 2019, 19 June. "The role of social capital and ethnocultural characteristics in the employment income of immigrants over time." *Statistics Canada's Insights on Canadian Society.* https://www150.statcan.gc.ca/n1/en/pub/75-006-x/2019001/article/00009-eng.pdf

Kazemipur, Abdolmohammad. 2013. "The economics of attachment: Making a case for a relational approach to immigrants' integration in Canada." *Journal of International Migration and Integration, 15*(4), 609–32. https://doi.org/10.1007/s12134-013-0284-6

– 2014. *The Muslim question in Canada: A story of segmented integration.* University of British Columbia Press.

– 2016. "Bringing the social back in: On the integration of Muslim immigrants and the jurisprudence of Muslim minorities." *Canadian Review of Sociology, 53*(4), 437–56. https://doi.org/10.1111/cars.12134

– 2017a. "Muslim immigration to North America: The rise of new challenges and the need for new perspectives." In Victoria M. Esses and Donald E. Abelson (Eds.), *Twenty-first-century immigration to North America: Newcomers in turbulent times* (pp. 206–32). McGill-Queen's University Press.

– 2017b. "Reckoning with the minority status: On fiqh al-aqalliyat al-Muslema (jurisprudence of Muslim minorities)." In Mario Peucker and Rauf Ceylan (Eds.), *Muslim community organizations in the West* (pp. 13–34). Springer.

– 2018. "Religion in Canadian ethnic landscape: The Muslim factor." In Shibao Guo and Lloyd Wong (Eds.), *Immigration, racial and ethnic studies in 150 years of Canada: Retrospects and prospects* (pp. 261–80). Sense Publishers.

Nagra, Baljit. 2017. *Securitized citizens: Canadian Muslims' experiences of race relations and identity formation post-9/11.* University of Toronto Press.

SECTION 3

Positioning Selves

Researching One's Own Community: Reflections from Montreal, Canada

HICHAM TIFLATI AND ABDELAZIZ DJAOUT

Introduction

Producing field-based knowledge is not an easy task. It can be very challenging for researchers to gain access and trust, establish rapport, overcome suspicion, and negotiate with community gatekeepers who may try to block certain avenues of research if they consider the focus to be too sensitive or irrelevant (Ryan et al. 2010). Gatekeepers may also seek to use the researcher to their advantage by allowing access only to "positive" material. Here, insiders might have the advantage of the assumed trust of the community based on their shared identities and interests. If participants belong to a community under scrutiny, being interviewed by outsiders or strangers may lead to the fear of being labelled or misunderstood.

Numerous researchers (Anderson 2006; Brigg and Bleiker 2009; Giampapa 2011; Palriwala 2005; Reed-Danahay 2009) have raised the political, cultural, emotional, and practical issues facing so-called native researchers, who are usually perceived as performing their identities. These insider researchers encounter numerous challenges in validating their personal experiences as a source of academic knowledge and in balancing their insider/outsider statuses, especially when navigating the field. They struggle with the dilemma of insider/outsider status even before starting their "official" fieldwork. Many native researchers believe that in order to produce academic and scholarly *knowledge*, the researcher and the research, the field and the fieldworker, and the subject and the object have to stay at a distance from one another in all stages of the research. In other words, they insist that the personal traces of the author must be erased from their work (Brigg and Bleiker 2009). This understanding is, in part, because personal experiences are seen both as marginal and as a source of knowledge due to the difficulty involved in validating them (Brigg and Bleiker 2009). Insiders are aware of how their status affects their research and findings. In short, they cannot escape the fact that their research requires that they are both the subject and object of enquiry (Reed-Danahay 2009).

At the other end of the spectrum, knowledge produced by researchers who share a common identity or experience with their informants cannot be assumed to be richer or truer based only on that commonality (Ryan et al. 2010). When participants are interviewed by someone from their community, who is likely known to them, they usually have concerns about negative judgments and, despite assurances of confidentiality, may worry about being the subject of local gossip. Furthermore, the researcher's status is usually framed around assumed identities. For example, participants may narrowly label Muslim researchers based on their origin, nationality, or sect (Sunni, Shi'a, etc.). Factors such as education, gender, sexual orientation, and class may at different times outweigh the cultural identity we associate with insider or outsider status (Dawson 2010). Our construction of the field through our inclusions and exclusions of informants is often based on pragmatic considerations of access to the research field (Palriwala 2005).

In this chapter, we first investigate the role native identities play in formulating the knowledge produced by native researchers. Second, we briefly present autoethnography before turning to the challenges of subjectivity-objectivity and insider-outsider dichotomies. Last, we discuss the challenges facing so-called insiders who produce academic knowledge and analyse data from familiar terrains. Acknowledging our experiences as "native" ethnographers, we critique the essentializing nature of the insider/outsider and observer/observed dichotomies.

Our Identities

We have both researched issues of integration, Islamophobia, discrimination, and belongingness of Muslim communities in Canada for more than a decade.[1] Irrespective of our self-declared statuses as academic researchers, and regardless of our professional qualifications, we have noted how our participation in religious practices makes our Muslim participants acknowledge our qualified "permanent" insider identity, which influences our positionality in the field (Dawson 2010). Our participants are aware that we are not provisional insiders who will temporarily assume or adopt their identities through participation; they know that we are permanent insiders who identify with their faith, culture, history, and tradition. One question we often ask ourselves is: How far we should be involved and how much we should share with our participants? On one hand, not getting sufficiently close to participants would defeat the purpose of our ethnographic-based research projects. On the other hand, getting too close to participants would also defeat the scholarly nature of our research. At the same time, we are conscious that, as native ethnographers, we might be regarded as presenting a performance of our own identities and, in a way, we have been initially careful to exclusively present ourselves and our communities in a positive manner (Ryan et al. 2010). More precisely, in our case, our immigrant identities are religiously, socially, and politically visible in our fieldwork. For instance, we participate in prayers, we speak the dialect, we share our perspectives about political issues in Quebec and "back home." Our identities are multiple and fluid, as are the identities of most of our participants, and through the complex relationships in the field, it does impact the research process as a whole.

We sometimes feel that some of our participants are, unashamedly, using us to promote what they want. In other words, they see us as a part of their project, as we consider them part of academic work. One leader, for instance, openly shared his ease in talking to us because, as he put it, "we are all Muslims and we will never say anything that will hurt the community." We see our self-positioning as North African–origin Muslims as an important link to accessing, understanding, and engaging in the lives of our participants (i.e., Muslim Quebecers) and with Muslim youth groups and organizations (i.e., Muslim Students' Associations, Islamic centres), that we engage with in our fieldwork. This includes the ways in which our identities are assigned and constructed within academia through discourses in our discipline and the procedures that are imposed on us through institutional discourses.

Native researchers sometimes experience conflict from their academic institutions as well. The Orientalist-informed approaches to studying the so-called East are still dominant in most universities; native researchers, particularly those who are racialized, are constantly questioned about their subjectivity, and even their sincerity, in producing academic knowledge. Being researchers and community members can also create serious challenges. For instance, we both work on questions related to radicalization within the Muslim community in Montreal. We have access to families and loved ones of those radicalized or would-be radicals. Nonetheless, our work is questioned in regard to both its subjectivity and the possibility of being seen by our subjects as "sell-outs" who are delivering data to the Canadian authorities. Participants may also have concerns about confidentiality as well as being judged (Ryan et al. 2010). In sum, our work is constantly questioned from all sides.

We navigate this challenge by what we call a methodology of "patience and transparency." We give our interlocutors the necessary time to get to know us, and we try to be as open as possible to let them appreciate the complexities and nuances of our positions as both Muslims and researchers. We strive to take a pedagogical and humble approach that privileges natives' perspectives. We understand that the fears and suspicions of our subjects are not coming from nowhere, but they are rooted in the misrepresentation, and overrepresentation, of Muslims and minorities in the media and the surveillance they experience.

Our social agency and that of our participants is a key role in understanding the research and its context (Reed-Danahay 2009). Many participants are very happy to share their experiences and feelings with us, believing that we also share their points of view because we share the same status (i.e., immigrant, minority, Muslim). The phrase "as you know" is commonly employed by many of our participants. It is an indication that, according to them, whatever they say is only a confirmation of what we already knew.

Postmodern Ethnography

Autoethnography

One more recent way that scholars have endeavoured to position themselves is through an autoethnographic approach. Autoethnography refers to scholarly knowledge that conveys the experiences of ethnographers as individuals who transcend the temporal and spatial context of their terrain (Anderson 2006). One of the commonly articulated approaches in autoethnography is that of the "native ethnographer," a title that calls into question the dualism of insider-outsider, of object-subject, and of the researcher's positionality vis-à-vis the knowledge they are trying to produce (Reed-Danahay 2009). An autoethnography is not an autobiography in which the author dominates the story; neither is it a narrative that removes the ethnographer's traces with their informants or the field. Rather, it is a method of social analysis that depends upon the ethnographer's capabilities to communicate their observations, reflexivity, reciprocity, and critiques (Reed-Danahay 2009). It falls squarely at the intersection of insider and outsider perspectives. According to Brigg and Bleiker (2009), by problematizing the object-subject separation that characterizes scientific legitimacy, autoethnography reintroduces the self as a methodological source for producing knowledge. The idea behind this methodological move is to bring the ethnographer into greater relation with the empirical reality and to place their experience at the centre of the phenomenon under study.

Although much recent emphasis on the uses of the term "autoethnography" refers to writing that conveys the emotional experiences of the ethnographer as individual, there has been less attention paid to other possible uses and meanings of this term (Reed-Danahay 2009). Autoethnography looks at the researcher's personal experiences in order to understand their cultural and religious backgrounds. It challenges traditional methods of doing research and reflecting on subjects, and it treats being in the field as a socially and politically conscious act.

Brigg and Bleiker (2009) assert that there are three basic elements that facilitate and guide autoethnographic research: (1) openness and vulnerability to the field as a source of knowledge; (2) a willingness to draw upon a range of different faculties (i.e., sensation, intuition, personal experiences); and (3) a process of selecting, analysing, and decolonizing the collected data that partly exposes rather than erases the traces of the non-Western authors. We have found these counsels very helpful to our research conducted between 2015 and 2018 on the families of the few Quebecers who joined ISIS.

Decolonizing Ethnographic Knowledge

According to Cohen, Manion, and Morrison (2018, 382), producing ethnographic knowledge is like trying to translate a foreign manuscript embodied in the informants' behaviour, full of ellipses, incoherencies, and tendentious commentaries. In colonial periods, ethnographies were the key tools of studying non-Western societies (Hitchcock and Hughes 1995, 120), as well as tools for imperialism and colonialism. Before the emergence of postmodernism, the "native" anthropologist or social scientist risked being seen as irrelevant or as supplying unnecessary knowledge for the community of scholars (Palriwala 2005). Postmodernism gave the "other" a voice and allowed them to speak and empower their own social groups. Today, postmodern ethnography is no longer considered the sole authority to speak on behalf of those labelled as unable to speak for themselves (Palriwala 2005). As has been well charted, in the processes of decolonization new methodological perspectives emerged, enabling critique of classical ethnography. Native ethnographers began claiming scholarship and challenging findings and standpoints in the literature. Critical voices emerged that challenged common assumptions related to the so-called West. The ideal example is that of Edward Said's (1978) book, *Orientalism*. For Said, Orientalism allowed the West to create vague generalizations and misrepresentations of the Orient, which became the assumed image of the East and Easterners.

Sensitive Research

Any research on Muslim communities in the so-called West is necessarily both political and sensitive. This sensitivity might concern not only the produced knowledge itself but, perhaps more importantly, the relationship between this knowledge and the social context or the specificity of the object under investigation (i.e., stigmatized communities, feminists, minorities). Likewise, all social research is sensitive; the question is therefore one of degree and not of kind. The researcher has to be sensitive to context, cultures, and participants and to the consequences of the research on participants. Recognizing the importance of reciprocity enables the fieldworker to give back to their informants, to serve their purpose, and to support their aims, but without compromising the research (Russell 2006). Research on marginalized groups should thus have concrete benefit for the informants so they do not continue to be exploited or marginalized (Cohen, Manion, and Morrison 2018, 393).

In-depth studies of ethnic-minority communities often reveal significant levels of heterogeneity arising from socio-economic status, immigration history, language skills, integration stage, and contribution to the host society, which oblige researchers to take on highly interactive tactics (Hitchcock and Hughes 1995, 39; Ryan et al. 2010). Researching Muslims, who have in many ways taken on the status of a suspect community, is more complicated today than ever. All research involving Islam and Muslims is political, which leads to researchers facing difficulties overcoming distrust while studying Islam and Muslims in post-9/11 Western societies. Muslim participants, who are over-researched, may also reject cooperation with outsiders, including researchers, out of fear of being judged, stereotyped, and labelled in a way that will put them in danger. For instance, while trying to recruit participants for projects related to radicalization and terrorism, many potential participants insisted on being given all details about the funding of the study, the level of confidentiality, the names of those in charge, and how/when the information will eventually be disseminated.

Subjectivity-Objectivity Dichotomy

Researchers are actors in everyday life: they play roles, interact with others, negotiate situations, and interpret findings. With the postmodern turn, as researchers no longer see objectivity as an option, one response has been to focus on their subjectivity and to turn it into a set of methodological concerns (Heshusius 1994). Objectivity is not a concept that has to do with the discovery of truth; rather, it represents a continuum of closeness to an accurate description and understanding of the observable phenomena (DeWalt and DeWalt 2010, 111). According to Hegelund (2005), the conventional meanings and dichotomy of subjectivity and objectivity are under attack by the postmodern ways of thinking. Hegelund observes that it makes no sense to discuss what objectivity and subjectivity really mean without analysing the different ways in which ethnographers are using these concepts. That said, recognizing the impact of the researcher's agency on the produced knowledge allows for a deeper understanding of their field site, participants, status within the field, and their own subjectivities (Russell 2006). Furthermore, Hegelund (2005) differentiates between two sorts of subjectivity: The first is when a researcher omits important knowledge because it does not fit their agenda. The second is when the researcher employs their particular authority in the process of collecting and analysing such knowledge. However, relying on one's subjectivity can be seen as a "subtle version of empiricist thought," which the native researcher is best situated to embark on because his field is a part of him and he is a part of it (Heshusius 1994, 19).

Methodology

Because of the risk of creating and using knowledge unconsciously, awareness of the process that we adopt in our research is of utmost importance (Hegelund 2005). Both of us research issues of integration, Islamophobia, discrimination, and belonging of Muslim communities in Quebec, Canada. We rely on a critical ethnographic approach (Anderson 2006), which enables us to probe the issues we explore in relation to marginalized voices within Muslim communities in Montreal. Critical ethnography, as its name suggests, takes a critical stance to traditional ethnography, which first emerged as a research methodology within the field of anthropology. While also depending on participant observation, critical ethnography allows for the interpretation of data and field settings from the perspectives of the participants. Its aim is not only to observe and describe, but more specifically to better the lives of the observed. We believe the critical ethnographic approach enables native researchers to probe the issues we explore. The key to pursuing and evaluating the researcher's agency as a legitimate source of knowledge is to recognize that autoethnographic claims are a necessary part of a larger struggle over the scholarly production of knowledge. Furthermore, we partly adopt methodologies, such as Jackson's (1997, 2004, 2011) interpretative approach, that privilege natives' world views in explaining and interpreting their personal experiences. This interpretive approach has three main key concepts: (1) interpretation, (2) representation, and (3) reflexivity. According to Jackson (1997, 189), the interpretive approach takes into account and recognizes the heterogeneous nature of worldviews and belief systems. He (2011) asserts that this approach privileges neither the individual nor the faith but focuses instead on the hermeneutical relationship between the two without neglecting the impact of external factors on either one. We believe the interpretative approach's main concepts help native researchers distance themselves from their fieldwork while balancing their academic and religious responsibilities.

Discussion

Our statuses as researchers are usually framed around assumed religious and cultural identities. Although we never confirm that we are from Muslim Sunni backgrounds, most participants categorize us as such based on our national origins (Moroccan and Algerian) and on previous knowledge of our statuses within Muslim communities in Montreal. Some of the assumptions about us are made on the basis of an assumed shared language (i.e., Moroccan and Algerian Arabic dialects) and culture. Moreover, participation in prayers, if it occurs, is never an attempt to demonstrate open-mindedness, a willingness to engage in participant observation with our objects, or a credentialing process to establish an empathetic status (Dawson 2010). Indeed, it is simply a part of our daily rituals that we might perform in the field, at our homes, or elsewhere. In other words, the dynamics involved in our ascription as "permanent insiders" emerge directly from particular interpretations of our ethnicities, our names, and the religious implications of our ritual participation (Dawson 2010).

Nonetheless, there are also those who regard us as outsiders and see our insider identities as incomplete. They do so on the grounds of our belonging at the same time to a secular and academic community. Yet our insider statuses improve as we gradually win more approval based on our culture, religion, kindness, and trustworthiness, which not only makes our work more enjoyable but also makes our participants more open to discussing potentially sensitive areas in subsequent conversations and situations (Purdy and Jones 2013).

We are insiders in many capacities: Not only are we North African Muslims and first-generation immigrants (as are the majority of the subjects in our studies), we are also seen as practising, "good" Muslims who advocate for the well-being of Muslims as minorities and oppressed communities across the world. We take pro-Palestinian positions, in their right to self-determination, and are personally affected by the excess and side effects of the "War on Terror" on Muslim communities. In a number of instances, our insider statuses have given us access to outstanding informants and knowledgeable insiders. Through our personal network within the Muslim community, we have had access to Muslim leaders and Islamic institutions. For instance, the friends and families of Quebecers who joined ISIS, and who refused to talk to many journalists and researchers, opened their homes and welcomed us in their personal spaces.

Validating Our Experiences in Our Work

As native researchers, we also struggle to validate our personal experiences as a source of knowledge (Brigg and Bleiker 2009). The main challenge is whether it is possible to be objective all the way from the definition of the object of study through the collection of data to the analysis of the findings and the production of knowledge, as the assumptions researchers carry around can sometimes completely blind them (Hegelund 2005). For instance, we do not believe that our so-called insider roles (if such a fixed position can truly exist) would automatically lead to a closer understanding of the "lived experiences" of our participants or of the field with which we are already familiar. The belief that one can actually distance oneself and then regulate that distance is sometimes referred to as alienated consciousness, which may lead to a kind of disenchantment of knowing (Heshusius 1994). While in the field (and despite the smooth access to it) we often find our personal experiences to be an obstacle to understanding because they are not usually validated in academia as scholarly knowledge.

In her edited volume *Islam in the Hinterlands: Muslim Cultural Politics in Canada*, Jasmin Zine (2014) asserts that, in situations where the "narratives and lived experiences of Muslims have been co-opted by those who do not share in this identity or the costs and implications of labeling and defining the experiences of others," this creates "academic forms of colonialism" (27). It seems to us that this point is an exaggeration. Studying a community from the outside is not always colonialism de facto. We must first define this notion and understand how an external narrative on a given tradition may or may not be a modern form of colonialism. Knowledge becomes colonialism when it is produced to oppress and reinforce stereotypes about the communities being studied.

Furthermore, we are sometimes caught in the dilemma of being empirical researchers trying to decode a field in which interpretation, understandings, and even solidarity can be seen as central notions (Hegelund 2005). Personal characteristics of the researcher may influence the level of participation that an individual may choose or be forced to adopt (DeWalt and DeWalt 2010, 30). As stated above, our self-identification as Muslim immigrants and its multiple representations both linguistically and culturally allowed for some degree of access and connection to the participants' personal and daily experiences. Still, as male researchers, we found that recruiting and interviewing females was more difficult. Men have been more accessible and flexible in their willingness to participate in our studies. While female participants did not object to being interviewed by male researchers, finding a place and time to arrange a meeting was difficult. Most female participants – mothers in particular – are busy looking after their families. Taking time off from their lives to participate restricted their availability to late evenings, when it may be inappropriate for a male researcher to visit their homes. Additionally, we do not believe that, in social sciences, facts speak for themselves or that we, as researchers, can produce knowledge without letting personal, political, moral, or religious judgments enter into our research and thereby distort the "truth." The only sure course for us is to express our values openly and honestly, rejecting the myth of moral neutrality and full objectivity (Hitchcock and Hughes 1995, 53). Our subjecthoods cannot be ignored. For instance, even though we are considered insiders in our research terrain, we are also messengers who record events and carry them to another destination, where they are read and reinterpreted. Neither the voyage nor the framing can be erased. To erase our agency is to erase important insights, which affect our understanding of the phenomena under study (Brigg and Bleiker 2009).

That being said, we have become convinced that to better understand the way we are producing knowledge, we have to be concerned with more than our findings. We feel it is important to answer truthfully personal questions asked by our participants about religious beliefs and practices, values, and opinions.

Participants constantly ask us about our sects (i.e., Sunni, Shi'a), beliefs, and political views. We also attempt to provoke questions regarding our place and our evolving personas in the research setting (Purdy and Jones 2013). We already resemble our participants as Muslims and North Africans. But we differ as researchers trained in the social sciences. Through the process of fieldwork, we come to resemble our participants more and more as we engage with them in their internal discussions and debates about the best ways to protect the interest of our communities. For example, we come to resemble our subjects in their position concerning how to counter the radicalization processes observed in our communities and, at the same time, resist and denounce the securitization of the Islamic religion and community.

We are referring here to the issue of "methodological" detachment from our objects, which refers to taking the right distance and employing the right epistemological tools during all stages of the research. Concurrently, the real issue for us is being objective not just as researchers but, more importantly, as conveyers of data. We learn that there is very rarely, if ever, a straightforwardly one-dimensional objective-subjective spectrum across which ethnographers can act (Dawson 2010). Furthermore, the irony is that once we believe we can be objective and we admire the distance we construct between our subjects, then we try to cross the distance (again) and go native, while insisting that we can be in charge of the situation (Heshusius 1994).

One frame of meaning can only be understood from the viewpoint of another (Jackson 2011). We have to enter, as researchers, into a dialogue with the field and its occupants as well as with ourselves, mainly about the role of Muslimness and Islamic institutions. This point is relevant to our involvement in the creation of meaning. The field may have completely different meanings for different ethnographers and in different times, as every ethnographer brings to the field their knowledge, assumptions, cultural differences, experiences, and insights, all of which affect their interpretation (Hitchcock and Hughes 1995, 229).

In order to better understand our participants, we have to be concerned with more than our data. In other words, we have to take into account their agencies as well as their well-being. Certainly, the relationships we form with each participant influence the nature of our interaction and the subsequent information shared between us. Moreover, participants interested by our research, who believed for instance that it would benefit their community, their school, or them personally, showed more concern and offered more help for our projects.

As Palriwala (2005) states, we do not start fieldwork "raw"; we build on past work and experiences. In fact, ethnographers are always doing fieldwork, trying to understand the culture and society we are living in. No scholar can have a thought or gain some form of insight out of nothingness. Knowledge is an inherently social phenomenon that adheres to social rules in which the powerful decide the norms. This is why many marginalized scholars, such as feminists, are often skeptical about tightly controlled academic disciplines (Brigg and Bleiker 2009). Furthermore, we have to manage the wide variety of practical, emotional, and intellectual challenges provoked by a range of interpersonal encounters (Dawson 2010). We also need to deal with the demands of our assumed roles in the field and to manage the "switch" from complete participants to academic researchers. This, however, is not the case for outsiders or provisional insiders. Aside from a little uncertainty and initial constraint, researchers with provisional insider identities can easily manage changes provoked by the shift from ritual co-participants to academic interviewers (Dawson 2010). At the same time, as native ethnographers, we have a difficult time recording sufficient levels of details. Many events and activities that would be novel and provide insights to outsiders are so commonplace to us that they are not well documented (e.g., prayers, holy days, religious celebrations). To navigate this, we have to rely on multiple visits and careful observation of the field sites. Furthermore, the researcher may choose to look at communities as a whole or at individual behaviours. Although communities are collections of individuals and groups that share some understandings of the world, individuals have their own perspectives and interpretations depending on their unique experiences and places in the social system (DeWalt and DeWalt 2010, 129; Hegelund 2005). That said, not all observations are synonymous with interpretation. We make reports that are capable of verification and exclude (as much as possible) inferences and subjective judgments. In other words, when communities open their arms to us and accept being part of our research, we undergo personal conversations and conversions that include a sense of being part of the adopted culture and initiation into its specificities (Palriwala 2005). We inevitably bring our biographies and our subjectivities to every stage of the research process. These biographies should never be seen as a regrettable disturbance to objective research but viewed as one element in the human interactions that comprise our object of study (Giampapa 2011, 137).

In qualitative approaches, the researcher takes on a highly interactive profile (Hitchcock and Hughes 1995, 39), tending to have a small field of focus and dividing the observed into pieces that can be aggregated into a variable, which draws the research into the complex world of the informants in order to capture their reality (Cohen, Manion, and Morrison 2018, 177). The observer translates the observed phenomena into a series of notes contained on a finite number of pages and then, consciously or not, makes a series of decisions about what to report, how to report it, and what to omit (DeWalt and DeWalt 2010, 182). Therefore, all observation is partial and selective. As we can observe and document everything, our observation has to be structured. Structured observation is useful for testing hypotheses, while unstructured observation provides a rich description of a situation that can lead to the subsequent generation of hypotheses (Cohen, Manion, and Morrison 2018, 192).

Additionally, many researchers choose to engage in participant observation. The latter has long enjoyed an established place within the methodological tool kit of ethnographic studies (Dawson 2010), and it remains the starting point in ethnographic research. Today, it continues to grow in popularity as a mode of qualitative data collection used by most empirically oriented disciplines. Through it, a researcher engages in the daily activities of a group of people in order to unlock details about their life and culture. It is not just a visual phenomenon; it is an activity of mapping the scene and documenting impressions, and it is the central and defining method of research in cultural anthropology (DeWalt and DeWalt 2010, 3).

Besides the literature review and the interviewing process that a researcher engages in, participant observation provides other advantages to research. DeWalt and DeWalt (2010) consider it both a data collection and an analytic tool. It enhances the quality of the data obtained during fieldwork and the quality of the researcher's interpretation of data. Moreover, "it encourages the formulation of new research questions and hypotheses grounded in on-the-scene observation" (DeWalt and DeWalt 2010, 28). Participant observation designates the conduct of an ethnographer who immerses themselves in a terrain so as to observe an activity, a ritual, or a ceremony while, ideally, taking part in it (Bourdieu 2003). It is a paradox because the ethnographer seeks to understand the native's viewpoint but not go native. They may be affected by gender, ethnicity, class, appearance, age, language, personality, temperament, attitude, interpersonal behaviour, and familiarity with the situation of the observer (Cohen, Manion, and Morrison 2018, 408; Dawson 2010), but participant observation raises many issues (e.g., confidentiality, trust, identity, risk) which resonate with the theoretical framing and the methodological implementation of empirical research in general.

Furthermore, we as researchers choose to rely on active participation through volunteering in Islamic schools and institutions as well as through using life narratives with community leaders and founders of Islamic schools and associations. Life-history narrative rather than question-and-answer interviews work best in enabling us to understand not just our field but also the challenges that the Muslim community encounters. These narratives contextualize the struggles of the community (i.e., in establishing and funding community centres) and shed more light on the experiences of being in Canada.

To say that we just have to turn to the data to find the objective truth is an oversimplification, as the arguments from the philosophy of science against this empiricist teaching convincingly demonstrate (Hegelund 2005). There is the risk that, since data and interpretation are unavoidably combined, the subjective views of the researcher might lead them to be selective and unfair to the situation in the choice of data and the interpretation placed on them (Cohen, Manion, and Morrison 2018). By omitting data, one paints a picture of the observed reality that is less true than it could have been (Hegelund 2005). Omission of crucial data would be a lack of objective correspondence. However, a level of subjectivity is always present. We deal with these risks by raising our awareness to prevent the influence of our subjectivities, even unconsciously, on our results. When findings seem prejudicial to our communities, we know that it is always better to present those kinds of results accompanied by our emphatic comments and remarks than to ignore them.

Conclusion

Recognizing that we are socially constructed beings directs the attention to what we research and to the ways in which we interpret and present our findings (Giampapa 2011). Fieldworkers, including community researchers such as ourselves, are not passive conveyers of data; we are involved in the process of constructing and interpreting the information recorded in the field (Ryan et al. 2010). We have our background of knowledge with us all the time, and because this cannot be switched off, it affects what we see, what we conclude (Hegelund 2005), and the ways in which we interpret our data. Our interests and academic backgrounds shape what we observe in a particular setting as well (DeWalt and DeWalt 2010, 90).

When studying Islam and Muslim communities, the real challenge for native researchers is keeping to their objective standards not only while researching but, more importantly, while interpreting and analysing their data. A distinction between data and the interpretation of data must then be made. The great tension in knowledge production is between maintaining a sense of the holism of the interview, that is, not losing the synergy of the whole, because the whole is always greater than the sum of the parts (Cohen, Manion, and Morrison 2018, 52). In summary, and according to Dawson (2010), there is very rarely, if ever, a straightforwardly one-dimensional outsider-insider spectrum across which academic research enables the researcher to change his or her positionality vis-à-vis the knowledge produced. What is more important is to clearly state where we are coming from and to be aware of the personal experiences and the hidden traits we bring with us to the field. That said, the reality about what is going on in the field should come both from the point of view of the researcher and from the point of view of the informants. Muslims not only are the observed but also have a say in what should be observed, how it should be observed, and how it should be interpreted. The researcher, insider or outsider, should consult with their informants before, during, and after completing fieldwork to verify findings with their points of view. Seriously considering their answers and interpretations is the most accurate approach to getting their insights about the research questions.

NOTE

1 From 2013 to 2016, the first author, Hicham Tiflati, coordinated a national project entitled *New Muslim Public Spheres in the Digital Age: Identity, Community, Diversity and Authority*, which involved four collaborating universities. He served as a research associate with Resilience Research Center at Halifax University on a Public Safety Canada's Kanishka Project, *Understanding Youth Resilience to Violent Extremism*, during which he worked closely with youth and organizations in the Muslim community in Montreal. This study, among the very first in the world to investigate the social ecologies of resilience with regard to violent extremism, attracted great interest in Canada and internationally. In 2015, he served with the Centre for the Prevention of Radicalization Leading to Violence (CPRLV) in Montreal as a research professional. During that time, he developed experience in analysing discourses pertaining to security and radicalization trends, was entrusted with unclassified and classified material, and was provided intelligence assessments, briefing notes, and recommendations based on the analysis of the data. Additionally, he was a senior researcher for a study at the University of Waterloo. This Defence Research and Development Canada (DRDC) project, entitled *Canadian Foreign Fighters*, examines the lives of Canadians who have gone overseas to fight in foreign conflicts or to join terrorist groups. He was also the co-investigator in a project at McGill University entitled *Educational Trajectories of Radicalized Females in Montreal*, funded by the Canadian Network for Research on Terrorism, Security, and Society (TSAS), wherein he worked in collaboration with Dr. Ratna Ghosh at the Department of Integrated Studies in Education. The second author, Djaout, worked on multiple projects as well. He was a researcher in a project directed by Professor Rachad Antonious titled *The Representations of Arabs and Muslims in Quebec's Major Print Media* and funded by Heritage Canada. This work resulted in a report submitted to Heritage Canada and several articles and book chapters. He also worked on a *Secularism and Identity in Quebec* project, which was under the supervision of Professor Micheline Milot and funded by the Centre d'études et de recherches internationales (Cérium). The project resulted in a collective publication in the Metropolis Centre's *Capsules Recherche*. Moreover, he participated in a project on *Interreligious Dialogue Québec*, under the supervision of Professor Denise Couture and funded by the Canada Research Chair on Islam, Pluralism and Globalization (IPG). Finally, as part of his doctoral research, he analysed public policies and media debates on radicalization and counter/deradicalization in Quebec and Canada and conducted several interviews with presumed radicals in the Greater Montreal area. This work was partly funded by the Religion and Diversity

Project, a network of international researchers who study the issues raised by religious diversity in Canada and abroad.

REFERENCES

Anderson, Leon. 2006. "Analytic autoethnography." *Journal of Contemporary Ethnography, 35*(4), 373–95. https://doi.org/10.1177%2F0891241605280449

Bourdieu, Pierre. 2003. "Participant objectivation." *Journal of the Royal Anthropological Institute, 9*, 281–94. https://doi.org/10.1111/1467-9655.00150

Brigg, Morgan, and Roland Bleiker. 2009. "Autoethnographic international relations: Exploring the self as a source of knowledge." *Review of International Studies, 36*(3), 779–98. http://doi.org/10.1017/S0260210510000689

Cohen, Louis, Lawrence Manion, and Keith Morrison. 2018. *Research methods in education*. Routledge Falmer.

Dawson, Andrew. 2010. "Positionality and role-identity in a new religious context: Participant observation at Céu do Mapiá." *Religion, 40*(3), 173–81. http://doi.org/10.1016/j.religion.2009.09.007

DeWalt, Kathleen, and Billie DeWalt. 2010. *Participant observation: A guide for fieldworkers*. Alta Mira Press.

Giampapa, Frances. 2011. "The politics of 'being and becoming' a researcher: Identity, power, and negotiating the field." *Journal of Language, Identity, and Education, 10*(3), 132–44. https://doi.org/10.1080/15348458.2011.585304

Hegelund, Allan. 2005. "Objectivity and subjectivity in the ethnographic method." *Qualitative Health Research, 15*(5), 647–68. https://doi.org/10.1177%2F1049732304273933

Heshusius, Lous. 1994. "Freeing ourselves from objectivity: Managing subjectivity or turning toward a participatory mode of consciousness?" *Educational Researcher, 23*(3), 15–22. https://doi.org/10.3102%2F0013189X023003015

Hitchcock, Graham, and David Hughes. 1995. *Research and the teacher: A qualitative introduction to school-based research*. Routledge.

Jackson, Robert. 1997. *Religious education: An interpretive approach*. Hodder and Stoughton.

– 2004. *Rethinking religious education and plurality: Issues in diversity and pedagogy*. Routledge Farmer.

– 2011. "The interpretive approach as a research tool: Inside the REDCo project." *British Journal of Religious Education, 33*(2), 189–208. https://doi.org/10.1080/01416200.2011.543602

Palriwala, Rajni. 2005. "Fieldwork in a post-colonial anthropology: Experience and the comparative." *Social Anthropology, 13*(2), 151–70. https://doi.org/10.1111/j.1469-8676.2005.tb00004.x

Purdy, Laura, and Robyn Jones. 2013. "Changing personas and evolving identities: The contestation and renegotiation of researcher roles in fieldwork." *Sport,*

Education and Society, 18(3), 292–310. https://doi.org/10.1080/13573322.2011.586688

Reed-Danahay, Deborah. 2009. "Anthropologists, education, and autoethnography." *Reviews in Anthropology, 38*(1), 28–47. https://doi.org/10.1080/00938150802672931

Russell, Ian. 2006. "Working *with* tradition: Towards a partnership model of fieldwork." *Folklore, 117*(1), 15–32. https://doi.org/10.1080/00155870500479877

Ryan, Louise, Eleonore Kofman, and Pauline Aaron. 2010. *Insiders and outsiders: Working with peer researchers in researching Muslim communities*. Routledge.

Said, Edward. 1978. *Orientalism*. Vintage Books.

Zine, Jasmin. 2014. *Islam in the hinterlands: Muslim cultural politics in Canada*. University of British Columbia Press.

Cooking Up Research: Positionality and the Knowledge Production of Islam(s)

RACHEL BROWN

The ethnographer may need to realise that what *he* or *she* observes is conditioned by who *he* or *she* is, and that different ethnographers – equally well trained and well versed in theory and method but of different gender, race, or age – might well stimulate a very different set of interactions, and hence a different set of observations leading to a different set of conclusions.

– Angrosino and Mays de Perez 2000, 689; emphasis in original

Introduction

"Are you just going to talk to women?" This was the beginning of an exchange with a faculty member during the question period of my PhD dissertation proposal defence, where the gender dynamics of my project were teased out. I responded to this enquiry saying that no, I would not speak with just women; I did not want to restrict the voices that would be represented in my data. Some looks of confusion and disappointment spread throughout the room. Implicit and explicit notions filled the room, that "foodwork" was solely women's work, that I as a female researcher would have better access to women's experiences, that looking at women's experience with food would be a welcome change to the historically male-dominant lens through which many studies of religion have gazed, that men, and especially Muslim men, would not have much to say about the everyday practice of foodways. I, as a young researcher, was slightly confused by the line of questioning and the kinds of assumptions being made. "Don't men eat too?" I thought to myself, and maybe said out loud. "Why would I *not* include their voices?" "Wouldn't I be directing the kind of results I would get about Islam, immigration and food by only speaking with women?" These questions were the beginning of my own process of critical reflexivity throughout my research on Islam(s) in Canada and France and the seeds of my inner positionality debate.

This chapter explores how positionality and specifically the choice of research topic affect how our research is perceived by others, as well as being generative of the knowledge we produce. The choices that the researcher makes, both intentional and not, about what to research and how, inevitably lead to certain pictures emerging as to what Islam "is" in Canada. I argue that there are implicit expectations, largely dictated by gender norms, that impact on the possibility of access to certain aspects of Muslim communities and individuals. For example, there tends to be an implicit expectation, by scholars and participants alike, that research focusing on food and Islam will focus on women's experiences. By choosing to focus on a topic such as the food practices of Muslims, does this immediately restrict the knowledge produced to the realm of Muslim women? Furthermore, does the gender identity and positionality of the researcher themselves impact on the knowledge produced? If there is an expectation that someone who self-identifies as, and is identified by others as, a woman must focus their qualitative research on Muslim women, how much does this expectation restrict, limit, and delineate the kinds of knowledge produced about Islam(s)? Finally, how does research that transgresses these implicit, and often explicit, expectations add to or challenge the conversation around positionality generally and the knowledge produced on Islam(s) more specifically? Through the process of critical reflexivity, I will explore how my own work, as a White, female, non-Muslim, non-migrant ethnographer researching Maghrebine Muslim migrants in Montreal, is illustrative of the ways that researcher positionality affects what knowledge is produced about Islam(s) in Canada. Drawing from my research journals, where I engaged in critical reflexivity throughout my project, I will decentre, challenge, and engage with past research on positionality and knowledge production, specifically in the realm of gender, and discuss what we can learn from this one study that might speak to future trends in the study, and knowledge production, of Islam(s) in Canada.

Positionality and Knowledge Production: Past Research

In 2017 I wrote in my dissertation,

> Someone with a different background, both personal and academic, with a different set of strengths and weaknesses, most likely would have wound up with an entirely different set of findings. These personal idiosyncrasies affected how I gathered my data, what I paid attention to, what I probed further on, what I missed, etcetera, and they affected how I understood that data and consequently communicated it in this ethnographic account. It is important to note how these identities that I carried with me into the field shaped, and were shaped by, my informants throughout this ethnographic endeavour. (Brown 2017, 32–3)

While researcher positionality, and the kind of reflexivity that is present in this quotation from my dissertation, seem like overly obvious and essential aspects of ethnographic writing, the push towards considering positionality is only thirty years old. Prior to the 1980s, it was expected, in an effort towards objectivity and reproducibility of results, that the ethnographic "self" was unseen and mostly unheard. Then a paradigm shift occurred. Now there is an acknowledgment that the researcher is no "longer simply observing, but observing from precise coordinates within space, time and individual biography and … these play a part in the way that our various interlocutors make sense of us in their worlds" (Simpson 2006, 128). Because of this acknowledgment, scholars suggest that there is a need for personal reflexive analysis "to be built into research design, conduct and writing up" (Dean et al. 2017, 276).[1] This reflexivity is not done at the expense of the social scientific approach, which emphasizes reproducibility, but instead helps to add nuance to the underlying themes that arise across studies.[2]

Critical Researcher Reflexivity and the Impact of Identities and Bodies

One need not look far to find multiple studies that show that researcher traits such as race, class, age, language, ethnicity, and gender impact data (Benstead 2014; Blaydes and Gillum 2013; Dean et al. 2017; Gawlewicz 2016; Gilliat-Ray 2010; Sherif 2001; Zempi 2016). Many of these studies acknowledge the impact of identity on data collection as well as its impact on data analysis. These studies, however, do not take the next step to tease out how this positionality inevitably shapes the information that is constructed about their topics. Knowledge production is often viewed under the paradigm that knowledge is universal and value-free and, alongside that, researchers are objective experts who remain detached and neutral in the process (Gawlewicz 2016). Like the paradigm shift in positionality presented above, there has been a paradigm shift in the study of knowledge production as well, such that there has been "a major shift towards situated knowledge produced in highly contextualized circumstances … and by non-neutral researchers embroiled in changing power relations" (Gawlewicz 2016, 29). If this is the case, critical reflexivity must go beyond how one's identities, values, and beliefs influence the collection of data and must reflect on how one's positionality structures how that data is then analysed and disseminated as knowledge.

When talking about positionality and knowledge production, the body matters. That is, "meaning-making is always informed and shaped by the subjective interaction of bodies in context" (Hoel 2013, 45). According to Gilliat-Ray (2010) "it is not sufficient to consider only the identity or biographical positionality of the researcher: one must ideally go further and reflect upon the ways in which the body of the researched and the researcher mutually construct and produce 'the field'" (414). It is not just the identities we claim but those read on our body, and on the bodies of our participants, that impact on research process and knowledge production.[3]

Beyond how our bodies are read, the embodied practice of remembering, or memory as an embodied reality, also plays a key role in knowledge production. Not only does researcher memory shape data collection, often through shifting positions on various insider and outsider spectrums (Coleman 2010), but it impacts on what gets written up; what knowledge is produced is dependent on the memory of the researcher. Collins (2010, 237) suggests that "narrative memory," the idea that "memory is largely a matter of being able to tell the right story at the right time," is essential in the writing up of ethnography. In fact, he says that what we hold on to in our memories is merely a skeleton of a story that we then tell in the way we want, often manipulating our own experiences to fulfil our needs (Collins 2010). What story we "remember" and the ways in which we tell that story – the meat that we put on the bones as it were – are inevitably shaped by our various and shifting identities, values, and beliefs. It is essential not only to acknowledge that fact but to tease out how any knowledge we produce is in many ways remembered, and therefore created, knowledge.

Positionality and the Knowledge Production of Islam(s)

Looking at the study of Islam(s) in general and in Canada specifically, we can see that while researchers are quick to acknowledge their positionality, usually along the religious insider and outsider spectrum, discussions around how this positionality, and various others, impacts on knowledge production are fewer. In the current global political climate, one may argue that there has been less pause to consider the positioned creation of knowledge around Islam(s) in an effort to just get the "knowledge of Islam(s)" out there in the first place. Juliane Hammer (2016) suggests that while the debates around normativity and positionality are incredibly important, these debates are not "at the forefront of methodological and theoretical reflections in much of Islamic and religious studies scholarship" (655).

When looking at studies that specifically address positionality and Islam(s), most of the focus is on religious insider identity, visibility of said identity, and the consequent impact on research process and data collection (Benstead 2014; Blaydes and Gillum 2013; Hoel 2013; Hopkins and Greenwood 2013; Sherif 2001). While these studies show how researcher positionality can impact on the kind of data we collect in a tangible way, what do they consequently tell us about what Islam(s) *is/are* in any real way? How do the interactions between researcher and research subject, which are clearly meaningful and significant, influence the picture of Islam(s) that we as scholars paint for others to see?

Critical Reflexivity and Knowledge Production of Islam(s) in Canada

For the remainder of this chapter I will engage in a critical reflexive engagement with my own research on Maghrebine Muslim immigrants in Montreal to discuss and challenge the previous research on positionality and knowledge production that I outlined above. I will begin with a short reflection on the shifting spectrums of insider and outsider researcher identity in research on Islam(s). Through critical reflection of my own positionality, I will show how the rhetoric around religious insider/outsider, while valuable, often does not take into account the impact of the intersectional identities of both researcher and participant and the resultant co-creation of knowledge that happens in the research encounter. I will then discuss how our choice of research topic within the study of Islam(s) in Canada, a choice that is always positioned, affects the knowledge production of Islam(s). Through this exploration, I will also show how my research challenges some of the ideas around positionality and knowledge production, specifically as it relates to expectations around the researcher's gender.

The Shifting Insider/Outsider Spectrums

Considerations of the researcher's insider or outsider identity on a variety of identity spectrums – gender, class, race, religion, and so on – are prevalent in studies which address critical reflexivity and positionality. Some studies do acknowledge that, because of intersectionality, there is more than one insider-outsider continuum at work in any given research project and that each of these spectrums shifts over time (Hellawell 2006; Zempi 2016). Corbin Dwyer and Buckle (2009) challenge the dichotomy between insider and outsider and suggest that most researchers, within their interactions with the participants/research topic, operate in a "space between" (see also Zempi 2016). This "space between" is a liminal, constantly shifting space, where a "circle of impact" is operative; that is, it's a place where the researcher impacts the research and the research impacts the researcher (Corbin Dwyer and Buckle 2009, 61); therefore, leading to a co-creation of knowledge.

Even with this kind of acknowledgment, that identities on any insider-outsider spectrum are fluid, many studies of critical reflexivity and positionality set up religion as an either/or, insider *or* outsider, dichotomy. Even those suggesting that we have multiple and changing insider/outsider status over the course of a research process still treat religion in sui generis ways, such that you are either in or out. For example, Zempi (2016) suggested that her Christian identity provided a "degree of commonality" but still saw her research from an outsider position because "Christianity and Islam are two different religions" (Zempi 2016, 4.2). My research adds an interesting angle to this dichotomy and supports the idea that our positionality, even in terms of our religious identity, is never fixed. In my own work, I addressed the benefits and drawbacks of being a "technical religious outsider." For example, when conducting my research, I reflected on the fact that because I was not Muslim I had no detailed, fixed notions about what Islam *was* or should *be*, or about which food practices were "essentially religious" and which were cultural, and because of this I posited that my informants could fully teach me about what these things were to them in their own terms. On the other hand, as a religious "outsider" I also reflected on the reliance on participant gatekeepers and could see the impact of impression management processes at work (Benstead 2014; Blaydes and Gillum 2013). In my field journal I wrote,

> They want to send me to "experts in Islam" and have a hard time grasping the fact that I want to just talk to them about their own personal experience. The participant asked the Muslim woman I was with to call the man [the expert in Islam] first and to set up a meeting for me. I also find this interesting about this experience, people always seem to have to vouch for me. (Author field journal [hereafter "AFJ"], 24 Feb. 2013)

In this, one can see how I, as the researcher, was reflecting on my outsider status and how it influenced how my participants were responding to me and my lines of enquiry. These responses may have been influenced by what Benstead (2014) calls "social desirability theory," that is, that "respondents engage in self-preservation and impression management by avoiding socially unacceptable views or conforming to socially-stereotyped views of the interviewer" (740). It was important to them to present the "right" Islam(s) to me as an "outsider," perhaps thinking that this is what I wanted to see or what people *needed* to hear above their own voices.

While I did reflect on my positionality as a religious outsider in my work, I spent more time exploring how these dichotomies between insider and outsider, when it comes to religion, are not as clear-cut as many suggest. My work instead challenged the idea of the religious identity of the researcher as a fixed reality that inevitably affects knowledge production in clear-cut ways. First, I could combat the power differential that is often present between an outsider and insider, especially an outsider who claims powered identities and an insider who claims minority or disempowered identities,[4] by allowing my own vulnerabilities to enter the researcher/participant relationship. For example, my gender and sexuality/relationship status often placed me in vulnerable positions in the field and in my interactions with my participants; there were occasions where my relationship status was questioned, where I was emotional about my divorce that was in process, where it was clear that I was a potential target for matchmaking, where I was left alone with male participants, and so on. According to

Gilliat-Ray (2010), putting oneself in vulnerable situations can tamp down some of the identities that might act as barriers to open, honest communication, barriers that are often lifted in insider research.

Furthermore, while I was not a complete religious insider, in the sense of claiming Muslim identity, my religious identity still provided me some insider benefits, what I labelled as "semi-spiritual-insider" status. I went into the field with some preconceived notions that my identity as a Christian may help in my research process, but I could not have anticipated how much this identity, and the outward claiming of such an identity, would impact the way that my participants responded to me. I discovered quickly that if I had not been a "person of the book" I probably would not have been given the same initial access or the depth of access that I was granted. Sharing the basic understanding of one God, the same basic spiritual history, gave me an immediate boost in trust points. I was not fully an insider, but I was also not completely an outsider. Concretely, my religious identity allowed me to engage in deep theological conversation with my informants. They were interested in learning about Christianity and thus would spend hours with me discussing the similarities and differences between the two traditions. These moments of interfaith dialogue between us inevitably led to me getting a longer and deeper glance into their daily lives, not to mention many more dinner invitations.

This is highly dependent on the research context in which I was operating (Quebec) where committed religious belief, no matter what the religious background, is often seen as a minority position. In this case, my identity as a "believing Christian" provided me with "spiritual street cred" amidst my participants – a credibility that I only benefited from once I clearly announced my religious identity, since it was not "read" on my body in the ways that other scholars have discussed (Benstead 2014; Blaydes and Gillum 2013; Gilliat-Ray 2010).[5]

While I hinted at what this all meant for the knowledge that I produced about Islam – i.e., that my lack of insider knowledge about Islam allowed my participants to largely dictate what I examined and presented, that my semi-spiritual-insider status gave me more access to the intimate details of my participants' lives and therefore to the kind of knowledge I was interested in gathering – this discussion, while a part of my dissertation, has not made its way into my scholarly output as of yet.[6] Even within the most commonly addressed aspect of positionality within the study of Islam(s) in Canada (religious identity), researchers, like myself, do not necessarily address in any concrete way the effects of their own shifting positionalities on the actual knowledge they produce about Islam(s). That is, the kind of knowledge I produced about Islam(s) in Canada changed and shifted as my own religious identity allowed my participants to change and shift their perspective towards me. Furthermore, if most studies of Islam(s) in Canada are done by religious "insiders," with all the assumptions that go along with that label from a standpoint that sees religious positionality as a binary category, the knowledge produced about Islam will be read differently than if most studies of Islam(s) in Canada are done by religious "outsiders." That is, the studies done by insiders may be viewed as producing more authentic or "true" knowledge about Islam than those done by "outsiders." If, on the other hand, scholars address their shifting and nuanced positionality vis-à-vis religion, we may be able to view the knowledge produced about Islam(s) in Canada in such a shifting and nuanced way as well. If insider/outsider status is on a spectrum and not a binary category, we can begin to see how the picture of Islam(s) in Canada that emerge from scholarly output is also shifting. This can help to support the idea that, like all other religious traditions, Islam is not a binary category, not a sui generis concept that the objective researcher can observe and present on paper to a "captive audience." If the researcher is positioned and their positionalities are shifting, then the kinds of knowledge about Islam that we get glimpses of are also shifting and nuanced.

Subject Matter

Again, while one can find some willingness to discuss researcher positionality and its impact on knowledge production within the study of Islam(s) in Canada, most of this discussion is around how various researcher identities, often religious, sometimes gender and racial, impact on data collection and interpretation. In this final section I will address how my research, specifically the choice of research topic, challenges previous work and assumptions around researcher positionality (specifically gender) and the study and knowledge production of Islam(s).

Setting of Research

The first way that my choice of research topic influenced the knowledge I inevitably produced about Islam(s) was through the setting of research. The exploration of foodways,[7] specifically domestic foodways, immediately placed the context of research within the domestic rather than institutional realm. This meant that most of my research in Montreal took place in people's homes. This in turn meant that the "picture" of Islam(s) in Canada that I witnessed, the one I inevitably remembered and the one that I therefore wrote about, was a domestic, lived, and intimate picture.

In an entry in my fieldwork journal I reflected on the setting of research and how one of my participants suggested that this might affect the knowledge I would gather on Islam(s) in Montreal and consequently the knowledge that I would produce on the subject.

> The overarching piece of advice that he gave me in terms of my research was to not really bother with trying to make the mosques my primary point of entry and

> observation. Instead he suggested that meeting with families, in people's homes would be the way to get the richest data. He said that the mosque communities are fairly closed off here in Montréal and that I will get pad answers from folks there. He suggested that in people's homes, after putting them at ease, I will get to see the real way that my subject gets played out. (AFJ, 1 Mar. 2013)

With a topic such as food, the domestic angle not only makes sense but is somewhat inevitable, especially when considering the qualitative nature of my work. If I had been exploring the theological underpinnings of food practice and the way "Muslim foodways" are taught, discussed, and disseminated within the community, perhaps the institutional context would have made more sense for this project. Here we see how various aspects of positionality work on one another in the "circle of impact" discussed by Corbin Dwyer and Buckle (2009). For me the domestic setting was inevitable because of my choice of topic and the methodology that I chose to follow, but my access to this setting was also highly dependent on another aspect of my positionality: my gender.

Food and Gender

When looking at the literature around food and gender, it becomes clear that there is an implicit assumption that domestic food work is women's work. According to Cairns et al. (2010), when talking about domestic cooking, "women rather than men primarily plan for, purchase, and cook food in the home" (591). Because of this, studies on the meaning of cooking and domestic food work have tended to focus on women (Szabo 2014). This focus is often left unquestioned, and researchers just operate under these assumptions when they choose to research food. Specific studies about food and gender "interrogate the historically naturalized connection between food and femininity that has served to legitimize women's disproportionate food labor and to reproduce gendered divisions between the public and private spheres" (Cairns et al. 2010, 592). While these studies may interrogate the connection between food and femininity, they tend to still find strict gender divisions present when it comes to domestic food practice (Cairns et al. 2010; Szabo 2014).

In my own work, I could also see how there were gender-influenced perspectives on food and food practices. The fact that I had twenty-two female participants and ten male participants in Montreal reflects the position that women have "more to say" about food than men. While men were quite willing to talk to me about their food practices, because of the snowball sampling method that I followed, women tended to introduce me to other women to interview, so methodologically it was more difficult to recruit male participants. When going back to my work and teasing out my field journals and interview experiences, I could see that talking with women about their food experiences gave a different perspective on food and Islam(s) as opposed to speaking with men. I wrote in one of my field journal entries that "younger men seem to have less to say about food and food practice than women" (AFJ, 11 Apr. 2013). I also reflected after another set of interviews where I interviewed three women and three men in one day that

> my first interview was with a woman and the following two were with men. I do find that talking to women about food seems to flow easier. It is easier to ask questions about preparation of traditional dishes because it is often them who are preparing. Although that could simply be a preconceived notion I have which influences how I view the question. (AFJ, 30 Apr. 2013)

Talking with women, whose experience with food was often domestic, daily, and mundane, versus talking with men, whose experience with food was often intellectual, also gave a different view of Islam(s). I saw this clearly in an interview that I conducted with a PhD student/scholar in which he discussed theological and textual perspectives on the food practices rather than the emotional, memory-driven perspectives I would get from women who are domestic cooks. My longest interview in Montreal was with a man who spoke with me for two hours about food, challenging the idea that men do not have much to say about food but also supporting the gendered relationship to food, as he spent most of the two hours talking about the rules and regulations and the theology behind the practices rather than the personal engagement with food practice. When considering these gendered perspectives, it becomes clear why a researcher choosing a topic related to food, and especially domestic food practices, would focus on women and women's experiences. This is perhaps more so if the researcher herself is a woman and researching within a community where some individuals have strict ideas around gender norms. Within this gendered cultural perspective that places women at the centre of household affairs, food as women's work, and separation between unrelated men and women as the norm, my positionality inevitably placed me firmly within these norms and expectations for my interactions with my participants. But did it *have* to be that way?

Decentring Assumptions of Researcher Positionality: Islam, Food, and Gender

Because my study was about food and, as argued above, food is often seen as the domain of women, as a woman, I could access events, places, and people related to domestic food practice that a male researcher may have had difficulty accessing. As Gilliat-Ray (2010) suggests, female researchers have easier access to female experience. When reflecting on positionality and the study of Islam(s) as it relates to gender specifically, some scholars have suggested that being a woman when interviewing women in a Muslim context is "particularly important because of *purdah* (gender segregation)" (Zempi 2016, 4.20). Gilliat-Ray (2010) states that this is dependent on "norms and ideals about physical proximity, eye-contact and demeanour between unrelated men and women," which "are strongly shaped by religious laws and social and cultural expectations" (419). I saw these norms and ideals in action during my time in the field and could see how my positionality as a woman inevitably impacted on my access – intimate access – to women's experiences. First, I could be in the kitchen helping to prepare meals, a task most likely unavailable to male researchers. During one Ramadan iftar experience, a rare iftar where I was seated at the table with all members of the family, both male and female, my participants and I had a lively discussion about gender norms and food preparation.

> We talked about the role of women versus men and how women prepare everything and men just sit back and take in the benefits of that. We talked about the fact that it is cultural and not religious but that men will use religious arguments for why it is that way. The participant's sister-in-law explained that the prophet actually did everything for himself. He made food, he cleaned, etc. and I retorted with "well if you are supposed to follow the lead of the prophet shouldn't men be doing the same thing?" They all laughed and the mother suggested that I might be thrown out of the window if I talk like that. (AFJ, 15 July 2013)

The fact that I was speaking with the men about their food experiences was an unexpected approach to studying food and Islam(s) in Canada. This interest in and look at the male perspective as it related to food helped to decentre and challenge the norms around gendered foodways. While Meah (2014) sought to respond "to the gender-bias that has tended to characterize much academic scholarship concerning food," by looking "at the experiences of men in those spaces where they have been assumed to be absent" (672), my process was not as intentional. I generally avoided questions about gender and the gender influence on food preparation. It wasn't my interest. Therefore, the kind of knowledge I produced about food practices and Islam(s) had little to do with gendered power structures in food practice, women as the gatekeepers of the tradition, and so on, and more about people's visceral engagements and interactions with their own food practice.

Although gender was not my orienting interest/question, my research revealed that people's engagement with their foodways was gendered, as I discussed above. What becomes interesting is how much of these gendered presentations of foodways were affected and influenced by my positionality. Was it that men had a more distant relationship to food than women, or was that the story I was being told because I am a woman? Could my gender allow for more intimate descriptions of home life, and the place of food within one's practice of

Islam(s), by the women I interviewed, while keeping my conversations with the men I interviewed on a scholarly, academic, and professional level? Did gendered norms, while not my interest, still impact on my research process and therefore on the knowledge I could produce about Islam(s)? The answer is clearly yes.

While I did try to get at the male experience through my participant observation, I was still somewhat restricted in my access to the lived male perspective on these food practices and was much freer to explore the female experience and perspective because of my positionality. By reflecting on my many iftar dinners during Ramadan, I could see how my participant observations of these moments were highly skewed to the female perspective (I only attended three iftars during the month of Ramadan where men and women were all eating together in the same room and at the same table). In one of my field journals I wrote about an experience during an iftar in a respondent's home that highlights many of the norms and ideals regarding gender segregation present and how they invariably influenced the kind of knowledge I had access to about Islam(s).

> Because it is Friday today we had a bigger group for dinner tonight. In total, we were nine women and I believe there were three or four men in the other room … I asked, feigning ignorance, why the men were in another room. My participant explained to me that first and foremost it was just the way that she was familiar with from her family of origin. She mentioned that if it was close family they may all eat together, but friends and unknown people usually meant that the men and women would be separate. She then explained that when men and women are together the women must be covered and they should pay extra close attention to what they say. So they prefer to be just with other women, that way they can take off the veil and *talk about whatever they want*. (AFJ, 12 July 2013)

My positionality clearly gave me access to a different kind of knowledge about Islam(s) in Canada than would have been possible for a male colleague. As my participant said, because we were all women together, they could "talk about whatever they want" rather than potentially feeling the need to engage in the kinds of impression management discussed by Benstead (2014). At another iftar, the potential for impression management, and the kind of conversation that one would have at the table with just women versus with men and women together, was further highlighted. Reflecting on that iftar I wrote,

> The meal was going to be with men and women in the same space, so my participant [the same participant who is quoted directly above] made a comment about the fact that conversation would be different. One of my favourite moments of the night was related to this. We were sitting at the table enjoying the iftar meal with some women who have been coming to her house for the iftars. One of the women is a convert from Mexico and her father joined in for the iftar at the mosque … My

> participant had explained to him through his daughter that normally when we are at home we sit in separate rooms from the men, so we can talk freely, etc. When we got tea for everyone at the table and he began to drink it he said that it was an aphrodisiac (in Spanish) and his daughter got a bit mortified and laughed and said "no Papa." My participant asked what he had said and she explained what he had said and justified it as a "latino culture" thing. Everyone was a bit shocked, but my participant brilliantly responded with a laugh "you see, that's why we don't eat with the men." We all laughed. (AFJ, 20 July 2013)

With participants who held to these gender norms, my positionality as a woman clearly allowed me to gain more intimate knowledge of their practice of Islam(s) as it relates to food.

Even if I were to focus just on women though, my identity as a woman did not immediately give me insider understanding of Muslim women's experience: "The collectivity 'Muslim women' is striated by a plurality of identities – such as race, ethnicity, age, language, class, education, sexual orientation and degree of practising Islam, to name but some examples" (Zempi 2016, 2.4). On the one hand, some of my female participants might have felt comfortable allowing me deeper access to their daily lives and to their thoughts about their food practices because I was a woman. On the other hand, others may have restricted their answers or engaged in more impression management because of my Whiteness, my Canadian, non-migrant identity, or my perceived/presented class or education. Relatedly, while some of my male participants may have restricted their answers because I am a woman and they did not feel it appropriate to allow me into their personal, intimate perspectives, others felt quite comfortable discussing all kinds of topics with me because I was not a Muslim, and in their eyes I was not bound by the same gender norms that we would have been restricted by had I been a Muslim woman. Therefore, simple ideas of insider and outsider positionality when it comes to gender need to be questioned and challenged. Studies that push these boundaries of positionality and consequently show how topics such as "the distribution of power in domestic kitchen spaces [are] more diverse, diffuse, dynamic and contingent than previously thought" (Meah 2014, 684) are increasingly important. Acting outside of the boundaries of expectation based on one's positionality as a researcher may be one way to diversify the knowledge that is produced about Islam(s) in Canada. For example, I acted outside the boundaries of expectation by speaking to both men and women about foodways and consequently got some insight into Muslim men's perspective on food, a data set that would be non-existent had I only spoken with women. Furthermore, while many people would label my study as "outsider research," I pushed the boundaries of insiderism, and my self-claimed semi-spiritual-insider status provided many of the benefits of "insider" research that are often documented: more transparency and faster responses from participants, acceptance, an easier starting point for access, assumptions of understanding and shared distinctiveness (Corbin Dwyer and Buckle 2009, 58). By pushing back at the boundaries around gender, age, race, religion, and so on, we can produce more nuanced pictures of Islam(s) than might be possible if we all act according to the binary expectations surrounding these positionalities.

Conclusion: Positionality and the Co-Creation of Knowledge of Islam(s) in Canada

Throughout this chapter I have argued for the need for more critical reflexivity on researcher positionality within the study of Islam(s) in Canada. I suggested that this critical reflexivity needs to go beyond a simple acknowledgment of one's positionality to a serious engagement with how our various, and often shifting, positionalities (and those of our research participants) impact on not only data collection but also knowledge production. Using entries from my field journals I showed how this kind of critical reflexivity is often present but not often reported on or engaged with in our scholarly writing. By purposefully engaging in this kind of critical reflexivity, I illustrated how ideas about insider and outsider positionality are more complicated than simply being "in" or "out." In fact, this, and all other aspects of one's positionality, should be seen more as a shifting spectrum rather than a binary position. If the researcher is positioned and their positionalities are shifting, then the kinds of knowledge about Islam(s) we get glimpses of are also shifting and nuanced. I also suggested that acting outside of the boundaries of expectation based on one's positionality as a researcher may be one way to diversify the knowledge produced about Islam(s) in Canada.

Furthermore, I claimed that our choice of research topic (within the broad subject of Islam(s) in Canada) highly influences the knowledge that we produce. By choosing to focus on food, a choice affected by my various positionalities, I painted a picture of Islam(s) in Canada that was curated, selective, and coloured in specific ways. Within the qualitative research process, people spoke to me about a great deal of other topics than food (i.e., the veil, work and/or the lack of work, family relationships). For example, after one interview I wrote in my field journal entry that "we had a long interview, and then spoke for another hour after the interview about the veil" (AFJ, 29 May 2013). On other occasions, I reflected in my field journal about people's frustration with their employment situation in Canada, about how family dynamics were different and affected by being in Canada, about moments of interfaith interaction and how that changed their understanding of Islam(s), and more. Yet I didn't write on these topics. I only wrote about food and how that impacted on the migrant experience, not how these other topics necessarily impacted on it or on my participants' practice of Islam(s) in Canada. Furthermore, while I did not restrict my examination to only women's perspectives, and thus challenged certain implicit expectations about gender positionality, my positionality, and the gendered expectations around it, meant that the bulk of my data, and the bulk of the knowledge about Islam(s) in Canada that I wrote about, were principally from a domestic, female perspective.

These arguments are seemingly straightforward for the qualitative researcher of Islam(s) in Canada and have been somewhat reflected in the literature. Since much of the knowledge production of Islam(s) in Canada has been qualitative, it makes sense that the conversation around researcher positionality takes up a prominent role in the discussion of what kind of picture of Islam(s) in Canada emerges within that research landscape. A question arises as to whether, and to what extent, researchers engaged in other methodologies in the study of Islam(s) in Canada need to participate in critical reflexivity in the way that researchers engaged in qualitative research do. Furthermore, how do various methodologies and approaches impact on knowledge production of Islam(s)? According to Dean et al. (2017), different methods bring out different data, so we need to discuss more frequently how these positionalities inevitably lead to certain knowledge being produced about Islam(s) in Canada over others.

For many of us that study Islam(s) in Canada, I think we often feel how I was feeling when I reflected in my field journal, "I am looking forward to getting my actual data totally transcribed and consequently analyzed. I am looking forward to seeing what actually shows up in the data and not just what I have been imagining in my head" (AFJ, 24 July 2013). These kinds of statements, the idea that I might see "what actually shows up in the data," as if there is some mysterious "truth" to be found there that was separate from my hand on it, need to be acknowledged and challenged. Rather than just trying to get some objective "truth" out there about Islam(s) in Canada, we should put effort towards the "co-creation of knowledge amongst researchers and the researched," which will be more "likely to generate strong, authentic and credible research outcomes" (Zempi 2016, 5.4). This co-creation of knowledge comes from a place of vulnerability of the researcher and participant, a willingness to acknowledge and work with both parties' shifting positionalities and to make sure that the knowledge produced is not just a one-sided endeavour, which results in an "unbiased" presentation from the "objective" researcher to the world.

Ultimately, if we do not pause, as researchers of Islam(s) in Canada, to critically reflect on how our own positionality in a variety of realms dictates what Islam(s) is/are in Canada, we are missing an essential aspect of our work. In fact, the focus of this current work, the knowledge production of Islam(s) in Canada, sets up the centrality of the discussion of researcher positionality in the study of Islam(s). We are knowledge producers, ideally co-producers with our participants, and therefore cannot ignore our hand in that production. All future research projects on Islam(s) in Canada should not only acknowledge the positionality present but also critically engage with how one's positionality (an ever-changing set of positionalities) facilitates, challenges, and decentres our ideas about what Islam(s) in Canada is/are.

NOTES

1 While acknowledging one's positionality is, I would argue, essential for all researchers who produce knowledge about any given topic, most of the past research on positionality and its impact looks at qualitative research projects and methodologies, and specifically methods that require researcher and participant to be in direct contact in some way. This chapter will therefore focus on these kinds of methods. An interesting question to consider is whether, and to what extent, researchers engaged in other methodologies in the study of Islam(s) in Canada need to participate in critical reflexivity as researchers engaged in qualitative research do.

2 For example, while researchers with varied positionality conduct research on the veil in Canadian Muslim communities, the underlying theme of "choice" is constant. In studies of food and religion, and specifically food in migrant communities, the underlying theme of food as means of connection to homeland and religious practice is constant regardless of the positionality of the researcher.

3 This "reading" of the researcher body and identities also impacts on and is impacted by ideas of power. The reason that researcher identities can impact on data collection is often related to the power, real or perceived, that a researcher has in the eyes of their participant(s). When there is a real or perceived power differential between the researcher and the participant, this often leads to the participant engaging in various forms of impression management, where they will consciously or subconsciously alter their responses in a way to fit with, or not challenge, the powered position/identity of the researcher. For more on positionality and power see Blaydes and Gillum (2013); Benstead (2014); Hoel (2013); and Zempi (2016).

4 Blaydes and Gillum (2013) argue that "respondents who are members of groups that have been subjected to discrimination in the past, such as African-Americans or women, might be especially likely to express views that are respectful to high-status interviewers' social groups, such as white males" (4). In the study of Islam(s) in Canada this is important, and researchers need to acknowledge how Muslims, as members of minority groups who are often the focus of discrimination, may engage in impression management with researchers who are in various positions of power over them. Zempi (2016) argues that this is particularly evident in the study of Islam(s) conducted by so-called outsiders, and that often Muslims will participate in the research out of a desire to dispel myths about Islam to "non-Muslims" – outsider researchers would have a reach to other outsiders and could dispel myths further (4.13).

5 Benstead (2014) suggests that "in a society with relatively secular elite and ascendant Islamist movements, religious respondents are more likely to edit their responses than secular respondents" (736–7). When reflecting on my own religious positionality,

I wonder if this could have been the case in my early days in Paris and Montreal, when respondents didn't "read" religiosity onto my body. Does knowledge of religiosity then lead to less editing? Can this effect only happen in qualitative ethnographic fieldwork, where more time is spent than delivering a survey, for example?

6 In the manuscript based on my dissertation research, which I am working on currently, I do address my positionality and its impact on the knowledge produced therein.

7 I use "foodways" in line with Marie Dallam's (2014) definition of the term. Dallam defines a foodway as "an expression of our 'ways' around food: how we grow or acquire it, how we prepare it, how we display or use it, and how and when we consume it. To talk about the foodways of a group, then, is to talk about what people consider food, what they do with food, what they think about the food and the eating, and their ideas about what the food means to them" (xviii).

REFERENCES

Angrosino, Michael V., and Kimberly A. Mays de Perez. 2000. "Rethinking observation: From method to context." In Norman K. Denzin and Yvonna S. Lincoln (Eds.), *Handbook of qualitative research* (2nd ed.) (pp. 673–702). SAGE.

Benstead, Lindsay J. 2014. "Does interviewer religious dress affect survey responses? Evidence from Morocco." *Politics and Religion*, 7, 734–60. http://doi.org/10.1017/S1755048314000455

Blaydes, Lisa, and Rachel M. Gillum. 2013. "Religiosity-of-interviewer effects: Assessing the impact of veiled enumerators on survey response in Egypt." *Politics and Religion*, *6*(3), 1–24. https://doi.org/10.1017/S1755048312000557

Brown, Rachel D. 2017. "Immigration, integration and ingestion: The role of food and drink in transnational experience for North African Muslim immigrants in Paris and Montréal." PhD diss., Wilfrid Laurier University. http://scholars.wlu.ca/etd/1901

Cairns, Kate, Josee Johnston, and Shyon Bauman. 2010. "Caring about food: Doing gender in the foodie kitchen." *Gender and Society*, *24*(5), 591–615. https://doi.org/10.1177%2F0891243210383419

Coleman, Simon. 2010. "On remembering and forgetting in writing and fieldwork." In Peter Collins and Anselma Gallinat (Eds.), *The ethnographic self as resource: Writing memory and experience into ethnography* (pp. 215–22). Berghahn Books.

Collins, Peter. 2010. "The ethnographic self as resource?" In Peter Collins and Anselma Gallinat (Eds.), *The ethnographic self as resource: Writing memory and experience into ethnography* (pp. 228–45). Berghahn Books.

Corbin Dwyer, Sonya, and Jennifer L. Buckle. 2009. "The space between: On being an insider-outsider in qualitative research." *International Journal of Qualitative Methods*, *8*(1), 54–63. https://doi.org/10.1177%2F160940690900800105

Dallam, Marie. 2014. "Introduction: Religion, food, and eating." In Benjamin E. Zeller, Marie W. Dallam, Reid L. Neilson, and Nora L. Rubel (Eds.), *Religion, food and eating in North America* (pp. xvii–xxxii). Columbia University Press.

Dean, Jon, Penny Furness, Diarmuid Verrier, Henry Lennon, and Cinnamon Bennett. 2017. "Desert island data: An investigation into researcher positionality." *Qualitative Research, 18*(3), 273–89. https://doi.org/10.1177%2F1468794117714612

Gawlewicz, Anna. 2016. "Language and translation strategies in researching migrant experience of difference from the position of migrant researcher." *Qualitative Research, 16*(1), 27–42. https://doi.org/10.1177%2F1468794114557992

Gilliat-Ray, Sophie. 2010. "Body-works and fieldwork: Research with British Muslim chaplains." *Culture and Religion, 11*(4), 413–32. https://doi.org/10.1080/14755610.2010.527615

Hammer, Juliane. 2016. "Gender matters: Normativity, positionality, and the politics of Islamic Studies." *Muslim World, 106*(4), 655–70. https://doi.org/10.1111/muwo.12164

Hellawell, David. 2006. "Inside-out: Analysis of the insider-outsider concept as a heuristic device to develop reflexivity in students doing qualitative work." *Teaching in Higher Education, 11*(4), 483–94. https://doi.org/10.1080/13562510600874292

Hoel, Nina. 2013. "Embodying the field: A researcher's reflections on power dynamics, positionality and the nature of research relationships." *Fieldwork in Religion, 8*(1), 27–49. https://doi.org/10.1558/firn.v8i1.27

Hopkins, Nick, and Ronni Michelle Greenwood. 2013. "*Hijab*, visibility and the performance of identity." *European Journal of Social Psychology, 43*(5), 438–47. https://doi.org/10.1002/ejsp.1955

Meah, Angela. 2014. "Reconceptualizing power and gendered subjectivities in domestic cooking spaces." *Progress in Human Geography, 38*(5), 671–90. https://doi.org/10.1177%2F0309132513501404

Sherif, Bahira. 2001. "The ambiguity of boundaries in the fieldwork experience: Establishing rapport and negotiating insider/outsider status." *Qualitative Inquiry, 7*(4), 436–47. https://doi.org/10.1177%2F107780040100700403

Simpson, Bob. 2006. "'You don't do fieldwork, fieldwork does you': Between subjectivation and objectivation in anthropological fieldwork." In Dick Hobbs and Richard Wright (Eds.), *The SAGE handbook of fieldwork* (pp. 125–38). SAGE.

Szabo, Michelle. 2014. "Men nurturing through food: Challenging gender dichotomies around domestic cooking." *Journal of Gender Studies, 23*(1), 18–31. https://doi.org/10.1080/09589236.2012.711945

Zempi, Irene. 2016. "Negotiating constructions of insider and outsider status in research with veiled Muslim women victims of Islamophobic hate crime." *Sociological Research Online, 21*(4), 70–81. https://doi.org/10.5153%2Fsro.4080. http://www.socresonline.org.uk/21/4/8.html

Fieldworking While Veiled: Autoethnography of a Brown + Muslim + Female Researcher in Quebec

ROSHAN ARAH JAHANGEER

Introduction

While leafing through some of the handwritten field notes from my fieldwork research in Quebec in October 2013, two sentences scrawled unremarkably on the bottom of a blank page in my notebook jumped out at me: "There were around 75–100 people in attendance, and community media as well. I was wearing a red leopard print hijab and black skinny jeans with my [navy] blue, leather stars, elbow patch sweater." It was an observation I wrote about what I had been wearing that day, written immediately after participant observation about the number and backgrounds of people in attendance at an event I attended. Rereading these sentences gave me pause: Why did I feel the need to write down this observation about my own clothing choices that day? Was this something that most ethnographers do? Was this something that male ethnographers do? What about female ones? Do other racialized ethnographers make these types of self-conscious reflections about their sartorial choices while inhabiting particular spaces?

Field notes are essential to an ethnographer. They routinely contain information regarding one's participant observation. They are detailed notes and "thick description" about the environment that one finds oneself in, including demographic information about participants. Ethnographers might handwrite brief field notes in a notebook and later flesh out their observations in a typed entry. However, when reading some of the other field notes I had written over the course of a thirteen-week research trip to Montreal from my home city of Toronto in 2013, I noticed that I would write such self-conscious observations more frequently as the weeks wore on.

As a brown Muslim woman who wears a hijab (or headscarf), my positionality is complicated through multiple layers of colonialisms, including settler colonialism (Patel 2019). I was born in Mauritius, a small island off the southern east coast of Africa that had been colonized by both the French and the

British, and immigrated to Toronto, Canada, with my parents as a child. Though I spoke French and Mauritian creole since childhood, English slowly became my dominant language while growing up in anglophone-majority Toronto. But I always maintained French as a second language through enrolment in French immersion schooling, albeit with a somewhat anglophone accent. Racially, I am South Asian, and like many other Mauritians, my ancestors migrated from India to Mauritius as indentured labourers during the mid-nineteenth century when Mauritius was still controlled by the British empire. Religiously, I identify as Sunni Muslim, and while I did not wear the hijab in my early teens and twenties, I do wear it now and have done so for many years. Therefore, my positionality is one of multiple intersecting identities of race, class, gender, sexuality, religion, ability, language, coloniality, and nationality, among others.

The way that my multiple identities intersect is critical to the research I do and to the knowledge I produce. Case in point is the subject of my current research and the reason for my 2013 research trip to Montreal: I study anti-veiling laws and how they circulate transnationally between France and Quebec. By anti-veiling laws, I refer specifically to proposed bills or laws that prohibit the wearing of hijabs or niqabs in certain spaces (e.g., schools), in certain professions (e.g., teaching, judiciary, prosecution, police), in certain contexts (e.g., while giving or receiving public services), or in public space altogether.[1] My point of entry into this topic proved to be very different from most researchers, because I had a personal connection to both un/veiling and to my francophone interlocutors, not only because I speak French but also because I am Muslim and face similar forms of discrimination as they do in my everyday life. My positionality affected both the way that I conducted my fieldwork research and the experiences I encountered while "in the field."

A Note on Methodology and Embodiment

Studying the impacts of the French law of 2004[2] which prohibits students from wearing "religious symbols" in public schools proved to be a challenge. Before travelling to Paris, France, for the first part of my fieldwork in 2012, I knew that I would not be able to volunteer in French public schools because I wear a hijab in my daily life. French public schools are deemed to be secular spaces; therefore, teachers and volunteers are considered as representatives of the French Republic and are thus required to keep their appearance "neutral" (translation: they must not wear any "religious symbols" on their bodies, including hijabs). This restriction affected my research design as I could not study the impacts of anti-veiling laws on public high school students directly; I had to do so indirectly, while interviewing young Muslim women who were over eighteen and who had already graduated from high school. While in Paris, it was also very difficult to meet with teachers, public servants, or politicians, because again, I would not be allowed to enter certain government offices or school buildings while wearing a hijab. On the rare occasion that I did meet with a teacher or public servant, we met in cafés, restaurants, or even, once, at a local park during their lunch break. There was also an issue of safety; I was very careful not to meet with groups or persons who had expressed Islamophobic remarks or taken anti-veiling positions publicly in the past. I took my own safety very seriously, and that meant not subjecting myself to those who I believed would be hostile towards me or my religion, even if they were potential interlocutors. Off the record, I often asked some of the local Muslim activists that I met with whether I should speak with certain groups or individuals, since they had more knowledge of the political field than I did. They would tell me, "Maybe, but you'll probably have to either remove or wear your hijab differently if you do meet with them or else they might get hostile." Removing my hijab or changing the way that I dress to cater to someone else's racism was not something I was willing to do for the sake of research. I was very clear from the start of my research trip to France about where my boundaries lay.

Taking into account one's personal safety is essential when planning fieldwork research, especially for female, racialized, and/or 2SLGBTQQIA[3] researchers who are more vulnerable to sexualized, racialized, and gendered harassment and violence than, say, a White cisgender male researcher might be (Kloß 2017). It is also important to acknowledge that instances of harassment or violence can and do occur during fieldwork, as such incidents are more common than what is normally represented within anthropological literature (Kloß 2017, 398).

After concluding the first part of my research trip to France, I returned to Canada and immediately set off for Montreal, Quebec, to continue the second part of my research. I confess that upon arriving back in Canada, I let my guard down because I was at home, somewhere I had imagined myself belonging.[4] I did not put up the same boundaries as I had in Paris, and it was not clear what challenges I would face on account of being a hijabi[5] in Montreal, particularly because in early 2013, the Quebec government had not yet proposed any anti-veiling laws that would restrict the wearing of hijabs in any context. However, the presentation of my hijab-clad body in the francophone Quebecois space and context became especially contentious during the 2013–14 debate over the Quebec Charter of Values (hereafter the PQ Charter).[6] The PQ Charter (i.e., Bill 60) was the law proposed by the Parti Québécois (PQ) in 2013 that sought to ban specifically identified "ostentatious religious symbols" in the public sector.[7] These so-called ostentatious symbols included hijabs, niqabs, kippas, turbans, and large crucifixes.[8] I had failed to consider the impact of the PQ Charter on women who looked like me, since I had previously travelled to Montreal without any major incidents in March and June–July and was returning for a third time in the fall – after the PQ Charter had been announced. By then, it was a markedly different political climate. Suddenly, the hijab that I had worn unremarkably on the streets of Montreal several times over the course of 2013 had become a flashpoint – an ostentatious marker that made me a target of various glares, remarks, and unsolicited attention.

I will illustrate a few episodes from the fieldwork research I conducted in Montreal, Quebec, in 2013, which was undertaken as part of my larger project on the transnational circulation of anti-veiling laws between France and Quebec. I will detail some of my experiences before and after the announcement of the PQ Charter. As the debate evolved, the locus of attention centred on Muslim women, particularly those who practised veiling. For example, in late 2013, the Commission des droits de la personne et des droits de la jeunesse (Human Rights and Youth Rights Commission), as well as several women's shelter groups across Quebec, pointed to a sharp rise in complaints of verbal and physical assaults against veiled women in particular (Peritz 2013). In addition, scores of Muslim women were left out of the debates, particularly Black Muslim women, and those who were included were vilified in the media (Jahangeer 2020; Mugabo 2014, 2016). This hypervisibility coupled with erasure led to a context whereby Muslim women experienced a hyper presence-absence: They were present in the debates, in that they were constantly spoken about by others, be they nationalists or liberals, but they were absent in that they were not expected to speak back or to participate in the debates on their own terms (Benhadjoudja 2018; Jahangeer 2020; Mugabo 2014, 2016).

With regard to my own presence in the field within this political context, the PQ Charter debate was a period when my body was hypervisible, which affected the way that my research unfolded. As has been noted by previous ethnographers, "the presence of the ethnographer is intricately entwined in the reality under study. In fact, participants in the scene respond to the presence of the observer (and the observer, in turn, responds to them), thus blending, as humans do, action and interaction" (Poulos 2012, 38). This two-way interaction between ethnographer and participant in terms of action and reaction became even more pronounced when there were few other hijab-wearing women present at a public event or in a public space. In the situations I describe here, my presence as an ethnographer was rendered as something of an anomaly, even a spectacle. This was the context in which I began writing down notes about myself while "in the field," as not only an observer but also an active participant in the phenomena I was observing.

The method that seemed most conducive to the type of detailed note-taking I began doing was autoethnography. Autoethnography, which mixes methods of autobiography and ethnography, relies on detailed memory-work and note-taking about significant events that impact the researcher. Although ethnography also uses these elements, it differs from autoethnography in that the latter uses researchers' own lived experiences as data, which they then use as the basis for further theoretical analysis (Crawley 2012, 146). As Crawley

(2012) explains, "Engaging both evocation and analysis, my favourite kind of format for autoethnography engages 'scenes' from one's reflected life experiences followed by theoretical analysis" (153). In doing so, autoethnography openly acknowledges the authors' memories as primary sources of data for reflecting on their life experiences "according to their specific research focus and data-collection criteria" (Chang 2008, 212). Similar to feminist standpoint theory, whereby knowledge is both situated and embodied according to one's social location, autoethnography rejects the idea of a neutral, passive, or objective observer, which numerous scholars have criticized for reproducing masculine, White, Christian-centric models of research and writing (Chang 2008; Crawley 2012; Kloß 2017). Instead, "autoethnography is one of the approaches that acknowledges and accommodates subjectivity, emotionality, and the researcher's influence on research, rather than hiding from these matters or assuming they don't exist" (Ellis et al. 2011). Because I had been noting my own emotional experiences in addition to details about the field I was observing, I felt that my hijab-clad body might reveal some of the power asymmetries at the heart of so-called debates surrounding "religious symbols" in Quebec, in addition to the "emotional politics" of doing fieldwork in an environment where Muslim and other racialized communities and their practices were under intense scrutiny.[9]

In what follows, I detail two instances of autoethnographic reflections where my hypervisibility as a hijab-wearing female Muslim researcher in the field served to disrupt the social field. I then reflect on the meaning of those disruptions and their implications for research as a racialized Muslim woman who veils in a context where veiling is oversaturated with symbolic meaning.

Field Note 1: "Be Careful."

In March 2013, the Université du Québec à Montréal (UQAM) hosted a public debate on the emergence of new racisms in Quebec. The event, which was aptly held in the same week as the International Day for the Elimination of Racial Discrimination, was organized by a prominent university-based research unit and was open to the public.

I attended the event with two friends, Suzanne, a Muslim feminist convert who was completing a PhD in communication studies at the time, and Manal, a longtime Muslim feminist activist who had worked in several Muslim community organizations in Montreal. There were between 150 and 200 people in attendance, most of whom seemed to be UQAM students, plus some community members who belonged to other organizations.

The panel was made up of two women and two men: an academic, a journalist with *La Presse*, and two activists from well-known faith-based and human rights NGOs in Quebec. The two men were racialized while the two women were both White French Canadian, and all of the panelists spoke in French. There were no racialized women on the panel.

The event was promoted as a "public debate," but as the speakers spoke one at time and did not seem to be responding to each other's points, it was more like a regular speaker's panel. Moreover, there did not seem to be much disagreement among the speakers, so it really did not seem like much of a debate. All of the speakers spoke on the general theme of the infiltration of what was termed "new racisms" in public debates, most arguing that these supposedly new forms of racism stemmed from deep systemic inequalities that have affected numerous minority communities in the past, most notably Black communities.

During the question period, I got up to pose a question after a number of others had already asked theirs. Feeling self-conscious, I made sure to ask both of the friends who had accompanied me to check over the question I had written down in French, in case there were any errors or anything that should not be asked in a public forum. Both read it and found nothing controversial, and they confirmed that my French was correct. So I asked my question in French (which is translated here):[10]

> Good evening. Thank you for all of your interventions. You had mentioned that there was no political party from the extreme right here in Quebec; however, there are still some similarities between the debates occurring in Quebec and those occurring in France on the subject of Muslims and Islam, particularly when it concerns veiled women. According to you, is there an influence from France or from French politics on the debates here in Quebec (I'm thinking particularly of the debates around Reasonable Accommodation,[11] Bill 94, and the discussions on halal meat …) and if there are similarities, how do these debates translate here in Quebec?

I had asked this question both because of my intellectual interest in France and Quebec and because I had travelled to France just a few months prior for the first part of my fieldwork; I had constantly found myself wondering whether I was experiencing déjà vu in Quebec since it seemed that so many of the same arguments were being recycled: for example, the argument that the Muslim head covering is inherently oppressive to Muslim women and that the face veil was equivalent to an "ambulatory prison."[12]

The first person from the panel to answer my question was the female academic. She started off by rephrasing my question and saying that, yes, there were some basic similarities between the debates on the veil that had taken place in France, Germany, the UK, Italy, Spain, and the Netherlands, and also Quebec, but that any such similarities were superficial. Then she said that to make comparisons between societies that are different can lead to an "analytical and political impasse." There seemed to be something she was implying in her remarks, something that I had heard in France as well: Basically, the argument goes that Quebec (likewise France) is so "exceptional" that it cannot be compared to any other place in the world, that its history and concepts (such as *laïcité*) are so different that not only are they untranslatable, but that other people would not understand them because they are not Quebecois (or French) themselves. Again, this line of argument can and has been debunked by numerous scholars (both Quebecois and French), so I will not spend time debunking it here.[13]

After several other members of the audience asked their questions and the event was over, people began leaving the room in single file. At this point, I turned off my recording – and as anyone doing fieldwork will tell you, this is usually when the most interesting things happen. As the female academic was leaving the room, she stopped near me and we made eye contact. I nodded and quietly said, "*Bonne soirée.*" There were several people walking past us towards the exit, and my friend Suzanne was standing to my left. The female academic walked right up to me and began speaking in French, in short, curt sentences:

"Are you doing your studies (here)?" she asked curtly, without preamble.

"Yes, but not here. At York," I replied, just as curtly.

"Doctorate?" she asked.

"Yes, doctorate," I answered. Neither of us were smiling.

"In what?" she continued.

"In political science," I answered. It had started to feel like an interrogation.

She persisted: "Is this the first time you've come to one of these symposiums?"

I replied, "No, it is not the first time, but this is the first time that I asked a question."

The female academic then dropped the neutral facial expression she had been wearing and began looking at me sternly while furrowing her brows, and this time, she lowered her voice:

"You should be careful," she said in a grave tone.

At first, I assumed she was being sympathetic and telling me to watch out for people who might discriminate against or try to discredit me or my work, so I began nodding to agree with her. But as she kept looking at me with the same stern look on her face, I understood that this was not her intended meaning.

I immediately sought to clarify what she meant and asked, "Yes, but in what sense?"

She turned to me again and, with a pointed glance, cryptically said, "One must be careful when making comparisons. We must pay attention to the particular context."

I paused while looking at her, trying to let her words sink in and to read between the lines. I was utterly baffled that a professor who did not know me or my work was giving me such a warning.

After a moment, I exclaimed, "Yes of course [one must be careful]. But it's still possible [to make comparisons]!"

She countered, "Yes, of course it's possible, but be careful nonetheless. It will take a doctoral thesis to be able to do it."

I immediately replied, with a look of confusion on my face, "But it is for a doctoral thesis!"

She immediately turned away to leave while saying dismissively, "Well then, good luck."

As soon as she was gone, I turned with wide, disbelieving eyes to my friend Suzanne, who had been standing next to me during the entire exchange and who was also a PhD candidate. Suzanne immediately exclaimed, "*Write it down!* Write down a field note right now!!!" I immediately sat back down and scribbled down our conversation in my notebook, word for word, in addition to whatever participant observation notes I had already written about the event in general.

I had felt incredibly frustrated and angry after my interaction with this female academic, which had felt very violent despite its seeming subtlety. It was one of the strangest interactions I had ever had with a professor, one that was both patronizing and condescending although in the subtlest of ways. Nothing that she had said to me was overt: In fact, the whole script of our interaction probably seemed very mild in comparison to what other students may have previously experienced. But the tone in her warning for me to "be careful" was what gave away her intention. It was definitely not out of concern for my well-being – it was more like something you would say to a little child, to be quiet and to not put their nose where it does not belong. It was not something you would say to a fellow scholar or even a scholar-in-training. Our interaction left me with a very bad and unsettled feeling long after it was over – as it was likely meant to.

In addition to writing about the interaction, I had also written down my friend's interpretation of the exchange, which, true to her training in communication studies, emphasized the power asymmetry of the conversation. She thought the dynamic was either something like *you're a student and I'm a professor*, or *I'm White and you're not*, or *I'm a Quebecoise and you're not*, or *I'm francophone and you're anglophone* – the implication being, you should stay away from things you have no business studying.

I wanted to add my own interpretation of our interaction. To me, she seemed to be saying, *This is a debate between us Quebecois: people like you are the source of this problem, so you Muslims should stay out of it.* This is not the first time such a hierarchical racialized dynamic has been upheld in Quebec, and indeed such dynamics and exclusions have been analysed by numerous scholars in the context of provincial debates over reasonable accommodations that had occurred several years earlier (Mahrouse 2010; Schaefli and Godlewska 2014).

However, at the time this interaction happened, I was probably one of the few hijab-wearing Canadian Muslim women of colour who were working on the issue of anti-veiling laws at the doctoral level. In many ways I was breaking a stereotype just by being present and by speaking and doing the research I was in the space of academia – which has historically been very White and male dominated, White women only having "broken in," so to speak, in the 1960s or later. Most academics, especially ones who are doing anti-racist feminist work or who work on questions of immigration, are usually pleasantly surprised to meet me because those who look like me and who do the work I do are rare.

This professor, however, did not seem pleased to meet me. She did not introduce herself or ask for my name. She did not ask what I was studying. Instead, she immediately assumed that I was not doing doctoral work and that I had no knowledge of the issue at hand. She did not ask if I had previously conducted research in France – which I had for at least five months prior to our meeting – or what my research was about. She did not seem pleased that I had asked a question at a public symposium. She seemed to dislike that I was making a comparison between France and Quebec, even as an intellectual exercise. It seemed as though she was saying that I had no place speaking about or researching Quebec because I was an outsider with no knowledge about the specific Quebec context. Moreover, the fact that I was a Muslim woman wearing hijab could not have escaped her notice. I later learned from a male Quebecois professor, who worked in a similar field, that this specific female professor had received complaints from former hijab-wearing students in the past about her behaviour and that she apparently had made it known that she disliked the hijab. Our interaction seemed to make a bit more sense after that.

Evicting Muslims from Public Life

As Razack (2008) argues in *Casting Out: The Eviction of Muslims from Western Law and Politics*, evicting Muslims from politics is not an exceptional occurrence. In Quebec, it has been argued that evicting researchers and activists of colour from participating in politics is also not an exceptional occurrence, as there have been numerous attempts to silence racialized activists and researchers from speaking about or even participating in Quebec politics (Benhadjoudja 2015, 2018; Jahangeer 2020; Mugabo 2014, 2016).

Délice Mugabo, a Muslim Black feminist and academic who had been heavily involved in the Quebec feminist movement as well as with the Quebec nationalist movement, writes about her experiences participating in a group that organized against the PQ Charter. The group, called Independantistes pour une laïcité inclusive (Sovereigntists for an Inclusive Secularism), had held informal meetings throughout 2012 and officially formed in February 2013, just one month prior to my first visit to Montreal. Mugabo writes that the group was organized to articulate a different vision of Quebec nationhood than the one presented through the PQ Charter, one that was more open to pluralism and diversity and that promoted a model of "open" secularism (Maclure and Taylor 2011, 27).[14] The group was composed of political activists from all three of the main sovereigntist parties in Quebec: the PQ, the Coalition Avenir Québec (Coalition for Quebec's Future, CAQ), and Québec Solidaire (Solidarity Quebec, QS).[15]

In her article, Mugabo details her experience at one of the meetings:

> At one meeting, a prominent white francophone academic known for his research on the Muslim North African community in Québec joined the group. I will call him Professor C. As we always did when new members arrived, the group's existing members took turns introducing ourselves to the new arrivals. My turn was last but my introduction did not go as planned. Professor C. boldly interrupted me after I had said my name: "I don't understand why you're here. You're Black. The [PQ] charter has nothing to do with Black people so why are you here?" I was speechless.
>
> After my initial shock, I told him that I am Muslim. He sighed in exasperation and replied, "Okay, okay, yes there are a few African people who are also Muslims but this is about Quebecers and Arab people; it has nothing to do with Black people." Still in disbelief, all I could say was that whether Black people are Muslim or not, living in Québec meant that Black people can participate in any discussion or debate about life in this province. Nobody at the meeting interjected against Professor C's comments. (Mugabo 2016, 162)

Mugabo's experience in this supposedly progressive space clearly demonstrates the ways that various types of Muslim people are ejected and discredited from participating in debates about themselves in the province of Quebec, whether it be debates among conservatives or debates on the "left" with those who presume to offer an alternative vision of Quebec nationalism and how *laïcité* fits into it. In Mugabo's case, it was because she is a Black Muslim (and presumably because she does not wear hijab and thus is not visibly Muslim to the casual observer) that she was dismissed as unqualified to participate in a debate that was deemed to be only between Quebecers and Arabs (according to Professor C). In my case, although visibly Muslim in terms of wearing a hijab, it was because I was presumably anglophone (although French is my mother tongue) and not Quebecois (although I am Canadian) that I was warned against comparing Quebec and France in a public forum.

As Mugabo (2014) further reiterated during a published interview with me regarding the PQ Charter, "Much of the debate over the Charter of Québec Values … concerned white francophone Quebecers deciding how they will manage their nation; POC [people of colour] were invited to offer anecdotes and to act as props for either one of the camps. WOC [women of colour] were not invited to the public discussion unless it was to repeat or to validate a predetermined agenda" (35). In other words, Muslims, especially Muslim women, can be spoken about by White Quebecers, but they cannot participate in those conversations or speak back in defence of themselves or their communities, lest they been seen as "sticking their noses where it does not belong." This situation is ironic because at the end of the day, those "debates" between Quebecers directly impact the lives and livelihoods of Muslim women along with other racialized groups in particular.

Leila Benhadjoudja (2018), another racialized Muslim researcher from Quebec, analyses the complex processes at play when Muslims participate in civil society in Quebec while not renouncing their affiliation with Islam. Either, on one hand, they are presumed to be in need of saving and as victims of false consciousness, or on the other hand, they are seen as a menace, a sign of the dangers of radical Islam and the return of religion to the public sphere:

> When Muslim women mobilize as Muslim women in civil society, by not renouncing their identification with Islam, their political subjectivity is either ignored or transformed into a threat. In effect, their political agency is perceived as a sign of society's "Islamization" or a return of the religious (understood as dangerous), and as a step backward for feminist gains. And when they wear a headscarf, in particular, Muslim women are represented as paradoxical figures anchored in an Orientalist colonial imaginary. (Benhadjoudja 2018, 114; my translation)

For racialized activists and scholars, being perceived as "paradoxical figures" of "an Orientalist colonial imaginary" is especially apparent when they try to participate in public debates that impact their bodies and their communities: Those who participate are delegitimized through various tactics, be it by disqualifying them on account of their race or the (in)visibility of their religion or both. Given this context, Benhadjoudja (2018) poses a provocative question: Can Muslim women speak in Quebec? And to follow up from the perspective of research: Can they conduct fieldwork? Can they produce knowledge? What kind of knowledge can they safely produce? What does safety mean in a context when your body, your entire subjectivity, becomes the target of government censure, a walking threat to the body politic?

Field Note 2: Walking "Ostentatiously" While Muslim

18 September 2013

It was late afternoon as I was walking south on Berri Street towards the Mont Royale subway station. Several people were heading home from a long day of work while exiting the station, many walking past me on the sidewalk in the opposite direction. Having grown up in the large metropolitan city of Toronto, I was not accustomed to making eye contact very often, so I initially looked straight ahead as I walked.

I was wearing a pink floral hijab that I had purchased at a market in the small town of Sarlat, in the South of France, when I went on a trip to visit my uncle and cousins the previous summer. I matched it with a short, sleeveless, blush-pink dress, worn layered on top of a black long-sleeve top and black skinny jeans, paired with the black combat boots that my older sister had gifted me on my birthday a few weeks earlier. As many scholars who study contemporary Muslim fashion have argued, experimenting with style, fabrics, and colours is one of the main ways that young Muslim women engage in forms of self-expression that mix local and global modes of dressing, producing a hybrid aesthetic that blends together Islamic ethics with mainstream fashion (Göle 1996; Lewis 2015; Tarlo 2010). Personally, dressing in "untraditional" ways while mixing both feminine (blush pink, florals) and masculine (black, combat boots) styles had become something like armour for me, a way of communicating my feminist political leanings while at the same time staying true to my Muslim heritage: a conscious way of dressing to subvert the stereotypes surrounding Muslim women.

As I kept walking towards the station while staring straight ahead, something caught my peripheral vision, so I turned towards it. A man approached me on the sidewalk from the opposite direction, directly to my left, and stared hard into my eyes.

This man is glaring at me, I suddenly realized, startled. He had white skin and white hair, peppered with grey flecks, and he was maybe in his late fifties to early sixties. I had no idea if he identified as anglophone or francophone, as we did not exchange words. However, he was looking straight at me with what I perceived as blazing hatred in his eyes as he passed by. His gaze was hard, brows furrowed, and lips drawn downward in a tight line, making direct, unflinching eye contact with me for several steps until we had both passed one another on the sidewalk. I was taken aback because his gaze was so unmistakably hostile that I felt the heat in it. It was late in the afternoon, the sun was shining even though the temperature was getting cooler, and there were people all around us. Had I been walking alone at nighttime, I would have reached for my phone and called someone for help. But the warmth of the afternoon sun and the surrounding crowd gave me (perhaps falsely) a sense of security.

Barely a few minutes later, as I was standing across the small street that leads to the entrance of the Mont Royal metro, this time I saw a woman standing opposite to me on the crosswalk. The light was red and as we both waited for it to change, she looked at me from across the street. I was once again met with a cold stare, though this time not as blatantly aggressive. But the woman's stare seemed hard and unflinching, not bothering to look away even as I caught her looking directly at me. She was a White woman with blond and white hair, perhaps in her fifties. After a long moment, I broke eye contact and looked away, not wanting to either engage with or interrogate her look. I had had enough for one day. As we passed by each other on the crosswalk, I whispered a quiet prayer of gratitude under my breath. *Thank God they didn't say anything to me*, I thought as I returned to my friend's apartment in Côte-des-Neiges, where I was staying overnight.

The following day, as I was getting ready to take the train from Montreal back to Toronto, I dressed in whatever clean clothing I had left, as I had only brought enough to last me a few days. My outfit consisted of black skinny jeans and a loose army-green shirt, paired with a shimmery black hijab. On top, I wore an army-green leather jacket – another hand-me-down from my older sister – as well as the combat boots she had gifted me. I had to take the subway to the central Montreal train station before catching the long-distance train to Toronto.

As I got onto the subway car, struggling a bit because I had been rolling my carry-on luggage and carrying a heavy handbag on my right shoulder, I spotted a single empty seat off to the far-right side of the car and went to sit down. After settling in, I looked around the rest of the relatively empty car (it was past the early-morning rush hour, so the train was mostly empty). To my left and diagonally across from me, there were two seats occupied by what appeared to be a Latino couple, a man and a woman with dark hair and lightly tanned skin. They were huddled close to one another and speaking to each other in hushed voices, too far for me to be able to hear what they were saying or even what language they spoke in. I looked over to them and we made eye contact for a moment. As they looked at me and then at each other, and then back at me, they began pointing. At me.

I quickly looked away, feeling a pang of panic at the sudden and unexpected attention. I have always been a bit shy and introverted, and I felt uncomfortable at times whenever I was the centre of attention. But in this context, and after the strange encounters I had had the previous day, I did not understand why I was being pointed at and wasn't sure I wanted to know. And yet, my curiosity got the best of me and I chanced another look back at the couple that had pointed at me.

Although they were still both looking directly at me, eyes round and staring, and speaking to one another in low voices, I saw that there was a small smile on both of their faces. Despite still feeling uncomfortable because I was being so obviously watched and spoken about, I didn't feel threatened in any way. It was not a hostile look, even if it was a little rude.

I looked away and did not look back again until I exited the subway car. I could see the couple's faces clearly as I passed them, both smiling at me as I left the car.

Weird, I thought. *Maybe they mistook me for someone else.*

The series of encounters I describe occurred a little over a week following the announcement of the PQ Charter on 10 September 2013. I had been to Montreal many times before this, by myself and with others, but encounters like these had never occurred. Although part of the experience had been unsettling at the time, it did not result in any lasting harm. No one had directly threatened me, swore at or insulted me, nor physically harmed me in any way. However, it did make me think of a number of Muslim women who had been subjected to various forms of violence – termed "gendered Islamophobia" – over the course of the Charter debate (Jahangeer 2020; Peritz 2013; Perry 2014; Zine 2006). Valérie Létourneau, a spokeswoman for the Regroupement des centres de femmes du Québec (Québec Grouping of Women's Centres),[16] was quoted as saying, "It's obvious. Since the debate over the [PQ] charter, the increase in intolerance is palpable. It's contributing to a climate of fear. Veiled women are finding it harder to leave their homes. It's taken serious proportions" (Peritz 2013). Since then, studies have shown a significant link between debates around secularism/"religious symbols" and violence against Muslim women in particular.[17] These forms of violence and their impacts on Muslim women are not taken into account whenever "debates" are proposed around secularism and the place of "religious symbols" in certain contexts. What is usually reiterated by politicians is that the public should have such debates in a "serene" and "non-emotional" way, as though secularism, neutrality, and gender equality were not being debated on the backs of Muslim women.

Conclusion

As a hijab-wearing Muslim researcher doing fieldwork in a political context where the government has targeted your embodied religious practice, your body becomes both hypervisible and dismissed. Even if the political debate centres around secularism, neutrality, gender equality, or some other abstract philosophical concept in university classrooms or parliamentary hearings – on the street, what they are really talking about is *you*. All eyes are on you and you feel it. It is not just in your imagination. And this gaze has implications for participant observation and the positionality of the "neutral" observer-researcher. The veneer of neutrality does not exist for you (not that it ever did).

At times, I drew unwanted attention because I spoke in French at a public debate with an anglophone accent; at other times it was because I walked down the street while wearing hijab in a "modern" way (Göle 1996). Nevertheless, in the context of the PQ Charter debate, which began in earnest in September 2013, my body and clothing choices became a flashpoint for several experiences that I had not anticipated. These experiences had implications for me in terms of the kind of research I could undertake and the kind of knowledge I produced.

For one, my research design changed to take into account what spaces I could enter and what individuals or groups I could speak with safely, both of which depended on an imprecise evaluation of who would not be hostile to me if I were to meet with them in person. Second, several unanticipated encounters occurred on account of the hypervisibility of my body in a space where a veiled body is expected to inhabit a submissive and oppressed subjectivity. Last, it influenced the people I did speak with and who my research ended up centring upon: Muslim women and activists, many of whom I befriended and who welcomed me with open arms. For the most part, I ended up interviewing Muslim women and those few academics and activists with whom I felt comfortable (most of whom were referred to me by friends and colleagues). I did not interview politicians, academics, or other public figures who were known to be hostile to veiling or to veiled women. This is because I did not want to expose myself to harassment, aggression, outright hostility, or Islamophobia. I put my personal safety first before "objectivity" or presumptions about "neutrality," because the former should (always) outweigh the latter. As Kloß (2017) argues, "I emphasize that fieldwork has to be considered as a gendered practice in which the (a)sexuality of the fieldworker directly influences his or her research, acquired data, and safety" (399). I would also add that the race and religion of the researcher, in sum, their intersectional positionality, and the political context they find themselves in, also influence the research, data, and safety of the researcher, in a myriad of anticipated and unanticipated ways.

I would like to conclude on a note of encouragement to graduate students and early-career researchers, especially those who identify as female, 2SLGBTQQIA, and/or racialized, who are considering conducting fieldwork while incorporating autoethnographic methods. Autoethnography can be a way for marginalized researchers to produce knowledge in a context where their bodies are or become the direct targets of government censure, legislation, and misrepresentation. Autoethnography is a way for marginalized researchers to speak back and to return the gaze on those who monopolize the public sphere, who silence us in public debate, and who act as gatekeepers of knowledge production. For instance, in debates around "religious symbols," Muslim women have mostly been the objects of other people's research, writing, analysis, and knowledge production. Yet using autoethnography as a method can help speak against such silencing and erasure, which is actually crucial for knowledge production. When our silenced experiences and perspectives are taken seriously, the conversation changes completely, which is all the more reason to keep researching and writing.

NOTES

1 See Jahangeer 2020 and Jahangeer forthcoming for a fuller theoretical elaboration of anti-veiling as a concept. Examples of anti-veiling laws include a 2004 French law

that prohibits students from wearing religious symbols in public schools (L'Assemblée Nationale de la République Française 2004); the 2010 French law that prohibits concealing one's face in public space (L'Assemblée Nationale de la République Française 2010); and Bill 21 (2019) in Quebec which prohibits teachers, judges, police officers, and prosecutors (among others) from wearing "religious symbols" while practicing their professions (National Assembly of Québec 2019); Bill 60 (2013) also proposed a similar ban on all civil servants, but it never became law (National Assembly of Québec 2013). In Quebec, Bill 94 (2010), Bill 60 (2013), and Bill 62 (2017) all proposed to ban those with their faces covered from giving or receiving social services.

2 See L'Assemblée Nationale de la République Française (2004).

3 I use the term used by the National Inquiry into Missing and Murdered Indigenous Women and Girls, which represents Two-Spirit, lesbian, gay, bisexual, transgender, queer, questioning, intersex, and asexual people, as well as those who identify as non-binary or gender nonconforming (National Inquiry into Missing and Murdered Indigenous Women and Girls 2019, 5).

4 Korteweg and Yurdakul (2014) define belonging as "the subjective feeling of being at home in one's country, of easily moving through its particular places and spaces, and the sense of comfort and joy in inhabiting a particular locale" (3).

5 A colloquial term used among Muslims to refer to a Muslim woman who wears a hijab. A similar term, niqabi, exists to refer to Muslim women who wear a niqab (see Razack 2018).

6 Although the PQ Charter did not pass in 2014 due to the PQ's election loss, the Quebec government passed Bill 21 (2019) several years later. See Jahangeer 2020, for a discussion of how Bill 21 follows the same logic as the PQ Charter.

7 The PQ is a sovereigntist political party formed in 1968, committed to achieving independence from Canada.

8 Except for the large crucifix that was displayed in the Salon Bleu of the Québec Legislature; both politicians and commentators had argued that this crucifix was not a religious symbol but rather a historic symbol of Quebec's heritage and thus should not be removed.

9 The other racialized communities affected included Sikh and Jewish communities, whose religious practices were also interpellated in the PQ Charter's naming of "ostentatious religious symbols."

10 All French-to-English translations are mine.

11 The Reasonable Accommodation debate (more formally known as the Quebec's Consultation Commission on Accommodation Practices Related to Cultural Differences) was established by the Quebec government in 2007–8. Its commissioners, Charles Taylor and Gérard Bouchard, broadly studied the issue of national identity, secularism, and interculturalism in the context of increasing public debates regarding whether minority religious and cultural practices could be accommodated by the

French Quebecois majority. For critiques of the Reasonable Accommodation commission, see Mahrouse (2010) and Schaefli and Godlewska (2014).

12 Remarks made by Christine St. Pierre, Quebec's Status of Women Minister (quoted in Kingston 2012).

13 See, for example, Amiraux and Koussens 2014; Baubérot 2012; Maclure and Taylor 2011; Milot 2009.

14 "Open" secularism, in contrast to a more "rigid" or "strict" secularism, is said to foreground the protection of religious freedom and freedom of conscience, while having a more flexible conception of the separation of church and state as well as state neutrality (Maclure and Taylor 2011, 27).

15 The CAQ is a centre-right political party formed in 2011 that defines itself as a modern nationalist party committed to defending Quebec's autonomy within Canada. Led by François Legault, it won a majority of seats in the 2018 provincial elections and currently forms Quebec's government. QS is a left-wing, social democratic, and sovereigntist political party, formed in 2006 and led by two spokespersons, Manon Massé and Gabriel Nadeau-Dubois.

16 This is the largest grouping of autonomous feminist community action in Quebec.

17 A recent study, led by Quebec's Commission des droits de la personne et des droits de la jeunesse (Human Rights and Youth Rights Commission) has examined this link in more detail between 2015 and 2018. See Asal et al. 2019.

REFERENCES

Amiraux, Valérie, and David Koussens. 2014. "De mauvais usage de la laïcité française dans le débat public québécois." In Sébastien Lévesque (Ed.), *Penser la laïcité québécoise: Fondements et défense d'une laïcité ouverte au Québec* (pp. 55–75). Presses de l'Université Laval.

Asal, Houda, Jean-Sébastien Imbeault, and Karina Montminy. 2019. "Les Actes haineux à caractère xénophobe, notamment islamophobe: Résultats d'une recherche menée à travers le Québec." Commission des droits de la personne et des droits de la jeunesse. Août. http://www.cdpdj.qc.ca/Publications/etude_actes_haineux.pdf

Baubérot, Jean. 2012. *La laïcité falsifiée*. La Découverte.

Benhadjoudja, Leila. 2015. "Le féminisme musulman au Québec: Quel enjeu pour la laïcité?" In Jean Baubérot, Micheline Milot, and Philippe Portier (Eds.), *Laïcité, laïcités: Reconfigurations et nouveaux défis*. Éditions de la maison des sciences de l'homme.

– 2018. "Les femmes musulmanes peuvent-elles parler?" *Anthropologies et Sociétés*, *42*(1), 113–33. https://doi.org/10.7202/1045126ar

Chang, Heewon. 2008. *Autoethnography as method*. Left Coast Press.

Crawley, Sara L. 2012. "Autoethnography as feminist self-interview." In Jaber F. Gubrium and James A. Holstein (Eds.), *The SAGE handbook of interview research: The complexity of the craft* (pp. 143–60). SAGE.

Ellis, Carolyn, Tony E. Adams, and Arthur P. Bochner. 2011. "Autoethnography: An overview." *Forum: Qualitative Social Research, 12*(1). http://www.qualitative-research.net/index.php/fqs/article/view/1589/3095

Göle, Nilüfer. 1996. *The forbidden modern: Civilization and veiling.* University of Michigan Press.

Jahangeer, Roshan Arah. 2020. "Anti-veiling and the Charter of Québec Values: 'Native testimonials,' erasure, and violence against Montréal's Muslim women." *Canadian Journal of Women and the Law, 32*(1), 114–49. http://doi.org/10.3138/cjwl.32.1.05

– Forthcoming. "Anti-veiling in France and Québec: Secularism, feminism and Islamophobia." PhD diss., York University.

Kingston, Anne. 2012, 17 January. "Veils: Who are we to judge?" *Macleans.* https://www.macleans.ca/society/life/who-are-we-to-judge

Kloß, Sinah Theres. 2017. "Sexual(ized) harassment and ethnographic fieldwork: A silenced aspect of social research." *Ethnography, 18*(3), 396–414. https://doi.org/10.1177%2F1466138116641958

Korteweg, Anna C., and Gökçe Yurdakul. 2014. *The headscarf debates: Conflicts of national belonging.* Stanford University Press.

L'Assemblée Nationale de la République Française. 2004, 15 March. "LOI n° 2004–228 du 15 mars 2004 encadrant, en application du principe de laïcité, le port de signes ou de tenues manifestant une appartenance religieuse dans les écoles, collèges et lycées publics." Légifrance. https://www.legifrance.gouv.fr/eli/loi/2004/3/15/MENX0400001L/jo/texte

– 2010, 11 October. "LOI n° 2010–1192 du 11 octobre 2010 interdisant la dissimulation du visage dans l'espace public." Légifrance. https://www.legifrance.gouv.fr/eli/loi/2010/10/11/2010-1192/jo/texte

Lewis, Reina. 2015. *Muslim fashion: Contemporary style cultures.* Duke University Press.

Maclure, Jocelyn, and Charles Taylor. 2011. *Secularism and freedom of conscience* (Jane Marie Todd, Trans.). Harvard University Press.

Mahrouse, Gada. 2010. "'Reasonable Accommodation' in Québec: The limits of participation and dialogue." *Race and Class, 52*(1), 85–96. https://doi.org/10.1177%2F0306396810371768

Milot, Micheline. 2009. "L'émergence de la notion de laïcité au Québec: Résistances, polysémie et instrumentalisation." In Paul Eid, Pierre Bosset, Micheline Milot, and Sébastien Lebel-Grenier (Eds.), *Appartenances religieuses, appartenance citoyenne: Un équilibre en tension* (pp. 29–71). Presses de l'Université Laval.

Mugabo, Délice Igicari. 2014. "Charter of Québec Values, intersectionality and being a Black feminist in Montréal: Interview by Roshan A. Jahangeer." *Upping the Anti: A Journal of Theory and Action, 16*, 28–41.

– 2016. "On rocks and hard places: A reflection on antiblackness in organizing against Islamophobia." *Critical Ethnic Studies, 2*(2), 159–83. https://doi.org/10.5749/jcritethnstud.2.2.0159

National Assembly of Québec. 2010, 24 March. "Bill 94, an act to establish guidelines governing accommodation requests within the administration and certain institutions." http://m.assnat.qc.ca/en/travaux-parlementaires/projets-loi/projet-loi-94-39-1.html

– 2013, 7 November. "Bill 60, charter affirming the values of state secularism and religious neutrality and of equality between women and men, and providing a framework for accommodation requests." http://www.assnat.qc.ca/en/travaux-parlementaires/projets-loi/projet-loi-60-40-1.html?appelant=MC

– 2017, 18 October. "Bill 62: An act to foster adherence to state religious neutrality and, in particular, to provide a framework for requests for accommodations on religious grounds in certain bodies." http://www2.publicationsduquebec.gouv.qc.ca/dynamicSearch/telecharge.php?type=5&file=2017C19A.PDF

– 2019, 16 June. "Bill 21: An act respecting the laicity of the state." http://www2.publicationsduquebec.gouv.qc.ca/dynamicSearch/telecharge.php?type=5&file=2019C12A.PDF

National Inquiry into Missing and Murdered Indigenous Women and Girls. 2019. *Reclaiming power and place: The final report of the National Inquiry into Missing and Murdered Indigenous Women and Girls.* CP32-163-2-1-2019-eng.pdf

Patel, Shaista. 2019. "The 'Indian Queen' of the four continents: Tracing the 'undifferentiated Indian' through Europe's encounter with Muslims, anti-Blackness, and conquest of the 'new world.'" *Cultural Studies, 33*(3), 414–36. https://doi.org/10.1080/09502386.2019.1584906

Peritz, Ingrid. 2013, 2 October. "Québec Muslims facing more abuse since charter proposal, women's groups say." *Globe and Mail.* https://www.theglobeandmail.com/news/national/quebec-muslims-facing-more-abuse-since-charter-proposal-womens-groups-say/article14672348

Perry, Barbara. 2014. "Gendered Islamophobia: Hate crime against Muslim women." *Social Identities, 20*(1), 74–89. https://doi.org/10.1080/13504630.2013.864467

Poulos, Christopher N. 2012. "Autoethnography." In Audrey A. Trainor and Elizabeth Graue (Eds.), *Reviewing qualitative research in the social sciences: A guide for researchers and reviewers* (pp. 38–53). Routledge.

Razack, Sherene H. 2008. *Casting out: The eviction of Muslims from Western law and politics.* University of Toronto Press.

– 2018. "A site/sight we cannot bear: The racial/spatial politics of banning the Muslim woman's niqab." *Canadian Journal of Women and the Law, 30*(1), 169–89. http://doi.org/10.3138/cjwl.30.1.169

Schaefli, Laura, and Anne Godlewska. 2014. “Social ignorance and Indigenous exclusion: Public voices in the province of Quebec, Canada.” *Settler Colonial Studies, 4*(3), 227–44. http://dx.doi.org/10.1080/2201473X.2013.866514

Tarlo, Emma. 2010. *Visibly Muslim: Fashion, politics, faith*. Berg.

Zine, Jasmin. 2006. “Unveiled sentiments: Gendered Islamophobia and experiences of veiling among Muslim girls in a Canadian Islamic school.” *Equity and Excellence in Education, 39*(3), 239–52. https://doi.org/10.1080/10665680600788503

The Interplay of Identity in Ethnographic Conversations: The Grammar of Recognition in Conversion Narratives

GÉRALDINE MOSSIÈRE

Introduction: Deciphering the Impacts of Being Muslim (or Not) in the Field

Quite expectedly, research on converts to Islam has flourished in the last two decades and is often qualitative rather than quantitative. This trend is due in part to the complexities of calculating the actual number of converts[1] but also to the impetus to understand the subtle dynamics underlying the conversion process. Embracing Islam may indeed seem curious to Western liberal readers. While most studies follow a methodological nationalism (Schiller 2005),[2] in my work I have compared converts in France and Quebec to grasp commonalities between the two national contexts, as well as to question the role of the specific social and political conditions from where my interviewees speak (Mossière 2013). My positionality as a non-Muslim played a role in orienting the conditions of this fieldwork, including shaping the narratives of my informants and the knowledge I produced following the ethnographic process. In public talks, I am regularly questioned by Muslim-background or converted people, who appeared to see it as their responsibility to verify what I say about Islam and Muslims. This questioning often relies on their own personal experience. In these instances, the underlying assumption is that, as a non-Muslim, I could never grasp the true experience of being Muslim.

In this chapter I consider how reality, however, is not so clear-cut. The boundary between Muslimness and non-Muslimness is more blurred than it might seem. While most scholars investigating the issue of converts to Islam do not belong to the Muslim world (Margot Badran, Tina Gudrun Jensen, Vanessa Vroon, Juliette Galonnier), some in fact are Muslims (Ali Köse) or converts themselves (Nicole Bourque, Anne Sofie Roald, Marcia Hermansen, Leon Moosavi). With respect to the non-Muslim scholars, gradual acquaintance and sometimes incorporation of Muslim practices and views promoted by in-depth ethnographic fieldwork led them to explore Muslimness in their scholarly work. In this chapter, I acknowledge and recognize that anthropologists are all influenced by the interviewees they engage with. In the course of my ongoing conversations with female converts to Islam, I recognized similarities between my own story and their narratives. In the field, I endorsed some of their ways of behaving, first for the sake of conducting effective fieldwork and later as a habitus-like integration of my informants' dispositions. At one point, I saw these behaviours as evidence of my authentic engagement in my fieldwork and as proof of having achieved rapport with my research subjects. In one instance, in the context of an email exchange with an imam introduced to me by a convert participant, the imam remarked that he felt he knew me and found me to be so "nice" that he could have mistaken me for a Muslim. I took this remark as a good sign.

The blurring of Sameness and Otherness that has for so long been the hallmark of social scientific thinking should not ignore the conditions of the encounter between the scholar and the informant as two situated alterities (Kilani 1995). The literature has emphasized how these interactions are fraught with issues of authority and power, as well as a quest for recognition and legitimacy. In this chapter, I consider how narratives of conversion to Islam delivered in the context of qualitative scientific studies (including my own) are framed by the conditions of the intersubjective encounter between the ethnographer and the new Muslim: namely, the normative social role and political status that each one embraces and assigns to the other. Drawing on Honneth and Voirol's (2006) theory of recognition as framed by Piettre and Monnot (2013) around issues of visibility (Voirol 2005) and recognizability (Butler 2010), I argue that the structure of the conversion narrative is built to display a socially and politically acceptable image of converts and conversion and that these representations follow a specific script. It is in the context of the ethnographic conversations that new Muslims articulate themselves, their identities, and their social and political positions according to a limited set of norms, references, and values they assign to the ethnographer and to the readers. The elaboration and constant negotiation of this grammar of recognition shed light on the methodological challenges of conducting empirical research among Muslim populations as an outsider. I then argue that this interplay shifts the process of production of knowledge about Islam to a critical study of Islam and how Muslims exist in their social and political environment – in this way, switching from scientific research to a political claim.

Drawing on fieldwork conducted since 2006 among converts to Islam in France and in Quebec, I first introduce narratives of conversion that share redundancies; I identify their common structure and components. I then discuss how these schemes borrow a commonly held language that more broadly governs the recognition and the non-recognition of minorities in public discourse. While this language is shaped by widely circulated tropes, it is also coloured by the conditions of the interview and the roles that each interlocutor assigns to the other, as well as the role that each assumes. I argue that such conditions of encounter between ethnographer and informant unevenly distribute the authority of knowledge production. In conclusion, I discuss the possibility of triangulating narratives with observations and thick descriptions in contexts where the presence of the scholar in converts' everyday lives is either turned down or considered highly suspect by respondents.

Many scholars argue that in spite of the standardized format of ethnographic interviews, interviewees might, throughout their narratives, develop their own singularity by using strategies to express their agency without necessarily displaying contradictions. Like Le Pape (2007), I contend that the narratives of Muslim converts should be considered not only as data but also as objects of enquiry that are part of the personal biography of the interviewee and of the sociopolitical dynamics that make the conversation possible. While this observation does not deprive the life narratives of their methodological interest for our projects, it shifts the focus of the research towards the making of the narrative plot first, and then the production of knowledge around the discursive analysis of sociopolitical issues. In the case of conversion to Islam, narratives are political. Their construction hinges on common tensions between, on the one hand, a desire to adopt Islam and conform to religious and social practices and belonging and, on the other hand, the management of this identity on subjective, political, and public levels.

Methodology

This chapter is based on data collected during two phases of fieldwork I have conducted among female converts to Islam in France and in Quebec. In the first phase, 2006–8, I collected seventy-eight narratives (forty in France and thirty-eight in Quebec); and in the second phase, 2016–18, I met fifteen of these women a second time (eight in Quebec and seven in France). As the interviews were semi-directed, the interview protocol was gradually adjusted. For the first interviews, I modelled my questions on the conversion pathway; respondents were invited to freely describe their subjective experience of embracing Islam.[3] Although this hermeneutic technique often entails a highly vivid and somewhat normalized monologue from converts, it allowed me as ethnographer to avoid the pitfalls of objectifying the converts' experiences using standardized categories of comprehension. By doing so, the interview remains limited to the experience of informants and to the meaning they attribute to it and wish to convey.

In the second phase of the project, I added questions on topics that had systematically emerged from the first narratives, such as the construction of gender and family relationships, the learning of Islamic practice, the (re)organization of social identity, and the shaping of female subjectivity in Islam. In addition, I paid special attention to examples and anecdotes that revealed areas of tension, conflict, and hesitation that may have led them to embrace Islam. At the end of the interview, most of the converts reported they appreciated the interview experience as an intimate space where they could narrate and build a retrospective of their own story. Common enthusiasm might also explain the unexpectedly high number of conversion narratives I succeeded in gathering, a point to which I will return.

Conversion Narratives: Standard and Common Schemes

Midway through analysing the conversion narratives of my seventy-eight interlocutors, I observed a common pattern emerging. These personal testimonies conformed to a standard narrative that circulates among the community of "sisters in Islam" and on social media. This high degree of conformity to a common conversion narrative emphasizes the illocutionary power of these discourses as they contribute to constructing how converts relate to their environment. The emergence of these narrative schemes in my fieldwork unexpectedly turned the ethnographic project into a research project on discursive analysis.

Narrative Plots and Pattern

Juliette is twenty-one, lives in a working-class area of Paris, and studies sociology. After three years as a Muslim, she describes her path as follows:

> I have always had a lot of affinities with Maghrebian people. At high school, we used to get on very well. Then, one of my girlfriends of Algerian descent started to practice [Islam]; she had always been a believer but she didn't practice. This girl really impressed me; she had a strong personality. As a teenager, she was cool but she didn't joke about specific things – respect for elders, virginity, principles like that, and I realized that it was Islam that gave her all this. Before, I thought that Islam was a religion for Arab people, but then I started to get interested, she gave me a few books, we used to talk a lot, about the *Qur'an*, etc. Then, in the group, the Maghrebian girls started to practise [Islam] and all French girls embraced Islam, approximately ten, and now we are like sisters of blood.

Amelie is thirty and lives in Montreal, where she works as a supervisor in a call centre while studying business administration. She had been Muslim for two years when we met, and she reported she always believed in God but never "really" practised any particular religion. Four years ago, she met Mourad, a newcomer to Montreal from Morocco. Although he claimed he did not practise Islam, Mourad abided by some Muslim values, like refusing cohabitation before marriage. Amelie was intrigued by his behaviour, which she qualified as "peaceful, joyful and calm" and associated with Islam. This appreciation pushed her to learn more about this religion. She later decided to get in touch with a Muslim woman because she "needed to know how one really goes about being Muslim as a woman. Because, want it or not, there are more prescriptions for women, it's harder for women."

These two conversion narrative excerpts from France and Quebec exemplify the two primary narrative schemes that converts used in describing their foray into Islam. This ideal path in Islam includes standard key steps that may be negotiated in diverse ways by interviewees, with variations and tensions that also reveal the idiosyncrasies and non-linearity of experiences. The narratives are usually structured around several stages that gather the following elements, to different degrees:

(1) A memorable or moving encounter with a key person of Muslim background, practising or not. This could be a friend, lover, neighbour, colleague.
(2) A personal quest for information on Islam by searching online or by reading the Qur'an (which may have a triggering effect) and/or a gradual awareness of the existence of God and of the veracity of Islam. This may involve a struggle with rational arguments to prove that Islam is the truth and, as such, there is no other choice but to embrace it.
(3) Fears and hesitations around the changes that adhering to Islam would require in everyday social relationships and personal life. These sometimes lead to a temporary step back or hesitation.
(4) The creation of new social ties with Muslim practitioners and gradual learning and embodiment of Muslim identity. This transition occurs through disembodying prior religious heritage, disciplining resistance, consolidating faith, and learning practices (prayer, Ramadan) through trial and error.
(5) A decision to embrace Islam and take the statement of faith (*shahada*) that is most often formulated in informal circumstances (as opposed to formal conversions that take place at mosques).
(6) The socialization in Islam through intensive learning of Muslim beliefs and practices (e.g., lessons in mosques) and constructing a common sense of belonging to the Muslim community (ummah). This mode of sociability that is more or less exclusive according to interviewees involves a community of "sisters" in Islam and a gradual change in social behaviours through disciplining social, ritualistic, and bodily practices embedded in daily life.
(7) The public announcement and informal exhibition of Muslim affiliation in non-Muslim social circles (e.g., family, work environment, public space).
(8) The management of possible conflicts in private and public spaces and negotiation of identity with the community of origin and of adoption. This may ultimately lead to veiling.

As narrated by converts, this progressive dimension of their path towards Islam is influenced by their familial, social, and political environment, which constantly jeopardizes their project of learning and asserting their chosen identity. Similar to other empirical studies on conversion to Islam, my interviewees are situated in various phases on this broad canvas within which they build diverse paths that vary according to their generation belonging, their personal characters or biographies, and their family situations or social milieu, but also upon the type of Islam they identify with (e.g., Sufism, Salafism). Although their conversion path may include a love or marital trajectory with a Muslim man, half of the women I met had embraced Islam before meeting their current partner. The vast majority of their spouses were first- or second-generation migrants from Maghreb or, in some cases, from West Africa.

In spite of this variety of profiles, the narratives I collected display common features that are corroborated by other studies (Bourque 2006; Galonnier 2015; Haddad 2006; Jensen 2008; Özyürek 2014; Puzenat 2015; Roald 2004; Rogozen-Soltar 2012; Sultan 1999; Van Nieuwkerk 2006; Vroon 2014). First, most of the women report they have always nourished a quest for mysticism or moral compass; they feel passionate about or highly committed to a cause; they are justice lovers; they are highly pragmatic; and they like to present themselves as rebels and nonconformists. Many of them experienced alterity in their own biographies, having either travelled a lot since early childhood, belonged to other religious minorities before embracing Islam, or had mixed identities as offspring of mixed unions.

Most recurring topics in their narratives concern their attraction to elements of Islam. These include the everyday discipline and logical dimension of Islamic prescriptions; the spiritual quest triggered by conversion to Islam; the lifestyle centred on family and traditional values; the importance of women as mothers and spouses; the force of community ties; and the sexual differentiation between men and women with respect to responsibilities and duties. Other recurring topics concern their criticism of "Western" ways of life. These include the decline of family values; the disruptive effect of individualism on society; liberalism in sexuality; the subjugation of female bodies as sexual objects; the culture of materialism; the uneven distribution of power and resources; and the hegemony of the West. These concerns, which have also been documented in Quebec, France and other European countries, and the United States,[4] are driven by a quest for moral values, codes of conduct, and identification of "true values."

Finally, narratives of conversion systematically represent the social relationships and civic status of converts by referring to the stigma surrounding Islam in public opinion and politics. They also refer to the dominant negative stereotypes associated with Muslim populations and discrimination around the veil. Interviewees in my fieldwork see the reactions of their close circle (to their announced conversion and embracing the veil) as more symptomatic and contentious than their religious choice itself. For example, Amelie (of Quebec), told me:

> Quebecois people, when they see a Muslim woman, they think she is oppressed or influenced by her husband or by her culture. People are not educated, it is not their fault, because they do hear no good about Islam. There is a little bit of work to do on this, especially for us as converts, Quebecois listen more to us, so we should give a little conference once and a while, be benevolent, help to get rid of some stereotypes.

The recurrence of the trope of stigma is likely related to the social and political ambience in Western societies, where politics and media are prone to reactivate the binary semantics of the Crusades. In contrast, interviewees explain their attraction to Islam as a fascination they feel for the exoticism of the Muslim world. They also identify with Islam as a set of everyday guidelines (as opposed to Catholic or other tenets), which they see as a sound meaning system in a fluid and uncertain world. All these arguments are organized within a broad narrative scheme that also includes the plots of personal biographies.

Narrative Structures and Their Variations

For the women I met, narrating their path towards Islam is an act of faith that recalls the *shahada* that marks their entry in Islam. As many authors have demonstrated, such narratives are framed within conventional linguistic forms (Harding 1987; Henry 1998; Hermansen 2006; Moosavi 2012; Wohlrab-Sahr 2006). By reinterpreting their personal and social experience in a specific narrative scheme, new Muslims put their identity to the test and strengthen it at the same time. Internet forums and lessons on Islam (where narratives of conversion circulate in open access) provide new Muslims the necessary semantics, arguments, and tropes. They also transmit to them the techniques of plotting conversion: These enable them to report their conversion on standardized canvases that are informed by the Muslim process to embrace Islam (Bourque 2006). Narratives are equally influenced by various dogmatic discourses, including those that aim at removing the interpretative biases around the Qur'anic message (*da'wa*) often conveyed by mass media, or the discourses that impart diverse authorities and powers that I captured through the networks of respondents I recruited. My data include converts affiliated with traditionalist mosques, others whose orientation is more reformist, and others showing allegiance to Sufi groups. Within these networks, I observed a diversity of religious postures. For example, Anna (of France), depicts herself as more "modern and less radical" than her sisters of the same Muslim university association, and she does not hide her Sufi sympathies.

Whether real or perceived, this power structure doubtless shapes narratives and semantics.

In the narrative schemes I identified, embracing Islam is part of a space-time matrix that encompasses an encounter with a Muslim person in the future convert's circle who is said to embody the values of Islam. These values may vary from one "agent of conversion" to another, ranging from flexible views inclined to interreligious dialogue to more rigorous or conservative postures. The conviction of having found the "real path" arises from the study of holy scriptures, which may be strengthened by other experiences, such as travelling in a Muslim country or watching the popular movie *The Message* (1976, directed by Moustapha Akkad). This whole process is usually validated through a dream or a consultation prayer. The timing of conversion matches a specific momentum that takes place in particular spaces of initiation. Women report that it is in the conviviality of mosques, the friendly welcome of practising Muslims, or the warmth of religious rituals (in particular during the month of Ramadan) that they recognize the "true way" they associate with "the source." In these spaces of intense sociability, which hold a vivid fascination for them, the attraction and pressure around conversion intermingle in such a way that some converts report "the mere feeling of embracing Islam." Most narratives suggest that the convert's quest is often achieved in an experience of reified alterity that is either concrete and local, or imagined and global: "I was alone and I realized that there were Muslims who were really Muslims and manifested it." However, this quest is not validated by people in their close social circle (e.g., family, friends, colleagues), who constantly question the authenticity of their choice (Le Pape et al. 2017).

This path towards Islam is not devoid of doubts, hesitations, or resistance. Interviewees describe it as a road that is more winding than straight, thereby making their narratives all the more convincing and realistic. For example, converts reveal tension between their deep conviction that Islam is "the truth" and their apprehension regarding the constraints of religious practices (e.g., wearing the veil, five daily prayers). Reporting the delicate conciliation between belief and practice turns the narrative of conversion into one of persuasion (of the self and of the interlocutor). Samantha (of Quebec) told me, "I was trying to get some documentation but inside of me, I understood it was compulsory because it is clearly written in the Qur'an, but I wanted to be convinced of the opposite, so I was buying books to find somewhere that I was not obliged to veil." Discouragement and doubts arise, especially when it comes to the complicated Muslim religious practices and bodily rituals (prayers, ablutions, etc.) and the gradual awareness that they are endorsing Muslim identity.

Paths towards Islam are therefore non-linear: some converts reported they took a break from Muslim practices during uncertain periods of life (travels, teenage years), before reactivating them during important periods, such as during pregnancy. In any case, embodying Muslim identity is presented as a target;

and once the Muslim practices are supposedly mastered and assumed, it becomes hard to move backward, because, as one woman put it, "It is easier to put the veil on than to take it off" (Marie-Eve, of Quebec). Some women say the feeling of autonomy and empowerment that came from having chosen to embrace this religion (as opposed to inheriting it) usually makes the prescriptions less constraining, and others evoke the relief of surrendering to God. The women also counter possible criticism of Muslim codes of conduct and prescribed practices by either rationally justifying them or interpreting their meaning; for instance, some interviewees presented the ban of alcohol as an issue of public security. However, the Qur'anic possibility that a man can punish his spouse is, according to these women, not yet understandable given the current limits of human knowledge.

Narratives that frame the embodiment of Islam as a gradual process seem to contradict converts' constant mentioning of an ontological and primordial Muslim identity that would precede the discovery of Islam and to which embracing Islam would allow them to return: "I realized that I was very Muslim, even without living in this environment or this way of life. But I had principles that were Muslim." Most women contended that they entertained Muslim values innately, even before knowing about Islam: "Already before, I didn't eat pork" or "Anyway, I have never liked mini-skirts." Through this rhetoric of continuity that addresses practices, dogma, and values, new Muslims emphasize their familiarity with the Muslim world view that was established well before embracing Islam: "I have always felt an unease with the idea that Jesus was the son of God" (Elizabeth, of France). Although a common thread, this narrative construction varies according to the converts' context, conditions of living, or phase of life. In fact, narratives clearly distinguish personality and social behaviours, arguing that the former has not changed, though if it had, it would be for the better:

> I wanted my mother to understand that I haven't changed. Because I truly haven't changed mentally; my heart is still the same, my intentions are still the same: thriving in life, etc. I am even doing better, less fearful. The first time my friends saw me with the veil, they asked, "What the heck is that?" But my personality has not changed. (Sandra, of France)
>
> Is this in relation to Islam? Or is it my personality? I guess both overlap. I have chosen Islam because my personality and the values I wanted to have correspond to the ones that are conveyed in Islam. (Pauline, of Quebec)

This conception of the self that is based on the premise of human beings' innate status of submission to God (*fitra*), which only pious believers can revert to, conforms to Muslim ethics. It contrasts with Christian theology that refers to a change of heart when one accepts Jesus, becomes Christian, and obtains salvation (Asad 1996). As opposed to Christian narratives of conversion, which centre on a breakdown structured around a past life of distress and a new life of salvation (Décobert 2001), narratives of entry into Islam follow a rhetoric of continuity that refers to an Islamic anthropology – involving not a conversion but a reversion towards an ontological Muslim identity.

As a result, in spite of the high emotions expressed by new Muslims about their path towards Islam, the women I met rarely reported a moving event or trauma that triggered their adopting Islam. They depict their entry into Islam as a fluid series of events, within which uttering the act of faith (*shahada*) represents only one step. This return to Islam parallels personal, familial (death of parents), romantic (mixed unions, affairs), or professional (career move, dismissal) experiences, while discovering Islam is framed in line with converts' life cycle (marriage, maternity, dismissal) or environments (ethnically diverse living milieu).[5]

In this way, the semantics of conversion based on Christian perspectives that informed my approach when I undertook fieldwork had no resonance with converts' view of their own experience in Islam as aligned with their biography. This discrepancy in terminology undoubtedly reinforced their need to deconstruct my perspective by referring to a "grammar of conversion." The latter relies not so much on a corpus of codes and rules that regulate narratives (Le Pape 2007) as on a set of techniques that allow them to present the narrative of conversion as the proof and achievement of their authenticity in Islam.

Although I have shown in previous work that Ricoeur's theory of narrative identity, including the dynamics of *idem* and *ipse*, may be useful to understand how converts' narratives produce Muslim identity (Mossière 2013), this is probably not enough. Following Foucault (2001) and Somers (1994), I contend that the self, as it is formed through narratives, reveals more the conditions of his or her production and the contingencies he or she has to negotiate than it does any ontological being. During fieldwork, it was indeed very clear that some respondents who volunteered for interviews were actually driven by the example of their "sisters in Islam," who sometimes pressured them with ideas about how Muslims should display themselves, claim the legitimacy of their new identity, and take their place in the public sphere. In other words, while the anthropological logic of the continuity of human beings structures my respondents' narrative canvases, deconstructing this scheme shows the various strategies that help make their choice of Islam socially and politically acceptable for the ethnographer, and more so for the public.

The Structure of Narratives and the Public Language of Recognition

As the converts embark upon the narration of their path in Islam, they enter a dynamic process of social recognition of their new identity. They know that such validation depends on subjective motives, including the variety of interpretations of Islam. The institutionalization of the self, therefore, hinges on the ritualization of narratives.

Grammar of Conversion and the Problem of Recognition

In his study of converts to Judaism, sociologist Tank-Storper (2007) compares the standardization of converts' narratives with the process of conformity they operate ex post that makes the individual experience fit into the institutional frame and the narrative canons of the new religious tradition. In discussing the grammar of conversion, political scientist Le Pape (2007) considers the skills converts have to acquire, notably the ability to judge which narrative version is appropriate to different publics and spaces, but also the mastery of the art of "talking about intimacy" and the ability to tolerate or manage criticism, controversy, and ridicule. Such ability to adjust the narration of conversion to the forms required by the social and political conditions gives most narrators the power of recognition, although every narrator is not equally empowered: "This is why, passing one's conversion means being able to show, in specific situations, the vigor of the self" (Le Pape 2007, 360).

Here, I would like to push Le Pape's proposition further by arguing that this process of conforming is built in relation not only to the religious institution or community but also to the rest of the society. The standardization of the narratives would therefore be related to converts' desire to make their experience and discourse ideologically and sociologically intelligible and acceptable to the surrounding society, of which the ethnographer is considered the emissary. The narrative plot hinges on this concern for the recognition of the subject by the Other. Indeed, the points of convergence I have observed among the narratives of converts with diverse social, national, or political backgrounds indicate that new Muslims face the constraint of displaying themselves according to precise identity categories, including identity rules of the community they claim to belong to and the guidelines of presentation of the self for a non-Muslim public. These constraints are articulated according to the expected representations of what it means to be Muslim and French/Quebecois (etc.), to be a veiled woman, to adopt a minority identity, or to belong to an ostracized group.

Honneth and Voirol's (2006) theory of recognition allows us to delineate new Muslims' grammar of conversion. The German philosopher Honneth and his Swiss colleague Voirol argue that issues of recognition have their own language in that they are endowed with a grammar that suits the claims of social agents. The centrality of language in achieving recognition draws on the idea of reciprocity, where representatives get to know themselves from the point of view of their interlocutors, because "subjects may only reach a pragmatic relationship with themselves if they learn how to understand them from the normative perspective of their conversation partner who sends them a certain amount of social requirements" (Voirol 2005, 113). Given that the subjects who are denied such recognition are likely to experience "the moral experience of social contempt" (Honneth and Voirol 2006), recognition is also a dialectical relationship stemming from a personal and moral desire that turns it into a struggle with the Other. Piettre and Monnot (2013) distinguish three specific domains of struggle: first, the struggle for recognition that includes the wording of expectations within the existing normative frame (Honneth and Voirol 2006); second, the struggle for visibility based on communication techniques and strategies (Voirol 2005); and third, recognizability that implies jeopardizing the existing normative rules and politics through which recognition is distributed. Following Butler's (2010) idea of reaching a "good life" and Fraser's (2011) concern for social justice, Piettre and Monnot (2013) contend that struggle for recognizability could grant social value, rights, and legitimacy to lifestyles that have been deprived of it or have been considered an alternative to dominant norms.

The structure of the conversion narratives I have collected is framed by a common language of recognition: as the latter follows the normative sets of norms and values that feature Western neoliberal societies, it also revisits its power structure, where it introduces subversive elements. The reliability of this narrative is established right away, as most converts start by asserting, "I know the real face of Islam," thereby contrasting their view with the image conveyed through the media. In the next sections, I show how this grammar of conversion hinges on two different types of normative rhetoric that allow the women to produce reliable knowledge on Islam that expresses their experience of conversion in a consistent and normative way.

The Rhetoric of Continuity

As explained above, most of the women I met associated Islam with their authentic way of being and living in the world. In this way they presented the changes in their social behaviour due to adopting Islam (getting married, having kids, etc.) as part of their natural life cycle: "I live my life naturally and it happens that it fits with Islam." Along with this natural predisposition to Islam, they also emphasize the role of circumstances and contingencies in their encounter with Islam, which suggests they also consider Islam as a destiny: "It is Islam that chose me and not me who chose Islam" (Anne Marie, of France). Yet conversion does not mark their arrival at what they identify as their inner state; rather, it starts as a move to turn faith into action or action into faith.

Converts' discourse regarding the adoption of a Muslim first name – which is not compulsory for new Muslims – reveals their desire to render consistent their inherited legacy and the ideology they have adopted. The women I met articulated these two concerns in various ways: On the one hand, those who keep their original first name emphasized the importance of maintaining symbolic and social ties with their group of origin. This is illustrated in an interview with one French woman who explained her discomfort over changing her name:

> When they [Muslims] call me Firdaws, I feel like I am betraying my parents, because in a way, it is like denying the inheritance they gave me. But I always told my parents that me being Muslim does not change anything about the fact that I am proud of the education they gave me, of the choices they made for me, etc. Because it is thanks to all this that I am the woman I am today and that I am able to make my own choices.

On the other hand, the women who adopt a Muslim first name either assert they have never been at ease with their previous name or evoke concern for integrity with their Muslim identity. One woman stated, "I have always felt more Leila than Nathalie." Women who change their names usually choose one that fits their personality or personal quest, or whose phonetics are close to their given name, such as Marie's taking of the name Maryam.

All of the women's discourses recalled that Islam is in line with and completes the monotheistic traditions that most of them are from, with Muhammad as part of the same prophetic lineage as Jesus and David. The women found common normative references in the holy scriptures (on which the three traditions rely) that they presented as universal and often compared with traditional social and moral models (family structure, gendered distribution of roles, abstinence and virginity until marriage). Hélène (of Quebec) explained how her Christian background made Islam so familiar to her:

> The imam was saying "Being Muslim means to believe in a unique God, with no associates." Okay, I believe this. So he said "It's believing in all the prophets." I believe in that, it's just that I don't know Muhammad yet. Well I believe in other Books, but I don't know yet the Qur'an. I believe in the invisible world, I believe in angels, I believe in the last day, a day when we're going to be judged according to the life we live here. I believed in that too, that our life is determined in advance, there's like a destiny there. I believed in that too. So there was nothing that I was hanging on to when I was listening to the class. It was something that struck me, it's like I'm a Muslim, but I don't know.

These narratives reproduce common tropes that are spread via short booklets, edited by publishers like Tawhid Editions, that circulate in Western mosques. Muslim testimonies that sprout up on the internet also echo these arguments.

A discrepancy emerges between the construction of this rhetoric of biographical and ideological continuity and the recurring claim made by new Muslims that Islam allows them a new start. Women whose pre-conversion lifestyle did not meet Muslim prescriptions, notably regarding sexuality, point out that in Islam, all transgressions committed before conversion are erased. Narratives show a clear break with Catholicism, from which most of the interviewees want to distance themselves – especially in Quebec, where the rejection of the Catholic Church has been common discourse since the 1960s.

The narratives display some fuzziness regarding the time frame of the conversion path; for instance, many converts cannot define the exact date of their entry into Islam. The redundancy of these patterns shows the standardization of the narratives I have collected. Nevertheless, converts' ability to frame their experience in these schemes varies according to how advanced they are on the conversion path; this includes the time they have spent in Islam, their degree of embodiment of Muslim practice, semantics, and way of thinking, as well as their diligence in learning (Allievi 1998; Jensen 2008). The reflexivity they develop with respect to their lived experience and the identity they ascribe to their interlocutor also play a part, as we shall see later. Incidentally, a recurring feeling of being unqualified and not "strong enough in Islam" led a few converts to refuse to participate into my research, others to come to interviews in a group, and many to mitigate the impact of their narratives with sentences like "I wouldn't like to say something stupid" or "I am going to do some research before answering your question." By and large, the longer women have been Muslim, the more standardized their narrative is. Yet this narrative scheme leaves some spaces open for converts to compose their own distinction. For example, some women define themselves more as believers than as Muslims, having also always nurtured a spiritual quest or believed in God without associating any practices to these beliefs – which Islam now allows them to do. Because the deconstruction of this narrative scheme jeopardizes the association converts build between continuity and linearity, it also informs us about the tensions that govern the path in Islam, namely the compatibility of so-called Muslim and Western world views.

The Rhetoric of Compatibility

Making the choice of Islam recognizable to the society of origin also implies showing how and where both paradigms can meet. Narrative elements are therefore organized so as to emphasize the compatibility between what they associate with Islam and what they associate with Western world views. Therefore, the choice of Islam as well as of Muslim identity are depicted in line with the values ascribed to the society of origin (agency, free will, and freedom of consciousness).

First, converts' narratives actively promote values of tolerance, openness to Otherness, freedom of consciousness, and individual rights in the context of the high cultural diversity of their society of living that they say they value. I thus heard many times: "Everyone can do what they want as long as they're happy." They relate this liberal discourse to an interpretation of Islam anchored in Tariq Ramadan's posture. This highly contested Islamic scholar, who enjoys high moral capital among converts, publicly campaigns for a reformed version of Islam that would be adapted to contexts where Muslim populations are a minority with the saying, "No constraint in any sense or another." When converts willingly assert that "each one makes their own choice," they express their commitment to this posture of mutual recognition, thereby trying to redraw and enlarge the identity possibilities allowed by their environment. As a result, they associate the tensions entailed by their conversion to Islam with resistances specific to the dominant society, where prejudices against Islam circulate, rather than with normative Muslim codes and tenets.

The complex issue of gender relations is another point of tension that tends to delegitimize new Muslims' claim for recognition, on the basis that the role and status of women in Islam disagree with the feminist orientation that forms one of the core pillars of contemporary Western societies. Ironically, the women's narratives plot the condition of women in Islam as one of their motives to convert. They articulate a Muslim feminist discourse that depicts Islam as a progressive religion regarding women at the time of the Prophet. With a rhetorical twist, women reverse the Western second-wave feminist argument by valuing the Muslim gendered distribution of tasks that spares them from having to contribute to the household's material needs. Many women say they take advantage of the option to not work in order to study or commit to charitable activities.

Narrative schemes also aim to unravel the trope of social contempt towards new Muslims, which often depicts converts' choice as inauthentic and their conversion as a constrained and uninformed choice, and which justifies women's conversion to Islam by their physical attraction to an Arabic dominant lover. To deconstruct this stereotype, women who entered Islam before meeting their husband (half of the women in my data) heavily stress the chronology of their path. Others enhance the role of sisters and other female converts in their decision to embrace Islam at the expense of their lovers, who are sometimes not even present at the *shahada* ritual. This insistence on deconstructing common associations between conversion and mixed union is reinforced by the repeated evocation of the serenity, peace, and self-realization converts have found in Muslim tenets and regular practices, like the testimony of Natasha (of Quebec):

> Islam has brought me more stability and serenity in my life. Maybe I was a bit lost; you always wonder, "The man I am with, is he the right one?" There is always a bit of uncertainty, even about the future, you are never sure of anything. While since I embraced Islam, I feel I put things more in God's hands, I trust in fate: "If it didn't happen, it's because fate wanted it to happen, that's how it is."

Likewise, this sense of self-realization is strengthened by the emphasis narratives place on the progression and constant work to become a "good Muslim." Converts describe their efforts to learn, adopt, and embody Muslim practices and stress that Allah values their endeavours and self-control more than the accuracy of the practices. By activating this rhetoric of well-being, self-cultivation, autonomy, and good will, women shift their choice of Islam from an undesirable political category of subjugation of the female subject to a domain of socially valued autonomy and achievement of the self.

Last but not least in the techniques of this grammar of recognition, the rhetoric of faith leads converts to describe their path in Islam as the synthesis of their religious, personal, family, health, and professional paths. In this understanding, everyday concerns and experiences of stigma and depreciation are interpreted through the Muslim paradigm lenses that transpose them into a spiritual domain. As converts downplay ritual constraints, they also spiritualize their meaning and impact with claims like "This makes me closer to my God" or, like Natasha's (of Quebec), who says Islam inspires all of her everyday behaviours: "You can do everything with the intention of pleasing God, so Islam relates to everything you do." Some women plot their conversion as a love story, in which the romantic encounter between the future new Muslim and Islam is a metaphor for her discovery of Islam. Such narratives sometimes intermingle with actual love stories between converts and Muslim-born men. Supported by this rhetoric of deep intimacy and serenity with an outside and almighty entity, conversion is thus presented as a profound, unique, and non-material experience that is out of her interlocutor's reach and, as such, out of the realm of critique and testing. The sense of mystery that emerges from this narrative scheme suggests that the mechanics that lead to the embrace of Islam can be grasped only by non-objective means. This idea is reinforced by the women's repetitive assertion that their path inspired their kinships' own religious experience, which led some parents or siblings to embrace Islam themselves or to turn back to Catholicism.

These observations show how conversion narratives navigate between two discursive levels that the sociologist Tank-Storper (2007) labels the "attestative" (or demonstrative) dimension of conversion, which establishes the path's consistency, and the problematic dimension, which displays the tensions related to the change of religion. In this section, I have shown how the interplay between these two dimensions contributes to the persuasive effect of conversion narratives. This strategy targets not only the public and surrounding society but also the ethnographer, who appears as the go-between for new Muslims and the oppositional public opinion.

The Interplay of Identity and Roles in Fieldwork and the Production of Knowledge

As Van Nieuwkerk (2006) compares narratives of conversion collected through face-to-face ethnographic research with those that circulate on the internet, she observes that the modes of representation of the self vary according to the platforms on which they take place. Narratives that circulate among large, anonymous, and virtual public spaces display standardized religious identities that abide by a missionary and normative ideology. In contrast, representations of the self that are articulated in the interactive context of empirical fieldwork are more diverse. Van Nieuwkerk concludes from her study that examining the way new Muslims build narratives informs us more about the conditions of production of meaning and experience of conversion than motives of conversion. In my research as well, in midst of the variety of biographical paths I have collected from the women I met, I found that narratives share the gender issue as a common plot whose aim is to liberate the vision of Muslim woman from the prejudices of oppression that are part of the Western imagination.

In this section, I argue that converts appropriate the narratives schemes to deconstruct common stereotypes, all the while adapting their testimony to the conditions of the ethnographic encounter. It is in the intersubjective space of dialogue with the Other, namely their interlocutor, that the process of identification and recognition takes place. For new Muslims, the exchange with the ethnographer is a social test of probation and recognition of their new identity, as well as an interpersonal exercise of their subjectivity in the making. As they tell their story to a public, of which the ethnographer is seen as the emissary, converts get the opportunity to articulate the self, their identity, and their social and political position. For each partner of the conversation, this experience of intersubjectivity is fraught with openness and resistance, and with negotiation and challenges of one's own posture and power, and the recognition of that of the other.

Building Identities through the Ethnographic Conversation

In her comparative study of converts in Sweden and in the United States, McGinty (2006) shows that, as they organize the experience of conversion within their new religious system and their personal biography, their narratives also work on the historicity of the individual and arrange the continuity of their representation. Likewise, my research demonstrates that plotting conversion narratives is as much an ideological (or dogmatic) exercise as an emotional and personal experience. This turns conversion narratives into unique, personal, and new products that are co-constructed within the interview space.

Most of the women I contacted to interview feared they could not legitimately talk about Islam as a Muslim – they first tried to redirect me towards one of their friends "who really knows Islam": "*She* is a real good Muslim, she studied a lot, she will be able to tell you." Yet the ones that accepted took care not to present a bad image of Islam, including abiding by the tenet of respecting their parents, who in most cases were hostile to or uneasy with their new religious affiliation. In fact, I soon observed that many women who agreed to meet me were actively encouraged by their fellow sisters in Islam, who saw the interview as an opportunity for the converts to learn how to express and frame their interest in Islam. After each interview, they spread the word on social media about how the conversation went, circulating the conditions of the interview and the questions I asked, as well as giving each other advice on how to conduct it. I usually made clear that interviews were one-on-one, but in one case, a French woman who was about to utter the *shahada* to become Muslim appeared with two other converts. These two women came with the obvious intention to support their new sister's testimony in Islam, as it was clear that the future new Muslim was very shy and unsure in her new identification to Islam.

In this case as in many others, the exchange with the ethnographer is a social test of probation and recognition of their new identity, as well as an interpersonal exercise of their subjectivity in the making. Whereas they were cautious and insecure at the beginning of the interview, most converts end the ethnographic conversation by emphasizing how they appreciated having the opportunity to think and talk about their experience with Islam, leading them to more awareness about their path and renewing their identification with Islam. A few of them compared the interview with a session of psychotherapy; others mentioned the catharsis effect of the ethnographic conversation, as it released the tensions their change of religion created with their social circle and realigned them with their religious choice.

The role of the interview in the construction of Muslim identity is, however, contingent on the specific time-space matrix in which it takes place. The ethnographic conversation can only provide a snapshot of interviewees' identification in a limited instance. This momentary effect appears more clearly when the ethnographer can meet interviewees several times, as I did with Samantha (of Quebec).

When I first met her, Samantha had just ended her relationship with a Muslim of North African descent. She firmly asserted she would not leave Islam after this separation. She reproduced a narrative that was shared by many respondents: She recalled the commonalities between Islam and Christianity and stressed the continuity between her Muslim beliefs and her identity heritage. During the second interview six months later, she said she did not really ascribe to the rigour of some prescriptions in Islam, which she in a way invalidated by shifting the description of her path from Muslim to "spiritual." She mentioned salsa, an activity she was fond of and that her sisters in Islam urged her to give up due to its incompatibility with their interpretation of Islam. One year later, Samantha had given up her practice of Islam and was highly critical of the unnecessary compulsory dimension of some Muslim rules that she saw as too pragmatic. According to her, the respect of certain moral values was what, above all, allowed her to maintain religious practices wholeheartedly and sincerely, framing a return to her Christian heritage that she considers more in line with her beliefs.

Although Samantha's profile is not typical of all the converts I met, the evolution of her discourse regarding her entry into Islam reveals how individual and social elements are intermingled to assemble and disassemble identification through narratives. As a part of the process of adopting the new religion, narratives allow converts to ritualize the tensions and conflicts aroused by their new identification and resolve them by navigating between the boundaries of the self and the social (Stromberg 1993). Yet narratives are also framed by the conditions of the intersubjective encounter, which makes their potential to promote knowledge on conversion experience the outcome of an insightful negotiation between two situated perspectives and roles that the ethnographer and the interviewee assign to each other.

Negotiating Roles in Fieldwork

The plot of conversion narratives does not rely as much on the adoption of the new religion as on the doubts, hesitations, and tensions that revolve around this decision. Women in interviews with me pointed out their initial resistance to, or lack of tolerance for, Islam with respect to the role and status given to women as well as the code of behaviour for gender relationships prescribed in the Qur'an. For instance, Denise (of Quebec) said, "Before, I was like you, I had prejudices on Islam; I would never have accepted to wear the veil." Others reported how shocked they first were as they read that in certain interpretations of the Qur'an, men are allowed to beat their wife in some circumstances. They went on to stress that this specific text has given rise to significant debate among Muslims and prominent figures, such as Amina Wadud, who disagree with this interpretation. By heavily stressing their early stereotypes of Islam, they related these ideas to their environment of origin to make their shift towards Islam more sound: "My colleagues do not understand, they actually do like we used to when we didn't know Islam, they judge" (Denise, of Quebec). At the same time, they made connections to my own profile, which, except for my religious identity, is similar to theirs: for example, we are female, White, of the same generation, and in the same stage in life. During interviews, I noticed we shared common references to comics we watched during childhood, sentimental experiences we had as teenagers, concerns around career-family conflicts. I often felt religious identity was the only barrier between us, making my posture all the more ambivalent. The possibility of erasing this frontier actually appeared a few times, for instance when our conversations were interrupted by the call for prayers and they invited me to join them.

Yet, because I made clear I was not Muslim myself and never really opened a door to embrace Islam, the reactions triggered by such a posture could indeed inform me about converts' capacity to embrace ideological challenges and perhaps unravel political and social issues related to conversion as a lived practice.

In fact, converts usually started the conversation by asking me about my beliefs and religious affiliations. My Catholic upbringing and my spiritual path seemed to reassure them, creating a sense of familiarity and intimacy conducive to confidence because some of the women had been involved in forms of Christianity before embracing Islam.

However, this strategy of ethnographic contact only allowed me to reach new Muslims who were open to non-Muslims. It is likely that many converts who declined my invitation to meet actually did so because they rejected interactions with non-Muslims. The flexibility my interviewees displayed with respect to my religious identity also sheds light on their own modes of negotiation between the identity they had prior to conversion, their identity after conversion, the identity of their kinship, and the identity of their peers in Islam. Such openness takes root in their desire to let the public know more about their decision to embrace Islam and to deconstruct stereotypes. Indeed, many of my interviewees emphasized the importance of my research and showed eagerness for the results to be disseminated. I sent an electronic copy of my thesis to all of them, and some of them browsed and circulated it. Whatever their motives, the interviewees seemed to attribute a status of "in-betweenness" to me that allowed me to navigate fruitfully on fieldwork. It granted me access to converts who usually value spiritual paths, all the while differentiating our religious affiliation and making clear the reasons for my presence with them.

Nevertheless, my posture evolved during fieldwork. At first, since I was aware of Muslims' suspicion around participating in any research or enquiry, I situated myself outside their social and political landscape: as French in Quebec and as Quebecoise in France. Converts therefore ascribed me a status of radical alterity and felt free to express political and normative discourses on prejudices and discriminations they were enduring in both geopolitical spaces: for example, the difficulties of penetrating the working market as veiled women in France, and the degradation of social mores and misconduct of the Catholic Church in Quebec. Later on, when the collection of data was ending, my presence seemed appreciated and more familiar to some convert women, and a few converts invited me to diverse activities and events in their everyday lives (e.g., weddings). Motives that justified such a symbolic capital varied according to the respondents: For a French immigrant in Quebec with nostalgia for her home country, my proximity was related to my French origin and accent; for the most educated Quebecois respondent of my data, it was related to my university level. In this phase of my work, some possibilities appeared to revisit narratives in the light of observations, as I will discuss in my conclusion. This dynamic interplay between my own posture and my interviewees' undoubtedly interfered with my ability and legitimacy to produce knowledge about them.

Challenging the Authority of Producing Knowledge

As a practice of communication, qualitative interviews depend on the conditions of transmission of the information collected, on the respective situations of the ethnographer and informants, and on the relationships between participants and with respect to third parties. What is more, interviews are contingent on the possible discrepancy between the postures that are assumed by each one and the roles ascribed to them. It is now widely acknowledged that the data collected within the space-time of interviews make ethnographers the custodians of a situated knowledge that they have the power to reproduce and articulate (Marcus 1986). The leverage effect produced by the possibility of diffusing this knowledge multiplies such power. Ethnographic writing that follows the collection of data is not free from this subjective relationship, because the diffusion of the scientific production of ethnographers exposes them and their work to the feedback of informants who nowadays have access to these scientific outputs.

Yet the production of knowledge is also influenced by the relationship between the one who knows and talks, on the one hand, and the one who determines the conditions of the encounter and the production of truth that follows them on the other hand. Consequently, the situation of ethnographers does not make them all-powerful, and the terms of the anthropological dialogue, as well as its incidental impossibility, also draw on the posture of the respondents. In the ethnographic encounter, informants are indeed expected to display through words and gestures the authentic perception they have of themselves; as a result, this power actually ascribes them the authority over the production of knowledge. As they abide by the free and voluntary prescriptive dimension of interviews, anthropologists are limited in the array of questions and answers that the rules of propriety and free consent allow. Likewise, they may have to answer to respondents' concerns and questions themselves. For example, all the women I've met asked me to situate myself with respect to either Islam or my personal beliefs; most of them were intrigued by my interest in the issue of conversion to Islam since I was not Muslim myself. What is more, the quality and consistency of the fieldwork material depend on the openness of respondents to convey a set of data that might be filtered, oriented, dogmatized, or ahistorical. Given these caveats, one can wonder: What truth does a narrative convey?

Most converts admitted they agreed to be interviewed by me because of an activist agenda that aims to rehabilitate Islam, to raise awareness among the dominant group about "what Islam really is," and to "educate people," not to mention their religious mission to spread the word of Islam (*da'wa*). For ethnographers, the role of spokesperson assigned to them by converts combines with the role of audience – in front of which converts try out the identity rhetoric they have learned to form the self. Although this function undoubtedly facilitates the collection of data, it also entails methodological biases, along with the uncomfortable sensation for ethnographers that they have been taken hostage by the interviewees, who appropriate the ethnographic exercise as a performative space in which to build and act out their new identity.

For example, I did a three-hour interview with Marion, during which I could barely discern her narrative within her dogmatic discourse and references to Qur'anic sura to support her statements. Afterwards, she emailed me to ask for another interview, writing, "After you left, I realized that I stayed a lot on the factual dimension and I haven't talked a lot about what attracts me for real in that religion: what I found in there, interested me and encouraged me to know more … yet I think this is essential in the process [of conversion]." For the second interview, Marion had prepared a point-form list with precise topics related to the virtues of Islam, about which she spoke in a long monologue.

In the intersubjective space that forms the ethnographic encounter, actors' intentions shape tensions, negotiations, and powers, as well as mutual trust. They also orient and circumscribe the range of knowledge the ethnography can produce. In my case, it definitely transposed my ambition to grasp the lived experience of embracing Islam in the everyday life into the formal realm of normative guidelines designed to behave and reveal oneself as "a good Muslim."

Conclusion: The Limits of Narratives in Studying Muslim Topics and the Possibility of Triangulation

In this chapter, I have scrutinized the grammar of recognition and the conditions of the ethnographic conversations on my fieldwork with converts to Islam to discuss the methodological challenges of conducting empirical research among Muslim populations as an outsider, paying attention to the intersubjective play that fieldwork entails. Following Bourdieu's (1994) insightful invitation to consider life narratives as a "superficial creation of meaning," wherein he labels them as "biographical illusion[s]," the conversion narratives I collected among new Muslims in France and in Quebec shed light on the distinction that Bauman (1986) draws between "lived event" and "narrated event." Conversion narratives form a literary genre that is codified and standardized; they are also a construction that narrators shape ex post as a result of the new religious paradigm that they have adopted. In this regard, conversion narratives provide significant information about the process of religious change. While the ethnographer cannot avoid considering the fictive dimension of narrative, the study of conversion narratives can inform us about how new Muslims give meaning to and assume their decision to change religion. It also indicates to what extend new Muslims abide by the norms of conversion and negotiate within the situated space of interaction that the ethnographic encounter creates.

During my research, recruitment was unexpectedly very successful, with forty respondents in France and thirty-eight in Quebec. My participants' enthusiasm for the project could be explained by the public audience it offered to converts to express their discourse as a politics fraught with determination, emotions, and deception. While my research project aimed to compare the processes of conversion to Islam in France and in Quebec, in this chapter, I chose to delineate the commonalities in the discourses I collected, leaving the task of specifying the variations between contexts for future research. As a political object, all narratives of conversion to Islam coincide in deconstructing stereotypes on Islam yet vary in means, ranging from anger to grief to irony:

> Can you describe your relationship with your husband?
>
> Yes, my man beats me, he drinks alcohol and gambles! Because this is what people who do not know too much about Islam love to hear. (Sandra, of France)

My discursive analysis of conversion narratives highlights the common tropes that ethnographic research might lead new Muslims to build and rely on as they negotiate contact with people from outside their everyday lives. Yet these findings also point out the strong need for new ethnographic methods to triangulate the narratives and situate converts' discourses. Observations are indeed helpful to connect narratives, intentions, and motivations to their real actions and their impact. Although nowadays respondents are usually reluctant to let the ethnographer be part of their environment, the observations I had the opportunity to make showed the pressures exerted by a surrounding Muslim community (family, sisters in Islam) between the converts and their experience of Islam.

Meeting the respondents at different intervals is another strategy to distinguish the normative from the biographical part of narratives. It leads converts to revisit their narrative as they embrace practices, beliefs, and belongings that make sense in their path. The vagaries of Melissa's path, for example, which gradually turned away from Islam in the course of my study, emphasized the methodological precautions and creativity that a study on Islam drawing on narratives should entail. When converts' narratives follow plotting techniques that frame their experience within the normative lenses required by the language of recognition, the discourse of apostates may also shed new light on the conversion process. Indeed, the apostates I have met tend to criticize how converts instrumentalize Islam to offset family insecurities or lack of personal individual or family valorization, or to conform to pressure from partners or in-laws. Because apostates' narratives are likely to be as constructed as the converts', the convergence of motives of conversion they question suggest the presence of "unacceptable reasons" to embrace Islam. By allowing us to identify the power relationships at work among new Muslims, the method of collecting narratives of people at the margins epitomizes the specific discourse that converts' narratives aim to answer. It is, therefore, likely to help deconstruct the subtle processes underlying fieldwork among Muslim converts.

NOTES

1 Unlike in Christianity, becoming Muslim does not require any official collective recognition. It is enough to recite the *shahada*, that is, to say that there is only one God and that Muhammad is his Prophet. This ritual can be performed in a private setting, including alone.
2 One exception to this is the study by McGinty (2006). Methodological nationalism is defined by anthropologist Nina Glick Schiller (2005) as an empirical methodology that delineates its object of enquiry within the spatial scale of a country (or a nation state).
3 I asked them: "Could you please share with me how you embraced Islam?"
4 France (Le Pape 2015; Mossière 2013; Puzenat 2015; Riva 2015), the UK (Bourque 2006; Köse 1996; Moosavi 2012; Suleiman 2013; Zebiri 2007), Belgium (Leman 2010), Switzerland (Leuenberger 2013), Netherlands (Van Nieuwkerk 2006; Vroon 2014), Germany (Özyürek 2014; Wohlrab-Sahr 2006), Norway (Roald 2004), Sweden (McGinty 2006), Denmark (Jensen 2008), Spain (Rogozen-Soltar 2012), Italy (Allievi 1998), USA (Winchester 2008), Quebec (Mossière 2013).
5 For example, a few converts travelled in Muslim-majority countries during their childhood or were brought up in migrant residential areas.

REFERENCES

Allievi, Stefano. 1998. *Les convertis à l'Islam: Les nouveaux Musulmans d'Europe*. L'Harmattan.

Asad, Talal. 1996. "Comments on conversion." In Peter Van der Veer (Ed.), *The globalization of Christianity* (pp. 263–73). Routledge.

Bauman, Richard. 1986. *Story, performance, and event: Contextual studies of oral narrative*. Cambridge University Press.

Bourdieu, Pierre. 1994. *Raisons pratiques sur la théorie de l'action*. Éditions du Seuil.

Bourque, Nicole. 2006. "How Deborah became Aisha: The conversion process and the creation of female Muslim identity." In Karin Van Nieuwkerk (Ed.), *Women embracing Islam: Gender and conversion in the West* (pp. 233–48). University of Texas Press.

Butler, Judith. 2010. *Ce qui fait une vie: Essai sur la violence, la guerre et le deuil*. Zones.

Décobert, Christian. 2001. "Conversion, tradition, institution." *Archives de Sciences Sociales des Religions, 116*, 67–90. https://doi.org/10.4000/assr.541

Foucault, Michel. 2001. *L'herméneutique du sujet: Cours au Collège de France 1981–1982*. Gallimard.

Fraser, Nancy. 2011. *Qu'est-ce que la justice sociale? Reconnaissance et redistribution*. La Découverte.

Galonnier, Juliette. 2015. "The racialization of Muslims in France and the United States: Some insights from White converts to Islam." *Social Compass, 62*(4), 570–83. https://doi.org/10.1177%2F0037768615601966

Haddad, Yvonne Yazbeck, Jane I. Smith, and Kathleen M. Moore. 2006. *Muslim women in America: The challenge of Islamic identity today.* Oxford University Press.

Harding, Susan F. 1987. "Convicted by the Holy Spirit: The rhetoric of fundamental Baptist conversion." *American Ethnologist, 14,* 167–81. https://doi.org/10.1525/ae.1987.14.1.02a00100

Henry, Christine. 1998. "Le discours de la conversion: Parcours de conversion." *Journal des Africanistes, 68,* 155–72.

Hermansen, Marcia. 2006. "Keeping the faith: Convert Muslim mothers and the transmission of female identity in the West." In Karin Van Nieuwkerk (Ed.), *Women embracing Islam: Gender and conversion in the West* (pp. 250–74). University of Texas Press.

Honneth, Axel, and Olivier Voirol. 2006. *La société du mépris: Vers une nouvelle théorie critique.* La Découverte.

Jensen, Tina Gudrun. 2008. "To be 'Danish,' becoming 'Muslim': Contestations of national identity?" *Journal of Ethnic and Migration Studies, 34*(3), 389–409. https://doi.org/10.1080/13691830701880210

Kilani, Mondher. 1995. *L'invention de l'autre essai sur le discours anthropologique.* Payot.

Köse, Ali. 1996. *Conversion to Islam: A study of native British converts.* Kegan Paul International.

Leman, Johan. 2010. "Crossing boundaries: Ethnicity and Islamic conversion in Belgium." *Ethnoculture, 2,* 27–44.

Le Pape, Loïc. 2007. "Qu'est-ce que la religion pour les Français? Ce que nous enseigne la conversion." PhD diss., École des Hautes Études en Sciences Sociales.

– 2015. *Une autre foi: Itinéraires de conversions en France; Juifs, chrétiens, musulmans.* Presses Universitaires de Provence.

Le Pape, Loïc, Myriam Laakili, and Géraldine Mossière. 2017. "Les convertis à l'islam en France, entre liens originels et recompositions croyantes." *Ethnologie française, 4*(168), 637–48.

Leuenberger, Susanne. 2013. "'I have become a stranger in my homeland': An analysis of the public performance of converts to Islam in Switzerland." In Samuel M. Behloul, Susanne Leuenberger, and Andreas Tunger-Zanetti (Eds.), *Debating Islam: Negotiating religion, Europe, and the self* (pp. 1181–1202). transcript Verlag.

McGinty, Anna Mansson. 2006. *Becoming Muslim: Western women's conversions to Islam.* Palgrave Macmillan.

Marcus, George E. 1986. *Writing culture: The poetics and politics of ethnography.* University of California Press.

Moosavi, Leon. 2012. "British Muslim converts performing authentic Muslimness." *Performing Islam, 1*(1), 103–28. https://doi.org/10.1386/pi.1.1.103_1

Mossière, Géraldine. 2013. *Converties à l'islam: Parcours de femmes au Québec et en France.* Presses de l'Université de Montréal.

Özyürek, Esra. 2014. *Being German, becoming Muslim: Race, religion, and conversion in the new Europe.* Princeton University Press.

Piettre, Alexandre, and Christophe Monnot. 2013. "Entre reconnaissance et visibilité: Les luttes des acteurs islamiques en suisse et en France." In Christophe Monnot (Ed.), *La Suisse des mosques: Derrière le voile de l'unité musulmane* (pp. 199–231). Labor et Fides.

Puzenat, Amélie. 2015. *Conversions à l'islam: Unions et séparations*. Presses Universitaires de Rennes.

Riva, Virginie. 2015. *Converties*. Seuil.

Roald, Anne Sofie. 2004. *New Muslims in the European context: The experience of Scandinavian converts*. Brill.

Rogozen-Soltar, Mikaela. 2012. "Managing Muslim visibility: Conversion, immigration, and Spanish imaginaries of Islam." *American Anthropologist, 114*(4), 611–23. https://doi.org/10.1111/j.1548-1433.2012.01518.x

Schiller, Nina Glick. 2005. "Transnational social fields and imperialism: Bringing a theory of power to transnational studies." *Anthropological Theory, 5*, 439–61. https://doi.org/10.1177%2F1463499605059231

Somers, Margaret R., and Gloria D. Gibson. 1994. "Reclaiming the epistemological 'other': Narrative and the social constitution of identity." In Craig Calhoun (Ed.), *Social theory and the politics of identity* (pp. 37–99). Blackwell.

Stromberg, Peter G. 1993. *Language and self-transformation: A study of the Christian conversion narrative*. Cambridge University Press.

Suleiman, Yasir. 2013. *Narratives of conversion to Islam: Female perspectives*. Cambridge University Press.

Sultan, Madeleine. 1999. "Choosing Islam: A study of Swedish converts." *Social Compass, 46*, 325–37. https://doi.org/10.1177%2F003776899046003008

Tank-Storper, Sébastien. 2007. *Juifs d'élection: Se convertir au judaïsme*. CNRS Éditions.

Van Nieuwkerk, Karin (Ed.). 2006. *Women embracing Islam: Gender and conversion in the West*. University of Texas Press.

Voirol, Olivier. 2005. "Les luttes pour la visibilité: Esquisse d'une problématique." *Réseaux, 23*(129–30), 89–120.

Vroon, Vanessa. 2014. "Sisters in Islam: Women's conversion and the politics of belonging: A Dutch case study." PhD diss., University of Amsterdam.

Winchester, Daniel. 2008. "Embodying the faith: Religious practice and the making of a Muslim moral habitus." *Social Forces, 86*(4), 1753–80. https://doi.org/10.1353/sof.0.0038

Wohlrab-Sahr, Monika. 2006. "Symbolizing distance: Conversion to Islam in Germany and the United States." In Karin Van Nieuwkerk (Ed.), *Women embracing Islam: Gender and conversion in the West* (pp. 71–94). University of Texas Press.

Zebiri, Kate. 2007. *British Muslim converts: Choosing alternative lives*. Oneworld Publications.

On Critical Muslim Studies and Islamophobia: An Interview with Jasmin Zine

MEHMET ALI BASAK

Biography

Jasmin Zine is a professor of sociology and religion and culture at Wilfrid Laurier University, where she co-founded the Muslim Studies Option. Zine is also an affiliated faculty member of the Islamophobia Research and Documentation Project (IRDP) at the University of California, Berkeley. Her research falls in the areas of Islamophobia studies, critical Muslim studies, race/anti-racism, postcolonial/anti-colonial studies, social justice education, decolonizing research, and critical ethnography. She served as co-chair of the Islamophobia sub-committee of the Ontario Anti-Racism Directorate (2018) and testified at the Canadian Heritage Parliamentary sub-committee meetings on Motion 103 (2017), addressing Islamophobia, systemic racism, and religious discrimination. In addition to her more traditional academic work, Zine is a public intellectual and politically active in responding to Islamophobia through public talks, radio programs, and op-ed articles. In 2018 Zine joined the Critical Muslim Studies Institute in Granada, Spain, as a faculty member. She also serves on the editorial board of the critical Muslim studies journal *ReOrient*.

Zine has researched Muslim communities in Canadian diasporas since the late 1990s. She has written numerous journal articles on Islamic feminism, Muslim women's studies, and Muslims and education and in the Canadian diaspora, as well as in anti-racism education. Her books include *Canadian Islamic Schools: Unravelling the Politics of Faith, Gender, Knowledge and Identity* (2008, University of Toronto Press), *Islam in the Hinterlands: Muslim Cultural Politics in Canada* (2012, University of British Columbia Press), and (co-edited with Lisa K. Taylor) *Muslim Women, Transnational Feminism and the Ethics of Pedagogy: Contested Imaginaries in Post-9/11 Cultural Practice* (2014, Routledge).

As a consultant, Zine has developed award-winning curriculum materials that address Islamophobia and anti-Muslim racism. She worked with the Office for Democratic Institutions and Human Rights at the Organization for Security and Co-operation in Europe (ODIHR/OSCE), the Council of Europe, and the

United Nations Educational, Scientific, and Cultural Organization (UNESCO) on developing international guidelines for educators and policymakers on combating Islamophobia and discrimination against Muslims. She was also an advisor on a 2017 national survey on Islamophobia in Canada conducted by Canadians for Justice and Peace in the Middle East (CJPME) and EKOS Research Associates (2018).

In her study of the "9/11 generation" of Muslim youth, Zine examines how Islamophobia and the ongoing War on Terror have affected the sense of identity, citizenship, and belonging of the 130 Muslim youth she interviewed across Canada. This six-year national study (2009–15) funded by the Social Sciences and Humanities Research Council (SSHRC) explored the impacts of 9/11, the "War on Terror," and domestic security discourses and policies on Muslim youth in Canada. The forthcoming book based on this study is entitled *Under Siege: Islamophobia and the 9/11 Generation* (McGill-Queen's University Press, 2022).

Zine was awarded an SSHRC Partnership Engage Grant in 2018 to examine and map the Canadian Islamophobia industry. This new study builds on research that Zine and her team of graduate researchers from Wilfrid Laurier University have been working on in partnership with the Bridge Initiative at Georgetown University, developing fact sheets on Islamophobia in Canada.

Interview

Mehmet Ali Basak [MAB]: Among your many pedagogical projects, you teach at the Critical Muslim Studies: Decolonial Struggles and Liberation Theologies summer school in Granada, Spain. You are also on the editorial board of the critical Muslim studies journal, *ReOrient*. In your opinion, why are these studies "critical"? How does this adjective signal a different politics or approach?

Jasmin Zine [JZ]: In my view, when the term "critical" is added to a concept it signals a reference to the social and political imperatives behind critical theory. Critical theory (with its intellectual legacy in the Frankfurt school) is distinguished from traditional theory through the explicit focus on gearing social enquiry (and inevitably social action) towards challenging the structures of domination and the promotion of freedom from oppression. Horkheimer (1993) argued that critical theory must explain what is wrong with current social reality, identify the actors to change it, and provide clear norms for critique of the status quo as well as achievable practical goals for social transformation. Therefore, when "critical" is attached to Muslim studies it signals a political and social commitment to these epistemic and practical goals.

As the premiere journal for critical Muslim studies, *ReOrient* outlines a series of epistemological orientations characterizing the field in its inaugural issue. They can be grouped into four broad currents (Sayyid et al. 2015): (a) a critique of Eurocentrism understood in a variety of registers (epistemological, cultural, geopolitical) that problematizes its deployment as a universal standard and referent; (b) a suspicion against positivist claims of creating neutral, transparent, and predictive knowledge; (c) a critique of Orientalism and the power/knowledge nexus; (d) a focus on decolonial thought as the means of delivering on the promise of the liberatory imperatives of critical theory. In framing the epistemic parameters for critical Muslim studies, the *ReOrient* editorial outlines the project as an "engagement with some of the key concerns and responses of decolonial thinking, in particular the project of writing a new history of the world without the telos of the West" (Sayyid et al. 2015, 7). These ideas form the core epistemic frames for articulating the field and capture the overlapping political challenges and investments out of which critical Muslim studies emerges.

MAB: In your intervention in a "Producing Islam(s) in Canada" podcast, you highlight that as a scholar you engage in Muslim studies rather than Islamic studies (Zine 2017a). How do you differentiate these two fields?

JZ: I co-founded the Muslim Studies Option at Wilfrid Laurier University in 2008. Working with my colleagues in the program, we wanted to develop and differentiate this field from Islamic studies, which is rooted in the historically based textual analysis of religious doctrine (Qur'an, Hadith, and Fiqh). Islamic studies also focuses on Islamic history and civilizations, historiography, Islamic law, theology, and philosophy. Muslim studies on the other hand addresses the realities of contemporary Muslim communities, societies, and diasporas and is sociologically and politically grounded in an epistemological and methodological focus on these concerns. As a discipline, Muslim studies engages with the cultural context of Muslim societies and communities that is rooted in their socio-historical dimensions and religious formations in a variety of global contexts. Instead of a focus on historically rooted religious texts (as in Islamic studies), Muslim studies is concerned with how these religious texts animate, shape, and inform Muslim social, political, and cultural development and is attentive to how the identities and lived experiences of Muslims are contested, negotiated, and challenged in the communities and nations in which they reside. Muslim studies draws from interdisciplinary fields, and those who locate their scholarship in this area may be part of disciplines such as religious studies, politics, sociology, education, women and gender studies, law, global studies, social work, literary and cultural studies, and so on. Methodological approaches in Muslim studies include qualitative/quantitative, ethnographic, discourse analysis, and other types of empirical research, as well as theoretical and philosophical engagements.

MAB: How does your understanding of anti-Islamophobia shape your academic work, as explained in "Unveiled Sentiments: Gendered Islamophobia and Experiences of Veiling among Muslim Girls in a Canadian Islamic School" (2006b), the IRDP (2017b), and your article in the *National Post* (2017c)? Additionally, can you tell us how you locate anti-Muslim racisms in your perception of Islamophobia?

JZ: I developed a definition of Islamophobia in 2002, which was published in an article in the *American Journal of Islamic Social Sciences* entitled "Anti-Islamophobia Education as Transformative Pedagogy: Reflections from the Educational Front Lines" (2004a). I was working on the development of anti-Islamophobia curriculum to respond to the rise in hate crimes and anti-Muslim racism after 9/11. At the time, while it was possible to find the conceptual and pedagogical tools to address issues of racism, classism, sexism, homophobia, ableism, and anti-Semitism, resources that addressed the discursive and pedagogical foundations for dealing with Islamophobia did not exist. The term "Islamophobia" did not have currency at the time. And yet, being able to name and define the experience of Muslims as the result of Islamophobia was critical to shaping the kind of interventions that were needed, so having a clear and actionable framework for understanding and addressing Islamophobia was important. Yet I found that Islamophobia was defined in ways that were too literal and incomplete, reducing it to an attitude of fear, mistrust, or hatred of Islam and its adherents. One of the blind spots of this definition was that it did not take into account that Islamophobia affects not just Muslims, but anyone perceived to be a Muslim. The first violent act of reprisal after 9/11 was against a Sikh man, Balbir Singh Sodhi, who was shot at a gas station because he was wearing a turban and misidentified as a Muslim. It's also believed that the shooting by a White supremacist at a Sikh gurdwara in Wisconsin in 2012 that took six lives was motivated by Islamophobia and that the temple had been misidentified as a mosque. Non-Muslim racialized groups are victimized in the cross hairs of Islamophobic hate because their Brown, turbaned bodies are misread in the climate of heightened anti-Muslim sentiments and hate crimes.

Another blind spot in the way Islamophobia was being understood and characterized was how it was reduced to "fear, mistrust or hatred." This interpersonal dynamic represented a very narrow conceptual framework that did not consider the social, structural, and ideological dimensions through which forms of oppression are operationalized and enacted. In my view, far from being based on "ignorance," Islamophobic attitudes are part of a rational system of power and domination. The idea that discrimination, be it based on race, class, gender, sexuality, ability, or religion, simply arises from "ignorance" allows those engaged in oppressive acts and policies to claim a space of innocence for their actions. By labelling Islamophobia as an essentially "irrational" fear, this conception denies the racial logics of social dominance and oppression, which operate on multiple social, ideological, and systemic levels that are mutually reinforcing and support and maintain relations of power. So, to capture the complex sociological dimensions through which it operates, I define Islamophobia as a *dynamic system of oppression against Islam and Muslims (or anyone perceived to be Muslim) that operates through (a) individual, (b) ideological, and (c) systemic practices of subordination which support the logic and rationale of specific power relations* (Zine 2004, 2022). For example, individual acts of oppression include such practices as name-calling, hate crimes, vandalism, or assault, while systemic forms of oppression refer to the structural conditions of inequality regulated through such institutional practices as racial and religious profiling, xenophobic state policies, or denying jobs or housing opportunities. These exclusionary practices are shored up by specific ideological underpinnings, among them recurrent Orientalist notions that pathologize Muslims as "terrorists" and impending threats to public safety or render Muslim women as "backward" and oppressed. In my view, Islamophobia is an overarching framework within which anti-Muslim racism exists as a specific manifestation that is evident through the violence and discrimination that is enacted against Muslims as a social category. But since these acts rely upon the demonization of Islam, one does not exist without the other. I resist attempts to take "Islam" out of Islamophobia as the vilification of Islam is one of the hallmarks of this form of oppression.

This recognition does not preclude legitimate critiques directed at Islam. Alt-right critics argue that the term "Islamophobia" silences criticism of Islam using the "free speech" argument to undermine use of the term. There is a clear difference between critique and vilification and demonization or between free speech and hate speech. Nonetheless, such criticism has led to moves to reframe the definition of Islamophobia as a form of racism to make it more intelligible, recognizable, and less contested. For example, the All Party Parliamentary Group on British Muslims (APPG) put forward the following definition of Islamophobia: "Islamophobia is rooted in racism and is a type of racism that targets expressions of Muslimness or perceived Muslimness." While I don't disagree with the idea that Islamophobia can be understood as a kind of racism, I have kept the reference to Islam in my definition of Islamophobia because I see that the roots of this form of oppression are not only about race (i.e., that Muslims are targeted as an identifiable racial group), but Muslims are targeted by Islamophobia due to the *racialization of religion* whereby certain phenotypical characteristics and features associated with racial groups are ascribed to specific religions. Islamophobia is a racialized phenomenon, but since Muslims are not one identifiable racial group, and indeed many Muslims are White but are still subject to Islamophobia, the dynamics of Islamophobic oppression are more broadly constituted.

Islamophobia has a longer genealogy and history than racism, which has its formation in the modern period. Islamophobia, on the other hand, dates back to the first Muslims who were persecuted for their beliefs in the seventh century and continued to ideologically and systemically underpins the era of European Crusades from the eleventh to thirteenth centuries and the Spanish Inquisition starting in the fifteenth century before the colonial expansion of the modern period and the formation of Orientalist scholarship and culture, which continues to shape the discursive foundations of the imperial present. Therefore, it is important to discern the complexities and historical specificities of Islamophobia as a multidimensional phenomenon.

Given the Quebec mosque shooting in 2017 where six Muslim men were shot after their evening prayers (Zine 2021a) and the recent terror attack in London, Ontario, on 6 June 2021, that took the lives of four members of a Pakistani Muslim family (Zine 2021b), it is even more imperative to address White nationalist Islamophobic violence in Canada, as well as liberal forms of Islamophobia, which further the normalization of anti-Muslim animus.

Employing an intersectional approach to Islamophobia studies, my ethnographic research on the experiences of Muslim women led to my coinage of the term "gendered Islamophobia" (Zine 2004a, 2006b), which is important in addressing how Islamophobia as a form of individual, ideological, and systemic oppression operates in specific ways to affect the lives, choices, and lived experiences of Muslim women, as well as shaping the discursive foundations for how their identities and subjectivities are understood and categorized through ongoing Orientalist tropes and idioms. In my co-edited book *Muslim Women, Transnational Feminism and the Ethics of Pedagogy: Contested Imaginaries in Post-9/11 Cultural Practice* (Taylor and Zine 2014), we examined the gendered foundations for neo-Orientalism as an ongoing trajectory of representational forms that shape our current political and discursive landscape within the politics of empire. In addition to the way in which Orientalist and Islamophobic representations serve to justify ongoing military campaigns related to the so-called "War on Terror," they also raise important ontological concerns for Muslim women and girls. Being exposed to a barrage of images in literature, cinema, and popular culture is a form of epistemic violence that not only structures the way others perceive and behave towards Muslim women and girls in their daily interactions (going to school, applying for jobs, seeking health care or social services, etc.) but also demarcates the boundaries of their own identities in ways they cannot control. Day-to-day forms of harassment and discrimination are often by-products of the stereotypes generated through the ubiquity of negative images and the dearth of equally salient counter-narratives to correct them. Policies banning Islamic attire (the hijab and the niqab) in Europe and Canada in civic spaces such as voting booths, citizenship ceremonies, courtrooms, and even soccer fields are based on misinformed ideas about Islam and Muslim women. Underlying these policies are negative stereotypes about veiled and oppressed Muslim women without agency and voice and the violent, repressive men they must be protected from. This is well represented by Spivak's (1994) famous formulation of "saving brown women from brown men." The multiple iterations of this vast repertoire of Orientalist and Islamophobic images shape popular sentiments in common-sense-making ways, and this in turn becomes reflected in the cultural politics and racist policies in many national contexts. Therefore, understanding Islamophobia requires an intersectional lens as well as the ability to grasp its historical and discursive genealogy and the contemporary manifestations that operate to shore up contemporary neo-imperial relations of power.

MAB: In most of your work you make candid observations about your own experiences as a Muslim Canadian. What are some of the strengths and drawbacks of framing some of your scholarly work vis-à-vis your personal experiences?

JZ: Every academic/researcher writes from a particular social location that raises questions surrounding the politics and ethics of their work and the knowledge they produce. The role of the body in knowledge production is critical to acknowledge and address the way it implicates and impacts scholarship. This is not just about insider vs. outsider research but about acknowledging and taking responsibility for ongoing academic forms of colonialism that exist in the study of Islam and Muslims. Given the wider understandings surrounding the destructive legacies of White settler colonialism in Canada (knowledge that has been facilitated through the Truth and Reconciliation Commission), there are few non-Indigenous scholars who (I hope) feel the sense of entitlement to go into Indigenous communities to conduct research and impose their meanings on a community that has already been subject to Eurocentric hegemony and political and epistemic domination. Yet this is not at all the case when it comes to the study of Muslim societies. I feel strongly about the need to decolonize research and reinstate discursive control to communities that have had to contend with their lives and experiences being labelled and defined by others who do not have "skin in the game." Being an ally requires humility and stepping back from spaces where you take up room that others need to occupy and lead. Muslims, like other marginalized groups, need to set their own agendas and determine the questions they feel are necessary to examine rather than be subject to the "imperialist fascination" of well-meaning academics who perform what bell hooks (1992) termed "eating the Other." So yes, I do situate my work within this decolonial frame, and I am open about the fact that as a Muslim I do not have the discursive impunity that non-Muslim scholars have where they can come and label and define our experiences (in ways that may or may not resonate with or correspond to how we make sense of our lives) and then can walk away and not be implicated by the knowledge they produce. What I write, theorize, and put out in the world through my research on Muslims affects me, my children, my family, my friends, and my community. My research speaks to the pressing needs of the community because I am part of it. I have trust, access, and insight in ways that non-Muslim academics do not. That is not to say that being a stakeholder makes this work easy. On the contrary, we are often in conflict with sectors of our communities (which are not monolithic or homogeneous) and have our own critiques of and deep-seated frustrations with the status quo. But these are "family matters" and part of a community process that we must negotiate. For example, when I examine Muslim Students' Associations (MSAs) on Canadian university campuses, I cannot ignore the fact that I was a member of the MSA over thirty years ago. My experiences give me insight into the structure, role, and history of these organizations and provides a connection between my experience and the youth I interview. I view this as a strength, though those who still operate from outmoded positivist approaches might see this as a form of "bias" instead. I don't really worry about these limited views; I know my social location and experience allow me to have relevant insights that inform my knowledge production in grounded and authentic ways. For example, developing a critical faith-centred epistemology in my book on Canadian Islamic schools (Zine 2008) came through my fieldwork and my ability to understand the subtext of the experiences my participants had from an Islamic point of view. I realized that purely secular understandings could not capture the complex and metaphysical meanings they attach to their experiences, and so the framework I developed came from this intrinsic understanding. I do not think this would have been apparent to me if I did not share similar sensibilities with my participants. So as a Muslim scholar and public intellectual, my analysis is immersed and grounded in my experience as a stakeholder and my ability to capture and respond to the needs of my community.

MAB: You conducted a national SSHRC-funded study where you interviewed 130 Muslim youth across Canada from 2009 to 2015. This research forms the basis for your forthcoming book *Under Siege: Islamophobia and the 9/11 Generation*. Based on your in-depth research and analysis, what do you see as some of the challenges of the "9/11 generation"?

JZ: The title says a lot in terms of what I have discovered about the 9/11 generation. Being "under siege" is an ontological status that is unique to this generation in that they are socialized into a world where they are subject to suspicion and surveillance by virtue of their religious identity and race. As millennials they do not know a reality before 9/11 and have been socialized into a world where they are treated as potential threats to the nation and as suspect citizens, or what I have termed "anti-citizens," in the West (Zine 2012). They also bear the burden of representation for their entire global community of 1.5 billion Muslims every time an incident of violence takes place anywhere in the world by a co-religionist. They (and other Muslims) are held to account for these actions and are called upon to explain and publicly denounce them. This is a heavy burden to bear and one that Muslim youth are cognizant of in their day-to-day lives, where they feel bound to counteract negative stereotypes about Islam and Muslims and single-handedly be the corrective to hundreds of years of Orientalist labelling.

I think a positive development is the way many youths are using the arts as a form of political resistance against the plethora of Islamophobic narratives in media, television, film, literature, and social media. Muslim youth are engaging in spoken word, visual art, theatre, filmmaking, music, and so on as a means to express themselves, to tell their stories, and to provide political commentary and critique. They are attempting to "reclaim the narrative" about their faith, identity, and experience in ways that are intersectional and speak to the diversity of their social locations and to create platforms to re-deploy new understandings on their own terms. These artistic ruptures are a positive intervention where Muslim youth are engaging and transforming the backlash they face in an Islamophobic climate into productive spaces of social change. Instead of being defined by the clichéd tropes and stereotypes that permeate the dominant media and public sphere, they are imagining and crafting possibilities for alternative narratives and futures.

REFERENCES

All Party Parliamentary Group on British Muslims (APPG). 2018. *Islamophobia defined: Report on the inquiry into a working definition of Islamophobia/anti-Muslim hatred.* https://static1.squarespace.com/static/599c3d2febbd1a90cffdd8a9/t/5bfd1ea3352f531a6170ceee/1543315109493/Islamophobia+Defined.pdf

CJPME. 2018. "Islamophobia in Canada: Still a grave problem." https://www.cjpme.org/islamophobia

hooks, bell. 1992. "Eating the Other: Desire and resistance." In *Black looks: Race and representation* (pp. 21–39). South End Press.

Horkheimer, Max. 1993. *Between philosophy and social science: Selected early writings.* MIT Press.

Sayyid, Salman, Ruth Mas, AbdoolKarim Vakil, and Uzma Jamil (Eds.). 2015. "ReOrient: A forum for critical Muslim studies." *ReOrient, 1*(1), 5–10.

Spivak, Gayatri Chakravorty. 1994. "Can the subaltern speak?" In Patrick Williams and Laura Chrisman (Eds.), *Colonial discourse and post-colonial theory: A reader* (pp. 66–111). Columbia University Press.

Taylor, Lisa K., and Jasmin Zine (Eds.). 2014. *Muslim women, transnational feminism and the ethics of pedagogy: Contested imaginaries in post-9/11 cultural practice.* Routledge.

Zine, Jasmin. 2004a. "Anti-Islamophobia education as transformative pedagogy: Reflections from the educational front lines." *American Journal of Islamic Social Sciences*, Special Issue: *Orientalism, Neo-Orientalism and Islamophobia, 21*(3), 110–19. https://doi.org/10.35632/ajis.v21i3.510

– 2004b. "Creating a critical faith-centered space for antiracist feminism: Reflections of a Muslim scholar-activist." *Journal of Feminist Studies in Religion, 20*(2), 167–87. https://doi.org/10.2979/FSR.2004.20.2.167

– 2006a. "Between Orientalism and fundamentalism: The politics of Muslim Women's feminist engagement." *Muslim World Journal of Human Rights, 3*(1). https://doi.org/10.2202/1554-4419.1080

– 2006b. "Unveiled sentiments: Gendered Islamophobia and experiences of veiling among Muslim girls in a Canadian Islamic school." *Equity & Excellence in Education, 39*(3), 239–52. https://doi.org/10.1080/10665680600788503
– 2008. *Canadian Islamic schools: Unravelling the politics of faith, gender, knowledge, and identity.* University of Toronto Press.
– 2012. "Introduction: Muslim cultural politics in the Canadian hinterlands." In Jasmin Zine (Ed.), *Islam in the hinterlands: Muslim cultural politics in Canada* (pp. 1–38). University of British Columbia Press.
– 2017a. "Producing Islam(s) in Canada." Sound Cloud Podcast. https://soundcloud.com/user-375255614/jasmin-zine
– 2017b, 6 March. "Rescuing Islamophobia from the melting pot of oppression." Islamophobia Research and Documentation Project. https://irdproject.com/rescuing-islamophobia-melting-pot-oppression
– 2017c, May. "Let's worry more about violent Islamophobes – and less about writers who fear being called 'Islamophobic.'" *National Post.* https://nationalpost.com/opinion/lets-take-the-violence-of-islamophobes-more-seriously-than-writers-worried-about-being-branded-islamophobic
– 2021a, 28 January. "Remembering the Quebec City mosque attack: Islamophobia and Canada's national amnesia." *The Conversation.* https://theconversation.com/remembering-the-quebec-city-mosque-attack-islamophobia-and-canadas-national-amnesia-152799
– 2021b, 8 June. "Muslim family killed in terror attack in London, Ontario: Islamophobic violence surfaces once again in Canada." *The Conversation.* https://theconversation.com/muslim-family-killed-in-terror-attack-in-london-ontario-islamophobic-violence-surfaces-once-again-in-canada-162400
– Forthcoming, 2022. *Under siege: Islamophobia and the 9/11 generation.* McGill-Queen's University Press.

SECTION 4

Future Trends

Mixed-Methods and Comparative Approaches to Studying Muslim Immigrant Women in Canada

CATHERINE HOLTMANN

Introduction

This chapter explores the opportunities and challenges of knowledge production using mixed-methods and comparative approaches in studying Muslim immigrant women. My reflections concern the scholarship regarding Muslim immigrant women's social support networks. I conducted a two-pronged study, which includes analysis of quantitative data from Statistics Canada's Longitudinal Survey of Immigrants to Canada (LSIC) along with analysis of qualitative data. I spoke with eighty-nine immigrant women who lived in the provinces of New Brunswick and Prince Edward Island in 2012. The mixed-methods approach capitalizes on the combined strengths of quantitative and qualitative methodologies and leads to findings concerning Muslim immigrant women's emotional struggles that are generalizable yet also provide rich details about their social support networks. A comparative approach – comparing the findings from qualitative data concerning Muslim immigrant women with their Christian counterparts – also has benefits by providing a broader perspective on the knowledge of Muslim women and highlighting both similarities and differences between Christians and Muslims. Public discourse tends to depict Muslim women as vastly different from other religious women in Canada, and my research shows that this is not the case. My research findings also provide the opportunity to think about the situation of Muslim women through deeper analysis of the intersections of gender, ethnicity, and class as they carry out their daily activities in an eastern Canadian context.

Before discussing the details of how the methodology of my study of Muslim immigrant women's social networks contributes to the knowledge about Islam in Canada, I outline the theoretical foundations of the research project. In sociology, method and theory are interrelated – in fact, one's theoretical conceptions play an important role in determining the methodological approach to a particular study. I describe the theoretical basis for my research by clarifying my conceptualization of religion and then follow this with a description of the intersectional framework.

Theoretical Foundations

Religions are dynamic systems of practice (Riesebrodt 2010) that continually change because they are embedded in particular cultural contexts which have impacts on the daily lives of religious people. This is certainly the case for women, like my Muslim research participants, who have a history of marginalization in patriarchal religious traditions. Women manage multiple identities (Ammerman 2003) and their associated practices. Muslim women choose to foreground or background religious identities depending on the demands of a particular context. Beaman (2014) argues that contemporary religious identities are not rigid or pure and draws on concepts of "contaminated diversity" and "collaborative adaptation" in order to break apart identity binaries (2017, 78). My research findings show the flexibility of Muslim women's identities as they adapt to diverse religious and secular influences.

In contemporary Canadian culture, there can be no doubt that the secular forces of capitalism and feminism have had an impact on Muslim women's religious identities and practices, as our contemporary economy propels all Canadian women to participate in the paid labour market in numbers equal to men. Secular and religious feminist movements support women's economic participation as a means of agency (Aune et al. 2008; Walby 1990). Many feminists assume that economic equality will lead to gender equality, and although the gender wage gap in Canada has narrowed, it stubbornly persists. One explanation for this persistence is the unequal division of household labour. Among dual-income couples in Canada, women continue to shoulder greater responsibility for unpaid household work, especially when it comes to the care of young children (Statistics Canada 2011). Doucet (2011) attributes this persistent form of gender inequality to ideological influences and to religion as a source of these influences. My work takes up the challenge of assessing the influence of lived religion on Muslim women's paid and unpaid labour.

To do so, I employ an intersectional framework for analysing data on Muslim immigrant women given that religions are gendered (Avishai 2016), racialized (Cobb et al. 2015), and classist (Sullivan 2012) systems of practice. In considering the gendered nature of Islam, I note that Muslim religious texts reflect the gender norms between men and women of their time (Chaudry 2013). Nason-Clark and Fisher-Townsend (2005) argue that conservative Christian groups promote a form of gender inerrancy or gender complementarity through which men are essentialized in their roles as fathers, leaders, and providers while women's primary roles are as mothers, caregivers, and nurturers. These groups claim that men and women are equal in dignity but have different natures (Holtmann

2018). Yet not all religious families live according to gender roles as promoted by religious leaders. Social science research among evangelical Protestants in the US reveals that couples tend to "do gender" in pragmatically equal terms while maintaining beliefs in gender traditionalism (Gallagher 2003). Rinaldo's (2013) study of Muslim couples in Indonesia highlights that as Muslim women become more active in the paid labour force, the division of unpaid labour in the home becomes the primary site in which couples utilize religious gender scripts. Scripts describing wives' obedience and husbands' authority in the home are a way to accomplish both gender and religion (Rinaldo 2013, 345–6). My study contributes to a growing body of research in Canada where Zine, among others (Hamdan 2009), asserts, "Muslim women navigate between both racialized and gendered politics that variously script the ways their bodies and identities are narrated, defined, and regulated" (Zine 2004, 168). Muslim women conform to and resist male-centred interpretations of Islam from within Canadian Muslim groups and secular narratives of their victimization from outsiders.

Christianity remains the religion of the ethnic majority in Canada – the descendants of White western European settlers. Muslims are a rapidly growing religious group, but public rhetoric concerning "barbaric cultural practices" implies that they have introduced violent interpersonal practices into Canadian society that are at odds with the values of gender equality and respect (CIC 2013, 36). This misrepresentation ignores, however, Canada's long history of colonial violence against Indigenous and immigrant peoples, largely supported by Christians, through the systematic destruction of and discrimination against their cultural practices. My findings provide evidence of the impacts of ongoing, intersecting racialization and religious discrimination of Muslim women.

Although the research on the economic inequality of religious groups in Canada is limited (Heaton and Cornwall 1989), there is evidence of widening class differences between Muslims and other religious groups. Religion has an influence on values such as "emphasis on education, the virtue of work, or honesty and other personal characteristics that are rewarded in the labour market" (Grant and Rosenstock 2011, 75). Yet there is evidence that despite how religious values may have led to their high levels of education and training, Muslim women are penalized in the labour market. Kazemipur's (2014) quantitative research reveals that although Muslim women's pre-migration employment rates are higher than for other immigrant women's groups, they are the lowest overall post-migration. Muslims have the lowest levels of income compared to other religious groups in Canada, and the gap grows in the years following immigration.

This evidence of religious contributions to the intersecting structures of gender, ethnicity, and class contributes to complex inequalities (Walby 2009) for Muslim women in Canada. By focusing my analysis on Muslim immigrant women, my research highlights the opportunities and challenges created by the religious structuring of gender yet takes into account that, in particular contexts, the consequences of the intersecting structures of ethnicity and class may amplify gendered differences.

Mixed Methods

A mixed-methods approach to social scientific research allows me to make some generalizations about Muslim immigrant women in Canada based on statistical analysis and to follow that up with some rich and specific details based on narratives from women living in the Maritime context.

Statistical Methods

The analysis of data from a probability sample drawn from the population of Canadian immigrants, such as that of the LSIC, allows me to make generalizations about the immigrant population and its subgroups.[1] Statistics Canada undertook the LSIC with the purpose of providing indicators of how immigrants are meeting the challenges of integrating into Canadian society over time. The target population for the survey consisted of immigrants from the following categories: economic class, family class, independent immigrants, and refugees who arrived in Canada between 1 October 2000 and 30 September 2001. Economic-class immigrants include skilled workers, investors, entrepreneurs, and self-employed persons. Family-class immigrants are sponsored by family members already living in Canada. Independent immigrants apply on their own and qualify for certain types of jobs or have other important assets. Refugees are people seeking protection in Canada (Statistics Canada 2007d, 8). The survey has a longitudinal design, with immigrants being interviewed at three different times: at six months after arrival, two years after arrival, and four years after arrival in Canada. The interviews were conducted in fifteen languages most frequently spoken by Canadian immigrants. The first wave includes data from 12,040 participants, but because of attrition by the end of the third wave of data collection, this number drops to 7,716 participants.[2] The subsample used for my research consists of the female participants who remained at the end of the third wave, a sample size of about 3,900.

I chose self-reported mental health status as the outcome of interest for the analysis. Just as positive feelings of trust and safety in the Canadian context have been used as indicators of the creation of social capital (Kazemipur 2009), negative feelings of loneliness and sadness can be used as a measure of a lack of social support in meeting the challenges of the immigration and settlement process. In each wave of data collection for the LSIC, participants were asked about their experience of mental health problems. In wave one, survey participants were asked, "Since you came to Canada, have you had any emotional or mental health problems?" In waves two and three, the question changed slightly and the participants were asked, "In the past 12 months, have you experienced any emotional problems? By emotional problems, I mean persistent feelings of sadness, depression, loneliness, etc."

Advanced statistical methods (Gibbens et al. 2010) allow me to distinguish between two types of change in immigrant women's mental health: (1) changes in an individual woman's mental health over time and (2) differences in changes in mental health between groups of immigrant women.[3] The first type of change can be characterized as positive or negative as well as constant or fluctuating. The second type of change is relational and helps to determine if there is a relationship between certain predictors and patterns of change in mental health. The two types of change are related because individual change takes place in the lives of women who are embedded in identifiable social groups. Individual changes in mental health trajectories are analysed according to group characteristics and illustrated as having a particular shape or smooth curve. Comparing mental health trajectories for different groups of immigrant women shows that there are some who pay a higher emotional cost during the settlement process than others, indicating that there may be problems in their access to or utilization of social support.

Variables based on the women's main activities are incorporated into the model. These include unpaid care work, study, and paid work.[4] Main activities have an impact on an immigrant woman's mental health because they influence her identity construction. Depending on how immigrant women manage the influences on their identities in the early years of settlement – religious and secular – a main activity may align or contrast with their values. Participating in the labour market or studying at a post-secondary education institution can provide immigrant women with better access to social support networks than performing care work in the home. As already mentioned, some Muslim groups promote gender roles in which women's identities and practices as caregivers are foregrounded. This is in contrast to secular pressures for Canadian women to identify primarily with their paid employment. These pressures are evident given that between 1950 and 2015, the labour force participation rate for Canadian women between twenty-five and fifty-four years of age rose from 21.6 per cent to 82 per cent (Moyser 2017). Table 1 shows that almost 70 per cent of the immigrant women in the sample were employed part-time or full-time prior to coming to Canada. This is due to immigration policies that prioritize highly skilled immigrants, yet it also indicates that participation in the labour market is not antithetical to the pre-migration identities of the majority of immigrant women.

I am interested in how religious characteristics predict differences in immigrant women's mental health trajectories according to their main activities.[5] There is only one LSIC survey question related to religion, which asks the respondents to identify their religion. Muslims had only one option – Islam.[6]

This poses a limitation in accounting for the impact of religious heterogeneity in the analysis of mental health outcomes. To overcome this discrepancy, I create interaction terms using information on ethnic origins. Variables on five religious affiliations – Christian, Muslim, Eastern religions (Hindu, Buddhist, and Sikh), Other, and No Religion[7] – are combined with nine ethnic categories of East/Southeast Asian, South Asian, West Asian, Arab, Eastern European, Western European, African, Latin American, and Other. Research shows that religion and ethnicity are closely intertwined (Bramadat and Seljak 2005) and that variability within a particular religious tradition can be associated with ethnic diversity.

The information on religion in the LSIC data does not provide an indication of the women's frequency of engagement with religious practices nor the importance of religion in their daily lives. The data do not provide information about immigrant women's lived religion or non-religion. For some Muslims, religion is a cultural identity and not a lived practice. The information on ethnicity is also problematic. The ethnic origins categories created by Statistics Canada are quite broad. For example, West Asian ethnic origins include Afghan, Armenian, Assyrian, Azerbaijani, Georgian, Iranian, Israeli, Kurdish, Pashtun, Tatar, and Turkish women (Statistics Canada 2007c). Thus, the group of West Asian Muslim women have a wide range of ethnicities lumped together. Creating ethno-religious interaction terms is a limited solution to the lack of information about Muslim diversity and the small proportion of Muslim women in the LSIC sample. These limitations concerning the ethno-religious identities of Muslim immigrant women are important to keep in mind when reading the results of my analysis. As Day and Lee (2014) suggest, "Any piece of research, such as a survey or an interview, has an ethical dimension, and research into the characteristics – inferred, imposed, or solicited – of people is one that is enormously vulnerable to misinterpretation and misrepresentation" (347).

Caution should also apply to the interpretation of Muslim immigrant women's mental health outcomes. It is difficult for most people to admit to experiencing sadness, loneliness, and depression, but there are cultural differences in the expression of emotions (Gudykunst and Ting-Toomey 1988). Cultural values may prohibit immigrant women, particularly Asians, from disclosing feelings of distress, especially in the early stages of the settlement process. Last, the measurement of women's main activities is also imprecise. Women were asked to identify the activity which occupies most of their time, but many women juggle multiple responsibilities at the same time, especially mothers.

Only two Muslim subgroups are of sufficient size to include in the analysis – South Asian and West Asian Muslims.[8] Table 1 provides a general description of the sample used for the analysis.

Table 1. Selected descriptive characteristics of immigrant women in LSIC data (N=3,897)

Age at arrival	%
Working age (26–65)	75.4
Young (16–25)	21.3
Senior (66+)	3.3
Family structure	
Without children	50.4
With children	49.6
Level of education at arrival	
University undergraduate degree or equivalent	55.5
High school	30.3
University graduate degree or equivalent	14.2
Employment status prior to migration	
Full-time employed	63.1
Not employed	30.6
Part-time employed	6.3
Ethnic origins	
East/Southeast Asian	34.5
South Asian*	25.0
Western European	9.8
Arab	7.0
Eastern European	6.3
Other	5.6
West Asian	5.4
African	3.2
Latin American	3.1
Religion	
Christian	39.5
No religion	22.5
Eastern religions (Hindu, Buddhist, Sikh)	18.7
Muslim	18.6
Other	0.7
Ethno-religious groups†	
East/Southeast Asian no religion	19.0
South Asian Eastern religions	16.0
East/Southeast Asian Christians	14.0
South Asian Muslims	7.1
West Asian Muslims	4.8

* South Asian ethnic origins include Bangladeshi, Bengali, East Indian, Goan, Gujarati, Kashmiri, Nepali, Pakistani, Punjabi, Sinhalese, Sri Lankan, Tamil, and South Asian (not included elsewhere).

† Only ethno-religious groups included in the analysis are listed in the table.

Statistical Findings

Figure 1 illustrates the mental health trajectories of all immigrant women according to their main activities, regardless of their ethno-religious identities. In looking at the relationship between main activities and immigrant women's mental health trajectories, figure 1 shows that all Canadian immigrant women, regardless of whether they provide unpaid care in the home, participate in the labour force, or pursue post-secondary education, are increasingly likely to report mental health problems. The horizontal axis depicts the years after arrival in half-year increments.

The vertical axis indicates the percentage of immigrant women reporting mental health problems. The smooth curves are the mental health trajectories labelled according to the women's main activities at four years. It is interesting to note that in figure 1, the rank order of the impact of immigrant women's main activities of employment, care work, and study on their mental health trajectories changes from that at the six-month mark to that at four years. Six months after arrival in Canada, women doing care work or studying are *less* likely to report mental health problems compared to women in the labour market. The highest likelihood of reporting mental problems six months after arrival is among employed immigrant women. But notice how the mental health trajectories associated with each main activity change over time. Women whose primary activity is studying are more likely to report mental health problems after four years in Canada than either women with paid employment or those doing care work, and the rate of increase in reporting, for women whose main activity is study, is the steepest of the three groups. The reporting of mental health problems for women doing care work also increases over time but at a lower rate than for students. While women who are employed experience the highest rates of mental health problems at six months after arrival, they become the group that is *least likely* to report mental health problems after four years. Employment is the least emotionally distressing activity for immigrant women (regardless of ethno-religious identity) after four years of living in Canada.

The intersection of immigrant women's main activities with ethno-religious identity markers reveals even more complex variability in their mental health trajectories. Figure 2 illustrates differences in the mental health trajectories for only the Muslim immigrant women. The graph in the upper-left quadrant shows the average mental health trajectories of all Muslim immigrant women according to their main activities. Unlike the results in figure 1, employment is generally not protective[9] of Muslim women's mental health at any point in the first four years after arrival. Muslim immigrant women who are employed after four years of living in Canada report mental health problems at higher rates than Muslim women doing care work or studying. Study is less emotionally distressing than employment for Muslim women over four years, and those doing care

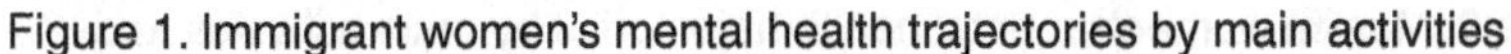

Figure 1. Immigrant women's mental health trajectories by main activities

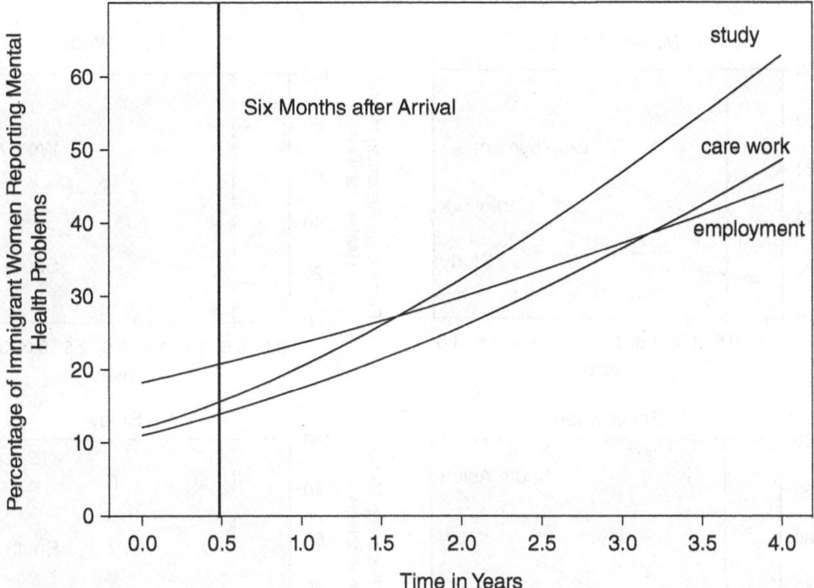

work at home have mental health trajectories that fall between these two. The remaining three graphs in figure 2 show that there are differences in this basic pattern among Muslim women depending on their ethnic origins.[10] The graph in the upper-right quadrant illustrates that West Asian Muslim women whose primary activity is care work are more likely than the average Muslim woman to report mental health problems over time. However, South Asian Muslim women for whom unpaid care work is a main activity report mental health problems at lower rates than the average Muslim woman. When it comes to the relationship between employment and mental health, South Asian Muslim women report mental health problems at higher-than-average rates for Muslim women both at arrival and over time, as shown in the graph in the lower-left corner of figure 2. West Asian Muslim women who are employed at six months after arrival in Canada are more likely than the average Muslim woman to report mental health difficulties, but over time their rates drop to below-average levels. The graph in the lower-right corner shows that over time South Asian Muslim women who study report mental health problems at higher-than-average rates, while for West Asian Muslim women, being students improves their mental well-being over time. In fact, the mental health trajectories of West Asian Muslim immigrant women who study improves over the initial four years of settlement.[11]

Figure 2. Muslim women's mental health trajectories by main activities and ethnicities

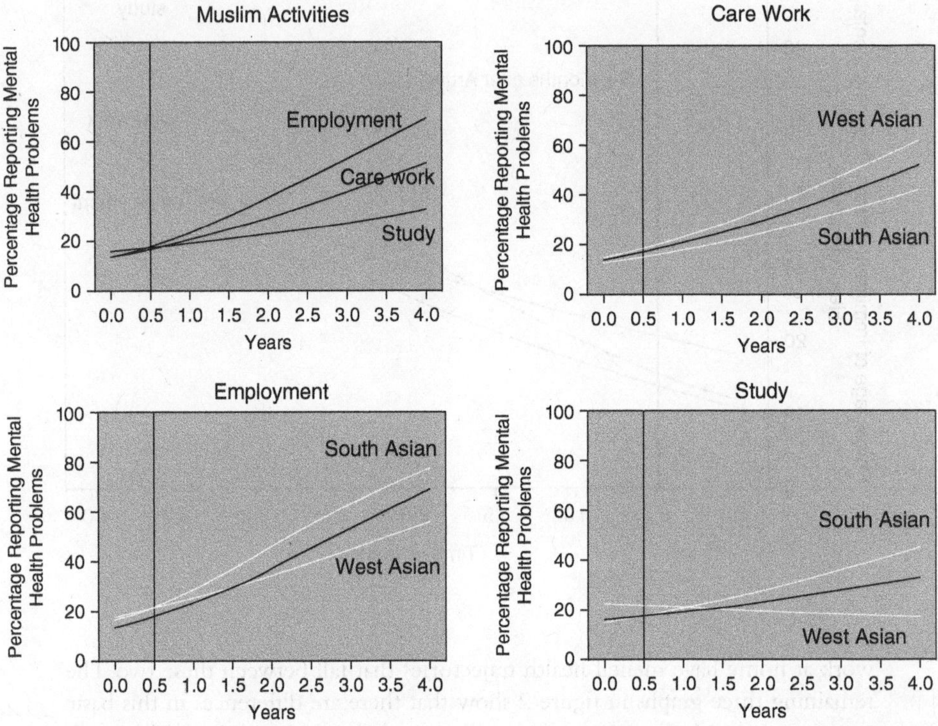

It is at the intersection of Muslim immigrant women's ethnic identities and main activities that interesting variations in mental health trajectories are found. Given the religious emphasis on Muslim women's identities as caregivers (Chaudry 2013), it might be assumed that engaging in unpaid care work would be protective of their mental health. Based on the analysis of the UK's 2001 census data, Hussain (2008) argues that responsibility for care work in the home and higher rates of economic inactivity for Muslim women in Britain are indications of their greater religiosity than other women in the UK.[12] My analysis shows that West Asian Muslim women with paid employment experience lower rates of mental health problems than other Muslim immigrant women with paid employment. In fact, West Asian Muslim women whose primary responsibility is for unpaid care work are more likely to report mental health problems over time than other Muslim immigrant women in Canada.[13] However, because the Canadian data provide no measures of the religious engagement of Muslim immigrant women, there is no evidence to support the assumption that care work is more aligned with some Muslim women's religious identities than paid employment. There is also no information about whether Muslim immigrant women choose to spend the majority of their time doing unpaid care work or whether other options are unavailable.

Secular feminist and capitalist social influences, among others, urge women to prioritize their identities as paid workers (Crompton and Vickers 2000; Kim 2015; Walby 1990). Given that a large proportion of the sample had been engaged in paid employment before coming to Canada (Statistics Canada 2007a), the assumption that being employed after arrival contributes to Muslim women's mental well-being is worthy of investigation. My larger study (Holtmann and Tramonte 2014) shows that Muslim immigrant women who are employed report higher rates of mental health problems over the first four years of settlement than Christian immigrant women. They also are more likely to report mental health problems than Muslim women who are doing unpaid care work or studying. West Asian Muslim women who are employed are less likely to experience mental health problems, but I do not have evidence to support the conclusion that they are more likely to foreground economic priorities than other Muslim immigrant women. The results of Kazemipur's (2014) analysis of 2001 Census and LSIC data provides some explanation for Muslim working women's elevated rates of mental health problems. He argues that it takes much longer for Muslim women to get their first paid job and that their education and work experience are more likely to be discounted by Canadian employers than for other immigrant women. Thus, employed Muslim women's poor mental health trajectories may be explained by stress due to the length of time it takes for them to find work and the dissatisfaction that comes from underemployment once a job is found. Kazemipur's analysis also shows that Muslim women are more likely to be unemployed than other immigrant women. Muslim immigrant women's experiences of employment, underemployment, and unemployment are the results of structural racism and Islamophobia. This context might help to explain why my results show that studying is protective of Muslim immigrant women's mental health. Perhaps the hope that a degree from a Canadian post-secondary institution will increase their chances of finding a good job helps to buoy their mental health.

None of the above explanations for the results of the statistical analysis of Muslim immigrant women's mental health trajectories in relationship to their ethnic origins and main activities considers the role that social support networks play in mitigating or augmenting their emotional distress. I undertook preliminary analysis of the relationship between the mental health trajectories of immigrant women and their participation in religious and cultural groups with the LSIC data. Women who participate in these groups are more likely to report mental health problems over time than those who do not. Yet it is impossible to tell whether immigrant women with mental health problems are more likely to join religious and cultural groups or whether these groups lack social support networks for women. Also, only a small proportion of immigrant women indicate that they participate in these groups, which means that the sample size was too small for further analysis.

I followed up the results of the statistical analysis of data from Muslim immigrant women with a qualitative study of Muslim immigrant women in the Maritimes,[14] seeking to find more detailed information about the intersection between their lived religious practices, their main activities, and the ways that social support networks contributed to their mental health during the settlement process.

Qualitative Methods

Qualitative data provide a rich description of the lived religious practices and social relationships that Muslim immigrant women rely on for emotional support during their early years in Canada. I use semi-structured questions about different aspects of immigrant women's lives (religious practices, family life, employment, education, health care, friendships, and support networks) so that they can tell me stories about their experiences. These stories reveal the complexity, ambiguity, and contradictions of social life. In 2012, I conducted focus groups and interviews with immigrant women who had arrived in the Maritime provinces of New Brunswick and Prince Edward Island since 2002. This timeline ensured that their experiences of the settlement process were relatively recent – similar to the women in LSIC. I recruited Muslim and Christian immigrant women so that I could compare the narrative experiences of these two groups with the results of the statistical analysis.[15] More specifically, I was interested in better understanding why Muslim immigrant women are more likely to report mental health problems in the early years in Canada when their main activity is employment compared to Christian women and why they are less likely to report mental health problems if they are mainly occupied doing unpaid care work in the home. I wanted to know what relationship these different activities have with the women's religious identities and practices as well as with their social support networks. In addition to recruiting women who had recently immigrated to the Maritimes,[16] I also sought women from a broad range of countries of origin in order to mirror the ethnic diversity in the LSIC sample. Thirty-one Muslim women from six different ethnic origins groups and fifteen different countries participated in the qualitative portion of the study, along with fifty-eight Christian women from five ethnic origins groups and twelve different countries.

Qualitative Findings

The qualitative sample of Muslim immigrant women is diverse in terms of ethnicity and class, which contributed to capturing the heterogeneity of women's lived religious practices and beliefs. Class differences are evident and have an influence on lived religious practices, especially for Muslim women who share the same country of origin. Muslim women originally from Pakistan provide good examples of how class differences relate to religious practices and social networks. At the time, Pakistani Muslim immigrants played a prominent role in several Maritime mosques and counted themselves among the founders. Thus, recent immigrants benefit from the social support networks that Pakistani Muslim women have established. They share common languages (Urdu and Pashto), and newcomer women get assistance from those who are already established. When they need information, they call someone on the phone; they understand announcements at social gatherings; and they can strike up conversations with strangers. Nahla,[17] a thirty-two-year-old woman with a master's degree in microbiology who immigrated five years prior to the interview, explains.

NAHLA: So when I came here we found out about the mosque and we go directly to the mosque. So the whole community sort of helps the new immigrant, it's not just like one person helping.

CATHY: So there's a real strong sense that the community gets together and helps the new ones?

NAHLA: Yes, yes, and by just asking them to come and have a dinner at your house. It's in a way letting them know that we're here for you so if you need us for anything just let us know. But it's hard to ask for help sometimes. I would say that because the reason being, not everybody is fortunate enough when they come here that they can have a very good lifestyle. But back home they're coming from really good families and highly educated and that's why they were able to immigrate to Canada – good solid financial backgrounds, let's just say that. So when they come here it's a little bit difficult for them to just approach someone and ask for help. So we do it in our own way.

CATHY: Ok, so that the community feels like they embrace everybody that comes, regardless?

NAHLA: Yes, yes but not in the Pakistani community that we need to help out financially but if somebody else. Our mosque is not just Pakistani and they're from Africa, people are from the Middle East and you know, the European Union – everywhere. So if the students need help, we would give money, we would give food, we would give clothes. So in a way we help out that way, so you can say we can help out immigrants by providing them what they need.

Nahla had invited me to her home for the interview. She is married to a physician, and it is evident from the size of her house and living room that they have "a very good lifestyle." Qualitative research enables me to visually observe elements of the Muslim women's class status in addition to the information that they provide through our conversation. Contrary to what Nahla says about members of the Pakistani community not needing help financially, I interviewed two other Pakistani Muslim women living in the same city who have a lower socio-economic status. For example, Abeera's family lives in a modest duplex and her husband drives a taxi because he cannot find work as a computer programmer. When I ask about her religious practices, Abeera explains that when breaking their daily fast during Ramadan, they eat alone at home. On Saturday evenings, they gather with other Muslim families at the mosque for a potluck to collectively break the fast. Abeera feels that the members of the mosque provide good social support for her family. When I ask the wealthier Pakistani immigrant women about their religious practices, they talk about the difficulties they experience in practising modesty when accessing services. They rely on their Pakistani social networks to find female hairdressers, aestheticians, and gynaecologists. Lower-income Pakistani women express less concern than their wealthier peers about contact with non-relative men in the public sphere. Both classes of Pakistani Muslim women engage in religious practices, but the extent to which these practices are public or private differs. In the Maritimes, wealthier Pakistani Muslim immigrant women are able to put boundaries on their social interactions in the public sphere while lower-income women are more reliant on the opportunities in the broader public sphere, especially in relationship to employment. This finding indicates that class differences between Muslim immigrant women who share the same ethnic origins contribute to diversity in their lived religious practices.

Ethnicity has an impact on Muslim immigrant women's access to social support networks. Muslim women whose experiences with employment, study, or doing unpaid care work cause them emotional distress differ in their access to social support networks that can help them cope. Differences in social support depend in large part on the size of ethnic groups in their city. Pakistani, Saudi, Iranian, and African Muslim immigrant women have access to formal and informal social support networks through mosques, cultural associations, and student societies in the Maritimes.[18] Muslim women from smaller ethnic groups have access to social support networks composed of other immigrant women which develop through use of services provided by immigrant settlement agencies. If the number of immigrants who share their ethnic identity is very small, however, then Muslim immigrant women are more vulnerable to mental health problems due to the difficulties in accessing social support.

The Iranian Muslim women in the study provide a good example of the influence of context on identity management and religious diversity. As mentioned,

Iranian immigrant social networks in the Maritimes are robust and include formal women's networks. During a focus group discussion, the Iranian women describe themselves as non-religious Muslims and share what they like about living in Canada:

NEDA: Here you are free – just for women. Sometimes I remember when I was in Iran, I wish sometimes that I can take off the hijab, just my hair a little to have in front of the sun. Sometimes I like to go swimming in the sea and I can't because in my country for women it is forbidden to swim in the sea – limited time and limited location for women.

DINA: This is because of Islamic rule. You know, Muslim women they have to cover their body in front of men. That is why it is compulsory in Iran.

LADAN: And one more thing that I'm going to add, like in our families, stuff is not like that. We have our parties, like we don't have to cover up, like we're like this. But in public, you cannot so there is less freedom. Like they can just arrest you if you don't have your scarf. It just makes you feel, well it's not comfortable, I guess. I prefer to be here instead of my own country.

As the conversation continues, the women discuss other Iranian immigrant women "who are really religious" and speculate how they might feel having lived under Islamic rule now that they are in the Maritimes.

DINA: I'm just thinking that, ok, what are the problems that Muslims can have here in a country that is not an Islamic country like Iran? Probably they have some problems with food because they have to eat halal food. And they don't have many places here to go for their activities … But it doesn't really matter what is your religion in Canada. No one even asks you what is your religion or no one asks you why you have hijab or you don't have hijab. Even when I go to the mall and I see a woman in a burqa, I look at her more than people from Canada! No one cares that she covers her face or her hair.

CATHY: So you think that you notice her more than Canadians notice her?

DINA: Yes.

SANAZ: I think, "Why did you come here?"

The non-religious Iranian Muslim women in this discussion appreciate that religious freedom in Canada means to be free from religious coercion by the state, but they find it difficult to understand why, given this freedom, Muslim women would choose to wear a burqa – a practice they describe as "really religious." Muslim immigrant women in the study from other ethnic origins also describe Muslim women who try to completely conceal their bodies in public as religiously strict or more religious than them. It is interesting that some Muslim women assess each other's level of religious engagement by means of outward appearances given that there are diverse ways in which they themselves live their religion. For many Muslim immigrant women, the Canadian context is the first time that they encounter religious diversity among Muslims. This presents an opportunity for them to better understand the breadth of Muslim women's lived religious practices and identities and support one another, or not, based on their commonalities as Muslim immigrant women who must cope with the challenges of settling into a new home.

None of the women indicate that being a stay-at-home mother made her unhappy. The emotional well-being of Muslim immigrant women whose primary activity is caring for their families at home depends on their access to ethno-religious social networks, given the potential for isolation. An example comes from Hanna, a thirty-seven-year-old mother of four young children. She and her husband, a physician, are originally from Jordan and settled in Canada five years ago after her husband completed his medical training in the US. Hanna knows of only two other Jordanian Muslim families in her region. She describes her family as middle-of-the-road Muslims in terms of their religiosity, but she is not able to regularly participate in social activities for families at the mosque because of the young age of their children. In response to my question about how she deals with loneliness, Hanna answers:

> When I had my fourth [child] it was really hard because I had no help. My husband had to go to work. My mother, God bless her, she came to help so that was great. During that time, she stayed for five months so that was a big help. So for pregnancy that was helpful and you could ask your family to help because they can come, but for one day sickness this is the worst thing ever! I was sick and my husband had to work. I was all by myself with three children in the house and it was really bad. It is hard.

When Hanna's older children began to attend school, she started to make friends with other mothers. She is beginning to feel more support from her non-Muslim neighbours.

However, the lack of access to social support experienced by Hanna is not so different from that of Orthodox Christian immigrant women in the study whose ethnic groups are also very small. At the time of the research, there was only one Greek Orthodox church in New Brunswick and PEI. Orthodox immigrant women from Ukraine and Romania, like some of their Muslim counterparts, often feel very isolated in the Maritimes because of the difficulty in having regular social interactions with women who share a common language and understanding of the role that their Eastern Orthodox practices play in their daily activities. Like Hanna, nearly all of the immigrant women in the qualitative study have a hard time making friends with non-immigrant Maritimers.

This finding shows that the social isolation that contributes to women's mental health problems in the Maritimes has a relationship to ethno-religious differences between immigrant women in general rather than simply to the unique religious differences of Muslim women.

Muslim immigrant women of all classes and ethnicities throughout the region express worry and concern about employment – for themselves, their husbands, and their children. It does take professional women time to find good jobs, and some are underemployed. Several women told me stories about experiences of discrimination in the workplace. An example is from Gulshan, a woman in her forties with five children who arrived with her family five years prior to our conversation. Gulshan was studying medicine before war forced the family to flee their home in Afghanistan.

> I work in Walmart, I'm still working there. I was a cashier. But one time an old man came and said to me, "Why do you wear this scarf?" I said, "It's my religion, I have to wear this." He said, "I think this is a humiliation for women if they wear this." I said, "OK, that's for you, but it's not for me. I'm proud of my scarf – I'm proud of what I am but I respect you for what you are. You should respect me." He told me so many things, "You are not strong. You do what they want." After that I said I don't want to be a cashier anymore and I change my position. Now I'm working in cosmetics. It's quiet there.

Gulshan's family had lived in Pakistan, Turkey, and Russia before coming to the Maritimes, and given her experiences living in multiple contexts and Canada's global reputation for valuing multiculturalism, she found this type of treatment particularly offensive. She said, "If in Canada you feel this – it's very bad!" Visible-minority Christian women also shared stories of discrimination, but their cases are clearly acts of racism, such as when Yun, a Korean Catholic woman, was driving and a young man yelled at her, "Oh, stupid Asian!" Muslim immigrant women who wear a hijab constitute a doubly visible minority. When discrimination happens, as shared by Gulshan at Walmart, it is because of her religious practice of modesty in the public sphere as a Muslim woman. Muslim women who choose not to wear a hijab (or niqab or burqa) are still subject to racism like their visible-minority Christian counterparts. Thus, the heterogeneity of lived religious practices of Muslim women explains some of the differences in mental health trajectories found for employed Muslim immigrant women in the quantitative portion of the study.

The emotional well-being of Muslim women in the Canadian Maritimes is also impacted by their husbands' experiences of employment. Some Muslim immigrant women are living in transnational family situations. They arrive in the Maritimes as intact families, but their husbands (or fathers) cannot find work commensurate with their professional expertise. The men return to work in their home countries or find work elsewhere while their wives and children remain in the Maritimes. This kind of transnational family situation is common in the qualitative sample yet is stressful in different ways for Christian and Muslim women. Many Christian women arrive knowing that they will be living in a transnational family. They choose to work in the Maritimes and send remittances to family members back in their country of origin, or they come alone to support their children's educational pursuits. In contrast, Muslim women usually arrive with their families intact and intend to settle here permanently but feel forced to live apart because of the challenges associated with their husbands' employment. Like their Christian counterparts, Muslim women in transnational families cope with loneliness, but unlike Christian women, they have greater challenges dealing with different sets of gender-role expectations depending on the context.

In Canada, Muslim immigrant women take on a greater share of family responsibilities. Sabia is a twenty-one-year-old student majoring in business administration who lives with her family – two sisters, a brother, and her mother. The family immigrated to Canada eight years prior to the interview and are originally from Saudi Arabia – where her father moved back for work. Sabia explains some of the changes in her life after arrival:

> Back home I had a driver, so he always parked you at the door, when you came out with groceries, he took them from you, I never carried my own groceries – ever. Coming here, parking the car, going far, because everyone parks close to the door in the wintertime, parking it far and then coming back in, taking the groceries and putting [them] back in the [house]. Scratching the car off – the snow – it would make me cry, I'd be crying doing all of that. If I was back home …

If she was back home in Saudi Arabia, Sabia would not be scraping snow off her car, but she would not be driving it either.[19] While the initial adjustment to daily life in the Maritimes is challenging, some immigrant Muslim women gain self-confidence in learning to drive or taking responsibility for managing family finances. Gender roles are markedly different in Canada and Saudi Arabia. Because of transnational family situations and frequent travel (Sabia flies to Saudi Arabia twice a year), Muslim women adjust their activities depending on the context.

Adjusting expectations that arise from new ways of acting, however, is more problematic. Muslim immigrant women appreciate how gender-role shifts lead to more autonomy within their family in Canada. This is the case for several Muslim women whose main activity was studying at university. A twenty-four-year-old graduate student, Kalley, was born in Iraq and lived in Libya and Dubai before moving with her family to Canada. Her father lives and works in Toronto while she and her three brothers live with their mother in the Maritimes. She spoke about how in the early years of her studies, her brothers, who are also students, kept a close eye on her.

> We all had the same friends, like our gang. But after that my brothers started to have different friends so they kind of pulled themselves out of the group and I'm the one left and I'm still friends with these people but I can't go out with them because my brothers don't want to go out with them anymore and it was hard.

Kalley's family believed that she should socialize only with other women when not in the presence of her brothers. Over time, she says that her family developed a more open attitude towards gender roles. She became a teaching assistant and has authority over Muslim male students in her engineering program. Kalley shares:

> I am way stronger right now. I am very independent. My dad didn't pay me money since we moved here. In Dubai, and the Arab countries, people and the kids will keep taking money from the parents, even when they are married. 'Cause my dad is the one – he is supposed to work and pay for us. Coming to Canada made me … I feel funny for the people taking money from their parents. Like I am old enough, I am strong enough to work and have my own money.

Her independence is judged negatively by some other Muslim students. "Everyone from the religious people – Saudis – they will judge us, as we are the bad girls 'cause we are friends with these guys … I don't care about those people. I just care about keeping my parents kind of happy about me … my parents are the most important thing in my life." Kalley thinks of herself as non-religious in contrast to other Saudi students, whom she describes as very religious – further evidence of heterogeneity among the Muslim women in the qualitative sample. She does not pray or wear the hijab, but she fasts, abstains from alcohol, and avoids pork. Kalley believes she has become less conservative since moving to the Maritimes and does not want to return to Iraq to live and work. She hopes to get a job in Canada after graduation so that she can maintain her independence along with the approval and support of her family.

Conclusion

Employing mixed-methods and comparative approaches have enabled my social scientific research on Muslim immigrant women to be both generalizable and richly descriptive. An intersectional framework guides my use of research methods to highlight the impacts that the intersecting structures of gender, ethnicity, and class have on Muslim immigrant women's experiences in the early years of settlement in Canada. The results illustrate that Islamic systems of practice and so-called secular pressures influence the structuring of gender, ethnicity, and class in the lives of Muslim immigrant women as they manage multiple and fluid identities. The statistical results emphasize the importance of considering the impact that ethnicity has on Canadian Muslim immigrant women's experiences of employment, study, and unpaid care work. Most Muslim immigrant women are increasingly likely to experience feelings of sadness, loneliness, and depression over the first four years in Canada, but these feelings may be mitigated for some Muslim women whose primary activity is caring for their families. Likewise, some Muslim immigrant women with paid employment are less likely than others to report mental health problems after the first four years in Canada.

Qualitative methods provide detailed explanations of how ethnic social networks differ in social support for Muslim immigrant women in the Maritimes. Muslim immigrant women who have regular opportunities to interact with others who share their ethno-religious backgrounds use these social support networks when coping with the challenges of underemployment and unemployment or the isolation of unpaid care work. Immigrant women who do not have regular access to social support networks, because of either their ethnic or religious background, are more likely to experience emotional distress when dealing with the demands of their job or caring for their families in a new social context in which Islamophobia and anti-Muslim racism is on the rise. This is particularly pertinent to the Maritime context because the proportion of Muslim immigrants in the population is relatively low compared to other regions of Canada.

The results of the qualitative analysis also highlight the importance of understanding class in relationship to Muslim women's religious practices. Class has an influence on Muslim immigrant women's ability to manage social interactions in the public and private spheres in the Maritimes. Lower-income Muslim immigrant women do not have the same resources as wealthy Muslim immigrant women to shield themselves from exposure to racial and religious discrimination in their public interactions. Muslim women who wear the hijab and are underemployed or with precarious employment are at a higher risk of experiencing the emotional distress of discrimination than their wealthier counterparts. Thus, Muslim women's ethnic social networks can play an important role in helping them to build emotional resiliency through solidarity.

According to my statistical findings, engaging in study at a post-secondary institution is most likely to contribute to Muslim immigrant women's emotional well-being over the first four years after arrival, despite the high levels of education that they bring with them to Canada. Student participants in the qualitative portion of the study affirm that their experiences in university increase their autonomy and independence. Their gender roles within Muslim families shift to meet the demands of being a student and of transnational relationships. Young

Muslim women want to maintain their independence along with their ethno-religious values as participants in the Canadian labour force.

Mixed-methods research provides challenges and opportunities for the production of knowledge concerning Canadian Muslim immigrant women. Among the challenges are the limitations in Statistics Canada data about Muslims, which fail to provide information about their religious diversity or the need to juggle responsibilities for childcare and employment or study. My statistical analysis highlights diverse relationships between affiliation with Islam, ethnicity, main activities, and mental health trajectories for immigrant women, but the results cannot be used to infer the causes of mental health problems. Qualitative data are able to provide rich details about the positive impact of social support networks on Muslim immigrant women's mental health, but the results are specific to the Maritimes – a distinct regional context compared with the rest of Canada. Yet the opportunities for better understanding Muslim immigrant women provided by the secondary analysis of a large probability sample are significant. The variety of mental health trajectories arising from the relationship between ethnicity and Muslim women's main activities validate a lived religion approach to research. Both the quantitative and qualitative results enhance our understanding of Muslim immigrant women's agency, particularly in relation to how they strategically use a variety of daily practices and identities in the face of complex inequalities. The statistical results highlight the increased likelihood of emotional distress for many Muslim immigrant women during the early years of life in Canada. It is clear that they face barriers, particularly in the labour market, but the problem-solving skills of Muslim women become apparent from the qualitative findings, which show that, for the most part, Muslim immigrant women engage with formal and informal social networks to support one another while managing identities influenced by religious and secular sources. Participating in the collective give and take of social support is evidence of their collaborative adaptation of identities in a new social context and an important part of Muslim immigrant women's lived ethno-religious practices.

NOTES

1 The goal of probability sampling procedures is to ensure that the sample is representative of the population from which it is drawn. In the case of LSIC, a stratified sampling method was used to ensure representation of immigrants according to the intended province of destination and the class of immigrant (family class, economic-skilled, economic-business, government-sponsored refugees, other refugees, and other immigrants).

2 The attrition rate for LSIC participants is estimated at a total loss between waves 1 and 3 of 44 per cent of the sample. At wave 3 the weights are adjusted to account for those immigrants who left Canada as well as those who still reside in Canada

(Statistics Canada 2007a). Nevertheless, the high rate of attrition is concerning because of the likelihood that information on some of the most vulnerable immigrant women who are not meeting the challenges of the settlement process is not in the data at wave 3.

3 My ability to use advanced statistical methods and interpret the results is due to the mentorship of and collaboration with my colleague at the University of New Brunswick, Dr. Lucia Tramonte, an internationally recognized leader in multidisciplinary statistical research on social inequality.

4 The LSIC questionnaire at each wave includes one closed-ended question about the respondent's main activity, and the interviewer prompt in the second wave defines this as how the respondent spends the majority of her time (Statistics Canada 2007b).

5 I focus on the results of analysis of data from Muslim immigrant women in this chapter. To see the findings comparing multiple groups of religious immigrant women, see Holtmann and Tramonte 2014.

6 The discrepancy between the choices for Christians and Muslims in the LSIC questionnaire (Statistics Canada 2007a) highlights how Statistics Canada's method of data collection perpetuates a limited knowledge of Islamic diversity in Canada.

7 The category of "no religion" includes those who do not identify with Statistics Canada religion categories. Many East Asian Canadians for example, when asked to identify their religion by Statistics Canada, will respond with "none," yet research reveals that their lives may be permeated with ancient religious practices and beliefs (Chuenyan Lai et al. 2005). For this reason, I chose to include the category "no religion" in the analysis.

8 The smaller the size of the group, the larger the error in the statistical estimations. Ideally, groups should be approximately the same size.

9 By "protective" I mean that this main activity does not decrease the rate of reporting mental health problems.

10 The dark curve in each of these three graphs shows the average mental health trajectory for *all* Muslim women engaged in this particular main activity.

11 Again, these results are interpreted with caution, given the small size of the groups of South and West Asian Muslim immigrant women engaged in unpaid care work, study, and employment in the sample. See the appendix in Holtmann and Tramonte 2014 for the complete growth model regression results for differences in post-migration activities, unstandardized logit coefficients, and standard errors.

12 Hussain's analysis also includes the high number of children in Muslim families.

13 The graph is not shown but available upon request.

14 The research participants were from New Brunswick and Prince Edward Island.

15 Research participants were recruited by contacting immigrant settlement organizations, churches, mosques, international student offices of universities, immigrant business owners, and snowball sampling.

16 The Muslim women had been living an average of four years and four months in the Maritimes, while the average length of time Christian women was only two years and four months.

17 This and all names of Muslim women in this chapter are pseudonyms.

18 More recently, many Syrian Muslims have come to the Maritimes as refugees. In 2016, New Brunswick accepted more Syrians per capita than any other province in Canada (Jones 2016), making Syrians one of the larger ethnic Muslim groups.

19 At the time of the interview it was illegal for a woman to drive a vehicle in Saudi Arabia. The kingdom's ban on women drivers was lifted on 24 June 2018.

REFERENCES

Ammerman, Nancy Tatom. 2003. "Religious identities and religious institutions." In Michele Dillon (Ed.), *Handbook of the sociology of religion* (pp. 207–24). Cambridge University Press.

Aune, Kristin, Sonya Sharma, and Giselle Vincett (Eds.). 2008. *Women and religion in the West: Challenging secularization*. Ashgate.

Avishai, Orit. 2016. "Theorizing gender from religion cases: Agency, feminist activism and masculinity." *Sociology of religion*, 77(3), 261–79. https://doi.org/10.1093/socrel/srw020

Beaman, Lori G. 2014. "Deep equality as an alternative to accommodation and tolerance." *Nordic Journal of Religion and Society*, 27(2), 89–111.

– 2017. *Deep equality in an era of religious diversity*. Oxford University Press.

Bramadat, Paul, and David Seljak (Eds.). 2005. *Religion and ethnicity in Canada*. University of Toronto Press.

Chaudry, Ayesha S. 2013. *Domestic violence and the Islamic tradition: Ethics, law and the Muslim discourses on gender*. University of Oxford Press.

Chuenyan Lai, David, Jordan Paper, and Li Chuang Paper. 2005. "The Chinese in Canada: Their unrecognized religion." In Paul Bramadat and David Seljak (Eds.), *Religion and Ethnicity in Canada* (pp. 89–110). University of Toronto Press.

Citizenship and Immigration Canada [CIC]. 2013. *Welcome to Canada: What you should know*. Ottawa, Ontario. https://www.canada.ca/content/dam/ircc/migration/ircc/english/pdf/pub/welcome.pdf

Cobb, Ryon J., Samuel L. Perry, and Kevin D. Dougherty. 2015. "United by faith? Race/ethnicity, congregational diversity, and explanations of racial inequality." *Sociology of Religion*, 76(2), 177–98. https://doi.org/10.1093/socrel/sru067

Crompton, S., and M. Vickers. 2000. *Canadian social trends: One hundred years of labour force*. Statistics Canada. Catalogue No. 11–008: 12.

Day, Abby, and Lois Lee. 2014. "Making sense of surveys and censuses: Issues in religious self-identification." *Religion*, 44(3), 345–56. https://doi.org/10.1080/0048721X.2014.929833

Doucet, Andrea. 2011. *Breadwinning mothers and caregiving fathers: A quiet revolution, a resilient problem, and one persistent puzzle.* 42nd Annual Sorokin Lecture, University of Saskatchewan.

Gallagher, Sally K. 2003. *Evangelical identity and gendered family life.* Rutgers University Press.

Gibbens, Robert D., Donald Hedeker, and Stephen DuToit. 2010. "Advances in the analysis of longitudinal data." *Annual Review of Clinical Psychology, 6*(3), 1–29. https://doi.org/10.1146/annurev.clinpsy.032408.153550

Grant, Hugh, and Michael Rosenstock. 2011. "Do Mennonites earn less than other Canadians? The role of religion in the determination of income." *Journal of Mennonite Studies, 24,* 73–92.

Gudykunst, William B., and Stella Ting-Toomey. 1988. "Culture and affective communication." *Scientist, 31*(3), 384–400. https://doi.org/10.1177%2F000276488031003009

Hamdan, Amani. 2009. *Muslim women speak: A tapestry of lives and dreams.* Women's Press.

Heaton, Tim B., and Marie Cornwall. 1989. "Religious group variation in socioeconomic status and family behavior of women." *Journal for the Scientific Study of Religion, 28*(3), 283–99. https://doi.org/10.2307/1386740

Holtmann, Catherine. 2018. "Who cares? Religious immigrant women, social networks, and family violence." In Catherine Holtmann and Nancy Nason-Clark (Eds.), *Religion, gender, and family violence: When prayers are not enough* (pp. 38–59). Brill.

Holtmann, Catherine, and Lucia Tramonte. 2014. "Tracking the emotional cost of immigration: Ethno-religious differences and women's mental health." *Journal of international migration and integration, 15*(4), 633–54. https://doi.org/10.1007/s12134-013-0302-8

Hussain, Serena. 2008. "Counting women with faith: What quantitative data can reveal about Muslim women in 'secular' Britain." In Kristin Aune, Sonya Sharma, and Giselle Vincett (Eds.), *Women and religion in the West: Challenging secularization* (pp. 165–82). Ashgate.

Jones, Robert. 2016, 20 June. "New Brunswick sets 3 populations records in first 3 months of 2016." CBC News. http://www.cbc.ca/news/canada/new-brunswick/new-brunswick-population-records-refugees-1.3643021.

Kazemipur, Abdolmohammad. 2009. *Social capital and diversity: Some lessons from Canada.* Peter Lang.

– 2014. *The Muslim question in Canada: A story of segmented integration.* University of British Columbia Press.

Kim, Minzee. 2015. "Women's employment, state legal protection of women's economic rights, and gender prejudice: Evidence from 52 countries." *Korea Observer, 46*(1), 181–210.

Moyser, Melissa. 2017. *Women and paid work.* Statistics Canada. Catalogue no. 89–503-X: 38.

Nason-Clark, Nancy, and Barbara Fisher-Townsend. 2005. "Gender." In Helen Rose Ebaugh (Ed.), *Handbook of religion and social institutions* (pp. 207–23). Springer.

Riesebrodt, Martin. 2010. *The promise of salvation: A theory of religion* (S. Rendall, Trans.). University of Chicago Press.

Rinaldo, Rachel. 2013. *Mobilizing piety: Islam and feminism in Indonesia.* Oxford University Press.

Statistics Canada. 2007a. *Longitudinal survey of immigrants to Canada,* Wave 3 Codebook. Ottawa, ON.

– 2007b. *Longitudinal survey of immigrants to Canada,* Wave 2 Questionnaire. Ottawa, ON.

– 2007c. *2006 Census Dictionary.* Ottawa, ON.

– 2007d. *Microdata User Guide: Wave 3, Longitudinal survey of immigrants to Canada.* Ottawa, ON.

– 2011. *General social survey 2010 – Overview of the time use of Canadians.* Ottawa, ON.

Sullivan, Susan C. 2012. *Living faith: Everyday religion and mothers in poverty.* University of Chicago Press.

Walby, Sylvia. 1990. *Theorizing patriarchy.* Basil Blackwell.

– 2009. *Globalization and inequalities: Complexity and contested modernities.* SAGE.

Zine, Jasmin. 2004. "Creating a critical faith-centered space for antiracist feminism: Reflections of a Muslim scholar-activist." *Journal of Feminist Studies in Religion, 20*(2), 167–87.

Influencing the Public Imaginary: The Case of a Montreal Islamic School

MELANIE ADRIAN

Introduction

Early one morning in February 2012, Montreal radio talk show personality Benoit Dutrizac hosted an interview with Djemila Benhabib, a known critic of Islamic schooling in France and Quebec and of Islam more generally. In that interview, Benhabib described a Montreal private Islamic school as practising "indoctrination worthy of a camp … in Afghanistan or Pakistan." The school, the commentator went on, is rigid and practising "gender apartheid."[1] Among other critiques, Benhabib went on to say that the school taught Qur'anic verses filled with hate and that the teachers would produce fundamentalist activists who, down the line, may commit "honour crimes" and make unreasonable requests of Quebecois society.

The interview was heard by the listening audience, which included members of the school. The school community was angry and humiliated by these remarks, which, they maintained, were untrue and slanderous (Montréal Muslim School v. Benhabib 2016, para. 166). Benhabib had neither visited the school nor been in touch with its leadership to ask about their curriculum. The school leadership asked Benhabib to retract some of her comments. When she refused, they sued her for defamation. They argued that her comments had hurt their reputation, caused security concerns, and decreased registrations. Benhabib held that although her comments may have been hurtful, they are legitimate – and indeed appropriate – in a democratic society. The Superior Court of Québec agreed with Benhabib. I argue in this chapter that while the court took note of Benhabib's history as a critic of Islam, it failed to adequately consider how Behabib's insinuations might negatively shape a public vision about the school community and Islam in Canada more generally. I further show that no one with a deep understanding of the varieties of religious expression spoke out to help craft a different narrative of this community.

Theoretical Orientation

What is striking about this case was how the law, as interpreted by this court and Justice Hallée specifically, upheld what some scholars have been arguing against for decades. Scholars such as Edward Said (1978), Muhammed Arkoun (1990), Talal Asad (2003), and Karim H. Karim (2012) have all, in varying ways, been locked in a debate that is largely opposed to Samuel Huntington's thesis in his article and subsequent book entitled *Clash of Civilizations* (Huntington 1996).

As is well known, Huntington's theory posited a world order based on the differences and conflicts between civilizations – specifically "Islam" and the "West" (Huntington 1996). I use quotations for these two concepts as it is these that Said took on – first in his book *Orientalism* (unrelated to Huntington) and later in an article directly responding to Huntington's thesis (Said 2001). Arguing that generalizations such as these are fictitious and problematic, the West, Said states, is an "ideological fiction" (Said 1978). In a later imprint of his book he asks more specifically,

> How can one today speak of "Western Civilization" except as in large measure an ideological fiction, implying a sort of detached superiority for a handful of values and ideas, none of which has much meaning outside of the history of conquest, immigration, travel, and the mingling of peoples that gave the western nations their present identities? (Said 1994, 347)

Said's point is that generalizations about "cultures" and "civilizations" uphold a set of values that are generated in a specific moment in time and sustain a specific set of values. It is particularly interesting to see which values are upheld in the case under consideration.

In an article by Karim H. Karim and Mahmoud Eid (2012) entitled "Clash of Ignorance," the authors also take issue with Huntington's thesis. They agree with Said that generalizations about cultures (and religions) – specifically Islam – portray them as monolithic blocks that function apart from one another. In fact, they argue, cultures and peoples have long-standing, mutually enriching relationships, and thus a clear demarcation between *their* values and *our* values is superficial and unhelpful. They also argue that this way of understanding complex international sociopolitical systems necessitates a vision that entails conflict between self and other – or us and them (Karim and Eid 2012).

The 2016 case of the *Montréal Islamic School v. Benhabib* is an example of how the provincial court upheld a type of Orientalist vision that further ingrained in the public imaginary a conflict between Islam and the wider Quebec society. To my knowledge, the case was never appealed.

Background to the Case

The Parties

Conceptualized in 1983 and founded two years later, the Montréal Islamic School (hereafter MIS) was started by a group of Muslim intellectuals and scientists. They wanted to establish a school that provided a good-quality education while paying heed to their specific cultural (Middle Eastern and North African), linguistic (Arabic), and religious (Islam) heritage. The school is privately funded but provincially accredited, meaning that they teach the full provincial curriculum in addition to three hours (total) of Arabic, Qur'an, and Islamic history weekly. According to their current website, the school focuses on self-discovery and integration into Canadian society (Écoles Musulmanes de Montréal 2018).

On her personal website, Djemila Benhabib describes herself as an author, journalist, teacher, and lecturer (Benhabib 2018). Benhabib was born in Ukraine to a Muslim Algerian father and a Greek Cypriot mother (Valiante 2016b). She grew up in Algeria, where she "suffered through an Islamic educational system," and has vowed to fight against what she calls "political Islam" (Valiante 2016a). She is closely associated with the Parti Québécois, the political party seeking Quebec independence, having unsuccessfully run for office on multiple occasions.[2] She has written several books, including one entitled *My Life Against the Koran: A Woman Testifies Against Islamists* (2009).

According to the case files, Benhabib had been engaged in fighting fundamentalist and political Islam for years, particularly as it regards the treatment of women and the imposition of the veil. She considers Qur'anic memorization harmful to children. She is known for her blunt, generalized, and often incorrect remarks about Islam. In an article published in the Canadian magazine *Chatelaine* in 2013, for example, she states,

> The Muslims did not invent anything. In the history of humanity, the domination of women has continued to be perpetuated. The Islamic veil expresses this pattern of domination. And philosophically, this schema, I refuse and reject it. (Montréal Muslim School v. Benhabib 2016)

Not only are such generalizations absurd, but they show that Benhabib's thinking about Islam lacks factual credence, nuance, and sophistication.

Furthermore, her comments fall into the trap of ignorance as outlined by Karim and Eid (2012). Their argument shows how one person's lived experience is important but does not, and cannot, be mapped onto the experience of a billion other practitioners of the same faith. Furthermore, at the time that she gave the radio interview, she had never visited MIS or contacted the school about their pedagogical orientations and structure. Her remarks were made on the basis of her observations of a pamphlet and the school website and lacked any first-hand knowledge.[3] These comments thus constitute, as Valérie Amiraux would argue, gossip rather than informed knowledge. Amiraux (2016) states, "Gossip is an informal form of personal communication built around those who are absent or are simply treated as such" (Amiraux 2016, 44). It is a type of communication that becomes a trusted source. Gossip creates a "kind of authority" (Amiraux 2016, 44). Using her status as a former insider who is in the "know" about how Islam and Muslim communities operate, Benhabib creates an aura of factuality that can be trusted by the listening audience.

The Radio Interview

The talk radio show covers all manner of subjects, and its host, Benoit Dutrizac, is known for his frankness. On the morning of 8 February, Benhabib was asked to come on the show. Her comments were wide ranging and, taken together, created a vision of the school that likened it to a militaristic and fundamentalist environment that indoctrinated its students with hatred and misogyny. Moreover, she claimed, MIS prepared future citizens to stand in opposition to Quebec society and values, rather than seeking integration and critical thinking. In all, Benhabib painted a picture of a school belonging *there*, not *here*. I quote parts of the interview at length to demonstrate how she depicts a school that does not belong, a school that teaches foreign values. The interview begins with her description of the school. She says,

> It's similar to an indoctrination worthy of a camp, um, of a military camp in Afghanistan or Pakistan. I mean, there's not much of a difference, in my opinion, between the indoctrination that is done in those schools in Montreal or … or where … or wherever the schools are happening, whether in Pakistan or Afghanistan. (Benhabib 2012)

By likening the school to a military camp in Afghanistan or Pakistan, Benhabib quite literally removes the school from being part of Quebec's society. The school is more foreign and dangerous than similar and is underwritten with images of warfare and violence associated with the term "military."

She continues by critiquing two suras – sura al-Waqi'a ("The Event") and sura ar-Rahman ("The All-Merciful") – that the school posted on its website. She says that "the surahs, in fact, that are imposed on the children … right from the first years of elementary school, are extremely violent and they are misogynistic and sexist" (Benhabib 2012).

Much has been written on these two verses, and it is outside the frame of this paper to discuss the varying interpretations (Faraz Rabbani 2017). I can only acknowledge that there are wide-ranging frames of reference within Islam in which to understand and interpret these verses. More generally, Abdul-Karim Soroush (1998), for instance, argues that like any other text, the interpretation of religious texts is "subject to expansion and contraction according to the assumptions preceding them and … these assumptions can be of a very different nature" (Soroush 1998, 245). He further suggests that "the text does not stand alone, it does not carry its own meaning on its shoulders, it needs to be situated in a context, it is theory-laden, its interpretation is in flux" (Soroush 1998, 245). Feminist scholars such as Leila Ahmed call for a variety of interpretations of Qur'an and Islam that meet the demands of today (Ahmed 1992). Building on the work of Fazlur Rahman and Farid Esack, Asma Barlas (2002) states that "exegetical literature in Islam is replete with competing views on hermeneutics and interpretation" (78). Amina Wadud, advocating for female-inclusive interpretations of the Qur'an, argues, "Contexts affect perspective and conclusions in textual contents … For example, the patriarchal context of Quranic revelation shaped both the text and its readers" (Wadud 2004, 328). All of these scholars suggest that any Qur'anic verse can have a changing understanding and application in the lives of Muslims in Quebec.

What is important to note is that in one sweeping overgeneralization that gives no nod to the diversity of interpretations and historical context, Benhabib casts what the children are taught from the Qur'an generally as anti-woman and violent. Thus, the school is described as one which is located in Montreal but is like a military camp from another place that teaches values that are anti-woman and not native to Quebec. Benhabib continues to describe the school:

> I think, well, it's extremely disturbing. Especially since, well, there's a very high rigidity, there's a separation of the sexes, there's a gender apartheid. There's the imposition of the Islamic veil. Ultimately, that doesn't tell me anything good about what is happening in those schools. (Benhabib 2012)

In addition to teaching foreign values, for Benhabib, the school is rigid, gender apartheid – a loaded political concept – is ongoing, and the Islamic veil is imposed. Benhabib is correct about the veil being mandated as part of the uniform requirement in the upper years, but the word "imposition" has a negative connotation as something that is unwelcome, a burden or nuisance.

In the first few minutes of the interview, Benhabib has cast the school as being foreign because of what it is like (military camp), because of what it teaches (hateful, sexist suras), and how it is organized (separation of the sexes). In short, the school is not teaching what it means to be Quebecois. She continues to describe what the mission of any school should be: free enquiry, critical engagement, choice. MIS is the opposite:

> The main mission of school is precisely to allow children to become students, which means to be discerning and to be free. That is, free, which means that they will be able, later, to choose; choose between the options that will be available to them and develop critical thinking skills, an open mind, tolerance, and so on. So, you see, in the particular conjuncture that exists in these schools, there's no room for criticism, there's no room for reflection, there's no room for sharing between men and women, quite the opposite. We're erecting walls of separation between the sexes, walls that are absolutely abominable, walls in which … and through which we maintain the hatred of women and the detestation of women. (Benhabib 2012)

In the last part of the interview then, Benhabib builds on this picture of a rigid, sexist, fundamentalist, militaristic school by suggesting that MIS is not educating for citizenship, that it is not teaching toleration, critical awareness and engagement, equality. Additionally, MIS is also

> creating fundamentalist activists who will demand, in a few years, accommodations and all kinds of crazy things; that we're not creating the citizens of tomorrow, rather the opposite. We're extremely far from citizenship, we're far from all the values that belong to our society. We are, as I was saying earlier, perhaps somewhere in Afghanistan or Pakistan … and where men will probably commit honour crimes against … against their sisters. (Benhabib 2012)

According to Benhabib, MIS is not just a threat to the values of Quebec society today but also a threat for Quebec society tomorrow. With these remarks, Benhabib presents the school as belonging to another time, another place, and another future. In doing this, she casts Islam as one unchanging and largely dangerous entity, generalities which distort knowledge about the lived particular and set up a zero-sum game that pits one group against another (Asad 2003).

The court was tasked with determining if Benhabib's comments were protected speech or if they infringed on the reputational integrity of the school. Specifically, the court was asked to decide if the remarks made by Djemila Benhabib in this radio program were defamatory and if they fell under protected speech (Montréal Muslim School v. Benhabib 2016, para. 27). Let us turn to the legal context.

The Law

In Canada, human rights are outlined in the Charters of Rights and Freedoms passed at both the federal and provincial levels. Section 2 of the Canadian Charter of Rights and Freedoms outlines fundamental freedoms, including the freedom of conscience and religion, freedom of thought, belief, opinion, and expression, including freedom of the press and other media of communication, freedom of peaceful assembly, and freedom of association. The Québec Charter of Human Rights and Freedoms, passed in 1975, states that "every person has a right to the safeguard of his dignity, honour and reputation" (Légis Québec 1975, chap. 1).

Note the terms "freedom of expression" and "reputation" in the above, as these were the two rights that conflicted in this case. The Islamic school sued Benhabib for defamation, which is harm to reputation. In order to be successful in this, they had to show, as I discuss below, that they suffered damages, a point to which I will return momentarily. I turn now to a discussion of the definition of defamation and subsequently the idea of the right to freedom of expression. I then address how these were operationalized in this case.

Defamation

The Québec Court relies on the Supreme Court and Québec Superior Court judgments to define defamation. Defamation, they cite,

> consists of the communication of words or writings that cause someone to lose his or her esteem or consideration or who, in turn, causes him or her to feel unfavorable or unpleasant. (chap. 6, para. 45)

Defamation can be caused by the meaning of ideas as they are expressed or by the insinuations that emerge from speech (chap. 1, para. 45). Importantly, feeling humiliated, insulted, or sad on a purely individual level is not enough to meet the definition of defamation. Defamation is not about an individual feeling badly. Speech that rises to the level of defamation must entail a social element, meaning that the ordinary citizen must understand the comments as a whole as causing disrepute to the affected party. In Quebec, the application for defamation is governed by the rules of civil liability of article 1457 of the Civil Code (Montréal Muslim School v. Benhabib 2016, para. 44). These rules outline that damages are awarded when someone causes harm or injury to another party (Montréal Muslim School v. Benhabib 2016, para. 26). Thus, defamation is largely decided on two fronts: if the ordinary citizen would perceive the affected party as less reputable and if the affected party can show harm done (Montréal Muslim School v. Benhabib 2016, para. 26).

In this case, freedom of expression is the competing right. Did Benhabib infringe on the reputation of the Montréal Islamic School, or did she have the right to make the claims she did during her radio interview?

Freedom of Expression

Freedom of expression is protected under the Canadian Charter of Rights and Freedoms and section 3 of the Québec Charter of Human Rights and Freedoms.

They are similar in their descriptions, and I cite the official translated version of the Québec Charter:

> Every person is the possessor of the fundamental freedoms, including freedom of conscience, freedom of religion, freedom of opinion, freedom of expression, freedom of peaceful assembly and freedom of association. (Légis Québec 1975, chap. 6, sec. 3)

There exists ample literature and case law that emphasize the importance of freedom of expression, linking a vibrant exchange of ideas to the development of democracy (Montréal Muslim School v. Benhabib 2016, para. 49–50; see also WIC Radio Ltd. v. Simpson 2008). In this case, Judge Hallée quotes then Court of Appeal judge Jean-Louis Baudouin, who warns that freedom of expression should not be amenable to the influx of political correctness. He cautions that even hurtful speech needs to be tolerated in order to allow the views of minorities to be heard.

In addition to the words that are used, the situation and history of the individual are important to give context. There are largely two guiding principles here. One, sentences and words should never be dissected and extracted from their circumstances but understood in relationship to them. Second, the history of the person making the comments, in this case Benhabib, is also considered. If the person has a reputation for audacity, the court considers this as part of the question of what the ordinary person would make of the statements.

On the issue of veracity, a distinction is made between a statement of fact and a statement of opinion. Opinion and commentary do not necessarily need to be fact-based, as these are an attitude of the mind and thus do not map onto the true-false dichotomy. In the journalistic context, truth is more valued. Benhabib was seen as making a commentary and not acting in her journalistic capacity for the purposes of this interview and case.

The Court's Assessment of the Case

As per established legal precedent, the assessment of the right to freedom of speech in this case looked at what was said – the actual spoken words – and the context and history of the speaker. Secondly, the court examined the case MIS put forward regarding the alleged reputational harm done to the school. Let us take each in turn beginning with the defamation piece.

Recall that in the case of defamation, the claimant must prove that their reputation was affected by the speech, that an ordinary citizen must understand the comments as a whole as causing disrepute to the affected party, and that the words and insinuation thereof are considered.

To prove harm to reputation, MIS called six witnesses, each of which maintained that the reputation of the school had suffered due to the broadcasting of this interview. The key witness was the chairperson of the board of directors of MIS. He stated that he and the community were humiliated and horrified at the remarks made on the show (Montréal Muslim School v. Benhabib 2016, para. 132). He testified that registrations had decreased, that the school was forced to heighten teacher supervision at lunchtime and install additional security cameras. One teacher stated how hurt he was at the remarks made during the interview (Montréal Muslim School v. Benhabib 2016, para. 143). Two alumni of the school testified that they had removed the name of the school from their CVs out of humiliation and anger.

The witnesses crumbled in pre-trial interrogation and again before the court. Benhabib's team showed that school registrations had not suffered (in fact, they remained consistent at the day care level, rose at the elementary level, and decreased at the secondary level since before the Benhabib interview aired) (Montréal Muslim School v. Benhabib 2016, para. 137). It was also demonstrated that the security cameras were installed in 2015 shortly after the *Charlie Hebdo* attack in Paris, after which the MIS was vandalized (Montréal Muslim School v. Benhabib 2016, para. 142). The teacher who had stated that he was hurt at the remarks later testified that he did not understand French sufficiently to follow the interview and that he had never listened to the interview in its entirety (Montréal Muslim School v. Benhabib 2016, para. 143). Neither of the alumni were told they had to produce their CVs for the court, which counted against them (Montréal Muslim School v. Benhabib 2016, para. 147).

The witnesses seemed unprepared for the type and style of testimony used in legal proceedings. In his pre-trial testimony, for example, the chairperson denied that the mission of the school was to primarily foster a close relationship with Allah, even though the website at the time promoted the school as helping students build a relationship with God. He maintained throughout that the primary task of the school was to provide a sound education in a comfortable environment for Muslim youth. One can see how both could be true, but the court was suspicious of his testimony (Montréal Muslim School v. Benhabib 2016, para. 113–14).

The Montréal Islamic School could not demonstrate, through reduction in registrations or other damage, that they suffered reputational harm. This is in large part what caused them to lose the case. This was so even though alumni reported reputational harm that prompted them to remove the name of the school from their CVs. Doubt was cast on this argument as the CVs were not produced. One might imagine that the court would see how, in using words such as "military camp" and "Afghanistan/Pakistan," Benhabib insinuated that this school was akin to a terrorist training camp. Or at least that the ordinary citizen might make these connections. But the court did not see it this way.

The issue of defamation was weighed by the court with the right to freedom of speech. Djemila Benhabib's statements were evaluated according to the particular context of the case and the information available at the time the statements were made. That is, the identity of Benhabib as a vocal critic of Islam, the context of her speech, and that she was making a commentary not claiming journalistic integrity were also considered.

Recall that cases relating to expression are guided by two principles: that words should never be extracted from their contexts and that the history of the commenter is considered. MIS argued that Benhabib used the terms "terrorist" and "boot camp" to describe the students and the school, noting not her actual words but what she insinuated. Neither of these statements were true. Although Benhabib likened the school to a "military camp" in Afghanistan or Pakistan, she never stated that these were terrorist boot camps. Additionally, Benhabib's lawyers rejected the MIS's claims that she used the word "terrorist," that the school was creating fundamentalist militants, and that the teachers teach extremist values. Benhabib held to critiquing extremist values and the suras more generally, not in relation to any individual at MIS.

Justice Hallée ruled in favour of Benhabib. The court held that MIS did not make a strong enough case to show that they suffered consequences as a result of Benhabib's comments. The court found that the school had not suffered attacks or threats or that their admissions were affected. Additionally, they considered Benhabib's history critiquing Islam and Islamic education and understood her comments in this context. The court acknowledged that Benhabib is a known public figure and that she had for several years been defending her strong views in favour of secularism and against the so-called fundamentalist application of the Qur'an, the wearing of the veil, and Qur'anic memorization (Montréal Muslim School v. Benhabib 2016, para. 97).

In sum, the court found that although her statements were harsh and, perhaps, hurtful, they are words that must be permitted in the context of a healthy democracy that holds speech as a central value. Additionally, the court found that the remarks were made in the context of a news program that encourages the debate of divergent opinions; while this may have caused humiliation, this is part of the right to freedom of speech.

Allow me to make two points on the above that will weave the theory and legal issues in this chapter together. One relates to how the case was adjudicated and the law interpreted. The second relates to how the media covered the case and how there was no credible counter-narrative to oppose the insinuations made by Benhabib. What this case proclaimed is that a Muslim minority can be critiqued – largely unfairly – but that if these remarks are made generally, it falls under protected speech.

In terms of how the law was applied, I note that limiting freedom of speech should entail a high bar considering its relationship with democratic principles and a flourishing public debate. In this case, however, the court gave disproportionate weight to Benhabib's context and history as a critic of Islam and failed to adequately consider the insinuations she made and what the ordinary citizen would understand from her speech. The court considered that she had a long history writing about her experiences with Islam. They considered that she gave her remarks on a radio show that is known to host controversy and that she was speaking in her personal capacity, not as a journalist, which reduced her obligation to speak the truth.

This perspective failed to consider the linkages Benhabib was making. Although it is true the terms "terrorist" and "boot camp" were missing, she likened the school to a "military camp" in Afghanistan or Pakistan. Although she did not direct her comments at any one individual, she stated that MIS was creating fundamentalist activists, that the school teaches extremist values and practises gender apartheid, and, most absurdly of all, that this school is modelled after cultures that will encourage men to commit honour crimes against their sisters.

Her comments were wide ranging and, taken together, created a vision of the school that likened it to a militaristic and fundamentalist environment that indoctrinated its students with hatred and misogyny. Moreover, she claimed, it prepared future citizens to stand in tension with Quebec society and values. In all, Benhabib painted a picture of a school belonging *there*, not *here*. What the court did not weigh adequately was how inappropriate, insulting, and damaging her words, and ultimately this judgment, would be to the understanding of Islam in Canada. It did not consider rising anti-Muslim discrimination, the effects of the national dialogue about Islamophobia, or the then-recent discussions around Bill 60 (Québec Charter of Values), which sought to limit religious expression – particularly Islamic veils – in Quebec (Environics Institute 2016). Thus, while the court considered the context of Benhabib's speech, it did not consider the context of everyday life for Muslims in Quebec.

Where Were the Scholars?

My second point relates to how the media wrote about this case and how experts intervene in such issues. In short, the media covered the case and reiterated its main themes, but there was a clear lack of expert intervention. It is obvious from the interview that Benhabib likens MIS to a military camp in Afghanistan and Pakistan. It is not a far reach for the ordinary citizen to interpret the words "military" and "camp" in Afghanistan/Pakistan to mean "boot camp" and "terrorist camp," as the claimants held. Their point was that they live in a context where boot camp is often equated with terrorism and Islam more generally. As Karim and Eid (2012, 12) state,

> Western media depictions of Muslims over the last few decades reveal a dramatic increase in the use of stereotypes and discriminatory rhetoric … Such coverage frequently relates the teachings of Islam to terrorism, destruction, and conflict.

In the case of the *Montréal Islamic School v. Benhabib*, the media did not relate Islam to terrorism. By covering the case, this point was already made.

I make these statements on the basis of an examination of news pieces in the *Toronto Star*, *National Post*, *Montréal Gazette*, CBC, CTV, Global News, *La Presse*, Radio Canada, *Journal de Montréal*, and *Le Soleil*. In my initial scan, I found personal blogs that mentioned Benhabib and decided to include these in the evaluation. I looked at articles/posts from February 2012 to one year following the termination of the case in 2016. In total I looked at eighteen blog submissions, six opinion pieces, and nineteen media pieces. Having read the trial records, I wanted to assess how the media had covered the event and what experts had to say about the case.

What I learned was that most of the articles were written after the case finished as a sort of case wrapper. All of the national and Quebec media pieces were published on or after the beginning of the court case. There were four interesting points of note. First, the case was taken up by the media only when the trial began in August 2016 and again when the judgment was handed down four months later. It was not on the radar when the interview was aired in February 2012. Second, all major Canadian news outlets in Quebec and across the country covered the case between two and four times.[4] While the angles of each article differed slightly, they generally reiterated the issue at hand: the comments Benhabib made about the school, including the association of terrorism to Islam (see, for example, *Global News* 2016). Third, the case also generated various personal blog, Facebook, and fundraising initiatives – all in support of Benhabib's freedom of speech. These included pages in Canada and France.[5] Fourth, and perhaps most disturbingly, no scholars or other experts on Islam wrote publicly in blogs, social media, or the press to critique the way in which Benhabib cast MIS in the media or elsewhere. No one pushed back on her generalizations and absurdities. That is, no one with expertise on the variations of religious expression and freedom of belief impacted this view of Islam.[6] Of all the ink that has been spilled critiquing Huntington's theory and his overgeneralizations of cultures and religions, none of it was used to balance out what the case and the court eventually held about this Muslim community.

In sum, a reasonable citizen might, after hearing how this school was described during the radio interview, the judgment, and media representations thereof, be concerned about what is happening in this private Islamic school in their neighbourhood. The confluence of factors that came together in this case – from the way the law was interpreted, to the inability of the claimants to show damages, to the lack of expert intervention to push back on some of Benhabib's claims (gossip) – framed a general picture of a violent, dangerous community that was a threat to Quebec society. It is precisely such overgeneralizations that won the case and that elucidate the dangers Said, Karim, Eid, and others have warned cast a narrow and unduly stable vision of culture and community. This vision has been inscribed into the Canadian public imaginary and subsumed into what we "know" about Islam.

Conclusion

This chapter has examined two competing rights – freedom of speech and against defamation – in the case of the *Montréal Islamic School v. Benhabib*. Recognizing that any limit on the freedom of speech should be carefully delineated given its close relationship to democracy, I argue that in this case the court got it wrong. In its judgment, the court gave disproportionate weight to Benhabib's context and history as a critic of Islam and failed to adequately consider that the insinuations she made about what and how this school taught might affect this minority community in a larger context of Islamophobia and anti-Muslim racism in contemporary Quebec. Although reprimanding Benhabib for her hurtful comments, the court allowed the statements about the school to stand.

In the last section of the chapter I looked at the counter-narratives offered by scholars and experts and found that although the case was covered by mainstream media outlets, no one with a general reference on or in Islam spoke up to offer a more academically informed perspective. This silence helped tailor a very specific knowledge on Islam. It engrained an increasingly negative image of Islam into the Canadian public imaginary.

Appendix: Selections from the Radio Interview

Madame Benhabib: Well, those surprises, uh … *it's similar to an indoctrination worthy of a camp, um, of a military camp in Afghanistan or Pakistan.*[7] I mean, there's not much of a difference, in my opinion, between the indoctrination that is done in those schools in Montréal or … or where … or wherever the schools are happening, whether in Pakistan or Afghanistan. So that's essentially what it was.

Monsieur Dutrizac: Aren't you exaggerating a little?

Madame Benhabib: Well, listen, yeah, okay, maybe I … I did exaggerate, but … *the suras, in fact, that are imposed on the children* … right *from the first years of elementary school, are extremely violent and they are misogynistic and sexist.* So …

…

… it's the Qur'anic verses that are the entity of the Qur'an, so there you go. So, the Qur'an, therefore, is made up of Qur'anic verses and among all those Qur'anic verses, well, there are some that are extremely hateful, for example, towards unbelievers. And among those suras that are extremely hateful to unbelievers, there's one of them that's on the website and that's taught to the children.

Monsieur Dutrizac: And what does it say?

Madame Benhabib: Well, it basically says that, well, people who don't believe in the resurrection will be scalded with hot water, they'll be put into a furnace, they will burn.

…

Madame Benhabib: Well, listen, that tells me that we're … *creating fundamentalist activists who will demand, in a few years, accommodations and all kinds of crazy things*; that we're not creating the citizens of tomorrow, rather the opposite. We're extremely far from citizenship, we're far from all the values that belong to our society. We are, as I was saying earlier, perhaps somewhere in Afghanistan or Pakistan. So, *I think, well, it's extremely disturbing. Especially since, well, there's a very high rigidity, there's a separation of the sexes, there's a gender apartheid. There's the imposition of the Islamic veil. Ultimately, that doesn't tell me anything good about what is happening in those schools.*

Monsieur Dutrizac: Also, you said that we're preparing the next generation, but there's nothing about citizenship, about integration, about the society in which we live. It's as if this school is completely apart and doesn't live in Québec.

Madame Benhabib: Yes. Absolutely. That's a … that's a great observation because, in fact, this school is completely disembodied. It certainly doesn't fit in the Québec political landscape, it's not rooted in the Québec society. It's extremely far from the values of our society. This school is modeled on another society, that is, a society where the separation of the sexes is normalized, where women must look down and walk behind men, where children have to … to recite Qur'anic verses, *and where men will probably commit honour crimes against … against their sisters.* So, that's how, uh … all the work is done upstream in schools to … to create walking disasters in the coming years.

…

Monsieur Dutrizac: And all that is … when we take them that young, we eliminate their capacity to think for themselves, to analyze what we teach them and to be open to the world.

Madame Benhabib: Yes, of course, because the main mission of school is precisely to allow children to become students, which means to be discerning and to be free. That is, free, which means that they will be able, later, to choose;

choose between the options that will be available to them and develop critical thinking skills, an open mind, tolerance, and so on. So, you see, in the particular conjuncture that exists in these schools, there's no room for criticism, there's no room for reflection, there's no room for sharing between men and women, quite the opposite. We're erecting walls of separation between the sexes, walls that are absolutely abominable, walls in which … and through which we maintain the hatred of women and the detestation of women.

Monsieur Dutrizac: Hum. Well, let's address this global phenomenon and get our kids to convert to this … to these sound values …

Madame Benhabib: … (laugh) …

NOTES

1 For a translated extract of the interview, see appendix 1. Translation by Audrey Monette, 2018.

2 For an interesting commentary on how Benhabib's secularism ran counter to questions about the crucifix in the Québec Legislature during the 2012 election campaign, see Chiasson 2002. On her unsuccessful runs for office, see Giuseppe Valiante, 2016, 23 August, "Slander trial looms for Québec author who criticized Muslim school," *CBC News*, https://www.cbc.ca/news/canada/Montréal/quebec-djemila-benhabib-muslim-schools-Montréal-slander-1.3731906.

3 Neither the pamphlet nor website was available for review at the time this chapter was written and thus what follows is based on court records.

4 I looked at the *Toronto Star*, *Globe and Mail*, *Montréal Gazette*, *National Post*, CBC, CTV News (Montreal) and Global News (Montreal), *La Presse* (Montreal), *Journal de Montréal*, Radio Canada, and *Le Soleil* (Quebec City) between 2012 and 2017.

5 For example, the editor of *Marianne* – a weekly Paris-based magazine with approximately 300,000 distribution per week – wrote an article in support of Benhabib (see Gozlan 2016).

6 I do not consider one self-described and self-taught "expert" on Islam who is an astrologer by training.

7 Emphasis added throughout the interview is mine.

REFERENCES

Ahmed, Leila. 1992. *Women and gender in Islam: Historical roots of a modern debate.* Yale University Press.

Amiraux, Valérie. 2016. "Visibility, transparency and gossip: How did the religion of some (Muslims) become the public concern of others." *Critical Research on Religion*, *4*(1), 37–56. https://doi.org/10.1177%2F2050303216640399

Arkoun, Mohammed. 1990. "Islamic cultures, developing societies, modern thought." In Hayat Salam (Ed.), *Expressions of Islam in buildings* (pp. 49–64). Aga Khan Trust for Culture.

Asad, Talal. 2003. *Formations of the secular*. Stanford University Press.

Barlas, Asma. 2002. *Believing women in Islam: Unreading patriarchal interpretations of the Qur'an*. University of Texas Press.

Benhabib, Djemila. 2012, 8 February. "Muslim schools in Montréal are recruiting: Djemila Benhabib comes to talk about it." Benoit Dutrizac. 98.5 FM. https://www.canlii.org/fr/qc/qccs/doc/2016/2016qccs6067/2016qccs6067.html?resultIndex=2#par19

– 2018. "Official Page of Djemila Benhabib." http://djemilabenhabib.com

Chiasson, Paul. 2002, 15 August. "Québec mayor slams foreign-born PQ election candidate: They're going to make our culture disappear." *National Post*. https://nationalpost.com/news/canada/quebec-mayor-slams-algerian-born-pq-election-candidate-theyre-going-to-make-our-culture-disappear

Écoles Musulmanes de Montréal. 2018. "Homepage." http://www.emms.ca

Environics Institute. 2016. *Survey of Muslims in Canada 2016: Final report*. https://www.environicsinstitute.org/docs/default-source/project-documents/survey-of-muslims-in-canada-2016/final-report.pdf

Faraz Rabbani, Shaykh. 2017, 14 October. "The great event: Surat al-Waqi'a explained." Video. SeekersHub Global. https://www.youtube.com/watch?v=Bx80AtaCGLA

Global News. 2016, 13 December. "Quebec feminist author found not guilty of slandering Montreal Muslim school." https://globalnews.ca/news/3124487/quebec-feminist-author-found-not-guilty-of-slandering-montreal-muslim-school

Gozlan, Martine. 2016, 2 October. "Djemila Benhabib: Le djihad tente d'imposer sa loi aux tribunaux." *Vigile Quebec*. https://vigile.quebec/articles/djemila-benhabib-le-djihad-tente-d-imposer-sa-loi-aux-tribunaux

Huntington, Samuel P. 1996. *Clash of civilizations and the remaking of world order*. Touchstone.

Karim, Karim H., and Mahmoud Eid. 2012. "Clash of ignorance." *Global Media Journal–Canadian Edition*, *5*(1), 7–27.

Légis Québec. 1975. *Charter of Human Rights and Freedoms,* Chapter 1 – *Fundamental Freedoms and Rights*. http://legisquebec.gouv.qc.ca/en/ShowDoc/cs/C-12

Montréal Muslim School v. Benhabib. 2016 QCCS 6067. (CanLII).

Said, Edward W. 1978. *Orientalism*. Random House.

– 1994. *Orientalism*. Vintage.

– 2001, 22 October. "The clash of ignorance." *The Nation*. https://www.thenation.com/article/archive/clash-ignorance

Soroush, Abdul-Karim. 1998. "The evolution and devolution of religious knowledge." In Charles Kurzman (Ed.), *Liberal Islam: A sourcebook* (pp. 244–51). Oxford University Press.

Valiante, Giuseppe. 2016a, 22 August. "Québec author faces slander trial for 'greatly tarnishing' Muslim school." *Star.* https://www.thestar.com/news/canada/2016/08/22/quebec-author-faces-slander-trial-for-greatly-tarnishing-muslim-school.html

– 2016b, 13 December. "Djemila Benhabib didn't slander Muslim school in Montreal, court finds." *Montréal Gazette.* https://montrealgazette.com/news/local-news/djemila-benhabib-found-not-guilty-of-slandering-muslim-school-in-montreal

Wadud, Amina. 2004. "Qur'an, gender and interpretive possibilities." *Hawwa: Journal of the Middle East and the Islamic World, 2*(3), 316–36. https://doi.org/10.1163/1569208043077297

WIC Radio Ltd. v. Simpson. 2008 SCC 40. (CanLII).

2(b) or Not 2(b): The Expressive Value of the Niqab

NATASHA BAKHT

Introduction

The rhetoric of religion has dominated public discourse and scholarly analysis of "the veiled woman." Muslim women who cover themselves with a niqab or full-face veil have borne the brunt of racist and discriminatory legislative prohibitions in many Western countries, including most recently in Quebec, Canada (Bill 21 2019; Bill 62 2015).[1] As these women speak out and judicially challenge public bans on their clothing, we are learning more about what compels them to wear garments that cover their faces. The reasons given by Muslim women for wearing the niqab (like the hijab or headscarf) are multifaceted, engaging spiritual, social, political, and personal interests (At Home in Europe 2011, 2015; Brems 2014; Clarke 2013).[2] Yet legal analysis of "the veil" has conflated these multiple dimensions, as evidenced by the framing of pleadings and decisions in the relevant cases involving niqab-wearing women and scholarship analysing legal proscriptions of the niqab (Fournier and See 2012, 73; Razack 2018, 173; Rochelle 2013, 51). When bans concerning women's clothing are legally challenged, the justifications relied on are typically restricted to the rights of religious freedom and sometimes equality or security of the person (Bakht 2015, 421; Chambers and Roth 2014, 383, 393). While much of the scholarship about niqab-wearing women that engages primary data is nuanced, recognizing the multiple influences in their lives and the various ways in which these motivations are enacted (At Home in Europe 2011, 2015; Bakht 2020; Brems 2014; Bouteldja 2014; Clarke 2013; Moors 2014; Østergaard et al. 2014), political debates, reports, and resolutions[3] about niqab-wearing women have for the most part emphasized the religious/cultural dimensions of the practice of face veiling (Bouchard and Taylor 2007, 3; Selby 2014, 443, 446, 451; Sharify-Funk 2011, 143), often inaccurately, to the exclusion of other expressive possibilities.[4]

We have yet to see much attention given to the argument that wearing a niqab embodies one's right to freedom of expression in Canada. This is surprising, given that there is clearly an expressive element to any choice of clothing, particularly where such a choice runs counter to a dominant culture. This chapter examines covered Muslim women's freedom to express themselves by wearing the clothing of their choice. It analyses section 2(b) of the Canadian Charter of Rights and Freedoms (1982) and its accompanying jurisprudence in the Canadian context to determine if such an argument is viable and, if so, what it might contribute to our understanding of niqab-wearing women as legal subjects. It may be that the production of knowledge about niqab-wearing Muslim women has to date only been understood in a context that is religious and not one that simultaneously advances an individualized or collective argument of expression.

The Freedom to Express Oneself

Freedom of expression is guaranteed under section 2(b) of the Canadian Charter of Rights and Freedoms (1982). In *Edmonton Journal v. Alberta (Attorney General)* (1989), Justice Cory stated, "It is difficult to imagine a guaranteed right more important to a democratic society than freedom of expression" (1336). In one of its earliest decisions on freedom of expression, the Supreme Court of Canada stated:

> Freedom of expression was entrenched in our Constitution and is guaranteed in the Québec *Charter* so as to ensure that everyone can manifest their thoughts, opinions, beliefs, indeed all expressions of the heart and mind, however unpopular, distasteful or contrary to the mainstream. Such protection is, in the words of both the Canadian and Québec Charters, "fundamental" because in a free, pluralistic and democratic society we prize a diversity of ideas and opinions for their inherent value both to the community and to the individual. (*Irwin Toy Ltd v. Québec (Attorney General)* 1989, 968)

Freedom of expression has largely been championed as a fundamental freedom in Canada, as the following quote from Justice Rand illustrates. It was "little less vital to man's mind and spirit than breathing is to his physical existence" (*Irwin Toy Ltd v. Québec (Attorney General)* 1989, 968).[5] In the jurisprudence, expression is defined broadly as any activity that conveys or attempts to convey meaning, as long as that meaning is not conveyed through violence or the threat of violence (*Irwin Toy Ltd v. Québec (Attorney General)* 1989; *R. v. Keegstra* 1990; *R. v. Butler* 1992). There is no limitation internal to the provision itself,[6] making it unnecessary to engage in complex decisions about what counts as "expression" or to identify categories of expression that have high or low value (*Irwin Toy Ltd v. Québec (Attorney General)* 1989).[7] Thus, the breadth of the concept means that almost all freedom of expression cases will turn on the application of section 1, whether the infringement of the right can be "justified in a free and democratic society" (Canadian Charter of Rights and Freedoms 1982, s. 1).

While Muslim women don the niqab for a variety of reasons, there is no doubt that wearing the niqab conveys meaning. The niqab introduces its wearer to the world as a primarily Muslim-identified woman. Such an introduction can open the door to a number of different assumptions and connotations, both positive and negative, but the conveyance of meaning is clear. Wearing the niqab can be an expression of faith, identity, modesty in dress, rebellion against parental upbringing, and protest against governmental restrictions on attire, among other perspectives. Any law that interferes with one's ability to freely participate in that expression is an infringement of freedom of expression, whether justifiable or not.

The expression protected under section 2(b) of the Charter (1982) extends beyond the mere content of the expression (*Ford v. Québec (Attorney General)* 1988, 749) to encompass individual self-fulfilment and personal autonomy (*R. v. Keegstra* 1990). "The personal belongings of an individual are an expression of that person's essential self. His or her books, diaries, pictures, clothes and other personal things are intertwined with that person's beliefs, opinions, thoughts and conscience" (*R. v. Sharpe* 1999, para. 27). Clothing is undoubtedly among the methods by which individuals express themselves and experience self-fulfilment. This is particularly true of types of clothing, such as the niqab, that identify the wearer as a member of a particular group or the holder of particular ideas or beliefs, religious or otherwise.

Complicating the Legal Discourse about "Veiled Women"

In the six countries where empirical research has been done about women who wear the niqab, the predominant reason given for wearing this article of clothing is religious. For the majority of women in Canada, France, the United Kingdom, Belgium, Denmark, and the Netherlands, the motivation for wearing the niqab is strongly religious, that is, to further one's spiritual journey, to become a better Muslim, or to deepen one's relationship with God (At Home in Europe 2011, 2015; Brems 2014; Clarke 2013; Inge 2016). I have conducted nine interviews of niqab-wearing women in Ontario and Quebec as part of a larger project examining the Canadian context as it relates to these women (Bakht 2020). Most of the women I interviewed engaged in thoughtful decision-making and prolonged individual study to acquire more Islamic knowledge and to determine whether donning the niqab was right for them. Some niqab-wearing women articulated that their face veil and modest dress in general are not a message to the outside world, but that wearing the niqab is something they do for themselves or for God. For example, a niqab-wearing woman in Denmark noted, "We do not do it for political reasons. I cannot be bothered to single out myself every day in a society that is predominately non-Muslim so I can make a political statement! That's really not going to motivate me for too long" (Østergaard et al. 2014, 61). The idea that the niqab is not meant to express a statement to others suggests that proselytism is not a motivation (Brems et al. 2014, 82). However, the perspective that the face veil expresses a personal spiritual journey advances a form of individual self-fulfilment and human flourishing that freedom of expression is meant to cultivate.

While religious reasons predominate, several examples suggest that women who wear the niqab may also do so for supplementary reasons. Just as Muslim women in the West who wear the hijab have stated that they wear the headscarf to articulate a religious identity, resist racism, express cultural difference, or make a fashion statement, among other significations (Bakht 2009, 116; Hoodfar 2003, 11; Lewis 2015, 2), several Canadian interviewees also gave a number of explanations for why they had chosen to wear the niqab.

For some, the niqab functioned as a powerful marker of Muslim identity, both proclaiming and forming this identity. One Canadian interviewee identified a clear message to those who might observe her:

> I feel like for me these days it's more just like an identity thing … I'm not just doing it for God … Mostly my intention is just to show that even as a niqabi I can do the same thing as you, right? Because the only people putting the barrier on my capabilities are people who don't understand niqab fully … I don't put these barriers on me … I don't feel like Muslim women should shy away from their identity or how they want to dress just because other people don't understand. (Ayesha in Bakht 2020, 21)

For this niqab-wearing woman, an important purpose in wearing the niqab is to dispel typical notions of the niqab-wearer as conservative and oppressed. The expressive value of the niqab is to counter widespread though inaccurate beliefs about niqab-wearing women as subordinated. In Wales, Sahar Al-Faifi has stated that while the niqab has become a part of her identity (proudly Welsh and unapologetically Muslim) as well as her faith, the third reason she wears the niqab is as a symbol of resistance to all of the stereotypes and negative perceptions about Muslim women. "What we hear a lot of the time is that Muslim women are isolated, are uneducated, are failing to integrate, but the truth is they haven't really spoken to women like me" (This Morning 2017).[8] As a molecular geneticist and licensed skydiver, Sahar's rejection of tired and contradictory narratives about Muslim women is expressed subversively through her niqab.[9]

Canadian niqab-wearer and university student Aima Warriach has stated, "I wear niqab as an act of defiance against the patriarchy that keeps telling me what to wear because somehow they know what it means to be liberated from 'Taliban like oppression'" (Sisters Project, n.d.). Similarly, a woman in France who admitted to not being a practising Muslim before France's niqab ban was passed said about wearing the niqab, "This is my way of saying 'no' to a government that has robbed me of my freedom" (Heneghan 2015). The intolerance towards niqab-wearing women that several democratic governments have demonstrated by prohibiting their presence in a variety of spaces has led to the rise of another signification of the niqab: as an expression of dissent and disapproval of governments that censor minority voices in favour of majoritarian values.

In other cases, the decision to wear the niqab, at least initially, was clearly the quintessential teenage rebellion against standards of so-called acceptable behaviour. One woman stated, "Honestly speaking, it was going to be an adventure for me. And I wanted to do something different, which is not the norm and I wanted to be a little different from everyone else" (Zakia in Bakht 2020, 19). In such instances, the expressive content of the niqab might be to define oneself in opposition to one's parents' generation, values, and beliefs.[10]

Contrary to popular perceptions that the face veil is inherently oppressive to women, that it is a "mobile prison" (Howard 2014, 207) that prevents women from being equal to men, several Muslim women have expressed feeling empowered by wearing the niqab. In particular, by wearing the niqab, they express a refusal to participate in social expectations of beauty ideals and body images for women (Fogarty 2018).

Each of these expressive interpretations for the niqab falls squarely within the purview of freedom of expression under section 2(b). Niqab-wearing women would simply identify the relevant meaning(s) being conveyed by their dress and how it "relates to the pursuit of truth, participation in the community, or individual self-fulfillment and human flourishing" (*Irwin Toy Ltd v. Québec (Attorney General)* 1989, 978).[11] This would not be a difficult task. Objectors to the niqab might argue that because the niqab subjectively represents something violent, radical, or fearful, it ought to be subject to the exception that violence as a form of expression does not qualify for protection. Such an approach, however, would incorrectly alter the focus of the enquiry from the applicant's expression to the subjective beliefs of the purported recipients of the expression. Where competing interests are at stake, these must be dealt with under section 1 to avoid improperly shifting the burden of proof to the applicant to prove why the expression is not violent.

The association of niqab-wearing women with violence or the incitement of hatred towards other people or lifestyles is patently false (Inge 2016, 5). Such declarations are merely roundabout ways of silencing and interfering with the equal participation of niqab-wearing women in public debate. Indeed, freedom of expression ensures that we can convey our thoughts and feelings of the heart and mind in non-violent ways without fear of censure. Because niqab-wearing women have deep convictions, they are often subject to a host of negative reactions from members of the public, including outright violence.[12] Rather than inciting violence, they are routinely subject to it precisely because they are committed to wearing face veils. Most of us cannot relate to such a commitment and the courage that it requires each and every day. But the research on niqab-wearing women clearly indicates that they do not impose their beliefs on others or expect compliance with their commitments. An affiant to the constitutional challenge of Bill 62 in Quebec, Salma Siddiquea (2017), notes, "Other followers of Islam have different beliefs and I respect that … I respect other people's choices. Even though these choices might run contrary to my faith, I do not think that other individuals are bad people just because they wear less clothing than me" (para. 5, 11).

Litigating Freedom of Expression?

Freedom of expression has not been a central focus of legal arguments in cases involving prohibitions of the niqab in Canada. In *R. v. N.S.* (2012),[13] the Muslim woman sexual assault complainant who wanted to wear her niqab while testifying in court relied on freedom of religion as the primary constitutional argument. Interveners who supported N.S.'s position made intersectional Charter arguments relying on freedom of religion, equality (section 15), and security of the person (section 7) to advance the important idea that a complex matrix of rights affects Muslim women who are prevented from wearing face veils when testifying as sexual assault complainants (Women's Legal Education and Action Fund 2011). Freedom of expression, however, did not feature in either the legal arguments or the decision of any level of court.

Ishaq v. Canada (Citizenship and Immigration) (2015) involved a challenge by permanent resident and niqab-wearer Zunera Ishaq to the federal government policy that required an uncovered face during the recitation of the oath of citizenship, a requirement to becoming a Canadian citizen. Ishaq argued that the policy infringed her section 2(a) rights since she would have to abandon either her religious beliefs or her dream of becoming a citizen. Moreover, it was argued that the policy was discriminatory on the grounds of sex and religion and thus contrary to section 15 of the Charter, as it disproportionately affected Muslim women and perpetuated stereotyping and prejudice. Though freedom of expression was certainly relevant, it was not argued. In deciding the case in favour of Ishaq, the Federal Court and the Federal Court of Appeal relied on the non-constitutional arguments put forth by the applicant. In preferring a course of judicial restraint, the court avoided making unnecessary constitutional pronouncements where the case could be decided on non-constitutional grounds (*Ishaq v. Canada (Citizenship and Immigration)* 2015, para. 66; *Ishaq v. Canada (Minister of Citizenship and Immigration)* 2015, para. 5).

In the legal challenge of Quebec's enactment of a law that prohibits people who wear face veils from either working in the public service or receiving public services (Bill 62 2015), the applicants decided to focus their submissions on how the law infringes niqab-wearing women's freedom of religion and equality rights.[14] Though freedom of expression is equally pertinent, it was not argued. One of the challenges of litigation is framing a persuasive argument within the page limit permitted by the court. This presumably plays some role in the strategic choice to limit the scope of all applicable rights, since one need only be successful on one constitutional ground in order to receive the typical Charter remedy of having a statute or policy declared unconstitutional. Because many niqab-wearing women identify with a religious basis for wearing the niqab and because religious freedom under section 2(a) has a low legal threshold, this route may seem the most obvious to lawyers in cases challenging niqab bans.

In 2015, Justice Eliana Marengo refused to hear Rania El-Alloul's case in Montreal because she wore a hijab and the judge decided this meant that she was not suitably dressed (Shulman 2015). When asked why she wore the headscarf, El-Alloul responded, "I'm Muslim" (*Rania El-Alloul c. Procureure générale du Québec* 2018, para. 13). The Court of Appeal of Québec eventually declared that "the provisions of the *Regulation of the Court of Québec* dealing with a dress code do not forbid the appellant from wearing a head scarf ... *if that practice results from a sincerely held religious belief* [emphasis added] and does not conflict with or harm an overriding public interest" (*Rania El-Alloul c. Procureure générale du Québec* 2018, para. 7). A justification relying on expression, whether for a hijabi or niqabi plaintiff, would likely not have garnered the same protection as a religious explanation because everyone's expression is limited in courtrooms to some extent. As Justice Marengo stated, "Decorum is important. Hats and sunglasses, for example, are not allowed" (*Rania El-Alloul c. Procureure générale du Québec* 2018, para. 14). Whether vague justifications that rely on supposedly neutral concepts such as decorum should continue to guide permissible dress in courtrooms is highly questionable in our increasingly diverse societies.

Legal submissions made by niqab-wearing women in New Zealand, England, Australia, and the United States have similarly not utilized the lens of freedom of expression to advocate their case. In the New Zealand criminal case *Police v. Razamjoo* (2005), which dealt with the question of whether witnesses for the prosecution could wear the burqa while testifying,[15] the competing interests were defined by the court as the witness's religious rights, the defendant's right to a fair trial, and the community's right to the public and open administration of justice. The witness's freedom of expression rights were neither argued nor considered. Freedom of expression was similarly not considered in an English criminal case involving a niqab-wearing defendant accused of witness intimidation who was not permitted to wear her niqab and, thus, opted not to testify and ultimately pleaded guilty to the offence (*The Queen v. D(R)* 2013).

In a civil case in New South Wales, Australia (*Moutia Elzahed and Anors v. Commonwealth of Australia and State of NSW* 2016), religious freedom was the only ground relied upon to unsuccessfully argue that the niqab-wearing witness be permitted to testify with her face covered in a case involving a police raid of her home. In the United States (*Muhammad v. Enterprise Rent-a-Car* 2006), Judge Paruk dismissed a niqab-wearing woman's small claims action from the bench because she refused to remove her face veil. The plaintiff in that case, Ginnah Muhammad, who was not represented by a lawyer, said, "I wish to respect my religion so I will not take off my clothes" (*Muhammad v. Enterprise Rent-a-Car* 2006, 6). Though she refused to take off her face veil before Judge Paruk, she was willing to do so before a female judge (*Muhammad v. Enterprise Rent-a-Car* 2006, 4). Judge Paruk responded that no female judge was available and then shockingly went on to explain to Muhammad that wearing the face veil was "not a religious thing … [but] a custom thing" (*Muhammad v. Enterprise Rent-a-Car* 2006, 4–5). Interestingly, though he took the initiative to educate Muhammad about her own religion, Judge Paruk did not consider other potential legal arguments, such as a freedom of expression claim.

In Sweden and Australia, niqab-wearing women have been forbidden from observing trials in courtrooms because their clothing could be perceived as "disturbing order" (Edwards 2014b, 284) or because of a potential risk of mistrial should they misbehave (Wahlquist 2018). In such cases, judges do not typically take submissions from the women involved, as they are not parties to the case. Rather, they simply make decisions based on the court's inherent powers to regulate the conduct of its procedures.[16]

In the two European Court of Human Rights cases involving unsuccessful challenges to public bans of the niqab in France and Belgium, both sets of applicants utilized a number of grounds to frame their arguments, including article 10, freedom of expression, of the European Convention on Human Rights (1950). Interestingly, before France's ban of the niqab was enacted, the National Assembly of France adopted a resolution that actually contemplated freedom of expression. The resolution "affirms that the exercise of freedom of expression, opinion or belief cannot be relied on by anyone for the purpose of flouting common rules, without regard for the values, rights and duties which underpin society" (*SAS v. France* 2014, para. 24). In a democratic society, freedom of expression is protected precisely so one can dissent, object, and resist the imposition of accepted wisdom. In attempting to thwart a freedom of expression justification from the very start, the National Assembly must have imagined this non-conformist who prefers other truths.

In point of fact, the applicant in *SAS v. France* (2014) was described "as a devout Muslim who wears the burqa and niqab in accordance with her religious faith, *culture and personal convictions* [emphasis added]" (para. 11). Despite quoting from the Commissioner for Human Rights of the Council of Europe, who noted that "dress, after all, may not reflect specific religious beliefs, but the exercise of broader cultural expression" (*SAS v. France* 2014, para. 37),[17] the European Court held that the applicant's claim mainly raised an issue with regard to the freedom to manifest one's religion or beliefs (para. 108)[18] and did no further analysis under article 10.

In *Belcacemi and Oussar v. Belgium* (2017), the European Court again paid little heed to the freedom of expression claim, finding that no distinct issue is raised after analysing articles 8 (respect for private life) and 9 (freedom of thought, conscience, and religion and freedom to manifest one's religion), interpreted separately or combined with article 14 (prohibition of discrimination) (para. 69). On the one hand, the court found that it had already responded to the issue of freedom of expression through its analysis of articles 8 and 9 (no violations were found). However, in its reasoning, the court insisted that the focus of the analysis ought only to be on the freedom to manifest one's religion, wherein the practice of religion dictates that women must veil. Other potential expressive goals appeared not to be on the court's radar.

To date, freedom of expression has not been successfully argued in a case pertaining to niqab-wearing women. These cases reveal that the idea of expression as it relates to niqab-wearing women falls so outside our understanding of these women that courts do not adequately consider the right to freedom of expression even when the applicants raise it. Critically, how these cases are argued and decided reflects and reiterates how Muslim women are viewed. These cases produce and reify knowledge about niqab-wearing women, limiting our full appreciation of who they are.

What Does the Lens of Freedom of Expression Add?

One might ask, what is lost in not pursuing a freedom of expression claim? Tactically, there may not be a significant advantage to advancing freedom of expression versus religious freedom, except in the case where the claimant fails to convince the court that she has a sincere religious belief. In such a case, freedom of expression may well be helpful. The Supreme Court of Canada has recognized the ways in which religion is lived by emphasizing its subjective nature (*Syndicat Northcrest v. Amselem* 2004) and focusing the religious freedom enquiry on the applicant's sincere belief rather than those views espoused in religious doctrine or by religious officials. One might nonetheless imagine a religious freedom applicant whose conduct may not meet the test in section 2(a) that permits some inconsistency in conduct (*R. v. N.S.* 2012, para. 13). For example, in *SAS v France* (2014), the applicant was characterized as deciding to wear the niqab when the mood struck her (Beaman 2016, 7). The court held:

> The applicant added that she wore the niqab in public and in private, but not systematically: she might not wear it, for example, when she visited the doctor, when meeting friends in a public place, or when she wanted to socialise in public. She was thus content not to wear the niqab in public places at all times *but wished*

> *to be able to wear it when she chose to do so, depending in particular on her spiritual feelings* [emphasis added]. (*SAS v. France* 2014, para. 12)

Importantly, a freedom of expression analysis would not require the expression to be consistent in order to be protected. The freedom to express oneself includes the freedom to change how one expresses oneself. Clothing has been enumerated as a form of expression (*R. v. Sharpe* 1999, para. 37), and individuals change their clothing on a regular basis and may even adopt radically different styles from day to day. The content of the expression is also irrelevant to its protected status (*Ford v. Québec (Attorney General)* 1988). Whatever form the expression takes, one has every right to alter the message and continue to enjoy the constitutional right to express oneself. This would suggest that one's choice to wear the niqab is no less validly protected by freedom of expression merely because one chooses to express oneself by not wearing it on occasion.

Theoretically, freedom of religion, like freedom of expression, is defined broadly in Canada with no internal limits to the right, and any balancing of other interests ought to be done at the section 1 stage of the justificatory analysis. In practice, this may not always be the case, as the Supreme Court's analysis in *NS* suggests (Bakht 2015, 423). However, generally speaking, both rights are expansive in their protective ambit. The jurisprudence under freedom of expression goes to some length to articulate that there is inherent value in all expression, "however unpopular, distasteful or contrary to the mainstream. Such protection is 'fundamental' because in a free, pluralistic and democratic society we prize a diversity of ideas and opinions for their inherent value both to the community and to the individual" (*Irwin Toy Ltd v. Québec (Attorney General)* 1989, 968). The broadmindedness of section 2(b) thus must also be extended to expressions of modesty in dress that offend, shock, or disturb sectors of the population or the state.

The only other doctrinal advantage that might be gained in litigating under freedom of expression is if this right is combined with other Charter rights. The cumulative effect of having an infringement of religious freedom and equality and security of the person and expression (as might well be argued in the Bill 62 and Bill 21 cases) is powerful. It suggests that the government has not been prudent in drafting a law that minimally impairs the rights of the applicants, as required by a constitutional analysis. An intersectional reading of such an approach would suggest that it is not merely the aggregate effect of the multiple rights violations but the complex and interlocking ways in which such niqab prohibitions affect the lives of niqab-wearing women, including as agents of expression.

My modest contribution to why freedom of expression might be a useful lens as it pertains to niqab-wearing women is less doctrinal and more about how we view these women. Despite being constitutionally protected, religious expression tends to be marginalized or diminished in the public imagination. Critics of religious speech have proposed numerous strategies for limiting the presence of religion in the public square (Blum 2018, 1). It is also not unusual to conflate conservative or "backward" ideas with people who hold religious perspectives. Because religion is typically inherited from one's parents, the assumption is that religious adherents are shielded from other ideas and that this is problematic.

Religious women in particular are framed in a way that requires them to invest considerable energy in establishing themselves as thinking and rational beings (Hoodfar 1993, 5). The presumption that niqab-wearing women are forced into this attire, that they are oppressed and ignorant, is ubiquitous. Religious women's choices are questioned in a way that other women's choices are not, undermining their agency and individuality. Even when the research on niqab-wearing women clearly demonstrates that most women make the conscious and personal decision to adopt the niqab, often in contravention of their families' wishes (for Canada: Bakht 2020, 18, 23; Clarke 2013, 29; for Belgium: Brems et al. 2014, 84; for the Netherlands: Moors 2014, 32; for England: Inge 2016, 89; Bouteldja 2014, 133; for France: Bouteldja 2014, 133; for Denmark: Østergaard et al. 2014, 61), their perspectives are nonetheless questioned or supplanted with nefarious aims. Despite the individual nature of the section 2(a) test, a freedom of religion approach arguably paints niqab-wearing women in the public imagination as a monolithic mass. It contributes to public perceptions of the religious institution acting as a barrier which these women literally hide behind. Although these ideas are highly disrespectful, and much scholarship identifies and criticizes these predispositions about religious women (Beaman 2008, 1–58; Zine 2012, 13), the bias nonetheless remains.

A freedom of expression analysis might temper this secular bias by permitting us to see niqab-wearing women not as just products of a religious upbringing or indoctrination but as active agents of expression. When one thinks of someone who is standing up for their right to express themself, the image that comes to mind is of someone who is bold and engaged in an activity that has deep meaning to them; it sparks notions of industriousness, of someone who is animated, who may even be forceful in defending their convictions. Rather than seeing them as disenfranchised women who are subjects of law, we might begin to understand niqab-wearing women as law's constituents. A freedom of expression analysis might make it possible for decision-makers to perceive niqab-wearing women in more dynamic and complex ways by considering their multilayered commitments, everyday experiences, relationships, expectations, aspirations, and ways of navigating hegemonic structures (Bouclin 2013, 1167). A freedom of expression lens might permit personal and idiosyncratic elements of niqab-wearing women's lives to be highlighted, focusing on the individual rather than the undifferentiated group.

Conclusion

Lawyers, judges, scholars, and even ordinary people tend not to challenge antiquated notions about niqab-wearing women that limit them to their religious beliefs. Expanding and questioning our knowledge about niqab-wearing women beyond being only religious adherents might reframe our understanding of Muslim women and better serve our relations with them. It is important that the production of knowledge about Muslim women who cover their faces with veils represents the full array of these women's experiences. Understanding them in a context that is only religious and not also expressive negates their distinctive and varied representations of themselves. Niqab-wearing women have deployed unique expressive representations in their chosen form of dress. These assertions, individually and collaboratively, enrich our understanding of these women and articulate alternative legal subjectivities that demand protection.

NOTES

I am grateful to Professor Anver Emon for encouraging me to write on this topic. I am also indebted to Vanessa Baker-Murray for her invaluable research and editorial assistance. Thank you to Professor Lynda Collins for a road trip discussing this issue and to Elaan for enduring the conversation. Thanks also to Justine Bouquier for assisting me in my understanding of the European Court decisions and to the editors of this volume for their insightful comments, which improved the chapter.

1 For example, in France, see *Loi no. 2010–1192* 2010. In Belgium, see *Loi du 1er juin 2011* 2011. In the Netherlands, see *Instelling* 2018. For Denmark, see *Guardian* 2018.
2 See for example At Home in Europe 2011; Brems 2014; Clarke 2013.
3 See for example National Assembly 2010. The Information Report under section 45 of the rules in the enquiry on the practice of the use of the full-face veil on national territory concluded that the face veil was an infringement of the three principles constitutive of the French Republic: liberty, equality, and brotherhood. Interestingly, the report interviewed only one woman who wore a face veil and demanded that she remove it during her hearing.
4 Some excellent scholarship about hijab-wearing Muslim women demonstrates the multiple resonances for their sartorial choices, including fashion and political and individual expression (Alvi 2003, 172; Bucar 2017, 2; Bullock 2007, 118; Hoodfar 2003, 11; Lewis 2015, 2). Hijab-wearing is recognized in scholarly works as an ever-changing social practice that is governed by personal aesthetic, moral, and political values rather than merely the dictates of religious doctrine.
5 Referencing Rank J in *Switzman v. Elbling and AG of Quebec* 1957, 306.
6 By contrast to European Convention on Human Rights 1950, art. 10.
7 Elliot (2011) has argued that an understanding of freedom of expression that results in all expressive content being protected (including threatening violence, telling deliberate lies, and participating in criminal conspiracies) should be rejected.

8 See also Fogarty 2018.

9 Niqab-wearing women are othered both as victims needing to be rescued from the men who suppress them and as aggressors intent on destroying national cohesiveness and security. See Fatah 2017; Razack 2004.

10 In Denmark, Khadija's decision to wear the niqab was "seen as a rebellion against the standards of her parents and family" (Østergaard et al. 2014, 61).

11 Once a freedom of expression claimant establishes that the activity falls within the sphere of conduct protected by the guarantee (it conveys meaning and is not a violent form of expression), the second step in the section 2(b) analysis is to determine whether the purpose or effect of the government action is to restrict freedom of expression. Taking Bill 62 as an example, the government of Quebec argued that the purpose of the law is to foster state religious neutrality, as indicated by the act's title (Bill 62 2015). Such a purpose is likely to pass the low threshold to qualify legislation as pressing and substantial (*R. v. Oakes* 1986). The claimant can still, however, claim that the effect of the government's action is to restrict her expression (*Irwin Toy Ltd v. Québec (Attorney General)* 1989, 978).

12 Niqab bans that prohibit Muslim women from dressing in the clothing that they choose have the effect of legitimizing discriminatory beliefs and conduct. Ordinary people are emboldened by the government's backing of these exclusionary ideas, and they act as vigilantes, taking it upon themselves to enforce the law on Muslim women (Peritz 2013, 2017).

13 The Supreme Court of Canada provided an analytical framework for lower courts to determine whether a woman could wear her niqab while testifying in court. For an analysis of this decision see Bakht 2015.

14 Catherine McKenzie, personal comm., 9 September 2018. McKenzie is the lawyer representing the plaintiffs in *National Council of Canadian Muslims (NCCM) v. Attorney General of Quebec.* With the enactment of Bill 21, the Coalition Avenir Québec government has invoked section 33 or the "notwithstanding clause" in the Charter, which immunizes the law from any constitutional challenge on the basis of sections 2 and 7–15 of the Charter. Because freedom of religion (s 2(a)), equality (s 15), or even freedom of expression (s 2(b)) are no longer viable bases for subjecting the exclusionary law to constitutional scrutiny, innovative, alternative methods of constitutional challenge are being explored.

15 The burqa is a garment worn by some Muslim women that covers the entire body and face, including the eyes with gauze. Most women in the West do not wear the burqa but the niqab, which leaves the eyes visible. References to the burqa in Europe and other Western countries are typically inaccurate.

16 In Canada see *MacMillan Bloedel Ltd v. Simpson* 1995, para. 15, 33; Jacob 1970, 27. In the United Kingdom see Civil Procedure Rules 1998, rr. 32.1(1)(c), 32.3, 39.2(3)(g). In Sweden see Swedish Code of Judicial Procedure 1998, c. 5, s. 9. In Australia see Court Procedures Rules 2006, s. 6901.

17 The commissioner was further quoted: "The political challenge for Europe is to promote diversity and respect for the beliefs of others whilst at the same time

protecting freedom of speech and expression. If the wearing of a full-face veil is understood as an expression of a certain opinion, we are in fact talking here about the possible conflict between similar or identical rights – though seen from two entirely different angles" (*SAS v. France* 2014, para. 37).

18 The court also found no violation of article 9 on the basis that where several religions coexist within the same population, it may be necessary to place limitations on the freedom to manifest one's religion in order to reconcile the interests of the various groups and ensure that everyone's beliefs are respected (*SAS v. France* 2014, para. 126). The court's acceptance of France's novel argument that the niqab breaches "the right of others to live in a space of socialisation which makes living together easier" (para. 122) has been roundly criticized. See, for example, Edwards 2014a.

REFERENCES

Alvi, Sajida Sultana. 2003. "Muslim women and Islamic religious tradition: A historical overview and contemporary issues." In Sajida Sultana Alvi, Homa Hoodfar, and Sheila McDonough (Eds.), *The Muslim veil in North America: Issues and debates* (pp. 145–80). Women's Press.

At Home in Europe. 2011. *Unveiling the truth: Why 32 Muslim women wear the full-face veil in France.* Open Society Foundations. https://www.opensocietyfoundations.org/sites/default/files/a-unveiling-the-truth-20100510_0.pdf

– 2015. *Behind the veil: Why 122 women choose to wear the niqab in Britain.* Open Society Foundations. https://www.opensocietyfoundations.org/reports/behind-veil

Bakht, Natasha. 2009. "Objection, Your Honour! Accommodating niqab-wearing women in courtrooms." In R. Grillo, R. Ballard, A. Ferrari, A.J. Hoekema, M. Massen, and P. Shah (Eds.), *Legal practice and cultural diversity* (pp. 115–33). Ashgate Publishing.

– 2015. "In your face: Piercing the veil of ignorance about niqab-wearing women." *Social and Legal Studies, 24*(3), 419–41. https://doi.org/10.1177%2F0964663914552214

– 2020. *In your face: Law, justice and niqab-wearing women in Canada.* Irwin Law.

Beaman, Lori G. 2008. *Defining harm: Religious freedom and the limits of the law.* University of British Columbia Press.

– 2016. "Living together v. living well together: A normative examination of the *SAS* case." *Social Inclusion, 4*(2), 3–13. http://doi.org/10.17645/si.v4i2.504

Belcacemi and Oussar v. Belgium. [2017] ECHR 241.

Bill 21. An Act respecting the laicity of the state. 1st Session, 42nd Legislature, Quebec (2019).

Bill 62. An Act to foster adherence to state religious neutrality and, in particular, to provide a framework for religious accommodation requests in certain bodies. 1st Session, 41st Legislature, Quebec (2015).

Blum, Jason N. 2018. "Public discourse and the myth of religious speech." *Journal of Contemporary Religion, 33*(1), 1–16. https://doi.org/10.1080/13537903.2018.1408259

Bouchard, Gérard, and Charles Taylor. 2007. *Seeking common ground: Quebecers speak out.* Bibliothèque et Archives nationales du Québec.

Bouclin, Suzanne. 2013. "YouTube and Muslim women's legal subjectivities." *Õnati Socio-Legal Series, 3*(7), 1158–83. https://ssrn.com/abstract=2356844

Bouteldja, Naima. 2014. "France vs. England." In Eva Brems (Ed.), *The experiences of face veil wearers in Europe and the law* (pp. 115–60). Cambridge University Press.

Brems, Eva. (Ed.). 2014. *The experiences of face veil wearers in Europe and the law.* Cambridge University Press.

Brems, Eva, Yaiza Janssens, Kim Lecoyer, Saïla Ouald Chaib, Victoria Vandersteen, and Jogchum Vrielink. 2014. "The Belgian 'burqa ban' confronted with insider realities." In Eva Brems (Ed.), *The experiences of face veil wearers in Europe and the law* (pp. 77–114). Cambridge University Press.

Bucar, Elizabeth. 2017. *Pious fashion: How Muslim women dress.* Harvard University Press.

Bullock, Katherine. 2007. *Rethinking Muslim women and the veil: Challenging historical and modern stereotypes.* International Institute of Islamic Thought.

Canadian Charter of Rights and Freedoms. 1982. Part I of the Constitution Act, being Schedule B to the Canada Act (UK), c. 11.

Chambers, Lori, and Jen Roth. 2014. "Prejudice unveiled: The niqab in court." *Canadian Journal of Law and Society, 29*(3), 381–95.

Civil Procedure Rules. [1998] (UK) S.I. 1998/3132, L17.

Clarke, Lynda. 2013. "Women in niqab speak: A study of the niqab in Canada." Canadian Council of Muslim Women. http://ccmw.com/wp-content/uploads/2013/10/WEB_EN_WiNiqab_FINAL.pdf

Court Procedures Rules 2006 (Australian Capital Territory). S.L. 2006–29.

Edmonton Journal v. Alberta (Attorney General). [1989] 2 SCR 1326.

Edwards, Susan S.M. 2014a. "No burqas we're French! The wide margin of appreciation and the ECtHR burqa ruling." *Denning Law Journal, 26*, 246–60. https://doi.org/10.5750/dlj.v26i0.931

– 2014b. "Proscribing unveiling – law: A chimera and an instrument in the political agenda." In Eva Brems (Ed.), *The experiences of face veil wearers in Europe and the law* (pp. 278–96). Cambridge University Press.

Elliot, Robin. 2011. "Back to basics: A critical look at the Irwin Toy framework for freedom of expression." *Review of Constitutional Studies, 15*(2), 205–48.

European Convention on Human Rights. 1950, November 4.

Fatah, Tarek. 2017, 24 October. "Fatah: Burkas, niqabs pose public safety risk." *Toronto Sun.* http://torontosun.com/opinion/columnists/burkas-niqabs-pose-public-safety-risk

Fogarty, Shelagh. 2018, 9 August. "Muslim woman hits back: 'My niqab isn't oppressive, it's a devotion to God.'" *LBC.* https://www.lbc.co.uk/radio/presenters/shelagh-fogarty/muslim-woman-hits-back-my-niqab-isnt-oppressive-it

Ford v. Québec (Attorney General). [1988] 2 SCR 712.

Fournier, Pascale, and Erica See. 2012. "The 'naked face' of secular exclusion: Bill 94 and the privatization of belief." *Windsor Yearbook of Access to Justice, 30*(1), 63–76.

Guardian. 2018, 31 May. "Denmark passes law banning burqa and niqab." https://www.theguardian.com/world/2018/may/31/denmark-passes-law-banning-burqa-and-niqab

Heneghan, Tom. 2015, 21 October. "Anniversary of France's niqab ban passes almost unnoticed." *Religion News Service*. https://religionnews.com/2015/10/20/anniversary-frances-niqab-ban-passes-almost-unnoticed

Hoodfar, Homa. 1993. "The veil in their minds and on our heads: The persistence of colonial images of Muslim women." *Resources for Feminist Research, 22*(3–4), 5–18.

– 2003. "More than clothing: Veiling as an adaptive strategy." In Sajida Sultana Alvi, Homa Hoodfar, and Sheila McDonough (Eds.), *The Muslim veil in North America: Issues and debates* (pp. 3–40). Women's Press.

Howard, Erica. 2014. "Islamic veil bans: The gender equality justification and empirical evidence." In Eva Brems (Ed.), *The experiences of face veil wearers in Europe and the law* (pp. 206–17). Cambridge University Press.

Inge, Anabel. 2016. *The making of a Salafi Muslim woman: Paths to conversion*. Oxford University Press.

Instelling van een gedeeltelijk verbod op het dragen van gezichtsbedekkende kelding in het onderwijs, het openbaar vervoer, overheids gebouwen en de zorg (Wet gedeeltelijk verbod gezichstbedekkende kleding). 2018, 26 April. Netherlands Parliamentary Paper 34 349.

Irwin Toy Ltd v. Québec (Attorney General). [1989] 1 SCR 927.

Ishaq v. Canada (Citizenship and Immigration). [2015] 4 FCR 297.

Ishaq v. Canada (Minister of Citizenship and Immigration). [2015] FCA 194.

Jacob, I.H. 1970. "The inherent jurisdiction of the court." *Current Legal Problems, 23*, 23–52.

Lewis, Reina. 2015. *Muslim fashion: Contemporary style cultures*. Duke University Press.

Loi du 1er juin 2011 visant à interdire le port de toute vêtement cachant totalement ou de manière principale le visage. 2011, 1 June. Belgium.

Loi no. 2010–1192 du 11 octobre 2010, JO. 2010, 11 October. France, 18344.

MacMillan Bloedel Ltd v. Simpson. [1995] 4 SCR 725.

Moors, Annelies. 2014. "Face veiling in the Netherlands: Public debates and women's narratives." In Eva Brems (Ed.), *The experiences of face veil wearers in Europe and the law* (pp. 19–41). Cambridge University Press.

Moutia Elzahed and Anors v. Commonwealth of Australia and State of NSW. [2016] NSWDC 327.

Muhammad v. Enterprise Rent-a-Car. 2006, 11 October. No. 06-41896-GC (Mich. 31st Dist. Ct.).

National Assembly. 2010, 26 January. Rapport d'information fait en application de l'article 145 du règle-mentau nom de la mission d'information sur la pratique du port du voile intégral sur le territoire national. http://www.assemblee-nationale.fr/13/pdf/rap-info/i2262.pdf

Østergaard, Kate, Margit Warburg, and Birgitte Schepelern Johansen. 2014. "Niqabis in Denmark: When politicians ask for a qualitative and quantitative profile of a very small and elusive subculture." In Eva Brems (Ed.), *The experiences of face veil wearers in Europe and the law* (pp. 42–76). Cambridge University Press.

Peritz, Ingrid. 2013, 2 October. "Québec Muslims facing more abuse since charter proposal, women's groups say." *Globe and Mail*. http://www.theglobeandmail.com/news/national/quebec-muslims-facing-more-abuse-since-charter-proposal-womens-groups-say/article14672348

– 2017, 27 October. "'It's going to encourage more hate': Women in Québec who wear niqab speak out against Bill 62." *Globe and Mail*. https://www.theglobeandmail.com/news/national/quebec-women-who-wear-the-niqab-fear-impact-of-bill-62/article36753623

Police v. Razamjoo. [2005] DCR 408 (DCNZ).

The Queen v. D(R). [2013, 16 September]. (Crown Court at Blackfriars) [unreported].

R. v. Butler. [1992] 1 SCR 452.

R. v. Keegstra. [1990] 3 SCR 697.

R. v. N.S. [2012] SCC 72.

R. v. Oakes. [1986] 1 SCR 103.

R. v. Sharpe. [1999] 169 DLR (4th) 536.

Rania El-Alloul c. Procureure générale du Québec and al. [2018] QCCA 1611.

Razack, Sherene H. 2004. "Imperilled Muslim women, dangerous Muslim men and civilised Europeans: Legal and social responses to forced marriages." *Feminist Legal Studies*, *12*(2), 129–74. https://doi.org/10.1023/B:FEST.0000043305.66172.92

– 2018. "A site/sight we cannot bear: The racial/spatial politics of banning the Muslim woman's niqab." *Canadian Journal of Women and the Law*, *30*(1), 169–89. http://doi.org/10.3138/cjwl.30.1.169

Rochelle, Safiyah. 2013. "Whether angel or devil: Law's knowing and unknowing of veiled Muslim women in the case of *R. v. N.S.*" Master's thesis, Carleton University. Carleton University Research Virtual Environment. https://doi.org/10.22215/etd/2013-09926

SAS v. France. [2014] ECHR 1 (GC).

Selby, Jennifer A. 2014. "Un/veiling women's bodies: Secularism and sexuality in full-face veil prohibitions in France and Québec." *Studies in Religion*, *43*(3), 439–66. https://doi.org/10.1177%2F0008429814526150

Sharify-Funk, Meena. 2011. "Governing the face veil: Quebec's Bill 94 and the transnational politics of women's identity." *International Journal of Canadian Studies*, *43*, 135–63. https://doi.org/10.7202/1009458ar

Shulman, Michael. 2015, 27 February. "Judge's refusal to hear case of woman in hijab left her in tears." CTV News. http://www.ctvnews.ca/canada/judge-s-refusal-to-hear-case-of-woman-in-hijab-left-her-in-tears-1.2256718

Siddiquea, Salma. 2017. In National Council of Canadian Muslims (NCCM) v. Attorney General of Quebec, [2017] QCCS 5459. Affidavit.

Sisters Project. n.d. "Aima." https://www.thesistersproject.ca/home/aima

Swedish Code of Judicial Procedure. [1998] D.S. 1998–000.

Switzman v. Elbling and AG of Quebec. [1957] SCR 285.

Syndicat Northcrest v. Amselem. [2004] SCC 47.

This Morning. 2017, 25 April. "Holly slams the proposed British burka ban." Video. https://www.youtube.com/watch?v=EtPzU41og-Q

Wahlquist, Calla. 2018, 18 July. "Victorian judge bans niqab in court's public gallery." *Guardian*. https://www.theguardian.com/australia-news/2018/jul/18/victorian-judge-bans-niqab-in-courts-public-gallery

Women's Legal Action and Education Fund. 2011. In R. v. N.S., 2012 SCC 72. Factum of the Intervener. http://www.leaf.ca/wp-content/uploads/2012/12/NS-SCC.pdf

Zine, Jasmin. 2012. "Introduction: Muslim cultural politics in the Canadian hinterlands." In Jasmin Zine (Ed.), *Islam in the hinterlands: Muslim cultural politics in Canada* (pp. 1–38). University of British Columbia Press.

Gendering Everyday Islam, Border-Crossings, and the Production of "Alternative Knowledge"

PARIN DOSSA

Introduction

The production of knowledge is a politicized endeavour, even more so in the case of Islam, which has been consistently subject to the Orientalist discourse (Said 1978). Particularly pertinent is the issue of gender, a potent symbol mobilized by the West for governance and militant intervention, as was the case with the 2001 US-led invasion of Afghanistan to purportedly "liberate" Muslim women. Rather than being a discrete entity, the subject matter of gender invokes entrenched inequalities based on race, religion, class, generation, and national heritage. My ethnographic engagement with Canadian Muslim women suggests that this intersectional context positions women to produce situated knowledges. Using the analytic of the everyday, I demonstrate how Canadian Muslim women complicate and interrogate a hegemonic understanding of Islam, subverting Orientalized images. Fluidity and movement embedded in border-crossings enable Muslim women to engage with an imaginative and alternative production of knowledge on Islam(s) in Canada and in the diaspora.

Using the case of Canadian Iranian women as an example, this chapter begins with a summary of Iranian migration to Canada post-1979 Revolution. I then explore the import of gendered everyday Islam, illustrating its significance in enabling women to acquire "mastery of the minutiae of everyday life as part of a deeper ethical project of self-transformation" (Liebelt and Werbner 2018, 2). Following a discussion on the burgeoning literature on everyday life (Das 2010; Ferrero 2018; Hirschkind 2014; Marsden 2005; Mendoza Carmona 2018; Selby et al. 2018), I present storied lives of two women, Sodabeh and Fahimeh, as they go about the everyday work of remaking a home in Canada.[1] I show that their work leads to the production of an alternative understanding of Islam. This form of knowledge is revealed in fragments, the importance of which cannot be dismissed lightly, as Das (2010) and Zine (2009) have illustrated. I argue that fragments constitute a tapestry with unfinished threads that require continual weaving. Rather than relaying textual or scripted knowledge on Islam, the women in my study sought to remake a home that connected to the outside world, locally and transnationally. For them the significance of such a connection lay in its potential for fostering social relations, a space and a place where their understanding of Islamic values could be recognized by society at large. I illustrate that it is only when Muslim women engage in a larger project, beyond self and community, that they can claim a sense of belonging in a country where they are structurally excluded. Such is the case with Muslims at large in the post-9/11 era.

Research Context: Iranian Women in Canada

The 1978–9 Iranian Revolution triggered waves of Iranian migration to Canada and other parts of the Western world (Dossa 2004; Mobasher 2012; Moghissi and Ghorashi 2010). Reasons cited by research respondents included factors such as persecution under an oppressive regime, gendered harassment by the morality police for improper donning of mandatory hijab, evasion of compulsory drafting of sons into the military, a deteriorating economic situation, and the search for better education and quality of life for the upcoming generation. Iranian immigrants were not prepared for the situation they encountered in their country of settlement. A primary concern raised was the deskilling process whereby their educational credentials and work experiences, acquired over several decades, were not recognized.[2] The women in my study considered this systemic exclusion. As forty-two-year-old Mahin expressed it, "Canadians do not understand how this exclusion changes our lives completely. Some of us came here for our children's education. Now we must go to school to obtain what they tell us is, 'Canadian experience.' Even if we upgrade our qualifications, we do not get hired for positions for which we are qualified." Mir's (2011) observation that citizenship as shared membership and rights of full participation is not realized for American Muslims captures Mahin's sentiments. Their experience of not getting a job in their area of expertise is the lens through which the women became aware of their exclusion within public spaces such as shopping, visits to physicians, and everyday interactions. Rather than exclusively engaging with acts of discrimination, study participants adopted a counter stance of what Mahin referred to as "reaching out." In the way of an example, she observed, "I said 'hello' to a Canadian [White] woman in the parking lot of Safeway. She did not respond. I told myself, 'She must not have had her coffee today. Next time she will respond.'" It is this approach of carving out an inclusive[3] space in everyday life that caught my attention. Given the complexity of having to straddle two cultures, I asked myself: How did respondents go about negotiating this delicate terrain? Of critical importance was the fact that they were keen to take their place in Canadian society by foregrounding transformative change, even if this transformation was not immediately realized. The respondents were convinced that reversal of the Orientalist discourse to which they were subject could best take place in the context of everyday life, where the project of remaking an Islamic home loomed large.

It is with this focus in mind that I conducted ethnographic research on Iranian women in metropolitan Vancouver. It is important to note that the women are from the Shi'a school of thought compared with the majority of Sunnis. Being from the minority group, the women felt that their distinction from the Sunnis was sharper; yet in general they sought to speak for Islam as a whole to strengthen their position as a racialized community in Canada. My first encounter with the participants took place in 2002 (Dossa 2004); thereafter I engaged with women from different sectors of life in 2007 (Dossa 2009), and more recently, I undertook further research between 2015 and 2017. As is the case with ethnographic research, I sought to explore multiple meanings of home, family, and religiosity in the wake of being Othered. My research involved in-depth conversations with individuals, focus groups, and participant observations of formal and informal settings; some of the work took place within the service sector while other research occurred in homes and cafeterias. Ongoing interviews, with the help of Farsi-speaking research assistants, enabled me to see the interrelationship between different topics brought to light by the women in their own terms, using Farsi or English as they preferred. Furthermore, themes from interview transcripts were reviewed between meetings for preliminary analysis of data. As I am a South Asian Muslim woman myself, some of the respondents shared intimate experiences with me, while others felt more reticent, perhaps assuming I would fill in the blanks. By and large, the women engaged in storytelling, a genre that allowed them to share or withhold information as they wished. In this chapter, I focus on the experiences of two women who migrated to Canada in the late 1980s. Their stories reveal that home is not a discrete space; its connection to the outside world is complicated and contradictory.

Analytic of Everyday Life

This study is informed by the analytic of everyday life conceptualized as an ongoing process of negotiations and interactions. Scholars have noted multiple ways in which everyday life reveals the workings of structural forces along with affirmation of subjectivities. Space of the everyday "has a normative moral power that cannot be and should not be underestimated" (Liebelt and Werbner 2018, 5). In the same vein, Abu-Lughod (1993) calls for re-valorization of the everyday as a means of recovering our common humanity. Based on our understanding of women's individual lives, she makes a strong claim for alternative ways of being whereby we "ask ourselves how we could contribute to making the world a more just place … a place where certain kinds of forces and values that we consider important could have a wider appeal" (2016, 49). Hence, it is important to recognize materiality and spirituality of everyday life, overlooked as too mundane.

There is renewed focus on everyday Islam post-9/11, a period when being a Muslim in the West is equated with Otherness. As Shirazi and Mishra (2010) have observed, "Since the 9/11 attacks, renewed Orientalist constructions of difference have permeated the representations of Muslims in media and popular culture" (179; cf. Zine 2004, 184). This attention has compelled Muslims from different walks of life to engage with and redefine what Islam means to them, highlighting its relevance to society, locally and transnationally (for example, Mirza 2013, Shirazi and Mishra 2010). Of special import is gendering of everyday Islam, a development brought about by two factors: Western perception of Muslim women as oppressed and in need of rescuing from a patriarchal culture, and Muslim women's interrogation of Islamic fundamentalist patriarchy – "the nexus of dual oppression" (Zine 2006, 239). Being a Muslim holds different meanings for women based on their positionality in terms of age, nationality, class, ethnicity, and other embodied intersectional attributes. This focus requires us to look at "situated ways racialized and gendered boundaries are produced and lived through a faith-based Muslim female subjectivity" (Mirza 2013, 6). *Beyond Accommodation*, the co-authored volume of Selby et al. (2018), is illustrative; the authors document how Muslims in Canada navigate and negotiate their religiosity in the context of everyday life.

Gendering everyday Islam has largely focused on young Muslim women on the assumption that they are in a better position than their male counterparts to negotiate multiple and often-contradictory realities in the 9/11 era. In their work on young American Muslim women, for example, Shirazi and Mishra (2010) argue that women's own interpretation of Islam makes it possible for them to transgress and subvert dominant meanings while negotiating new ones. Citing the example of three professional Muslim women residing in Britain, Mirza (2013) explores ways in which they "negotiate the affective 'postcolonial disjunctures' of racism and Islamophobia" (5), challenging and transforming hegemonic discourse on race, gender, and religion. Recognizing that their status as "naturalized citizens" in post-9/11 America is problematized, young Muslim women in Mir's (2011) study assume multiple and shifting identities. Likewise, citing the example of hijab, Ahmed (2005) observes, "By taking on the hijab, young American Muslim women made visible their Muslimness and resisted connotations of inferiority attached to the Muslim Other" (127); in other situations, they sought to pass as non-Muslims. This is because Muslim women are in a position "to draw on meaningful diasporic communities of belonging across a number of nation states" (Mirza 2013, 9) to reconfigure their identities. Through voice or performance, young Muslim women challenge the stereotypes of being constructed as voiceless and subdued. Regardless of their mode of representation, their collective efforts amount to "just to make sure people know I was born here" (Mir 2011). By and large, studies on young Muslim women have focused on identity politics negotiated in the context of everyday Islam, along with their positionality as diasporic subjects. In this chapter, I focus on first-generation Iranian women: a grandmother and a mother. This choice is informed by their different trajectories of migration unfolding on the terrain of everyday lived spaces. Here, the production of alternative knowledge on Islam is informed by the fraught process of remaking a home. In short, study participants' understandings of everyday Islam were grounded in their search for a home, not conceived as a discrete unit but considered in terms of local and transnational connections. For them, home was a place of connectivity, a nexus point of activities that brought together kin and non-kin networks. Indeed, this constituted a feminist task that requires recognition. It is through the work of these women that the outside and the inside are intricately connected, ultimately leading to a reimagined diasporic home. It is in this context that the women claimed their own nuanced and unique ways to live Islam, utilizing border-crossing knowledge.

As a dynamic tradition and a religion, spanning temporally over 1,400 years and spatially across the globe, Islam does not exist within its own orbit. It has invariably addressed societal concerns. Zine (2004) has aptly noted that knowledge on Islam

> can enter academic dialogues and inquiries not as static dogma but as contextualized and historicized paradigm of thought that is referenced in metaphysical realities. They are not intended to operate as new grand narratives but, instead, can function in dialogical manner with other discourses and paradigms that may have a more secular foundation. (184)

Global migration has created space for the reinterpretation of Islamic traditions embedded in between the boundaries of nation states. For Sodabeh and Fahimeh, living in Canada means that what they have to say has implications as to how this nation state is structured and could be reconfigured through their situated understanding of lived Islam "here" (country of settlement) and "there" (homeland). Towards this end, both the women subvert and transform dominant meanings of home while negotiating new ones even though this is a fractured experience.

Sodabeh: "Please Solve the Housing Problem"

I met Sodabeh at the Iranian coffee hour, which constituted part of the mall walking program organized by a seniors' committee on the North Shore—home of the Canadian Iranian community.[4] Like other elderly women and men,

Sodabeh was concerned that they did not have a place that they could call home. Her family was dispersed following the Iranian Revolution: two of her children are in the United States, one child lives in Australia, and the other two (a daughter and a son) live on the North Shore. Both these families have children; hence there is not much space in their three-bedroom condominium for Sodabeh and her husband. Sodabeh and her husband live by themselves in a rented apartment. My conversations with families revealed that while it was preferable for the elderly to live with their married sons, this arrangement proved to be difficult in Canada. The main issue identified was that of space. Couples felt that the two- or three-bedroom condominiums could not accommodate their parents as their children required their own space to study. Behazin (a research participant) put it this way: "In Iran our door was open. Visitors dropped in and because of the number of people in and out, we hardly felt cramped. But here, there is no open door for people to drop in. Things are different here." Not having an open door meant little time for socialization, an activity that included realization of Islamic values and ethics lived in everyday life. Sodabeh was concerned that if she had lived with her grandchildren, they would have learnt from her experiential knowledge on what it is like to live, as she said, "the Islamic way." In Canada, she had to work to create space where the Islamic way of life could be activated within what she perceived as a home with connections to the outside world.

Sodabeh observed:

> My son has two children, a boy and a girl. The children had one room and we had one room. They are growing up and they need to have separate rooms. They have homework and they need space to study. We felt out of place. In Iran it was different. We owned a house and our children lived with us. We sold it at a cheap price as we had to leave the country. When you have your own house, you can have visitors. In our son's apartment, it is not easy to have friends. We feel isolated and lonely. It is better if we live in senior's housing. I heard there are Iranian seniors living there. We are living by ourselves in an apartment, but the rent is too high.

Later she continued,

> There are so many issues. In Iran, we played a role in raising our grandchildren. We taught them values. What is good and what is bad. They learnt from us about the struggles of life, about religion and lessons from the great poets of Iran.

Sodabeh does not make explicit reference to Islam per se. For her it constitutes part of everyday life beginning with greetings such as *Salaam* (peace), *Inshallah* (if Allah wishes), and *Khuda Hafiz* (may God be always with you), among others. More importantly, for her and the women in my study, Islamic values could best be realized through action and conversations. Everyday examples included visiting a sick neighbour, paying respects to the family of a deceased person, and being kind and helpful. The latter was the general principle, but it does not mean that it was followed to the letter. Hierarchical relationships are at work in all societies. The women remembered the Islamic norms because of their "absence" in their country of settlement. As Renna (a research participant) put it, "Neighbours are strangers."

Convinced that seniors' housing would be the best arrangement for her and hehusband, Sodabeh approached B.C. Housing. Her initial experiences were not positive. She asked for assistance three times to fill out the required forms at the service centre for immigrants, but she did not receive any help. Sodabeh stated, "I know some English, but I did not understand the meaning of the questions," itself not an unusual situation even for English-speaking seniors. Eventually a seniors' centre helped her with the application. It is interesting to note that she did not seek assistance from her children. She repeatedly informed me that "they are busy and should not be bothered." Not having access to the children on a day-to-day basis constitutes a rupturing of everyday life with its grounding in the home. The unavailability of children is attributed to neoliberalism with its emphasis on individualism, self-care, and orientation towards nuclear families (for example, Foley 2008; Ganti 2014). Recognizing the busyness of her family, Sodabeh turned to other sources conducive to fostering social relationships. She would often go for walks hoping to meet people. Consider the following narrative fragment: "I make it a point to go out every day."

Sodabeh goes out in the mornings. She said it was for the purpose of shopping to search for bargains. This meant she would go to different stores. When I accompanied her on one occasion, she informed me,

> It is important that I go out. This way I can meet people. I say "hello" to the cashiers. Some of them are nice and talk to me; others are not. If I go to an Iranian store, I talk to the owner for some time. We exchange news on Iran. Sometimes, I meet my Iranian friends on the street. We talk about life in Canada and the life we left behind.

As I got to know Sodabeh, I realized that going out and meeting people was one way in which she created space for the realization of core Islamic values as she understood them. She observed, "Being kind and helpful to others, sharing your understanding of life with others and being there to give a listening ear to someone gives meaning to my life. This is my way of practising Islam in everyday life." Sodabeh was disappointed when she realized that she had not been informed that her neighbour's mother had passed away. "If I had known, I would have gone to her house and taken her a dish even if she is a Canadian [women in my study referred to "White people" as Canadians and themselves as Iranians, revealing the gap between the two groups]. Human beings are human beings. I will go and say Salaam to her and offer prayers. I think she will like this."

Continuing the narrative, Sodabeh says:

> B.C. Housing gave me an apartment in a condominium that was built behind the Earl's Restaurant and I did not like it. It was far from the bus stop as my husband and I have arthritis and we are not able to walk too far, especially when we must carry our shopping; and the place was on a quiet area and it was on the first floor and I got scared as someone could get into our house easily. Also, the apartment smelled like urine as the previous tenant was a senior without the control of urine. I asked the manager to change the carpet, but they did not accept that. So, I did not accept the apartment. After that we have not heard from them. It is now three years that we have applied for B.C. Housing.

Remembering is a politicized act undertaken to critique the system. Sodabeh's struggles for housing, which for her was a home with social connections, makes her remember the life she left behind. She observed that in Iran they had a car, a house, and a villa. They had to abandon the life they had known for almost a lifetime because "the new regime fired my husband as he worked for the Shah's government." Her daughter was harassed by the morality police as she did not "cover herself properly." The couple was forced to sell their property at a loss. Furthermore, they lost money given to a broker who had promised to facilitate their move to Turkey. Their forced migration to Canada was and remains painful as "my husband has not been able to secure any kind of work."

Sodabeh feels that in Canada, she must undertake shopping trips to save money. She and her husband go shopping several times in a week.

> I go to different stores for shopping. I look for items on sale so sometimes I go to Save-on-Foods, or Safeway or Super Value at Park Royal Mall. I buy fruits and vegetables from Chinese stores. There are two Chinese stores around us, one close to Save-on-Foods and the other close to Park Royal Mall. Both have fresh fruits and vegetables and the prices are reasonable. I usually look at the flyers and compare prices. I usually don't go to Iranian stores as the prices are high and we cannot afford them. Sometimes I buy bread [Iranian] and Rose Tea from an Iranian store. This store is close to Save-On-Food as the price is less than other stores. Today I told my husband that our income is not enough and that we could no longer afford to buy skinless and boneless breast chicken. I buy whole chicken and then clean it up. This is extra work for me.

For Sodabeh, shopping was also a means to interact with people, regardless of their nationality or race. Commenting on photos of family and friends during one of my visits, she observed how she missed socializing on a day-to-day basis. As I learnt from my conversations with other women, female-centred socialization was significant as it was through this activity that they exchanged notes on issues such as children's education, health, and celebration of festivals such as Idd (or Eid, a religious festival that occurs twice a year) and Nurooz (New Year), along with concerns of everyday life. These conversations did not exclude references to the Qur'an as situations required them. Death or illness of a person evoked phrases such as "May Allah rest his/her soul in peace" and "may he/she be blessed." Sodabeh and other women in my study emphasized how much they missed social interactions that I learned were not merely instrumental but also a means of affirming their Muslim/Iranian identities in Canada. The women considered this an important aspect of their lives. "If you do not know who you are in this new country, what values will you impart to others?" Sodabeh's search for a home can be understood in this context. For her and her cohort, Islam could best be realized through social interactions where core values of this tradition are activated interactively, not in isolation.

The settlement programs fall under the category of therapeutic interventions underpinned by the need to "integrate" newcomers into the fabric of Canadian society. This politicized agenda leaves limited room for a repertoire of knowledge and skills embedded in evolving religious traditions and cultures like Islam. My reading of Sodabeh's search for a home suggests that she sought to reverse an inward-looking orientation of nation states, where hegemonic traditions and ways of life are foregrounded at the expense of subduing other traditions. The production of knowledge on Islam(s) with its border-crossing insights must be recognized if we are to write a different narrative, one where minority cultures and traditions are acknowledged in terms of their contribution to such sectors as health, education, and social service programs.

Following scholarship on acknowledging the everyday worlds of socially marginalized women (for example, Long 2013), I give central space to Sodabeh's work of shopping a couple of times a week to stretch her budget. Considering her arthritic condition, her age, and her use of public transport, her shopping can indeed be considered "work." In a later conversation, Sodabeh talked about the people she met while shopping:

> I like to go shopping as it is here that I meet people. When I am in my apartment, I do not meet anyone. We watch television. I see my neighbour in the elevator, but she does not talk to me. When I am shopping, I talk to the cashier. When I first came to Canada seventeen years ago, I could not talk to the cashier. I would just give her the goods with the money. She would give me the change. But now I can talk in English. The other day, it was her birthday. Some people were greeting her. I also said happy birthday in English and then in Farsi. She was happy that I also greeted her in Farsi.

During her shopping trips, Sodabeh exchanged notes with her peers on what may appear to be mundane matters, such as prices of products and best places to shop. On some occasions, the women talked about home remedies for colds and coughs and issues related to their children and grandchildren, revolving largely around struggles to maintain an Iranian way of life and adapt to their unfamiliar environment where racism looms large. The women I conversed with informed me that cumulatively the notes exchanged made a difference in terms of their identities as Muslims or Iranians. Identity politics surfaced in their conversations. The women explored the often-asked question, Where are you from? They noted that depending on the questioner, they would say, "I am an Iranian," "I am a Muslim," "I am a global citizen," or "I am a Canadian." Adoption of shifting identifies assisted the women in claiming a sense of belonging while circumventing judgments from outsiders. Only when they felt comfortable that they foregrounded their goal and that was "to be a good person," an understanding grounded in Islamic values.

Sodabeh's last words to me were: "Please solve the housing problem." For Sodabeh and her cohort, home was not a discrete entity. Her remembrance (embodied memories) included a milieu. She portrayed a mental map of her home as being connected to other homes in her neighbourhood; she also mapped connections to a place where she shopped, the office of her doctor, and the schools that her grandchildren attended. Consider her portrait of everyday life in Iran:

> I always kept busy in the house. There was so much work, cooking and cleaning and shopping. Our son and his two children lived with us. My daughter-in-law worked part-time. I was happy. I did not know where my day went. Sometimes I would be cooking, and a neighbour would come by to get yogurt culture. Then we would sit and chat. I would go to my neighbour's house if I ran out of an ingredient like sugar or flour. When my husband came home from work, we would go to the nearby store to pick up groceries. We had parties and celebrations. I was happy until the Revolution took this life away from us.

Sodabeh's account assumes significance in the diaspora. Her recall of her everyday life is in relation to her home in Canada. One's sense of belonging in a new place begins in the home. My visits to the homes of other women revealed a hybrid formation. Depending on the material resources of the family, their homes contained items categorized under modern consumption: modern furniture, kitchen gadgets, electronics such as TV and DVD player and computer. At the same time, their homes included Iranian decor such as carpets, paintings, and beautifully woven tablecloths and other coverings. Invariably, I was served Iranian tea with nuts and raisins brought from Iran by a friend or relative or purchased from an Iranian store. The combination of Iranian and Canadian decor symbolizes creativity in terms of making a home away from home. Yet, as I learnt from Sodabeh's testimonial narrative (capturing the situation of her cohort), this reconfigured home is not a discrete unit. Sodabeh is concerned that her home in Canada does not have an external avenue for fostering sociality. "I have no one to talk to unless I go out and the places where I go are food stores where I see people and maybe talk to them."

My reading of Sodabeh's narrative suggests a deep-level search for a home – an aspect missed by service organizations that seek to assist immigrants to settle down in a new country. Sodabeh wishes to establish a home that extends into the world of sociality, not a place of fear from potential attacks. Her agency comes into place first through assuming the position of a protagonist (she authors her own narrative) and second through shopping several times a week. She looks for items on sale and acquaints herself with produce stores near her house. She shops at several places to save money, but the element of meeting and talking to people is not totally absent. At times when she is shopping, she meets her Iranian friends. She loves going to the Iranian store even for one or two items, as it is here that she can speak Farsi to the shopkeeper and other customers. Sodabeh's reimagining of home in a broader sense may be explained with reference to the moral economy. This means that her work in stretching her budget is intertwined with her social need to meet and interact with people, not excluding mainstream persons. For Sodabeh, home and its reimagining amounts to giving a human face to the market economy, an aspect that she and her cohort considered the "norm" in their country of birth. Sodabeh's reimagining of home in Canada is that of a place that connects to external spaces – shops, streets, and neighbours. On the other hand, B.C. Housing's perception of home is that of a place of shelter. The gap between the two images needs to be addressed if we are to ensure that the humanity of displaced persons is not compromised. Maintaining one's humanity is a function of being able to activate one's cultural and religious traditions dynamically in the context of an interactive and intersubjective milieu. This is what Sodabeh seeks to achieve in her efforts to reimagine a home, a home that would allow her (not excluding her progeny) to be a good person not in an abstract way but through activation of Islamic values that could ultimately have a wider appeal.

"Home Is Neither Here nor There"

The above was Fahimeh's observation during our conversation at the English as a Second Language (ESL) program, run by a settlement agency. Fahimeh worked here as a part-time translator with minimal wages and no benefits. She migrated to Canada in 1985 with her husband and two children aged ten and twelve. The family was admitted to Canada under the independent immigrant category, as both she and her husband Ali are medical professionals and fluent in English.

She is a psychiatric nurse and he is a paediatrician. Contrary to what they were told by the immigration officials, they were not able to get jobs in their areas of expertise. Their respective professional organizations informed them that without Canadian qualifications they would not be able to practise in Canada. Fahimeh was shocked: "If we both went to school to requalify, who will support us? We have just come into the country. We need to settle down. We came here for our children's education." Realizing that they would not be able to work in their destination country, the couple were compelled to make a difficult choice. Ali returned to Iran and continued practising his profession. Fahimeh stayed behind to take care of the children. Ali visited his family once or twice a year; one of the visits took place during Nurooz (the Persian New Year). As the children became more acculturated to the way of life in Canada, Fahimeh felt lonely.

> My children had activities and they started going out with their friends. There were times when I felt very lonely and even depressed. I would go to the mall and buy clothes. The week after, I would go back and return the clothes. I was just killing time. I started looking at newspapers. I saw that they [settlement services] needed a part-time translator – someone who spoke Farsi as well as English. I applied and was hired. I thought maybe I can change my career. This job required me to work with ESL teachers, the seniors and multicultural health workers. The pay was very little. I worked for twenty hours a week. I have not been able to progress in this work. Besides, I find myself doing extra work for which I am not paid. The women [Iranian] get hold of me in the corridor. They have questions about services, bus routes and doctors. It is endless. I find it difficult to say "no." I tell myself, "perhaps this is the work of a psychiatric nurse in this country."

Fahimeh's experiences were not unique. Some of the women in my study had parallel stories of husbands returning to Iran and wives taking on the nurturing role in the diaspora. While one may envision this as women continuing with their traditional role, this was not the case. The women undertook the most critical task of reimagining home in a new country. Reconstitution of a home entailed a creative process whereby memories and core values from homeland and destination countries are negotiated, are juxtaposed, or exist in a state of tension. Emerging contradictions were not necessarily resolved but lived with. It is in this context that we can view women's self-identified role as bearers of religious and cultural traditions, viewed dynamically in the context of everyday life. The hardship of families living apart cannot be underestimated. Life in Iran was less stressful for the returning husbands, as many had kin networks in place. The experiences of women in the diaspora proved to be more complex. Their primary role of nurturing entailed straddling two disparate cultures – Iranian and Canadian – in the wake of systemic and structural racism.

Fahimeh worked for seven years as a translator, after which time she felt exhausted. "I could not continue. What I was in Iran [meaning a professional] and what I am now. I am doing mindless work here." Her children had grown up and the family had acquired citizenship status. Fahimeh was relatively free to move back and forth between Iran and Canada. She recalled cooking a variety of meals and freezing them for her husband in Iran and freezing them for her children in Canada during her sojourn in these two places. Her home, she noted, was "there" and "here." Once the children completed high school, Fahimeh and Ali sent them to a university in the United States. "We wanted them to have the best education so they do not have to struggle like we did. If they have qualifications from the United States, they could work anywhere in the world. We want them to become global citizens."

At the beginning of my research, I had explained to Fahimeh that my work would be enriched if she invited me to accompany her on some of the tasks she performed every day; shopping was one of them. Fahimeh was accompanied by her daughter, Rehana, on the day I joined her. At the cashier at a superstore, there was a woman with a baby seated on a buggy fully filled with groceries. Although Fahimeh was in the front with only a few items, she let her go first. The woman thanked her. It was a silent gesture of goodwill. For Fahimeh, small gestures mattered. Such acts embodied "important values on living and life. For me, they come from my religion and culture." During my subsequent conversations with Fahimeh, I learned that she wanted Rehana to learn what constitutes a good person. When I asked her to further explain its meaning she said,

> I want my children to know that one day we are going to die. I would like them to be kind and help people when they can. These are deeper values not apparent in this society. There is pressure to buy and buy to no end. This kind of life does not contain values. You only think of yourself and not of others. In Islam, the most important aspect is to look at the world around you. To see if you can make it a better place. To keep in mind that there are people who may need your help even if this means just listening to them.
>
> You know, the lifestyle I see here is also becoming the lifestyle in Iran. I tell my children to think. If they read the Qur'an or the work of great Iranian poets, it will help them to see that that there is more to life than just earn to spend on yourself.

When I engaged Fahimeh on the question of Islamic practices such as halal meat, prayers, hijab, alcohol, and fasting, she said:

> I don't think I would like to tell my children what they should practice. In our home in Iran these practices were followed as a matter of course by everyone within our families, neighbourhoods and communities. Here, there are no "families" or

> neighbourhoods. Nobody is going to judge you if you eat halal meat or observe prayers. I think, people must decide for themselves as to what is important. And this decision must be informed by what makes you a good person. If you eat halal meat and if you observe fasting, it is no good if you are not kind to other people. What is important is your interactions with others.

During my last visit to Fahimeh, she informed me that she was planning to move back to Iran and that their children would visit them during the holidays. She added, "But Canada is our home. We have an apartment and once a year our whole family gathers here. We are Canadian citizens." She ruled out the possibility of living in Iran because her children had become acculturated to life in the so-called Western world. Identifying characteristic features from both the countries, Fahimeh observed, "In Canada [Vancouver] we can enjoy a good life as there is less traffic and not much pollution. We can live comfortably here. In Iran we have our families and memories that are with us. You cannot completely leave your home. It always remains with you in your heart, don't you think?"

My reading of Fahimeh's narrative brings to light two interrelated scripts: structural constraints and reimagining a transnational/diasporic home. As we have observed, she was separated from her husband for long periods of time. She related that there were a couple of times when he could not visit the family as scheduled during Nurooz – the most celebrated event in Iran, also the time for extended family to get together. My short visits to Iran (in 2003 and 2006) indicated that there were occasions when the changing global scenario was discussed in the form of a question: In this consumerist world, how do we continue to practise our faith and impart values to our children? This question assumed greater importance in the West, where the challenges of being a racialized minority were immense. Simply put, collectively the issue is how we maintain our religious or cultural practices and adapt to a world where Muslims are not well received, especially in the post-9/11 era. As Fahimeh's children grew up, they became distant: "I could not relate to my children. They were behaving like Canadian kids. They wanted to go to parties and eat Canadian food. I insisted that we speak Farsi at home but between them they would talk in English using words that I could not relate to. I felt that they lived in a different world, part of the time." Fahimeh's sentiments were shared by other study participants. At issue was emotional distance. She relayed that when Ali insisted that their children continue their education in the United States, Fahimeh was unhappy, as she felt that they would be Americanized, which for her meant individualized. Ali felt that after what the couple had gone through, living separately, it was necessary that their children acquire global credentials that would enable them to work "in any part of the world." The price, for Fahimeh, was heavy. It distanced her from the children in varying degrees, but it also compelled her to explore the meaning of a transnational home.

When I met Fahimeh during one of her visits to Vancouver, she observed, "My children are well educated. Having lived apart, I now feel close to them. They visit Iran and they also come to Vancouver when we are here. Canada is our home in some ways. It is a base from which we can travel to Iran and other countries in the world. My son will be taking up a job in Australia. We will visit him there." In response to my question on how much she had to give up (her career and her husband for long periods of time), she said, "Yes. I had to give up the most. But now we can move around. Our home is here and there."

Fahimeh's reimagining of home has taken the form of establishing family life beyond national borders, a position that resonates with Rouse's observation on the back-and-forth movement of Mexicans from their home country to the United States. Conceptualizing this movement as "transnational migrant circuit," he observes, "and they may send their children back to Mexico to complete their education or to visit during school vacations at least in part because they want to endow them with the bilingual and bicultural skills necessary to operate effectively on both sides of the border" (Soto 2012, 30). For Fahimeh, endowing her children with bilingual and multicultural skills is not enough. She is keen that her children acquire what she referred to as "values and ethics," which she simplified (in the form of a refrain) as being kind, generous, and a good person. In a transnational setting (Iran, Canada, and the United States), Fahimeh felt that it was a challenge to what we may refer to as the production of knowledge on Islam(s) within the boundaries of a nation state such as Canada. She noted, "Every time I talk to my children on the phone, I remind them of the importance of our values and that they must not be forsaken in our material world. Being a good person is what we have inherited from our parents. If we do not have values, how can we live in today's world? You know, it is a struggle. It is difficult to maintain values when we live in different places."

What Fahimeh has foregrounded can be referred to "as a space of possibility," to borrow Mattingly's (2010) term. Her comments echo Fahimeh's efforts to remake a home "here" and "there":

> Despite the immense power of oppressive social structures, reality is not summed up by their existence. It is not more real to disclose our imprisonment within everyday life than to disclose the possibilities for transformation that this life also admits. Ordinary people can and do still act, even in their ordinary contexts. They sometimes do struggle to remake their lives in the most remarkably barren social circumstances. And sometimes these struggles make a difference. (Mattingly 2010, 33).

Conclusion

Making a difference is how I understood the project undergirding this volume. My research suggests that this goal is a fraught endeavour because of structural factors that constrain and limit the contributions of racialized minorities, exacerbated in the case of Muslims unduly targeted as the Other in the aftermath of 9/11. We may note that anti-Muslim sentiments shape the agendas of political parties in the Western world, exemplified by former president Donald Trump, whose 2017-imposed travel ban was targeted at Muslims. What is not recognized is that the displacement of Muslims from their homelands is brought about primarily by Western intervention to promote its political agendas. This script remains buried. The West in alliance with regional powers such as Saudi Arabia is barely implicated for its acts of killing, maiming, and displacing thousands of Muslims so much so that we have lost count of lives lost in countries such as Afghanistan, Iraq, Syria, Libya, Palestine, and Yemen. This is one part of the narrative framed as "rescue mission" to which scholars like Abu-Lughod (2016) take objection, claiming that such a mission does not advance social-political rights of Muslim women. The second part comes into play with the migration of displaced Muslims to the West, though only a handful (typically the most privileged) are selected based on strict immigration policies. The question that arises for consideration is this: How do Muslim immigrants fare in a country responsible for their uprootment, not overlooking local factors in their homelands? In her response to the highly charged situation following 9/11, Sunera Thobani (2003, 399) noted, "I am here because you were there." Rather than being passive in the wake of Orientalism and Islamophobia, Muslim immigrants' responses have been as follows. First, they have sought to reverse the homogenized construct of a static and supposedly "barbaric" religion of Islam. Muslim female scholars have been particularly vocal, identifying themselves as belonging to a dynamic religion, unfolding contextually and situationally on the plane of everyday life (for example, Thobani 2003; Zine 2004, 2006). Second, Muslim women have struggled to claim citizenship rights, nationally and transnationally. The latter comes into play as it is within in-between spaces of nation states that the generation of "alternative" knowledge on Islam(s) takes place, reinterpreted and reconfigured in relation to the larger society.

The above context has informed my focus on the production of Islam(s) in Canada. My ethnographic research with first-generation Iranian women highlighted two themes. First, not all the women were comfortable making direct references to the Qur'an and other Islamic texts. This reluctance is because the women wanted to distance themselves from what they perceived as extreme forms of Islam advocated by the Islamic Republic of Iran, an iconic example of which is mandatory veiling. Second, study respondents were aware of the negative images of Islam circulating in popular culture, mainstream media, and state institutions. Respondents thus did not focus on textual Islam. Instead the women emphasized the importance of being "a good person," which in their view reflected Islamic values such as being kind, generous, and helpful – values that they perceived could best be realized in the context of sociality and intersubjectivity. The women saw their task as that of remaking a home connected with the outside world, not unlike Long's (2013) study of two Palestinian British women who engaged with a similar project of diasporic dwelling, "an ongoing attempt to draw these interior and exterior worlds into a desired alignment: an attempt which is enabled and constrained by the physical spaces and social surroundings in which we live and within which we attempt to make a home" (5).

The notion of a "home away from home" is not an uncommon concept in a world of mobility and migration. But the women in my study were acutely aware of their "forced" migration to Canada. They had not planned to leave the country of their birth, where they had lived, worked, socialized, celebrated ritual and life cycle events, and mourned the deaths of kin and kith. Racialized minorities do not enjoy substantive citizenship entitlements in Canada. It is from this socially marginalized position that the women undertook the task of reimagining an interconnected home within which Islamic values could be realized in everyday life. Their work was ruptured owing to their less than amicable reception in the host country. Nevertheless, their efforts within these ruptured spaces must be recognized; the women do not merely speak for themselves but speak for society at large. This is a politicized move of significance as the women are engaged in reversing the societal pressure towards integration. Deploying what they consider to be Islamic values (being kind, generous, and helpful – a good person), they make the effort towards including others while suggesting structural transformation. The house is then a home (Sodabeh), and a home is the unit that exists in between the spaces of nation states (Fahimeh). Their reimagining of home echoes Boehm's (2012) analytical insights on transnational Mexicans. She notes,

> The narratives and lives of transnational Mexicans illustrate the challenges to creating home and structuring family within a world of movement … Among transnational Mexicans, expressions of home and configurations of family are made up of parts and totalities, inconsistencies and continuities, divisions and connections. (51)

The process of reimagining home that the women envision reaches out and draws together border-crossing experiences; this move constitutes a past that is remembered and reimagined and a future that is hoped for as a possibility. They seek to forge and maintain connections for themselves and the world at large. As such, they invite others to weave an expanding tapestry of connectedness and solidarity where humane values (Islamic and others) could be activated even if these are on a small scale, embedded in realities of everyday life.

NOTES

1 To maintain anonymity, names and identifying markers have been modified.

2 For a broader understanding of structural and systemic exclusion, refer to Dossa 2004; Mir 2011; Mirza 2013; Thobani 2003.

3 It is interesting to note that it is racialized Iranian women seeking to include "White Canadians" rather than the other way around.

4 The first wave of Iranian Muslims was drawn towards the North Shore (Vancouver) because in their words, "the mountains reminded us of Tehran," the city they came from (Dossa 2004).

REFERENCES

Abu-Lughod, Lila. 1993. "Finding a place for Islam: Egyptian television serials and the national interest." *Public Culture, 5*(3), 493–513. https://doi.org/10.1215/08992363-5-3-493

– 2016. "The cross-publics of ethnography: The case of 'the Muslim woman.'" *American Ethnologist, 43*(4), 595–608. https://doi.org/10.1111/amet.12377

Ahmed, N. 2005. "Women in between: The case of Bangladeshi women living in London." In K.B. Tapan (Ed.), *Transnational migration and the politics of identity* (pp. 99–129). SAGE.

Boehm, Christopher. 2012. *Moral origins: The evolution of virtue, altruism, and shame.* Soft Skull Press.

Das, Veena. 2010. "Engaging the life of the Other: Love and everyday life." In Michael Lambek (Ed.), *Ordinary ethics: Anthropology, language, and action* (pp. 376–99). Fordham University Press.

Dossa, Parin. 2004. *Politics and the poetics of migration: Narratives of Iranian women from the diaspora.* Canadian Scholars' Press.

– 2009. *Racialized bodies, disabling worlds: Storied lives of immigrant Muslim women.* University of Toronto Press.

Ferrero, Laura. 2018. "Gendering Islam through migration: Egyptian women's gatherings in a mosque in Turin (Italy)." *Contemporary Levant, 3*(1), 20–31. https://doi.org/10.1080/20581831.2018.1455350

Foley, Ellen. 2008. "Neoliberal reform and health dilemmas." *Medical Anthropology Quarterly, 22*(3), 257–73. https://doi.org/10.1111/j.1548-1387.2008.00025.x

Ganti, Tejaswini. 2014. "Neoliberalism." *Annual Review of Anthropology, 43*, 89–104. https://doi.org/10.1146/annurev-anthro-092412-155528

Hamdan, Aisha. 2007. "A case study of a Muslim client: Incorporating religious beliefs and practices." *Journal of Multicultural Counseling and Development, 35*(2), 92–100. https://doi.org/10.1002/j.2161-1912.2007.tb00052.x

Hirschkind, Charles. 2014. "Everyday Islam: Commentary by Charles Hirschkind." Curated Collections. *Cultural Anthropology.* Retrieved 14 December 2014 from https://journal.culanth.org/index.php/ca/everyday-islam-charles-hirschkind

Liebelt, Claudia, and Prina Werbner. 2018. "Gendering 'everyday Islam': An introduction." *Contemporary Levant, 3*(1), 2–9. https://doi.org/10.1080/20581831.2018.1449932

Long, Lucy M. 2013. "Culinary tourism." In David M. Kaplan (Ed.), *Encyclopedia of food and agricultural ethics* (pp. 1–8). Springer. https://doi.org/10.1007/978-94-007-6167-4_416-1

Marsden, Magnus. 2005. *Living Islam: Muslim religious experience in Pakistan's north-west frontier.* Cambridge University Press. https://doi.org/10.1017/CBO9780511489549

Mattingly, Cheryl. 2010. *The paradox of hope: Journeys through a clinical borderland.* University of California Press.

Mendoza Carmona, Blanca Edurne. 2018. "Transforming 'everyday Islam' through feminism and higher education: Second-generation Muslim women in Spain." *Contemporary Levant, 3*(1), 44–55. https://doi.org/10.1080/20581831.2018.1455345

Mir, Shabana. 2011. "'Just to make sure people know I was born here': Muslim women constructing American selves." *Discourse: Studies in the Cultural Politics of Education, 32*(4), 547–63. https://doi.org/10.1080/01596306.2011.601552

Mirza, Heidi Safia. 2013. "'A second skin': Embodied intersectionality, transnationalism and narratives of identity and belonging among Muslim women in Britain." *Women's Studies International Forum, 36,* 5–15. https://doi.org/10.1016/j.wsif.2012.10.012

Mobasher, Mohsen M. 2012. *Iranians in Texas: Migration, politics, and ethnic identity.* University of Texas Press.

Moghissi, Haideh, and Halleh Ghorashi (Eds.). 2010. *Muslim diaspora in the West: Negotiating gender, home and belonging.* Ashgate. https://doi.org/10.1177/009430611348470З1

Nesbitt-Larking, Paul. 2008. "Dissolving the diaspora: Dialogical practice in the development of deep multiculturalism." *Journal of Community and Applied Social Psychology, 18*(4), 351–62. https://doi.org/10.1002/casp.956

Said, Edward. 1978. *Orientalism: Western conceptions of the Orient.* Kegan Paul.

Selby, Jennifer A., Amélie Barras, and Lori G. Beaman. 2018. *Beyond accommodation: Everyday narratives of Muslim Canadians.* University of British Columbia Press.

Shirazi, Faegheh, and Smeeta Mishra. 2010. "Young Muslim women on the face veil (niqab): A tool of resistance in Europe but rejected in the United States." *International Journal of Cultural Studies, 13*(1), 43–62. https://doi.org/10.1177%2F1367877909348538

Soto, Lilia. 2012. "On becoming Mexican in Napa: Mexican immigrant girls negotiating challenges to transnational identities." *Social Identities, 18*(1), 19–37.

Thobani, Sunera. 2003. "War and the politics of truth-making in Canada." *International Journal of Qualitative Studies in Education, 16*(3), 399–414. https://doi.org/10.1080/0951839032000086754

Zine, Jasmin. 2004. "Creating a critical faith-centered space for antiracist feminism: Reflections of a Muslim scholar-activist." *Journal of Feminist Studies in Religion, 20*(2), 167–87.

– 2006. "Unveiled sentiments: Gendered Islamophobia and experiences of veiling among Muslim girls in a Canadian Islamic school." *Equity and Excellence in Education, 39*(3), 239–52. https://doi.org/10.1080/10665680600788503

– 2009. "Unsettling the nation: Gender, race and Muslim cultural politics in Canada." *Studies in Ethnicity and Nationalism, 9*(1), 146–63. https://doi.org/10.1111/j.1754-9469.2009.01036.x

Dancing between Academia and Activism: An Interview with Katherine Bullock

SARA HAMED

Biography

Katherine Bullock is a University of Toronto lecturer in the political science department who describes herself as a traditionalist-feminist Muslim convert. Her work is a synthesis and at times oscillation between academia and activism, demonstrating both the tensions and synergistic potential of these two worlds. On both of these fronts, Bullock is a constructive critic of her immediate as well as broader Muslim community, while simultaneously working to dispel negative stereotypes about Muslims and Islam, primarily in the West.

For Bullock, the Qur'an and Sunnah are increasingly misinterpreted by both Muslims and others, resulting in restrictive religious practices (i.e., exclusion of women from public, community involvement) and media stereotypes. In her view, setting the record straight requires countering misreading of the texts with proper interpretations, as well as demonstrating the detrimental effects of such problematic renditions. As a Muslim social scientist, Bullock attempts the latter in her research. In the wake of the current geopolitical climate, Bullock is especially concerned with giving voice to Muslim experiences in national debates, particularly on issues pertaining to Muslim women, youth, politics, and the media. Her first full-length monograph, *Rethinking Muslim Women and the Veil: Challenging Historical and Modern Stereotypes* (2002), blends academic research with personal anecdotes to demystify the practice and offer alternative, positive perspectives that respond to common critiques of veiling. Beyond the veiling debate, Bullock's *Muslim Women Activists in North America: Speaking for Ourselves* (2005c) captures the autobiographical experiences of Muslim women activists from Canada and the United States, presenting them as role models for marginalized Muslims as well as figures challenging media stereotypes of the veiled, submissive Muslim woman. Each chapter of the book is a narrative contribution by one of eighteen women, chronicling challenges and triumphs experienced in their activist lives within and outside their respective Muslim communities. Collectively, the book is both a critique of stereotypical visions of Muslim women and patriarchal interpretations of women's roles in Islam and a call to activism in the face of social injustices in the wider North American context. Likewise, in "Becoming Holistically Indigenous: Young Muslims and Political Participation in Canada" (Bullock and Nesbitt-Larking 2013), Bullock and co-author Nesbitt-Larking construct a study to offer data about Canadian Muslims' civic and political engagement. Using semi-structured interviews with twenty Canadian Muslim youth, they demonstrate that the media and policy stereotypes of marginalized, young Muslim persons vulnerable to fundamentalism are unsubstantiated. Instead of disloyalty, their interviews demonstrate that Muslim youth engage and define politics variously in Canada, showing an across-the-board civic commitment. Another example of this type of work is elaborated in "To Make a Difference: Oral Histories of Two Canadian Muslim Women and Their Organisational Lives" (2017). Here, Bullock challenges typical archetypes of Muslim women (i.e., oppressed, submissive, passive, etc.) with the testimonials of two "traditionalist-feminists" who defy archetypal moulds and offer a new way of understanding the possible roles of Muslim women in Islamic organizations in Canada. By relying on their specific oral histories to interrupt long-standing stereotypes, Bullock emphasizes the weight and validity of their experiences. Similarly, in "Visible and Invisible: An Audience Study of Muslim and Non-Muslim Reactions to Orientalist Representations in *I Dream of Jeannie*" (2015), Bullock uncovers that Canadian Muslims in the study more easily recognize Orientalism than do their non-Muslim counterparts, a finding that she suggests may reflect broader Canadian and North American trends. These and other studies spearheaded by Bullock are pioneering works on Islam and Muslims in Canada.

Like her academic contributions, Bullock's activism is multipronged and extensive, beginning in 1994 when she first converted to Islam. More recently, in 2007, she co-founded the Tessellate Institute, a think tank dedicated to archiving and disseminating research on the experiences of Muslim Canadians, and currently serves as research advisor. Furthermore, she is the recent past (and first female) president of the Islamic Society of North America–Canada (ISNA) – one of the earliest Muslim organizations in the country, working to promote Muslim community life in accordance with the Qur'an and Sunnah. In addition, she is president of a Canadian publishing house called Compass Books, which aims to meet a growing demand for quality English materials about Islam and Muslims.

Interview

Sara Hamed [SH]: In *Muslim Women Activists in North America: Speaking for Ourselves*, you point to the contemporary Muslim preoccupation with dispelling negative stereotypes, which you argue can distract from other important issues within and beyond the Muslim community (Bullock 2005b, xvi). In my reading, your work continuously challenges these stereotypes, aiming to set the record straight about, for example, the meanings of jihad and representations of Muslim women. Can you tell us more about how you navigate – in your writing and activism – this seemingly inevitable tendency towards apologia, while simultaneously addressing the often-overlooked social problems you cite as festering in the North American context (substance abuse, poverty, homelessness) (Bullock 2005b, xvi)?

Katherine Bullock [KB]: Let me first suggest that dispelling negative stereotypes is not quite the same thing as apologia.[1] A negative stereotype is a misguided generalization of a people, so correcting a stereotype is about setting the record straight; apologia is a defence or justification of one's beliefs and can carry the impression of being "an opinion" rather than "setting a record straight" with unbiased "facts." In the academic world, to be "apologetic" is to be not properly "scholarly" by being biased, rather than working towards "truth." I would say that most of my work does try to present correctives to negative stereotypes. Unfortunately, the politicized climate of studying and living Islam in Canada does sometimes force one into apologia mode, and both of these requirements – correcting stereotypes and apologia – can be time-consuming distractions when there are important socio-economic and political issues facing Muslim communities here.

I was first alerted to the issue of tending towards apologia as a new convert in 1994. While researching for my PhD thesis, I came across a short article by Leila Ahmed. In it she describes visiting a conference in the United States from the Middle East, where she thought the three Arab women speakers were presenting an "unwarrantably rosy picture of women in Islam" (Ahmed 1982, 521). After she'd lived in America for a while, she came to

> see perfectly why the women making the presentation took the stand they did. For if one is of Arabic or Islamic background in America, one is almost compelled to take that stand [because] Americans by and large know nothing at all about the Islamic world … [and because] Americans "know," and know without even having to think about it, that the Islamic peoples … are backward, uncivilized peoples totally incapable of rational conduct. (521–2)

When I wrote my chapter for the book I edited on Muslim women activists, I had come to a similar experience. This issue of apologia affects Muslim activism and community engagement in many ways. Consider this: a Muslim activist, who has a family and works full-time and has around five hours a week to spare on community-related volunteering, has to spend those precious five hours on attempting to dispel stereotypes (op-eds, letters to the editor, and lectures at local community groups on whether or not Islam oppresses women). Meanwhile, legal assistance is needed for those experiencing discrimination in the workplace, on the streets, in malls, and so on. Abused women need assistance leaving domestic violence and rebuilding their lives; new immigrants and refugees need language and culture training, job search and settlement assistance (housing/doctor/food etc.). Youth need programs to help them learn about their religion and sustain a positive Muslim identity in a secular world. There is alcohol and drug abuse. And the list goes on. If community groups are always busy trying to dispel stereotypes, where is the energy for the harder community matters?

The good news is that in the thirteen years since that book was published, there has been a surge in more specialized community groups addressing different aspects of this complex puzzle: advocacy organizations focusing on human rights and media discourse; settlement organizations; youth-focused endeavours; women's groups and shelters; training and job placement for professionals; social service organizations. Now it is easier for activists to choose more focused avenues for their five hours a week volunteering.

In terms of my more personal navigation, one of the conscious decisions I took early on was never to spend spare time writing negative letters to editors about biased reporting in the media. I decided if I were ever to write to the media, with such precious spare time I would only write thank-you and supportive letters to any journalist who came out with a good and balanced piece.

In addition, although this has definitely changed over the last decade, when I wrote that book, there was a very strong community pressure never to discuss negative aspects of our community (the "dirty laundry") in public. I recall being a new Muslim in 1994 and speaking out against the Taliban at a mosque lecture. Afterwards I was approached by someone who said, at least they were trying, that I shouldn't criticize my fellow Muslims, especially when the West was against Islam. For a new Muslim, these were very confusing pressures. It took me many years to realize this was a wrong approach. As I wrote in my chapter for that book, I argued for a new approach – to recognize and speak up against community errors when needed. I pointed out that Westerners admire those who stand up for justice. Now, if I do speak publicly on "dirty laundry" topics, I recall the Qur'anic verse "stand out firmly for justice, as witnesses to God, even as against yourselves (4:135)." At the time (the 1990s), only "progressive" Muslims were pointing out publicly injustices in our community. But I believe that more traditional Muslims also have this obligation. So, in public lectures, I tried to shy away from apologia and speak what was true – e.g., rather than saying "Islam means peace, and there is no violence in Islam," I would say, "Yes, there are Muslims who use the Qur'an to justify violence, but they are wrong and misreading the text for X or Y reason." Others have also come to the same conclusion, and now we see more traditional Muslim organizations and scholars advocating against injustice within (and without) the Muslim community. This is a big change.

As I write, looking back, I can see that this conundrum is part of what pushed me to establish the Tessellate Institute. During the 2005 Ontario debates over faith-based arbitration, I was interviewed by the media enough to grasp the low level of understanding about Islam, Islamic law, and Muslims in Canada that prevailed in public discourse. Often, I would have to "defend" Islam as not being an "oppressive" religion, rather than talking at a more sophisticated level about the complex issues involved. I realized the need for top-quality academically sound material available to the intellectual classes and the wider public in general. So that is where I focused my activist energies for the next ten years.

SH: In the aforementioned text, you characterize the Muslim community as "in a stagnated state of decline and mess" (Bullock 2005b, xvii), partly because Muslim women are denied public roles in their communities as well as in the broader society. In your view, is this state of decline unique to Canada? North America? Is it meant to be a global characterization? Can you elaborate on this stagnation (i.e., what other reasons may have produced this state) and speak to the relationship between this decline and "the restrictive interpretations of the role of Muslim women"? What remedial role do you think your work can play? Do you use particular methodologies in your work to address this particular concern?

KB: If I were to write the introduction to that book today, I might not use that phrase. Not only is it a simplistic understanding of the forces that contribute to underdevelopment globally, overlooking other crucial factors such as global capitalism, elite corruption, and geopolitics, but it obfuscates the differences between being a Muslim woman in the global South versus in North America. When I wrote that introduction, at the stage of knowledge I was at the time, I was referring mostly to Muslim women in Muslim-majority countries and their underdevelopment in terms of political, social, and economic empowerment. I blamed their state on the lack of implementation of proper Islamic guidelines by government leadership, overlooking socio-economic-political and geopolitical factors. I saw the North American communities as similar to the extent that they were being created by immigrants with "cultural baggage" that was biased against Muslim women's empowerment, and thus I related their restricted lives to certain interpretations of Islam. My work attempted to demonstrate the error, Islamically, of these interpretations that would restrict women's role only to look after "hearth." In a way, I had unknowingly fallen into the "culture trap," best described by Mamdani (2011), as assuming that everything Muslims do is motivated by their religious Text or Culture, rather than other factors, such as socio-economic-political context, including global forces of hegemony.

Now I would say that correcting interpretations of Text is only one aspect, albeit important, of a complex and larger puzzle addressing Muslim women's disempowerment. Since I am a social scientist, and not a scholar of Islam qualified to do textual interpretation, my work in this area is slightly derivative. I rely on the scholarship of others with respect to textual interpretation and women's political, social, and economic empowerment, and I use qualitative interviews, or sociological analysis, to demonstrate empirically the detrimental consequences of women's exclusion from community life.

It is clear to me that the Qur'an envisions a public role for women beyond certain responsibilities to the family that are only vaguely alluded to. I think, for example, of "The Believers, men and women, are protectors one of another: they enjoin what is just, and forbid what is evil: they observe regular prayers, practise regular charity, and obey God and His Messenger. On them will God pour His mercy: for God is Exalted in power, Wise" (9:71). What I have learnt in my activism, and without being essentialist, is that women and men have different life experiences and perspectives that are needed for community development. A society is better off when both men and women are involved. I do not mean to belittle the work of women who focus their attention on the home and do not find the bandwidth to contribute beyond that. Feminists have long understood the crucial role this free labour, this care work, plays in creating wealth. A part of the problem, as I wrote in that book, is the "restrictive interpretations" of the Qur'an that intersect with Muslim cultural practices which say that this is all a woman ought to do. Doing the dishes, the laundry, or supervising children – this is only one aspect of a woman's ability, talents, intelligence, and skill set. These are also chores that can be shared in a household. It is to stunt a woman and her community not to give her space and opportunity to make other contributions to community life.

SH: How do you envision the importance of the Tessellate Institute, which seeks to "explore and document the lived experiences of Muslims in Canada" (Tessellate Institute 2014)? How do you see (or do you see) its contributions alongside your research at the university? To what extent is the knowledge produced by the institute different than the academic knowledge you produce? Can you tell us more about how your academic work informs the institute's activities?

KB: The Tessellate Institute (TTI) is a pioneering organization within the ecology of Canadian Muslim organizations. Muslims tend to focus on building mosques, Islamic schools, and relief organizations. Social services and advocacy are new fields in the last decade that are receiving more community support. Research institutes receive much less support. As I said before, it was during the 2005 faith-based arbitration debates in Ontario that I really understood the need for an organization like TTI. So many claims and assumptions were being made about Muslim women, Islamic law, and Muslims' place in Canadian society. There was a need for intellectual resources to inform the debate, instead of the anecdotes and apologia that dominated the discourse. So TTI was certainly born of a desire to correct stereotypes, but it always had a broader vision than that.

In addition to serving as a Muslim think tank, TTI also helps ensure that public policy is based on empirical realities – "evidence-based policy" – which have long been missing when it comes to policies relevant to Muslims and indeed most Othered communities. Moreover, there is a need for Muslims to be leaders in any discourse about them, defining what issues face the Muslim community, discussing possible solutions, and identifying what governments should best do to govern a multicultural society that includes Muslims. Thus, TTI provides opportunities for Muslim voices to contribute to national debates and builds capacity to do so, especially among researchers and artists.

Now, there are many academics in Canadian universities, both Muslim and non-Muslim, who produce relevant knowledge for policymakers. Policymakers do draw on academic work, though less so than we might wish. So there is an important role to play for research produced outside the academy, such as the work TTI produces. Usually the formatting and presentation of the data is different – i.e., there are short executive summaries; there is less emphasis on "original contribution to the field" and lesser emphasis on theory and methodology in TTI outputs. Such research is more accessible to politicians, bureaucrats, journalists, and businesspeople, who shape policy more than academics.

Dancing between academic and TTI research has been interesting. I didn't realize when I started TTI the slightly antagonistic relationship that exists between the think tank world and academia, with the latter often discounting the former's research as "biased" and not properly "objective," and the former often regarding academia as "ivory tower, not relevant to the real world." I view "objectivity" as an aspiration rather than an actuality in research. We all wear blinders and come from certain places; we all speak for certain ideas, even in academia. What matters is to consider other perspectives and opinions in one's work. Over the years, successive TTI boards have committed to striving towards "objectivity" in our research, while at the same time recognizing the pitfalls of such a "positivist" concept and seeing it as a never achieved ideal. Moreover, knowing that we are a Muslim organization, living as Muslims in Canada, we are not going to produce work that, for example, supports the idea that Muslims should give up their identity in order to become Canadian. We, therefore, seek to ground our work in the lived experiences of Muslims in Canada, in order to advance ideas that will allow for synthesizing Muslim identities with "Canadian" identities.

TTI has also acted as an alternative to an academic career for me, though not in a financial way. Because I wanted to work only part-time while my children were small, I was obliged to take contract lecturer positions in a university. Unfortunately, academia is quite hostile to the mother-academic, in that there are no part-time positions that will accumulate to tenure. But I thought I'd keep my foot in the door and go full-time when the children were older. I didn't realize that contract faculty are looked down upon by hiring committees. More than a couple of years as a sessional, the chances of getting a tenure-track position are next to zero. So I thought I'd be able to pave my own path and create myself a full-time job by establishing a research institute! I was inspired by two colleagues at the time, serving with me on the board of the Association of Muslim Social Sciences (AMSS, now the North American Association for Islamic and Muslim Studies). Both had founded Muslim think tanks in the USA. Little did I know that in Canada a board member cannot be paid for their work for the organization, especially if it's a charity! TTI gave me an institutional framework within which to pursue my research interests, but all my work for it has been as a volunteer. (I stepped down from the board in 2018.)

So TTI has been a major avenue for me to explore questions of interest to me. Indeed, for me there has been a seamless flow from one to the other. To provide an institutional framework for qualitative work or grant applications, the research has been done under TTI auspices: a report based on the research is written for TTI publications, and then academic papers, which are written according to academic norms including literature reviews, methodology, and theory sections, are published. At times I believe my research work in TTI has been a little too abstract for the normal subject matters of policy-related research, although fully in line with the concept of "lived experiences of Muslims" – I think for example of the audience research we did, which looked at audience reactions to *I Dream of Jeannie* and *Aladdin* (Bullock 2015). This research is incredibly important because it helps establish the effects of film and television's negative portrayals of Muslims and makes a modest contribution towards tracing the complex relationship that exists between celluloid portrayal and anti-Muslim racism in actuality. Eventually, one hopes, the film and television industry will realize these issues and change their representations (I write this just after the release of *Crazy Rich Asians*). But government regulation of the cultural industry does not usually encompass such issues of "representation," so this research is less useful in policymaking circles.

SH: You write of "practicing Islam properly" (Bullock 2005a, 63) and of "the Islamic perspective" (63). Can you speak to the scholarly discourse on the study of Muslims and Islam, namely the debate on what constitutes "Islam," "islams," "Islamic," etc. (e.g., the work of Samuli Schielke 2010; Talal Asad 1986; Shahab Ahmed 2015). How do you discern "Islam" and "the Islamic" in your scholarly work? Do you see anything distinctly Islamic about the knowledges you work to produce? Is this framework productive, in your view?

KB: As alluded to earlier, this is the debate over Text and Context and how they inform each other. The distinction I have followed in my work is to conceptualize as "Islamic" anything connected closely to the religious, or spiritual, aspects of the faith, and to use the idea of the "Muslim" as connected to the way Text is interpreted or played out in Context. The Qur'an, the Sunnah, the traditional religious sciences of interpretation, *tafseer*, or fiqh; these are how I see the concept of "Islamic." It is in this sense that I do not see myself as an "Islamic" scholar, not having been trained in any of the religious sciences. I am a Muslim social scientist, who tries to be informed by religious principles (Text) in her lifestyle and work, who researches and writes about Muslim attempts to live as Muslims in twenty-first-century Canada (Context).

Of course, as I write this, I recognize immediately the nuances and grey areas in which there is overlap. How is a *tafseer* produced, for instance, except from a situation of Context, a Muslim in a time and place thinking and wondering about the meaning of the Text? And yet, as I wrote before about the concept of objectivity, I am convinced that the Text is not a completely elastic discourse. There are parameters and boundaries that can constitute, or be arrived at, even if there are always debates about such parameters. I consider aiming for the boundaries to be attempting "objectivity," endeavouring to be non-partisan, neutral, considering all sides of the issue and not following one's own desires or wishes in interpreting Text. The Qur'an says:

> He it is Who has sent down to you the Book: in it are verses basic or fundamental (of established meaning); they are the foundation of the Book: others are allegorical. But those in whose hearts is perversity follow the part thereof that is allegorical seeking discord and searching for its hidden meanings but no one knows its hidden meanings except God and those who are firmly grounded in knowledge say: "We believe in the Book; the whole of it is from our Lord"; and none will grasp the Message except men of understanding. (Qur'an 3:7–9).

This is why not everything Muslims do is "Islamic." And this is why we need a distinction between Text and Context, or between Islamic and Muslim.

Such a discussion is also crucial, especially in the current context of the War on Terror, because this politicized discourse interprets everything Muslims do as generated by Text. To understand violent acts by Muslims in London, England, Tony Blair read the Qur'an. Mamdani (2011) brilliantly points out how such a culturalist understanding of human behaviour completely disregards other motivating factors, such as political or socio-economic circumstances. To which we can add irrational human emotions, such as anger or revenge.

SH: In reference to the faith-based arbitration question in the province of Ontario in 2005, you lament the media's antics – simplifying the debate, mislabelling stakeholders, and sensationalizing the issue – in a chapter in *Debating Shari'a* (Bullock 2012). In this instance, it seems that while various media outlets manipulated your voice and stripped it of nuance, your academic voice expressed later in that chapter allowed you the opportunity to clarify your position and reflect on the experience. Can you comment more generally on how you see your various voices (academic, activist, and public intellectual) intersecting and diverging, and the challenges and advantages of wearing multiple hats? In your view, what forms of knowledge do your academic and activist contributions produce? Are they different? If so, how?

KB: The biggest advantage of being both an academic and an activist is the way activism grounds you in the community with real-life experiences. Choices must be made, positions argued for. It's not the same as sitting in a seminar room debating theories and options from different angles. Activism also provides the empirical testing ground for academic theories about, say, integration, or "Muslim perspectives" on particular issues. Academics may speculate that Muslims think x or y about an issue, but if you sit in on a meeting and hear Muslims talking passionately and debating issues, you experience the debate from a closer point of view.

At the same time, there is an advantage to being an activist with an academic ability. Academia helps hone the thought process, teaching precision in definitions, understanding the scope of an issue, recognizing the wider context. The methodologies and theories of interpretation can help develop an in-depth understanding of an issue that can then help shape an activist response. I feel truly blessed to be able to draw on both arenas.

The biggest disadvantage of being both, unfortunately, is in the realm of academia, which often has a culture of hierarchy and snobbery with respect to activist work. Academic culture often disdains the knowledge of the activist as being "biased," "not objective," or "too partisan." Although many social science disciplines, like anthropology and sociology, have rightly problematized for a few decades the concept of "objectivity" – the idea that the world is an object that can be viewed from a neutral point in space – there remains the sense, especially in my field of political science, that an activist is too ensconced in their world to produce "non-partisan" work. This is most especially true of Islam and Muslim studies. Being not only an activist but also a practitioner of the faith, in the secular academy, can render the work produced suspect in the eyes of many academics.

I faced this issue many times when trying to give lectures about my thesis work, which was about Muslim women's choices, perspectives, and experiences of wearing hijab or niqab. I wear the hijab myself, which seems to render me suspect as a lecturer. When giving a talk about my thesis and later book, I found that instead of being received as an "academic" lecture, meaning a non-emotionally involved, non-committed, "non-partisan" lecture about interviews with Muslim women, I would get asked questions such as why did I convert to Islam, and why did I wear the headscarf? This was most pronounced in the United States but not absent in Canada. Moreover, since the headscarf signals publicly my spirituality (i.e., a belief in God), this also renders me suspect as a lecturer, or "producer of knowledge," about Islam and Muslims. If a non-Muslim says something about Islam, this is taken more trustfully, more authentically than if I do. Thus, to speak publicly wearing these many hats is an exceedingly complicated affair.

This is one of the reasons I chose to stop writing about hijab after my book on the topic came out. My decision to wear a headscarf is a private one and not really anyone's business. The thesis/book was an attempt to give a platform for Muslim women to speak their own truths about hijab to a Western culture that often silences them, but academics are not usually obliged to entwine their personal lifestyle choices into their work. And as I write that, I know of course this isn't exactly true – feminist scholarship, after all, was born of that nexus. Many paradigmatic changes in the academy that have introduced new perspectives to the issues of social injustice have been born of scholar-activists. But there is so much more to being a Muslim woman than the hijab, so I decided not to spend the rest of my life focused on a topic imposed upon me by outsiders that would oblige me publicly to "explain/defend" myself all the time. Also, for me, the religiously mandatory nature of hijab is so clear that the research problem should be "why don't Muslim women wear hijab?," not all these studies that focus on "why do Muslim women wear hijab?" The "problem" of hijab is not a truly indigenous issue. It exists at the intersection of Western critiques of Islam as an "oppressive religion" and Muslim attempts to be prosperous and contributing members of the twenty-first-century world.

SH: As someone who studies Muslims in Canada but has had important international experiences, do you consider Canada to be part of the phenomenon that has been termed the Islamic Revival? If so, is there anything exceptional or particular about the Canadian context?

KB: The Islamic Revival came to Canada with Muslim emigrants arriving in the late 1970s/early 1980s. These emigrants found small local Muslim populations with basic institutions serving their needs; they were doing their very best under the circumstances. Many of the newer immigrants who became active in Islamic organizations were inspired by Revival activist teachers, such as the Egyptian Hasan al Banna or the Pakistani Maulana Maududi. They sometimes found what is called "folk Islam," or a Muslim culture rapidly assimilating to the wider culture, such as "sock hops" at an Islamic conference or folk dancing in the masjid. Some conflicts ensued between these newer immigrants and the earlier generations, many of whom remain quite bitter about how they feel the new immigrants imposed authoritarian and patriarchal interpretations of Islam on their local mosque. New associations have in general pushed out the earlier ones. It is in this way that Canada has been part of the phenomenon of the Islamic Revival. It is very complex; we cannot make easy lines between "progressive" older immigrants and "fundamentalist" newer immigrants, because traditional Muslim cultures have practised patriarchy for centuries, and in some ways these new activist immigrants challenged patriarchy. For example, an activist immigrant woman might be empowered to become a board member, whereas traditional culture might not endorse women's attendance at the masjid. And at the same time, as far as I have been able to tell, early Muslim associations did empower women to be at the masjid and take leadership roles.

There is a difference between the Revival in a Muslim country and immigrants inspired by Revivalism in a minority context. In the majority context, Revivalists usually seek to capture political power. In the minority context, such Muslims seek to adapt for the Canadian context Revivalist inspirations about God's continued relevance in the modern era, the solutions of Islamic teachings on the family, interest, racism, economics, charity, and so on – not on turning Canada into an "Islamic State," fearmongering by right-wing populists notwithstanding. But as far as I know, in that Anglo-European–North American context, Canada is not particularly exceptional in this regard. There is an immense diversity in ethnic, sectarian, and ideological background, which gives rise to an impressive number of masjid and Islamic organizations, some inspired by Revival, some opposed to Revival.

SH: You mention on more than one occasion that your activist experiences have taught you that one cannot always resist the powers that be, which may ultimately dictate the success of a cause (e.g., Bullock 2005a, 58). How does this knowledge play out in your academic and non-academic considerations, for example funding proposals? Looking back at Canadian scholarship on Muslims and Islam over the last ten years, what do you make of its emphases and silences?

KB: A significant proportion of the literature on Muslims in Canada is driven by the larger geopolitical environment. I don't think this is particularly unique to scholarship on Muslims. There have always been trends, even fads, in research, determined by the political discursive environment of the day. For Muslims, it has been Muslim women and the veil, oppression, integration/assimilation, radicalization, and images in the media. As I said, this means that much research on Muslims is driven by externally generated questions and concerns.

A few years ago, I was hired as an interviewer for a project on converts to Islam. It was an international study comparing Canada, Singapore, and Australia. The principal researcher spent three years trying to get a grant to fund this research. Eventually he figured out how to pitch it to the Canadian Kanishka project, which was about counterterrorism in Canada. Since there were some converts joining ISIS or conducting terror attacks in the West, but not all converts, he argued we need to understand "conversion to Islam" per se so we could understand why a few would commit violent attacks. I did a lot of soul searching before I joined this project. As a convert myself, how could I justify studying conversion through the lens of counterterrorism? Why would the Canadian government care about converts? After several conversations with the principal researcher and his project manager, I became convinced that he was an empathetic scholar, genuinely interested in conversion sociologically, and that he had a free hand to develop his research study and control the data collected and interpreted. He would have to write one report to the government to fulfil the conditions of the grant. I suppose it was some kind of game he had to play in order to get money. It was very hard to recruit interviewees.

As a sessional lecturer in the academy, without the proper institutional support, I do not apply for grants. But under the Tessellate Institute we have been successful in receiving a few grants to advance our work. One of the biggest differences from the two granting streams that have affected my work is that non-academic grants do not fund pure research. There always has to be an impact element, such as a workshop, focus groups, or an event. In addition, the project has to advance research goals set out by the funding authority, so that the project is already shaped in advance by someone else's agenda.

NOTE

1 I am deeply grateful to my colleague Nabeel Ahmed, the new president of the Tessellate Institute, for his insightful comments on an early draft of my responses to these questions, one example of which is pointing this out.

REFERENCES

Ahmed, Leila. 1982. "Western ethnocentrism and perceptions of the harem." *Feminist Studies*, *8*(3), 521–34. https://doi.org/10.2307/3177710

Ahmed, Shahab. 2015. *What is Islam? The importance of being Islamic*. Princeton University Press.

Asad, Talal. 1986. *The idea of an anthropology of Islam*. Center for Contemporary Arab Studies, Georgetown University.

Bullock, Katherine. 2002. *Rethinking Muslim women and the veil: Challenging historical and modern stereotypes.* International Institute of Islamic Thought.

– 2005a. "Activism as a way of life." In Katherine Bullock (Ed.), *Muslim women activists in North America: Speaking for ourselves.* University of Texas Press.

– 2005b. "Introduction." In Katherine Bullock (Ed.), *Muslim women activists in North America: Speaking for ourselves.* University of Texas Press.

– (Ed.). 2005c. *Muslim women activists in North America: Speaking for ourselves.* University of Texas Press.

– 2012. "'The Muslims have ruined our party': A case study of Ontario media portrayals of supporters of faith-based arbitration." In Jennifer Selby and Anna Korteweg (Eds.), *Debating shari'a: Islam, gender politics and family law arbitration* (pp. 257–76). University of Toronto Press.

– 2015. "Visible and invisible: An audience study of Muslim and non-Muslim reactions to Orientalist representations in *I Dream of Jeannie.*" *Journal of Arab & Muslim Media Research, 8*(2), 83–97. https://doi.org/10.1386/jammr.8.2.83_1

– 2017. "To make a difference: Oral histories of two Canadian Muslim women and their organisational lives." In Mario Peucker and Rauf Ceylan (Eds.), *Muslim community organizations in the West: History, Developments and Future Perspectives* (pp. 183–204). Springer Fachmedien Wiesbaden.

Bullock, Katherine, and Paul Nesbitt-Larking. 2013. "Becoming 'holistically Indigenous': Young Muslims and political participation in Canada." *Journal of Muslim Minority Affairs, 33*(2), 185–207. https://doi.org/10.1080/13602004.2013.810116

Mamdani, Mahmood. 2011. "Good Muslim, bad Muslim: A political perspective on culture and terrorism." In Frédéric Volpi (Ed.), *Political Islam: A critical reader* (pp. 109–25). Routledge.

Schielke, Samuli. 2010. *Second thoughts about the anthropology of Islam, or how to make sense of grand schemes in everyday life.* Zentrum Moderner Orient Working Paper no. 2.

Tessellate Institute. 2014. "What is TTI?" http://tessellateinstitute.com/what-is-tti

Contributors

Melanie Adrian is an associate professor in the Department of Law and Legal Studies and holds the inaugural Chair of Teaching Innovation at Carleton University. She is the author of *Religious Freedom at Risk: The EU, French Schools, and Why the Veil Was Banned* and serves as senior editor of the *Oxford Encyclopedia of Islam in North America.* Her op-eds have been published in the *Globe & Mail* and the *Ottawa Citizen.* Adrian was named to the Order of Ontario in 2019.

Sadaf Ahmed is a PhD candidate at the Department for the Study of Religion at the University of Toronto. Her ethnographic research on Muslim parenting and bereavement is a lens to explore current formations of Islam in contemporary Canada.

Schirin Amir-Moazami is Professor of Islam in Europe at the Institute of Islamic Studies at Freie Universität Berlin. Her research interests include political secularism and secularity, critical political theory, body politics, and the politics of knowledge production. She has published on public controversies related to Muslim bodily practices and regulations of religious plurality in France and Germany. She is co-editor of the web-based essay series "Provincializing Epistemologies." Amir-Moazami recently published an edited volume on the politics and epistemologies of knowledge production on Islam and Muslims in Europe, entitled *The Inspected Muslim*, and she is finishing a monograph entitled *Interrogating Muslims: The Liberal-Secular Matrix of Integration in Contemporary Germany*, to be published with Bloomsbury Press.

Natasha Bakht is a professor of law at the University of Ottawa and the Shirley Greenberg Chair for Women and the Legal Profession. Her scholarship explores the intersection between religious freedom and women's equality. She is the author of *In Your Face: Law, Justice and Niqab-Wearing Women in Canada* (Irwin Law, 2020).

Amélie Barras is Associate Professor in the Department of Social Science at York University (Toronto). She conducts research on the intersection between law, religion, and politics. She has published on the politics of secularism in Turkey and France, including *Refashioning Secularisms in France and Turkey: The Case of the Headscarf Ban* (Routledge, 2014). She also writes on Reasonable Accommodation and Islam in Canada. Her publications on the topic include a book written with Jennifer A. Selby (Memorial University) and Lori G. Beaman (University of Ottawa): *Beyond Accommodation: Everyday Narratives of Muslim Canadians*. Finally, her newest project documents the work of faith-based nongovernmental organizations at the United Nations' Human Rights Council.

Mehmet Ali Basak is a PhD candidate at the University of Ottawa. Basak's research is centred upon anthropology of Islam and Muslim societies. Drawing upon one year-long fieldwork in Turkey, in his doctoral project Mehmet attempts to shed light on the transformation of religion in the everyday lives of Turkish people by focusing on nonreligious practices and beliefs within the newly emerging conceptual framework of "nonreligion."

Lori G. Beaman, PhD, F.R.S.C., is Canada Research Chair in Religious Diversity and Social Change, professor of religious studies at the University of Ottawa, and director of the "Nonreligion in a Complex Future" project. Her publications include *The Transition of Religion to Culture in Law and Public Discourse* (2020) and *Deep Equality in an Era of Religious Diversity* (2017).

Rachel Brown is the Program Coordinator and Religious Studies Teaching Fellow at the Centre for Studies in Religion and Society at the University of Victoria. She holds a PhD in religious diversity in North America from Wilfrid Laurier University and specializes in religion and migration, food practice, contemporary Islam, and lived religion.

Katherine Bullock is a Lecturer in the Department of Political Science, University of Toronto at Mississauga. Her teaching focus is political Islam from a global perspective, and her research focuses on Muslims in Canada, their history, contemporary lived experiences, political and civic engagement, debates on the veil, media representations of Islam and Muslims, and Muslim perspectives on basic income.

Lara Deeb is Professor of Anthropology at Scripps College and the author of An Enchanted Modern: Gender and Public Piety in Shi'i Lebanon (Princeton University Press, 2006), co-author of Leisurely Islam: Negotiating Geography and Morality in Shi'ite South Beirut (with Mona Harb, Princeton University

Press, 2013), and co-author of Anthropology's Politics: Disciplining the Middle East (with Jessica Winegar, Stanford University Press, 2015).

Abdelaziz Djaout has an MBA in marketing and also completed two doctoral programs in sociology and religious studies. He has been a research assistant on several studies on Muslims living in Quebec. He is currently teaching administration at the CEGEP in Granby (Quebec) and is also an invited professor in strategy at the African Institute of Management in Dakar (Senegal).

Dr. Parin Dossa is a Professor of Anthropology at Simon Fraser University. Her teaching and research interests include migration and diaspora, gender, health, and social palliation, ethnographic methods, and structural violence in war and peace. Her books include *Racialized Bodies, Disabling Worlds: Storied Lives of Immigrant Muslim Women* (2009), *Politics and Poetics of Migration: Narratives of Iranian Women from the Diaspora* (2004); *Afghanistan Remembers: Narratives of Violence and Culinary Practices* (2014); *Social Palliation: Canadian Muslims' Storied Lives on Living and Dying* (2020), and first author of *Transnational Aging and Reconfigurations of Kin Work* (2016).

Paul Eid is a Professor of Sociology at Université du Québec à Montréal (UQAM). His areas of research and expertise include immigration, interethnic relations, racism and discrimination on the labour market, racial profiling, ethnic and religious identity building among second-generation youth, and the role played by religion in the public domain.

Anver M. Emon is Professor of Law and History, Canada Research Chair in Islamic Legal History, and Director of the Institute of Islamic Studies at the University of Toronto. He is the author of numerous studies on Islamic law and history, including *Islamic Natural Law Theories* (Oxford University Press, 2010), *Religious Pluralism and the Empire of Law* (Oxford University Press, 2014), and co-author with Urfan Khaliq of *Jurisdictional Exceptionalisms: Islamic Law, International Law and Parental Child Abduction* (Cambridge University Press, 2021).

Sara Hamed is a doctoral candidate at the Department for the Study of Religion at the University of Toronto. Her research is based in the Greater Toronto and Hamilton area in Canada, bringing together the anthropology of Islam, institutional theory, and rhetorical studies.

Catherine Holtmann is Professor of Sociology and Director of the Muriel McQueen Fergusson Centre for Family Violence Research at the University of New Brunswick. Her research includes the areas of gender and religion, domestic violence, and immigrants. She is the principal investigator of the Muslim

Family Safety Project in partnership with the Arab Cultural Centre in Fredericton and a co-investigator on the project Violence Against Women Migrants and Refugees: Analyzing Causes and Effective Policy Response. She is the editor of *Exploring Religion and Diversity in Canada: People, Practice and Possibility* (Springer, 2018).

Aaron W. Hughes is the Philip S. Bernstein Professor in the Department of Religion and Classics at the University of Rochester.

Amir Hussain is Chair and Professor of Theological Studies at Loyola Marymount University, the Jesuit university in Los Angeles. From 2011 to 2015, Amir was the editor of the *Journal of the American Academy of Religion*, and he is currently the Vice President of the American Academy of Religion. He is also the editor in chief of the *Oxford Encyclopedia of Islam in North America*. His most recent book is *A Concise Introduction to World Religions*, 4th edition (Oxford University Press, 2019).

Roshan Arah Jahangeer is a PhD Candidate (ABD) in the Department of Politics at York University in Toronto, Canada, and an Instructor in the School of Gender, Sexuality, and Women's Studies. Her dissertation research focuses on the transnational circulation of anti-veiling laws between France and Quebec and on secularism, feminism, and islamophobia. Her research foregrounds (settler-) colonialism, intersectionality, religion, race, and gender.

Karim H. Karim is Chancellor's Professor at Carleton University and Director of the Centre for the Study of Islam. He previously served as Director at the Institute of Ismaili Studies (UK) and Carleton's School of Journalism and Communication. Karim's publications are widely cited, and he won the inaugural Robinson Prize for the internationally acclaimed *Islamic Peril: Media and Global Violence*.

Abdie Kazemipur is Professor of Sociology and Chair of Ethnic Studies at University of Calgary. Among other things, he studies the integration of Muslim minorities in the West and the religious developments in Muslim-majority societies in the Middle East. He is the author of *The Muslim Question in Canada* (University of British Columbia Press, 2014), and *Sacred as Secular: Secularization Under Theocracy in Iran* (McGill-Queen's University Press, 2022).

Sahver Kuzucuoglu holds a master's degree in Religion and Culture, has a second master's in Cultural Analysis and Social Theory, and is currently a PhD candidate in Religious Studies at Wilfrid Laurier University. Sahver has worked for many years as interpreter/translator in the settlement of new Canadians in Southern Ontario, fuelled by her passion for volunteerism, community, decoloniality, pluriversality, and intercultural dialogue. Her current research areas include Turkish cultural studies, Sufism, and the identity negotiation of the "minority within a minority."

Géraldine Mossière is an anthropologist who teaches in the Institut d'études religieuses at the University of Montreal. She conducts empirical research on religion and migration by focusing on new religious mobility and subjectivities. She has worked and published on women converts to Islam in Quebec and in France, as well as on identification process among young converts to Islam in Quebec (see *Converties à l'islam: Parcours de femmes au Québec et en France*, Presses de l'université de Montréal, 2013). Mossière also examines the role of Islam as a new mode of sociability as well as a resource for identity construction for young people who feel attracted to Islam (SSHRC Insight Grant (2016–22)), and she is interested in the emergence of new religious authorities among converts to Islam.

Rehan Sayeed is a PhD student in the Department of Anthropology at McGill University. Ethnographically focused in the Greater Toronto Area, his work explores the theological and pedagogical dimensions of Islamic seminaries (madrassas) and their place in contemporary discourses of citizenship and Islamophobia.

Jennifer A. Selby is Associate Professor and Graduate Coordinator of Religious Studies and affiliate member of Gender Studies at Memorial University of Newfoundland. Her ethnographic-based research examines secularism in contemporary France and Canada, with attention to gender. She is most recently co-author of *Beyond Accommodation: Everyday Narratives of Muslim Canadians* (University of British Columbia Press, 2018). In addition to her work on the executive committee of the Canadian Corporation for Studies in Religion, Selby is co-chair of the Anthropology of Religion section within the American Academy of Religion.

Meena Sharify-Funk is an Associate Professor for the Religion and Culture Department at Wilfrid Laurier University. Her research interests include Islamic and Sufi thought and identity, Muslim women in North America, Islamic hermeneutics, and the role of cultural and religious factors in peacemaking.

Jason Idriss Sparkes teaches Religion and Global Studies at Wilfrid Laurier University. In his research, he applies a decolonial and transdisciplinary approach to examine Muslim traditions of being, knowing, and behaving west of Mecca, with a focus on Sufism.

Hicham Tiflati, PhD, is Humanities Professor at John Abbott College and Quebec regional director for the Centre for Civic Religious Literacy. Hicham has worked closely with families and individuals affected by terrorism and done fieldwork in Germany, Turkey, Morocco, and Canada. His research focuses on radicalization, disengagement from violent extremism, Muslim identity construction, and Islamic schooling. He has academic and research interests in topics such as deradicalization, CVE, Muslim identities, citizenship, and the role of religious education in (re)shaping identities.

Jasmin Zine is a Professor of Sociology, Religion, and Culture/Muslim Studies at Wilfrid Laurier University. Her forthcoming book, *Under Siege: Islamophobia and the 9/11 Generation* (McGill-Queen's University Press) is based on a six-year study funded by the Social Sciences and Humanities Research Council (SSHRC). She has been working on another SSHRC-funded study that maps the Canadian Islamophobia industry. Dr. Zine is a co-founder of the International Islamophobia Studies Research Association (IISRA).

Index

Page numbers in *italic* represent figures and tables.